SIXTH EDITION

Theories of Personality

Richard M. Ryckman
University of Maine at Orono

Brooks/Cole Publishing Company
I(T)P® *An International Thomson Publishing Company*

Pacific Grove • Albany • Bonn • Boston • Cincinnati • Detroit • London • Madrid • Melbourne
Mexico City • New York • Paris • San Francisco • Singapore • Tokyo • Toronto • Washington

Sponsoring Editor: *Marianne Taflinger*
Marketing Representative: *Carolyn Crockett*
Editorial Assistant: *Laura Donahue*
Production Editor: *Tessa McGlasson*
Manuscript Editor: *Bernard Gilbert*
Permissions Editor: *Fiorella Ljunggren*
Design Coordination: *E. Kelly Shoemaker*
Cover/Interior Design: *Sharon Kinghan*

Cover Illustration: *Ron Mura*
Art Editor/Interior Illustration: *Lisa Torri*
Photo Editor: *Kathleen Olson*
Marketing Team: *Gay Meixel / Romy Fineroff*
Typesetting: *Shepard Poorman Comm. Corp.*
Cover Printing: *Phoenix Color Corp.*
Printing and Binding: *Quebecor / Fairfield*

COPYRIGHT © 1997 by Brooks / Cole Publishing Company
A division of International Thomson Publishing Inc.
I(T)P *The ITP logo is a registered trademark under license.*

For more information, contact:

BROOKS/COLE PUBLISHING COMPANY
511 Forest Lodge Road
Pacific Grove, CA 93950
USA

International Thomson Publishing Europe
Berkshire House 168-173
High Holborn
London WC1V 7AA
England

Thomas Nelson Australia
102 Dodds Street
South Melbourne, 3205
Victoria, Australia

Nelson Canada
1120 Birchmount Road
Scarborough, Ontario
Canada M1K 5G4

International Thomson Editores
Campos Eliseos 385, Piso 7
Col. Polanco
11560 México D. F. México

International Thomson Publishing GmbH
Königswinterer Strasse 418
53227 Bonn
Germany

International Thomson Publishing Asia
221 Henderson Road
#05-10 Henderson Building
Singapore 0315

International Thomson Publishing Japan
Hirakawacho Kyowa Building, 3F
2-2-1 Hirakawacho
Chiyoda-ku, Tokyo 102
Japan

Printed in the United States of America

10   9   8   7   6   5   4   3

Library of Congress Cataloging-in-Publication Data

Ryckman, Richard M.
    Theories of personality / Richard M. Ryckman.—6th ed.
      p. cm.
    Includes bibliographical references and index.
    ISBN 0-534-33976-X
    1. Personality.   I. Title.
BF698.R96 1996
155.2—dc20
                             96-5593
                             CIP

For Cailey, Catherine, Laine, Maris, and Matthew:
They speak to the angels.

Contents

PART THREE   TRAIT PERSPECTIVES   *271*

Preface

Theories of Personality serves essentially the same primary purposes in its sixth edition as in the first, published nearly 20 years ago. It reviews the basic concepts and principles of the major theories of personality and assesses how well they meet criteria for judging their scientific worth. The text also introduces students to research studies that test the validity of the theories. It presents issues that challenge contemporary personality psychologists and discusses some of the major new developments in the discipline.

The material is accessible to undergraduates who have had little or no exposure to the field of personality psychology. In this edition, I have included many more case studies that show how the theories are applied to the treatment of personality disorders. There are also many more examples from everyday life and unusual topics to stimulate interest among students of both traditional and nontraditional ages. Each major theoretical position is introduced by an overview of the theorist's basic concepts and principles; comparisons of the theories thus follow easily.

Although the goals of the text remain intact, there have been many changes in most of the theories in the past 20 years, particularly as advocates of the theories have tried to increase their validity and applicability to the solution of human problems by elaborating upon and modifying some of the concepts. In this edition, I try to convey the intellectual excitement generated by the ongoing work with these theories. I also attempt to show in the final chapter how they continue to inspire the creative efforts of a new generation of personality psychologists, and thus further our understanding of human personality and functioning.

Organization

The book is divided into seven parts. Part One, "An Introduction to the Discipline," addresses the problem of establishing an acceptable definition of personality and considers the reasons for studying individual differences from a scientific perspective. Chapter 1 provides basic information about the scientific process and the interrelatedness of theory and research. This edition features extended coverage of theory construction and testing. The chapter also explains the criteria by which scientists judge the worth of a theory; students can thus evaluate the theories in succeeding chapters.

Part Two, "Psychoanalytic and Neoanalytic Perspectives," covers Freud and his psychoanalytic theory and the neoanalytic theories of Jung, Adler, Horney, Erikson, and Kohut. In the Freud chapter, materials on the free association technique will stimulate student interest. The theory of psychosexual development is described, and the latest research evidence for the character types is examined.

The chapter on Jung includes the structure and functions of the psyche, and extended coverage of the latest research that supports the validity of the theory of psychological types.

To round out the discussion of Alfred Adler's theory about psychological health, this edition includes detailed descriptions of healthy and unhealthy individuals. Recent research on birth order is highlighted, and the battle between Zajonc and Markus and their critics about the relation of intellectual development to birth order is described in detail, as an illustration of the connection between issues raised by Adler and today's theoretical work.

In the chapter on Karen Horney, her psychoanalytic theory of self-realization is presented in detail, and her seminal views on the role of hypercompetitiveness in U.S. society in creating neurotic individuals are examined, along with the validating research evidence.

In the chapter on Erik Erikson, links are made between his theory of psychosocial development and contemporary elaborations of his position; for example, Erikson's work on identity status in adolescence is extended by the recent work of Marcia and Waterman, and his thinking about intimacy in young adulthood is extended by Orlofsky. Both constructs are reviewed, together with current validating evidence. This chapter also features research tests of Erikson's theory about generativity in middle adulthood and ego integrity in late adulthood.

An entirely new chapter on Heinz Kohut's self psychology, the latest theory to build upon classical psychoanalysis, outlines Kohut's unique interpretations of phenomena initially examined by Freud. A particular focus is Kohut's creative discussion of the long-lasting damage to the self induced by unempathic parents, who fail to provide their children with the support and understanding necessary to personal growth; such children tend to develop a pathological narcissism, characterized by an unrealistic grandiosity and exhibitionism, which results in ineffective personal functioning. The use of empathy and several new forms of transference to treat patients with various psychological disorders is considered. Finally, Kohut's imaginative account of healthy narcissistic development is presented.

Part Three, "Trait Perspectives," covers the major theories of Allport, Cattell, and Eysenck. In the Allport chapter, his devotion to constructing a humanistic theory of personality is demonstrated, and the tremendous impact of his ideas on contemporary personality psychology is explored.

In the chapter on Raymond Cattell, the measurement principles underlying his theory of personality are clarified by means of a brief account of two forms of factor analysis—the R and P techniques. A case study demonstrates how unique individual traits can be measured. Cattell's latest efforts to account for the effects of situational variables on personality expression are also presented. The chapter concludes with Cattell's controversial ideas about a morality with a purportedly scientific basis.

In the chapter on Eysenck, there is extended coverage of the interaction between heredity and environment as it relates to intellectual development, especially IQ. New materials detail Eysenck's explanations of genius and the links between genius and psychopathology.

Part Four, "Cognitive Perspectives," is devoted to George Kelly's theory of personal constructs. His theory is presented in detail. In this edition, the most recent research testing his views on schizophrenia is presented.

Part Five, "Humanistic/Existential Perspectives," covers Maslow, Rogers, and May. The links between Maslow's thinking and today's theorizing and research are revealed both in the latest studies of fear of success in men and women, and in the association of Maslow's key concept of peak experiences with Csikszentmihalyi's concept of flow.

Part Six, "Social-Behavioral Perspectives," includes Skinner,

Rotter, and Bandura. The chapter on Skinner contains a careful review of basic concepts and operant-conditioning principles. Recent research examples show the successful application of these concepts and principles to the treatment of behavioral disorders. The chapters on Rotter and Bandura have been updated to include recent research evidence for the locus-of-control and self-efficacy constructs.

Part Seven, "The Role of Personality Theories in Contemporary Personality Psychology," highlights the heuristic value of the theories. The many ways in which they act as stimulants to the thinking and research efforts of personality psychologists are noted in Chapter 18. For example, interest in the Big Five factors of personality derives from the efforts of Allport, Cattell, and Eysenck, and the recent trend to incorporate more cognitive constructs into conceptualizations of personality owes much to the legacy of Allport, Kelly, and Bandura. The chapter concludes with a look at some of the newer areas of development in the discipline.

Helpful pedagogical features in Chapters 2–17 include: *evaluative comments* that assess the scientific worth of each theory; *discussion questions*; a list of *suggested readings* that instructors can use in substituting or adding pertinent materials; and a *glossary,* whose items are **boldfaced** in the text.

Acknowledgments

This edition has benefitted immensely from the comments of my undergraduate and graduate students. Their curiosity, honesty, and provocative questioning have helped me tremendously. Special thanks to Marc Lindner for his comments on the Kohut chapter, and to Kathy McAuliffe, who helped with the graphics. I also owe a debt to my colleagues Marie Hayes, Michael Robbins, Laurence Smith, and Allan Stubbs for sharing their expertise and for their many useful suggestions.

The following reviewers made many helpful recommendations that led to several substantial changes and additions in various chapters: Teresa Dill-Standiford, Trenton State College; Lena K. Ericksen, Western Washington State University; Richard K. Kimball, Worcester State College; Robert J. Leider, Chicago Institute of Psychoanalysis; Carolyn Mangelsdorf, University of Washington; and Connie Veldink, Everett Community College.

It is also a pleasure to acknowledge the fine staff at Brooks/Cole. Senior editor Marianne Taflinger has skillfully guided the book to completion. I commend Tessa McGlasson, production editor, Bernard

Gilbert, copyeditor, and Kelly Shoemaker and Sharon Kinghan, designers, for their excellent work.

Finally, I want to thank my brother, Reggie, for his continual encouragement. Once again I express my love and appreciation to my wife, Leona, and our sons, Robert and Mark, for their concern and support.

Richard M. Ryckman

PART ONE

AN INTRODUCTION TO THE DISCIPLINE

Personality psychology has been blessed with an array of creative thinkers, whose insights have been of immense value in helping us understand how personality functions. Although all of the theories have certain strengths, not surprisingly each of them also has its limitations. The phenomena encompassed by human personality are simply too complex and diverse for any one individual to unite them in a single, coherent theoretical framework; thus, no one theorist can ever hope to construct a completely adequate theory of personality. The goal is to create theories that are more and more adequate or scientifically useful. Therefore, adherents of the various approaches often exert substantial efforts to overcome the limitations, and improve the scientific quality, of current theories. Others seek to construct new theories; for them, the current theories serve to stimulate new creative efforts.

To help you understand the strengths and weaknesses of the current theories of personality, we begin by discussing the major concepts used in the construction of scientific theories, the principal research procedures used to test them, and the criteria ordinarily used by investigators to assess the worth of a theory. Exposure to this basic information in Chapter 1 should enable you to evaluate the scientific usefulness and adequacy of the theoretical positions presented in succeeding chapters. It also should help you to comprehend the materials in the final chapter, which focuses on the contributions made to the discipline by the theories.

Personality and the Scientific Outlook

Virtually all of us are interested in knowing more about ourselves and other people. In our attempts to make sense of our experiences, we often engage in naive analyses of people's behavior. We wonder, for example, why one of our friends refuses to date a young man or woman we find particularly attractive. We are puzzled by the student who is fascinated by astronomy, whereas we find it difficult to listen attentively for more than ten minutes to a lecture on the topic. We are at a loss to explain why presidential assassins acted as they did, whereas countless others with similar or even greater frustrations and personal problems did not. We are frustrated in our attempts to explain why a quiet, self-effacing civilian with no previous military experience, who is well-liked by neighbors and relatives, should suddenly decide to buy a semiautomatic weapon, enter a local fast-food restaurant dressed in Army combat fatigues, and begin to slaughter customers. In each of these instances, we seek to generate explanations for the actions we observe: we want to know *why* these people behaved as they did. The answers to that general question are also sought by psychologists who work in the discipline of personality psychology. In seeking explanations for individual differences in behavior, they construct theories designed to explain and therefore help us better understand a wide variety of behavioral differences in many situations. Their efforts are aimed at understanding human motivation and behavior throughout the entire developmental process—from individual differences in activity level at birth to the different attitudes of young and elderly people toward dying. Clearly the range of behavior under consideration is so great, and the phenomena examined are so complex, that no investigator, no matter how knowledgeable or creative, can study every aspect of them.

Each investigator brings to the discipline a particular perspective on the subject matter; that is, the investigator's own theoretical orientation guides his or her efforts. These perspectives range from Eysenck's strong emphasis on the biological or inherited determinants of personality to Rotter's stress on the ways in which social-learning experiences affect behavior. The upshot is that each investigator generates a particular definition of personality, along with working assumptions regarding how personality operates. Many laypersons assume that the existence of competing theories in a scientific discipline indicates that the science is immature and has not accumulated a substantial body of knowledge about its subject matter (Kuhn, 1970, p. 4). However, prominent thinkers in the philosophy of science argue that it is rare for any single theory to achieve unquestioned leadership or dominance in a discipline, even in the so-called mature or hard sciences, such as physics, chemistry, and biology (Laudan, 1977, p. 134; Mayr, 1994, p. 332). In fact, a theory's scientific usefulness in solving problems is often judged by comparison with competing theories. In general, theories that are more useful and effective tend eventually to replace those that are less useful and effective (Laudan, 1977, p. 120; Smith, 1985, pp. 213–215).

DEFINING PERSONALITY

For the layperson, personality is often defined in terms of social attractiveness. The person with a good personality is one who impresses others with his or her ability to get along well with people. Beauty pageant contestants are typically judged not only on their physical attractiveness and talent, but also on their personality, here defined in terms of popularity with judges and other contestants, as well as social poise and sophistication. Some students also talk about each other in these terms: Jill is said to have a great personality, meaning that Jill behaves in ways that the perceivers find acceptable; Burt is said to have no personality, meaning that they find Burt's behavior highly objectionable. Personality is sometimes also treated as a consolation prize: Bob encourages Matt to date an ugly female because she has a great personality; Jane encourages Linda to date an ugly male because his personality makes up for his looks.

A definition of personality in terms of social attractiveness is inadequate in two major respects. First, it limits the number of behaviors and the kinds of behavior considered as aspects of personality; that is, only those kinds of behaviors that the perceivers select in making judgments about the attractiveness or unattractiveness of the perceived are regarded as part of personality. Second, it carries the absurd implication that some individuals, who obviously have unique learning histories and unique, biologically based temperament traits, are devoid of personality.

Despite the plethora of definitions, investigators generally agree that **personality** is the dynamic and organized set of characteristics of a person that uniquely influences his or her cognitions, motivations, and behaviors. It can also be thought of as a **psychological construct**—a complex abstraction that encompasses the person's unique genetic background (except in the case of identical twins) and learning history and the ways in which these factors influence his or her responses to various environments or situations. Thus, many investigators regard the study of personality as primarily the scientific analysis of individual differences that help to account for why and how people react uniquely, and often creatively, to various environmental or situational demands. The primary focus of interest in the discipline is to create theories that offer explanations for each individual's unique ways of responding to his or her physical, social, and cultural environments. These explanations then lead to predictions that are tested and buttressed by **empirical evidence.** Such theories increase our understanding of individuals and help us to predict their actions accurately.

Our ability to accurately predict an individual's behavior, because we have an adequate explanation of the factors that produce it, may prove very useful. For example, suppose that scientists learn, by verifying a theory of test anxiety, that one key factor in generating high test anxiety is a lack of adequate preparation for the exam. They also find that taking the exam in a large, crowded, stuffy classroom of several hundred students creates severe test anxiety, an inability to concentrate, and poor performance. An instructor could use this knowledge to help improve the student's performance on the next test, by changing the conditions that produced the poor performance. The instructor, for instance, could work with the student prior to the test to insure that he or she knew the materials well and could also provide a separate room for the student to take the test alone. These changes might well reduce the student's test anxiety and increase his or her chances of performing more effectively.

THE SCIENTIFIC STUDY OF PERSONALITY

Personality psychologists use the scientific approach to study individual differences because they believe it is the most effective way to gather accurate information about personality functioning. They also hope that such knowledge can be used to benefit people. In the final analysis, psychologists are convinced that a scientific orientation will lead us more directly and surely to beneficial, accurate information than will orientations that rely almost exclusively on rational speculation, mysticism, intuition, or common sense. This conviction does not mean that those alternative ways of knowing have no value and can never be used to help us understand human behavior; insights stemming from the work of philosophers, novelists, poets, and theologians certainly have their place in the totality of human self-knowledge. The discipline of personality psychology, however, is scientific in outlook.

In general terms, science is an enterprise concerned with the description, explanation, prediction, and control of events. The outcome of all the efforts by countless investigators is the accumulation of systematized knowledge based on the observation of phenomena or events. Science is grounded in human values and concerns, from which investigators select certain problems for study. At its best, this process excites their imagination and taxes their ingenuity. It is often frustrating—for example, when one's **hypotheses** (theory-based predictions) are disconfirmed—but rarely dull. To the investigator, it is definitely not the passionless, automatic, and impersonal activity imagined by the uninitiated.

Scientific researchers are interested in developing adequate theories that will organize our thinking and enable us to describe, explain, and predict phenomena in a given domain. Thus, a **theory** is a conceptual system constructed by an investigator to help make sense out of existing information and also to aid in the prediction of as yet unobserved relationships between events.

In its essence, science involves the interaction between two major processes: theory and research. A brief overview of the scientific method, including the manner in which theories are constructed and tested through empirical research, will help you to evaluate critically the specific theories presented later in this book.

BUILDING SCIENTIFIC THEORIES

Inductive versus Deductive Approaches

Inductive theories are created from a solid data base of empirical observations. They consist essentially of summary statements of observed relationships among events and contain a minimum of deductive logic (Marx, 1964, pp. 17–18). An example is the **law of effect**: performances followed by reward are strengthened, whereas those followed by punishment are weakened. This is a theoretical summary statement derived from empirical observation of the behavior of animals (mainly rats and pigeons) under reward and punishment conditions.

Advocates of the inductive approach believe that trying to create and test theories too far in advance of data collection frequently leads to useless experimentation, wasting the time and energy of researchers (Skinner, 1950, p. 194). By useless experimentation, they mean research that has little predictive accuracy or value. Such theories, they contend, contain constructs that are poorly defined and measured and that are often inaccessible to examination; thus, they generate little real knowledge. Focusing on those behaviors and performances that can be directly observed, in their view, yields substantial knowledge that increases our understanding of phenomena (Skinner, 1969, preface).

Although the inductive approach has merit, it also has limitations. Philosophers of science have contended that researchers using this approach actually do some intuitive theorizing prior to data collection, because tentative hypotheses are needed to determine what data are to be collected at a given point in an investigation (Hempel, 1966, p. 13). Also, there is no rule that can tell us when, if ever, we have collected sufficient data to justify making a theoretical generalization or summary statement (Richards, 1987, p. 50).

Most personality theorists have preferred to create and test **deductive theories.** They believe the inductive approach is too restrictive and conservative and that theories are not simply derived from facts, but are invented to account for them (Hempel, 1966, p. 13).

They also contend that deductive theories can be precisely stated and tested. Theorists who rely on this strategy use their imagination and creativity to invent hypotheses as tentative answers to problems. These hypotheses must be formulated in very precise terms in order to be testable. Thus, the deductive approach is to some extent inductive, in the sense that it involves the acceptance of a hypothesis on the basis of data that confirm it (Hempel, 1966, pp. 17–18).

Ideally, deductive theories consist of **postulates** and a set of interrelated and internally consistent **propositions,** from which specific hypotheses are derived logically and made testable by means of **operational definitions**; that is, the constructs in the hypotheses are defined in terms of the specific procedures or operations used to measure them. For example, a person's characteristic level of self-esteem may be measured by scoring his or her answers to a series of items on a questionnaire. Operational definitions are important because they allow other investigators to know precisely how the characteristics were measured, and so provide an objective basis for communication among investigators who use the constructs in their own theorizing or who want to replicate the results of another investigator's efforts.

Although sometimes considered a trivial aspect of science, **replication** is critical and necessary, because the outcomes of any research effort are considered not as facts in any absolute sense but rather as probability statements. On the basis of replication findings, investigators are better able to evaluate the worth of any one hypothesis. Successful replication tends to increase confidence in the findings; failure to replicate causes investigators to question the empirical validity of the relationship, on the assumption that the measurement procedures used to assess the constructs in the hypothesis were reliable and valid. One outcome of persistent failure to replicate is that investigators may be forced to revise their theories and perhaps make new predictions.

S-R Laws versus R-R Laws

The aim of scientific inquiry and of testing hypotheses is to establish reliable relationships between variables, or **laws.** When a particular hypothesis receives strong and repeated empirical support in research conducted by a variety of investigators who use multiple operational definitions of its constructs, scientists are likely to conclude that the relation is lawful.

In psychology, researchers seek to establish **S-R laws** and **R-R laws.** S-R (stimulus-response) laws are established when the occurrence of certain stimulus conditions results in certain outcomes or responses. S-R laws are causal: other things being equal, as the stimuli vary, the responses will vary; if the stimuli do not vary, the responses will not vary. S-R laws are typically generated by laboratory experimentation and are associated with the experimental method of research.

S-R laws allow investigators to predict and control behavior. For instance, let us conjecture that subjecting people to great stress before an exam results in their performing very poorly and that this relation between stress and test performance has been confirmed repeatedly by a variety of investigators who use multiple operational definitions of stress (for example, telling people that failing the test indicates low intelligence, or that failure on the test will be conveyed immediately to their parents, or that failing the test means they will not be accepted into graduate school) and of performance (score on a math test, or a verbal test, or a test of mechanical ability). Discovery of this lawful relation means that, if we can create stressful conditions, we can predict poor test performances. This law would enable teachers, for example, to control performance outcomes to a degree by eliminating stressful conditions prior to the test (as by assuring test takers that failure on the test will not have any of the highly negative consequences previously suggested). Under these conditions (other things being equal), grades should be improved somewhat.

R-R (response-response) laws, in contrast, are noncausal. The relationships established between variables are typically correlational in nature and are associated with the correlational method. For example, if we give people a paper-and-pencil measure of test anxiety and generate a distribution of scores on the measure, we can then use these scores to predict test performance. We could hypothesize that level of test anxiety (R_1) will be related negatively to performance (R_2). That is, we could predict that, the higher the student's test anxiety, the poorer will be his or her performance on the test. Acquisition of responses (scores) on the test anxiety measure (R_1) will ordinarily precede in time the acquisition of performance responses (R_2).

Both S-R and R-R laws can be used to predict behavior (performance on the test), but only S-R laws can be used to control behavior, because only S-R laws involve the active manipulation of environmental events or stimuli (S) as a means of producing responses (R). R-R laws simply state a reliable relationship between a variable at time 1 (R_1) and another at time 2 (R_2). Preventing people from filling out the test anxiety measure will not have any effect on the quality of their performance (Staats & Staats, 1963, pp. 20–26). Personality psychology needs both S-R and R-R laws to account adequately for personality functioning (Cronbach, 1957, p. 681).

TESTING THE THEORIES: RESEARCH METHODS

A wide variety of research techniques or procedures are available to investigators. We will focus on three major methods of empirical testing: the experimental method, correlational techniques, and case studies.

Experimental Method

In order to test hypotheses based on theory in a precise and rigorous manner, personality psychologists conduct laboratory experiments. In the **experimental method,** the investigator actively manipulates or systematically alters certain variables and checks their effects on other variables. The variables actively manipulated are called **independent variables**; the others are called **dependent variables.** In the traditional and strictest sense, such experiments demand the use of an **experimental group,** in which the independent variable is manipulated, and a **control group,** in which it is not; this permits a more accurate assessment of the effects of independent variable manipulation on the dependent variable.

By way of example, let us examine an experimental test of a specific theory: Leon Festinger's theory of **cognitive dissonance.** A major postulate in this theory of attitude change is that attitudes are learned from other people and through various media. This fundamental assumption is presented as self-evident. It is a working assumption that focuses and guides Festinger's theorizing, the kinds of propositions he sets forth, the hypotheses he generates, his choice of research methods to test the hypotheses, the kinds of data analyses he uses, and his interpretations of the data. The major propositions are that people tend to strive for consistency in their beliefs and behavior and that inconsistent or "nonfitting" cognitions about themselves or other people, inanimate objects, or events in the environment give rise to an aversive psychological state called dissonance (Festinger, 1957). Cognitions refer generally to opinions, beliefs, attitudes, behaviors, or feelings about one's environment or oneself. Festinger assumes that, once a dissonant state is generated, there will be pressures to reduce it or avoid its increase.

For example, a heavy smoker should experience dissonance when she reads that people who smoke heavily are ten times more likely to become cancer victims than are nonsmokers. She can reduce the dissonance in a variety of ways: (1) by telling herself that smoking is so enjoyable it is clearly worth the risk; (2) by reasoning that the results in the report are correlational in nature, implying that some smokers will never get cancer; (3) by arguing that smoking helps calm her nerves and that without it she would turn to other potentially self-destructive activities, such as overeating or excessive drinking; (4) by maintaining that the dangers of smoking have been exaggerated; or (5) by reducing or stopping her smoking. Such dissonance-reducing behaviors are ways of rationalizing or justifying one's actions to oneself *after* the behavior in question has occurred.

Adapting Festinger's theoretical approach, Aronson and Mettee (1968) hypothesized that, if individuals had their self-esteem lowered through an experimental manipulation, they would feel low and worthless and would therefore act consistently by behaving in a low and worthless way. Conversely, if they had their self-esteem raised by an experimental manipulation, they would feel good about themselves and worthwhile and therefore would refrain from acting inconsistently by behaving in a low and worthless way.

To test these hypotheses, the experimenters first asked all subjects to complete the same personality test. Subjects were told that the test would be evaluated by a professional counselor and that they would receive feedback about their personalities, based on their test scores, during the next laboratory meeting. Subjects were then assigned randomly to one of three conditions. In the first condition, subjects had their self-esteem heightened by receiving false feedback from the counselor indicating that they were intellectually very mature for their age. In the second condition, other subjects had their self-esteem lowered by receiving false feedback indicating that they were very selfish and materialistic. In the third condition, control subjects were told that their test had not been evaluated yet because of a backlog of work at the counseling center. All subjects then participated in a game of cards (blackjack) in which they had an opportunity to cheat if they wanted to do so.

Aronson and Mettee predicted that the subjects with lowered self-esteem would be more likely to behave in a low and worthless way by cheating at cards than would those with heightened self-esteem.

Their data strongly confirmed this prediction. Subjects with low self-esteem cheated most; control subjects cheated less; and subjects with high self-esteem cheated the least.

In this study, as in all ethically conducted research in psychology, subjects gave **informed consent** to their participation after the experimenter had warned about all aspects of the research that could conceivably have detrimental effects on them. They were told that they could not be informed in advance about the exact nature of the experimental manipulation because it might invalidate the results; that something might occur during the study that could make them temporarily unhappy; that they could quit the experiment at any time; and that the exact nature of the manipulation and the purpose of the experiment would be explained fully during a **debriefing** session immediately following the experimental session. Thus, all subjects had the option to participate or withdraw (Elmes, Kantowitz, & Roediger, 1995, pp. 57–61). Responsible research psychologists consider it important to establish an excellent rapport with study participants through the use of informed consent and debriefing procedures, because they think that data so obtained are more likely to be honest and devoid of distortion (see Jourard, 1968; Jourard & Landsman, 1980).

Correlational Method

Much of the research in personality psychology is correlational in nature; that is, it seeks to establish relationships between two variables. Is a person's ego strength (or emotional stability) related to his or her chronic anxiety level? Is there a relationship between ego strength and dominance? The **correlational method** expresses the direction and size of the relationship by a statistical device called the **correlation coefficient** (also known as Pearson's product-moment coefficient).

The direction of the correlation coefficient tells us how scores on one variable are associated with scores on the other. Positive correlations indicate that low scores on one variable are associated with low scores on the other or that high scores tend to be associated with high scores. For example, high scores on the ego-strength scale—a test designed to measure a person's ability to cope with stress effectively in the face of criticism and/or failure—are associated with high scores on a **self-report** scale of dominance, which measures a person's ability to exercise control over self and others (Campbell, 1991). Thus, dominant people tend to be high in ego strength, whereas submissive individuals tend to be low in ego strength. In short, submissive individuals are less emotionally stable. Negative correlations indicate that high scores on one variable are associated with low scores on another. An example of a negative correlation is Campbell's finding that people high in ego strength tend to have low anxiety levels, whereas individuals low in ego strength tend to have higher anxiety levels.

The size of a correlation indicates the degree of the relationship between two variables. A perfect positive correlation would be written as +1.00; a perfect negative relationship as −1.00; and a complete lack of association as .00. Perfect positive or negative correlations are, of course, rare.

Correlation coefficients do not provide us with any information about which variable *causes* the other. If we found a +.60 correlation between students' ego strength and their achievement test scores, we could not conclude that their higher scores were the result of their high ego strength. The positive correlation between the two variables could have been produced by a third variable, such as greater problem-solving ability; that is, increased problem-solving ability may cause increases in both ego strength and achievement test scores. One of the primary advantages of the experimental over the correlational method is that it allows us to make causal inferences with a higher degree of confidence.

A good example of correlational research in personality psychology is an early study by Singer (1964) designed to determine the relationship, if any, between students' use of manipulative strategies and their academic grades. This study was based on the undergraduate belief that some students get high grades by manipulating their professors. Singer asked large numbers of students to fill out a paper-and-pencil test, called the Machiavellianism Scale, designed to measure individual differences in the use of manipulative strategies in a wide variety of situations. This scale was based primarily on information adapted from Machiavelli's *The Prince,* in which a 16th-century statesman offered advice to monarchs on the proper ways to rule. Items in the scale included the following. (1) It is wise to flatter important people. (2) Never tell anyone the real reason you did something unless it is useful to do so. (3) The best way to handle people is to tell them what they want to hear (Christie & Geis, 1970).

After obtaining the test scores, Singer proceeded to correlate them with grade-point averages. He found a correlation of +.39 for the men in his sample, but not for women; this suggests that men who use manipulative strategies get higher grades. The kinds of strategies used were left unspecified. The positive correlation might be explained in other ways, however. For example, bright people might tend to be more manipulative, in which case brightness—higher academic ability—would contribute to their higher grades. This alternative was ruled out by using a partial correlation technique that allowed the investigator to hold ability test scores constant. The initial correlation was still obtained.

Thus, there remained a positive association between Machiavellian skills and high grade averages for men, but no such relationship for women. Does this mean that women do not use manipulative strategies to attain their goals? Singer proposed that women probably manipulate, too, but that they use strategies revolving around physical attractiveness rather than verbal deceit. Singer tested this idea by compiling faculty ratings of the physical attractiveness of the women in his study and then correlating these ratings with grade-point averages, with academic ability held constant. The results showed a significant correlation of +.37 for first-born women, but a nonsignificant correlation of −.04 for later-borns. Why did he find the relationship for first-borns but not for later-borns? That question could not be answered precisely and directly, but further study did show that first-born women tended to sit at the front of the class, to see the instructor after class, and to visit the instructor in the office more frequently than did later-borns. The general conclusion, then, was that college men and women probably do use manipulative strategies to secure their goals but that the kinds of strategies used differ by sex.

These results also imply that the professor is a poor soul at the mercy of students. As Singer notes, "He is seemingly caught in a maelstrom of student intrigue and machination. The picture is bleak" (1964, p. 150). However, it should be noted that, when faculty members were administered the Machiavellianism Scale, their scores were higher than the students'; in other words, the professors were even more manipulative than were their students. Perhaps, as Singer points out, the battle is not all that one-sided.

Finally, we should note that psychologists use many other correlation techniques in their research, some of which are considerably more sophisticated than the Pearson product-moment coefficient. Examples include **partial** and **multiple correlation** techniques, as well as a variety of factor analytic methods. (See Chapter 9 for the rudiments of factor analysis.)

Case-Study Method

The intensive study of an individual's life over a long period of time is called a case history, or **case study.** Such studies are frequently used in clinical and medical settings to provide descriptions and explanations of a person's actions and experiences, as well as a prescription for the treatment of the individual's problems (Runyan, 1982, p. 443). Personality studies using the experimental method examine average or typical differences between individuals, whereas the case-study procedure provides a rich—that is, complex and integrated—view of the uniqueness of the person. It accomplishes this goal by describing both the consistencies and the inconsistencies of the person's behavior, as well as the ways in which characteristic experiences are organized. Because it focuses on the unique characteristics of the individual, the data it yields are often, but not always, impossible to apply to people in general. The procedure also lacks the systematic control of variables inherent in laboratory experiments. This lack of control is a major source of weakness, because it makes causal inferences impossible. Yet the case-study method has considerable strength, because it can lead to serendipitous findings that, in turn, may lead to new testable hypotheses and research, and the development of more adequate theory.

A good example of the case-study method is Freud's analysis of Leonardo Da Vinci's personality, with special focus on his alleged homosexuality. The famous genius of the Renaissance had been accused and acquitted by authorities of forbidden sexual relations with other boys while he was an apprentice in the house of his master, Verrocchio. From this information and a few other biographical fragments, Freud brilliantly reconstructed much of Leonardo's unconscious life in an attempt to determine the truth or falsity of the accusation. Since Freud assumed that early childhood experiences were critical determinants of later personality development, he focused on Leonardo's only written account of his early life. As Leonardo described the flight of the vulture, he interrupted himself to discuss an early memory:

> It seems that it had been destined before that I should occupy myself
> so thoroughly with the vulture, for it comes to my mind as a very
> early memory, when I was still in the cradle, a vulture came down to

me, opened my mouth with his tail and struck me many times with his tail against my lips. (cited in Freud, 1947, pp. 33–34)

Freud's interpretation was that the

"tail," or "coda," is one of the most familiar symbols, as well as a substitutive designation of the male member, in Italian no less than in other languages. The situation contained in the fantasy, that a vulture opened the mouth of the child and forcefully belabored it with its tail, corresponds to the idea of fellatio, a sexual act in which the member is placed into the mouth of another person. Strangely enough, this fantasy is altogether of a passive character; it resembles certain dreams and fantasies of women and of passive homosexuals (who play the feminine part in sexual relations). (Freud, 1947, p. 381)

Freud then described this fantasy as an elaboration of another situation that he assumed everyone had experienced—namely, the pleasurable sensations derived from sucking our mother's nipples during infancy. Thus, Da Vinci's fantasy suggested to Freud that Leonardo may have been a passive homosexual whose sexual life had been inhibited by an extraordinarily close relationship with his mother in the absence of his father. "Mother," according to Freud, was depicted in Egyptian hieroglyphics by the picture of a vulture, so that Leonardo's fantasy was a memory of a time when his own mother (the vulture) held him close and kissed him passionately on the lips many times. Since the erotic feelings of the young Leonardo for his mother could not continue to develop consciously, they were repressed: in this process, Leonardo put himself in her place and then mirrored her behavior in the selection of a sexual object. Furthermore, Leonardo sublimated much of his sexual feeling by taking pretty boys into his employment as apprentices. He selected strikingly handsome boys and nursed them as his mother had protected and cared for him during his childhood.

Some people concluded Freud had proved scientifically that Leonardo Da Vinci was a homosexual because of certain early memories that the artist had reported. This conclusion is wrong. Freud has presented an interesting and ingenious but **post hoc explanation** of the dynamics of Leonardo's alleged homosexuality, based on certain information about his early life. Although Freud's intriguing formulations are intellectually stimulating, a retrospective analysis does not prove anything scientifically. Freud's own biases could have caused him to select only certain experiences from Da Vinci's life. Another investigator could analyze the same case but focus entirely on other aspects of Da Vinci's early childhood experiences and come to an entirely different conclusion.

Scientists generally prefer to conduct studies that make **a priori predictions,** that is, studies that utilize explanations to make predictions before the data are collected.

Finally, despite the arbitrariness of Freud's retrospective explanations, not all case studies are based on retrospective reports. Often they are based on data from sources less subject to the limitations of retrospective reporting, including systematic **longitudinal studies** of the individual (Runyan, 1982, p. 442).

CRITERIA FOR EVALUATING SCIENTIFIC THEORIES

Comprehensiveness   There seems to be general agreement among theoreticians that a theory that encompasses and accounts for a wider range and diversity of data is better and more useful than a theory that explains only a more limited range of phenomena. Thus, a good theory should meet the test of **comprehensiveness.** For example, all else being equal, a theory that explains both mature and romantic (immature) love is preferable to one that explains only romantic love. The reason is that science is generally interested in accumulating knowledge that is organized and integrated and explains the interrelationships between a variety of phenomena.

Since no theory can cover all the phenomena related to human personality, decisions must be made concerning the importance of the events to be studied. For example, is it more important that the theory adequately describe and explain eyelid conditioning or human aggression? The answer seems obvious: an understanding of aggression would allow us to account for behaviors that have important implications for human welfare, whereas an understanding of eyeblinking would not seem to tell us much worth knowing. Yet we should exercise some caution in making this judgment until we hear the other side of the argument. Many scientists maintain that in science there is no unambiguous criterion that allows us safely to exclude phenomena from study on the basis of triviality. What may be a trivial undertaking to one investigator may be an important area of research to another. Furthermore, and more importantly, work on a seemingly trivial problem may bear fruit at some future time. In the eyeblink example, an understanding of the parameters or characteristics that control eyeblinking could give us information about the principles of classical conditioning, principles that can be used to explain the origins of many irrational fears and phobias.

As you can see, there is no clear-cut answer to this problem. One prominent personality theorist, Salvatore Maddi, has suggested that investigators can minimize the risk of triviality by relying on naturalistic observation of human behavior—that is, by studying people in their daily surroundings and, to a lesser extent, in therapeutic settings (Maddi, 1989, pp. 616–617). On this basis, we can make tentative judgments about the worth of personality theories in terms of comprehensiveness.

Precision and testability   Besides being comprehensive, a good theory should contain constructs that are clearly and explicitly defined. Scientists want explanations that are stated in clear language. A theory that is couched in muddied language is difficult to comprehend and not very useful. It lessens the chances for clear and effective communication among scientists and hinders scientific progress. Besides having constructs that are clearly defined, a good theory should also contain **relational statements** or propositions that are consistent and logically related to one another. It is generally recognized that, in the early stages of theorizing, investigators may rely heavily on analogies and metaphors as an aid to thought—examples include Jung's "shadow," which lurks around in the darkness of the collective unconscious, and Freud's treatment of the ego as a battlefield where mortal combat takes place between the forces of the id and superego—but in the final analysis these may create inconsistencies and ambiguities that hamper understanding. An adequate scientific theory should meet the criterion of **precision.**

Not only must the constructs and relational statements in the theory be defined precisely, but the hypotheses containing them must be capable of being studied empirically; that is, they must be linked at some point with external reality. The link between conceptualization and observation is accomplished by means of operational definitions. In brief, a good theory is also judged by the **testability** of its hypotheses.

Parsimony   A good theory should be parsimonious, or economical; that is, the theory should contain only those constructs, relational statements, and assumptions necessary for the explanation of the phenomena within its domain. The inclusion of unnecessary constructs or assumptions can lead an investigator to waste great amounts of effort studying meaningless relationships. A theory that contains more constructs and assumptions than necessary fails to meet the test of **parsimony.** Conversely, however, the parsimony criterion cannot be met simply by minimizing the number of constructs and assumptions. Such a theory would be too simplistic and would not do justice to the complexity of the phenomena. Instead, a theory is parsimonious only if it adequately accounts for the complexity of the phenomena to be explained.

Empirical validity   A good theory must have **empirical validity**; that is, it must have data that support it. This is a key function of theory. Empirical validity is determined by testing hypotheses—that is, by making observations to determine if the investigator's predictions are accurate. Of course, establishing the theory's empirical validity is far from easy. First, theories are never proven (or disproven) in any absolute sense. They are only indirectly tested, on the basis of hypotheses derived from them. Second, research findings obtained by testing hypotheses are always determined statistically, that is, in terms of probability. For example, researchers may want to know if a relationship or correlation between two variables that they predict is real or whether it could simply have been a chance occurrence. The concept of **statistical significance** is used to answer this question. A statistically significant result is one that has a low probability of occurring by chance alone. Traditionally, a result is considered statistically significant if the probability that it is a chance finding is 5 in 100 or less (written $p < .05$). A probability of 1 in 100 (written $p < .01$) would mean that there is even less likelihood that the result is due to chance alone. If it is unlikely that a result is due to chance, then that result must be due to factors that are not chance, but rather are systematic. Systematic factors or variables are those that are embedded in the hypothesis. For example, Kaczor, Ryckman, Thornton, and Kuehnel (1991) were interested in testing the hypothesis that students higher in hypercompetitiveness would attribute more blame to a rape victim for her own victimization than would students lower in hypercompetitiveness. The correlation between the two factors or variables was .35, $p < .01$; in other words, male and female subjects higher in hypercompetitiveness assigned more blame to the rape victim for the occurrence of the crime than did subjects lower in hypercompetitiveness. The likelihood that this result is due to chance is only 1 in 100; thus, this is regarded as a systematic result and not a chance finding.

Along with statistical significance, successful replications of findings in various studies increase our confidence in those findings. Conversely, successive failures to replicate make us even less certain that the relationship exists.

Third, determining the validity of a hypothesis depends on the reliability and validity of the measures used to assess the constructs. Theorists sometimes argue that their constructs have been measured poorly or not at all and, therefore, failure to confirm hypotheses should not invalidate the theory. Such claims may or may not be legitimate. On the one hand, the measurement procedures may be unreliable and error-ridden. On the other hand, a few theorists and their advocates have such strongly vested interests in their own formulations that they dismiss out of hand any evidence to the contrary, on the grounds of inadequate measurement. Such self-serving statements run counter to the ideals of science, however, and in the long run are overruled by the body of evidence accumulated by independent researchers.

Heuristic value   A good theory has **heuristic value,** in that it stimulates and provokes investigators to do further theorizing and research. The heuristic value of theories may spring from several sources. For example, a theory may arouse researchers' intellectual curiosity; in seeking answers to the questions it raises, they pursue new paths that may prove enlightening and useful. Another theory may be so reasonable that investigators simply accept it at first and seek to utilize and test it. However, with the subsequent collection of large amounts of disconfirming data, researchers may seek to revise it in order to increase its predictive accuracy. Thus, new theory and research may result. Finally, investigators may examine another theory and think it inadequate, wrong, or absurd in its explanation of phenomena. Their disbelief, resistance, and even hostility may lead to a concerted effort to demonstrate its falsehood, thereby generating new conceptualizations and explanations of the same phenomena.

Applied value   Finally, a good theory has **applied value**; that is, it leads to new approaches to the solution of people's problems (Kelly, 1955, p. 24). This criterion is not universally endorsed by scientists, especially by those who work in experimental psychology. Yet it seems particularly germane to the area of personality. There can be little question that an adequate theory of personality will focus on abnormal as well as normal development and that helping people to overcome their problems is an overriding concern of virtually all personality psychologists.

Equipped with information about the essential ingredients of the scientific process and the standards used to evaluate scientific theories, we are now in a position to examine the major theoretical approaches to personality.

DISCUSSION QUESTIONS

1. Why is the definition of personality in terms of social attractiveness inadequate for use by psychologists?
2. How would you define personality more adequately?
3. What is science? In what ways does the scientific enterprise involve the use of theory and research?
4. Why do most psychologists use the scientific approach to study individual differences?
5. Discuss some of the inadequacies of the common-sense approach to the study of behavior, as compared to the scientific approach.
6. Discuss the importance of operational definitions and replication in the study of personality.
7. What are the basic elements of the experimental method?
8. What is the correlational method, and when and how is it used in the investigation of scientific problems?
9. Explain the differences between the experimental and case-study methods.
10. List and describe six criteria commonly used by investigators for the evaluation of scientific theories. Can you think of any others?

GLOSSARY

a priori predictions   Predictions about the outcome of an investigation that are made *before* the data are collected.

applied value   Criterion or standard for judging the scientific worth of a theory: an adequate theory is capable of providing creative solutions to problems that are of interest and concern to people. For example, a theory might specify the different kinds of parental discipline that lead to the development of physically and psychologically healthy or unhealthy children. If the theory has considerable data to support it, then parents could adopt the kinds of discipline (for example, praise for their children when they exhibit helpful behavior, encouragement for cooperative behavior during play activities) that lead to healthy development and avoid or eliminate the kinds of discipline (for example, physical and verbal abuse, praise for aggressive behavior) that lead to unhealthy development. Such a theory therefore would have high applied value: it would help people to raise children who are psychologically healthy.

case study   Research technique involving the intensive study of a single person in order to understand his or her unique behavior.

cognitive dissonance   Painful motivational state created within a person when two or more thoughts, attitudes, or behaviors are mutually inconsistent.

comprehensiveness   Criterion or standard for judging the worth of a scientific theory: theories are judged as more adequate and useful if they encompass and account for a wide range and variety of phenomena.

control group   In an experiment, the group that does not receive the experimental treatment. A control group is designed to provide baseline data against which the effects of the experimental manipulation on the dependent variable can be accurately judged.

correlation coefficient   A numerical index of the size and direction of an association between two variables.

correlational method   General procedure for establishing an association or relationship between events. Statistics involving correlations can vary in complexity from simple correlation coefficients to complicated factor analyses.

debriefing   Informing subjects of the true nature and purpose of a study after it is completed.

deductive theories   Theories in which specific hypotheses are derived from abstract propositions and then tested by the collection of data.

dependent variables   Changes in behavior that occur as a result of the manipulation of conditions by an experimenter.

empirical evidence   Observations of phenomena made by investigators.

empirical validity   Criterion or standard for judging the worth of a scientific theory: the theory's hypotheses are tested by the collection of data to determine whether or not they are accurate. Confirmation of the hypotheses tends to lend support to the theory; disconfirmation of the hypotheses, if repeated, tends eventually to decrease confidence in the theory.

experimental group   The group of subjects who experience the intentional alteration of factors in an experiment.

experimental method   Scientific method for studying cause-and-effect relationships between variables. It involves the manipulation of independent variables and observation of the effects of the manipulation on dependent variables.

heuristic value   Criterion or standard for judging the scientific worth of a theory: an adequate theory should be challenging; it should stimulate new ideas and new research.

hypotheses   Tentative theoretical statements about how events are related to one another, often stated as predictions about how the operation of one set of events will affect the operation of others.

independent variables   The variables actively manipulated by the experimenter so that their effects on individual behavior can be observed.

inductive theories   Generalizations or summary statements about phenomena derived from a set of facts.

informed consent   The practice of telling subjects about the nature of their participation in a proposed experiment and then obtaining their written agreement to participate.

law of effect   The principle that a behavior becomes more probable when it is followed by a positive reinforcer, whereas it becomes less probable when it is followed by a punisher.

laws   Systematic and highly reliable associations between variables.

longitudinal studies   Studies in which data are collected on the same individuals over time so that investigators can determine the direction and extent of changes in their behavior.

multiple correlation   Statistical technique by which it is possible to determine the relationship between one variable and a combination of two or more other variables simultaneously.

operational definitions   Procedures or operations used to define particular constructs. For example, intelligence could be operationally defined in terms of a person's scores on a verbal reasoning test.

parsimony   Criterion or standard for judging the scientific worth of a theory: an adequate theory should be as parsimonious, or economical, as possible, while still adequately accounting for the phenomena in its domain.

partial correlation   A correlational technique that allows an investigator to assess the relationship between two events by eliminating, or "partialing out," the influence of a third variable.

personality   The term used by personality psychologists to describe the uniqueness of the individual. Personality involves judgments regarding who the person truly is and how she or he differs from other people. Particular biological tendencies and social and cultural learning experiences combine to determine the person's uniqueness.

post hoc explanation   Explanation of a phenomenon given *after* its occurrence. The explanation presumes that certain factors caused the phenomenon, but there is no evidence that they actually did so.

postulates   The fundamental or core assumptions of a theory. They are taken as self-evidently true in order to provide a clear and focused direction for theorizing and research. They specify which phenomena will be addressed by the theory and which won't be addressed. For example, one theory of aggression could postulate that aggression is learned behavior, whereas another could postulate that it is genetically based. Reliance on the assumption that it is learned would lead the theorist and investigators to focus their energies and attention on the environmental conditions that produce it and not on its instinctive origins. Reliance on the assumption that it is genetically based would focus attention on its biological roots and not on its environmental causes.

precision   Criterion or standard for judging the scientific worth of a theory: an adequate theory should contain constructs and relational statements that are clearly and explicitly stated and measured.

propositions   General relational statements that may be true or false. They are not tested directly; instead, hypotheses are derived from them. The hypotheses—specific propositions containing constructs that are operationalized—can be tested and confirmed or disconfirmed through empirical testing.

psychological construct   A highly complex abstraction that encompasses a variety of components or dimensions. For example, intelligence is a construct that encompasses reasoning ability, spatial ability, mechanical ability, mathematical ability, and so forth.

relational statements   Theoretical propositions or hypotheses that link or relate constructs. For example, the constructs of frustration and aggression might be linked as follows: increases in frustration lead to increases in aggressive behavior.

replication   Duplication or repetition of an experiment or study to determine whether or not the original findings are reliable.

R-R laws   Highly reliable, but noncausal, linkages between variables.

self-report   An individual's written or oral description of his or her own behavior.

S-R laws   Causal connections between variables such that manipulation of one variable produces changes in another.

statistical significance   A numerical index of the probability that a particular result occurred by chance.

testability   Criterion or standard for judging the scientific worth of a theory: an adequate theory must contain hypotheses that can be defined clearly, measured precisely, and confirmed or disconfirmed in terms of observable events.

theory   A number of interrelated conceptual statements that are created by investigators to account for a phenomenon or a set of phenomena.

SUGGESTED READINGS

Elmes, D. G., Kantowitz, B. H., & Roediger, H. L., III (1995). *Research methods in psychology* (5th ed.). St. Paul, MN: West.

Heiman, G. A. (1995). *Research methods in psychology.* Boston, MA: Houghton Mifflin.

Liebert, R. M., & Liebert, L. L. (1995). *Science and behavior* (4th ed.). Englewood Cliffs, NJ: Prentice Hall.

REFERENCES

Aronson, E., & Mettee, D. K. (1968). Dishonest behavior as a function of differential levels of induced self-esteem. *Journal of Personality and Social Psychology, 9,* 121–127.

Campbell, J. F. (1991). The primary personality factors of Hawaiian middle adolescents. *Psychological Reports, 68,* 3–26.

Christie, R., & Geis, F. L. (1970). *Studies in Machiavellianism.* New York: Academic Press.

Cronbach, L. J. (1957). The two disciplines of scientific psychology. *American Psychologist, 12,* 679–684.

Elmes, D. G., Kantowitz, B. H., & Roediger, H. L., III (1995). *Research methods in psychology* (5th ed.). St. Paul, MN: West.

Festinger, L. (1957). *A theory of cognition.* Evanston, IL: Row, Peterson.

Freud, S. (1947). *Leonardo Da Vinci: A study in psychosexuality* (A. A. Brill, Trans.). New York: Random House.

Hempel, C. G. (1966). *Philosophy of natural science.* Englewood Cliffs, NJ: Prentice Hall.

Jourard, S. (1968). *Disclosing man to himself.* New York: Van Nostrand Reinhold.

Jourard, S., & Landsman, T. (1980). *Healthy personality: An approach from the viewpoint of humanistic psychology.* New York: Macmillan.

Kaczor, L. M., Ryckman, R. M., Thornton, B., & Kuehnel, R. H. (1991). Observer hypercompetitiveness and victim precipitation of rape. *Journal of Social Psychology, 131,* 131–134.

Kelly, G. A. (1955). *The psychology of personal constructs* (Vol. 1). New York: Norton.

Kuhn, T. S. (1970). *The structure of scientific revolutions* (2nd ed.). Chicago: University of Chicago Press.

Laudan, L. (1977). *Progress and its problems: Towards a theory of scientific growth.* Berkeley: University of California Press.

Maddi, S. R. (1989). *Personality theories: A comparative analysis* (5th ed.). Pacific Grove, CA: Brooks/Cole.

Marx, M. H. (1964). The general nature of theory construction. In M. H. Marx (Ed.), *Theories in contemporary psychology* (pp. 4–46). New York: Macmillan.

Mayr, E. (1994). The advance of science and scientific revolutions. *Journal of the History of the Behavioral Sciences, 30,* 328–334.

Richards, S. (1987). *Philosophy and sociology of science: An introduction* (2nd ed.). Oxford: Basil Blackwell.

Runyan, W. (1982). In defense of the case study method. *American Journal of Orthopsychiatry, 52,* 440–446.

Singer, J. E. (1964). The use of manipulative strategies: Machiavellianism and attractiveness. *Sociometry, 27,* 128–150.

Skinner, B. F. (1950). Are theories of learning necessary? *Psychological Review, 57,* 193–216.

Skinner, B. F. (1969). *Contingencies of reinforcement.* New York: Appleton Century Crofts.

Smith, L. (1985). Problems and progress in the philosophy of science: An essay review. *Journal of the History of the Behavioral Sciences, 21,* 208–216.

Staats, A. W., & Staats, C. K. (1963). *Complex human behavior: A systematic extension of learning principles.* New York: Holt, Rinehart & Winston.

PART TWO

PSYCHOANALYTIC AND NEOANALYTIC PERSPECTIVES

Only a few people in human history have generated work so creative and provocative that it shapes the course of human values and thought. Copernicus, the eminent 16th-century Polish astronomer, was one such individual; his discovery that the Earth was not the center of the universe forced us to reexamine our beliefs about our own omnipotence and omniscience. Darwin, the English naturalist of the 19th century, was another; his work forced us to realize that we too are part of the natural world and are governed to some extent by our biology.

Sigmund Freud belongs in this august company, because he compelled us to acknowledge that we are often driven to act impulsively and irrationally by unconscious conflicts of a sexual and aggressive nature. Scholars in the humanistic tradition of Western thought, which emphasized rationality and the virtues of ethical conduct, were shocked to learn that human beings are often irrational and that they continuously engage in internal struggles to keep their sexual and aggressive impulses in check. Freud bared the baseness of the human soul for everyone to see, and some people have never forgiven him. He removed us from our pedestals and forced us to examine the dark side of our natures.

At first, he was publicly reviled and scorned. Eventually, however, investigators in many disciplines began to explore the validity of his theory. Today, Freud's influence is worldwide. Scholars in literature are fond of using psychoanalytic constructs or concepts to explain the motives of fictional characters. Psychological anthropologists focus on child-rearing practices in various cultures and often use a Freudian model to understand adult personality. Philosophers and sociologists have used the Freudian concepts of repression and anxiety in their analyses of problems confronting modern society. Freudian concepts have also been adopted by laypeople. We are all aware of the importance of Freudian slips and the ways in which the unconscious influences behavior. Sometimes we talk glibly about ego trips, phallic symbols, penis envy, and Oedipal conflicts; we might speak of getting it all out when we are angry. In short, Freudian thinking has had a revolutionary impact on our lives. Whether we ultimately accept or reject his view of human behavior and functioning, Freud has clearly earned his place in history.

In Chapter 2, we review the basic concepts of Freud's theory. We examine his attempts to construct a theory of personality based on interpretations of self-reports by his patients. We describe the basic constructs (the unconscious, preconscious, and conscious; the life and death instincts; the id, ego, and superego), how they interact to produce internal conflicts, and the various defense mechanisms used to protect the ego and reduce the anxiety generated by these conflicts. We review Freud's theory of psychosexual development, with special emphasis on the origins and nature of the various character disorders. We then consider the research evidence for the theory of psychosexual development and show how Freud's theory can be applied to cases involving psychopathology, including obsessive-compulsive neurosis. We conclude this chapter—as we do each of the chapters that follow—with an analysis of the strengths and weaknesses of the theory.

In Chapter 3, we turn to Carl Jung, and examine the nature of the individual psyche—all the interacting systems within the human personality that account for the mental life and behavior of the person, and the life process energy that motivates the person to action. Although both Freud and Jung used the term *libido* to describe the energy that propels the person into action, Jung's conceptualization was much broader than Freud's. Jung thought of libido not simply as sexual impulses that try to force their way into consciousness, but as forces that are generated by continuous conflicts within the psyche and that can split and move erratically through the psyche in unpredictable ways; at times these forces result in bizarre and impulsive behavior. This conceptualization adds a certain mystery to the person; if a person's behavior is determined by autonomous forces, which often operate capriciously, outside observers cannot pinpoint its causes.

Following the discussion of Jung's libido, we examine the major structures of the psyche and describe the evolution of the self as the conflicts between the various oppositional forces are resolved via transcendence. Jung believed that, in the attempt to evolve toward selfhood, people adopt different orientations or attitudes toward life and utilize different psychological processes or functions to make sense of their experiences. Eventually he combined the attitudes and functions in a theoretical scheme of psychological types and discussed the ways in which introverted and extraverted individuals try to deal with the world and their own conflicts. We present this theoretical scheme in considerable detail, review the current research evidence based on it, and then examine Jung's views of disordered behavior and therapy.

In contrast to Freud and Jung, Alfred Adler presented a simplified scheme to account for the development of personality. Adler, whose work is the subject of Chapter 4, came to believe that all individuals felt inferior and strove to overcome these feelings and to become superior. Neurotic strivings were associated with attempts to achieve personal superiority at the expense of others, whereas healthy strivings entailed a quest for perfection or completion via efforts to improve the lot of others. Although Adler emphasized human rationality and consciousness in making decisions and the ways in which our goals inspire us to improve ourselves, his position was not totally optimistic. Never able to break completely with his Freudian origins, he concluded that our lifestyles are formed to a considerable extent by the end of our fifth year, with the implication that fundamental change is very difficult to achieve after early childhood.

Despite his adherence to this aspect of Freudian theory, however, the general tone of Adler's writings is optimistic. In Chapter 4, we see his essential humanism, his socialist political orientation, and his persistent attempts to help oppressed people. In particular, we focus on Adler's concept of social interest—his belief in an innate human need to help others and his vision of an ideal society in which cooperation, harmony, and equality would be the rule. We then outline his other major concepts and review his theory of personality development, with special emphasis on his birth-order concept and the research based upon it. Finally, we examine his view of abnormal development and the application of Adler's theory to the treatment of psychopathology.

In Chapter 5, we present the major concepts and principles of Karen Horney's revisionist view of Freudian theory. Her theory posits disturbed relationships between parents and their children as the primary cause of neurosis. Neurotics are pictured as insecure individuals with rigid, compulsive needs and strivings that are designed to reestablish the safety of their environments. Unfortunately, these strivings are almost invariably unsuccessful; for the individual, the result is conflict and pain on an unconscious level and also inefficient problem solving. According to Horney, neurotics are alienated from their real selves and from other people. They identify with a false, idealized self in order to avoid the pain of acknowledging their limitations. In Chapter 5, we chronicle the development of this alienation process and the therapeutic procedures Horney used to reduce alienation and to release the individual's potential for growth.

In Chapter 6, we examine the concepts and principles of Erik Erikson's psychoanalytic ego psychology. Erikson's theory systematically extends Freud's view of the role played by the ego in personality development and functioning. In contrast to Freud, Erikson saw the ego as often operating autonomously from id motivations—as an entity with nondefensive functions that helps people adapt constructively to the demands of their surroundings. Our primary focus is on Erikson's dynamic theory of ego development and functioning; we pay particular attention to the crises experienced by adolescents as they try to establish their identities and by young adults who are seeking to establish intimate and long-lasting relationships. In Erikson's view, the major disturbance during adolescence is role confusion based on an inability to decide on an occupational identity. In young adulthood, the primary disturbance centers on a sense of isolation based on an inability to love and cherish another person in a personal relationship. We present considerable research support for Erikson's theorizing about these crises, as well as the rapidly accumulating evidence concerning his views about middle and late adulthood. We also consider his techniques for assessing personality, review his pioneering efforts in the psychohistorical analysis of important historical figures, and examine the application of his theory of ego development to the treatment of abnormal behavior.

Finally, in Chapter 7, we review the newest variant of psychoanalytic theory—the self psychology of Heinz Kohut. Unlike Freud, Kohut did not see human beings as driven relentlessly by sexual and aggressive instincts. Instead, he believed that pathological sexual and aggressive behavior occurs as a result of damage to the self, which originally occurs early in family life. In Kohut's view, unempathic parents who fail to provide adequate nurturance, support, and understanding seriously hinder children's ability to develop a self that is realistic and capable of initiating creative action.

Whereas Freud thought that the basic direction of development was set by the end of the fifth year, Kohut took a broader view: he argued that changes in the self can occur throughout the life span. However, he focused mainly on developmental changes from infancy through adolescence. In the developmental process, Kohut's emphasis is on the ways in which narcissism can give rise to either a healthy or an unhealthy adult personality. In Chapter 7, we are most concerned with his explanation of psychopathology in terms of narcissistic personality disorders. Thus, we present his views on narcissism in detail, and review the research support for them. We also present Kohut's discovery of the self-object transferences, which provide a new, in-depth understanding of the origins and cure of a variety of psychological disorders.

CHAPTER 2

Freud's Psychoanalytic Theory

BIOGRAPHICAL SKETCH

Sigmund Freud was born in 1856 in the town of Freiburg, Moravia (now Czechoslovakia), of Jewish parents. His father was a wool merchant who married twice. Sigmund, the oldest son of the second wife, had five sisters and two brothers. He was a serious boy who excelled in his studies throughout his early schooling. He could repeat verbatim a page in a book he had read and record almost the entire content of scientific lectures after he heard them. He read voraciously the works of great playwrights, poets, and philosophers, including Goethe, Shakespeare, Kant, Hegel, Schopenhauer, and Nietzsche. His love of books, in fact, led him to run up a debt at a bookstore that he had no means to settle—an indiscretion for which his father, hard-pressed for money, could find no sympathy (Puner, 1947, pp. 46–47).

Upon entering the University of Vienna, he reluctantly decided on a medical career and was graduated in 1883. He maintained that he never felt comfortable playing the "doctor game," but he was impressed with the scientific attitude of people in the medical profession. Freud yearned to solve the great problems of the world and to learn all he could about human nature (Jones, 1963, pp. 3–4, 22); he perceived that science provided the means of satisfying such yearnings.

During his medical school days, Freud came under the influence of the eminent physiologist Ernst Brucke and worked as his assistant on neurological problems in lower animals. Although quite content in his work at Brucke's laboratory, Freud soon realized that his chances for advancement were poor and that the monetary rewards would always be minimal. Since he was seriously interested in a lovely young woman at the time and believed he should be earning enough money to support her before he committed himself to marriage, Freud, with Brucke's friendly encouragement, left the laboratory and entered private medical practice. Shortly afterward, in 1885, he applied for, and obtained, a postgraduate traveling stipend to work with the renowned French neurologist Jean Charcot in Paris on the treatment of nervous disorders. Elated, he wrote to his fiancée, then living in Hamburg:

> Oh, how wonderful it is going to be. I am coming with money and am staying a long while with you and am bringing something lovely for you and shall then go to Paris and become a great savant and return to Vienna with a great, great nimbus. Then we will marry soon and I will cure all the incurable nervous patients and you will keep me well and I will kiss you till you are merry and happy—and they lived happily ever after. (Jones, 1963, p. 50)

In fact, Freud and Martha Bernays were married in 1886 and lived happily for more than half a century.

Upon his return to private practice, Freud developed a mentor relationship with a physician named Breuer and, under his influence, began using hypnosis. Breuer had treated a young woman, Anna O., for a group of physical symptoms—including paralysis of the limbs and disturbances of sight and speech—that had arisen in connection with the death of her father. Breuer found, to his astonishment, that the woman's symptoms disappeared if she talked about them while in a hypnotic trance. In this state, she would relive the terrifying experiences that gave rise to her symptoms and express the accompanying emotions fully. This physical expression of emotion he labeled a **catharsis.** Eventually Freud and Breuer severed their relationship because of Freud's insistence that the basis of such disorders was sexual (Jones, 1963, pp. 147, 165).

Freud used the cathartic method in his treatment for several years but, finding that many patients could not be hypnotized, he began asking them to concentrate on a particular symptom and to try to recall any early experiences that might explain its origins. Between 1892 and 1895, he gradually developed the method of free association, in which he asked his patients to express every thought that occurred to them, no matter how irrelevant, unimportant, or unpleasant (Jones, 1963, pp. 157–158). Although the patients' recollections seemed aimless and accidental, Freud felt intuitively that there must be some definite force controlling them. Thoroughly trained in medicine and neurology to accept the principles of **determinism** and causality, Freud could not bring himself to believe that his patients' thoughts were unrelated. In addition, Freud was impressed by the unwillingness of many patients to disclose memories that were painful to them. He labeled this opposition **resistance** and came to believe that his patients were repressing certain important memories. His job, then, was to probe their unconscious and uncover the reasons for their active resistance.

In the course of his analyses, Freud also discovered that patients insisted on tracing the origins of their traumatic experiences to early childhood. To his surprise, he found that many of these memories involved sexual experiences. Until this time, most people believed that childhood was a time of innocence, devoid of sexual urges. Freud disagreed strongly:

> We do wrong entirely to ignore the sexual life of children; in my experience children are capable of all the mental and many of the physical activities. Just as the whole sexual apparatus of man is not comprised in the external genital organs and the two reproductive glands, so his sexual life does not begin only with the onset of puberty, as to casual observation it may appear to do. (Jones, 1963, p. 172)

Freud at first believed that the early childhood seduction scenes described to him by his patients were literally true. Eventually, however, he began to have doubts. He found it difficult to believe, for example, that all his female patients' fathers were sexually perverse. He also found that literal acceptance of these accounts and subsequent suggestion to the patients of how they must deal with them did not always have therapeutic benefits. He wrote in a letter to a friend that he had to renounce his explanations of hysteria and his hopes of becoming a famous physician. But he eventually faced up to the situation and revised his **libido theory**; he concluded that the descriptions were not literally true but fantasies that were nevertheless psychically real and valid in their own right (Jones, 1963, pp. 172–173).

Freud also discovered that patients often mentioned their dreams. He found that dreams provided the best means of unlocking the secrets of the unconscious, and could yield invaluable information about the nature of the person's conflicts and the mechanisms by which they were concealed from awareness (Jones, 1963, p. 129). In 1900, Freud published *The Interpretation of Dreams,* in which he contended that dreaming was neither an idle activity nor as chaotic as it seemed. Rather, he proposed, dreams serve as wish-fulfillment devices, and their latent content can be used to help a patient understand his or her problems.

In 1902, Freud founded the Vienna Psycho-Analytical Society, a small group of scholars from various disciplines who met in his office to discuss their work. As the membership grew, meetings were held in larger, more formal settings. The period 1905–1906 was highly productive for Freud; he published several books, including *Jokes and Their Connection with the Unconscious, The Psychopathology of Everyday Life,* and *Three Essays on the Theory of Sexuality,* as well as some articles. *Three Essays,* in particular, made Freud almost universally unpopular. The book was labeled "shockingly wicked," and Freud was branded as a man with an obscene and evil mind. The principal focus of the criticism was Freud's assertion that children are born with sexual urges and that their parents are selected as their first sexual objects. Freud believed that he was right, however, and that eventually his arguments would be accepted (Jones, 1963, pp. 240–243).

By 1910, Freud had gained an international reputation, but internal dissension concerning his libido theory had arisen within the Psycho-Analytical Society. The defections began with Adler and Stekel; they were followed by Jung and others. Disagreeing fundamentally with Freud, Adler minimized the importance of the sexual factor in determining behavior and elevated the concept of a struggle for power in its place. He also deemphasized or discarded the concepts of repression, the unconscious, and infantile sexuality. Such major differences led inevitably to a separation between the two men. The split with Jung was much more distressing for Freud, who had been closer personally to Jung and believed him superior to Adler in intellect and knowledge (Jones, 1963, pp. 313–314, 318).

Jung was disturbed by Freud's uncompromising treatment of sexuality in his public discussions of patients' neuroses.

> We should do well not to burst out with the theory of sexuality in the foreground. I have many thoughts about that, especially on the ethical aspects of the question. I believe that in publicly announcing certain things one would saw off the branch on which civilization rests; one undermines the impulse of sublimation. . . . Both with the students and with the patients, I get on further by not making the theme of sexuality prominent. (Jones, 1963, pp. 318–319)

Eventually, Jung deemphasized the sexual factor in the development of neurosis. He considered libido, or sexual energy, as a designation of general tension and rejected Freud's belief that the Oedipal conflict involved incestuous yearnings on the part of the child. But despite the defection of some of his disciples, whose positions came to be known as the **neoanalytic perspective,** Freud's fame continued to grow, and the Psycho-Analytical Society flourished.

World War I had a profound impact on Freud's thinking and research. Acutely distressed by the mass killing and suffering, he eventually came to attribute these experiences to a universal death instinct. Despite his pessimism about the future of humankind, however, Freud continued to elaborate his ideas in a long series of books, including *Totem and Taboo* (1913), *Introductory Lectures on Psychoanalysis* (1917), *Beyond the Pleasure Principle* (1920), *The Ego and the Id* (1923), *Future of an Illusion* (1927), *Civilization and Its Discontents* (1930), *New Introductory Lectures on Psychoanalysis* (1933), and *An Outline of Psychoanalysis* (published posthumously in 1940). In the early 1930s, Hitler came to power and anti-Semitism flourished. Freud's books were burned in Berlin, and his supporters urged him to flee Vienna. With the Nazi invasion of Austria in 1938, Freud reluctantly left his home and took up residence in London. He died there on September 23, 1939. During the last few years of his life, Freud suffered from cancer of the jaw and mouth. Despite more than 30 operations, he persisted in his work until the very end.

CONCEPTS AND PRINCIPLES

The Role of Conscious, Preconscious, and Unconscious Forces in Personality

Freud's fundamental assumption about our mental life was that it is divided into three parts: the **conscious,** the **preconscious,** and the **unconscious.** The conscious refers to those ideas and sensations of which we are aware. It operates on the surface of personality and plays a relatively small role in personality development and functioning. While it is true that psychologically healthy people have a greater awareness of their experiences than do unhealthy ones, still Freud believed that even relatively mature people are governed, to a degree greater than they would care to admit, by unconscious needs and conflicts.

The preconscious contains those experiences that are unconscious but that could become conscious with little effort. For example, you may have forgotten the foods you had for supper yesterday, but you could probably recall them readily if you were asked to list them for a dietician who is trying to help you lose weight. The preconscious exists just beneath the surface of awareness.

In contrast, the unconscious operates on the deepest level of personality. It consists of those experiences and memories of which we are not aware. Such mental states remain out of awareness because making them conscious would create tremendous pain and anxiety for us. The unconscious could include sexual abuse that we experienced during early childhood at the hands of a parent, relative, or family friend. It could consist of incestuous feelings, strong emotional reactions of anger or rage toward certain authority figures, or painful feelings of shame and humiliation growing out of competitive experiences. A key point is that such repressed memories do not simply disappear once they have been thrust from awareness; they continue to operate outside awareness, and seek expression in various defensive, disguised, and distorted ways. Thus, unconscious ideas, memories, and experiences may continually interfere with conscious and rational behavior.

Finally, while it is impossible to make these unconscious experiences fully conscious, their existence can be clarified through the use of psychoanalytic therapeutic procedures. In a sense, if therapy works, the person becomes more conscious or aware of the nature of these forces than he or she was at the beginning of therapy (Freud, 1960a, pp. 3–8).

Instincts: The Driving Forces in Personality

Rooted in the unconscious are the instincts, which, in Freud's view, largely govern our behavior. Instinctual drives are initiated when bodily needs motivate people to seek gratification, so that bodily processes can return to their prior state of equilibrium or homeostasis. Painful feelings are associated with instinctual stimulation, and pleasurable feelings are associated with a decrease in this stimulation.

Instincts have four basic characteristics: (1) a *source* in some bodily deficit; (2) an *aim*—gratification of the need; (3) an *impetus* that propels the person to act; and (4) an *object* through which the instinct achieves its aim. As Freud perceived it, many objects in the external world can provide gratification of our biological needs. Also, instincts are changeable; that is, they can move from object to object in their attempt to gain maximum gratification. For example, a college man may find a new girlfriend to love if his relationship with his current companion is not satisfying; a woman who has hostile feelings toward her boss, but is unable to express them because she fears the loss of her job, may come home and behave aggressively toward her family. Instincts can even turn inward on the individual, as when a person's aggressive feelings toward others are turned toward self and result in acts of self-mutilation or even suicide. Sexual impulses can also be turned inward, as when an individual becomes self-absorbed and narcissistic and utilizes masturbation as the primary sexual outlet.

Life instincts   Freud theorized that each person has instinctive urges that seek to preserve life. Each of us is motivated to satisfy our hunger, thirst, and sexual needs. Without food and water, we could not survive; the typical consequence of efforts to achieve sexual satisfaction is procreation, which helps perpetuate the species. The energy associated with these instincts he termed **libido.** Originally, Freud maintained that libido was associated only with the sexual instincts but later, revising his position, he viewed libido as the psychic and pleasurable feelings associated with gratification of the life instincts (Freud, 1952b).

Death instincts   In addition to the life instincts, Freud postulated the existence of opposing death instincts. He believed that "the goal of all life is death" (Freud, 1952b, p. 652)—that human beings strive to return to an inorganic state of balance that preceded life, in which there is no painful struggle to satisfy biological needs. The life instincts operate, however, to ensure that death is delayed as long as possible, so that human beings can obtain many other satisfactions before attaining this nirvana.

A major derivative of the death instincts is aggression, whereby individuals try to destroy others or themselves. Freud believed these aggressive impulses to be very strong; accordingly, his view of human nature was extremely negative.

> The . . . truth . . . is that men are not gentle, friendly creatures wishing for love, who simply defend themselves if they are attacked, but that a powerful measure of desire for aggression has to be reckoned as part of their instinctual endowment. The result is that their neighbor is to them not only a possible helper or sexual object, but also a temptation to them to gratify their aggressiveness on him, to exploit his capacity for work without recompense, to use him sexu-

ally without consent, to seize his possessions, to humiliate him, to cause him pain, to torture and kill him. *Homo homini lupus* [Man is to man a wolf]; who has the courage to dispute it in the face of all the evidence in his own life and in history? (Freud, 1952a, p. 787)

Not surprisingly, Freud remained pessimistic about the future of the species. Interestingly, however, he never postulated an energy source, corresponding to libido, for the death instincts.

The individual versus society   Freud recognized that society would not survive for long if its members were allowed to express all their impulses. Stronger individuals would take advantage of weaker ones, by using their superior force to gain their ends. Social instability could easily result from allowing people to mate indiscriminately whenever the urge arose. Thus, even though people may wish to act out their sexual and aggressive impulses, society does not permit them to do so—and rightly so, in Freud's view. Indeed, society is often harsh in its demand that people renounce their impulses, and threatens punishment if they disobey. Eventually parents and others instill society's values so that people feel guilty if they do something wrong and become anxious if they even contemplate behaving inappropriately. Yet despite these internal checks on their behavior, people's urges continually seek expression; the result is a never-ending conflict between the individual and society. In Freud's view, individuals must eventually learn to resolve this conflict by seeking realistic ways of gratifying their impulses through behavior that is in line with the prescriptions of society.

Structural Theory of Personality

To understand the dynamics of an individual's conflicts, Freud postulated constructs that allowed him to describe the ways in which these conflicts originated and influenced behavior. To this end, he proposed three systems of the mind—id, ego, and superego—that compete for the limited amount of psychic energy available, energy that has its starting point in the instinctual needs of the individual. (See Figure 2.1.)

Id   Freud considered the **id** to be the original aspect of personality, rooted in the biology of the individual (Jones, 1963, p. 2), and to consist of unconscious sexual and aggressive instincts. These instincts might operate jointly in different situations to affect our behavior.

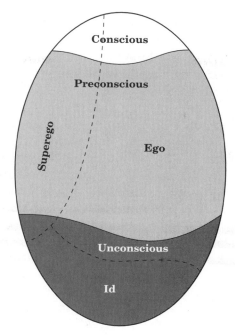

FIGURE 2.1   Structure of the mind. (Adapted from Jacobi, 1962, p. 126.)

For example, we might find ourselves hating and acting aggressively toward parents whom we dearly love, or we might feel sexually attracted to an arrogant and obnoxious person with whom we are continually arguing.

Freud likened the id to a "seething cauldron" that contains powerful and primitive urges and desires. He believed that these urges insistently and indiscriminately seek expression in external reality. Thus, the id is amoral and unconcerned with the niceties and conventions of society. It operates according to the pleasure principle: the aim of these impulses is always immediate and complete discharge and satisfaction. The **pleasure principle** maintains that people always strive to maximize pleasure and minimize pain.

Ego   Clearly we do not live in a social vacuum and cannot simply do whatever we wish whenever we want something. Adults who act impulsively are called immature or childish; mature conduct demands that we control our impulses in a wide variety of situations. For Freud, this control becomes possible when the **ego** is differentiated from the id. The ego, in his view, is the organized aspect of id, formed to provide realistic direction for the person's impulses. It comes into existence because the needs of the person require appropriate trans-actions with the environment if they are to be satisfied. The ego, therefore, develops partially to carry out the aims of the id. At the same time, it functions to keep the impulses of the id in check until a suitable object is found.

Superego   The **superego** is the construct Freud used to describe the individual's internalization of societal values. These values are instilled in the person primarily by parents, who teach which behav-iors are appropriate or inappropriate in given situations. The super-ego thus represents a set of learned ideals. Freud eventually described the superego as having two major components, **con-science** and the **ego-ideal.** Conscience is acquired through the use of punishment by the parents; the ego-ideal is learned through the use of rewards. When we do something wrong, our conscience makes us feel guilty; when we obey our parents and win their approval by performing in socially accepted ways, we feel proud. The main func-tions of the superego are to inhibit the urges of the id, to persuade the ego to substitute moralistic goals for realistic ones, and to strive for perfection.

Although the superego serves positive functions—preventing the individual from expressing primitive urges publicly, encouraging the individual to set goals leading to a career as a productive citizen—it also has a negative side. The superego may be too harsh and demand-ing. For example, a child who incorporates parental views of sex as dirty and sinful may, in adulthood, be afraid to approach members of the other sex and be incapable of forming an intimate relationship with anyone. Or a person may learn from parents that one must al-ways love one's neighbors—an impossible task, according to Freud, because many people are not worthy of respect and love. Adherence to such an exceedingly high standard, in Freud's opinion, inevitably creates problems for the individual.

Defense Mechanisms

The ego tries to exert control over both an id that is concerned only with gratification of its instinctual urges and a superego that con-stantly seeks perfection. While total, permanent control over the id and superego can never be established, there are times when the ego is able to bring these two agencies under some control, so that the individual can function effectively. To this end, the ego seeks to find realistic outlets for the person's id impulses—for example, to transform aggressive urges into more socially acceptable activities, such as competing athletically with others. Control over the superego may be established when the ego convinces the person to give up perfectionism (for example, the belief that he or she must achieve all A grades, be a great athlete, or have a perfect family) and to substitute more realistically attainable goals in these life areas.

As Freud saw it, the ego resembles a battlefield where the armies of the id and superego continually clash. Although much of the ego operates in consciousness, some of its processes are unconscious and serve to protect the person against anxiety caused by the conflicting demands of the id and superego (Freud, 1960a, p. 7). The person needs protection from **anxiety** because it is a highly unpleasant state that signals a danger to the ego (self). The danger may be that the person's instinctual impulses are out of control and are threatening to overwhelm him or her; or the danger may arise because the individual fears punishment from his or her conscience for thinking about doing something that the superego considers wrong; or the threat may come from an outside source in the environment (for example, the death of a parent, severe injury in a car accident, the rejection by a boyfriend or girlfriend). In the face of these dangers, the person's ego unconsciously attempts to regain control by activating defensive processes.

These defense mechanisms serve a useful purpose in that they protect the person against pain. Also, they are normal and universally used (Freud, 1937, p. 237). For example, we very often engage in denial when we are told of the death of a loved one. Our disbelief allows us to cope with the shock and to assimilate it in a more gradual and less painful manner. However, Freud believed that defense mechanisms can be potentially pathogenic when they are used indiscriminately, compulsively, and in ways that continually contradict the reality of the situation (Cramer, 1991, p. 10).

The primary defenses are as follows.

Repression   **Repression** is an attempt by the ego to keep undesirable id impulses from reaching consciousness. In the course of analyzing dreams, Freud discovered that certain thoughts were blocked from consciousness—repressed—because they were too painful to acknowledge, and that attempts to make patients aware of these experiences met with resistance. In Freudian terms, the battle for supremacy between the ego and the id involved an opposition between energy forces. The driving forces he called **cathexes**; the restraining forces, **anticathexes.** In other words, certain unconscious wishes or ideas were energized and strove for expression in consciousness but were met by other ideas energized by restraining forces seated in the ego. If the ego forces dominated, the wishes would be repressed—that is, forced back into the unconscious. If the id forces dominated, the person would act out his or her socially unacceptable impulses. For example, a woman who hated her father might repress her hostility and anger, and thus be totally unaware of her actual feelings. If these feelings broke through to the surface, the individual might physically attack her father. The battle would be centered on her attempts to express her feelings and the ego's attempts to repress them because their expression could lead to serious problems. The ego would attempt to protect the individual by forcing her to keep her unpleasant thoughts repressed. Freud considered repression the most fundamental of all defense mechanisms. As he put it, "the theory of repression is the pillar upon which the edifice of psychoanalysis rests" (Freud, 1938a, p. 939).

Repression occurs entirely on an unconscious level and involves preventing unpleasant experiences that are repulsive to the ego from reaching consciousness. Repressed memories are not under the conscious control of the person.

Suppression **Suppression** involves the individual's active and conscious attempt to stop anxiety-provoking thoughts by simply not thinking about them. If a high school student finds herself thinking sexual thoughts about her teacher, she may actively suppress them because of her moral training. The thoughts would then be stored in the preconscious and could be reactivated and made conscious by the student through an exertion of her will.

Denial **Denial** refers to a person's refusal to perceive an unpleasant event in external reality. For example, a loved one dies and the grieved partner refuses to accept it. Or parents repeatedly tell a child to leave the playground and come home and the child ignores them.

Often, parents unwittingly teach children to use such a defense. They inform their little son that he is "a big boy" and that he is "just as strong as father." They reassure him after he is hurt that he is really "all right" or they tell him that he really "loves to play the piano" despite his protestations to the contrary. As a result, he may learn to apply such thinking to painful experiences (Freud, 1946, pp. 90–91).

Displacement   **Displacement** refers to the unconscious attempt to obtain gratification for id impulses by shifting them to substitute objects if objects that would directly satisfy the impulses are not available. For example, a young boy who is insulted by a strong teenager may not be able to retaliate for fear that the adolescent might physically hurt him. Instead, he may vent his anger on someone smaller and weaker than he is. In this case, a substitute object is sought so that the impulse can be gratified, even though aggressing against the weaker child will not be as satisfying as aggressing against the teenage antagonist.

Sublimation   **Sublimation** is a form of displacement in which the unacceptable id impulses themselves are transformed, rather than the object at which they aim. The unacceptable impulses are displaced by ones that are socially acceptable (Freud, 1946, p. 56). A woman with a strong need for aggression may channel her energies into activities that are socially acceptable, becoming, for example, an outstanding scientist or first-rate novelist. By so doing, she can demonstrate her superiority and domination of others, but in a way that contributes to society. In like manner, poets and painters may satisfy some of their sexual needs through their art. Freud believed that creative sublimations of human instincts are necessary if civilized society is to survive. He also believed, unfortunately, that such creativity is available only to the few people with special gifts and talents. Furthermore, in his rather pessimistic view, even the creative elite will suffer because sublimated activities could not fully satisfy their primitive sexual and aggressive impulses (Freud, 1952a, pp. 773–774).

Regression   In **regression,** there is a movement from mature behavior to immature behavior. That is, when the ego is threatened, the person may revert to an earlier, more infantile form of behavior as a means of coping with the stress. For example, a 6-year-old boy might start sucking his thumb or clinging to his mother on the first day of school. Or a woman who learns that she has not been promoted to a higher paying job in the company may storm into her supervisor's office and have a temper tantrum. Or a man who is having marital difficulties may leave the home he shares with his wife and move back into his parents' house.

Projection   When a person protects the ego by attributing his or her own undesirable characteristics to others, we might infer that **projection** has taken place (Freud, 1938c, p. 625). For example, a student who is very stingy might claim that other people are stingy. A girl who hates her mother may be convinced that her mother hates her. A student who cheats on examinations may continually assert that other students received high grades because they cheated.

Reaction formation   The conversion of an undesirable impulse into its opposite is known as **reaction formation.** Freud considered it a lower form of sublimation (Freud, 1938d, p. 625). A man who hates his wife and yet is exceedingly kind to her would be a pertinent example. He could be said to be killing her with kindness.

Rationalization   **Rationalization** is the justification of behavior through the use of plausible, but inaccurate, excuses. For example, a young athlete, dropped from the team because of lack of ability, comes to the conclusion that he did not really want to be on the team because it is going to lose so many games.

Intellectualization   **Intellectualization** is a process that allows individuals to protect themselves against unbearable pain. It involves a dissociation between one's thoughts and feelings. For example, a woman may conjure up an elaborate rationale to explain the death of her young husband. By citing reasons and focusing on the logic of her argument, she may avoid, for a while at least, the tremendous pain associated with such a traumatic experience.

Undoing   Sometimes a person who thinks or acts on an undesirable impulse makes amends by performing some action that nullifies the undesirable one, a defense mechanism known as **undoing.** Such actions are typically irrational and can be seen in various superstitious rituals and some religious ceremonies. By performing the undoing act, the person is convinced that the wrong he or she committed has been rectified. For example, a boy who has continual thoughts about masturbation and believes that they are evil may wash his hands frequently as a means of cleansing himself.

Compromise formation   **Compromise formation** involves the use of contradictory behaviors to gain some satisfaction for an undesirable impulse. The barbed compliment would be an example. Jill, who really hates Kathy, comments: "My, what a pretty dress. How did *you* ever manage to select it?" Or a student remarks to a professor, "Good lecture; I never expected it from *you*."

Other defense mechanisms postulated by Freud, including identification and fixation, will be reviewed in the section on psychosexual development.

PERSONALITY DEVELOPMENT

The Theory of Psychosexual Development

Having reviewed the major structural components of personality, we turn now to Freud's usage of these constructs in his scheme of **psychosexual development.** The theory, it should be noted, is biological in nature; it is based on the inevitable unfolding of a series of stages in which particular behaviors occur. Normal development involves the coursing of libidinal or sexual energy through a variety of earlier stages to a final stage, aptly called the genital stage. Immediately preceding the genital stage is the latency period, in which sexual energy is considered to be dormant. Abnormal development occurs if, in early childhood, the person undergoes traumatic experiences—almost invariably sexual in nature—that prevent the flow of significant amounts of libidinal energy through the various stages. The result is **fixation** at a particular stage, making the person more vulnerable to crisis later in life. When subjected to stress, this person may regress, and display infantile behavior. For each stage at which conflict occurs, Freud postulated a corresponding adult character pattern.

Oral stage   The infant is practically all id, according to Freud, and cannot initially distinguish between the self and the environment. An infant is controlled by biological impulses and is basically selfish. The focus of pleasurable sensations or "sexual" impulses during the first pregenital stage is the mouth (Freud, 1969, p. 10); Freud labeled it the **oral stage.** Pleasurable sensations occur as the infant takes in food and water. The parents' behavior is critical in determining whether or not the infant will experience personal difficulties later in life. These difficulties may occur as a result of parental overindulgence or underindulgence of the infant's needs during the first year or so. For example, if the mother resents nursing and weans the baby abruptly, a portion of the libidinal energy available to the individual becomes fixated around this conflict, while the remaining energy flows through to the next stage.

Anal stage   During the second and third years, pleasurable sensations are focused on the anal cavity: the chief pleasures for the child involve retention or expulsion of feces (Freud, 1957, p. 324). During this **anal stage,** ego processes are being differentiated from the id and the child begins to assert his or her independence. This independence does not, however, involve rational decision making, in which the child weighs the conflicting evidence and comes to reasonable conclusions. Rather, it is a negativistic independence, in which the child rejects out of hand whatever is being offered by the parents. If the child is asked, "Will you please put on your shoes?" the answer is an immediate "No." If the child is then asked, "Do you want a candy bar?" the answer, once again, is a resounding "No"—even though the child may be hungry and may have begged for candy only moments earlier. It is a period, in short, for a contest of wills and the assertion of ego control.

According to Freud, the primary contest revolves around toilet training. In this culture and others, cleanliness is a virtue, and parents typically place heavy stress on regulating defecation and urination. Children can resist these demands by retaining the waste matter or by expelling it inappropriately—for example, by wetting or soiling their pants. Conflicts during this stage precipitate particular kinds of behavioral difficulties in adolescence and adulthood.

Phallic stage   During the fourth and fifth years, sexual tension is focused on the genital area. At this **phallic stage,** both boys and girls are considered to derive pleasure from self-manipulation (Freud, 1957, p. 327). Boys, according to Freud, develop a longing for sexual contact with the mother. In the most general sense, they seek affection and love from the mother. At the same time, however, the child is increasingly aware that there is a sexual relationship between his parents and that the father is his rival. But the father is bigger and stronger physically, and the boy is fearful that he will be punished for his desires—specifically, that his penis will be cut off. The child alleviates this castration anxiety by **identification** with his father. In this way, his sexual desire is shunted into more socially acceptable channels. These strong, conflicting feelings and the process by which they are more or less adequately resolved Freud named the **Oedipal complex,** a term borrowed from Sophocles' tragedy *Oedipus Rex,* in which the Greek king, Oedipus, unwittingly kills his father and commits incest with his mother. The superego is an outgrowth of the resolution of this complex, as the child takes on the values of his parents and their attitudes toward society.

Freud believed that the kinship ties and practices of various primitive societies supported his ideas about the Oedipal conflict in males (Freud, 1950, pp. 144–145). On the basis of anthropological and historical evidence, he speculated that brothers within a primitive clan banded together to kill their father, their chief rival for the affection of the women. After committing the deed, they realized that a new social organization was necessary if they were ever going to live in harmony and avoid mutual destruction in a frantic effort to possess the women. As a consequence, a law against incest was adopted. Freud theorized that all cultures had instituted two taboos: a law against incest and a law protecting the totem animal. He saw the totem animal as a symbol of the father, and worship of it as a means of allaying the clan's sense of guilt over the original patricide. In Freud's view, worship of the totem animal also symbolized a covenant between tribal members and their fathers: the father promised them protection and care, and the members promised to respect the father's life. Freud saw this covenant between tribal members and their fathers as analogous to the male child's eventual identification with his father as a means of resolving his own basic conflict over the mother.

According to Freud, the conflict process for females is very different. He postulated that a girl, lacking a penis, envies boys and seeks to obtain one. At first, girls try to compensate for this deficiency by emulating boys and by masturbation of what Freud calls their "stunted penis" (clitoris). Although the mother is their first love object, they come to resent her for bringing them into the world without a penis and begin to love their father because he has the desired object. They then identify with the mother as a means of vicariously obtaining the desired object (Freud, 1969, pp. 44–51). Although initially they seek the father's penis, this fantasy is then transformed into the wish to have a baby—specifically, a male baby who will bring the longed-for penis with him. Since these desires can never be fulfilled, Freud considered all girls to have relatively inadequate superegos. These "mutilated little creatures," as he called them, had little sense of objectivity and justice. (Some of Freud's supporters called this special conflict process in girls the Electra complex—in Greek mythology, Electra induced her brother to murder their hated mother—but Freud himself was reluctant to use the term, perhaps because the analogy seemed weak and at variance with his own description of the process.)

To many people, the Freudian proposal concerning the mechanisms and outcomes of the Oedipus complex, especially for girls, is patently absurd. Freud has been severely criticized for maintaining that the Oedipal conflict is biologically based and occurs universally in all human beings, and there is some cross-cultural evidence that contradicts his contentions. In some cultures at least, the resentment of the boy toward his father is based on the father's powerful position in the family and not on sexual jealousy.

Advocates of the women's movement point to Freud's chauvinistic outlook toward women—an attitude common to the strongly patriarchal society in which he lived. Viennese women in Freud's time were second-class citizens, subject to all the degrading treatment meted out to members of minority groups. His concept of penis envy is particularly galling to women because it implies that anatomy is destiny and that constructive personal growth is virtually impossible. If you are inherently inferior, it makes little sense to expend great amounts of effort trying to improve yourself.

Karen Horney, a prominent neoanalyst, took particular issue with Freud's concept of penis envy many years ago. Her arguments are, in general, echoed by leading feminists today. Horney maintained that the Freudian position is bogged down in faulty biology. She asks why a biologically healthy female would show such psychological qualities. Further, she maintains that the Freudian interpretation does not allow for the social and cultural factors that affect the psychology of women. Penis envy is presumed to manifest itself in the behavior of the "castrating female"—ambitious, competitive, seeking to dominate and humiliate men. Tendencies toward dictatorial power and egocentric ambition, Horney noted, are characteristics of neurotic men as well as neurotic women (Horney, 1937, p. 204). These problems stem, she suggested, from an excessively competitive society in which status is conferred upon those who are achievement-oriented, dominant, and ambitious. What normal women actually envy is the status of men and the psychological and physical rewards associated with it. (Horney's position is discussed in greater detail in Chapter 5.)

Finally, psychotherapist Max Hammer has questioned the validity of Freud's contention that all women desire a male child. He asked married and single college students and married noncollege adults, "If you knew for sure that you could have only one child, would you prefer that child to be a male or a female?" (Hammer & McFerran, 1988). Most women in all three groups tended to prefer girls over boys. Hammer suggests that this preference for girls may be a result of the women's movement and its impact on females. On the basis of these data, he argues that such preferences are not biologically determined, as Freud contends, but are more likely to be culturally determined. Of course, strict Freudians would probably disagree with any such conclusion based on individual self-reports; they might argue that the women who said they preferred a girl were unconscious of their actual wishes. Although there is no way actively and directly to disconfirm the Freudian contention, it does not seem reasonable to expect that every woman in the world has such desires, given the incredibly complex and varied motivational life of human beings.

Latency stage   Freud postulated a **latency stage,** from the sixth year to puberty, during which sexual development is assumed to be at a standstill (Freud, 1969, p. 10). He believed that the person's characteristic ways of behaving are established during the first five years of life and that radical personality change is extremely difficult, if not impossible, thereafter. At this point in their development, children turn to the world of school and peers and begin to learn the social and technical skills that will allow them eventually to take their place as responsible and effective citizens in their society.

Genital stage   With the advent of puberty, sexual tension increases dramatically. The reproductive organs have matured, and both sexes are now capable of procreation. Previously, the aims of the sexual instincts have been predominantly autoerotic, but now the goal is to mate with an appropriate sex object. At this **genital stage,** an adequate heterosexual adjustment depends on the amount of libidinal energy available to the person. If there have been no severe traumatic experiences in early childhood, with corresponding libido fixations, an adequate adjustment is possible. When adulthood is reached, the person typically marries and settles into family life.

For Freud, the normal person is one who makes satisfactory adjustments in two major areas—love and work. While this pronouncement appears simplistic, it becomes more profound when we realize that any person must have many outstanding qualities to attain success in these two areas. For example, to be able to love another person, one must be secure in one's own identity, generous, caring, compromising, trusting, and so forth. To be able to work productively, one must be responsible, dependable, motivated, persistent, ambitious, and so on. An inadequate adjustment, on the other hand, involves libidinal fixations and the development of specific character disorders (Freud, 1969, pp. 12–13).

Character Types

The oral character   Persons who are fixated at the oral stage have problems later in life that are related primarily to receiving or taking things from the external world. The **oral receptive character** is a result of overindulgence in infancy. The individual has become habituated to receiving support and encouragement from other people and thus is excessively dependent on others for gratification (Blum, 1953, p. 160). Such people tend to be trusting, accepting, and gullible; they admire strength and leadership in others but make little attempt to fend for themselves. They also tend to be rather incompetent—most of their gratification is derived from what others do for them and not from what they themselves accomplish—and to be overly optimistic. This type of person inevitably experiences conflicts with others because not everyone is nurturant and supportive like mother. How long can one expect others to remain friends if one keeps demanding all of their time, effort, and affection without reciprocating in approximate measure?

Fixation may also occur when parents underindulge or severely frustrate the needs of their infants. In this case, the person learns to exploit others and may develop sadistic attitudes (Fenichel, 1945, p. 489). This type of **oral aggressive character** tends to envy others their success and to try, through the use of manipulative strategies, to dominate them. Again, it is difficult to imagine liking and supporting a person who is continually manipulative and exploitative in interpersonal relations.

The anal character   **Anal eroticism** stems from difficulties during toilet training, when children are locked in a battle over power and control with their parents. If the parents are highly punitive and demanding, children may decide to defiantly keep their prized possessions from the parents. The **anal character,** according to Freud, is delineated by a particular constellation of traits: obstinacy, parsimony, and orderliness. Obstinacy in anal characters means that they are stubborn, defiant, and resistant to control by others. They are also overly conscientious, rigid, fiercely independent, and doggedly persistent in the performance of even the most trivial duties. Parsimony in this character type suggests that they are frugal and stingy with regard to possession, money, and time, all of which are not to be wasted. The trait of orderliness is reflected in their need to live by routine. They are meticulous, perfectionistic, and sticklers for precision (Pollak, 1979, pp. 226–227).

The phallic character   The difficulties experienced by the **phallic character** stem from inadequate resolution of the Oedipus complex. In males, it is a reaction to severe castration anxiety; they behave in a reckless, resolute, and self-assured manner (Blum, 1953, pp. 163–

164). Overvaluing of the penis is reflected in excessive vanity and exhibitionism. Such males have to prove that they are real men. One way of doing so is by repeated conquests of women; the Don Juan type of male fits this description. For women, the primary motive is penis envy. Consequently, they are continuously striving for superiority over men. Such women are considered to be castrating females.

The genital character   Freud viewed the **genital character** as the ideal type. Such people are sexually mature and capable of orgasm; their libidinal energies are no longer dammed up because they have found appropriate love objects (Blum, 1953, p. 164). In Freud's view, the key to happiness is the ability to love and be loved. Sexual love is one aspect of intimacy that provides us with happiness and joy. Although establishing intimacy is central to happiness, Freud reminds us that it also makes us vulnerable—to rejection by the loved one and also to the eventual loss of the loved one. Yet Freud believed that love was necessary for healthy functioning and that love had to be pursued despite the suffering that it inevitably entailed.

Genital characters are also capable of sublimating their id impulses by expressing them in the form of productive and creative work. The creative activities that bring happiness differ for each individual. Some pursue happiness by refining their intellectual skills and by seeking truth, as in the case of the scientist; others seek it through direct action, as demonstrated by the artistic grace and agility of the ballet dancer. Thus, each person has to find the course that is best for him or her (Freud, 1952a, pp. 772–776).

Research Evidence for the Theory of Psychosexual Development

We may agree that Freud created an interesting and provocative theory of human development, but the question of its empirical validity remains open and subject to examination. Even though the theory is relatively vaguely stated, hypotheses for scientific testing may still be derived from it.

The Evidence for Character Types

Freud's theory suggests that certain clusters of personality traits exist in mature adults. Hypothesized traits in the oral receptive character, for example, include excessive optimism, dependency, impatience, talkativeness, and an intense curiosity. For the anal character, key characteristics are an opposition to influence from others, minute attention to detail, and a love of independence. For the phallic character, typical traits include recklessness, pride, vanity, self-assurance, and courage (Kline, 1972, pp. 7–12). There is considerable evidence for the oral receptive character, some evidence for the anal character, and no support for the phallic character. However, the lack of support for Freud's ideas about the phallic character may be attributed to the absence of a reliable and valid measure of such a character orientation and a consequent failure to test his ideas.

A good example of empirical support for the oral receptive and anal character types is provided in a study by Tribich and Messer (1974). In accordance with psychoanalytic theory, they predicted that, if oral receptive people are submissive and dependent in general and even more so in the presence of authority figures, they should conform more to influence by these individuals than would anal characters.

To test this hypothesis, Tribich and Messer first measured orality in college men by administering a projective test called the Blacky Pictures. This test contains 12 cartoons depicting the adventures of a dog named Blacky. Subjects (all men) were asked to make up stories about Blacky, and their responses were then scored by trained assessors. A subject, for example, might look at one of the pictures and tell a story that involved Blacky "sucking vigorously at his mother's breast." Or he might look at another picture and say that he believed it meant that "Blacky will grow up to like eating more than anything else." (These are two actual responses of a subject in the experiment.)

Once the subject's level of orality was determined, he was brought individually to a laboratory where he was introduced to a high-status authority figure (a psychiatrist). Each subject was then told that, once the room was completely dark, a point of light would be shown; his task was to judge how far the point of light had moved in inches. He was told it would move between 1 and 23 inches. Before responding, however, the subject would hear the authority figure's judgment of how far it had moved. Over a series of trials, the high orals' responses were much closer to the authority figure's than were those of the low orals, thereby confirming the investigators' prediction. Earlier studies (Kagan & Mussen, 1956; Masling, Weiss, & Rothschild, 1968) had also found that oral types tend to conform highly to the judgments of others.

Psychoanalytic theory claims not only that oral receptive characters are highly dependent on others, but also that they have strong needs for contact, affiliation, and nurturance. Research has provided evidence of their needs for company and emotional support by showing that oral receptive types tend to experience aversive arousal when socially isolated (Masling, Price, Goldband, & Katkin, 1981). Specifically, these researchers found that people with oral dependency needs showed more anxiety when performing tasks alone in a soundproof chamber than when they performed them in the presence of others. Masling, O'Neill, and Katkin (1982) showed further that oral subjects forced to interact with a cold, impersonal individual experienced more stress than did oral subjects who interacted with a warm, personal individual. Low-oral subjects, in contrast, showed no differences in stress level between the cold and warm interaction conditions.

In terms of their needs for contact, Juni, Masling, and Brannon (1979) found that people high in orality used greater physical contact as a means of helping others solve a problem than did people low in orality. Specifically, high- and low-oral individuals participated in an experiment on problem solving. As part of the experiment, they were asked to coach (by any methods they chose) another subject (who was blindfolded) through a maze as fast as they could. The investigators found that high-oral individuals touched the blindfolded subjects more often as a means of coaching them than did low-oral subjects and that the blindfolded subjects tended to successfully complete the maze more quickly under the guidance of the high-oral individuals.

Freudian theory also predicts that withdrawal of others' support can result in depression under extreme circumstances. Dozens of studies with both clinical and nonclinical populations show that oral dependency is related directly to depression. Another research finding consistent with psychoanalytic theory is that high-oral individuals rely too heavily on oral activities (for example, drinking, eating, and smoking) to cope with anxiety; that is, orally dependent individuals tend to be obese, to have elevated levels of cigarette smoking, and to be more likely to be alcoholic (Bornstein, 1992, pp. 14–16).

While the prevailing view of the orally dependent person from a psychoanalytic stance is predominantly negative, some recent studies in the research literature show that such individuals also have certain positive personal qualities. For example, in comparison to low orals, high orals are found to be more interpersonally sensitive, are more likely to seek medical attention when physical symptoms appear, and are more likely to ask teachers for guidance when confronted with difficult tasks. Since guidance from teachers usually leads to better understanding, such behavior promotes strong academic performance (Bornstein, 1992, p. 18; Bornstein, 1994, p. 629).

Also, high orals' strong desire to please and win the approval of authority figures can motivate them to perform well for teachers and parents who are highly supportive. Thus, these individuals can achieve effective test performances when their need to please others exceeds their fear of rejection if they fail (Bornstein, 1993, pp. 74–76).

Finally, there have been a few tests of Freud's ideas concerning the anal character. Several studies, for example, have found that anal characters tend to be rigid and dogmatic, and to use their time in a niggardly, thrifty, and cautious manner (Pollak, 1979, pp. 235–237). Tribich and Messer (1974) also found that subjects high in anality were more resistant to influence by others than were low-anal subjects. In more recent research by Fischer and Juni (1982), subjects higher in anality were more reluctant to disclose information about themselves than were subjects lower in anality.

Character Types and Child Rearing

The second hypothesis that can be derived from Freud's theory of psychosexual development is that the character types are the outgrowth of specific child-rearing practices. At the present time, there are only clinical data to support the theory; there are no experimental data to check these clinical assertions (Masling, 1986, p. 101). Accordingly, the evidence in support of this part of the theory is weak.

ASSESSMENT TECHNIQUES

To understand the personalities of his patients, Freud primarily employed the case-study method: first, detailed and exhaustive examination and analysis of their lives and past experiences; and then utilization of this information to help them overcome their problems. Freud explored lines of inquiry that focused on the physiological determinants of behavior and on hypnotic phenomena but, after considerable experimentation, he came to rely on three major techniques: free association, dream analysis, and transference.

Free Association

Freud's technique of **free association,** as we have seen, involved the patients' self-reports of whatever thoughts and memories occurred to them without any kind of self-censorship. The patients were told to report *all* thoughts, no matter how trivial, unimportant, mortifying, embarrassing, and illogical they seemed to be. Freud called this attempt at completely uncensored reporting the "fundamental rule" of psychoanalysis. During these sessions, Freud sat behind the patient, out of sight but in a position to watch facial expressions and gestures; in this way, he ensured that he did not elicit behavior from the patients by his own gestures and facial expressions. He wanted the patients' responses to be spontaneous and not controlled by him (Ford & Urban, 1963, p. 168). Freud believed that, when resistance occurred, the analysis was definitely moving in the right direction— that is, uncovering the actual source of the patients' problems. Through the use of free association, Freud discovered that patients' problems typically stemmed from traumatic experiences in early childhood.

Freud provided an interesting nonclinical example of the use of free association to uncover an unpleasant secret (Freud, 1960b, pp. 8–11). While on vacation, Freud renewed his acquaintance with a young academician, who was familiar with some of Freud's theories but highly skeptical about their validity. The man was very depressed about the state of the world in general and about his own bleak prospects for success in academic life. Not only were few academic positions available, but his Jewish heritage virtually guaranteed his professional failure because of the anti-Semitism prevailing in academic life.

The incident involved a **parapraxis,** which is basically a cognitive failure such as a slip of the tongue, a mishearing of a word, or the forgetting of an obvious word or thing. The young academician wanted to emphasize his outrage at the injustice by quoting a line from Virgil's *Aeniad,* in which the wronged Dido prays for revenge on Aeneas. The line was: "Exoriar(e) aliquis nostris ex ossibus ultor" (Let someone arise from my bones as an avenger). However, he omitted the word "aliquis" (someone). Immediately aware of his error, he tried to correct it but, even though he thought about it for a long while, he just could not remember it. Finally, he very reluctantly asked Freud to supply it, which Freud did. Feeling humiliated by his failure, the man tried to retaliate by reminding Freud of his "absurd" theory that even senseless mistakes had meaning. He then challenged Freud to prove his theory by revealing the latent meaning of the missing word, *aliquis.*

Freud promptly accepted the challenge, but only on condition that the young man report each and every thought that he had as he free-associated. The man accepted and began his free associations: "There springs to mind the ridiculous notion of dividing the word *aliquis* like this: *a* and *liquis*." Freud asked, "What occurs to you next?" The young man replied, "Reliquien [relics], liquefying, fluidity, fluid." He then asked, "Have you discovered anything yet?" Freud replied, "No. Not by any means yet. But go on." The man laughed scornfully and said, "I am [now] thinking of [Saint] Simon of Trent whose relics I saw two years ago in a church at Trent. I am thinking of the accusation of ritual blood-sacrifice which is being brought against the Jews [again today]." In the 15th century, the Jews were accused of killing Simon, a 2½-year-old child, who was subsequently declared a martyr and a saint. Only centuries later did the Catholic church exonerate the Jews and acknowledge that confessions of the crime had been extracted by torture (Erdelyi, 1985, p. 39).

The man's next association was that he had recently read an article in an Italian newspaper entitled "What Saint Augustine Thinks of Women." And then the man said that he was thinking that both Saint Augustine and Saint Januarius were calendar saints and that there was a miracle involving Saint Januarius' blood. Freud asked the man to explain the miracle of the blood, and he replied:

> They keep the blood of St. Januarius in a phial [vial] inside a church at Naples, and on a particular holy day it miraculously *liquefies*. The people attach great importance to this miracle and get very excited if it is delayed as happened once at a time when the French were occupying the town. So the general in command . . . took [the priest in charge of the church] aside and gave him to understand with an unmistakeable gesture toward the soldiers posted outside that he *hoped* that the miracle would take place very soon. And in fact it did take place. (Freud, 1960b, p. 10)

Then the man paused and hesitated to go on, saying that his next thought was too intimate to report. Finally, after some prodding, he reluctantly continued: "I have suddenly thought of a lady from whom I might easily hear a piece of news that would be very awkward for both of us." Freud immediately delivered his interpretation in the form of a question: "That her periods have stopped?" The young man was amazed and asked, "How could you guess that?" Freud replied:

> That's not difficult any longer; you've prepared the way sufficiently. Think of *the calendar saints, the blood that starts to flow on a particular day,* the disturbance *when the event fails to take place, the open threats that the miracle must be vouchsafed, or else.* . . . In fact you've made use of the miracle of St. Januarius to manufacture a brilliant allusion to women's periods. (Freud, 1960b, p. 11)

The man's subdued reaction was: "I certainly was not aware of it." Freud then expanded his interpretation, explaining that the prefix *a* in *aliquis* often means no, while *liquis* means liquid. He thought the young man was trying to reject from consciousness the frightening idea "aliquis," no liquid; that is, he was trying to avoid the thought, "No menstruation—she's pregnant!" (Erdelyi, 1985, p. 41).

The young man sheepishly acknowledged that he thought his Italian girlfriend was pregnant. Freud then observed that he was also in a quandary about whether to marry her or to encourage her to have an abortion. The idea of the abortion, Freud maintained, was suggested by the young man's thoughts regarding the sacrifice of Simon as a child. Through his analysis, Freud was able to reveal, to the young man's amazement and satisfaction, the underlying meaning of his forgetting.

Dream Analysis

Another major technique used by Freud to unravel the secrets of his patients' unconscious was **dream analysis.** Freud's task, as he saw it, was to analyze and interpret the symbols present in the manifest content of their dreams, in an attempt to discover the latent or hidden meanings. As a result of his extensive clinical experiences, Freud believed that these symbols had universal meanings. Sticks, tree trunks, umbrellas, and snakes, for example, were thought to symbolize the penis; boxes, doors, and furniture chests represented the vagina. Despite their universal nature, Freud also believed that all symbols had to be judged and interpreted in terms of the unique conflicts of the individual. Also, these symbols typically had multiple meanings, which made analysis highly difficult.

In Freud's view, dreams are always disguised attempts at wish fulfillment. The wishes are unconscious motives that are unacceptable to the individual and are nearly always erotic in nature. During sleep, these impulses seek expression but are subject to censorship. As a result, they seek expression indirectly (via displacement) by taking on disguised symbolic forms. This indirect expression is seen in the manifest content of the person's dreams. Often the events in the manifest content appear totally unrelated to the actual wish. Detailed analysis by Freud, however, eventually revealed the connection, as seen in the following case study.

Freud's patient, a young woman, told him that her sister had two sons, Otto and Charles, and that, unfortunately, Otto had died recently. Otto was the patient's favorite, but she claimed that she was fond of Charles as well. She then told Freud that the evening before her appointment, she had had a dream in which she "saw Charles lying dead . . . in his little coffin, his hands folded; there were candles all about; and, in short, it was just as it was at the time of little Otto's death, which gave me such a shock" (Freud, 1938b, pp. 229–230). She then asked Freud what this strange dream meant. Did it mean, she asked, that she was so evil as to wish that her sister would lose the only child she had left? Or did it mean that she really wished that Charles had died instead of Otto, whom she loved so much more? Freud reassured her that neither interpretation was correct.

In the course of the analysis, Freud discovered that the young woman had been orphaned at an early age and had gone to live with her sister. A number of years later, the sister introduced her to a very attractive man. She and the man had planned to marry, but somehow the sister had intervened, and now the man no longer paid visits to the house. Although she had many other suitors, the young woman was unable to extend her affections to other men.

The object of her interest was a professor with literary talents who often gave public lectures. The young woman always managed to get tickets to hear him speak, and would sit unobserved in the audience. If she learned that her friend was going to a concert, she attended also, in the hope of seeing him. The last time she saw him was at little Otto's funeral, when he offered her and her sister his condolences. Even under those circumstances, she could not suppress her feelings of affection for the professor. The motive of her dream about little Charles then became clear: it signified nothing more than her wish to see the man again. Thus, even though the dream initially seemed strange and inexplicable, Freud was able to ferret out the hidden wish, and thus helped the woman by making her real motivation clear to her.

Transference

Besides free association and dream analysis, Freud relied heavily on **transference** to facilitate movement toward cure for his patients. In the course of treatment, Freud discovered that patients inevitably began to relive their old conflicts and interactions with authority figures (most notably, their parents) in their relationship with him. In general, he maintained, patients begin to see their therapist as a reincarnation of important figures in their past. As a result, they transfer to their therapist the kinds of feelings and behaviors previously directed toward these early authority figures.

In Freud's view, this transference phenomenon could be of inestimable value in helping therapists cure their patients. Yet it could also be a possible source of danger if the patients decided to act out their old feelings of hostility and anger toward their parents.

In general, according to Freud, the transference process is characterized by **ambivalence**; that is, patients typically have attitudes of both affection and hostility toward their parents, and these positive and negative feelings are displaced onto the therapist. Freud found that positive feelings were displaced onto him first and that negative feelings followed later. In **positive transference,** the patients developed a special affectionate interest in him. They trusted him completely and praised him lavishly. Among his female patients, some fell passionately in love with him and made sexual demands of him. Others revealed a wish that he treat them as he would a favorite daughter. In all cases, the women were highly jealous of anyone who was close to him. In his male patients, Freud also found evidence of sexual feelings toward him, although rarely in the direct form expressed by his female patients.

In his analysis of the transference process, Freud focused on the many cases where his female patients expressed their love and affection toward him. He believed that these affectional overtures were a major sign of resistance on the part of the patients; that is, expressions of love were most likely to occur at a point in the analysis where patients had to admit or remember some particularly distressing and heavily repressed part of their past. Thus, they expressed their love for the therapist in order to avoid coming to grips with traumatic, early sexual experiences in their own lives. Freud believed that these patients unconsciously were trying to destroy his credibility as a therapist by bringing him down to the level of a lover. If they could achieve their goal, they would no longer have to listen to, or believe, his interpretations concerning the sources of their conflicts. They could, therefore, avoid the pain associated with the confrontation of their repressed memories.

But how is the therapist to react to these irrational affectional overtures? Freud thought it made little sense for the therapist to sever the therapeutic relationship, because that would leave the repressed materials intact and the patient uncured. Nor should the therapist ever yield to the temptation of sexually consummating the relationship, for ethical reasons. Freud held the highest professional standards and argued strongly that the therapist should never violate the patient's trust. Even if the therapist had feelings of affection for the patient and was therefore experiencing a **countertransference,** he should not act on those feelings. Instead, he should continually bear in mind that his primary commitment was to the welfare of the patient and her cure. To accomplish these goals, the therapist should work patiently with her in an attempt to confront and eventually understand the reality that her feelings toward him had their origins in infantile sexual fixations. He should also make every attempt, through self-analysis, to understand the basis of his own feelings toward her. Increased self-understanding, Freud believed, helped him to understand her conflicts and wishes better and facilitated her movement toward a cure (Freud, 1958, pp. 159–171).

Under conditions of positive transference, patients typically made progress toward a cure. They were receptive to his interpretations, understood them, and were fully engrossed in the analysis. Difficulties soon arose, however, because positive transference was followed by **negative transference.** At this point, patients showed intense anger and hostility toward him, and viewed his interpretations with great distrust. Freud pointed out to his patients that their feelings did not arise from the present situation and that they were instead simply repeating negative experiences that had occurred earlier in their lives. To the extent that they accepted this explanation and explored its possibilities, they were likely to attain insight into their problems and to make progress toward the attainment of psychological health.

THEORY'S IMPLICATIONS FOR THERAPY

Psychopathology refers to disordered behaviors, ranging from ineffective coping with everyday problems (**neurosis**) to a serious inability to relate to other people (**psychosis**). In response to the anxiety created by the stifling of their instinctual impulses, neurotics and psychotics have resorted to various defense mechanisms. Normal growth has been arrested; as a result, their functioning is ineffective and stereotypic. To cure such individuals, it is necessary to reduce their conflicts and defenses by relieving their anxieties. The energies directed away from the maintenance of defenses then become available for constructive growth.

Through the use of free association, dream analysis, and transference, **psychoanalysis** can help these individuals to understand the sources of their conflicts and to see that these internal struggles have weakened the ego and prevented them from coping effectively with the demands of external reality—to see that they are repeating old behaviors and using ineffective strategies in current situations. Successful therapy results in increased self-understanding and a more accurate assessment of reality. What is unconscious is made more conscious, the ego is strengthened, and the patient is then able to function more effectively in everyday life (Freud, 1969, pp. 31–35).

To illustrate the process, let us examine an actual case of a person suffering from an **obsessive-compulsive disorder,** to see how Freud diagnosed the problem and helped the patient.

The patient, a young man with a university education, entered therapy because he suffered from a number of obsessions and compulsions (Freud, 1963, pp. 19–105). The young man told Freud that, during his childhood, his primary fears were that his father might die and that a woman whom he loved would be hurt or killed. In addition, he reported compulsions to cut his own throat. His attempts to cope with these recurrent fears absorbed considerable energy, and it was not surprising that his sexual life was less than adequate. He reported performing coitus irregularly and masturbating only rarely.

Freud secured a promise from the man to report everything that occurred to him, even if it was unpleasant or seemed senseless or irrelevant. According to Freud, the man was unfamiliar with the analytic emphasis on sexual matters but began a discussion of his problems by recalling sexual experiences in his childhood. In these episodes, he fondled the genitals of a willing young family governess and watched another family governess undress as she prepared for her bath. He reported further that he enjoyed these experiences immensely; he especially enjoyed looking at the nude woman. At the same time, however, he had an uncanny feeling that his parents knew his thoughts and that he could be punished by his father for them. In general terms, then, we have a case in which strong instinctual impulses are experienced but are warded off because the person anticipates superego-generated guilt feelings. Freud noted that the patient used other ego defense mechanisms to protect himself.

In the course of therapy, the patient mentioned a recent experience he had had with a military officer during training maneuvers. He reported that he disliked and dreaded this officer, who was obviously fond of cruelty and advocated corporal punishment. During a conversation, the officer had told the patient of a horrible method of torture used by the military in other countries. The patient resisted telling Freud about it, but eventually reported that it involved putting a number of ravenous rats into a pot that had been turned upside down and attached to the person's buttocks. The rats then bored their way into his anus. Despite the patient's reluctance to repeat the story, Freud noticed that he showed horrified pleasure as he told it. The patient further mentioned that, as he related the captain's story to Freud, he had the idea that the punishment was happening to the woman he loved. Subsequently, the patient was forced to admit that the idea occurred to him that the punishment was being applied to his father as well. Why did the patient have these cruel and hostile feelings toward two people he loved?

Further probing by Freud eventually revealed the source of the patient's wish that his father and loved one be subjected to the rat punishment. First, the patient's father had been a noncommissioned officer who had been extremely cruel and violent at times. Freud suggested that the patient disliked the officer who first related the rat-punishment story because he resembled the patient's father. At base, then, the patient hated his father. Freud then turned to the unraveling of these feelings. He believed that the problem lay in the sphere of sexuality and that some traumatic experience was responsible for the patient's feelings toward his father.

An examination of the patient's masturbatory history provided Freud with an important clue concerning the nature of the patient's conflicts with his father. The patient did not masturbate to any great extent during puberty, but a compulsion to do so started when he was 21, shortly after his father's death. At the same time, the patient had fantasies that his father was alive and would reappear at any moment. Between 12:00 and 1:00 in the morning the patient would interrupt his work, take out his penis, and look at it in the mirror. Freud conjectured that it was during this period that the patient expected his father's ghost to appear. Since the father would then witness his son's exposure and would disapprove of it, Freud inferred that the patient's actions were defiant. Further probing revealed that the father had caught the patient in a sexual act connected with masturbation during his early childhood and had beaten him severely for it. The patient had then repressed all memories of the event. Thus, the patient had perceived his father as trying to interfere with his sexual satisfaction, and wished secretly for his death.

Freud found that rats had many meanings for the patient, but three were especially important. First, the patient recalled that, once when he visited his father's grave, he saw a rat gliding over the grave. He assumed that the rat had been inside his father's grave and had just finished eating part of the corpse. Second, rats were regarded as dirty and greedy, and were mercilessly and cruelly persecuted by people. He felt that he was much like the rat because, as a child, he had bitten people when he was in a rage—a rage sometimes generated by his father's physical beatings. Third, rats were like children, in the patient's earliest recollections of them, and he was very fond of children. Unfortunately, though, his loved one could not have children, and this may have been the primary reason for his ambivalent feelings toward her.

Freud conjectured, finally, that the rat could be considered a symbol of the male sex organ. This organ could also be symbolized as a worm, and as a child the patient had had an illness in which large round worms had burrowed in his anus. Freud came to the conclusion that the rat obsession was related to anal eroticism. Thus, Freud eventually revealed to the patient the multiple sources of his anal conflicts and, with the patient's consent, concluded that he was cured.

EVALUATIVE COMMENTS

We are now in a position to evaluate Freud's theory in terms of how well it meets the six criteria outlined in Chapter 1 for judging the worth of scientific theories.

Comprehensiveness   Freud was an astute and original thinker who created a highly comprehensive theory. The range and diversity of behavior and experience described and interpreted are remarkable. Freud sought to understand not only various kinds of emotional and behavioral disorders, but many other phenomena, including humor, marriage, war, death, friendship, myths and fairy tales, incest, societal mores, dreams, slips of the tongue, "bungled actions," suicide, bed-wetting, creativity, competition, and absentmindedness. In short, Freud developed a system that explicitly sought to explain virtually all of human behavior. His theory remains, to the present day, the most comprehensive conceptual system ever created by a personality investigator.

Precision and testability   A major problem with Freudian theory is the relative vagueness of its concepts, the imprecision and ambiguities of its propositions or relational statements, and the difficulties it presents in deriving clear and testable hypotheses. When research is based on such loose theorizing, it is impossible to know whether the results really support the theory; when results are contrary to the theorizing, advocates can claim that the hypotheses were not validly derived from the major theoretical propositions.

A related criticism is that much of the theory is presented in metaphors, or in terms that do not lend themselves to precise scientific testing—for example, the life and death instincts. Frequently, explanations for observations are offered after the fact. The theory postdicts well, but has real difficulty in predicting in advance how people will behave. Much of the evidence for it is post hoc and secured through uncontrolled case-study methods. In addition, Freud did not record the patient's observations as he heard them, thereby opening the door to criticism that his memory of these events was distorted. Finally, the universal conclusions that Freud drew about human behavior on the basis of extensive observations of a few patients seem incredible and naive. They can be better understood, however, if we realize that the theory is strongly rooted in biology.

Clearly, Freud's theory does not satisfactorily meet the precision and testability criterion.

Parsimony   Freud's theory also fails to meet the parsimony criterion. Although it utilizes a number of assumptions and concepts to account for the phenomena in its domain, its proposed explanatory scheme is highly restricted in nature: sex and aggressive tendencies are the sole determinants of behavior. Nowhere in the theory, for example, does Freud discuss how needs for competence, exploration, or altruism influence personal development and behavior. Thus, the motivational base of the theory is limited and does not allow for different and more adequate explanations of behavior.

Similarly, the structure of human personality is divided into only three components, and the interactions among these three facets are presumed to account for all the underlying conflicts that hinder personality functioning.

Finally, Freud presented a generally pessimistic and one-sided view of human nature. People are seen as essentially irrational and controlled by amoral forces. Although he recognized fully that human beings can act rationally, he chose to focus almost entirely on the irrational side of human nature in his work.

Empirical validity   There have been literally thousands of investigations of various aspects of Freudian theorizing. These investigations can be divided generally into two categories: evidence for

Freud's theory of psychotherapy and evidence for his theory of psychosexual development.

In regard to the theory of psychotherapy, Eysenck (1952) conducted an early massive review of the clinical literature to assess the effectiveness of psychoanalysis in curing people. After examining more than 7,000 case histories of patients, he concluded that psychoanalytic therapy did not significantly facilitate the recovery of neurotic patients. Although 66% of patients treated to completion by means of psychoanalysis were much improved or cured, Eysenck found that 72% of patients who were *not* treated by means of any formal therapy were also much improved or cured within two years of the onset of their illnesses. Thus, approximately two-thirds of patients recovered or improved to a marked extent whether they were treated psychoanalytically or not. Although numerous critics have attacked Eysenck's conclusions on both theoretical and methodological grounds, reviews of all the evidence suggest that Eysenck's argument is still essentially valid today (Erwin, 1980; Franks, Wilson, Kendall, & Foreyt, 1990; Grossarth-Maticek & Eysenck, 1990; Stunkard, 1991).

The evidence in support of Freud's theorizing on psychosexual development is more promising, as we have seen. In addition, there is evidence that, the less adequate are an individual's defenses against sexual and aggressive impulses, the greater is the likelihood of psychopathology; this finding is consistent with Freud's theorizing (Silverman, 1976). There is also evidence that sexual conflicts are present in many neurotics and that some of these disturbances arise from experiences during early childhood. It is apparent that these early experiences have a marked impact on later personality functioning in some cases. Preliminary evidence also exists for Freud's hypothesis that, under stress, subjects may fail to suppress unacceptable thoughts and thus they may show up in slips of the tongue (Baars, Cohen, Bower, & Berry, 1992, p. 311). All in all, the research evidence in support of Freud's theory of neurosis is greater than many of his critics are willing to admit.

Heuristic value   Freud's theory continues to have tremendous heuristic value (Bornstein & Masling, 1994). Current supporters think that the future of psychoanalysis looks bright indeed, especially with the creation of new, more objective measurement procedures that allow Freudian hypotheses to be tested in more precise and unequivocal ways (Michels, 1988).

As a creative scholar, Freud continues to serve as an inspiration to other professionals, by showing them the kinds of contributions that can be made to our knowledge of behavior through painstaking and courageous investigation. Professional psychologists in a variety of specialty areas—especially cognitive, developmental, and social psychology—show an ongoing interest in many of his ideas. For example, researchers in developmental psychology are still intrigued and influenced by his ideas on moral development, sex-typing, identification, parent-child relations, aggression, and dependency (Miller, 1993, p. 146). Furthermore, his once-controversial ideas—(1) that unconscious states exist and influence behavior; (2) that people are frequently motivated to distort information about themselves and others when threatened; (3) that people typically act on the basis of many goals and thus must regulate multiple feelings and emotions simultaneously; and (4) that early experience plays an important role in subsequent development—are now generally acceptable to psychologists; that is, there is abundant research evidence demonstrating the validity of Freud's views on these matters (Masling, 1992, p. 262; Miller, 1993, p. 146; Wakefield, 1992, p. 78; Westen, 1992, p. 377; Westen, 1994, p. 645).

Scholars in disciplines outside of psychology—for example, in literature, art, sociology, history, anthropology, religion, philosophy, criminology, political science, and the physical sciences—all continue to make use of Freudian concepts (Bornstein & Masling, 1994).

Much of the continuing fascination with Freud's theory lies in the unusual and complex picture of human beings that it paints. Men and women are not simply rational animals, but curious mixtures of the irrational and rational. They often feel threatened by society and are continually searching for acceptable ways to express their innermost feelings. In an attempt to deal with their conflicts, they use various defense mechanisms that, while temporarily protective, prove damaging in the long run. Through painful confrontation with reality in a therapeutic setting, the limitations of their personalities are revealed and, with the help of the therapist, heroic attempts to overcome them are made. It seems clear that such drama was destined to excite and interest observers of human behavior and experience. This is a major part of Freud's legacy.

Applied value   In addition to his seminal contributions to therapy and the treatment of emotional disorders, Freud's insights have been applied by psychological anthropologists to cross-cultural phenomena. These investigators continue to use psychoanalytic ideas about child-rearing in their efforts to explain personality development (Haviland, 1994, pp. 379–380). Freud's ideas have also been employed by sociologists and social psychologists to help them understand the dynamics of family life and the functioning of small groups. In addition, Freudian concepts have been used fruitfully by historians, theologians, novelists, and economists. Thus, the psychoanalytic position continues to have considerable applied value.

DISCUSSION QUESTIONS

1. In what ways do the interactions between and among the id, ego, and superego create difficulties for the individual?
2. What are the primary defense mechanisms, as envisioned by Freud? Give possible examples of the operation of such mechanisms from your own experience.
3. Cite some examples of the ways in which defense mechanisms can be used to help people adjust to their environment.
4. What do you think might happen to a society in which id impulses were left unchecked by the superego?
5. How would you explain the behavior of a person who overeats continually in terms of the Freudian model of psychosexual development?
6. Do you agree that cleanliness is a virtue in contemporary society? If so, what are the possible reasons that people value it? If not, cite your reasons.
7. Do you think that Freud's concept of penis envy has any merit?
8. Research has shown that, in comparison to low-orals, high-orals are more interpersonally sensitive, more likely to ask for help when attempting to solve difficult problems, and more likely to seek medical attention when physical symptoms appear. What other positive qualities might dependent or high-oral persons have?
9. Do you agree with Freud that the normal individual is satisfactorily adjusted in two major areas—love and work?
10. Do you agree with Freud that the two major human motives are sex and aggression? State your reasons.

GLOSSARY

ambivalence   Mixed feelings of one person toward another, characterized by alternation between love and hate.

anal character   An individual fixated at the anal stage, who derives pleasure from his/her control over retention of feces. As an adult, this person is characterized by stinginess, orderliness, stubbornness, and the hoarding of possessions.

anal eroticism   Feelings of sexual pleasure that have their source in the person's control over expulsion and retention of feces.

anal stage   Second pregenital stage of psychosexual development, in which primary gratification centers around the anal cavity.

anticathexes   Restraining forces within the personality that are designed to keep unwanted impulses from reaching consciousness or awareness.

anxiety   Painful feelings experienced when the ego is threatened.

catharsis   Reliving earlier traumatic experiences emotionally, to reduce disturbing physical symptoms. This term dervies from the Greek word meaning purification.

cathexes   Driving energy forces that attach themselves to an idea or behavior.

compromise formation   Defense mechanism that involves the use of contradictory behaviors to attain some satisfaction for an unacceptable impulse.

conscience   Punitive aspect of the superego. Once the person has incorporated societal values by forming a conscience, violation of that conscience makes the person feel guilty or ashamed. Such feelings are punishing.

conscious   A state of the mind characterized by awareness of one's experiences.

countertransference   The tendency of the therapist to react with personal feelings toward the patient on the basis of the therapist's own needs and conflicts. These feelings might involve attraction and lust, but other possibilities include dislike and even revulsion toward an aggressive and/or hostile patient because of the therapist's own insecurities. Analysis of these needs and conflicts could lead the therapist to better self-understanding, which, in turn, could lead to an increased understanding of the patient and movement toward a cure.

denial   Primitive defense mechanism in which the person protects the self against threats from the environment by refusing to recognize their existence.

determinism   Philosophical doctrine that all behavior is caused by the operation of other events and does not occur freely or at random.

displacement   Defense mechanism in which the person seeks gratification of thwarted impulses by shifting the impulses from the original, frustrating object to a substitute object.

dream analysis   Psychoanalytic technique used to probe the unconscious through interpretation of the patient's dreams.

ego   Agency postulated by Freud to help the individual satisfy basic urges in ways deemed appropriate by society.

ego-ideal   Positive aspect of the superego, comprising the standards of perfection taught to the child by the parents.

fixation   Defensive attachment to an earlier stage of psychosexual development. Fixation prevents the learning of new behaviors, the acquisition of new interpersonal relationships, and progress in development.

free association   Therapeutic technique pioneered by Freud in which the therapist encourages patients to report, without restriction, any thoughts that occur to them.

genital character   A mature individual who is sexually developed and capable of relating to members of the other sex.

genital stage   Final stage of psychosexual development, in which an attempt is made to conduct a mature love relationship with a member of the opposite sex.

id   Reservoir of unconscious forces or urges that blindly seek gratification.

identification   In Freudian theory, the defensive process whereby an individual takes on the characteristics of another person in order to relieve anxieties and reduce internal conflicts.

intellectualization   Defense mechanism in which individuals protect themselves against pain by isolating their thoughts about painful events from their feelings about them.

latency stage   Psychosexual period during which libidinal energy lies dormant and the primary focus is on the development of interests and skills through contact with childhood peers and teachers.

libido   In Freudian theory, the basic energy source contained in the id that propels behavior. Freud considered it to consist of sexual impulses; Jung conceptualized it as a more general life-energy process consisting of sexual, creative, spiritual, and self-preservative instincts.

libido theory   The view that the child has unconscious sexual urges that seek expression through intimacy with the parent of the opposite sex.

negative transference   Phenomenon that occurs during psychoanalytic therapy in which the patient redirects toward the therapist unconscious feelings of anger and hostility retained from experiences with authority figures in childhood.

neoanalytic perspective   Theoretical positions that have their origins in Freudian psychoanalytic theory but have evolved new concepts and ways of examining and understanding human personality that are significant departures from Freud's original theory.

neurosis   Behavioral disorder characterized by underlying conflicts and anxieties that prevent the individual from coping effectively with everyday problems.

obsessive-compulsive disorder   A disorder characterized by repetitive thoughts and actions that the patient cannot control.

Oedipal complex   The process during the phallic stage in which the male child desires sexual contact with the mother, feels threatened by the father, and eventually resolves the conflict by identifying with the father.

oral aggressive character   An individual who becomes fixated in the oral stage because of underindulgence during feeding, when newly emerging teeth are used to bite the caregiver as a means of obtaining nourishment. As an adult, this person is characterized by envy, manipulation of others, and suspiciousness.

oral receptive character   An individual who becomes fixated in the oral stage because of overindulgence during feeding (before the emergence of teeth). As an adult, this person is characterized by gullibility, admiration for others, and excessive dependence.

oral stage   First pregenital stage of psychosexual development, in which primary gratifications center around the mouth.

parapraxis   Malfunction in language—such as a slip of the tongue, a bungled word, misreading, mishearing, or forgetting words or things—that indicates the presence of underlying conflicts.

phallic character   An individual fixated at the phallic stage who, later in life, needs to prove continually his or her sexual adequacy. The male phallic character needs to prove his adequacy through sexual conquests. This person is characterized by brashness, excessive vanity and pride, and exhibitionism. The female phallic character needs to prove her adequacy by continually ridiculing and humiliating men. This person is characterized by a domineering and contemptuous attitude toward men.

phallic stage   Third pregenital stage of psychosexual development, in which primary gratifications are derived from manipulation of the genitals.

pleasure principle   The rule by which the id operates; the id seeks to achieve pleasure and avoid pain.

positive transference   Phenomenon that occurs during therapy in which the patient redirects toward the therapist unconscious feelings of love and affection retained from experiences with authority figures (usually the parents) in early childhood.

preconscious   A state of the mind in which the person is currently unaware of some idea, memory, or event, which can, however, be made conscious with some effort.

projection   Defense mechanism in which a person attributes his or her own undesirable characteristics to others.

psychoanalysis   Theory of personality development, functioning, and change created by Freud. It places heavy emphasis on the roles of biological and unconscious factors in the determination of behavior.

psychopathology   Disordered behaviors, such as neuroses or psychoses, that interfere with realistic and effective functioning or behaving.

psychosexual development   Theory devised by Freud to account for psychological and personality development in terms of individuals' attempts to come to grips with key biological impulses.

psychosis   Severe behavioral disorder characterized by an inability to relate effectively to other people.

rationalization   Defense mechanism in which individuals provide plausible but inaccurate justifications for their behavior.

reaction formation   Defense mechanism in which an impulse or behavior is converted into its opposite.

regression   Defense mechanism in which a person reverts to infantile behavior as a means of alleviating stress.

repression   Basic defense mechanism by which unpleasant, highly painful experiences situated in the unconscious are prevented from entering consciousness.

resistance   A patient's unwillingness to report anxiety-provoking memories and conflicts. Freud believed that resistance was a symptom of an underlying conflict.

sublimation   Form of displacement in which a socially acceptable goal replaces one that is unacceptable.

superego   Agency postulated by Freud to represent the individual's incorporation of the moral standards of society and the ways in which these internalized standards control his or her behavior via reward and punishment.

suppression   A form of defense in which threatening thoughts are removed by actively and consciously deciding not to think about them. The person can exert control over their removal and their reactivation.

transference   Phenomenon postulated by Freud to account for the patient's development of positive and negative feelings toward the therapist during treatment—feelings presumed to have originally been directed toward another person (usually one of the parents).

unconscious   In Freudian theory, the depository of hidden wishes, needs, and conflicts of which the person is unaware.

undoing   Defense mechanism in which a person makes amends for a socially unacceptable act by performing a related socially acceptable act that nullifies the misdeed.

SUGGESTED READINGS

Bornstein, R. F. (1993). *The dependent personality.* New York: Guilford Press.

Cramer, P. (1991). *The development of defense mechanisms: Theory, research, and assessment.* New York: Springer-Verlag.

Freud, S. (1957). *A general introduction to psychoanalysis* (rev. ed.; J. Riviere, Trans.). New York: Permabooks.

Gay, P. (Ed.). (1989). *The Freud reader.* New York: Norton.

REFERENCES

Baars, B. J., Cohen, J., Bower, G. H., & Berry, J. W. (1992). Some caveats on testing the Freudian slip hypothesis. In B. J. Baars (Eds.), *Experimental slips and human error: Exploring the architecture of volition* (pp. 289–313). New York: Plenum Press.

Blum, G. S. (1953). *Psychoanalytic theories of personality.* New York: McGraw-Hill.

Bornstein, R. F. (1992). The dependent personality: Developmental, social, and clinical perspectives. *Psychological Bulletin, 112,* 3–23.

Bornstein, R. F. (1993). *The dependent personality.* New York: Guilford Press.

Bornstein, R. F. (1994). Adaptive and maladaptive aspects of dependency: An integrative review. *American Journal of Orthopsychiatry, 64,* 622–635.

Bornstein, R. F., & Masling, J. M. (1994). Introduction: From the consulting room to the laboratory: Clinical evidence, empirical evidence, and the heuristic value of object relations theory. In J. M. Masling and R. F. Bornstein (Eds.), *Empirical perspectives on object relations theory.* (pp. xv–xxvi). Washington, DC: American Psychological Association.

Cramer, P. (1991). *The development of defense mechanisms: Theory, research, and assessment.* New York: Springer-Verlag.

Erdelyi, M. H. (1985). *Psychoanalysis: Freud's cognitive psychology.* New York: W. H. Freeman.

Erwin, E. (1980). Psychoanalytic therapy: The Eysenck argument. *American Psychologist, 35,* 435–443.

Eysenck, H. J. (1952). The effects of psychotherapy: An evaluation. *Journal of Consulting Psychology, 16,* 319–324.

Fenichel, O. (1945). *The psychoanalytic theory of neurosis.* New York: Norton.

Fischer, R. E., & Juni, S. (1982). The anal personality: Self-disclosure, negativism, self-esteem, and superego severity. *Journal of Personality Assessment, 46,* 50–58.

Ford, D. H., & Urban, H. B. (1963). *Systems of psychotherapy: A comparative study.* New York: Wiley.

Franks, C. M., Wilson, G. T., Kendall, P. C., & Foreyt, J. P. (1990). *Review of behavior theory: Theory and practice* (Vol. 12). New York: Guilford Press.

Freud, A. (1946). *The ego and the mechanisms of defense* (C. Baines, Trans.). New York: International Universities Press.

Freud, S. (1937). Analysis terminable and interminable. In J. Strachey (Ed.), *Standard edition of the complete psychological works of Sigmund Freud* (Vol. 23, pp. 216–237). London: Hogarth Press.

Freud, S. (1938a). The history of the psychoanalytic movement. In A. A. Brill (Ed.), *The basic writings of Sigmund Freud* (pp. 931–977). New York: Random House.

Freud, S. (1938b). The interpretation of dreams. In A. A. Brill (Ed.), *The basic writings of Sigmund Freud* (pp. 179–549). New York: Random House.

Freud, S. (1938c). Totem and taboo. In A. A. Brill (Ed.), *The basic writings of Sigmund Freud* (pp. 807–930). New York: Random House.

Freud, S. (1938d). Three contributions to the theory of sex. In A. A. Brill (Ed.), *The basic writings of Sigmund Freud* (pp. 553–603). New York: Random House.

Freud, S. (1950). *Totem and taboo* (J. Strachey, Trans.). New York: Norton.

Freud, S. (1952a). Civilization and its discontents. In R. M. Hutchins (Ed.), *Great books of the Western world* (pp. 767–802). Chicago: Encyclopaedia Britannica.

Freud, S. (1952b). Beyond the pleasure principle. In R. M. Hutchins (Ed.), *Great books of the Western world* (pp. 639–663). Chicago: Encyclopaedia Britannica.

Freud, S. (1957). *A general introduction to psychoanalysis* (rev. ed.; J. Riviere, Trans.). New York: Permabooks.

Freud, S. (1958). Observations on transference-love. In J. Strachey (Ed.), *Standard edition of the complete psychological works of Sigmund Freud* (Vol. 12, pp. 159–171). London: Hogarth Press.

Freud, S. (1960a). *The ego and the id* (J. Riviere, Trans.; J. Strachey, Ed.). New York: Norton.

Freud, S. (1960b). *The psychopathology of everyday life* (A. Tyson, Trans.; J. Strachey, Ed.). New York: Norton.

Freud, S. (1963). Notes from a case of obsessional neurosis. In P. Rieff (Ed.), *Three case histories* (pp. 15–105). New York: Collier Books.

Freud, S. (1969). *An outline of psychoanalysis* (J. Strachey, Trans. & Ed.). New York: Norton.

Grossarth-Maticek, R., & Eysenck, H. J. (1990). Prophylactic effects of psychoanalysis on cancer-prone and coronary heart disease-prone probands, as compared with control groups and behaviour therapy. *Journal of Behavior Therapy and Experimental Psychiatry, 21,* 91–99.

Hammer, M., & McFerran, J. (1988). Preference for sex of a child: A research update. *Individual Psychology, 44,* 481–491.

Haviland, W. A. (1994). *Anthropology* (7th ed.). New York: Harcourt Brace.

Horney, K. (1937). *The neurotic personality of our time*. New York: Norton.

Jones, E. (1963). *The life and work of Sigmund Freud* (L. Trilling & S. Marcus, Eds.). Garden City, NY: Anchor Books.

Juni, S., Masling, J., & Brannon, R. (1979). Interpersonal touching and orality. *Journal of Personality Assessment, 43,* 235–237.

Kagan, J., & Mussen, P. (1956). Dependency themes on the TAT and group conformity. *Journal of Consulting Psychology, 20,* 29–32.

Kline, P. (1972). *Fact and fantasy in Freudian theory*. London: Methuen.

Masling, J. (1986). Orality, pathology and interpersonal behavior. In J. Masling (Ed.), *Empirical studies of psychoanalytic theories* (Vol. 1, pp. 73–106). Hillsdale, NJ: Erlbaum.

Masling, J. (1992). What does it all mean? In R. F. Bornstein and T. S. Pittman (Eds.), *Perception without awareness* (pp. 259–276). New York: Guilford Press.

Masling, J., O'Neill, R., & Katkin, E. S. (1982). Autonomic arousal, interpersonal climate, and orality. *Journal of Personality and Social Psychology, 42,* 529–534.

Masling, J., Price, J., Goldband, S., & Katkin, E. S. (1981). Oral imagery and autonomic arousal in social isolation. *Journal of Personality and Social Psychology, 40,* 395–400.

Masling, J., Weiss, L., & Rothschild, B. (1968). Relationships of oral imagery to yielding behavior and birth order. *Journal of Consulting and Clinical Psychology, 32,* 89–91.

Michels, R. (1988). The future of psychoanalysis. *Psychoanalytic Quarterly, 57,* 167–185.

Miller, P. H. (1993). *Theories of developmental psychology* (3rd ed.). New York: W. H. Freeman.

Pollak, J. M. (1979). Obsessive-compulsive personality: A review. *Psychological Bulletin, 86,* 225–241.

Puner, H. W. (1947). *Freud: His life and his mind*. New York: Dell.

Silverman, L. H. (1976). Psychoanalytic theory: The reports of my death are greatly exaggerated. *American Psychologist, 31,* 621–637.

Stunkard, A. J. (1991). Review of Schwartz, H. J. (Eds.), *Bulimia: Psycho-analytic treatment and theory* (Madison, CT: International Universities Press, 1988). *Psychiatric Annals, 19,* 279.

Tribich, D., & Messer, S. (1974). Psychoanalytic character type and status of authority as determiners of suggestibility. *Journal of Consulting and Clinical Psychology, 42,* 842–848.

Wakefield, J. C. (1992). Freud and cognitive psychology: The conceptual interface. In J. W. Barron, M. N. Eagle, and D. L. Wolitzky (Eds.), *Interface of psychoanalysis and psychology* (pp. 77–98). Washington, DC: American Psychological Association.

Westen, D. (1992). Social cognition and social affect in psychoanalysis and cognitive psychology: From regression analysis to analysis of regression. In J. W. Barron, M. N. Eagle, and D. L. Wolitzky (Eds.), *Interface of psychoanalysis and psychology* (pp. 375–388). Washington, DC: American Psychological Association.

Westen, D. (1994). Toward an integrative model of affect regulation: Applications to social-psychological research. *Journal of Personality, 62,* 641–667.

CHAPTER 3

Jung's Analytical Psychology

Carl Jung was born in Kesswil, Switzerland, in 1875. According to Jung, his father, a pastor in the Swiss Reformed church, was a weakling who was dominated by his wife. Jung described his mother as an insecure woman who frequently contradicted herself and treated members of the family inconsistently—sometimes loving and kind, sometimes harsh and aloof. When Jung was 3 years old, his mother entered a hospital for several months, with an illness Jung attributed to marital difficulties (Storr, 1991, pp. 1–2). He reported in his autobiography that the separation from his mother had a profound impact on him: he developed an ambivalent attitude of love and hate toward her. This conflict is reflected in his later works, in which women are frequently portrayed as destroyers and dominators as well as protectors, and as unreliable and not to be trusted.

> I was deeply troubled by my mother's being away. From then on, I always felt mistrustful when the word "love" was spoken. The feeling I associated with "woman" was for a long time that of innate unreliability. That is the handicap I started off with. Later, these early impressions were revised: I have trusted men friends and been disappointed by them, and I have mistrusted women and was not disappointed. (Jung, 1963, p. 8)

During his early school days, Jung lacked companionship, probably because he was far more advanced intellectually than any of the other children. He reported that he was not athletically inclined and did not engage in typical rough-and-tumble play with his peers. Instead, he spent much of his time in solitary pursuits, in long walks during which he gloried in the mysteries of nature. Jung reports that he became fully aware of his own existence during one of his walks to school. With this awareness, he reveled in the knowledge that he was an autonomous being who controlled his own life, instead of being continually controlled by others.

> I was taking the long road to school . . . when suddenly for a single moment I had the overwhelming impression of having just emerged from a dense cloud. I knew all at once: now I am myself! . . . Previously I had existed, too, but everything had merely happened to me. Now I happened to myself. Now I knew, I am myself now, now I exist. Previously I had been willed to do this and that: now I willed. This experience seemed to me tremendously important and new: there was "authority" in me. (Jung, 1963, pp. 32–33)

In this recollection we can see the beginnings of Jung's later focus on the importance of inner experience.

Another incident during his early school days made a marked impression on Jung and may explain his later reliance on the concept of the unconscious. In an English class, Jung was assigned a composition that interested him very much. He spent a great deal of time and effort on it, and hoped it would receive one of the highest marks in the class. Instead, his teacher accused him, in front of his classmates, of having copied it. Jung clung to his innocence, but the teacher persisted in his accusations and threatened to have Jung dismissed from school. For days afterward, Jung thought about the incident and tried to muster proof of his innocence, but there was no way of proving he had written the composition himself. At this point, his grief and rage threatened to get out of control. Suddenly, he reported, he experienced an "inner silence," and something deep down inside him (his unconscious) began to speak:

> What is really going on here? All right, you are excited. Of course the teacher is an idiot who doesn't understand your nature—that is, doesn't understand it any more than you do. Therefore he is as mistrustful as you are. You distrust yourself and others, and that is why you side with those who are naive, simple, and easily seen through. One gets excited when one doesn't understand things. (Jung, 1963, pp. 65–66)

The picture that emerges is that Jung was a sensitive and highly intelligent boy who neither understood nor was understood by his parents, teachers, and peers. As a result, he withdrew as much as he could from people and began to rely on his own inner experiences to help him understand the world.

During his teens, Jung decided to become an archaeologist, but his family was too poor to send him to a university that included this specialty in its curriculum. Instead, he entered the nearby University of Basel and majored in medicine. He decided to specialize in psychiatry, because it seemed to provide an opportunity to reconcile two important opposing tendencies within himself: an interest in natural science and a preoccupation with religious and philosophical values. This concern with conflict between opposites became a dominant theme in his later theorizing (Storr, 1991, p. 5). In 1900, having obtained his medical degree, Jung took a position as an assistant in a Zurich mental hospital. There he became interested in the etiology of schizophrenia. He found that the fantasies and delusions of these patients were in many respects similar to the myths and fantasies that guided people in contemporary and ancient cultures. Jung believed that the materials his patients revealed to him went beyond the recollection of their personal childhood and adult experiences; he postulated the existence of a *collective unconscious* (Storr, 1991, pp. 8–9).

In 1906, he published *The Psychology of Dementia Praecox,* a psychoanalytic treatment of schizophrenia. He sent a copy of the book to Freud. A year later, he went to Vienna to meet Freud, and began a collaboration that lasted until 1913. The many reasons for the final split, catalogued in Jung's *Psychology of the Unconscious,* include his basic disagreement with Freud over the importance of the sex instinct. Jung could not accept Freud's belief that such an urge was virtually the only determinant of behavior. He also grew tired of Freud's concern with the pathological side of human nature. Jung wanted to develop a psychology that dealt with human aspirations and spiritual needs; he argued that the way to self-realization was through the rediscovery of the spiritual self (Storr, 1991, pp. 12–13). In this respect, he was an important forerunner of the humanist movement.

Between 1913 and 1917, Jung went through a mental crisis in his own life that was precipitated by the break with Freud. Jung felt he could no longer rely on Freud's approach to therapy and that he needed to develop a new attitude or orientation toward treatment. He decided to let his patients tell him everything about their fantasies and dreams and tried not to interpret their self-reports in Freudian terms. Then Jung himself began to have dreams of a frightening nature. For example, he dreamed of dead bodies placed in crematory ovens, bodies that were then discovered to be alive. He also dreamed of monstrous catastrophes befalling Europe and felt vindicated when World War I broke out (Jung, 1963, pp. 170–176).

This flight into grotesque fantasies and dreams soon caused Jung to resign his lectureship at the University of Zurich. He did so consciously and deliberately because he "felt that something great was happening to me." In short, Jung began an attempt to probe the secrets of his unconscious and to unlock the mystery of his own personality. He was obsessed with understanding both sides of his personality: the inner world of subjective experience and the unconscious; and the outer world of contact with other people and material objects. Since he was already successful in his academic and writing career (his outer world), an exploration of his unconscious and inner world beckoned. In other words, Jung felt that his development was too one-sided; he was overdeveloped in terms of the outer world but underdeveloped in terms of his knowledge of the inner world. He began a quest for wholeness, for an integrated personality in which both sides of his nature would be brought into balance. Part of this journey of self-exploration also involved an acceptance of the inevitability of death and the fact that its occurrence was beyond the control of his ego. As a result, Jung eventually adopted a religious attitude toward life, in the sense that he had a greater appreciation of life and its mysteries. This inward turning and self-analysis at the middle stage of life is clearly reflected in his description of the individuation, or self-realization, process. This process is difficult and painful. In Jung's view, the person is "forged between hammer and anvil." Self-realization involves acknowledging everything you wish not to acknowledge about yourself and finding out and trying to actualize your unique potentials.

It was only toward the end of World War I that Jung emerged from his inward journey. In his opinion, the principal factor in the resolution of his crisis was that he began to understand his mandala drawings, which symbolized the self. The rest of his life was relatively uneventful, except for a period during World War II when some critics accused him of being a Nazi sympathizer. Jung vigorously denied the charges and was eventually exonerated (Stevens, 1994, pp. 113–122). He spent much of his time traveling and lecturing throughout the world and died on June 6th, 1961, at the age of 85 (Fordham, 1966, p. 145).

CONCEPTS AND PRINCIPLES

Jung's **analytical psychology** may be the most unusual theory in the entire body of work on personality. Although it provides numerous insights into personality functioning, it is very difficult to understand. In many respects, it is complex, esoteric, and obscure. Part of the problem is that Jung read widely in a number of different disciplines and drew upon materials from psychology, psychiatry, literature, physics, chemistry, biology, archaeology, philosophy, theology, mythology, history, anthropology, alchemy, and astrology in his attempts to understand human functioning. Since few investigators or readers have the background necessary to evaluate the materials he utilized, it has been easier to ignore or dismiss his theorizing than to grapple with its incredible array of complex ideas. Still another difficulty lies in Jung's own failure to write clearly. He often used conventional terms in idiosyncratic ways without fully explaining the arbitrary shifts he had made in their meanings. With these difficulties clearly in mind, we present a review of the basic ideas of the theory.

The Psyche

Jung referred to the total personality as the **psyche.** He conceived of it as a nonphysical space that has its own special reality. Through the psyche, energy flows continuously in various directions—from consciousness to unconsciousness and back, and from inner to outer reality and back. Jung considered this psychic energy to be real and to be interchangeable with libido. To him, libido is a general **life process energy,** of which sexual urges are only one aspect (Jung, 1969, p. 17). Psychic energy, like physical energy, is an abstraction representing something real that cannot be touched or felt but that we know exists through its effects. Just as physical energy manifests itself in the heating and lighting of the rooms in our homes, so psychic energy manifests itself in our various feelings, thoughts, and behaviors.

Most important, psychic energy is considered an outcome of the conflict between forces within the personality. Without conflict there is no energy and no life. Love and hatred of a person can exist within a psyche, creating tension and new energy that seeks expression in behavior. Other values may also conflict, such as a desire to have premarital intercourse despite the strong disapproval of significant others. The number of potential conflicts is virtually unlimited. Jung also maintained that the various structures of the psyche are continually opposed to one another. For example, ideas in consciousness and ideas residing in the unconscious may conflict with one another. Further, the shadow—that is, the unconscious and often evil side of our nature—may conflict with the ego, while ego processes may operate to keep unpleasant memories from awareness. Thus, he conceived of the psyche as a general entity that operates according to the **principle of opposites.**

Once energy is created, it moves in a variety of directions (Progoff, 1953, p. 63). It can be dissipated in outward behavior, or it can continue to move within the psyche, first in one direction, then in another. It may split and move unsystematically through the psyche, go into the unconscious, attach itself to other energy sources, and manifest itself in bizarre psychological forms—for example, in hallucinations, delusions, or unaccountable moods. In other words, some of the libidinal energy that courses through the psyche operates autonomously, and hence unpredictably, with various results.

Libido also operates according to the principles of equivalence and entropy. These psychological formulations are based on the first and second laws of thermodynamics in physics. The **principle of equivalence** states that "for a given quantity of energy expended or consumed in bringing about a certain condition, an equal quantity of the same or another form of energy will appear elsewhere" (Jung, 1969, p. 18). In other words, an increase in some aspect of psychic functioning is met by a compensatory decrease in functioning in another part of the psyche, and a decrease in some aspect of psychic functioning is met by a compensatory increase in functioning in another area of the psyche. An increase in concern with occupational success might mean an equivalent loss of concern with one's spiritual life, and vice versa. In the area of sexuality, an erotic feeling for a person that cannot be freely expressed would be repressed but would continue to be active at the same level of intensity in the unconscious. In another person, the expression of the same feeling might be sublimated or transformed into creative work. Jung's position is similar in this respect to Freud's notion of displacement.

The **principle of entropy** refers to the process within the psyche whereby elements of unequal strength seek psychological equilibrium. If energy is concentrated in the ego, for example, tension will be generated in the psyche to move energy from the conscious to the unconscious in order to create a balance. Consider the example of an outgoing student who acts as if life consists only of beer parties and endless social activities. Suddenly, he becomes bored and restless and begins to reflect on the meaning and direction of his life. He begins to explore inner experiences that were previously unconscious. As a result of these contemplations, he may reduce his social activities and increase the time he devotes to his studies, thereby becoming a more serious student, though still not a social isolate. The critical point is that any one-sided development of the personality creates conflict, tension, and strain, whereas a more even distribution produces a more fully mature person.

The aim of individual development is self-realization, the integration of all aspects of the psyche. In such a state, there is an increased understanding and acceptance of one's unique nature. This balanced state involves the evolution of a new center (the self) to replace the old one (the ego). The ego is not useless or obsolete in the final system; it exists, but in balance with the other aspects of the psyche.

Ego   Jung described the **ego** as a "complex of representations which constitutes the centrum of [the] field of consciousness and appears to possess a very high degree of continuity and identity" (Jung, 1923, p. 540). In Jung's terminology, a **complex** is a collection of thoughts that are united, often by a common feeling. Ego is a complex that is not synonymous with the psyche, but is only one aspect of it (Jung, 1969, p. 324). Nor is ego identical with consciousness. Instead, the ego, which is at the center of consciousness, is a unifying force in the psyche. It is responsible for our feelings of identity and continuity as human beings. Thus, the ego contains the conscious thoughts of our own behavior and feelings, as well as memories of our experiences.

The personal unconscious   The **personal unconscious** is the region next to the ego. (See Figure 3.1.) It consists of all the forgotten experiences that have lost their intensity for some reason, possibly because of their unpleasantness. It also includes sense impressions that are too weak to be perceived consciously (Jung, 1969, p. 376). These unconscious materials are accessible to the person's consciousness under certain circumstances. For example, they could be elicited by a skillful therapist with the help of the patient.

Collective unconscious   Lying still deeper within the psyche is the **collective unconscious,** characterized by Jung as "a deposit of world processes embedded in the structure of the brain and the sympathetic nervous system [which] constitutes, in its totality, a sort of timeless and eternal world-image which counterbalances our con-

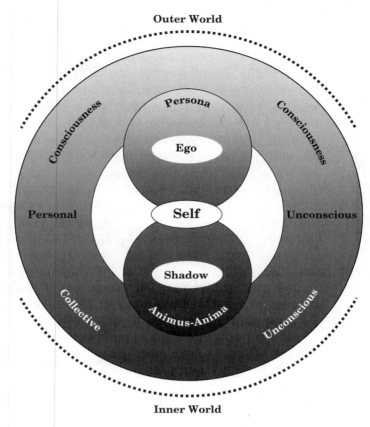

FIGURE 3.1   Structural components of the psyche. (Adapted from Jacobi, 1962, p. 126.)

scious momentary picture of the world" (Jung, 1969, p. 370). In other words, it is the storehouse of latent memories of our human and prehuman ancestry. It consists of instincts and archetypes that we inherit as possibilities and that often affect our behavior.

Archetypes

Archetypes are themes that have existed in all cultures throughout history. At various points in his writings, Jung referred to such themes as "imagoes" (images), "primordial images," "root-images," "dominants," and "behavior patterns." According to Jung, such collective memories are universal in nature because of our common evolution and brain structure.

This concept has often been misunderstood. Writers usually refer to it as one of Jung's original contributions to psychology, although Freud had already utilized a similar concept that he called the racial unconscious. More importantly, Jung did not accept the idea, espoused by the French naturalist Lamarck, that a person's characteristics are inherited directly. Instead, he argued that we inherit pathways that carry with them a tendency or predisposition to respond to certain experiences in specific ways (Progoff, 1953, p. 70). These tendencies emerge—sometimes spontaneously and sometimes when the person is under stress—in the form of archetypal motifs or themes.

For example, Jung proposed that men and women in every culture have inherited a tendency to respond to ambiguous and threatening situations with some form of an all-powerful being that we call God.

> God is an absolute, necessary function of an irrational nature, which has nothing whatever to do with the question of God's existence. The human intellect can never answer this question, still less give any proof of God. Moreover, such proof is superfluous, for the idea of an all-powerful divine Being is present everywhere, unconsciously if not consciously, because it is an archetype. (Jung, 1964, p. 81)

Jung contended that a person who renounces the idea of God will experience personal difficulties. Human beings must come to grips with such an idea if they are ever to achieve greater understanding of themselves. Thus, Jung would probably characterize atheists as people who have developed in a one-sided fashion and who are bound to experience difficulties eventually because they have failed to acknowledge this nonrational aspect of their nature. Searching for a rational answer in an irrational realm is a doomed quest. Jung seems to suggest that we accept the idea of an all-powerful being on faith; yet, he also seems to contradict himself by suggesting that, since the idea of God has a reality within the psyche as an archetype, it is potentially knowable. This difficulty disappears if we keep the distinction between internal and external reality clearly in view. Jung maintained that we can never offer objective proof of God's existence—that is, tangible, material proof shared by others in the external world—but that the idea of God still has validity, in a subjective or inner-reality sense, because of its roots in universal human experience.

The idea of God is not like the idea of a chair, with its clearly discernible properties. God is a universal symbol; such symbols, though real, can never be completely understood (Jung, 1958c, p. 118). We may gain valuable information about their reality through persistent self-analysis, but we will never know them completely. They take different forms; they have a shadowy existence, a mysterious quality about them that at some point, perhaps, we must come to accept. In brief, their reality is so complex and bewildering that rational inquiry is helpful only to a point. Beyond that, movement toward a balanced psyche demands faith and an acceptance of the unknown and unknowable.

Archetypes are, essentially, thought forms or ideas that give rise to visions projected onto current experiences. For example, one of the primary archetypes is the mother-child relationship, which is characterized by the mother's protection of the child. Dissolution of this bond must ultimately occur if the person is to attain adulthood. Jung suggests that the bond is broken in many primitive cultures when young men undergo rituals of rebirth (Jung, 1964, p. 208). We do not have many comparable rituals in our culture; as a result, many men have never resolved their basic dependency on their mothers. In married life, they may project the mother image onto their wives by acting in childish, dependent, and submissive ways; or they may react in an opposite manner by acting in hypermasculine ways and rejecting any offers of help from their spouse.

Not all archetypes are equally developed within the psyche. Those that are well formed exert a strong influence on personality functioning; those that are not well developed exert only minimal influence. Other major archetypes in the Jungian system include the persona, shadow, anima and animus, self, and introversion/extraversion. Although introversion and extraversion are considered by many theorists not to be archetypes, Jung believed that they were. They were innate dispositions, but ones often molded by experience (Jung, 1923, p. 286).

The persona

The **persona,** in Jung's theory, is "a compromise . . . between the demands of the environment and the necessities of the individual's inner constitution" (Jacobi, 1962, p. 19). It is the mask we wear in order to function adequately in our relationships with other people. This mask may take as many forms as the roles we play in our daily routines. It also aids in controlling evil forces in the collective unconscious. Presumably, the persona is an archetype because it is a universal manifestation of our attempt to deal appropriately with other people.

But the persona also has negative features. We can learn to hide our real selves behind these masks. Our personas can become split off from potentially enlightening forces in the personal and collective unconscious. We may become so committed to a particular role that we lose sight of our individuality. "We all know the professor," writes Jacobi (1962), "whose individuality is exhausted in playing the professor's role; behind this mask one finds nothing but a bundle of peevishness and infantilism" (pp. 19–20). In the Jungian view, so inflexible a man needs to become more accepting of his own and other people's feelings, recognize and accept the limits of his rationality and intellect, and become more receptive to archetypes such as the wise old man—the embodiment of wisdom and understanding—who might teach him something about human fallibility. Of course, the professor might argue that such a view is sheer nonsense, that he is feeling fine and functioning well; Jungians would probably retort that the professor is simply rationalizing. The point is that, in Jung's system, excessive identification with the persona may have harmful effects on personal development.

The shadow

Jung chose the term **shadow** to indicate the dark, sinister, Mr. Hyde side of our natures. In contrast to the persona's affiliation with the ego and consciousness and its role in personal adaptation to the external world, the shadow represents the evil, unadapted, unconscious, and inferior part of our psyches. It has two main aspects—one associated with the personal unconscious, the other with the collective unconscious (Dry, 1961, p. 95). In relation to the personal unconscious, the shadow consists of all those experiences that the person rejects on moral and/or aesthetic grounds. For example, our egos may reject our sadistic impulses, or we may repress socially unacceptable sexual or aggressive impulses. Jung believed that the shadow incorporated both Freud's sexual instinct and Adler's will to power.

In terms of the collective unconscious, the shadow consists of universal personifications of evil within our psyches. The devil, in its various forms, would be a prime example. Jung maintained that we may never understand this unadapted side of our personality fully because we can never bring ourselves to confront absolute evil. Nevertheless, the shadow exists in all of us, and it manifests itself in a variety of ways—unaccountable moods, pains of unexplained origin, urges toward self-destruction, and desires to harm others. It should be clearly understood that we do not, at base, have control over these impulses. Jung believed that these repressed feelings operate independently in the unconscious, where they join forces with other impulses. The result may be a complex with sufficient force to erupt into consciousness and momentarily subdue the ego. For example, a dignified and sophisticated executive may suddenly become highly abusive toward his colleagues during an important meeting. His arguments may become totally irrational, irresponsible, and unrelated to the issue under consideration.

Finally, as with all of Jung's concepts, the shadow has positive as well as negative features. Some examples are the murderer who decides impulsively to spare his victim because the victim reminds him of a loved one; or the selfish woman who spends virtually all her time making money and then generously decides to donate a large percentage of her earnings to a local charity. More generally, the positive side of the shadow may be seen when a person feels unaccountably vital, spontaneous, and creative.

Anima and animus

Like Freud, Jung believed that all men and women have elements of the opposite sex within them. Each man has a feminine side, and each woman has unconscious masculine qualities. This concept is based, at least partially, on the fact that both men and women have varying amounts of male and female hormones. The feminine archetype in man Jung called the **anima**; the masculine archetype in woman he labeled the **animus.** Like all archetypes, the anima and animus can function in either constructive or destructive ways. Jung states that, when the anima operates positively in man, it serves as "his inspiration": "her [anima's] intuitive capacity, often superior to man's, can give him timely warning [presumably about harmful events], and her feelings, always directed towards the personal, can show him ways which his own less personally accepted feeling would never have discovered" (Jung, 1964, p. 199). The negative aspects of the anima are seen when men act in moody, "bitchy," and "catty" ways. The animus in women has positive manifestations when it produces arguments based on reason and logic. The negative side of the animus can be seen in these behaviors:

> In intellectual women [it] encourages a critical disputatiousness and would-be high-browism, which . . . consists essentially in harping

on some irrelevant weak point and nonsensically making it the main point. Or a perfectly lucid discussion gets tangled up in the most maddening way through the introduction of a quite different and if possible perverse point of view. Without knowing it, such women are solely intent upon exasperating the man and are, in consequence, . . . completely at the mercy of the animus. (Jung, 1964, p. 220)

Despite Jung's claims that the anima and animus are universal phenomena, the descriptions sound suspiciously like our cultural stereotypes of the sexes. The masculine archetype includes those characteristics traditionally associated with the role of man—reason, logic, forceful argument, and social insensitivity, among others. The feminine archetype reflects traditional feminine behavior, including such attributes as emotionality, social sensitivity, intuition, vanity, moodiness, and irrationality. Although Jung did catalogue the presumed negative characteristics of the animus, his detailed arguments about the weaknesses of the anima suggest a patriarchal bias that we have already seen in the writings of Freud.

Jung notes that these archetypes may operate in dreams and fantasies, but often they are projected onto real-life objects. For example, the anima in a man could be projected onto his lover, producing a discrepancy between them that could be harmful to both parties. Perhaps he sees his lover as the universal mother, a compassionate and sensitive being who will always protect him and look out for his interests. In actuality, however, she may be an insensitive boor who is concerned only with exploiting him sexually. In a woman, the animus may take the form of the evil conqueror who, when projected onto a kindly and sensitive suitor, will inevitably produce conflicts and problems. To differentiate these universal images from their real-life counterparts is extremely difficult, but is essential if each of us is to progress toward selfhood.

The self

The **self** is an archetypal potentiality in all of us. Jung sees it as an innate blueprint that, theoretically at least, is capable of being realized. This "destiny within us" involves a process that Jung called the "way of individuation" (Jacobi, 1962, p. 100)—a "process by which a [person] becomes the definite, unique being that he in fact is. In doing so he does not become 'selfish' in the ordinary sense of the word, but is merely fulfilling the peculiarity of his nature, and this . . . is vastly different from egotism or individualism" (Jung, 1964, p. 183).

Thus, the self is the final goal of our striving. In this sense at least, it is similar to the goal of perfection in Adler's system, discussed in the next chapter. The movement toward self-realization is a difficult process, one that Jung believed could not be attained by young people. It takes time and considerable effort to resolve the many conflicts between opposites within the psyche, so that the few people who come closest to the attainment of selfhood will be at least in middle age. With the attainment of balance, a new center or midpoint, the self, evolves within the personality, replacing the old one, the ego. The ego now becomes a satellite of the self, much like the earth in rotation around the sun. Consciousness does not replace unconsciousness within the psyche. Instead, the principle of opposites remains in force, with consciousness and unconsciousness balancing each other.

The self thus becomes a unifying force with a **transcendent function**: it provides stability and balance to the various systems of the personality. As individuals explore the unconscious aspect of their individual psyches, they learn more about this side of their nature and its functions and begin to feel more comfortable with it. A woman, for example, begins to understand how her shadow operates to make her moody or impulsive; a man begins to understand how his anima forces him to idealize his girlfriend and ignore her faults. This understanding involves a resolution, not a solution, of the individuals' conflicts. Through their new understanding, they transcend these conflicts and begin to live more productively with themselves and with others.

Much of Jung's interest in **symbols,** such as shadow and anima, stems from his search for ways in which the self has been described and expressed in various religious and occult systems, psychologies, arts, and philosophies throughout history (Progoff, 1953, p. 153). Even medieval alchemy figured in Jung's search for unique expressions of the self. He saw the alchemists' transmutation of base metals into gold as analogous to the "transformation of personality through the blending and fusion of the noble with the base components, of the differentiated with the inferior functions, of the conscious with the unconscious" (Jung, 1964, p. 232).

To Jung, the most important representations of the self were the **mandalas,** or magic circles, found in the writing and art of all cultures (see Figure 3.2). These mandalas represent the synthesis or union of opposites within the psyche that occurs when individuals attain self-realization. According to Jung, the oldest mandala is a paleolithic sunwheel drawing based on the principle of four (Jung, 1958a, p. 326). Mandalas are also found in Buddhism, Taoism, and

FIGURE 3.2   Mandala of awakening consciousness. (Adapted from Jacobi, 1962, p. 114.)

other Eastern religions. In these religions, the golden flower is often placed in the center of the mandala, to signify the "heavenly heart . . . the realm of the greatest joy . . . and the altar upon which consciousness and life are made" (Jung, 1958a, p. 320). In the Middle Ages, European mandalas often included Christ with four evangelists around him (Jacobi, 1962, pp. 128–131). According to Jung, many of his patients spontaneously reported mandalas in their dreams and also painted them during therapy sessions. Thus, drawing upon materials from an incredible variety of sources, Jung believed he had discovered a universal synthesizing phenomenon that transcended personal experience.

The Theory of Psychological Types

Jung proposed that, in their attempt to evolve toward selfhood, people adopt different ways of relating to experience; that is, they adopt different attitudes toward life and utilize different psychological processes or functions to make sense out of their experiences. Jung described those basic attitudes and functions in his theory of psychological types.

Extraversion/Introversion

The two fundamental attitudes in Jung's typology are **extraversion** and **introversion.** Extraversion refers to "an outgoing, candid, and accommodating nature that adapts easily to a given situation, quickly forms attachments, and, setting aside any possible misgivings, often ventures forth with careless confidence into an unknown situation." Introversion, in contrast, signifies "a hesitant, reflective, retiring nature that keeps itself to itself, shrinks from objects, is always slightly on the defensive, and prefers to hide behind mistrustful scrutiny" (Jung, 1964, p. 52). Jung points out that people are not purely introverted or extraverted; rather, each person has both introverted and extraverted aspects. Moreover, both attitudes involve complex variations, including **dominant characteristics** (conscious) and **inferior characteristics** (unconscious). The dominant side compensates for the inferior side, and vice versa. If too much libido is invested in the dominant side, for example, energy forces are set up and activated in the unconscious, typically with harmful results for the individual.

Jung's typology is based on his idea of the flow of libido within the psyche. Energy can flow outward toward life, or inward toward subjective experience. For Jung, however, extraversion and introversion are not to be simply equated with outward libidinal flow, or progression, and inward flow, or regression. Instead

> movement can occur in two different forms; either extraverted, when the progression is predominately influenced by objects and environmental conditions, or introverted, when it has to adapt itself to the conditions of the ego (or, more accurately, of the "subjective factor"). Similarly, regression can proceed along two lines, either as a retreat from the outside world (introversion), or as a flight into extravagant experience of the outside world (extraversion). (Jung, 1969, pp. 40–41)

Thus, extraversion and introversion each have their own special dynamics, and both attitudes have progressive and regressive properties. As with all of Jung's concepts, introversion and extraversion can have both good (healthy) and bad (unhealthy) consequences for our development. Thus, for example, introversion may have progressive effects when a person creates a unique and useful product, such as a first-rate novel. It may have regressive effects when it leads to excessive brooding and indecisiveness at a time when a person needs to make a firm judgment. Witness the student who is doing poorly in a course and hesitates to ask a more competent classmate or the instructor for help; failure in the course may well be the outcome. Extraversion may have progressive effects when it leads a person to make sensible decisions, for example, by asking for assistance. It may have regressive effects when it leads someone to act injudiciously, for example, by unthinkingly accepting virtually every pronouncement of authority in order to secure approval. Such a person is so committed to the "object" (the authority figure) as to accept his or her comments uncritically. Witness the student who changes careers on the advice of neurotic relatives.

The Four Functions

Alongside the basic attitudes of introversion and extraversion, Jung postulated four functions, or ways in which people relate to the world: sensing, thinking, feeling, and intuiting. Sensing is the initial, concrete experiencing of phenomena without the use of reason (thinking) or evaluation (feeling). Thinking proceeds from this point to help us understand events through the use of reason and logic. It gives us the meaning of events that are sensed. Feeling gives us an evaluation of events by judging whether they are good or bad, acceptable or unacceptable. Finally, in the mode of intuiting we rely on hunches whenever we have to deal with strange situations where we have no established facts (Progoff, 1953, p. 100).

Jung called thinking and feeling the **rational functions** because they involve making judgments about experiences. Sensation and intuition he labeled the **irrational functions** because they involve passively recording experiences without evaluating or interpreting them. Although many of us associate thinking with rationality and feeling with irrationality, Jung makes the point that both thinking and feeling involve assessing the worth of an experience. Thinking is primarily concerned with truth or falsity, whereas feeling measures the degree to which we like or dislike something. There is a further semantic difficulty in that Jung does not want the term *irrational* to convey the idea of excessive or mindless emotionality. Instead, he used the term to mean modes of relating to experience that are unrelated to reason. Perhaps nonrational would have been a more suitable designation.

The rational and irrational functions are articulated, or differentiated, to varying degrees within the psyche. As Jung envisioned it, one function of the rational or irrational pair is dominant, superior or well-developed, and conscious and its counterpart inferior or under-developed and unconscious; the members of the remaining pair exist in a kind of twilight zone, partly conscious and partly unconscious. The superior function is the most highly differentiated, followed by the auxiliary pair; the inferior function is least differentiated. For example, in a thinking person, reason and logic are well-developed and conscious, and the person's feeling function is underdeveloped and unconscious. In this person, sensation and intuition are the auxiliary pair which means that each or both of them can be complementary or supportive of the thinking function. Each member of the auxiliary pair or both of them can become conscious at certain times and serve the superior function of thinking. Thus, in a highly scholarly person who relies on reason and logic to solve problems, her intuition can at times aid her thinking process by suggesting a vision of the correct solutions. Another example would be the person with strong mechanical skills who utilizes his sensation function to solve problems. A focus on the ways in which concrete objects can be manipulated helps him to use his reasoning abilities to solve problems. In this case, one could talk about the thinking person as having a practical intellect. Inventors often tinker with mechanical things in this way for long periods of time before finally seeing the logical connections that help them reach their goals.

Finally, it should be noted that any one of the functions can be dominant; that is, there are thinking, feeling, sensing, and intuiting kinds of individuals. Of course, each of these types lacks full development. The "whole" or integrated person would be capable of utilizing all the functions in dealing with experiences.

The Typology

Out of the two basic attitudes and four functions, Jung fashioned an eightfold classification **theory of psychological types.** In reality, there are 16 possible personality types, if we consider that either member of the auxiliary pair can exist in a somewhat differentiated and conscious form. In his classic work on the subject, however, Jung focused his attention on eight of the possibilities—namely, introverted and extraverted thinking, feeling, sensing, and intuitive types.

The extraverted thinking type According to Jung, the **extraverted thinking type** is characterized by a need

> to make all his life-activities dependent on intellectual conclusions, which in the last resort are always oriented by objective data. . . . This kind of man [lives by an] intellectual formula. By this formula

are good and evil measured and beauty and ugliness determined. . . . If the formula is wide enough, this type may play a very useful role in social life, either as a reformer or a ventilator of public wrongs . . . or as the propagator of important innovations. But the more rigid the formula, the more does he develop into a grumbler, a crafty reasoner, and a self-righteous critic. (Jung, 1923, pp. 346–347)

Such a person also has repressed feelings in his or her pursuit of ideas and ideals and tends to deny "aesthetic activities, taste, artistic sense, cultivation of friends, etc." (Jung, 1923, p. 348). Jung maintains further that a person who is developing in such a negative fashion may appear concerned about the welfare of other people but in reality is concerned only with the attainment of personal goals—for example, the self-serving activist who exploits the friendship of other people to further his or her aims.

The introverted thinking type   The **introverted thinking type,** "like his extraverted counterpart, is strongly influenced by ideas, though his ideas have their origin not in objective data but in his subjective foundation. He will follow his ideas like the extravert, but in the reverse direction: inwards and not outwards" (Jung, 1923, p. 383). The subjective foundation of the introverted thinker is the collective unconscious. Creative ideas spring from this source and not from outside sources such as traditional moral authority. As a result of this focus on internal forces, the introverted thinker appears cold, aloof, and inconsiderate of others. In addition, he or she tends to be inept socially and inarticulate in attempts to communicate ideas.

The extraverted feeling type   Jung described the **extraverted feeling type** as one who lives according to "objective situations and general values" (Jung, 1923, p. 356). The feelings and behavior of such individuals are controlled by social norms—that is, by the expectations of others. As a consequence, their feelings change from situation to situation and from person to person. Jung believed that women were the best examples of this type. A prime example would be a college woman who breaks her engagement because her parents object to the man. Her feelings toward the young man are based on her parents' judgments. If they like him, fine; if they do not, she feels compelled to reject him. In such people, thinking is largely repressed.

On the plus side of the ledger, Jung believed that extraverted feeling women could make satisfactory marriages. "These women are good companions and excellent mothers, so long as [their] husbands and children are blessed with the conventional psychic constitution"

(Jung, 1923, p. 357). By "conventional psychic constitution," Jung seems to mean conformity to the rules and regulations prescribed by society for the well-adjusted family.

The introverted feeling type   According to Jung, women are also the prime examples of the **introverted feeling type.** "They are mostly silent, inaccessible, and hard to understand; often they hide behind a childish or banal mask, and their temperament is inclined to melancholy. They neither shine nor reveal themselves" (Jung, 1923, p. 389). Although they appear unfeeling toward other people, in reality they are capable of an intense emotion, originating in the collective unconscious, that can erupt in religious or poetic form.

The extraverted sensing type   Jung visualized men as the prime examples of the **extraverted sensing type.** This type is primarily reality-oriented and typically shuns thinking and contemplation. Experiencing sensations becomes almost an end in itself. Each experience serves as a guide to new experience. Such people are usually outgoing and jolly and have a considerable capacity for enjoyment, some of which revolves around good food. In addition, they are often refined aesthetes, concerned with matters of good taste in painting, sculpture, and literature, as well as food and physical appearance. Such an individual who becomes overenamored of an object—for example, food or physical appearance—develops into a "crude pleasure-seeker or . . . unscrupulous, effete aesthete" (Jung, 1923, p. 365). The novelist Rabelais's fictional character Gargantua presents a perfect example of the negative aspects of extraverted sensing types:

> He spent his time like other small children: namely, in drinking, eating and sleeping; in eating, sleeping and drinking; in sleeping, drinking and eating. He was forever wallowing in dirt, covering his nose with filth and begriming his face. . . . He used to piddle on his shoes, brown up his shirt-tails, wipe his nose on his sleeve and clear his nostrils into his soup. . . . Often he coughed up, figuratively and literally. Fat? Another ounce of wind and he would have exploded. Appreciative? He would piss, full bladdered, at the sun. Cautious? He used to hide under water for fear of the rain. (Rabelais, 1936, p. 36)

The introverted sensing type   In Jung's view, **the introverted sensing type** is an irrational type guided by the "intensity of the subjective sensation—excited by the objective stimulus" (Jung, 1923, p. 395). These people seem to overreact to outside stimuli. They may take innocuous comments from others and interpret them in imaginative or bizarre ways. They may also appear rational and in complete control of their actions because they are unrelated to objects in the environment, including other people. Such types may also treat the objective world (external reality) as mere appearance, or even as a joke. Libido from primordial images affects their perception of events. Positive manifestations of libido are found in creative persons; negative manifestations are seen in psychotics.

The extraverted intuitive type   Exploiting external opportunities is the chief concern of the **extraverted intuitive type.** In Jung's words, they have a "keen nose for anything new and in the making" (Jung, 1923, p. 368). Politicians, merchants, contractors, and speculators are examples of this type; women are more likely to have such an orientation than are men (Jung, 1923, p. 369).

On the positive side, these people are the initiators and promoters of promising enterprises, and often inspire others to great accomplishments. But there are also serious dangers for people with this orientation. Although they may enliven and encourage others, they do little for themselves. And because they are impatient and always seeking new possibilities, they often do not see their actions through to completion.

The introverted intuitive type   An intensification of intuition in the **introverted intuitive type** often results in estrangement from external reality. Such people may be considered enigmatic even by close friends. On the positive side, they may become great visionaries and mystics; on the negative side, they may develop into artistic cranks who espouse idiosyncratic language and visions. Such people cannot be understood easily, and their ability to communicate effectively is further limited because their judgment functions (thinking and feeling) are relatively repressed.

Research Evidence for the Theory of Psychological Types

To assess the validity of Jung's proposed typology, investigators needed to construct a scale that measured the various concepts. The first personality inventory developed by Jungian analysts was called the Gray-Wheelwright. It has since been largely replaced by the more popular **Myers-Briggs Type Indicator** (MBTI), an inventory consisting of 166 items in a forced-choice format. Considerable work has been done to establish the reliability and validity of the MBTI. Sample items used to identify introverts and extraverts and the sensing, thinking, feeling, and intuitive types are presented in Table 3.1.

TABLE 3.1   Sample items from the Myers-Briggs Type Indicator (MBTI)

Introversion (I)–Extraversion (E) items

1. When you have to meet strangers, do you find it
   a. pleasant, or at least easy (E), or ✓
   b. something that takes a good deal of effort? (I)
2. Are you naturally
   a. a "good mixer" (E) or ✓
   b. rather quiet and reserved in company? (I)
3. In a large group, do you more often
   a. introduce others (E) or ✓
   b. get introduced? (I)

Sensing (S)–Intuition (N) items

1. Do you usually get along better with
   a. imaginative people (N) or ✓
   b. realistic people? (S)
2. Do you get more annoyed at
   a. fancy theories (S) or ✓
   b. people who don't like theories? (N)
3. Would you rather be considered
   a. a practical person (S) or
   b. an ingenious person? (N) ✓

Thinking (T)–Feeling (F) items

1. Which of these two is the higher compliment
   a. he is a person of real feeling (F) or ✓
   b. he is consistently reasonable? (T)
2. Do you think it is a worse fault
   a. to show too much warmth (T) or
   b. not to have enough warmth? (F) ✓
3. Do you more often let
   a. your heart rule your head (F) or
   b. your head rule your heart? (T) ✓

SOURCE: Adapted from Briggs & Myers, 1943, 1944, 1957, 1976.

In their research with the typology, Fling, Thomas, and Gallaher (1981) have shown that undergraduate volunteers for a meditation research study were more likely to be introverted than extraverted, more feeling than thinking, and more intuitive than sensing, in comparison to a comparable sample of nonvolunteer undergraduates.

Research summarized by Myers and McCaulley (1985, pp. 244–248) shows further that occupational interests among college students are related in many instances to the Jungian typology. For example, introverts have strong interests in mathematics, computer programming, library science, chemistry, and engineering, whereas extraverts gravitate toward sales, public relations, acting, and restaurant and hotel management. Students who are primarily intuitive show strong interests in becoming musicians, psychologists, artists, writers, and photographers, whereas sensing types lean toward food-service work, police and detective work, and craftwork. Thinking types prefer law, medicine, and dentistry, whereas feeling types are more interested in becoming preschool teachers, nurses, and priests.

Jung's typology also predicts the management styles of executives from different cultures. Specifically, Furnham and Stringfield (1993) found that Chinese managers who worked for a highly successful, international airline were more introverted, thinking, and sensing and less intuitive than were their European counterparts at the same airline. These differences in personality type were related moderately to managerial styles: Chinese managers were more concrete and practical, and less innovative, than were the European managers. The European style focused more on the spontaneous development of ideas through the use of intuition and on outgoing, informal relationships with employees. Chinese managers, in contrast, tended to be less creative and more authoritarian in their relationships with their employees. According to Furnham and Stringfield, these differences in personality and managerial style would make it difficult for the managers in one culture to work effectively with employees in the other culture if they were transferred or sought employment in companies in other cultures. They suggest the need for all managers to be trained in the skills, preferences, and practices of other cultures, so as to ensure healthy working relationships.

Other research has provided additional evidence in support of Jung's typology. Carlson and Levy (1973) found that introverted thinkers were more effective in memorizing emotionally neutral stimulus material (a number or series of digits) than were introverted and extraverted feeling types or extraverted thinkers. Extraverted feeling types were more accurate than were the others in remembering new, emotionally toned material (a series of pictures of a female model portraying different emotions). A number of other predictions derived from Jung's theory were also confirmed, including a finding that extraverted intuitive types were overrepresented among volunteers in the social services, as compared with a matched sample of nonvolunteers.

Interesting research by Carlson (1980) has shown a considerable difference in the kinds of memories that introverted thinkers and extraverted feelers report as significant moments in their lives. Introverted thinking and extraverted feeling adults were asked to describe their most vivid past experiences that made them feel joyful, excited, or ashamed. In line with Jung's theory, extraverted feelers most often mentioned memories that involved experiences with other people (social experiences), while introverted thinkers most often mentioned experiences that they had had while alone (individual experiences). Joyful experiences recollected by introverted thinkers included: (1) graduating from junior college; (2) awakening in the hospital and seeing my new baby; (3) shooting my first rabbit (age 10). In contrast, extraverted feelers reported: (1) meeting my girlfriend in a group attending the Rose Parade; (2) having my boyfriend propose marriage; (3) being chosen the most popular counselor at a church camp. Exciting experiences for introverted thinkers included: (1) anticipating a trip to San Francisco; (2) beginning a new job in a program for the mentally retarded. Extraverted feelers reported: (1) cheering for a friend at a cross-country track meet; (2) embarking on a small business venture with my spouse. Shameful experiences for introverted thinkers included: (1) drinking too much and then becoming "too candid" at a party; (2) getting plastered and throwing up at a party. Extraverted feelers reported: (1) being arrested for shoplifting with a friend (age 12); (2) calling my mother an "old hag" and being reprimanded by my father.

Thus, some complex Jungian concepts can be translated into terms that allow for empirical testing and verification and, in fact, the research provides considerable support for the Jungian scheme of psychological types.

PERSONALITY DEVELOPMENT

Self-Realization

Jung conceived of personal development as a dynamic and evolving process that occurs throughout life. A person is continually developing, learning new skills, and moving toward **self-realization.** Although Jung had little to say about the developmental process in childhood, it is clear that he did not accept Freud's view that the individual's personality was relatively fixed by the end of early childhood. Neither did he accept Freud's view that only past events determine a person's behavior. For Jung, behavior was determined not only by past experiences but also by future goals. Although, according to Jung, people can progress toward selfhood by developing differentiated psychological functions, they can also move backward. Such backward movement, however, is not necessarily detrimental; some retreats into the psyche can provide the impetus for creative growth.

The movement toward self-realization is often a difficult and painful process. It involves continual attempts by the individual to understand his or her experiences, to develop healthy attitudes, and to reconcile the opposing forces within the psyche through transcendence. The person is often beset by crises, and Jung believed that many individuals experience their most severe crises during the middle years. Adequate resolution of these crises helps move people toward a more accurate perception and a fuller understanding of themselves. The ultimate outcome is individuation; that is, the person becomes all he or she is capable of becoming as a human being.

Neurosis and Psychosis

Progress toward self-realization is not automatic. If the person grows up in an unhealthy and threatening environment, where the parents use harsh and unreasonable punishment, growth is likely to be stifled. Repressed evil forces within the psyche may also erupt without warning to produce personality dysfunction. Under these conditions, the outcome may be neurosis or psychosis.

In Jung's view, neurosis and psychosis differ primarily in the severity of their consequences. Both result from one-sided development in which repressed forces create problems in functioning. In all eight psychological types discussed earlier, intense repression of one of the four functions would probably result in a form of neurosis. For example, when thinking is repressed in the introverted feeling type, Jung argued, the thinking function may eventually project itself onto objects, thus creating problems for the person. Because the thinking function is archaic and undifferentiated, the person's judgment about the object or objects is bound to be gross and inaccurate. Such a person is unable to reason accurately about the intentions of others. As a consequence

> other people are [assumed to be] thinking all sorts of mean things, scheming evil, contriving plots, secret intrigues, etc. In order to forestall them, she herself is obliged to start counterintrigues, to suspect others . . . and [to] weave counterplots. Beset by rumours, she must make frantic efforts to be top dog. Endless clandestine rivalries spring up, and in these embittered struggles she will shrink from no baseness or meanness, and will even prostitute her virtues in order to play the trump card. Such a state of affairs must end in exhaustion. (Jung, 1923, p. 391)

The resulting form of neurosis is neurasthenia, a disorder characterized by listlessness and fatigue.

Jung saw psychosis as an extension of neurosis that occurs when repressed and unconscious forces overpower consciousness. In his view, consciousness is a secondary phenomenon derived from unconsciousness; it is a fragile entity that can be swallowed up by unleashed forces in the unconscious. In such instances, the person collapses; the ego, attacked by elements of the collective unconscious, loses control. Jung provides an illustration of the onset of psychosis in the case of a quiet young man who imagined that a woman was in love with him. When he discovered that his love was unrequited, he

> was so desperate that he went straight to the river to drown himself. It was late at night, and the stars gleamed up at him from the dark water. It seemed to him that the stars were swimming two by two down the river, and a wonderful feeling came over him. He forgot his suicidal intentions and gazed fascinated at the strange, sweet drama, and gradually he became aware that every star was a face and that all these pairs were lovers who were carried along locked in a dreaming embrace. An entirely new understanding came to him: all had changed—his fate, his disappointment, even his love receded and fell away. The memory of the girl grew distant, blurred; but instead, he felt with complete certainty that untold riches were promised him. He knew that an immense treasure lay hidden for him in the neighboring observatory. The result was that he was arrested by the police at four o'clock in the morning, attempting to break into the observatory. What had happened? His poor head had glimpsed a Dantesque picture whose loveliness he could never have grasped had he read it in a poem. . . . For his poor turnip-head it was too much. He did not drown in the river but in an eternal image, and its beauty perished with him. (Jung, 1959, p. 126)

In Jung's scheme, the collective unconscious also has its attractive elements and can sometimes lure a person into its essentially fathomless inner reality.

ASSESSMENT TECHNIQUES

Like Freud, Jung relied primarily on the case study as a personality assessment technique. He also showed his Freudian roots by utilizing dream analysis and by making use of patients' self-reports about significant early experiences. Yet, in a number of important respects, Jung's use of these techniques differed from his mentor's.

Dream Analysis

In Jung's view, dreams are involuntary and spontaneous eruptions of repressed materials that are rooted in both the personal and collective unconscious. However, their manifest content is not always a disguised attempt at wish fulfillment of sexual and/or aggressive needs. Instead, dreams are more often attempts at resolving current problems and conflicts, and provide dreamers with a means of furthering their own development in a healthy direction. For example, Jung reported the case of a young man who dreamt that his father was behaving in a drunken and disorderly manner. In reality, the son stated, his father was a highly virtuous man, and he and his father had an ideal relationship. Jung interpreted the dream to mean that the son's admiration for his father prevented him from having the confidence in himself to develop his own personality. He was, in fact, too close to his father and therefore was unable to develop his own identity. It was almost as if the dream were telling the son that his father was not so virtuous after all and that there was no need for the son to feel inferior (Fordham, 1966, p. 103).

According to Jung, dreams are also compensatory in nature. They are efforts at adjustment, attempts at rectifying deficiencies in personality. People who are very shy, for example, may have dreams in which they are the life of the party. Failures in business may dream of great financial ventures and successes. Mediocre actors may dream about receiving a standing ovation for their performance in a Broadway play. Although initial research did not support the idea of compensation in dreams (Domino, 1976), another study by Cann and Donderi (1986) is more strongly supportive. According to Jung, individuals high in neuroticism are one-sided in their development and dissociated from their collective unconscious. Individuals low in neuroticism, in contrast, are more balanced in their development and are not dissociated from their collective unconscious. Low neurotics are able to adapt to life by keeping in touch with their collective unconscious, whereas high neurotics are not able to make this compensatory adaptation—at least not as readily as low neurotics. Thus, according to Jungian theory, high neurotics should report fewer archetypal dreams—that is, dreams that are highly unusual, bizarre, and emotionally intense—than do low neurotics; this is exactly what Cann and Donderi found.

Cann and Donderi (1986) also found that intuitives recalled more archetypal dreams than did sensing types, whereas introverts recalled more dreams based on their everyday experiences than did extraverts. These findings tie in nicely with Jungian theory. Jung believed that intuitive individuals are closer to material in the collective unconscious than are sensing individuals. Intuitives, with their imaginative and creative tendencies, tolerance for complexity and change, and interest in dreams, find it easier to deal with the metaphorical characteristics of archetypal dreams. Sensing types, in contrast, have a more practical and concrete orientation that may lead them to find archetypal dreams very disturbing and difficult to process. He maintained that intuitive individuals' greater sensitivity to archetypal dreams assists their progress toward self-realization. Jung believed further that the introversion-extraversion dimension was focused more on conscious, everyday events. Extraverts focus primarily on the outer environment, whereas introverts emphasize the internal representation of these events and their storage in memory. Thus, introverts should be superior to extraverts in recalling everyday dreams. A recent study by Jacka (1991) using Australian students replicated the Cann and Donderi results.

Finally, Brown and Donderi (1986) tested the implications of Jung's idea that dreams are attempts at resolving current conflicts and furthering personal growth. If a particular dream helps in the resolution of a problem, the dream should not recur. Conversely, if the dream does not help resolve the problem, the dream should occur again. Thus, recurrent dreams, according to Jung, indicate that the conflict has not been resolved. Recurrent dreams should, therefore, be associated with stress, anxiety, and a lack of psychological well-being. Brown and Donderi tested this Jungian hypothesis and found strong support for it. Subjects who reported recurrent dreams were more neurotic, anxious, and depressed than were subjects who reported no recurrent dreams.

Method of Amplification

Dreams are replete with symbols that typically have multiple meanings and are very difficult to interpret. To reveal their meanings as far as was possible, Jung utilized the **method of amplification.** Unlike free association, which involves starting with a particular symbol and moving further and further away from it, the method of amplification involves adhering to a given symbol and giving numerous associations to it. In the process, the symbol's multiple meanings become clearer and provide patients with insights into their problems. These associations are given by both the patient and the analyst. Often the associations provided by the analyst determine the direction of the patient's own associations (Jacobi, 1962, p. 82). Patients usually provide the subjective or personal meanings of the symbols, whereas the therapist provides the universal meanings of the symbols as revealed in mythology, religion, alchemy, art, history, and so forth (Jacobi, 1962, p. 87).

Jung believed that analysis of a single dream could prove misleading, but analysis of a series of dreams could provide a means of achieving more accurate interpretations of the problems confronting the patient. The in-depth analysis of a series of dreams also allowed the patient and therapist to move from the personal meanings embedded in the symbols to their deeper meanings as archetypal images.

Word Association Test

In conjunction with dream analysis, Jung utilized an experimental technique called the **word association test,** in which he presented patients with stimulus words and asked them to respond with whatever words occurred to them. Jung recorded the time that elapsed between the initial presentation of the stimulus and the eventual response and used the time latency as an indicator of possible areas of resistance and conflict within the person. The longer the time interval, he assumed, the greater was the likelihood that important complexes or areas of conflict within the psyche were being tapped. In addition, areas of conflict were assumed to be present if the patient: (1) repeated the stimulus word several times as though it had been not heard; (2) misheard the word as some other word; (3) gave a response of more than one word; (4) gave a meaningless reaction (a made-up word); or (5) failed to respond at all. Jung also required his patients to recall all their responses to the word stimuli following a rest interval. Failure to reproduce the words and reporting distorted reproductions were also considered to reflect underlying conflict (Jacobi, 1962, p. 38).

Painting Therapy

Another technique used by Jung in conjunction with dream analysis was painting therapy. He relied heavily on paintings by his patients as a means of further encouraging them to express their unconscious feelings or thoughts. Pointing out that these paintings had little artistic merit, he helped patients to see that they must be expressions of their innermost selves. The painting exercises were conducted to help patients clarify the symbols seen in their dreams and to force patients to cope actively with their problems. In Jung's view, painting had real therapeutic effects. It moved patients off dead center and started them on the road to self-realization.

THEORY'S IMPLICATIONS FOR THERAPY

Jung believed that neurosis was a severe disorder in which the person's growth toward self-realization was halted. Yet, in his view, neurosis had a positive aspect to it as well. It was a warning sign that the person's personality was desperately in need of broadening and that this could happen only if the therapist and patient utilized the correct therapeutic procedures.

Jung believed that the forms of neurosis in young and middle-aged people were radically different:

> The life of a young person is characterized by a general expansion and striving towards concrete ends; and his neurosis seems mainly to rest on his hesitation or shrinking back from this necessity. But the life of an older person is characterized by a contraction of forces, by the affirmation of what has been achieved, and by the curtailment of further growth. His neurosis comes mainly from his clinging to a youthful attitude which is now out of season. Just as the young neurotic is afraid of life, so the older one shrinks back from death. (Jung, 1954, p. 39)

Thus, in Jung's view, therapy has to be tailored to the age of the person. For the most part, Jung confined his efforts to treating the problems of the middle-aged. His analytical therapy is really a "psychology of the afternoon."

The middle-aged people who visited Jung had special problems. Unlike many neurotics who suffer because they lack a strong ego, the men and women treated by Jung were usually highly successful people, often of outstanding ability. Yet they were restless and discontented. At this stage in their development, they typically began to ask themselves whether there might not be more to life than material success. They began to search for the meaning of their existence (Storr, 1991, pp. 79–80). This search involved an exploration of their unconscious as a means of correcting an overdeveloped consciousness. In other words, they made an effort to rediscover those aspects of themselves that had been neglected. They began to realize that they must stop their relentless pursuit of success in order to rediscover the spiritual meaning of their existence. They must cultivate their inner life, come to grips with its secrets, and assimilate them into consciousness. They must also come to accept the inevitability of death.

Jung viewed therapy as the process by which patients were able, through exploration of their inner lives, to broaden their personalities and to develop a spiritual or religious attitude toward their existence. It was not only patients, however, who gained insights into themselves as a result of analysis. Therapists were equally involved in the process and could derive positive benefits. Jung maintained that both analysts and patients had many limitations and that both were struggling toward self-realization. Consequently, he believed, therapists must give up all claims to superior knowledge, as well as desires to unduly influence their patients, if substantial progress toward self-realization is to be achieved.

In his view, the therapeutic process has four key stages: confession, elucidation, education, and transformation (Jung, 1954, p. 55). Confession is a necessary first step in the healing process, because it forces the individual to acknowledge his or her limitations to another. The person also becomes aware of his or her universal ties to humankind, in the sense that all men and women possess certain weaknesses. The cathartic process also leads to the patient's reliance on the therapist; that is, transference occurs. In the process of understanding this transference, the patient brings to the surface certain contents of the unconscious that the therapist clarifies; this is elucidation. During this stage, the person learns the origins of his or her problems. In the third stage, education, the person incorporates the insights into his or her personality in order to adapt to the social environment. Finally, transformation occurs when the dynamic interplay between therapist and patient leads to exciting changes that move beyond adaptation to the environment and toward self-realization.

Self-realization is an ideal state and not something to be actually attained. It is the process that is important, not the achievement of the goal. By undergoing this painful struggle to reconcile the conflicting sides of their nature, patients become more integrated, whole personalities. They do not become perfect human beings; they become, instead, what they are destined to become—individuals with unique sets of strengths and limitations. Self-realization involves the acceptance of these limitations. It is a religious experience in the sense that reconciliation of the opposites within individuals may occur when they subordinate themselves to a higher authority, who, they believe, will make all things well in the end (Storr, 1991, p. 90). However, this religious attitude does not necessarily entail allegiance to a particular orthodox creed. It may involve subordination to a set of rules or moral principles that help resolve their conflicts.

Finally, self-realization is not a state of total passivity. Rather, the person accepts the reality of each situation and adapts accordingly. He or she may work to control and change those situations in life that can be realistically shaped but knows that not every situation is controllable or should be controlled. There are some situations in which an accepting attitude is healthiest.

EVALUATIVE COMMENTS

At this point, let us utilize our six criteria to evaluate the scientific worth of Jung's theory.

Comprehensiveness   Jung's position comes close to matching Freud's in the sheer number and diversity of phenomena it examines. In many instances, however, it is not as detailed in its treatment of the phenomena in its domain as is Freud's. Nonetheless, Jung's theory is quite comprehensive; at various points, it addresses such diverse phenomena as marriage, creativity, religion, education, and the occult.

Precision and testability   Jung's theory fails generally to meet the criterion of precision and testability. Many of its relational statements are vague and riddled with inconsistencies. Many of its concepts are also highly ambiguous. For example, archetypes are metaphysical concepts that have multiple meanings and few clear referents in external reality. As Jung himself put it:

> They can only be roughly circumscribed at best. . . . Every attempt to focus them more sharply is immediately punished by the intangible core of meaning losing its luminosity. No archetype can be reduced to a simple formula. It is a vessel which we can never empty and never fill. It has a potential existence only, and when it takes shape in matter, it is no longer what it was. It persists throughout the ages and requires interpreting ever anew. The archetypes are the imperishable elements of the unconscious, but they change their shape continuously. (Jung, 1958b, p. 145)

Compounding this inherent vagueness, Jung argued that some of our behavior is controlled by "autonomous forces" in the collective unconscious—forces that operate unpredictably. For instance, a man and a woman may be having an enjoyable discussion about the virtues of the sexes when they suddenly find themselves embroiled in a bitter controversy about the inherent superiority of one sex over the other. Jung might account for this unexpected shift in behavior by maintaining that the negative aspects of the anima in the man and the animus in the woman had projected themselves onto their behavior. The man might begin to argue in a "womanish" way and become completely irrational and emotional about the innate superiority of men, whereas the woman might become "mannish" and begin to argue dogmatically and in a domineering fashion about the natural superiority of women. The bitter argument might continue unabated for an hour or so and then suddenly subside. Jung would maintain that the man was anima-possessed and the woman animus-possessed. The point at which such possessions occur is completely unpredictable.

To scientists, such an assumption is totally unacceptable, because it violates their belief that all behavior is caused by previous events. Although Jung believed that determinism is a useful concept in the explanation of behavior, he also maintained that it has its limitations. In his view, people live by aims as well as by causes. Furthermore, Jung maintained that some behavior is produced according to a **principle of synchronicity**—that sometimes two events occur together in time, but one event does not cause the other. For example, a man may dream of his uncle's death and then learn the next day by telephone that his uncle has just died. Clearly, dreaming about the death did not cause it. But neither was the nearly simultaneous occurrence of the events a chance happening. Instead, Jung believed that the co-occurrence was a meaningful coincidence. In his view, it is possible that an archetypal death image in some form had knowledge of the uncle's death and that it had penetrated the man's dream to make him aware of its impending occurrence. Jung believed that archetypes could readily move through and embrace the past, present, and future. Jung left unexplained the underlying mechanism and process that tell how archetypes are capable of transcending space and time boundaries, but he was convinced of the reality of this mysterious process.

Despite the ambiguity in Jung's work and his advocacy of acausal explanations for some phenomena, scientists are becoming increasingly interested in testing some of Jung's complex and original ideas.

Parsimony   Jung's theory also fails to meet the parsimony criterion. There seem to be more concepts than are necessary to explain phenomena. A wide range of archetypes may be invoked to explain a specific behavior. If a person behaves aggressively, for example, it could be the result of the activation of his or her shadow, animus or anima, mother archetype, father archetype, and so forth. It could be the result of the operation of one of these archetypes, several of them, all of them, or none of them; there is no systematic explanation of why or how one takes precedence over another. Alternatively, it could be due simply to the operation of unknown and uncontrollable forces within the psyche.

Empirical validity   Although Jung's theory is difficult to test, his position has recently generated some interest, and a number of studies have been conducted. Most of these investigations have focused on his theory of psychological types, and the evidence for its validity has been consistently supportive.

Heuristic value   Jung's theory has considerable heuristic value. Although it has not been accorded high status by most scientists, it has been accepted by professionals from a variety of disciplines, including history, literature, art, anthropology, religion, music, and certain segments of the clinical psychology community. The ties with religion have been especially close because, to Jung, spiritual concerns were the highest human value. He felt that people in Western societies are too overdeveloped in the rational realm and grossly underdeveloped in the spiritual area. Accordingly, Jung believed that many of us need to turn inward and to meditate in a search for the meaning of our existence. Not too surprisingly, Jung has enjoyed considerable popular success among idealistic middle-class students surfeited with material possessions and shaken by a crisis of faith in religious, political, and business authority figures who abuse their power.

Applied value   Jung's theorizing about the nature of psychopathology and its treatment has had a highly positive impact on the work of many therapists. The theory has also proved useful to members of many other disciplines, including theologians, artists, photographers, and historians. The Myers-Briggs Type Indicator, an outgrowth of Jung's theorizing about psychological types, has also been used to good advantage by vocational counselors and by personnel managers in many businesses, as they try to place job applicants within their companies in positions that maximize performance effectiveness and personal satisfaction.

Interestingly, Jung's ideas about the need in many troubled people for a spiritual reawakening had a profound impact on the cofounder of the Alcoholics Anonymous movement, Bill W. Bill acknowledged his debt to Jung in a letter written a few years after he had cofounded the organization. According to the letter, he became convinced that he could change his own alcohol dependency after he had spoken to a former patient of Jung's. This man had given up his excessive drinking after undergoing a spiritual metamorphosis while in therapy with Jung, who had pointed out that the patient's craving for alcohol was the equivalent of his spiritual thirst for wholeness, expressed through a union with God. Jung had worked with the patient to transform his life by finding a new meaning for his existence (W., 1988, pp. 276–281). Thus, it seems clear that Jung's theory has had considerable practical impact on people from many walks of life.

DISCUSSION QUESTIONS

1. What is the psyche? How does psychic energy originate, and how does it affect the person's behavior?
2. In the chapter, some examples were given to show how the principle of equivalence operates in the personality. Can you think of any additional examples?
3. Do you believe that the collective unconscious exists?
4. One example of an archetype is the mother-child relationship. Can you think of any other experiences that are universal in nature?
5. How would you define the shadow? Is it possible to measure it objectively?
6. What kinds of individuals believe in the existence of evil forces within a person that control his or her behavior?
7. What is the nature of the relationship between the anima and animus and our cultural sex-role stereotypes?
8. Have you ever had a transcendent experience that helped you resolve a personal problem? Describe it as best you can, and tell how it helped you overcome the difficulty.
9. Can you think of examples of mandalas that are part of our culture?
10. Are you primarily an introvert or an extravert? In what ways?

11. Cite examples that show the negative qualities of introversion and extraversion.
12. What are superior and inferior functions? What are some of the problems an individual could experience if his or her thinking function was undifferentiated?
13. List the characteristics of the eight personality types postulated by Jung. What personality type are you?
14. Do you agree with Jung that neurosis in young people is due to their avoidance of setting and striving toward concrete external goals?
15. In what ways is Jung's position compatible with contemporary religion? Would you agree that there is a need for spiritual awakening among young people and adults?

GLOSSARY

analytical psychology   Jung's unique brand of psychology, which emphasizes the complex interplay between oppositional forces within the psyche and the ways in which these internal conflicts affect personality development.

anima   The feminine archetype in men, including both positive and negative characteristics of the transpersonal female. In a positive sense, the anima involves a sense of warmth and intuitive understanding; in a negative sense, it involves moodiness and irritability.

animus   The masculine archetype in women, including both positive and negative characteristics of the transpersonal male. In a positive sense, the animus involves an ability to reason and use logic to solve problems; in a negative sense, it involves an uncritical and dogmatic adherence to certain ideas and an irrationality in solving problems.

archetypes   Universal themes or symbols that can be activated by forces operating in the psyche, thereby generating visions that are projected onto current experiences.

collective unconscious   The depository of instincts and archetypes that go beyond personal experience. These transpersonal experiences are the residue of human evolutionary development and can be activated under the proper conditions.

complex   Collection of thoughts united by a common feeling.

dominant characteristics   In Jung's theory, developed, differentiated, and conscious parts of the psyche.

ego Force in the personality responsible for feelings of identity and continuity.

extraversion One of two basic attitudes postulated by Jung, characterized by an outgoing and relatively confident approach to life.

extraverted feeling type Individual characterized positively by an acceptance of the standards of society and negatively by a change in emotions from situation to situation, along with an indiscriminate yielding to the expectations of others.

extraverted intuitive type Individual characterized positively by a quick grasp of the creative possibilities in various ventures and negatively by impatience and flightiness.

extraverted sensing type Individual characterized positively by an appreciation for the arts and negatively by crude pleasure seeking.

extraverted thinking type Individual characterized in a positive way by an ability to organize masses of facts into a coherent theory and in a negative way by a selfish and exploitative attitude toward others.

inferior characteristics In Jung's theory, underdeveloped, undifferentiated, and unconscious parts of the psyche.

introversion One of two basic attitudes postulated by Jung, characterized by a retiring and reflective approach to life.

introverted feeling type Individual characterized positively by intense feelings of sympathy for others who have experienced misfortune and negatively by shyness and inaccessibility.

introverted intuitive type Individual characterized positively by the ability to envision the future and negatively by an inability to communicate effectively with others.

introverted sensing type Individual characterized positively by the intensity of subjective sensations and negatively by oversensitivity and obtuseness.

introverted thinking type Individual characterized positively by imagination and an ability to think originally and boldly and negatively by social ineptness.

irrational functions Modes of apprehending the world without evaluating it. For Jung, sensation and intuition were the irrational (nonrational) functions.

life process energy All of the urges that are derived from conflict between forces in the psyche.

mandala Symbolic representation of the self or of the world.

method of amplification Therapeutic technique in which the patient and analyst continue to reassess and reinterpret the same symbols in an attempt to broaden their understanding of them.

Myers-Briggs Type Indicator (MBTI)   A paper-and-pencil test designed to measure the various psychological types postulated by Jung.

persona   Archetype consisting of the role human beings play in order to meet the demands of others. The persona also allows them to express their innermost feelings in ways acceptable to other people.

personal unconscious   In Jung's theory, the region that contains all of the personal experiences that have been blocked from awareness.

principle of entropy   In Jungian theory, the idea that energy is automatically redistributed in the psyche in order to achieve equilibrium or balance.

principle of equivalence   The idea that energy expended in one part of the psyche will be compensated for by an equal amount of energy in the same or different form in another part of the psyche. Thus, energy is neither created nor lost but simply shifted from one region of the psyche to another.

principle of opposites   The idea that the energy that propels personality and behavior is derived from the interplay between opposite forces within the psyche.

principle of synchronicity   Belief that there is an acausal order in the world that has meaning and that goes beyond causality.

psyche   A construct postulated by Jung to represent all of the interacting systems within human personality that are needed to account for the mental life and behavior of the person.

rational functions   Modes of making judgments or evaluations of events in the world. For Jung, thinking and feeling were rational functions.

self   In Jung's theory, an archetype that leads people to search for ways of maximizing the development of their potential.

self-realization   Process that involves the healthy development of people's capabilities, enabling them to fulfill their own unique natures.

shadow   The inferior, evil, and repulsive side of human nature.

symbol   In Jung's psychology, a representation of a psychic fact. Each symbol was thought to have multiple meanings and to be incapable of being understood completely.

theory of psychological types   Theory proposed by Jung in which people can be classified into eight types, on the basis of a combination of attitudes and functions.

transcendent function   The process by which a conflict is resolved by bringing opposing forces into balance with each other through understanding.

word association test   Therapeutic technique in which patients are presented with stimulus words and asked to give responses to them. Greater time latencies in responding are assumed to reflect the existence of underlying problems.

SUGGESTED READINGS

Jacobi, J. (1962). *The psychology of C. G. Jung*. New Haven, CT: Yale University Press.

Jung, C. G. (1953). *Collected works* (H. Read, M. Fordham, & G. Adler, Eds.). Princeton, NJ: Princeton University Press.

Jung, C. G. (1963). *Memories, dreams, reflections*. New York: Pantheon.

Stevens, A. (1994). *Jung*. New York: Oxford University Press.

Storr, A. (1991). *Jung*. New York: Routledge.

REFERENCES

Briggs, K. C., & Myers, I. B. (1943, 1944, 1957, 1976). Myers-Briggs Type Indicator. Palo Alto, CA: Consulting Psychologists Press.

Brown, R. J., & Donderi, D. C. (1986). Dream content and self-reported well-being among recurrent dreamers, past-recurrent dreamers, and nonrecurrent dreamers. *Journal of Personality and Social Psychology, 50,* 612–623.

Cann, D. R., & Donderi, D. C. (1986). Jungian personality typology and the recall of everyday and archetypal dreams. *Journal of Personality and Social Psychology, 50,* 1021–1030.

Carlson, R. (1980). Studies of Jungian typology: II. Representations of the personal world. *Journal of Personality and Social Psychology, 38,* 801–810.

Carlson, R., & Levy, N. (1973). Studies of Jungian typology: I. Memory, social perception, and social action. *Journal of Personality, 41,* 559–576.

Domino, G. (1976). Compensatory aspects of dreams: An empirical test of Jung's theory. *Journal of Personality and Social Psychology, 34,* 658–662.

Dry, A. M. (1961). *The psychology of Jung*. New York: Wiley.

Fling, S., Thomas, A., & Gallaher, M. (1981). Participant characteristics and the effects of two types of meditation vs. quiet sitting. *Journal of Clinical Psychology, 37,* 784–790.

Fordham, F. (1966). *An introduction to Jung's psychology*. Middlesex, England: Penguin Books.

Furnham, A., & Stringfield, P. (1993). Personality and occupational behavior: Myers-Briggs Indicator correlates of managerial practices in two cultures. *Human Relations, 46,* 827–848.

Jacka, B. (1991). Personality variables and attitudes toward dream experiences. *Journal of Psychology, 125,* 27–31.

Jacobi, J. (1962). *The psychology of C. G. Jung*. New Haven, CT: Yale University Press.

Jung, C. G. (1923). *Psychological types*. New York: Harcourt.

Jung, C. G. (1954). The practice of psychotherapy. In *The collected works of C. G. Jung* (Vol. 16). London: Routledge & Kegan Paul.

Jung, C. G. (1958a). Commentary on secret of the golden flower. In V. S. de Laszlo (Ed.), *Psyche and symbol* (pp. 302–351). Garden City, NY: Doubleday Anchor.

Jung, C. G. (1958b). The special phenomenology of the child archetype. In V. S. de Laszlo (Ed.), *Psyche and symbol* (pp. 132–147). Garden City, NY: Doubleday Anchor.

Jung, C. G. (1958c). The psychology of the child archetype. In V. S. de Laszlo (Ed.), *Psyche and symbol* (pp. 113–131). Garden City, NY: Doubleday Anchor.

Jung, C. G. (1959). The relations between the ego and the unconscious. In V. S. de Laszlo (Ed.), *The basic writings of C. G. Jung* (pp. 105–182). New York: Modern Library.

Jung, C. G. (1963). *Memories, dreams, reflections*. New York: Pantheon.

Jung, C. G. (1964). *Two essays on analytical psychology*. New York: Meridian.

Jung, C. G. (1969). *The structure and dynamics of the psyche* (2nd ed.). Princeton, NJ: Princeton University Press.

Myers, I. B., & McCaulley, M. H. (1985). *A guide to the development and use of the Myers-Briggs Type Indicator*. Palo Alto, CA: Consulting Psychologists Press.

Progoff, I. (1953). *Jung's psychology and its social meaning*. London: Routledge & Kegan Paul.

Rabelais, F. (1936). The five books of Gargantua and Pantagruel. In J. LeClarog (Trans.), *The complete works of Rabelais*. New York: Random House.

Stevens, A. (1994). *Jung*. New York: Oxford University Press.

Storr, A. (1991). *Jung*. New York: Routledge.

W., Bill (1988). *The language of the heart: Bill W's Grapevine writings*. New York: The AA Grapevine, Inc.

CHAPTER 4

Adler's Individual Psychology

BIOGRAPHICAL SKETCH

Alfred Adler was born in Vienna in 1870, of Jewish parents. His father was a grain merchant, whose work allowed the family to live an affluent, middle-class life. Adler was the third of seven children, five boys and two girls, of whom the oldest was a boy and the second a girl. As a child, he was very delicate and sickly. He had rickets and suffered from spasms of the glottis that put him in danger of suffocation whenever he screamed or cried. Other experiences made him acutely aware of the possibility of death: he was 3 years old when his younger brother died in a bed next to his; a year later, Adler himself contracted pneumonia and almost died; and twice during his early childhood he was run over in the street. His physical weakness led his parents, especially his mother, to pamper him. Because his doctor prescribed fresh air, his parents encouraged him to play outdoors with other children. He had many pleasant memories of play experiences with his peers and showed a lifelong fondness for the company of others. He also worked extraordinarily hard, apparently in an effort to compensate for his initial weakness.

During his early schooling, he was a mediocre student; he did so poorly in mathematics that he had to repeat a grade. Adler's reaction was to work diligently on mathematical problems at home until he had mastered them. Some time later, his mathematics teacher wrote a problem on the blackboard that no one (not even the teacher) could solve. Young Adler announced that he could solve it. Disregarding his teacher's sarcastic remark, "Of course, if no one else can, you will surely be able to," Alfred strode to the board amidst the laughter of his classmates and solved the problem. From that moment on, he was the best pupil in the class (Orgler, 1963, pp. 1–3).

Adler attended the Vienna Medical School, where he came under the influence of a famous internist who stressed that the physician must always treat the whole patient, not just the ailment. The internist was also fond of saying, "If you want to be a good doctor, you have to be a kind person." They were two lessons Adler never forgot. During his university days, he also acquired a socialist political orientation. Adler was attracted to the humanistic side of socialism—its stress on equality, cooperation, and democracy. He became an unflagging champion of the common person and fought against oppression of the masses all through his life.

Once he had received his medical degree, Adler established a private practice in a lower-middle-class Vienna neighborhood near a famous amusement park. His patients included artists and acrobats from the park shows. Some of these extraordinary physical specimens told Adler that they had achieved their powers as a reaction to weakness and illness in childhood. It was these experiences that later led Adler to focus on the concept of overcompensation.

Adler's association with Freud apparently grew out of his defense of Freud's view on dreams, which had been attacked by critics in the local press. In 1902, Adler was elected the first president of the Vienna Psycho-Analytic Society. However, he never established a warm personal relationship with Freud nor with most of the other members of the group. Adler was not a person to worship at the feet of the master, and his forthright questioning and criticism of some of Freud's concepts led to his resignation from the society in 1911.

Soon after, Adler formed a group called the Society for Free Psycho-Analytic Research, a title chosen to show his obvious displeasure with what he considered Freud's dictatorial ways. In 1913, Adler changed the name of the association to the Society for Individual Psychology, to reflect his concern with understanding the whole personality—the individual as an indivisible entity. Unfortunately, the term also suggests a study of the individual as contrasted with the study of group behavior. But Adler's theory is, in many respects, sociopsychological in nature; for Adler, the individual can be understood only in terms of participation with other members of society.

During World War I, Adler worked as an army doctor in a Vienna hospital. Witnessing the savage effects of the war on people—effects generated by lack of trust and cooperation—he developed his concept of social interest. He returned to his writing and research with renewed purpose, and focused much of his energies on disseminating information to the ordinary person about the need for cooperation, love, and respect among people. He was also instrumental in helping to establish in the Vienna school system some 30 child-guidance clinics that provided counseling for the entire family. By the early 1920s, Adler had gained international recognition and acceptance. In the late 1920s and early 1930s, he authored a number of popular books, including *The Practice and Theory of Individual Psychology* (1927), *Understanding Human Nature* (1927), *The Science of Living* (1929/1969), *The Education of Children* (1930), *What Life Should Mean to You* (1931), and *Social Interest: A Challenge to Mankind* (1933). During the same period, he also began accepting invitations to lecture in various European cities and, later, in the United States. He succumbed to a heart attack while on a European lecture tour in Aberdeen, Scotland, in May 1937 (Furtmuller, 1973).

CONCEPTS AND PRINCIPLES

Individual psychology, according to Adler, is a science that attempts to understand the experiences and behavior of each person as an organized entity. He believed that all actions are guided by a person's fundamental attitudes toward life. True to his interest in improving the lot of humankind, he sought to correct faulty or mistaken attitudes by means of the knowledge derived from his theory. Thus, in addition to collecting basic information about human behavior, Adler was very much interested in applying such knowledge in a practical way.

The Struggle for Perfection

Out of Adler's efforts to understand "that mysterious creative power of life—that power which expresses itself in the desire to develop, to strive and to achieve—and even to compensate for defeats in one direction by striving for success in another" came a simple, yet interesting, set of theoretical propositions (Adler, 1969, p. 1). According to

Adler, an understanding of human personality was possible only in light of an understanding of the person's goals. In contrast to Freud, who was a strict determinist, Adler adopted the **teleological position** that current behavior is directed by future goals. People have a purpose in life—to attain perfection or completion—and are motivated to strive toward fulfillment of their own unique potentials. This movement toward perfection, Adler proposed, is driven by feelings of inferiority—a continual struggle from "minus to plus." Thus, according to Adler, we are all engaged in a "great upward drive."

The related concept of **fictional finalism** is based on the writings of the philosopher Hans Vaihinger, who maintained in *The Philosophy of "As-If"* that people create the ideas that guide their behavior. Adopting this view, Adler believed that people strive for perceived or imagined goals that give direction to their behavior. These goals are not tangible; they are imagined ideals. In his later writings, Adler abandoned the term *fictional finalism* and instead used the term *guiding self-ideal* (Watts & Holden, 1994, pp. 161–163).

In his earliest writings, the final goal of this struggle was domination—aggressive, all-powerful control over others. Humans were seen as selfish and concerned only with self-aggrandizement. Later, Adler revised his thinking and defined the ultimate goal as **superiority.** Individuals can formulate this goal so that it guides them along either a constructive or destructive path. The destructive path leads them to seek to dominate and exploit others. Adler talks about it as a striving for a goal of personal superiority. It is a striving that sees others as enemies or obstacles in the person's path, which must be removed, overcome, or destroyed; according to Adler, only neurotics strive for such a mistaken goal. In contrast, the constructive path leads people to relate to others with cooperation and good will; healthy people, in Adler's view, act in accordance with social interest. The striving for superiority by healthy people involves movement toward perfection or completion. In other words, Adler believed that each person was continually striving to complete his or her development, to realize all of his or her potentials, and to become a complete and unique person. He thought that such a goal could be attained only by cooperative efforts. When each of us seeks to contribute to the welfare of others, we all benefit. Through cooperation, each individual is helped to grow as a human being and to survive. (See Figure 4.1.)

Finally, Adler believed that the development of healthy or unhealthy goals is shaped to a considerable extent by experiences in the first five years of life.

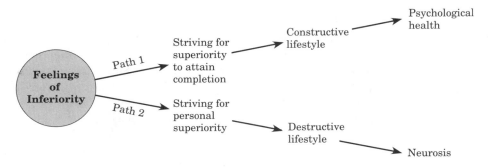

FIGURE 4.1   Developmental paths to psychological health or neurosis.

Creative Evolution and Social Interest

The essence of Adler's position is that people's mental health depends directly on their efforts to contribute to the betterment of the community. As he saw it, the species could not exist for long without sustained cooperation among its members. The life of each infant depends, for example, on the willingness of adults to extend themselves and to minister to the needs of these helpless creatures. The survival of the species also depends on the willingness of individuals to relate to one another on an intimate basis and to engage in procreative acts. In a complex society, the needs of the members can be gratified only through a division of labor and the coordination of effort among workers. Thus, without cooperative effort and good will, humanity would perish.

Adler discussed the necessity for such cooperation in the context of the evolution of the species. He proposed that there is a creative evolution in all living things that aims at the goal of perfection. Active, continuous movement and adaptation to the external world has always existed—a compulsion to create a better adaptation to the environment, to master it. All of us are in the midst of this creative evolution, according to Adler. We benefit tremendously from the massive efforts and contributions of our ancestors as we continue to strive in our own unique ways to improve the living conditions of all. The ultimate goal, in Adler's view, is the creation of an ideal community.

We are all born with the potential for social feeling or interest, Adler believed, but it can only come to fruition with proper guidance and training. He defined **social interest** as "a striving for a form of community which must be thought of as everlasting, as it could be thought of if mankind had reached the goal of perfection" (Adler, 1973c, pp. 34–35). By striving for others' goals, we help ourselves as well. This striving also implies respect and consideration for all human beings. "We remain open to the other and welcome him as a host would a guest, according to his own meaning, whose life is respected as equally valid as one's own" (Brennan, 1969, p. 10).

Researchers have created several useful measures of social interest and have begun to test Adler's ideas about the personality characteristics and behavior of individuals with a strong sense of social interest. Consistent with Adler's theorizing, investigators have found that people higher in social interest are more altruistic, trustworthy, socially adjusted, nurturant, and helpful than are people lower in social interest. Individuals high in social interest also report less depression, anxiety, loneliness, narcissism, and hostility toward others (Watkins, 1994, pp. 72–89). Other research showed that college students who were higher in social interest had emotionally closer relationships with friends and relatives than did students lower in social interest (Watkins & St. John, 1994, p. 167). Also, Australian mothers who were higher in social interest reported being more satisfied with their parental role and having more positive social relationships (Rodd, 1994, p. 64). In love relationships, research has indicated that people with a strong sense of social interest do not manipulate their partners for their own selfish purposes. Instead they treat their partners with respect and consideration (Leak & Gardner, 1990, p. 57).

Feelings of Inferiority and the Striving for Superiority

While he was still involved in the practice of medicine, Adler noted that individuals with defective organs typically tried to compensate for their weaknesses by intensive training. A girl with a speech impediment might try to overcome her problem by intensive and persistent practice until one day she is able to excel; perhaps she becomes a national news broadcaster. Or a boy with puny legs might strive to become an outstanding distance runner. According to Adler, it is not the defect itself that produces the striving, but the person's **attitude** toward it. The individual is free to interpret the deficiency in many ways, or even to ignore it; if it is ignored, it will not result in overwhelming striving behavior.

Adler later expanded the concept of **organ inferiority** to include exaggerated strivings caused by feelings of unmanliness. **Masculine protest** is the term he used to describe these compensation behaviors. In Adler's thinking, superiority tends to be equated with traditionally masculine behaviors such as assertiveness, independence, and dominance; inferiority tends to be equated with traditionally feminine behaviors such as passivity, submissiveness, and dependence. His thinking was presumably based on the roles enacted by males and females in Viennese society at the time. Adler himself was not a male chauvinist. In line with his egalitarian orientation, Adler abhorred the thought of treating anyone, male or female, as inferior and argued vigorously that such bias had to be eliminated (see Adler, 1927, pp. 120–148). He used the concept of masculine protest to show that women were placed in an inferior position by society and that, as a consequence, they often tried to overcome feelings of inadequacy by aping masculine behavior; he cited cases of women who spouted obscenities, swaggered, and acted tough. Lesbianism he considered to be an extreme manifestation of the masculine protest. On the other hand, compensatory behavior could also be seen in women who acted in an exaggeratedly feminine manner. These superfeminine women may have adopted this lifestyle as a means of luring men, whom they can then dominate and humiliate.

Adler applied his concept to men as well as women. Men who felt insecure could also acquire exaggerated ways of behaving to prove that they were real men. The Don Juan type would try to prove his manhood by countless seductions. In either sex, such manifestations were neurotic in character.

Adler eventually broadened the concept of organ inferiority even further; he argued that all of us experience feelings of psychological and social inferiority, beginning with our earliest participation in family life. Our parents and most others are not only bigger physically than we are, but also more sophisticated and adept at solving problems. Out of these inevitable feelings of inferiority comes a striving for superiority. Inferiority feelings can be primarily constructive or destructive. Acknowledging that we all feel inferior at some point in our lives can serve as a basis for mutual help and cooperation to overcome problems in living. But if we dwell excessively on our inferiorities, real or imagined, we are less likely to trust others or ourselves. As a consequence, we are likely to operate on the "useless side" of life, relying on **overcompensation** to make up for our deficiencies and developing an exaggerated sense of superiority that others find loathsome.

Style of Life and the Creative Self

Two concepts—the style of life and the creative self—are closely interrelated in Adlerian theorizing. The **style of life,** originally called the life plan or guiding image, refers to the unique ways in which people pursue their goals. An actor seeks to attain perfection through study and stage and film appearances. A scholar tries to become superior by intensive reading, studying, and thinking and by discussing ideas with her colleagues. Our unique styles of life are formed to a considerable extent during the first five years of life; later experiences are then assimilated and interpreted in accordance with these early patterns of behaving. These styles emerge as reactions to our inferiorities, real or imagined. Once established, they are difficult to modify.

The concept of the **creative self** appears to be an outgrowth of Adler's concern with the mechanistic implications of his style-of-life construct. Adler was probably dissatisfied with the idea that individuals acquire unique behavior patterns strictly through a stimulus-response kind of learning, because it implies that people are passive recipients who do not interpret or act upon their experiences. The concept of the creative self implies that people create their own personalities, by actively constructing them out of their experiences and heredities. In the final analysis, people are responsible for their destinies. Healthy people are generally aware of the alternatives available to them in solving problems and choose to act in a rational and responsible manner. Neurotics, in contrast, may have goals that are largely unconscious and are often unaware of the alternatives available to them in a given situation.

PERSONALITY DEVELOPMENT

Parental Influence in Early Childhood

Adler believed that both parents play crucial roles in discouraging or encouraging the development of their children's distinctive styles of life (Ansbacher & Ansbacher, 1956, pp. 372–381). The parents' responsibility is to nourish the child's increasing awareness with accurate conceptions of work, friendship, and love. In Adler's view, these are the three basic problems of life, and the healthy or courageous person is the one who confronts and attempts to cope with them.

The mother's role is particularly important, because she is usually the first person to have extended, intimate contact with the child. She introduces the child to social life. If she loves the child, she is more likely to be interested in teaching the skills necessary to secure his or her welfare. If she is dissatisfied with her role, she may be preoccupied with trying to prove her own personal superiority, by showing that her child is more intelligent and good-looking than all others and that he or she crawled, stood, and walked sooner than anyone else. Unfortunately, most children react adversely to such pressure, and the typical result is hostility and resentment.

For the father, the primary task is to prove that he is a worthwhile human being, by contributing to the welfare of his wife, his children, and his society. Furthermore, he must treat his wife as an equal and cooperate with her in meeting the problems of life. Of course, she must also value him as an equal. If she is afraid of losing the affection of her children and forces him to be the sole administrator of punishment for their misdeeds, she is not fulfilling her obligations as a wife and mother and is acting, instead, on the useless side of life. She is guilty of pampering her children because of her own weaknesses and of exploiting her husband. The same argument would apply to a husband who pampers his children.

Birth Order

Adler believed that each child is treated uniquely by its parents, and that this special treatment is typically, but not inevitably, related to the child's order of birth within the family. The eldest child tends to be the center of attention in the family before the birth of other siblings. With their births, he or she is placed in the position of the "dethroned monarch," forced to share parental affection and attention with others. As a consequence, the oldest child may feel resentment and hostility toward the younger ones. Such negative feelings are likely to occur if the parents have not properly prepared the child for the arrival of a sibling or siblings. If they have made adequate preparations, the oldest child may adopt a protective and supportive attitude instead, and often plays the part of father or mother with the younger ones and feels responsible for their welfare.

According to Adler, the oldest child understands best the importance of power and authority because he or she has had to undergo their loss within the family. Consequently, the oldest child will be highly supportive of, and dependent on, authorities in later life and will be a person who tends to support the status quo. Such a person is likely to be politically conservative. The second child is likely to view the older brother or sister as a competitor to be overcome. If the older child is protective and supportive of the younger sibling's attempts to excel, healthy development is more probable; if the older child resents the second child and acts maliciously, movement toward neurosis for the younger one is more likely. Adler also suggested that the second child may set unrealistically high goals, thereby virtually ensuring ultimate failure.

The youngest child is typically regarded as the baby of the family and tends to commandeer most of the family's attention. Adler believed that parents are likely to pamper and spoil the youngest members of their families (Mairet, 1964, p. 107). The result is a person who is excessively dependent on others for support and protection, one who wants to excel in everything he or she does but often fails.

The only child has no sibling rivals and is likely to be the center of attention in the family, provided his or her birth was a welcome event. If the child was unwanted, neglect or active rejection by the parents may occur. In most instances, the only child will be pampered by the parents, especially the mother. Later, the child may experience considerable interpersonal difficulty if he or she is not universally liked and admired.

Research Evidence: Intellectual Development

It would be encouraging to report that tests of Adler's **birth-order effects** have produced strong support for his major arguments. However, with the exception of his ideas about first-borns, recent reviews of the research literature have yielded data that are often inconsistent with Adler's theorizing (Blake, 1989; Watkins, 1992). Thus, caution should be exercised in interpreting these studies and their results.

Adler suggested that, because of the loss of power and authority suffered with the birth of a second child, first-borns spend their lives trying to regain their lost position through outstanding achievement. First-borns, in short, want to rule over others (Ansbacher & Ansbacher, 1956, p. 379). They try to establish themselves in a position of power over others and are found to be more dominant and aggressive than later-borns (Watkins, 1992, p. 362). Thus, we would expect first-borns to excel in intellectual activities and to attain higher levels of achievement and eminence.

There is abundant support for these predictions. Belmont and

Marolla (1973), for example, found a positive correlation between birth order and intellectual performance for nearly 400,000 subjects—the entire male population of the Netherlands who attained 19 years of age during the period from 1963 to 1966. First-borns outstripped later-borns in intellectual achievement in families where the number of children ranged from two to nine. Breland (1974) demonstrated that this positive relationship between birth order and intellectual performance held true for nearly 800,000 candidates for National Merit Scholarships.

Other investigations have found that first-borns are overrepresented among college students, graduate students, university faculty, and eminent people in science and government. Wagner and Schubert (1977), for example, found that oldest sons were overrepresented among United States presidents, but not among unsuccessful presidential candidates. Zweigenhaft (1975) also found first-borns overrepresented in the U.S. Congress, and Melillo (1983) showed that first-borns were overrepresented among women with doctorates (Ph.D., Ed.D., D.S.W., or M.D.). First-borns also were overrepresented among world leaders, whereas middle- and last-borns were underrepresented (Hudson, 1990). The most recent data indicated that United States governors who were in office in 1988 tended disproportionately to be first-borns, as were prime ministers in Australia in this century (Newman & Taylor, 1994).

Zajonc and Markus (1975) are strong supporters of the idea that first-borns exhibit greater intellectual development than do later-borns and offer a theory to explain the relationship. Their theory posits that children's mental growth is a function of the intellectual environment in which they mature. As the number of children in the family increases, their intellectual growth decreases because, as the family becomes weighted with younger, less intellectually developed members, the quality of the intellectual atmosphere deteriorates.

At the same time, first-borns are thrust into the role of teacher; they are expected to tutor their less-skilled brothers and sisters in a variety of activities. As a result, they have to learn more themselves, and their intellectual development is accelerated. The demands placed on younger children are less rigorous, since younger children do not usually have the wherewithal to educate their older siblings. Consequently, the younger children's intellectual development tends not to be as great, and the youngest child in particular suffers from a lack of opportunity to tutor others.

Zajonc and Markus contend that the massive data in the studies by Belmont and Marolla and by Breland offer substantial empirical support for their theory. Critics, however, point out that other attempts at gathering supportive data have failed (Steelman, 1985; Retherford & Sewell, 1991). Steelman (1986, p. 374) criticizes the studies cited by Zajonc and Markus for their failure to control adequately for the socioeconomic status (SES) of the parents—that is, their educational, occupational, and income levels. There is considerable research evidence that the socioeconomic status of parents is positively associated with a child's intellectual development: the higher the socioeconomic status of the family, the greater the intellectual development of the child. At the same time, higher-SES families tend to have fewer children than lower-SES families. Thus, the data showing greater intellectual development in first-borns than in later-borns may simply reflect the fact that the first-borns tested came from smaller, higher-SES families, whereas the later-borns came from larger, lower-SES families. In other words, socioeconomic status rather than birth order may have been the determining factor in intellectual development.

In a blistering rejoinder, Zajonc (1986) has accused Steelman of failing to cite numerous studies showing that first-borns have greater intellectual growth than later-borns no matter what the socioeconomic status of their families. Steelman (1986), in turn, insists that empirical support for Zajonc's theory is weak. Its basic premise is that interactions with intellectually stimulating persons sharpen intelligence; yet no research has focused on the actual interactions between older and younger siblings and their parents to determine the truth or falsity of Zajonc's premise. Furthermore, children interact with other adults (teachers, friends of the family) and with peers; they also read books and watch television. Research that examines all these types of interaction may lead to a more adequate theory about birth order and intellectual development and push researchers beyond the stalemate that currently exists.

Children with no siblings are in a unique position. Although they have no opportunity to tutor brothers and sisters, they nevertheless have the individual attention of their parents, who may spend large amounts of time instructing them. As a matter of fact, Falbo and Cooper (1980) have found that mothers with a single child of preschool age do spend more time with them during a typical week than do mothers with more children. Also, Lewis and Feiring (1982) found that, during mealtimes, one-child families engaged in more parent-child conversation, with a greater exchange of information, than did families with two or three children. Finally, other research has shown very clearly that only children are more intellectually advanced than later-borns from large families, and are as advanced as first-borns from small families (Falbo, 1977; Falbo & Polit, 1986).

Research by Falbo and Polit (1986) indicated further that only children are as sociable and as psychologically well-adjusted as children from other types of families. Falbo (1978) also found that only children were more likely than were first- or last-born children to be cooperative in a mixed-motive game where either player had the option of acting competitively or cooperatively. These findings call into question Adler's assertion that only children tend to be socially maladjusted because they do not have an opportunity to learn adequate social skills through frequent interactions with brothers and sisters (Adler, 1937).

Additional Research Evidence: Other Traits

A study by Ivancevich, Matteson, and Gamble (1987) suggests that the tremendous striving for achievement by first-borns may exact a high price. They found that first-born (and only-child) college students—black and white, male and female—had higher Type A personality test scores than did later-borns. Type A behavior is characterized by an excessive competitive drive and a strong time urgency. Type A individuals engage in an unremitting attempt to complete more and more tasks or participate in more and more events in less and less time. The result is often physical breakdown and heart attacks. A more recent investigation by Phillips, Long, and Bedeian (1990) obtained the same results with a sample of professional accountants; that is, first-born accountants had higher Type A scores than did later-borns.

Adler also maintained that the youngest child was likely to be the most pampered member of the family (Ansbacher & Ansbacher, 1956, p. 380). As a result of this pampering, he thought, such individuals would be excessively dependent on others and would seek easy, immediate solutions to problems. Excessive dependence, furthermore, would be seen most clearly in families in which the youngest child was a male and his older siblings were sisters rather than brothers. In such cases, the last-born was likely to have a conflict between needing independence and seeking dependence on others, who provide a convenient, hassle-free source of gratification. Because alcoholics frequently use the bottle as a quick and easy solution to their immediate problems, we might expect the youngest members of families to be overrepresented among alcoholics. In a review of studies examining the birth-order position of alcoholics, Barry and Blane (1977) found a higher incidence of alcoholics among last-borns in 20 out of the 27 studies. This finding does not mean, of course, that every last-born will become an alcoholic. Rather, it suggests that last-born individuals in general show a higher incidence of alcoholism than do first- or middle-born children and only children.

Spacing and Gender

Finally, although Adler proposed that a child's order of birth in the family provided clues about the direction of his or her development, he did not believe that it was the order of birth per se that caused the behaviors associated with it. Instead, it was the unique set of experiences within the family that had important implications for development (Ansbacher & Ansbacher, 1956, p. 377). Although the child's order of birth served as a rough indicator of likely experiences, this crude assessment device could be misleading. For example, if the eldest child in a family was disadvantaged because of brain damage suffered during birth, the second child might be treated by the parents as if he or she were actually the eldest. Or, if two children were born much later than their three older siblings, the parents might treat them as if they were first- and second-borns, even though they were actually the fourth- and fifth-borns in a family of five children. Thus, the spacing of siblings may have important implications for how children are treated and how they develop. This factor is often ignored by birth-order researchers.

Another factor with important consequences for development, according to Adler, is the sex of the siblings within the family. In Adler's view, a boy brought up in a family of girls will be more likely to experience special difficulties. He may feel that he is very different and may grow up feeling isolated. As a result, he may fight to assert his difference and assume an air of masculine superiority; or he may give in and develop a more feminine orientation. Similarly, a girl raised in a family of boys is apt to develop either very masculine or very feminine qualities, depending on the kind of treatment she receives and how she interprets it (Ansbacher & Ansbacher, 1956, p. 382). Unfortunately, researchers have often failed to take the sex composition of the family into account in their research. The failure to control for this factor (and others) may explain, at least in part, why the research results on birth order are generally not very supportive of Adler's theorizing.

Development of a Destructive Lifestyle

Out of this incredible welter of family experience and the person's interpretation of it emerges a guiding goal and a distinctive style of life. As hinted earlier, the three major sets of environmental factors that may give rise to severely destructive or neurotic life goals are: (1) organ inferiority; (2) neglect or rejection; and (3) pampering. Adler believed that pampering was especially damaging. Neurotic individuals are those who feel very acutely their own inferiority and who compensate for these feelings by establishing unrealistically high goals that they believe will enable them to demonstrate personal superiority over others. Neurotics are grossly inaccurate in their self-evaluations; they continually underestimate or overestimate their own worth. They are continually tense and fearful, especially of decisions, tests, and defeats. In the final analysis, they are terrified of being unmasked and recognized by others as inferior. Such people do not act in accordance with social interest; they are not courageous. Instead, they continually adopt safeguarding or defensive strategies to protect themselves.

Development of a Constructive Lifestyle

The person who develops a healthy or constructive style of life, according to Adler, has experienced a family life in which the parents treated him or her with respect and consideration. Under such conditions, Adler believed, the person was likely to learn the importance of equality and cooperation between people and to develop goals in accord with social interest. Adler left the nature of these goals unspecified: they could range from principles such as "honesty is the best policy" and "do unto others as you would have them do unto you" to specific occupational goals such as professor, doctor, silversmith, auto mechanic, used car salesperson, or television repair person. Adler believed that individuals could fill any of these roles in accordance with social interest—that is, by expending maximum effort and utilizing their abilities for the welfare of society. Thus, the auto mechanic is as worthwhile as the physician, if each is operating in accordance with social interest.

Adler also maintained that the healthy person could change his or her fictional finalisms or guiding self-ideals if circumstances demanded it. Would such a person act dishonestly and steal a loaf of bread to feed a starving child? Adler would probably answer, "Yes, but only if the individual had exhausted every other avenue in trying to solve the problem." The healthy person lives by principles, but is realistic enough to modify them under exceptional circumstances.

Adler's Four Major Lifestyle Types

Adler employed a simple classification scheme to help people understand the nature of destructive and constructive lifestyles more fully. He provided this typology reluctantly, because he did not consider human beings as types but believed each person had a unique style of life (Ansbacher & Ansbacher, 1956, p. 166). Nevertheless, he believed that such a typology had some educational value, and he presented it with that disclaimer.

Ruling, getting, and avoiding types all have destructive lifestyles, whereas socially useful types have constructive lifestyles.

The ruling type   Individuals of the **ruling type,** according to Adler, lack social interest and courage. When threatened, they try to reduce feelings of anxiety by acting in antisocial ways. Their striving for personal superiority is so intense that they typically exploit and harm others; they need to control others in order to feel powerful and significant. As children, ruling types want to exclude stronger children and play only with weaker children, so that they can dominate. When they fail to get their way, they throw themselves on the floor, hold their breath, or scream, kick, or yell in the hope that their parents will succumb.

When they become adults, ruling types want to be conquerors; they want to lord it over their spouses. They expect their spouses to cater to their every need and to pay constant attention to them. As parents, they order their children to obey "because I said so!" As teachers, they are arrogant and vain; they like to threaten their students: "If you don't do this, you'll go to the principal's office!" Ruling types may also try to control people through the use of money, in the belief that everyone has a price (Mosak, 1977, pp. 218–219). Adler cited juvenile delinquents, suicidal individuals, and drug addicts as prime examples of the ruling type.

The getting type   Individuals of the **getting type** are relatively passive and make little effort to solve their own problems. Instead, they rely on others to take care of them. Children of many affluent, permissive parents are given whatever they demand; growing up in such an environment, they have little need to do things for themselves, and little awareness of their own abilities to be productive or to give to others. Lacking confidence in themselves, they attempt to surround themselves with people who are willing to accede to their requests. Getting types frequently use charm to persuade others to help them (Mosak, 1977, p. 78).

The avoiding type   People of the **avoiding type** lack the confidence necessary for solving crises. Instead of struggling with their problems, they typically try to sidestep them, thereby avoiding defeat. Such individuals are often self-absorbed; they are inclined to daydream and create fantasies in which they are always superior (Adler, 1930, pp. 142–143).

The socially useful type   People of the **socially useful type** grow up in families where the members are helpful and supportive of each other, treat each other with respect and consideration, and are disinclined to handle stress and problems through conflict and aggression (Leak & Williams, 1989, p. 365). Instead they have the courage to face their problems directly as a means of solving them. As adults, their orientation to family members is based on respect, affection, and friendship and not on manipulation and game playing (Leak & Gardner, 1990, p. 57).

Socially useful people are psychologically healthy. They face life confidently and are prepared to cooperate with others, contribute to the welfare of others, and build a better community. In short, they act in accordance with social interest.

Crandall (1975) has constructed a reliable and valid measure of social interest and has proceeded to test some of Adler's major ideas about people with a high degree of social interest. He reports, for example, that individuals high in social interest are less self-centered, less hostile and aggressive, and more cooperative and helpful to others than are people low in social interest. They are also better adjusted psychologically than are individuals with low social interest (Crandall, 1980, pp. 484–487). More recent research by Leak, Millard, Perry, and Williams (1985), using multiple measures of social interest, generally corroborates Crandall's findings. Their study found that people high in social interest perceived a life goal of "making a lot of money" as unimportant; highly important life goals were "having a happy family," "being a community leader," and "working to correct social and economic inequalities."

Implications for Our Competitive Society

Much of Adler's theorizing has an authentic ring to it, especially in the context of our highly competitive and power-oriented culture. Many of us can see ourselves and others engaged in a race to outdo each other—a perpetual quest for more prestige and status than our neighbors have.

> Everyone tries to be more . . . to reach higher and, as a consequence, we are all neurotic, in a neurotic society which pays a premium to the overambitious search for prestige and striving for superiority. This search inspires a desire for self-evaluation and personal glory, thereby restricting our ability for cooperation and our sense of human fellowship. Yet underneath we are all frightened people, not sure of ourselves. . . . It is this doubt of oneself, expressed in a feeling of inadequacy and inferiority, which restricts our Social Interest and which is at the root of all maladjustment and psychopathology. (Dreikurs, 1963, p. 245)

From a very early age, children are taught the importance of winning and of avoiding failure. Comparisons between individuals are continuously made and, although warnings are sometimes given not to feel bad or think less of oneself after losing and not to downgrade a defeated opponent, such distinctions are tremendously difficult to maintain. As a consequence, people with superior skills tend to feel smug and personally superior to others, while the inept tend to feel unworthy and inadequate. Even successful persons are not spared these feelings of inadequacy, for they have been taught by their parents and others never to be satisfied with their accomplishments.

The harmful effects of excessive competition are manifested in a variety of ways. For example, there have been recent instances where, to increase the chance of winning prizes, children and their parents have cheated in 4-H competitions by giving illegal steroids to the children's pet cattle so that the animals would grow bigger and stronger. Also, recall the pathetic incident a few years ago in which, to increase her chance of winning, a skater hired a man to hurt a rival so that she couldn't skate. Or think of the woman in Texas who, to increase her daughter's chance of becoming a high school cheerleader, hired a hit man to kill the mother of her daughter's rival for a place on the squad. The woman figured that the rival would be so depressed and dispirited by her mother's death that she would not try out for the school's cheerleading team. Finally, consider those students who routinely cheat on examinations to achieve higher grades than their classmates and do not feel guilty about it, and the perhaps equal number of academics who have lied and cheated in similar situations and who now pontificate on the deceptions practiced by their students.

Adlerian theory seems to take the moral position that competition is bad. This assumption, however, is worth questioning. Can competition have positive consequences? Can competition be compatible with social interest? It appears that the answer to both these questions is yes.

A closer examination of Adler's theory shows that it postulates not only a negative striving for personal superiority but also a positive striving for superiority in the sense of realizing one's potential. Thus, an argument could be made that healthy individuals engage in a sort of private competition—setting standards, achieving them, and setting new standards. Competition, in this restricted sense, may well produce outcomes that contribute to the welfare and happiness of others. Competition of this sort is clearly compatible with Adler's idea that the attainment of perfection involves overcoming resistances in the environment (Adler, 1973c, p. 75).

Most competitive activities, however, involve interpersonal comparisons and evaluations. But, even here, an argument can be made for the compatibility of competition with social interest. Such an outcome could theoretically be obtained if people competed *with* rather than *against* one another. After all, the etymology of the word competition shows that its root meaning comes from the Latin *competere*, meaning "to strive together with." The basic meaning says nothing about striving against anyone. Competition with one another should generate feelings of accomplishment or defeat, but without the accompanying feelings of personal superiority or inferiority in relationship to others. Perhaps such an outcome is possible where there is mutual respect and esteem between opponents. There would still be a winner and a loser, but neither party would feel compelled to gloat after winning or to feel inferior after losing. Both parties would also benefit from the testing of their skills. The winner would be likely to improve as a result of the contest, while the loser would learn something from the failure that could be used to enhance performance in the future.

Recent research by Ryckman, Hammer, Kaczor, and Gold (1996) provides support for these arguments. These investigators studied competitors who were primarily concerned with using their competitive experiences as a means of enhancing their personal development and realizing their potential. They found that these competitors were not primarily focused on winning, but rather on enjoyment and mastery of various tasks through competitive experiences. Individuals with such competitive attitudes were most concerned with self-discovery and self-improvement and task mastery. Their focus was not on derogation of others in order to enhance the self; their competitors were not seen as obstacles standing in their way, but rather as helpers who provide them with opportunities for personal learning and discovery. Personal development competitors want to win, but not at all costs and at other people's expense. It should not surprise you to learn that personal development competitors were highly self-actualizing.

Finally, interpersonal competition can also serve to energize and motivate individuals, who find themselves pushed beyond previous levels of performance and forced to find creative solutions to seemingly insoluble problems. For example, many inventions that have served to better the lives of the members of society are the products of healthy competition between individuals and research teams in the marketplace of ideas. Such competitive outcomes are surely compatible with social interest.

ASSESSMENT TECHNIQUES

Like Freud, Adler sought to understand the individual's personality by focusing on early childhood experiences. He used three major techniques: early recollections, dream analysis, and birth-order analysis.

Early Recollections

Adler believed that reports by patients of their earliest memories provided valuable insights into their unique styles of life. He maintained that patients were very willing to discuss these memories. Often the memories were based on actual experiences, but sometimes they were fanciful. Whether real or imaginary, Adler thought they still revealed important meanings, and gave glimpses into the person's strivings for superiority (Ansbacher & Ansbacher, 1956, pp. 351–352).

To illustrate the importance of these memories, Adler reported the recollections of a woman whose father gave her a pony when she was 3 years old. He also gave her older sister a pony on the same occasion. Mounted on her own pony, the sister took the reins of the patient's pony from her father and proceeded triumphantly down the street. However, the patient's pony, hurrying after the other, went so fast that the patient fell down in the dirt. Later in life, she told Adler, she surpassed her sister as a horsewoman, but she never forgot this early humiliating experience (Ansbacher & Ansbacher, 1956, pp. 354–355).

Adler first noted that the woman mentioned her father and not her mother in recalling this incident. He interpreted this to mean that, as a child, the woman was not particularly satisfied with her home life and that perhaps her mother favored her older sister. This information could prove useful in her treatment.

Next Adler observed that the older sister appeared to triumph in the incident; this implied an unhealthy competition between the two sisters. The younger sister (the patient) believed that she was continually being humiliated in the relationship. When she reported that she later surpassed her sister as a horsewoman, Adler concluded that she felt the need to triumph over her. However, her victory did not in the least diminish her feelings about the original experience. Thus, the patient's memory simply reinforced her attitude: "If anyone is ahead of me, I am endangered. I must always be the first." In Adler's view, such striving is typical of second children, who are always trying to overtake the pacemaker, the oldest child. This unhealthy attitude toward life, along with others, was causing the patient needless pain. By revealing to the patient her basic attitude, Adler enabled her to begin making changes that would lead to a more satisfying outlook on life.

Besides therapists' use of case studies to illustrate the importance of early recollections in exploring people's striving for superiority, researchers have begun to examine how early recollections can reveal facets of individuals' personality traits and self-concept. For example, Chaplin and Orlofsky (1991) analyzed the contents of the earliest memories reported by alcoholics and nonalcoholics. They found that the earliest recollections of alcoholics reflected less social interest, a more passive and powerless orientation to life, greater depressive feelings, and a more negative self-concept. Their memories were also more rife with beatings, abandonment by one or both parents, and emotional deprivation. After undergoing Adlerian therapy for their substance abuse, these alcoholics began to realize that they could produce positive changes and could gain control over their drinking (Chaplin & Orlofsky, 1991, pp. 365–367).

Dream Analysis

Adler also utilized dream analysis as a major technique for understanding each patient's personality. Unlike Freud, however, he did not focus on sexual interpretations of manifest dream content. Instead, he believed that a person's dreams are determined by his or her goal of superiority. More specifically, dreams reflect the individual's unconscious attempts to achieve personal goals in accordance with his or her unique style of life. The student who is courageous and unafraid of examinations, for example, may dream of climbing a mountain and enjoying the view from the top, whereas the student who is a quitter and wants to postpone examinations may dream of falling off the mountain (Adler, 1969, p. 70). Each student's dreams are controlled by his or her unique style of life.

For Adler, dreams also provide glimpses of the future, and thus suggest potential solutions to the person's problems. For example, Adler cites the case of a man who was very disappointed in his wife. His primary complaint was that she did not take adequate care of their two children. Adler saw the complaint as a symptom of a deeper, underlying hostility toward her because he believed she had not married him out of love.

In the course of analysis, the man reported a dream in which he had three children, the youngest of whom got lost and could not be found. The man interpreted his dream as a warning not to have more children because his wife would neglect them. While acknowledging the plausibility of this interpretation, Adler pointed out that the dream about a third child might suggest instead a desire to reconcile with his wife and develop a more satisfying relationship with her (Mairet, 1964, pp. 164–166).

Birth-Order Analysis

Adler's third technique for understanding the patient's personality was birth-order analysis. Adler believed that a correct analysis of the effects of patients' birth positions on their subsequent behavior would help win their confidence. This emphasis on unavoidable childhood circumstances also helps patients to stop blaming themselves for developing a faulty style of life (Forer, 1977, p. 110). Reducing self-blame and resistance, in turn, enables patients to adopt more constructive goals and behavior.

THEORY'S IMPLICATIONS FOR THERAPY

Neurotics and psychotics, according to Adler, are individuals who have developed faulty styles of life, usually as a result of parental pampering, neglect, or rejection during early childhood. In many instances, parental behavior was erratic, mixing pampering and rejection. As a consequence of such treatment, Adler believed, children become highly anxious and insecure. To cope with their feelings of inferiority, they begin to develop protective devices—most often, a strong striving for personal superiority. Neurotic individuals begin to believe that they actually are superior to others and to act in ways consistent with that belief. They strive to be perfect, to avoid failure at all costs. They belittle others, and perceive them as competitors who must be defeated in order to achieve personal satisfaction. Psychotics, too, view others with suspicion, but they validate their worth not so much through comparison with others as through the use of private logic and reasoning and delusions of grandeur.

According to Adler, the goal of therapy is the reorganization of patients' mistaken beliefs about themselves and others, the elimination of faulty goals, and the implementation of new goals that will help them realize their potential as human beings. "The patient must be guided away from himself, toward productivity for others; he must be educated toward social interest; he must be brought to the only correct insight, that he is as important to the community as anyone else; he must get to feel at home on this earth" (Adler, 1973d, p. 200).

The therapist acts as the patient's guide to facilitate movement toward these ends. First, they jointly seek to understand the childhood origins of the patient's difficulties—to understand why the patient feels the need to be superior to others. Encouraged by the therapist, the patient moves away from competitive self-centeredness and comes to realize that psychological health is contingent on developing a cooperative attitude toward others and seeking to contribute to the welfare of society. The patient begins to see that he or she is a worthwhile part of the community and to appreciate the joy of accepting responsibility for one's actions. As a result, the person is no longer a taker but a giver. Slowly, the patient moves toward a reorganization of perceptions and begins to behave differently toward others.

EVALUATIVE COMMENTS

We turn now to an assessment of the scientific worth of Adler's theory in terms of our six criteria.

Comprehensiveness   Adler addressed himself to a wide range of phenomena involving disordered behavior; in this respect, his position rivals Freud's. He discusses at length the etiology and cure of many different kinds of neurosis and psychosis. But Adler also sought to understand the ways in which political, educational, and religious institutions affect personality development. He tried not only to assess the impact of the destructive elements of these institutions on the individual but also to outline the ways in which they could be restructured to promote psychological health and well-being. In general, then, Adler's theory is comprehensive in nature, although, like Freud's theory, it has a very limited motivational base.

Precision and testability   Generally, the concepts in Adler's theory are global in nature and poorly defined. He postulated, for example, a proof complex that is "found in many people who want to prove that they also have a right to exist or that they have no faults" (Adler, 1973b, p. 75). How would one go about measuring this proof complex? The same difficulty arises in seeking to operationalize such Adlerian concepts as redeemer complex, exclusion complex, predestination complex, and creative power.

   The relational statements of the theory are also vaguely stated. Witness a hypothesis such as this: "The law of movement and its direction originate from the creative power of the individual and use, in free choice, one's experiences of one's body and of external effects, within the limits of human capacity" (Adler, 1973a, p. 51). How much creative power is needed to affect the person's unique movements? How much movement occurs if the creative power of the person is utilized? How do you define movement? Creative power? It is interesting to note that Adler believed that this hypothesis had already been empirically validated.

Parsimony   Adler made a diligent effort to construct a scientific theory that was understandable to the ordinary person. The result was a commonsense psychology that utilizes only a few constructs. But although parsimony of explanation is considered a virtue in scientific psychology, the set of constructs must be adequate to the task of accounting for human behavior in all its complexity. Because Adler postulated a master motive—the striving for superiority—his position has a reductionist quality that fails to do justice to the great diversity of reinforcers that motivate us. Also, because there are only a few constructs in the theory, they must be applied in highly general and imprecise ways. As we have seen, constructs are defined so loosely that it is often unclear what dimensions they encompass and how they are related to everyday situations.

Empirical validity   Empirical support for Adler's theory is generally not very strong. However, this situation may well change in the near future, now that investigators have begun to construct reliable and valid measures of some of his key constructs—most notably, social interest (Crandall, 1975; Greever, Tseng, & Friedland, 1973; Leak, Millard, Perry, & Williams, 1985). Other researchers have tried to construct and validate a measure of Adler's typology of the lifestyles of healthy and unhealthy children and adults (Kannarkat & Bayton, 1979; Stiles & Wilborn, 1992; Wheeler, Kern, & Curlette, 1986). The current interest in operationalizing such key concepts and establishing their reliability augurs well for eventual hypothesis testing.

Heuristic value   Clearly the chief contribution of Adler's theory is the number of subsequent investigators of human personality who have been influenced by it. Adler's position has contributed to theory in the areas of existential psychology and psychiatry, neo-Freudian psychoanalysis, personality diagnosis including dream interpretation, the practice of psychotherapy, and the theory of positive mental health (Ansbacher & Ansbacher, 1973, p. 3). Adler has directly influenced such prominent psychologists and psychiatrists as Albert Ellis, Carl Rogers, Abraham Maslow, and Rollo May (Ansbacher, 1990, pp. 45–53; Ellis, 1973, pp. 111–127) and has had considerable impact on the experimental work of Julian Rotter. (See Chapter 16.)

Applied value   In addition to its considerable heuristic value, Adler's theory focuses on phenomena that are of particular relevance in a highly competitive and achievement-oriented society. In short, it is a theory that addresses itself to problems and issues that matter in a culture such as ours. His theory has had considerable applied usefulness in the areas of psychopathology, psychotherapy, education, and family life.

DISCUSSION QUESTIONS

1. Do you agree with Adler that all of us have an innate need for achievement? Does any cross-cultural evidence cast doubt upon Adler's contention?

2. Adler maintained that we all have had feelings of inferiority. Do you agree? If so, what were the primary sources of these feelings for you and your friends?

3. What, in Adler's view, is the relationship between a person's attitude and his or her behavior?

4. What is the masculine protest? How is the concept relevant in explaining the behavior of both men and women?

5. Do you agree with Adler that our behavior is guided by our goals? What are some of the major goals of college-educated people in North America today?

6. Adler's view of the healthy society is based upon his concept of social interest. What is social interest? Does the concept differ in any way from the concept of enlightened self-interest?

7. One of Adler's most interesting concepts is that of birth order. Do you agree with him that a person's order of birth can have a dramatic impact on personality development because parents tend to treat older and younger children differently? How many children are there in your family? Have your parents treated you and your siblings differently? If you are an only child, do you think that fact has made any difference in the way your parents reacted to you?

8. Do you think that your friends would classify you generally as more of a ruling type, a getting type, an avoiding type, or a socially useful type? Why?

9. Is competition necessarily destructive? How is social interest compatible with competition?

10. Is it possible for people to treat each other as equals in a largely capitalistic society such as ours?

GLOSSARY

attitude   Learned tendency to respond to an object in a consistently favorable or unfavorable way.

avoiding type   An unhealthy person who lacks the confidence to confront problems and avoids or ignores them.

birth-order effects   Adler's belief that how each child is treated by parents depends on the child's order of birth within the family and that, in consequence, birth order is an important correlate of personality development.

creative self   Term used by Adler to reflect his belief that people have the ability to create actively their own destinies and personalities.

fictional finalism   Imagined goal that guides a person's behavior; also called the guiding self-ideal by Adler in his later writings.

getting type   An unhealthy person who attains personal goals by relying indiscriminately on others for help.

individual psychology   Theory advanced by Adler that seeks to understand the behavior of each person as a complex, organized entity.

masculine protest   Attempt by an individual, male or female, to compensate for feelings of inferiority by acting as though superior to others.

organ inferiority   Biologically based defect that gives rise to feelings of inadequacy.

overcompensation   Exaggerated attempts by individuals to overcome their feelings of inferiority by acting as though they were superior to others.

ruling type   An unhealthy person who strives for personal superiority by trying to exploit and control others.

social interest   Innate tendency in human beings to help and cooperate with one another as a means of establishing a harmonious and productive society.

socially useful type   A healthy person who actively and courageously confronts and solves his or her problems in accordance with social interest.

style of life   The individual's distinctive personality pattern, which is basically shaped by the end of early childhood.

superiority   The striving to attain perfection. Adler categorized superiority into two types: (1) personal superiority, which he considered harmful because it implies seeking satisfaction at the expense of others; and (2) strivings for superiority in the sense of perfection, which he considered healthy because they imply a striving for fulfillment of individual potential through helping others and being helped by them.

teleological position   The belief that goals determine behavior—or, more generally, that behavior is directed and shaped by a designing force.

SUGGESTED READINGS

Adler, A. (1927). *The practice and theory of individual psychology*. New York: Harcourt, Brace & World.

Adler, A. (1969). *The science of living*. Garden City, NY: Doubleday Anchor. (Original work published 1929)

Ansbacher, H. L., & Ansbacher, R. R. (Eds.). (1956). *The individual psychology of Alfred Adler*. New York: Basic Books.

Ansbacher, H. L., & Ansbacher, R. R. (Eds.). (1973). *Superiority and social interest: A collection of later writings*. New York: Viking.

REFERENCES

Adler, A. (1927). *Understanding human nature*. Garden City, NY: Doubleday Anchor.

Adler, A. (1930). *The education of children*. South Bend, IN: Gateway.

Adler, A. (1937). Position in family constellation influences life style. *International Journal of Individual Psychology, 3,* 211–227.

Adler, A. (1969). *The science of living*. Garden City, NY: Doubleday Anchor. (Original work published 1929)

Adler, A. (1973a). Advantages and disadvantages of the inferiority feeling. In H. L. Ansbacher & R. R. Ansbacher (Eds.), *Superiority and social interest* (pp. 50–58). New York: Viking.

Adler, A. (1973b). Complex compulsion as part of personality and neurosis. In H. L. Ansbacher & R. R. Ansbacher (Eds.), *Superiority and social interest* (pp. 71–80). New York: Viking.

Adler, A. (1973c). On the origins of the striving for superiority and of social interest. In H. L. Ansbacher & R. R. Ansbacher (Eds.), *Superiority and social interest* (pp. 29–40). New York: Viking.

Adler, A. (1973d). Technique of treatment. In H. L. Ansbacher & R. R. Ansbacher (Eds.), *Superiority and social interest* (pp. 191–201). New York: Viking.

Ansbacher, H. L. (1990). Alfred Adler's influence on the three leading cofounders of humanistic psychology. *Journal of Humanistic Psychology, 30,* 45–53.

Ansbacher, H. L., & Ansbacher, R. R. (Eds.). (1956). *The individual psychology of Alfred Adler*. New York: Basic Books.

Ansbacher, H. L., & Ansbacher, R. R. (Eds.). (1973). *Superiority and social interest: A collection of later writings*. New York: Viking.

Barry, H., III, & Blane, H. T. (1977). Birth order of alcoholics. *Journal of Individual Psychology, 33,* 62–79.

Belmont, L., & Marolla, F. A. (1973). Birth order, family size, and intelligence. *Science, 182,* 1096–1101.

Blake, J. (1989). *Family size and achievement*. Berkeley: University of California Press.

Breland, H. M. (1974). Birth order, family configuration, and verbal achievement. *Child Development, 45,* 1011–1019.

Brennan, J. F. (1969). Autoeroticism or social feeling as basis of human development. *Journal of Individual Psychology, 25,* 3–18.

Chaplin, M. P., & Orlofsky, J. L. (1991). Personality characteristics of male alcoholics as revealed through their early recollections. *Individual Psychology, 47,* 356–371.

Crandall, J. E. (1975). A scale for social interest. *Journal of Individual Psychology, 31,* 187–195.

Crandall, J. E. (1980). Adler's concept of social interest: Theory, measurement, and implications for adjustment. *Journal of Personality and Social Psychology, 39,* 481–495.

Dreikurs, R. (1963). Individual psychology: The Adlerian point of view. In J. M. Wepman & R. W. Heine (Eds.), *Concepts of personality* (pp. 234–256). Chicago: Aldine.

Ellis, A. (1973). *Humanistic psychotherapy*. New York: McGraw-Hill.

Falbo, T. (1977). The only child: A review. *Journal of Individual Psychology, 33,* 47–61.

Falbo, T. (1978). Only children and interpersonal behavior: An experimental and survey study. *Journal of Applied Social Psychology, 8,* 244–253.

Falbo, T., & Cooper, C. R. (1980). Young children's time and intellectual ability. *Journal of Genetic Psychology, 173,* 299–300.

Falbo, T., & Polit, D. F. (1986). Quantitative review of the only child literature: Research evidence and theory development. *Psychological Bulletin, 100,* 176–189.

Forer, L. K. (1977). The use of birth order information in psychotherapy. *Journal of Individual Psychology, 33,* 105–113.

Furtmuller, C. (1973). Alfred Adler: A biographical essay. In H. L. Ansbacher & R. R. Ansbacher (Eds.), *Superiority and social interest* (pp. 330–394). New York: Viking.

Greever, K. B., Tseng, M. S., & Friedland, B. U. (1973). Development of the social interest index. *Journal of Consulting and Clinical Psychology, 41,* 454–458.

Hudson, V. M. (1990). Birth order of world leaders: An exploratory analysis of effects on personality and behavior. *Political Psychology, 11,* 583–601.

Ivancevich, J. B., Matteson, M. T., & Gamble, G. O. (1987). Birth order and the Type A coronary behavior pattern. *Individual Psychology, 43,* 42–49.

Kannarkat, J. P., & Bayton, J. A. (1979). Validity of Adler's active-constructive, active-destructive, passive-constructive, and passive-destructive typology. *Journal of Research in Personality, 13,* 351–360.

Leak, G. K., & Gardner, L. E. (1990). Sexual attitudes, love attitudes, and social interest. *Individual Psychology, 46,* 55–60.

Leak, G. K., Millard, R. J., Perry, N. W., & Williams, D. E. (1985). An investigation of the nomological network of social interest. *Journal of Research in Personality, 19,* 197–207.

Leak, G. K., & Williams, D. E. (1989). Relationship between social interest and perceived family environment. *Individual Psychology, 45,* 362–368.

Lewis, M., & Feiring, C. (1982). Some American families at dinner. In L. M. Laosa & I. E. Sigel (Eds.), *Families as learning environments for children* (pp. 115–145). New York: Plenum.

Mairet, P. (Ed.). (1964). *Alfred Adler: Problems of neurosis: A book of case studies.* New York: Harper & Row.

Melillo, D. (1983). Birth order, perceived birth order, and family position of academic women. *Individual Psychology, 39,* 57–62.

Mosak, H. H. (1977). *On purpose: Collected papers of Harold H. Mosak.* Chicago: Alfred Adler Institute.

Newman, J., & Taylor, A. (1994). Family training for political leadership: Birth order of United States state governors and Australian prime ministers. *Political Psychology, 15,* 435–442.

Orgler, H. (1963). *Alfred Adler: The man and his work.* New York: Liveright.

Phillips, A. S., Long, R. G., & Bedeian, A. G. (1990). Type A status: Birth order and gender effects. *Individual Psychology, 46,* 365–373.

Retherford, R. D., & Sewell, W. H. (1991). Birth order and intelligence: Further tests of the confluence model. *American Sociological Review, 56,* 141–158.

Rodd, J. (1994). Social interest, psychological well-being, and maternal stress. *Individual Psychology, 50,* 58–68.

Ryckman, R. M., Hammer, M., Kaczor, L. M., & Gold, J. A. (1996). Construction of a personal development competitive attitude scale. *Journal of Personality Assessment, 66,* 374–386.

Steelman, L. C. (1985). A tale of two variables: A review of the intellectual consequences of sibship size and birth order. *Review of Educational Research, 55,* 353–386.

Steelman, L. C. (1986). The tale retold: A response to Zajonc. *Review of Educational Research, 56,* 373–377.

Stiles, K., & Wilborn, B. (1992). A life-style instrument for children. *Individual Psychology, 48,* 96–106.

Wagner, M. E., & Schubert, H. J. P. (1977). Sibship variables and United States presidents. *Journal of Individual Psychology, 33,* 78–85.

Watkins, C. E., Jr. (1992). Birth order research and Adler's theory: A critical review. *Individual Psychology, 48,* 357–368.

Watkins, C. E., Jr. (1994). Measuring social interest. *Individual Psychology, 50,* 69–96.

Watkins, C. E., Jr., & St. John, C. (1994). Validity of the Sulliman scale of social interest. *Individual Psychology, 50,* 166–169.

Watts, R. E., & Holden, J. M. (1994). Why continue to use "fictional finalism"? *Individual Psychology, 50,* 161–163.

Wheeler, M. S., Kern, R. M., & Curlette, W. L. (1986). Factor analytic scales designed to measure Adlerian life style themes. *Individual Psychology, 42,* 1–16.

Zajonc, R. B. (1986). Family factors and intellectual test performance: A reply to Steelman. *Review of Educational Research, 56,* 365–371.

Zajonc, R. B., & Markus, G. B. (1975). Birth order and intellectual development. *Psychological Review, 82,* 74–88.

Zweigenhaft, R. L. (1975). Birth order, approval seeking, and membership in Congress. *Journal of Individual Psychology, 31,* 205–210.

CHAPTER 5

Horney's Social and Cultural Psychoanalysis

BIOGRAPHICAL SKETCH

Karen Horney (pronounced *horn-eye*) was born in 1885 in Blankenese, a village on the north bank of the Elbe River approximately 12 miles west of Hamburg, Germany. Her father, Berndt Wackels, was a sea captain employed by one of the large shipping lines located in Hamburg. Horney's mother, Clotilde van Ronzelen, was a member of a prominent Dutch-German family. Captain Wackels, 18 years her senior, had four children from a previous marriage. Their first child was a son, Berndt, followed four years later by Karen.

As a child, Karen had ambivalent feelings toward her father. He took her on several boat trips with him throughout the world and instilled in her a love of the sea and of travel and a cosmopolitan outlook on life. She loved him deeply, but felt intimidated by his stern, self-righteous manner. Wackels was a God-fearing, religious fundamentalist who strongly believed that women were inferior to men. He restricted Karen's activities, while granting freedoms and privileges to her brother. He vehemently opposed her ambitions, especially her educational goals. For example, Karen decided at age 13 that she wanted to study medicine, but her father said he would not pay for her education. Bitter at her father's opposition, she complained, "He, who has flung out thousands for my stepbrother . . . , who is both stupid and bad, first turns every penny he is to spend for

149

me 10 times in his fingers" (Paris, 1994, p. 7). But fortunately her mother was more encouraging and protected her from her father's authoritarianism, so that Karen was able to pursue her goal of medicine. Apparently, though, neither parent gave Karen much affection. Thus, wracked by doubts about her self-worth, she uncritically accepted the protection of her mother and became a clinging, highly compliant daughter, presumably as a means of feeling safe and wanted. Horney's feelings of inadequacy were heightened by her perception that she was physically unattractive, although others did not see her that way. She reacted strongly to this negative self-image by investing all of her energies in her studies. Looking back many years later, she said, "If I couldn't be beautiful, I decided I would be smart."

An excellent student, Horney entered medical school in Freiburg in 1906; she was the only woman in her class. In this male-dominated atmosphere, she sometimes felt that she had to prove she was as competent as, if not more competent than, her male friends and associates. Yet her social life during this period was full, exciting, and rewarding. She was introduced to Oskar Horney, a student majoring in economics, and married him while still in medical training. After finishing his studies, Oskar went to work in an investment firm and was promoted rapidly to manager of company operations. In the meantime, Karen was finishing her medical studies, while trying simultaneously to fulfill the roles of homemaker and mother to a newly born daughter (the first of three daughters).

The conflicts inherent in these activities, coupled with the death of her mother and emerging difficulties in her marriage, plunged Horney into depression, and she entered therapy with psychoanalyst Dr. Karl Abraham. Disappointed with the results of her therapy, Horney began to question the basic tenets of psychoanalysis. For several years, she participated in weekly evening sessions with other analysts at Dr. Abraham's home, to discuss psychoanalytic concepts, principles, and therapeutic practices. These informal sessions led to the formation of the Berlin Psychoanalytic Institute, of which Horney remained an active member from 1918 until 1932.

During this period, she also became more outspoken about the limitations of orthodox psychoanalysis. She believed strongly that Freud had placed too much stress on the role played by the sexual instincts in the development of neurosis and not enough on the cultural and social conditions that fostered pathology. For Freud, neurosis was essentially an outgrowth of the person's inability to cope with sexual impulses and strivings; for Horney, neurosis was primarily the result of disturbed human relationships. In her view, neurosis and sexual disturbance were often, but not inevitably, intertwined. When they were, it was the neurosis, based upon faulty character structure, that produced impaired sexual functioning; for Freud, it was impaired sexual functioning that was the primary cause of neurosis. Horney believed further that each culture generates its own unique set of fears in its members. In one culture, fears might be created by nature—for instance, living at the base of an unpredictable volcano or in the scorching desert; in another, by war-like neighbors. In our culture, the heavy emphasis on competition and the achievement of individual success sometimes leads to a fear of failure or of being inferior to others. The normal person, according to Horney, is capable of adjusting to these threatening conditions and of making the best use of what the culture has to offer. The neurotic, in contrast, is unable to adjust and uses defenses rigidly and indiscriminately to lessen his or her fears and to feel safe.

Interwoven with the problems generated by living in a particular culture are the problems and fears created by the unique social or interpersonal conditions of a person's life. Mistreatment by parents, siblings, peers, authority figures, and others may all contribute in complicated fashion to maladjusted functioning. Thus, in Horney's judgment, sociocultural conditions have a tremendous impact on the individual's development and functioning. Emphasizing the role of the socialization process in the onset of neuroses, and deemphasizing (but not eliminating) the role of biology, Horney began to reinterpret much of Freud's thinking, including his libido theory, his theory of psychosexual development, and his theory of therapy. Her new theory germinated under the stimulation of debates with her colleagues and students at the Berlin Psychoanalytic Institute and can be seen in its evolutionary form by reading her books in chronological order: *The Neurotic Personality of Our Time* (1937), *New Ways in Psychoanalysis* (1939), *Self-Analysis* (1942), *Our Inner Conflicts* (1945), *Neurosis and Human Growth* (1950), and the posthumous *Feminine Psychology* (1967).

In 1932, Horney left the Berlin Psychoanalytic Institute and came to the United States, where she became associate director of the Chicago Psychoanalytic Institute. Two years later, she moved to New York, to establish a private practice and to work and teach courses at the New York Psychoanalytic Institute. While in New York, she had many opportunities to meet and exchange ideas with prominent social scientists, including Erich Fromm, Clara Thompson, Margaret Mead, H. S. Sullivan, Ruth Benedict, and John Dollard. It was also here, in 1937, that she divorced her husband. She continued to refine her theories, to write books and journal articles, and to give lectures on her ideas to various professional societies. Her ideas, unfortunately, rankled some of her more orthodox Freudian colleagues at the New York Psychoanalytic Institute, and eventually she felt obligated to resign. Several other members resigned in sympathy with her. Shortly afterwards, she helped found the American Institute for Psychoanalysis as a vehicle for promoting her own theories. She succumbed to cancer in 1952 after a lengthy illness (Rubins, 1978).

CONCEPTS AND PRINCIPLES

Hypercompetitiveness: The Unfailing Center of Neurosis

According to Horney (1937), **hypercompetitiveness** is an indiscriminate need to compete and win and to avoid losing at any cost as a means of maintaining or enhancing one's feelings of self-worth. It also includes feelings and thoughts of manipulation, aggressiveness, exploitation, and derogation of others across a myriad of situations. Horney maintained that such an exaggerated competitive attitude was a central feature of American culture and had a highly detrimental impact on the individual's development and functioning.

> Our modern culture is based on the principle of individual competition, [and] the . . . individual has to fight with other individuals of the same group, has to surpass them and, frequently, [to] thrust them aside. The advantage of the one is frequently the disadvantage of the other. The psychic result . . . is a diffuse hostile tension between individuals. [This] competitiveness, and the . . . hostility that accompanies it, pervades all human relationships. Competitive stimuli are active from the cradle to the grave [and present] a fertile ground for the development of neurosis. (Horney, 1937, pp. 284–287)

According to Horney, hypercompetitive individuals have typically grown up in families where they were verbally and physically abused by their parents. As a result, they feel powerless and insignificant; these feelings are largely unconscious. To overcome their self-perceptions of inadequacy and inferiority, they begin to fantasize about attaining unlimited success and power. An incessant and indiscriminate striving for personal superiority permeates virtually every area of their lives. These individuals are possessed by a grandiose sense of self-importance and an exhibitionism designed to win attention, recognition, and admiration. They seek self-aggrandizement through indiscriminate competition. Ruthlessly single-minded, they come to perceive others as malevolent, and believe that their best chance for survival is to regard everyone with distrust. In their self-defeating quest for superiority, they become hostile, dogmatic, arrogant, aggressive, and derisive toward others. Their sexual life consists largely of attempts to subdue and humiliate their partners, as further proof of their own superiority (Horney, 1937, pp. 195–197).

To assess the validity of Horney's theorizing about hypercompetitiveness, investigators needed to construct a scale that measures it, and to establish its reliability and validity (Ryckman, Hammer, Kaczor, & Gold, 1990). Sample items and the scoring procedure for the scale appear in Table 5.1.

Using this instrument, researchers did find empirical support for Horney's ideas. College men and women who scored higher in hypercompetitiveness were generally less psychologically healthy than were college men and women lower in hypercompetitiveness. Specifically, individuals higher in hypercompetitiveness were found to be lower in self-esteem and higher in narcissism, exhibitionism, neuroticism, mistrust, and dogmatism than were people lower in hypercompetitiveness (Ryckman, Hammer, Kaczor, & Gold, 1990; Ryckman, Thornton, & Butler, 1994). They were also found to be indiscriminate in their pursuit of success; often they would take on so many roles and tasks that they inevitably fell short of their goals and felt perpetually dissatisfied. Furthermore, men with hypercompetitive attitudes were more macho (hypermasculine) and believed more strongly that women were sexual objects undeserving of respect than did men who scored lower on the hypercompetitive scale. In the light

---

TABLE 5.1   Sample items from the Hypercompetitive Attitude Scale

---

1. If I can disturb my opponent in some way in order to get the edge in competition, I will do so.
2. I can't stand to lose an argument.
3. I find myself being competitive even in situations which do not call for competition.
4. I compete with others even if they are not competing with me.
5. Winning in competition makes me feel more powerful as a person.

Note: Subjects respond to each item on a 5-point scale: never true of me (1), seldom true of me (2), sometimes true of me (3), often true of me (4), and always true of me (5). Higher scores indicate greater hypercompetitiveness.

SOURCE: Adapted from Ryckman, Hammer, Kaczor, & Gold, 1990, pp. 630–639.

of these findings, Kaczor, Ryckman, Thornton, and Kuehnel (1991) predicted that hypercompetitive men would have hostile attitudes toward rape victims—in particular, that such men would see rape victims as losers in a competitive and violent physical struggle for dominance and superiority with their assailants. They predicted and found that such individuals did indeed tend to blame rape victims for their own victimization more than did men with lower hypercompetitive attitudes.

The Etiology of Neuroses in the Family

In Horney's view, because parents generally adopt the values of society, their relationships with their children are often implicitly hypercompetitive and give rise to neuroses. Attitudes and behaviors of hypercompetitive parents that cause disturbed relationships include "direct or indirect domination, indifference, erratic behavior, lack of respect for the child's individual needs, lack of real guidance, disparaging attitudes, lack of reliable warmth, having to take sides in parental disagreements, isolation from other children, injustice, discrimination, unkept promises, hostile atmosphere, and so on" (Horney, 1945, p. 41). Rarely, if ever, does only one of these factors operate to produce pathology in a particular person; behavior is invariably multidetermined, with several factors operating jointly to produce disturbance.

The operation of these negative factors creates **basic anxiety** in children—a feeling of being isolated and helpless in a potentially hostile world. They dread their social environment, which they perceive as unfair, unpredictable, begrudging, and merciless. These children also feel that their freedom is being taken away, and happiness prevented, by parents and other adult authority figures. Thus, their self-esteem and self-reliance are continually being undermined. Fear is instilled in them by intimidation and isolation, and their natural exuberance and curiosity is stifled by brutality or overprotective love (Horney, 1939, p. 75).

The Use of Neurotic Strategies To Cope with Feelings of Basic Anxiety

To cope with the feelings of insecurity, isolation, and hostility that accompany basic anxiety, children often resort to certain defensive attitudes. These protective devices provide a temporary alleviation of pain and make them feel safe (Horney, 1942, p. 45). Horney discussed these defenses as neurotic needs or strivings designed to reestablish the safety of their environments. They are distinguished from normal needs by their compulsiveness, rigidity, and indiscriminate usage and by the fact that they are unconscious (Horney, 1945, pp. 30–31). Horney outlined and described ten neurotic needs (Horney, 1942, pp. 54–60).

The neurotic need for affection and approval   Although we all wish to be liked and appreciated by people of whom we are fond, neurotics show an indiscriminate hunger for affection, regardless of whether they care for the person concerned or whether the person has any positive feelings toward them. They are overly sensitive to any criticism or indication that the attention they want and need from others is not forthcoming. They will sever a budding relationship with someone who does not accept an invitation for supper, even if the person is unable to attend for reasons beyond his or her control. They may also terminate a relationship if someone disagrees with them about some trivial issue. Such individuals also have strong inhibitions about expressing their wishes or asking for favors, and they are incapable of saying no to the demands of others. Salespeople can readily convince them to buy household appliances that they really do not need; on a date, they can be persuaded to have premarital sex even if it is a violation of their moral principles and causes them considerable anguish afterward (Horney, 1937, pp. 35–38).

The neurotic need for a partner who will take over one's life
Many neurotics are excessively dependent on others. They feel very lonely and inadequate without the presence, benevolence, love, and friendship of a partner. Driven by the strong need for a partner, they select one without much prior reflection and consequently discover that he or she does not meet their expectations. Whereas a genuine and mature partnership involves mutual caring, sharing, and love, neurotics are incapable of such behavior and typically become associated with others who are bound by the same limitations. Thus, their relationships are disturbed and unsatisfying (Horney, 1939, p. 251).

The neurotic need to restrict one's life within narrow borders
Neurotics are generally not risk takers. They are afraid of expressing their wishes for fear of disapproval and ridicule. Even in situations where spontaneity and expansiveness are valued and accepted (for example, parties or athletic contests), neurotics may be unable to as-

sert themselves. Therefore, they may avoid such situations by claiming that they are boring and not worthwhile. They may avoid accepting jobs as teachers or as business executives because they are afraid that they will fail and face public humiliation. As a result, many neurotics feel safe only by living a highly circumscribed life in which routine and orderliness are paramount. Safety is also achieved through compulsive modesty and submission to the will of others.

The neurotic need for power   In normal individuals, the need for power manifests itself in the realistic realization of their physical strength, reasoning capacities, maturity, and wisdom. Their striving for power is typically associated with a worthy cause, such as the betterment of their family, professional group, or country. In power-oriented neurotics, however, striving springs not from strength, but from anxiety, weakness, and feelings of inferiority. Neurotic striving for power serves as a protection against helplessness, one of the key elements of basic anxiety. Because neurotics hate any appearance of weakness, they avoid situations where they would have to ask for help or where they would be expected to yield to the wishes of others. Their feelings of insignificance cause them to conjure up a rigid ideal image of themselves that makes them believe they should immediately, and with little effort, be able to master any situation, no matter how objectively difficult. Their belief in their own superiority implies that they should control the direction and outcomes of their relationships. These tendencies to control, however, may be masked or repressed to such a degree that they (and others) are unaware of them. The neurotic may appear to be highly generous and supportive of others' freedom, while in fact unconsciously striving to control others' lives in very subtle ways. If control is not possible, such neurotics may experience depression, severe headaches, or stomach upsets.

Power-oriented neurotics want to be right all the time; they become irritated at being proven wrong, even in trivial matters. Also, they need to be able to predict what will happen in the future and exhibit a strong aversion to any situation involving uncontrollable factors. Power-oriented neurotics see self-control as a virtue and feel contempt for anyone who cannot control his or her emotions. Thus, their own relationships are severely impaired, both because they must control their emotions at all times and because they view signs of affection from their partners as indications of weakness. Furthermore, their relationships are permeated by conflict, because they must always be right and must never give in (Horney, 1937, pp. 160–171).

The neurotic need to exploit others   Exploitative neurotics are hostile, distrustful individuals who need to exploit others in order to feel safe. They may steal other people's ideas, jobs, or partners to obtain relief from their feelings of insecurity. They lead a parasitic kind of existence; they expect others to do favors for them and to lend them money. They live as though they had a right to expect good things to happen to them and to blame others for bad things.

A frequent correlate of their need to exploit others is the fear that others will cheat or exploit them. As a consequence, such neurotics live in constant fear that others will take advantage of them. They may react with anger that borders on rage if there is the slightest delay in getting back work tools lent to a neighbor or if a cashier makes an honest mistake and overcharges them slightly (Horney, 1937, pp. 183–186).

The neurotic need for social recognition and prestige   Normal individuals take pride in being popular and in being recognized by others for their accomplishments. Yet their lives do not revolve totally around these events, nor do they devote virtually all of their energies to the attainment of recognition and prestige. Pathological individuals, however, are often driven by the need to be admired and respected by others. They evaluate all things—ideas, people, possessions, groups—in terms of their prestige value. To them, it is imperative that they have prominent friends, belong to prestigious groups, read the latest books, see the latest plays and films, and have spouses who enhance their prestige (Horney, 1937, p. 172). Their primary fear is loss of status.

The neurotic need for personal admiration   Neurotic individuals are filled with self-contempt and loathing. As a means of avoiding these painful feelings, they are driven to create an idealized image of themselves. This essentially unrealistic image operates largely on an unconscious level and varies depending upon the neurotic's prior experiences and character structure. Some neurotics unconsciously strive to be exquisite human beings, devoid of flaws and limitations. They act as though they were paragons of virtue or intelligence and are thereby forced to deny the fact that they are not always generous, loving, caring, or brilliant. Such neurotics are not concerned primarily with recognition of their status and material possessions, but with having others admire their idealized selves; they want to be seen as saints or geniuses (Horney, 1945, pp. 96–99).

The neurotic ambition for personal achievement   Related
to the needs for prestige, social recognition, and personal admiration
is the neurotic's need for personal achievement. Although it is
perfectly normal for people to want to be best in their chosen occupation, neurotics are characterized by indiscriminate ambition and
striving to be best in too many areas. This type of neurotic may want
to be simultaneously a great painter, an outstanding physician, a
prominent musician, and a world-renowned architect. Because they
expect too much and are obligated to divide their energies, they are
doomed to failure and are inevitably disappointed. Moreover, their
indiscriminate strivings force them to seek not only their own superior achievement but also the defeat of others. Such neurotics have
the hostile attitude that "no one but I shall be beautiful, capable,
[and] successful" (Horney, 1937, p. 192). Indeed, ambitious neurotics
act as if it were more important for them to defeat others than to
succeed themselves. In reality, their own success is of the utmost importance to them but, because they are not very likely to be highly
successful, they must at least feel superior by tearing others down
(Horney, 1937, pp. 188–194).

The neurotic need for self-sufficiency and independence   At
times, we all have a need for privacy and solitude. When the stresses
associated with our daily interpersonal interactions become too overwhelming, we sometimes retire to the privacy of our rooms, or take a
vacation, or distract ourselves by engaging in a variety of constructive solitary activities—perhaps jogging, reading, or woodworking.
When we are refreshed, we rejoin the fray and are usually better
able to cope with the situation. In contrast, many neurotics are permanently estranged from others. They are afraid to express emotional feelings toward others lest they be placed in a vulnerable
position and learn negative things about themselves, which would be
shattering. Consequently, they avoid long-term obligations such as
marriage.

  By remaining distant from others, neurotics also maintain
their illusion of personal superiority. In their fantasies, they are
clearly superior to others, and they jealously guard this illusion by
avoiding interpersonal comparisons and especially competition.
They are convinced that others should simply recognize their
greatness. Thus, their imagined superiority over others is unlikely
to be tested against reality by actual performance (Horney, 1945,
pp. 73–80).

The neurotic need for perfection and unassailability The need for perfection, Horney believed, typically has its origins in early childhood. Perfectionistic neurotics often have self-righteous, authoritarian parents who exercised unquestioned control over their lives and who instilled in them the need to attain lofty goals and to apply excessively high standards to their actions. Such individuals were often criticized and ridiculed for failure to measure up to these unrealistic standards. Unfortunately, these neurotics adopt their parents' values and spend much of their lives trying to act in ways that leave them beyond reproach and criticism. Obviously, no human being can be completely moral and virtuous in every respect, and so there is a tendency for them to maintain an appearance of perfection and virtue (Horney, 1939, pp. 215–219). In their minds, they equate knowing about moral ideals with being a good person (Horney, 1950, p. 196). Seeing themselves as fair, just, and responsible (although they often are not), they demand respect from others and are hypersensitive to any suggestion that they may have flaws and limitations.

The Three Basic Neurotic Trends

Although Horney believed that her descriptions of the ten needs were valid, she also perceived certain similarities and commonalities among them. As a result, she classified them into three basic types: compliant, aggressive, and detached.

Compliant types   All the traits and needs associated with **moving toward people** are manifested by **compliant types.** They have neurotic needs for affection and approval, for a partner to control their lives, and for a life contained within restricted borders. These types, as Horney saw it, need to be liked, wanted, loved, appreciated, protected, and guided by others (Horney, 1945, p. 51). As a result, they tend to be self-effacing and submissive and to devalue their own talents and abilities. Compliant types try desperately to live up to the expectations of others as a means of receiving approval. Any criticism, rejection, or desertion by others is terrifying, and they will make the most pitiable efforts to win back the positive regard of the person threatening them (Horney, 1945, p. 54).

Aggressive types   People who have neurotic needs for power, exploitation, social recognition and prestige, personal admiration, and personal achievement are **aggressive types.** These needs are all associated with **moving against people.** Whereas compliant types assume everyone is nice, aggressive types believe that others are essentially hostile and untrustworthy. Aggressive types believe, in the Darwinian sense, that only the fittest survive and that the strong annihilate the weak. Thus their primary aim is to be tough, or at least to appear tough. They regard all feelings, their own as well as others', as "sloppy sentimentality" (Horney, 1945, pp. 64–65). They make especially poor marriage partners because their prime concern is not the expression of positive and joyous feelings toward the partner but the acquisition of a mate who can enhance their own prestige, wealth, or position.

Aggressive neurotics are driven to demonstrate continually that they are the strongest, the smartest, or the shrewdest. They are highly competitive and extremely hardworking; they invest all of their intelligence and zest in their work and its success. Yet their apparent interest in their work may be misleading because, for them, work is only a means to an end—enhancing their prestige and wealth.

Detached types   Indiscriminate needs for self-sufficiency and perfection characterize **detached types.** These needs are associated with **moving away from people.** Detached types tend to shroud themselves in secrecy. They are reluctant to divulge even the most trivial details of their lives—even where they were born or how many siblings they have—and most of their activities are solitary. They prefer to work, eat, and sleep alone in order to prevent being disturbed by others. In their favor, detached types are not conforming automatons. They will fight for their beliefs and to maintain their integrity. Unfortunately, their independence has a negative aspect to it: it is aimed at *never* being influenced or obligated (Horney, 1945, p. 77).

The Basic Conflict in Neurosis

The three basic neurotic trends in Horney's scheme are not mutually exclusive. Neurotics have within them all three elements, although one typically predominates. Each neurotic trend has a set of needs associated with it. As mentioned earlier, people characterized by moving toward people have excessively strong needs for approval and affection; people characterized by moving against people crave recognition and admiration from others; and those characterized by moving away from others have an inordinate desire to be independent and self-sufficient. In each neurotic individual, one trend typically predominates, and the gratification of the associated needs is pursued relentlessly and endlessly; the other two trends and their associated needs are repressed. Although repressed, however, these needs continue to exist. Since they are not being gratified, the person is in continual turmoil. For example, an individual who moves toward people in virtually every situation, in an attempt to obtain love and approval, will find it virtually impossible to satisfy personal needs for independence and recognition. An individual who moves indiscriminately against people, in order to obtain recognition and prestige, will find it nearly impossible to receive affection and love from others. After all, a person can't systematically exploit people and expect to be showered with love and approval in return. And an individual who moves indiscriminately away from people will be very unlikely to win their love and approval or to satisfy personal needs for recognition. Isolation and secrecy are incompatible with social approval and recognition.

In Horney's view, the three fundamental attitudes and their associated needs are present to some degree in every neurotic individual. The tension created because these attitudes and their associated needs are incompatible and create contradictory tendencies within the person constitutes the **basic conflict** of neurosis. These contradictory attitudes create turmoil and conflict on an unconscious level, sap the person's energies, and result in fatigue and inefficiency in solving problems. In normal persons, the three trends are also present, but they complement each other and make for inner harmony. Nonneurotic people are much more flexible: they can alternatively give in to others, fight others, or keep to themselves, as appropriate. In contrast, neurotic individuals are driven to fight, to comply, to be aloof, regardless of whether or not their behavior is appropriate to the circumstances (Horney, 1945, pp. 34–47).

To illustrate how the three contradictory attitudes operate on an unconscious level to create basic conflict in the neurotic, let us examine the case of one of Horney's patients, a woman named Clare.

Clare, a 30-year-old magazine editor, entered therapy because she was easily overcome by a paralyzing fatigue that interfered with her work and social life. She could do routine work, but could not finish any difficult tasks. Clare had been married when she was 23; her husband died three years later. Since his death, she had established a relationship with another man, which continued throughout the period of psychoanalysis. According to Clare, both relationships were satisfying sexually, as well as otherwise.

In the course of the analysis, Horney discovered that Clare had a compulsive modesty, a need to force others to recognize her superiority, and a compulsive dependence upon her partner. Clare was unaware of any of these trends in herself at the outset of therapy.

Horney made the diagnosis of compulsive modesty by listening carefully to Clare's reports about herself. She continually described herself as not very intelligent, attractive, or gifted and tended to dismiss any evidence to the contrary. She claimed that others were clearly superior to her. If others disagreed with her, she automatically assumed that they were right. She recalled that, when her husband started an affair with another woman, she said nothing in opposition, although the experience was deeply painful. She even managed to consider his behavior justified, on the grounds that the other woman was more attractive and affectionate. Clare also found it impossible to spend money on herself. She could not bring herself to buy dresses or books or to take trips. And even though she was an executive, it was impossible for her to give orders. If she was forced to do so, she did so in a very apologetic way.

The consequences of this self-effacing trend were discontent and a general lowering of self-confidence. Clare was basically unaware of her discontent and was truly surprised when she had crying spells. Eventually, she began to realize that intense anxiety lurked behind her facade of modesty. The realization came when she was about to offer other company executives a suggestion for improving her magazine. About to make her recommendation, she experienced intense panic. When she made the suggestion anyway, a sudden attack of diarrhea forced her to leave the room during discussion of the idea. When she returned, she found the discussion moving in her favor, and her panic subsided. When her plan was finally accepted, she felt elated.

The next day, she came to Horney's office for a session and told the therapist of her experience. When Horney remarked that the adoption of the suggestion was a triumph, Clare became annoyed and rejected her congratulations. It had been presumptuous of her to offer such a plan; who was she to know better than the others? But gradually Clare began to realize that, by suggesting a plan, she had ventured forth from her narrow lifestyle and taken a risk. She also realized that she was ambitious and did have a strong desire for social recognition and success. These needs had been repressed, but they were continually operating on an unconscious level and striving for expression. The facade of modesty was a means of making her feel safe. It prevented her from having to test her ideas and abilities in direct competition with others and, most importantly, from having to cope with anticipated failure or rejection. The result of these insights was that Clare began to have more confidence in herself.

Clare also was highly dependent on men, although she did not realize it initially and claimed that there was nothing wrong in her relationships. Analysis revealed that she was totally devoted to her current male friend; her thoughts centered around a call or letter or visit from him. Hours spent without him she considered boring and empty, and she felt totally miserable about incidents that she interpreted as utter neglect by him. She had fantasies about him, in which he was a great and masterful man and she was his slave. In her dreams, he gave her anything she wanted and made her into a famous writer.

The main feature of her compulsive dependence was an entirely repressed parasitic attitude—an unconscious wish to have the partner supply the content of her life, take responsibility for her, solve all her problems, and make her into a great person without any effort on her part. This neurotic striving alienated her from him because the inevitable disappointments she felt when he could not fulfill her unrealistic expectations prompted her to become deeply irritated and angry with him. For fear of losing him, much of this anger was repressed, but some of it emerged in occasional explosions. Eventually, through analysis, Clare began to understand her deep dependency on her friend and the reasons for her hostility and anger. Her fatigue appeared only occasionally, rather than continually, as it had before. She also became more capable of productive writing, although she still suffered occasionally from writer's block. Her relationship with her partner became more spontaneous and honest. Her behavior became less compulsive and defensive, and both she and Horney were pleased with the substantial progress she had made at the time the analysis was terminated (Horney, 1942, pp. 75–88).

PERSONALITY DEVELOPMENT

Horney's Critique of Freud

Horney agreed with Freud that adult personality structure and functioning are influenced tremendously by early childhood experiences. Like him, she also believed that unconscious processes play an important role in the formation of character and that the use of defenses is an inevitable outgrowth of people's attempts to cope with inner conflicts and anxiety. She also agreed that the removal of these defenses is essential for adequate and effective functioning. Despite this common ground, Horney disagreed with Freud that the inherited set of sexual and aggressive strivings is more important than the environment, that the important experiences in the formation of character are primarily sexual in nature, and that, in adulthood, people are doomed to repeat compulsively ways of behaving learned in childhood (Horney, 1939, p. 33). Finally, Horney believed that Freud's theory of psychosexual development was essentially invalid. In particular, she strongly criticized Freud's explanations of the role played by the Oedipal conflict and penis envy in the formation of female character and his theory of female masochism.

Do Women Really Want to Be Men?

According to Freud, many abnormalities seen in women grow out of their frustrated wishes to be men. He maintained that the most upsetting event in the development of girls is their discovery that boys have penises and they do not. They react to this discovery with what Freud called **penis envy**—the wish to have a penis, too, and envy toward the more fortunate male sex. Since their supposed deficiency is an unalterable fact, they transfer the wish for a penis to a wish for a child, particularly a male child who will bring the penis with him. They then identify with their mothers, hoping to become mothers themselves some day, as a means of indirectly obtaining the desired object.

In Freud's view, women's most significant attitudes and wishes derive their energy from penis envy. Thus, happiness during pregnancy results from symbolic possession of the penis (the male child in the womb). Menstrual cramps are caused by fantasies in which the father's penis has been swallowed. Women who try to surpass men or to disparage them are characterized as castrating females. Defloration during sex may arouse hostility toward the partner because it is experienced as castration. Women's physical modesty is seen ultimately as a wish to hide the deficiency of her genitals (Horney, 1939, pp. 101–104).

In sum, the Freudian view of development leads to the unequivocal conclusion that women are inferior creatures. Feminine inferiority feelings are simply an expression of contempt for their own sex because of their lack of a penis. Furthermore, little can be done to eliminate this self-loathing because the perceived defect is biologically based and cannot be altered. Anatomy is destiny, according to Freud.

Horney's criticism of Freud's view was a complicated one. She considered Freud a genius who had identified an important phenomenon in women, but she questioned his attribution of the phenomenon completely to instinctual sources. She thought that penis envy did derive to some extent from anatomical differences between the sexes, but that more important sources were the cultural and social forces in a patriarchal society that indoctrinates both sexes with the assumption of male superiority and female inferiority.

Anatomically, she maintained that penis envy has its origins in the girl's desire to urinate like a boy. She believed that fantasies of omnipotence are more easily associated with the jet of urine passed by the male. As evidence, she cited a game played by European boys, in which they would stand at right angles to each other and urinate to make a cross, concentrating their thoughts simultaneously on a particular person and wishing he or she would die. This experience is laden with feelings of magic and power. The significance of the cross is heightened by its religious connotation and the idea that X marks the spot. In addition, males are able to look at themselves in the act of urinating, thereby satisfying their sexual curiosity, whereas females are unable to see or perform in the same way because their genitals are hidden. Thus women, according to Horney, may actively envy males because of the ready visibility of their genitals. Finally, a male derives pleasure from holding his penis while urinating, and this may be construed as permission to masturbate. Females, in contrast, are often forbidden to touch or manipulate their vaginas and clitorises (Horney, 1967, pp. 39–41).

Socially and culturally, Horney maintained, our whole civilization is essentially masculine. Its laws, religion, morality, science, and art are the creation of men. Men are clearly in the dominant or superior position, while women occupy an inferior place. Unfortunately, in Horney's judgment, women have adapted themselves to the inferior status assigned to them by men and judge themselves as inferior (Horney, 1967, pp. 55–57). This perverse adaptation results not only in self-hatred, but in contempt for other women and resentment and hostility toward men. Thus, they lack faith in women's capacity for any real achievement and minimize success whenever it occurs. Even motherhood appears as an unfair burden to women who have adopted the masculine disregard and disrespect for the accomplishments of women. Feeling that they have been discriminated against by fate, women also make unconscious claims for compensation. In their fantasies, they reject the feminine role and wish for all the qualities and privileges that in our culture are regarded as masculine—strength, courage, success, sexual freedom, and independence (Horney, 1939, p. 108).

Thus, Horney saw penis envy not as a castration complex—felt loss of the penis and fantasies of its symbolic replacement—but rather as a justifiable envy of qualities associated with masculinity in our culture. According to Horney, women must realize that their inferiority feelings are based upon unconscious acceptance of an ideology of male superiority, and that their feelings about themselves can only be changed if efforts are made to make society itself more democratic and egalitarian. Anatomy is not necessarily destiny, in Horney's opinion, although it does play a part.

Do Women Really Enjoy Suffering?

Before discussing Horney's criticisms of Freud's **female masochism,** we must first examine carefully the definition of this phenomenon, which has generated considerable confusion (Caplan, 1984). Some authorities define it as a wish to suffer pain and to be subjected to pain by force: the pain is pursued because it is pleasurable in itself. Others see it as a condition in which sexual gratification depends upon suffering physical pain and humiliation: the pain is endured because it is a prerequisite for pleasure. This second definition seems closest to Freud's conception, because he discussed the topic in terms of a *fusion* of life instincts (the drive toward pleasure) and death instincts (the drive toward death, or pain).

Freud identified masochism with femininity. He maintained that women were sexually passive by nature. This passivity caused them to repress their aggressiveness and was a manifestation of their drive toward death, "bind[ing] erotically the destructive tendencies which have been turned inwards" (Freud, 1952, p. 855). Thus, sexual intercourse involves masochistic gratification for women, because it fuses pleasurable sensations with pain (penetration of the vagina). Childbirth also mixes pleasure with pain and is presumed to give women unconscious masochistic satisfaction. In addition, the orthodox psychoanalytic view holds that girls' early sexual wishes and fantasies concerning the father involve a desire to be mutilated and castrated by him. Women may also fantasize about being raped, beaten, and humiliated. In short, the standard Freudian view of women is of an inferior and incompetent creature who takes secret pleasure in being abused physically and psychologically.

Horney's view of female masochism was very different from Freud's, although she believed his position had merit in some respects. Compatible with Freud's view, for example, was her belief that certain biological differences between the sexes could provide a basis for female masochism. Specifically, women's idea of their own inferiority could be created by men's greater size and strength, reinforced by their knowledge that they can be raped and by the pain that accompanies menstruation, intercourse, and childbirth. But Horney believed that these anatomical and physiological differences were not sufficient in themselves to create female masochism. These conditions simply *prepared* women to adopt a masochistic role; it is society itself that shapes women's behaviors and experiences and leads them to define themselves in masochistic terms. "The problem of feminine masochism cannot be related to factors inherent in the anatomical-physiological-psychic characteristics of woman alone, but must be considered as importantly conditioned by the culture-complex or social organization in which the particular masochistic woman has developed" (Horney, 1967, pp. 232–233). Society influences women's conception of themselves as inferior in several ways: (1) by blocking their strivings for achievement in male-dominated occupations; (2) by fostering their economic dependence on men; (3) by restricting their activities to life spheres that are built upon emotional bonds, such as family life, religion, and charity; and (4) by fostering an estimation of themselves as beings who are, in general, inferior to men (Horney, 1967, p. 230).

Although feminists today endorse Horney's view of female masochism as grounded primarily in social and cultural experiences, they challenge her arguments about the contributions of anatomical and physiological differences.

> The fact that men often have greater physical strength than women might well lead some women to feel physically inferior, but that is worlds away from leading women to *want* to suffer, which is masochism. Next, the possibility that women can be raped need not lead women to enjoy pain, any more than the possibility that men can be stabbed, murdered, or raped needs to lead men to enjoy pain. To suggest that biological differences in intercourse lead women to be masochistic reflects, first of all, a mistaken assumption that intercourse has to take place—for biological reasons—with the woman beneath the man, and it reflects furthermore a narrow focus on penile penetration as the essence and totality of sexuality, to the exclu-

sion of other aspects of sexuality and sensuality. For many women the moment of penetration is not the crux of their experience of sexuality, and since there are various opportunities for pleasure, and specifically for sexual pleasure, in women's lives, the focus on penetration as the foundation of a woman's personality, thus supposedly leading her to become generally masochistic, seems curious. (Caplan, 1984, p. 136)

Thus, modern feminists believe that, although Horney made a significant departure from the focus on biological factors as proof of women's innate masochism, and made a significant contribution to our understanding of masochism itself, she did not go far enough. Similarly, they reject her view of penis envy as having a basis in anatomical differences between the sexes. In brief, feminists agree with Horney's assessment of the cultural and social origins of female masochism and penis envy, but disagree with her view that these phenomena are partially rooted in biology.

Horney's Humanistic View of Development

As we have seen, Horney believed that the unique social and cultural experiences of children are crucial in determining their adult personalities, and that harsh and arbitrary treatment of children by parents lays the foundation for neurosis. Healthy development, she believed, was predicated on warm, fair, considerate, supportive, and respectful treatment by the parents. In her **humanistic view of development,** Horney maintained that everyone was special and had a unique set of potentials that would flourish under wise parental guidance. These intrinsic potentialities she called the **real self.** With proper support, she believed, everyone could develop toward self-realization; that is, they could develop the depth and clarity of their own feelings, thoughts, wishes, and interests, the ability to tap their own resources and gifts, the faculty to express themselves, and the ability to relate to others spontaneously (Horney, 1950, p. 17). Unfortunately, however, many people do not receive proper guidance. Instead they are treated arbitrarily and with a lack of respect, and the result is alienation from the real self.

Alienation and the Idealized Self

Horney maintained that unfavorable environmental conditions impair the realistic inner confidence of people and force them to evolve defenses. Because their energies are directed toward the development of defenses in order to feel safe, attempts to develop their real selves are overridden. To the extent that safety is paramount, people's innermost feelings and thoughts recede in importance and become blurred. They are no longer the masters of their destiny, but are driven by their neurotic needs. Alienation from their real selves causes people to seek a sense of stability and identity, a sense that they are significant and worthwhile.

The answer for neurotics is to create an **idealized image** of themselves. Such an image endows them with unlimited abilities and powers. In their imaginations, they become heroes, geniuses, supreme lovers, saints, and gods. These images provide an avenue for dealing with their basic conflicts. According to Horney, neurotics eventually try to actualize the **idealized self** by achieving success, glory, and triumph in the outside world. They are relentlessly and painfully driven to be perfect; they believe that they should be able to do everything, know everything, and like everyone. Horney calls this compulsive need the **tyranny of the shoulds**:

> He should be the [epitome] of honesty, generosity, considerateness, justice, dignity, courage, unselfishness. He should be the perfect lover, husband, teacher. He should be able to endure everything, should like everybody, should love his parents, his wife, his country; or, he should not be attached to anything or anybody, nothing should matter to him, he should never feel hurt, and he should always be serene and unruffled. He should always enjoy life; or, he should be above pleasure and enjoyment. He should be spontaneous; he should always control his feelings. He should know, understand, and foresee everything. He should be able to solve every problem of his own, or of others, in no time. He should be able to overcome every difficulty of his as soon as he sees it. He should never be tired or fall ill. He should always be able to find a job. He should be able to do things in one hour which can only be done in two to three hours. (Horney, 1950, p. 65)

Neurotics cling to these impossible standards because their attainment promises to satisfy all their inner conflicts and to eliminate all pain and anxiety. Unfortunately, self-idealization does not work. When neurotics compare the **actual self** (the self as it is at the moment) against the measuring rod of the idealized self, the actual self inevitably falls short. Poor performance during lovemaking, for example, belies the belief that they are great lovers. Hesitation and stammering while asking the boss for a promotion is clearly at variance with their view of themselves as articulate speakers. Working at a menial job is a constant reminder that they have not achieved high occupational status and success. As a result of the discrepancies that they experience between their actual and idealized selves, neurotics are filled with self-contempt and hatred. Although they are aware of the results—feeling inferior, tormented, guilty—they are completely unaware that they themselves have brought about these painful feelings and self-evaluations (Horney, 1950, p. 116). Thus, self-hate is essentially an unconscious process. Rather than examine themselves critically, neurotics are prone to externalize their hatred and to see it as emanating from other people or institutions or from fate.

Externalization: Keeping the Idealized Self Intact

The tendency of neurotics to experience internal processes as if they occurred outside the self and to hold external factors responsible for their difficulties is called **externalization.** In part, externalization involves projection—that is, the tendency to attribute one's own failings and shortcomings to others. It also involves perceiving feelings in others rather than in oneself. Thus, neurotics tend to believe that others are angry with them when actually they are angry with themselves. They attribute good feelings in themselves to the weather or to fate, successes to good luck, and so forth. Most importantly, the neurotic's self-contempt is externalized. In the aggressive type, the tendency is to despise others. Aggressive neurotics feel superior to others and reinforce their feelings of superiority by seeing others as inferior and worthy of contempt. In the compliant type, the tendency is to see others as filled with contempt for them. Horney believed that this projection is particularly damaging; it makes the compliant type of neurotic shy, inhibited, and withdrawn (Horney, 1945, p. 118).

In effect, externalization consists of the obliteration of the actual and real selves. It is designed to ensure survival of the idealized self. It does not work very well, however, and neurotics are forced to rely on other defenses for support.

Auxiliary Approaches to Artificial Harmony

Horney described seven defenses used by neurotics to help them cope with their inner conflicts and with disturbances in their interpersonal relationships (Horney, 1945, pp. 131–140).

Blind spots   Many laypeople have wondered how neurotics are unable to perceive the overwhelmingly blatant discrepancies between their actual and idealized selves. Neurotics seem to have **blind**

spots, areas in which obvious contradictions are blotted out or ignored. The reason, according to Horney, is that neurotics are often inordinately numb to their own experiences (Horney, 1945, p. 133).

Compartmentalization   The defense called **compartmentalization** involves the separation of beliefs or actions into categories (compartments), so that they do not appear inconsistent with one another. For example, a Ku Klux Klan member may convince himself that he is a Christian by maintaining that his Christian beliefs of love and tolerance extend only to humans; since, in his view, black people are clearly animals and, therefore, inhuman, he can continue to hate and persecute them without feeling the conflict between his actions and his beliefs.

Rationalization   The form of self-deception called **rationalization** uses plausible excuses to justify one's perceived weaknesses or failures. For example, aggressive neurotics view feelings of remorse and sympathy for others as weakness. Therefore, an aggressive neurotic who sends flowers to his longtime colleague's widow as an expression of sympathy might justify his action by claiming that he sent them only because it was his duty as a fellow employee.

Excessive self-control   The neurotic's compulsive need to restrict expression of emotions is termed **excessive self-control.**

> Persons who exert such control will not allow themselves to be carried away, whether by enthusiasm, sexual excitement, self-pity, or rage. In analysis they have the greatest difficulty in associating freely; they will not permit alcohol to lift their spirits and frequently prefer to endure pain rather than undergo anesthesia. In short, they seek to check all spontaneity. (Horney, 1945, p. 136)

Because the most destructive actions are violent ones prompted by rage, most of the neurotic's energy is directed toward controlling rage. However, the suppression of rage leads to an unconscious buildup of even more rage, which, in turn, requires even more self-control to choke it off.

Arbitrary rightness   Doubt and indecision characterize the neurotic. Because these feelings are intolerable, neurotics employ **arbitrary rightness**: that is, they attempt to settle all disputes by declaring dogmatically that they are correct.

Elusiveness   Neurotics who use **elusiveness** as a means of protection can never be pinned down to any statement; they deny ever having made the statement or claim that the other person misinterpreted their meaning. Elusive neurotics are continually equivocating and are unable to give a concrete report of any incident. As a result, the listener is confused as to what really did happen.

Horney maintained that this same confusion of truth reigns in the lives of neurotics. At times they are overly considerate; at others, ruthlessly inconsiderate. They can be highly domineering in some respects, self-effacing in others. Because of these inconsistencies, it is sometimes difficult for an analyst to guide them to an accurate identification of their underlying conflicts.

Cynicism   The protective device of **cynicism** involves a denying and deriding of moral values. Neurotics tend to be Machiavellian in their outlook. They believe that people are not to be trusted, and that they can do whatever they please as long as they are not caught. They are people of expedience, not principle.

In summary, all of these irrational defenses help (at least temporarily) to maintain the neurotics' idealized conception; in so doing, they make healthy growth virtually impossible.

Empirical Evidence: Irrational Beliefs and Psychopathology

A common theme in Horney's theorizing about neurosis is that abnormal people have numerous irrational beliefs about themselves and others that create and increase their suffering and encourage ineffective ways of behaving in relationships with others. Thus, neurotics believe that they are paragons of virtue, brilliant thinkers, and great lovers; blame other people, fate, or institutions for their failures; claim to be invariably right; and convince themselves that no one can be trusted. They are driven by moral absolutes (the tyranny of the shoulds) that require them to act as though they were completely honest, courageous, and unselfish.

Horney's assertions concerning the link between irrational beliefs and psychopathology are supported by considerable correlational evidence. Studies have found that, the greater the number of irrational beliefs held by individuals, the more likely they are to be depressed (Dobson & Breiter, 1983; LaPointe & Crandell, 1980; Lewinsohn, Steinmetz, Larson, & Franklin, 1981; Nelson, 1977; Thorpe, Barnes,

Hunter, & Hines, 1983), socially inept (Hayden & Nasby, 1977), poor at solving problems (Schill, Monroe, Evans, & Ramanaiah, 1978), and unhappy in their marriages (Eidelson & Epstein, 1982).

Comparing couples in marital therapy with couples not in therapy, Eidelson and Epstein (1982) found that those experiencing marital difficulties held a variety of dysfunctional beliefs. They believed, for instance, that disagreement with their spouses was destructive and indicative of a lack of love or even imminent divorce, even though conflicts based upon interpersonal differences are an inevitable part of any relationship. Unhappy couples also believed that partners who truly know and care about each other should be able to sense each other's needs and preferences without explicit, direct communication; as a result, they put less effort into clear communication, and so suffered disappointment and escalation of conflict. Unhappy couples believed that they could not change themselves, nor could their partners change. Such an extreme belief led to feelings of helplessness and diminished satisfaction with the relationship. Finally, unhappy couples believed that they must be perfect sex partners (recall Horney's point that many neurotics believe that they are great lovers), and, accordingly, experienced anxiety and inhibition in the sexual sphere.

To change these irrational thoughts and move toward improved mental health, Horney maintained, therapists need to actively challenge the beliefs and to replace them with more realistic thoughts and feelings. Cognitive therapists generally agree with Horney's contention, and there is some evidence that such therapy is effective (Ellis & Greiger, 1977; Smith, 1983). D'Alelio and Murray (1981), for example, used this type of cognitive therapy to reduce test anxiety in college students. Therapists taught groups of test-anxious students to identify and challenge the distracting and irrational thoughts that were interfering with their examination performance and to replace them with more constructive thoughts. For example, a student who reported the self-defeating statement, "Since I don't know the answer to the first question, I won't know the others and will fail," would be taught to challenge this statement and replace it with coping statements such as, "Just because I don't know the answer to the first question doesn't mean I don't know the others. I will skip this question and come back to it later. I won't spend time worrying."

This kind of cognitive therapy was administered in group sessions by different therapists. Each group met for 1.5 hours once a week, some for four weeks and others for eight weeks. The groups that trained for eight weeks showed the greatest reductions in test anxiety and worrying, followed by the four-week groups; the least reductions were found in the control groups of subjects who received no training. (Control subjects were offered similar therapeutic treatment at the end of the semester.) Unfortunately, although the students who went through the therapy sessions showed reductions in test anxiety and worrying, their grade-point averages did not improve during the school year. But a similar study by Holroyd (1976), using more highly motivated subjects, did find an increase in grade-point average from the end of the fall semester to the end of the spring semester following cognitive therapy (an average of 1.25 points for the treatment groups), while the control groups showed no statistically significant gains (actually, a slight decrease of three-tenths of a point).

ASSESSMENT TECHNIQUES

Horney agreed with Freud that free association and dream analysis could help therapists identify the sources of neurotics' problems; she disagreed with him, however, in interpreting what they revealed. Whereas Freud continually interpreted patients' free associations and dream reports in terms of thwarted sexual or aggressive strivings, Horney's interpretations focused on the disturbances her patients experienced in their interpersonal relationships and on the neurotic trends they used to cope with their basic anxieties and fears.

Horney also saw the personal relationship between analyst and patient differently than did Freud. Freud believed strongly that psychoanalysis was a science. He perceived himself as an objective observer whose role was to collect data and present them to the patients for their consideration and use. Accordingly, the analyst must refrain from making value judgments about the patients' personal qualities and experiences, so as to allay patients' fears of condemnation and encourage freer expression of their thoughts and feelings. Horney, however, thought it impossible for an analyst to refrain from making value judgments during the course of therapy. In her opinion, patients could sense that the analyst was indeed making such judgments, and trying to hide the fact only served to make the relationship worse. Instead, the analyst should be more honest and open with patients and more active and directive in offering suggestions. Such an approach, she believed, would facilitate the growth of the relationship and lead more readily to a cure.

THEORY'S IMPLICATIONS FOR THERAPY

Neurotics are alienated from their real selves and from others. They have identified with an idealized self and so have become pretenders who are afraid of having their limitations exposed by others. Horney believed that they will only have a chance to realize their potential when they are able to relinquish their illusions about themselves and their illusory goals. Removing the obstructions to growth, however, is a long and difficult process, for neurotics are strongly committed to defending their illusions. Aggressive types, for example, hope that analysis will remove all impediments to their achieving unqualified triumphs and unquestioned sainthood. Thus, they think only of perfecting their idealized selves, whereas the analyst seeks to help remove their idealized selves and to promote the growth of their real selves.

For Horney, therapy is a human relationship, and all the difficulties that neurotics have in their relationships with other people operate during the therapeutic process. Patients may become argumentative, sarcastic, or assaultive. They may be evasive, refuse to discuss a subject, or talk with emotionless intelligence about their problems, as if such problems were unimportant. They may react with rage and become abusive toward the analyst. Yet many of these behaviors are signposts directing the therapist's inquiries; that is, they provide clues that point to the presence of underlying conflicts. Patients tend to be highly threatened by the therapist's inquiries and to experience considerable anxiety. For the patients, this anxiety is terribly painful, but for the therapist it may also have a positive meaning. It may indicate that the patients are now strong enough to take the risk of confronting their problems more directly. According to Horney, the therapist's inquiries help patients become more aware of all the obstructive forces operating within them. She believed, however, that this self-knowledge must not remain at an intellectual level only; it must become an emotional experience as well. In her view, intellectual insight is important, but it does not have sufficient impact on the patient to promote change. Only when patients feel the intensity of the unconscious forces operating within them are they motivated to relinquish their illusions.

Once patients have given up their illusions, the therapist focuses on helping them find their real selves. Through free association and dream analysis, their real selves may begin to emerge. Patients are reinforced for any sign of greater independence in their thinking, of assuming responsibility for themselves, and of being interested in the truth about themselves. They are also encouraged to seek their own identities through self-analysis outside of the therapeutic setting. The analyst takes care to point out any signs of progress made by patients in their human relationships. These glimpses of growth have a highly positive impact on patients, who experience a sense of fulfillment that is different from anything they have known before. This acts as the best incentive for them to work harder at their own growth, toward greater self-realization. As they grow, they begin to realize that there are other problems in the world besides their own. They begin to extend themselves to others—their family, community, nation, and world. They become more willing to accept responsibility not only for themselves, but for others as well. They begin to find the inner certainty that comes from a feeling of belonging through active and unselfish participation (Horney, 1950, pp. 333–365).

EVALUATIVE COMMENTS

We turn now to an evaluation of Horney's theory in terms of our six criteria.

Comprehensiveness   Because of its focus on abnormal rather than normal phenomena, Horney's theory is limited in its comprehensiveness. In discussing the etiology and cure for different types of neuroses, however, she devotes considerable attention to the impact of complicated social and cultural forces on their development and maintenance. Thus, the explanatory base for her theory is much richer than Freud's. Possibly the most original aspect of her theory is the concept of the idealized self and the discrepancy between this idealized self and the real self. Here we see her humanistic interest in understanding not only the forces that produce and maintain neurosis, but the prerequisites of positive growth and optimal personality functioning.

Precision and testability   Many of Horney's concepts are abstract and difficult to define precisely. To her credit, Horney made a strenuous effort to define her terms; nonetheless, some of them remain relatively imprecise and unclear. Given these definitional ambiguities, it is very difficult to design adequate tests of the theory.

Parsimony   Horney's theory is clearly not overly simple. Her explanations of the origins and development of neurosis are rich and complicated and seem generally adequate to the task. Thus, her theory seems parsimonious.

Empirical validity   Although there have been only a few direct tests of Horney's theory, some of the research by prominent cognitive therapists, especially Albert Ellis and his colleagues, relies heavily on several of Horney's concepts and formulations. Their research evidence generally supports Horney's views, albeit indirectly.

Heuristic value   Horney's ideas about the tyranny of the shoulds are highly original and are utilized by Ellis in dealing with the sources of depression (Ellis, 1987, p. 123). Although cognitive therapists and researchers use many kinds of therapeutic procedures that cannot be directly traced to Horney's theory of psychotherapy, Ellis's **rational-emotive therapy** is in many respects an outgrowth of Horney's recommendations concerning the treatment of patients. Also Horney's theorizing about human growth and self-realization mark her as an important early contributor to the development of humanistic psychology.

Applied value   In addition to its heuristic value, Horney's theory has had an important impact on the work of cognitive therapists, who help to alleviate the suffering of many clinical patients.

DISCUSSION QUESTIONS

1. Horney believed that competitiveness and neuroticism were positively associated. Is competition necessarily destructive? What distinguishes healthy from unhealthy competition?
2. Why is this country so obsessed with competition and achievement?
3. Horney thought that each person had a real self consisting of worthwhile, intrinsic potentialities that awaited further development. Have you been able to identify such potential strengths in yourself? What are they?
4. Do you know many people who think they are invariably right? How do you cope with them?
5. How are Horney's views on the development of women consistent with the teachings of feminists today?

6. Why are the spontaneity and expansiveness that characterize the healthy person missing in the neurotic?
7. Is it always unhealthy or inappropriate to blame others for your failures, as Horney suggests?
8. Under what conditions or situational circumstances is it healthy to distort reality?
9. Do you agree with Horney that it is impossible for a therapist to avoid making value judgments during therapy sessions with patients?
10. Assuming that Horney's sociocultural explanations of penis envy and female masochism are valid, in what ways could penis envy and masochistic attitudes lead to mistrust and hostility between the sexes?

GLOSSARY

actual self The self as it is at the moment, including all of the person's actual strengths and weaknesses.

aggressive types Neurotic individuals who protect themselves against feelings of insecurity by exploiting others in order to feel superior.

arbitrary rightness A protective device in which people are convinced that they are invariably correct in all their judgments.

basic anxiety The painful psychological state in which a person feels isolated and helpless in a potentially hostile world.

basic conflict The turmoil created within neurotics because the three major trends are incompatible with one another. As the person indiscriminately pursues the predominant trend and the fulfillment of the needs associated with it, he or she is unable to satisfy the needs associated with the two trends that are repressed.

blind spots Defense mechanism in which painful experiences are denied or ignored because they are at variance with the idealized self.

compartmentalization Defense mechanism by which neurotics alleviate tensions by separating beliefs and actions within themselves.

compliant types Neurotic individuals who cope with feelings of basic anxiety by indiscriminately seeking the approval and affection of others through excessive conformity.

cynicism   Defense mechanism in which the person claims to believe in nothing so that he or she cannot be hurt or disappointed by others.

detached types   Neurotic individuals who protect themselves by continual avoidance of others.

elusiveness   Defense mechanism whereby a person refuses to take a position on anything so that he or she can never be proven wrong and criticized or ridiculed by others.

excessive self-control   Defense mechanism whereby a person exercises willpower, consciously or unconsciously, to keep emotional impulses under control.

externalization   Defense mechanism whereby a person experiences inner emotions externally and blames others for his or her own weaknesses and failings.

female masochism   For Freud, a perversion in which women experience a blending of pleasure and pain during certain activities and fantasies. He believed that male masochism occurred only in males with feminine (passive) natures.

humanistic view of development   An optimistic view of development that sees each person as having intrinsic and unique potential for constructive growth.

hypercompetitiveness   An attitude in which a person aims at self-aggrandizement by denigrating others, who are perceived as competitors.

idealized image   Fantasies of neurotic individuals in which they visualize themselves as perfect beings.

idealized self   The defensive identification of neurotics with their idealized images.

moving against people   A major neurotic trend that seeks to control basic anxiety through domination and exploitation of others.

moving away from people   A major neurotic trend that protects the person against basic anxiety by utter detachment and extreme self-sufficiency.

moving toward people   A major neurotic trend that protects the person against basic anxiety by self-effacement and obliteration.

penis envy   In Horney's view, essentially a sociocultural phenomenon in which women are indoctrinated to see themselves as inferior and men as superior. As a result, they unconsciously strive to emulate masculine goals and values and to obtain the advantages and privileges that accrue to members of the male sex.

rational-emotive therapy   A cognitive-restructuring therapy in which the faulty beliefs of neurotics that lead to emotional disturbance are identified, challenged, and then replaced with more constructive, rational ways of thinking.

rationalization   A defense in which people ward off anxiety by offering plausible, but inaccurate, excuses for their conduct.

real self   The unique set of potentials for constructive growth within each person.

tyranny of the shoulds   Concept used by Horney to describe the moral imperatives that relentlessly drive neurotics to accept nothing less than perfection from themselves.

SUGGESTED READINGS

Horney, K. (1937). *The neurotic personality of our time*. New York: Norton.
Horney, K. (1945). *Our inner conflicts*. New York: Norton.
Horney, K. (1950). *Neurosis and human growth*. New York: Norton.
Horney, K. (1967). *Feminine psychology*. New York: Norton.

REFERENCES

Caplan, P. J. (1984). The myth of women's masochism. *American Psychologist, 39,* 130–139.

D'Alelio, W. A., & Murray, E. J. (1981). Cognitive therapy for test anxiety. *Cognitive Therapy and Research, 5,* 299–307.

Dobson, K. S., & Breiter, H. J. (1983). Cognitive assessment of depression: Reliability and validity of three measures. *Journal of Abnormal Psychology, 92,* 107–109.

Eidelson, R. J., & Epstein, N. (1982). Cognition and relationship maladjustment: Development of a measure of dysfunctional relationships beliefs. *Journal of Consulting and Clinical Psychology, 50,* 715–720.

Ellis, A. (1987). A sadly neglected cognitive element in depression. *Cognitive Therapy and Research, 11,* 121–145.

Ellis, A., & Greiger, R. (1977). *Handbook of rational-emotive therapy*. New York: Julian Press.

Freud, S. (1952). New introductory lectures on psychoanalysis. In R. M. Hutchins (Ed.), *Great books of the Western world* (Vol. 54, pp. 807–884). Chicago: Encyclopedia Britannica.

Hayden, B., & Nasby, W. (1977). Interpersonal conceptual structures, predictive accuracy, and social adjustment of emotionally disturbed boys. *Journal of Abnormal Psychology, 86,* 315–320.

Holroyd, K. A. (1976). Cognition and desensitization in the group treatment of test anxiety. *Journal of Consulting and Clinical Psychology, 44,* 991–1001.

Horney, K. (1937). *The neurotic personality of our time*. New York: Norton.

Horney, K. (1939). *New ways in psychoanalysis*. New York: Norton.

Horney, K. (1942). *Self-analysis*. New York: Norton.

Horney, K. (1945). *Our inner conflicts*. New York: Norton.

Horney, K. (1950). *Neurosis and human growth*. New York: Norton.

Horney, K. (1967). *Feminine psychology*. New York: Norton.

Kaczor, L. M., Ryckman, R. M., Thornton, B., & Kuehnel, R. H. (1991). Observer hypercompetitiveness and victim precipitation of rape. *Journal of Social Psychology, 131,* 131–134.

LaPointe, K. A., & Crandell, C. J. (1980). Relationship of irrational beliefs to self-reported depression. *Cognitive Therapy and Research, 4,* 247–250.

Lewinsohn, P. M., Steinmetz, J. L., Larson, D. W., & Franklin, J. (1981). Depression-related cognitions: Antecedent or consequence? *Journal of Abnormal Psychology, 90,* 213–219.

Nelson, R. E. (1977). Irrational beliefs in depression. *Journal of Consulting and Clinical Psychology, 45,* 1190–1191.

Paris, B. (1994). *Karen Horney: A psychoanalyst's search for self-understanding*. New Haven, CT: Yale University Press.

Rubins, J. L. (1978). *Karen Horney: Gentle rebel of psychoanalysis*. New York: Dial.

Ryckman, R. M., Hammer, M., Kaczor, L. M., & Gold, J. A. (1990). Construction of a hypercompetitive attitude scale. *Journal of Personality Assessment, 55,* 630–639.

Ryckman, R. M., Thornton, B., & Butler, J. C. (1994). Personality correlates of the hypercompetitive attitude scale: Validity tests of Horney's theory of neurosis. *Journal of Personality Assessment, 62,* 84–94.

Schill, T., Monroe, S., Evans, R., & Ramanaiah, N. (1978). The effects of self-verbalizations on performance: A test of the rational-emotive position. *Psychotherapy: Theory Research and Practice, 15,* 2–7.

Smith, T. W. (1983). Changes in irrational beliefs and the outcome of rational-emotive psychotherapy. *Journal of Consulting and Clinical Psychology, 51,* 156–157.

Thorpe, G. L., Barnes, G. S., Hunter, J. E., & Hines, D. (1983). Thoughts and feelings: Correlations in two clinical and two nonclinical samples. *Cognitive Therapy and Research, 7,* 565–574.

CHAPTER 6

Erikson's Psychoanalytic Ego Psychology

BIOGRAPHICAL SKETCH

Erik Homburger Erikson was born in 1902 near Frankfurt, Germany. His parents were Danish. Erikson never knew his natural father, who abandoned Erik and his mother before Erik was born. Although Erikson (1975, p. 27) maintained that his parents were legally married at the time of their separation, one prominent biographer thinks they were not and that Erik was probably an illegitimate child (Roazen, 1976, p. 96). In any event, soon after the abandonment, his mother left Denmark for Germany to be near friends and to await the birth of her child.

A few years after Erik's birth, she took him to a local Jewish pediatrician, Dr. Theodor Homburger, for treatment of a minor illness. The mother and doctor soon became friends, eventually fell in love, and were married. Erik was given his stepfather's name and taken to live in the doctor's home. To ensure that Erik would be comfortable in his new life, his mother and stepfather decided not to tell him his natural father had abandoned him. Still, he quickly developed an acute sense that something was wrong: although his mother and stepfather were Jewish, his own physical appearance was clearly Scandinavian—tall, with blue eyes and blond hair. Adding to his confusion about his identity, he was called *goy* (non-Jew) by members of his parents' temple, but identified as a Jew by his classmates. Later, when he found out the truth about his heritage, his identity crisis worsened. Although he kept his stepfather's surname until well into adulthood, he eventually took the surname Erikson, for reasons that remain obscure—perhaps to affirm his Scandinavian heritage and establish his identification with the Danish father who had abandoned him (Roazen, 1976, pp. 98–99).

His early life was apparently serene in most other respects. Erik attended primary school from age 6 to 10 and a humanistic gymnasium (roughly equivalent to high school) until he was 18. He did not take well, however, to the strict and formal academic atmosphere, and he was not a good student (Coles, 1970, p. 14). His aversion to formal education continued throughout his life; he never earned a university degree.

Rejecting his stepfather's pleas to become a physician, Erikson left home after graduation and wandered through Europe, where he was free of attempts by his family and friends to convince him to make something of himself. During this moratorium, Erikson was wracked by doubts concerning his choice of an occupation. A year later, he returned home and enrolled in an art school to prepare for a career as an artist. He stayed for approximately a year, became restless again, and traveled to Munich, where he enrolled in another art school. After two years in Munich, he moved to Florence, a city he loved. There, he completely gave up sketching and simply wandered about the city; he was eager to learn about its culture and history. It should be noted that during this period he was not considered odd or sick by his family or friends, but simply as a wandering artist engaged in a natural struggle to find himself (Coles, 1970, pp. 14–15).

After his stay in Florence, he returned home and, at 25, prepared to settle down to study and teach art for a living. At that point, however, fate intervened. Erikson was asked by a former high school friend, Peter Blos, to join him as a teacher at a small, experimental American nursery school in Vienna. While at the school, Erikson met Anna Freud and her famous father, Sigmund, and was introduced into their circle of friends. Anna Freud was trying to convert a psychoanalytic interest in the childhood experiences of adults into a concern with understanding the dynamics of childhood itself (Coles, 1970). Erikson shared her pioneering interest and was eventually trained by her as a child analyst.

Though fully accepted by the psychoanalytic group surrounding Freud, Erikson was still unsure that he wanted to earn his living as a psychoanalyst. He still wanted to paint and draw. As his clinical experience with children grew, however, he began to see a connection between psychoanalysis and art. He observed that children's dreams and play involve important visual images that only later are translated into words in therapy (Coles, 1970, pp. 22–23). Also, Freud himself was becoming increasingly interested in the application of psychoanalysis to art, and this fact made a deep impression on Erikson (Coles, 1970, p. 24). Finally, Erikson began to think seriously about a career as an analyst, because he had acquired a new set of responsibilities. At a party he had met a young woman of mixed Canadian-American background, Joan Serson, and promptly fallen in love with her. A few months later, they were married. He finished his training at the Vienna Psycho-Analytical Society over the next four years and was elected a member in 1933.

Later that year Erikson, his wife, and their two young sons emigrated to the United States and settled in Boston. The first child analyst in Massachusetts, Erikson held positions at Harvard Medical School, Massachusetts General Hospital, and the Harvard Psychological Clinic. His thinking and his professional development were profoundly influenced by the Harvard intellectual community—most notably by anthropologists Margaret Mead, Gregory Bateson, Ruth Benedict, and Scudder Mekeel and psychologists Kurt Lewin, Henry Murray, and Lawrence Frank. In 1936, Erikson left Cambridge for New Haven, where he accepted a position at the Yale University Institute of Human Relations. In 1938, his third child, a daughter named Sue, was born. That same year, stimulated by conversations with his anthropologist colleagues, Erikson left New Haven to observe the behavior of Sioux children living on the Pine Ridge Reservation in South Dakota.

In 1939, Erikson moved to California, where he became affiliated with the Institute of Child Welfare at the University of California at Berkeley. Continuing his analytic work with children, Erikson devised "experimental play situations" designed to demonstrate the hopes, fears, struggles, defeats, and victories of growing children, as he sought to understand the crucial events in the life process. During this period, he also went north to observe the children of another Native American people, the Yurok. His anthropological work convinced him that the members of these cultures were not savages or sick simply because they utilized rituals and ceremonies to express their underlying needs; their rituals and ceremonies simply differed from the ones used in our own culture. He also refused to label their behavior neurotic or anal, as some analysts were prone to do; he rejected the idea that their unusual ritualistic behavior could be explained only by reference to unresolved conflicts surrounding toilet training during early childhood. Instead, he began to see that the Yurok and Sioux went through a series of developmental crises similar to the ones that people in our own society experienced and that successful resolution of these crises strengthened the members and moved them toward psychological health (Evans, 1967, p. 62). Thus, Erikson's anthropological experiences led him to recognize the limitations of Freud's theory of infantile sexuality and to replace it with a more general lifespan theory of ego development, in which he posited that the development of the person is marked by the unfolding of a series of stages that are universal to humankind.

In 1950, Erikson published *Childhood and Society,* a text that soon brought him international recognition as a leading spokesman of ego psychology. In it he presented the details of his theory of human development, which was based on his many years of cross-cultural research and clinical experience. He showed convincingly how various developmental stages unfold and how the ego changes, grows, and synthesizes a myriad of experiences. He also expanded on Freud's theory of infantile sexuality by placing and analyzing its basic propositions within a broader historical and sociocultural context. In brief, Erikson for the first time integrated psychoanalysis with history and anthropology.

While the *Childhood and Society* manuscript was in press, Erikson became involved in a political struggle between the University of California faculty and Regents. In the anti-Communist hysteria of the McCarthy era, the Regents passed a requirement that all faculty members sign a loyalty oath swearing that they were not members of the Communist party and did not support any party or organization that advocated the violent overthrow of the government. Erikson courageously refused to sign the oath. Instead, he resigned his university position and wrote an explanatory statement that was read to the members of the American Psychoanalytic Association. The letter read in part:

Dear Sirs:

I deeply appreciate the privilege of a free hearing before a committee of colleagues. With you I shall not play hide-and-seek regarding a question which must be implicit in what you wish to ask me and which must be explicit in what I shall have to say: I am not and have never been a Communist, inside "the party" or outside, in this country or abroad. One may say, then, why not acquiesce in an empty gesture if it saves the faces of very important personages, helps to allay public hysteria, and hurts nobody? My answer is that of a psychologist. I do believe that this gesture, which now saves face for some important people, will, in the long run, hurt people who are much more important: the students. Too much has been said of academic freedom for the faculty; I am concerned about certain dangers to the spirit of the student body, dangers which may emanate from such "compromises" as we have been asked to accept.

For many students, their years of study represent their contact with thought and theory, their only contact with men who teach them how to see two sides of a question and yet to be decisive in their conclusions, how to understand and yet to act with conviction. Young people are rightfully suspicious and embarrassingly discerning. I do not believe they can remain unimpressed by the fact that the men who are to teach them to think and to act judiciously and spontaneously must undergo a political test; must sign a statement which implicitly questions the validity of their own oath of office; must abrogate "commitments" so undefined that they must forever suspect themselves and one another; and must confess to an "objective truth" which they know only too well is elusive. Older people like ourselves can laugh this off; in younger people, however—and especially in those more important students who are motivated to go into teaching—a dangerous rift may well occur between the "official truth" and those deep and often radical doubts which are the necessary condition for the development of thought.

I realize that the University of California is a big place with many purposes. In many departments the danger which I have outlined will not interfere with the finding and teaching of facts. Mine is a highly specialized place in an area of knowledge still considered rather marginal to true science. My field includes the study of "hysteria," private and public, in "personality" and "culture." It includes the study of the tremendous waste in human energy which proceeds from irrational fear and from irrational gestures which are part of what we call "history." I would find it difficult to ask my subject of investigation (people) and my students to work with me if I were to participate without protest in a vague, fearful, and somewhat vindictive gesture devised to ban an evil in some magic way—an evil which must be met with much more searching and concerted effort.

In this sense, I may say that my conscience did not permit me to sign the contract after having sworn that I would do my job to the best of my ability. (Coles, 1970, pp. 157–158)

In 1951, Erikson moved east once more and worked at the Austen Riggs Center in Stockbridge, Massachusetts, an institute for psychoanalytic training and research. In 1958, he published a psychohistorical account of the life of theologian Martin Luther, *Young Man Luther: A Study in Psychoanalysis and History.* His work became increasingly popular among psychologists, historians, psychiatrists, anthropologists, philosophers, theologians, and biologists, as well as among students, and he was invited to lecture in colleges and universities all over the world (Coles, 1970, p. 255).

In 1960, Erikson returned to Harvard, where he taught an extremely popular undergraduate course entitled "The Human Life Cycle." (According to Erikson, his students irreverently dubbed it "From Womb to Tomb.") Erikson remained at Harvard until his retirement in 1970. Among the noteworthy texts he authored during this period were *Insight and Responsibility* (1964), *Identity: Youth and Crisis* (1968), and *Gandhi's Truth* (1969), a brilliant account of the life of India's nonviolent political leader, Mahatma Gandhi, which earned Erikson both the National Book Award and a Pulitzer Prize. He also published *In Search of Common Ground* (1973), *Dimensions of a New Identity: The 1973 Jefferson Lectures in the Humanities* (1974), *Life History and the Historical Moment* (1975), *Toys and Reasons: Stages in the Ritualization of Experience* (1977), *Identity and the Life Cycle: A Reissue* (1979), *The Life Cycle Completed* (1982), and *Vital Involvement in Old Age* (1986).

In 1978, Harvard awarded Erikson an honorary doctorate, and in 1982 he established the Erik H. and Joan M. Erikson Center to provide a forum for interdisciplinary studies of the life cycle. He continued his professional contributions through writing and consulting with various groups across the United States until shortly before his death in 1994 (Kroger, 1989, p. 12). His final days were spent in a nursing home in Harwich, Massachusetts, on Cape Cod. Following his death, Mrs. Erikson received letters of condolence from people throughout the world. Among them was a very warm and personal letter from the President of the United States, who praised Erikson's many professional contributions and concluded that Erikson had clearly "made a tremendous difference in our world" (Wallerstein, 1995, p. 174).

CONCEPTS AND PRINCIPLES

Ego Psychology: Liberalizing the Psychoanalytic Position

Erikson's position represents a systematic extension and liberalization of Freud's view of the role of the ego in personality functioning. Freud saw the ego as a relatively weak agency that operated in the service of the powerful id. In his judgment, ego functioning was primarily concerned with satisfying the person's biological needs by seeking realistic outlets that did not offend the moral prescriptions of a largely punitive superego, or inhibiting the id's urges when suitable objects for impulse gratification were not available.

In contrast to this traditional view, Erikson proposed that the ego often operates independently of id emotions and motivations. In his view, portions of the ego are neither defensive in nature nor concerned with the control of biological urges. Instead, the ego often functions to help individuals adapt constructively to the challenges presented by their surroundings. This new perspective examines ego function in relation to society. It provides a more positive view of personality, in which the ego has organizing and synthesizing functions that help people resolve inner conflicts as well as environmental challenges. Within this elaborated framework, the ego is a powerful agency that typically operates to promote health.

Ego psychology thus emphasizes the integration of biological and psychosocial forces in the determination of personality functioning. It gives special attention to the unique interpersonal, cultural, and historical context within which people face a common series of developmental crises. Each culture, in Erikson's view, has evolved unique ways of helping individuals resolve their crises so that their egos can be strengthened. Thus, the focus in Erikson's psychology is on the emergence of a strong ego identity as individuals resolve the crises inherent in the developmental process.

The Epigenetic Principle

Like Freud, Erikson postulated that human development is governed by the **epigenetic principle**—that development occurs in a series of stages, universal to humankind, that unfold in a predetermined sequence. Unlike Freud, however, he placed much greater emphasis on the growth and positive functioning of the ego. He posited further that ego development occurs throughout the lifetime, not just in early childhood. Erikson believed that, at critical points in the maturational process, people everywhere have

> a readiness to be driven toward, to be aware of, and to interact with a widening social radius and . . . that society, in principle, tends to be so constituted as to meet and invite this succession of potentialities for interaction and attempts to safeguard and to encourage the proper rate and the proper sequence of their unfolding. (Erikson, 1963, p. 270)

Each stage, according to Erikson, is marked by a particular psychosocial **crisis,** or turning point—a crucial period in which a decisive turn one way or another is unavoidable (Erikson, 1964, pp. 138–139). Crises are moments of decision between progress or regression in development. Erikson optimistically believed that the general tendency in human nature is toward the resolution of crises in a way that moves people toward a strong self-identity. He maintained that "such developmental and normative crises differ from imposed, traumatic, and neurotic crises in that the very process of growth provides new energy even as society offers new and specific opportunities according to its dominant conception of the phases of life" (Erikson, 1968b, pp. 162–163). Whether these crises are resolved satisfactorily depends to a considerable degree on the quality of the individual's psychosocial experiences. It also depends on the person's active attempts to analyze and integrate experiences and to utilize emerging abilities and skills. Thus, Erikson did not see people as passively buffeted around by outside forces. Rather, he saw them as actively seeking to deal with their experiences in a constructive, growth-promoting way.

Positive resolution of each crisis contributes to a progressive strengthening of the ego, whereas negative resolution results in the ego's weakening. A positive resolution at one stage also increases the chances that individuals will be able to resolve the crises at later stages. Conversely, an inability to resolve a crisis at a given stage reduces the chances of successful adaptation during succeeding stages. Thus, the stages are interrelated and interdependent (Erikson, 1963, p. 272); each one builds on the stages that precede it.

In describing ego strength, Erikson used the term **virtue,** meaning "inherent strength or active quality." Virtues are human qualities or strengths that emerge from successful resolution of the crises associated with various developmental stages (Erikson, 1964, p. 113). In Erikson's view, each stage provides the opportunity for the establishment of a unique strength or virtue. The establishment of each virtue, however, is not an irreversible achievement, nor does it make the individual impervious to new conflicts later in the developmental process (Erikson, 1963, pp. 273–274). Finally, crisis resolution is never completely positive or negative (Evans, 1967, p. 15); rather, each conflict resolution carries with it both positive and negative learning about events and people. Positive crisis resolution occurs when the ratio of positive to negative learning is weighted in favor of the positive.

PERSONALITY DEVELOPMENT

The Stages of Ego Development

Erikson postulated eight stages of ego development. The first four are closely wedded to Freud's oral, anal, phallic, and latency stages, although Erikson placed less emphasis than did Freud on the sexual bases of the conflicts in these stages, and more on the individual's social experiences. The remaining four stages show little reliance on Freud's theorizing. Table 6.1 presents a schema of the various stages.

Oral-Sensory Stage: Basic Trust versus Mistrust

The first stage corresponds closely to Freud's oral stage and occurs during the first year of life. Pleasurable sensations center around the mouth, and the focal activity is feeding. The infant lives and loves through its mouth. The mother is the one who typically ministers to the infant's needs, and healthy development in the infant depends on the quality of her care. The mother's attitude toward her child-care function is shaped by the society in which she lives. If the society downgrades the status of motherhood, the result will likely be a caretaker who resents her role; if society praises and extolls the virtues of motherhood, her attitude is likely to be healthy and constructive.

In Erikson's view, if the mother acts in a loving and consistent way, the infant is likely to develop a sense of **basic trust.** As they interact, the infant comes to recognize the mother by sight, her touch, the sound of her voice, and even her smell. All of the senses are part

TABLE 6.1	The eight stages of ego development		
Stage	**Estimated age**	**Ego crisis**	**Ego strength**
1. Oral-sensory	Birth–1	Basic trust vs. mistrust	Hope
2. Muscular-anal	2–3	Autonomy vs. shame and doubt	Will
3. Locomotor-genital	4–5	Initiative vs. guilt	Purpose
4. Latency	6–12	Industry vs. inferiority	Competence
5. Adolescence	13–19	Identity vs. role confusion	Fidelity
6. Young adulthood	20–24	Intimacy vs. isolation	Love
7. Middle adulthood	25–64	Generativity vs. stagnation	Care
8. Late adulthood	65–death	Ego integrity vs. despair	Wisdom

SOURCE: Adapted from Erikson, 1950, 1963.

of the interaction process between the two. The infant's first social achievement is his or her eventual willingness to let the mother out of sight without becoming unduly anxious, on the basis of an inner certainty that she will return to feed and care for the infant. Such certainty provides the rudiments of an ego identity because it depends on the infant's recognition that people are dependable (Erikson, 1963, p. 247). The basic trust that develops between mother and child is not totally one-sided; it is truly an interpersonal experience. Not only does the mother's dependability foster trust in the infant; the infant, too, begins to act in a trustworthy way. As the infant develops teeth, he or she is driven to bite. The infant must learn not to engage in this behavior, however, lest the mother withdraw in anger and pain. If the infant learns properly, the mother will come to trust her child, and both parties can engage in a relaxed and mutually gratifying set of experiences.

In contrast, a sense of **basic mistrust** is created if the mother acts in an unreliable, aloof, and rejecting way. The mother's lack of dependability and care is likely to frustrate, anger, and enrage the infant, who becomes more demanding and unpredictable. The feeling of being deprived also leaves a residue of mistrust that continues to have effects later in the developmental process.

If the interpersonal experiences with the mother are generally more positive than negative, the child develops an attitude toward others that is more trusting than mistrusting. The healthy person is not completely trusting, however; such a person would be too naive, gullible, and easily hurt by others. A certain amount of mistrust is healthy. Some people are dangerous, and precautions must be taken to ensure survival.

If this stage has a positive resolution, in which more trust than mistrust emerges, the outcome is a sense of confidence and **hope.** The beginnings of hope established during the first stage of life can be dashed later if new pressures or conflicts arise, or they can be strengthened substantially by subsequent positive experience. Society, in Erikson's judgment, provides an opportunity for the perpetuation and strengthening of trust through its religious institutions. Trust, in his view, becomes the capacity for faith. Whereas Freud viewed religious beliefs as unhealthy delusions that prevented people from dealing constructively with reality, Erikson saw religious institutions as "giving concerted expression to adult man's need to provide the young and the weak with a world-image sustaining hope" (Erikson, 1964, p. 153). Erikson's view of organized religion, however, was not entirely positive. He did recognize that, all too often, the church has exploited the most infantile strivings in human beings, for its own self-aggrandizement (Erikson, 1964, p. 153).

Muscular-Anal Stage: Autonomy versus Shame and Doubt

Erikson's second stage is closely related to Freud's anal stage and occurs during the second and third years of life. During this period, the child's muscles begin to mature, and he or she starts to learn how to exercise control over them. This is the period during which toilet training occurs in our society. Youngsters must learn to control their anal sphincter muscles so that elimination of waste materials can be accomplished in a manner deemed appropriate by society. Erikson pointed out that intense conflicts over whether to hold on or let go do not arise in all societies. In many agrarian cultures, for example, parents ignore anal behavior and leave it to older children to take toddlers out to the bushes so that they can perform the elimination function. The toddlers learn by imitating the behavior of the older children. In our society, however, the scene is set for intense conflict, according to Erikson, because we have as our ideal the always clean, punctual, and deodorized body (Erikson, 1968b, pp. 107–108). Thus, children must be trained to obey, and this leads to a conflict of wills and a power struggle between parents and children. Ironically, just as children have learned to trust their parents and the world, they must now learn how to assert their independence. They must become self-willed and take chances with their trust in order to establish what they can do by themselves (Evans, 1967, p. 19).

A sense of **autonomy** and self-control is engendered if parents guide their children's behavior gradually and firmly. When this is the predominant treatment, children experience an increased sense of pride in their accomplishments and good feelings toward others. The virtue that emerges is **will,** defined as "the unbroken determination to exercise free choice as well as self-restraint" (Erikson, 1964, p. 119), a gradual increase in the power to exercise judgment and decision.

If parents are either too permissive or too harsh and demanding during this stage, children experience a sense of defeat that can lead to **shame and doubt** concerning their ability to make effective judgments and to exercise control over their lives. One result may be the neurotic attempt to regain control by compulsive action (Erikson, 1963, p. 252).

Individuals who develop a sense of control over their lives tend later to support society's legal institutions to the extent that they are equitable in the administration of the law. They see that only through adherence to the law can they and others preserve their own freedom, independence, and sense of rightful dignity (Erikson, 1963, p. 254).

Locomotor-Genital Stage: Initiative versus Guilt

The third stage, ages 4 and 5, bears some resemblance to Freud's phallic stage. If the resolution of conflict in the previous stage has been successful, children feel that they are now individuals in their own right. During the third stage, their **initiative** is sparked, and they must find out what kind of people they may become (Erikson, 1968b, p. 115). Children at this stage become curious about their parents, their friends, and their surroundings. Now that their developing bodies allow them to locomote more freely, they independently seek out more contact with others beyond the family circle. They engage in play and other experimental activities with their peers. Their language becomes refined, and they ask incessant questions about innumerable things. Their imaginations are very active, and they fantasize about being adults. There is also a great deal of playacting, as children start trying out a variety of adult roles (Erikson, 1968b, p. 115).

At this age, children are intrusive. Like Freud, Erikson believed that, besides exploring their environments and trying out new roles, children show an overconcern with sexual matters. They attempt (largely in fantasy) to possess the parent of the opposite sex, with an accompanying feeling of rivalry toward the parent of the same sex. If children are punished severely for these advances, they develop a sense of **guilt**. If, on the other hand, the parents act in an understanding way and guide the children's motives and desires into socially acceptable activities, they develop a sense of **purpose**. This virtue involves thinking big, identifying with parents, and beginning to set major life goals.

Play activities greatly affect the development of these goals. Children playact being mothers or fathers and achieving success as doctors, nurses, teachers, astronauts, and so forth. According to Erikson, boys and girls engage in different kinds of play activities and fantasies; he attributed this, in part, to biology. He found, for example, that boys and girls made different kinds of constructions. Boys tended to build high towers and large buildings and to use animals, human figures, and cars. Girls, in contrast, rarely built towers; when they did, they made the towers lean against the background. Girls usually made simple enclosures with low walls that they called houses. According to Erikson, children's toy constructions closely parallel the morphology of their sex organs. In males, the penis, which is erectable and intrusive in character, is represented by high buildings and towers that stand out in comparison to other objects in a setting. In females, the vagina is represented by static house interiors and low enclosures. Erikson believed, further, that the boys' tendency to picture upward movement (high towers) and mobility (fast cars) could be the expression of their need to prove themselves strong and aggressive and to achieve high standing, whereas the girls' representations of house interiors could reflect their need to concentrate on the anticipated tasks of taking care of a home and rearing children (Erikson, 1963, pp. 97–107).

Needless to say, these interpretations did not endear Erikson to feminists (such as Weisstein, 1975), who thought he was claiming that anatomy is destiny. If accepted, they believed, this view would result in restriction of opportunities for women, who would be kept in a subservient position. These feminist critics maintained that the differences between the sexes could be better explained as the result of cultural conditioning, rather than as an expression of genetic endowment.

Erikson's response was that he had been misunderstood and quoted selectively by feminists. He did not say that *only* anatomy is destiny, but that anatomy is *one* determinant of behavior.

> Am I saying, then, that "anatomy is destiny"? Yes, it is destiny, insofar as it determines not only the range and configuration of physiological functioning and its limitation but also, to an extent, personality configurations. The basic modalities of woman's commitment and involvement naturally also reflect the ground plan of her body [but] a human being, in addition to having a body, is *somebody,* which means an indivisible personality and a defined member of a group. . . . In other words: anatomy, history, and personality are our combined destiny. (Erikson, 1968b, p. 285)

In Erikson's view, society, culture, and biology jointly determine our behavior. Our bodies predispose us to certain activities, but this does not mean we must perform only these activities and no others. Women's bodies are built for childbearing and nursing. Yet women have other capacities, too; some of these lead to careers that would be considered masculine in the historical period and society in which we live. (The same argument would apply to men entering so-called women's occupations.) Erikson would have welcomed a breaking down of these cultural stereotypes; at the same time, however, he maintained that women still have maternal feelings, desires, and unique capabilities because of their biology and that repression of these maternal characteristics because of societal pressures could restrict their personal growth. In his opinion, feminists have placed too much emphasis on the cultural and social determinants of behavior and, in their zeal to lift the oppression of women, have denied the positive aspects of their bodies and the fact that they alone can contribute to society as mothers and teachers of the very young (Erikson, 1975, pp. 225–247).

Latency Stage: Industry versus Inferiority

Erikson's fourth stage loosely parallels Freud's latency period and occurs from ages 6 to 12. During this period, there is a lull in sexual desires and feelings, and children turn from home to school life, whether school is classroom or jungle or field (Erikson, 1963, p. 258). It is a period of learning new skills and of making things. Children develop a sense of **industry,** which means that they are busy learning how to complete jobs (Evans, 1967, p. 28). Teachers become important in their lives; by introducing them to the technology of the culture, teachers prepare children for the future and for careers.

The danger in this period is that children may fail to learn new things and, as a result, develop feelings of **inferiority.** Failure to learn may be caused by an insufficient resolution of the conflicts in the preceding stage. Children may still want their mothers more than they want knowledge; or they may still compare themselves to their bigger and better-skilled fathers, and experience acute feelings of inadequacy. In Erikson's view, parents can help to minimize these feelings by gradually preparing children for the rigors of the school environment and by encouraging them to trust their prospective mentors. Erikson believed that a positive identification with their teachers is necessary if children are to develop a strong ego. Society needs teachers who are trustworthy and encouraging and who know how to emphasize what children can do (Erikson, 1968b, p. 125). The positive outcome of such sensitive treatment by teachers is that children develop the virtue of **competence,** giving them a healthy preparation for their roles as workers in later life.

Adolescence: Identity versus Role Confusion

The fifth stage of development occurs from ages 13 through 19. Individuals who have adequately resolved the conflicts inherent in the prior stages bring into adolescence a growing sense of self-identity.

The parents have made their child feel that he or she is *somebody*. Young people know that they are an integral part of the family, and yet they also have a budding sense of independence and personal efficacy. They recognize their own competence, can take initiative, and are able to see a variety of tasks through to completion. Thus, they enter adolescence with a variety of loosely related segments of identity based on experiences in the earlier stages. Mixed in with the individual's sense of positive identity, according to Erikson, is a negative identity consisting of all the things the individual has done for which he or she has been punished and for which the individual feels guilty or ashamed. It also includes feelings of incompetence and inadequacy based on past failures (Evans, 1967, pp. 35–36).

During adolescence, these prior identifications are questioned and then restructured by an ego that seeks to integrate them with strong, emerging sexual feelings and the social roles that are available to the individual.

> The integration now taking place in the form of ego identity is . . . more than the sum of the childhood identifications. It is the accrued experience of the ego's ability to integrate all identifications with the vicissitudes of the libido and with the opportunities offered in social roles. The sense of ego identity, then, is the accrued confidence that the inner sameness and continuity prepared in the past are matched by the sameness and continuity of one's meaning for others, as evidenced in the tangible promise of a "career." (Erikson, 1963, pp. 261–262)

Identity is a multifaceted concept. At base, however, it refers to a conscious sense of direction and uniqueness, derived from a variety of psychosocial experiences that are integrated by the ego—including all our previous identifications learned as a participant in a variety of groups (family, church, school, and peer) and all our self-images (Evans, 1967, p. 36). It involves the sense that we have made an adequate sexual choice and have found a suitable partner to love. It also encompasses our connection with the future when we opt for specific careers and become recognized by others as responsible members of society. A large part of our identity rests on what we do for a living, on the support we receive from society, and on our internalization of the ideals of our class, our nation, and our culture (Erikson, 1964, p. 93). Identity consists, therefore, of the things we are, the things we want to become, and the things we are supposed to become. It also consists of the "things which we do not want to be or which we know we are not supposed to be" (Evans, 1967, p. 32).

Identity is not achieved once and for all during adolescence. However, adolescence is the period during which an **identity crisis** is normative. It is a **moratorium** between childhood and adulthood in which individuals attempt to solve special problems. If these problems are not resolved satisfactorily, a frantic search for identity may be started anew, even in old age.

In Erikson's judgment, the identity crises experienced by youths stem from **role confusion** concerning who they are and what they will become. For many youths, adolescence is a period of torturous self-consciousness characterized by awakening sexual drives and rapid growth of the body, by doubts and shame over what they are already sure they are and what they might become.

The most disturbing part of life during this period, according to Erikson, is youths' inability to decide on an occupational identity. Empirical support for his contention is provided by a recent survey of adolescents' opinions conducted by Violato and Holden (1988). The investigators asked a large sample of adolescents to indicate how often they worried about a variety of topics, including their careers, alcohol use, smoking, grades, sexual impulses, personal appearance, and their interactions with family, parents, and friends. The areas of greatest concern and worry were careers and grades, followed by personal appearance, then interactions with family, friends, and parents, sexual impulses, and lastly, alcohol use and smoking behavior (Violato & Holden, 1988, p. 106).

Although they have a strong need to commit themselves to a set of goals and principles that would give direction and meaning to their lives, many adolescents find it extremely difficult to make satisfactory choices. Erikson maintains that in such an unsettled period, confused youths try to establish their identities by overidentifying with an assortment of heroes.

> To keep themselves together, they temporarily overidentify . . . with the heroes of cliques and crowds. On the other hand, they become remarkably clannish, intolerant, and cruel in their exclusion of others who are "different," in skin color, cultural background . . . and often in entirely petty aspects of dress and gesture arbitrarily selected as *the* sign of an in-grouper or out-grouper. It is important to understand . . . such intolerance as the necessary *defense against a sense of identity diffusion,* which is unavoidable at a time of life when the body changes its proportions radically . . . and when life lies before one with a variety of conflicting possibilities and choices. Adolescents temporarily help one another through such discomfort by forming cliques and by stereotyping themselves, their ideals, and

their enemies. . . . It is difficult to be tolerant if deep down you are not quite sure that you are a man (or a woman), that you will ever grow together again and be attractive, that you will be able to master your drives, that you really know who you are, that you know what you want to be . . . and that you will know how to make the right decision without, once [and] for all, committing yourself to the wrong friend, sexual partner, leaders, or career. (Erikson, 1968a, p. 200)

The behavior of many young people, according to Erikson, is characterized by **totalism**—a setting of absolute boundaries in one's values, beliefs, and interpersonal relationships (Erikson, 1964, p. 92). Adolescents embrace simplistic ideologies and follow them with little questioning; they may accept, for example, the values mouthed by celebrities in the drug culture, by delinquent gangs and fanatic religious cults, and by political groups that seem to provide simple answers to difficult and threatening problems. Erikson cautioned against simply labeling such behavior as pathological; instead, we should try to understand it as an alternative way of dealing with experience. Although such behavior has destructive outcomes that cannot be condoned, it also has survival value for many young people (Erikson, 1964, p. 93).

Erikson's view of young people and their development is generally optimistic. He believed that some of their confusion and failure to act constructively is not their fault; rather, rapid political, cultural, and technological changes have led to the questioning of established values that no longer seem to work. Adolescent confusion can also be traced to adults, who are unclear about their own values and, therefore, cannot provide proper guidance. Lastly, young people rightfully protest when adults behave in corrupt and evil ways and are themselves not worthy of emulation. Erikson stressed that adults need young people as much as young people need adults. Young people are the caretakers of the future; through their protests, they also force the older generation to restructure its own value system.

The successful resolution of the crisis of adolescence leads to a sense of **fidelity,** which Erikson called "the ability to sustain loyalties freely pledged in spite of the inevitable contradictions of value systems" (Erikson, 1964, p. 125). Young people are now much more honest with themselves and with significant others. They select friends, mates, and coworkers and commit themselves to these people. They develop a loyalty to a vision of the future, and they move to meet it (Erikson, 1975, p. 209). They are ready to take their place in a technological society not just as guardians of traditions and customs but as rejuvenators and innovators of the culture. Youths who have not adequately resolved their conflicts may develop a **negative identity,** in which they act in scornful and hostile ways toward roles offered as proper and desirable by the community (Erikson, 1968b, pp. 172–173). Their loyalties are to groups, people, and ideologies that are destructive to themselves and to society.

Young Adulthood: Intimacy versus Isolation

The sixth stage spans the ages of 20 to 24. Having established a stable self-identity during adolescence, healthy young adults are able to enter into intimate relationships with others, and they are eager and ready to strengthen their personal identity. They seek to commit themselves to partnerships, and they have the strength to abide by such commitments even when significant compromises and sacrifices are necessary (Erikson, 1963, p. 263).

Erikson pointed out that the establishment of intimate relationships is not to be confused with "intimacies" (Roazen, 1976, p. 103); that is, the intimacies involved in sexual intercourse are not to be mistaken for true **intimacy**—the ability to establish close relationships with others. Erikson believed that a truly intimate relationship is possible only between partners who have clearly established identities and loyalties. Because adolescents are still struggling to establish their identities, it follows that they cannot love (be intimate) in the truest sense. Mature love, for the young adult, involves "mutuality of mates and partners in a shared identity, for the mutual verification through an experience of finding oneself . . . in another" (Erikson, 1964, p. 128).

Healthy intimate relationships are beneficial to both the person and society. According to Erikson, such relationships meet the following standards:

1. a mutuality of orgasm
2. with a loved partner
3. of the opposite sex
4. with whom one is able and willing to share a mutual trust
5. and with whom one is able and willing to regulate the cycles of
   a. work
   b. procreation
   c. recreation
6. so as to secure to the offspring, too, all the stages of a satisfactory development (Erikson, 1963, p. 266).

Young adults who cannot develop a capacity for intimacy and productive work experience a sense of **isolation.** Isolation is the inability to take chances with one's identity by sharing true intimacy (Erikson, 1968b, p. 137). Such individuals are self-absorbed and engage in interpersonal relationships on a very superficial level. In young adults who develop their capacity for intimacy more than their sense of isolation, the result is the emergence of the virtue of **love.**

Middle Adulthood: Generativity versus Stagnation

The seventh stage spans the middle years, from ages 25 to 64. Healthy adults have a strong ego identity and have established a career and mature relationships with others. Their primary responsibility, in Erikson's judgment, is the establishment and guidance of the next generation. **Generativity** encompasses not only the production and rearing of children, but also the creation of products, ideas, art, and other items that can be used to benefit others (Evans, 1967, p. 51; Van de Water & McAdams, 1989, p. 435). The crisis centers on the question of whether adults are going to be productive or whether they are going to stagnate. **Stagnation** involves a lack of productivity, boredom, and interpersonal impoverishment (Erikson, 1968b, p. 138). If the capacity of adults for generativity exceeds their sense of stagnation, the virtue of **care** emerges. The older generation is thus concerned with helping the younger generation to develop in constructive ways. Although it is clear that generativity includes having children as a means of ensuring the survival of society, Erikson stressed that people can be generative even if they do not have children. Childless individuals can contribute to the higher development of society through productive work and through active demonstration of concern with the betterment of young people.

Late Adulthood: Ego Integrity versus Despair

The final stage lasts from the age of 65 to death. It is a time of intense reflection, involving reminiscence, the recollection of memories and dreams, and attempts to reconstrue the meaning of life while coming to terms with impending death (Walaskay, Whitbourne, & Nehrke, 1983–1984, p. 62). Healthy people are those who have adapted to the triumphs and disappointments of their lives, who have been the originators of others or the generators of products and ideas. They are able to look back at their lives and conclude that they were special and had meaning. They are also able to accept the inevitability of death as a necessary part of the life cycle and not fear it. In brief, elderly people who are functioning well see a unity and meaning in their lives. They have **ego integrity.**

In contrast, individuals who are unable to accept the inevitable failures in their lives and who have led selfish, uncaring lives experience **despair,** because they realize life is now short and there is no time to start a new life or try out new paths to integrity (Erikson, 1963, p. 269).

Finally, the virtue of **wisdom** is associated with a meaningful old age. According to Erikson, "wisdom is detached concern with life itself in the face of death itself" (1964, p. 133); wisdom affirms the integrity of experience despite a decline in bodily functioning. It allows the person to envisage human problems in their entirety and to communicate to the younger generation a constructive living example of the final period in the life of a unique human being (Erikson, 1964, pp. 133–134).

Research Support for the Theory of Ego Development

Empirical verification of Erikson's complicated theorizing about ego development requires extensive longitudinal studies in order to assess changes in development as people proceed through the life cycle. Such research is costly and difficult. Consequently, there has been relatively little research to date aimed at verifying Erikson's elaborate explanations of the ways in which the eight stages of development operate and influence one another. In addition, empirical verification of the theory is difficult, because the hypotheses are often not clearly stated and many of its constructs are highly abstract and difficult to measure adequately. Despite these difficulties, researchers have been able to create acceptable measures of some of the stages of ego development and have conducted important research based on extensions and refinements of Erikson's theorizing.

Industry in the Latency Stage

Research is just beginning to test Erikson's ideas about children's learning to be industrious through school experiences. Kowaz and Marcia (1991), for example, have created an individual differences measure of industriousness and examined how scores on this factor are related to several aspects of children's cognitive, motivational, and behavioral functioning in the classroom. They found that highly industrious children were more motivated to succeed in school and obtained higher grades than children who were low in industriousness. Furthermore, these results showed that highly industrious children had stronger preferences to make and do things rather than to engage in fantasy by making things up. They also were more content with their school experiences than were their less industrious peers. These results are generally supportive of Erikson's astute observations.

Ego Identity in Adolescence

Marcia (1966) has identified four distinct positions, or statuses, implicit in Erikson's theorizing about identity development in adolescence: (1) identity diffusion; (2) foreclosure; (3) moratorium; and (4) identity achievement. These statuses are defined in terms of the two dimensions of crisis and commitment. *Crisis* refers to an active period of struggle that individuals experience as they seek to resolve questions that arise in the selection of a career, a partner, and a set of values or principles to follow. *Commitment* involves making firm decisions in these areas and then pursuing goals consistent with those decisions.

Individuals with **identity diffusion** lack firm commitments and are not actively in crisis. They may never have experienced crisis, or they may have experienced a period of struggle in the past and been unable to resolve it by making a decision. Lacking a clear sense of identity, such people may exhibit a range of negative emotional states, including pessimism, boredom, unfocused anger, personal confusion, and feelings of helplessness and hopelessness (Waterman, 1985, p. 13). Individuals in **foreclosure** have never experienced a crisis but have nevertheless made firm commitments to certain goals, beliefs, and values. A good example is the first-year college student who is uncritically following her parents' wishes and pursuing a degree in medicine without examining whether this goal is actually the best for her in terms of her needs and abilities. Individuals in moratorium are currently in a state of crisis and are actively considering alternatives in an attempt to arrive at a decision. Finally, individuals with a status of **identity achievement** have undergone a period of crisis and, as a consequence, have developed firm commitments.

In addition to clarifying and making explicit Erikson's four phases of ego-identity development in adolescence, Marcia (1966) created an elaborate interview procedure to measure them. This instrument allows investigators to identify the interpersonal relationships of individuals who occupy particular identity statuses and to assess the implications of each status for personality functioning and performance. It has also spurred the construction of several other, less complicated measures of the ego-identity construct (Bourne, 1978; Rosenthal, Gurney, & Moore, 1981).

Several investigations have examined the particular family relationships and parenting styles experienced by individuals occupying each of the identity statuses. In general, this research shows that foreclosures have the closest relationships with their parents. They rate their parents most favorably, and strongly endorse parental authority and values. These individuals do not actively explore alternatives and exhibit a lower ego identity. In contrast, identity diffusers report the most distance between themselves and their parents. They perceive their parents as indifferent and rejecting. Moratorium adolescents have ambivalent feelings toward their parents, which stem from differences in opinion concerning the goals and values considered worthy and appropriate for pursuit by teenagers. In times of crisis, these young people are unlikely to turn to their parents for support and advice. Once the crisis has been resolved and identity achieved, however, warmer relationships are typically established (Waterman, 1982, pp. 351–352; Marcia, 1993, p.33).

The research on identity status generally assumes that a progressive strengthening in the sense of identity occurs during adolescence and into adulthood. Marcia (1966) posits a progression from low to high ego maturity as follows: diffusion, foreclosure, moratorium, and identity achievement. Within this overall progression, however, different people follow different sequential patterns. While one person in the moratorium phase moves progressively toward identity achievement, another person may move regressively from moratorium status to ego diffusion. Or an adolescent in a foreclosure state may simply remain there into adulthood. Some possible developmental pathways are illustrated in Figure 6.1.

Most studies in this research literature suggest that men and women undergo similar patterns of identity development (Archer, 1989, p. 135). The sexes may differ, however, in some of the goals that are an integral part of their emerging identities. Male identity has been found to center primarily on the attainment of a career, whereas female identity has a multiple and varying base, which revolves around career and/or marriage and/or childbearing. Females also engage in more active reflection regarding an identity based on personal relationships than do males (Waterman, 1993, p. 62).

In some interesting research on female identity, O'Connell (1976)

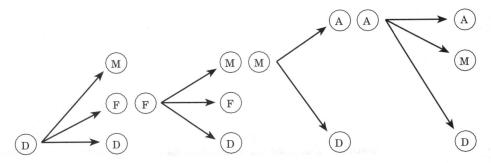

FIGURE 6.1   Possible sequential development patterns. **D**, identity diffusion; **M**, moratorium; **F**, foreclosure; **A**, identity achievement. (Adapted from Waterman, 1982, p. 343.)

has shown that the traditional woman defines herself in terms of the man she marries and the children she raises. Thus, to a considerable degree, her sense of identity is a reflection of her roles as wife and mother. Her worth and self-esteem are derived from her participation in the lives of significant others. Although her sense of reflected identity is strong, her personal identity, which is based on her own unique endowments, capabilities, and needs, is weak. O'Connell found, however, that a strengthening of personal identity does occur once the traditional woman's childbearing duties diminish and her children reach elementary school age.

For the nontraditional married woman, whose identity centers around career goals, the sense of personal identity is strong and remains strong, according to O'Connell, throughout the childbearing, preschool, and elementary school stages. Whereas the traditional woman experiences a moratorium during adolescence before marriage and childbearing, the nontraditional woman experiences no such moratorium during the period from adolescence to adulthood.

Researchers have devoted considerable attention to the information-processing and problem-solving strategies and abilities of college students in each of the four identity statuses. This research area is also concerned with the academic motivation, goals, and achievements of these students.

Several studies have shown that identity achievers and moratorium individuals tend to construe most personal problems as manageable and solvable. Accordingly, they confront their problems directly, by actively seeking out relevant information and considering alternatives when attempting to deal with them. They also process greater amounts of information and report feeling more certain of their ideas. In making decisions, identity achievers are more reflective and rational, as are moratorium individuals.

Foreclosures, in contrast, focus their attention so narrowly when trying to solve their problems that they fail to attend to relevant information. Their rigidity keeps them from assimilating novel information and/or from considering alternative courses of action that could help successfully resolve personal difficulties. They are intolerant of ambiguity and defensive, and possess authoritarian belief systems. When confronted by stressful problems, foreclosures tend to rely on others for help in solving them.

Finally, identity diffusers characteristically avoid dealing with their problems, possibly to reduce painful ambiguity. Thus, they tend to procrastinate and to delay making decisions for as long as possible. Under stress, they are rather disorganized in their thinking (Berzonsky, 1992; Berzonsky and Neimeyer, 1988; Blustein & Phillips, 1990; Marcia, 1966, 1967, 1994; Read, Adams, & Dobson, 1984; Schenkel & Marcia, 1972).

In research on academic motivation, Adams and Fitch (1983) have shown that identity achievers are more attracted to scholastic or academically oriented departments than to departments that emphasize social activities and the material benefits of pursuing degrees (such as high-paying jobs upon graduation). Consistent with these data is a study by Marcia and Friedman (1970), which shows that identity achievers choose more difficult academic majors than do identity-diffuse students. Students with strong identities more often chose to major in engineering, chemistry, pharmacy, biology, or mathematics, whereas identity-diffuse students preferred to major in sociology, anthropology, education, or physical education. Waterman and Waterman (1970) found that students with clear commitments to occupational goals evaluated their educational experiences more favorably than did students who were unclear about their occupational goals. Identity achievers also got higher grades than did college students of other statuses (Marcia, 1993, p. 27).

Marcia (1966) found that, as Erikson's theorizing would predict, college men who had successfully resolved their identity crises—and, therefore, had a clear sense of ego identity—performed better on an intellectually challenging task than did students with diffuse identities. Students with strong ego identities responded with a less severe loss of self-esteem to failure on tasks that they believed to be associated with academic success (Marcia, 1967). Identity achievers showed greater cultural sophistication and tolerance for outgroups, as well as higher levels of logical and moral reasoning, than did members of the other statuses (Cote & Levine, 1983; Rowe & Marcia, 1980; Waterman, 1982). Identity achievers also showed a greater openness to the opinions of other group members, presumably because of their secure sense of self and their highly flexible cognitive systems (Slugoski, Marcia, & Koopman, 1984, p. 658).

Erikson's idea that adolescence is characterized by psychosocial growth was supported by research showing that the number of students who achieved identity for both occupation and ideology—that is, a set of values and principles to guide one's life—increased significantly from the first year to the senior year of college (Waterman, Geary, & Waterman, 1974; Adams & Fitch, 1982). By the second half of their senior year, most students had achieved strong identities.

Finally, in a recent study focusing on noncollege adults from Finland, people with stronger ego identities had a more positive orientation toward the future than did individuals with weaker ego identities; that is, identity achievers felt more optimistic about their future and had clearer plans and goals than did individuals who were more ego diffuse (Pulkkinen & Ronka, 1994, p. 265).

Intimacy in Early Adulthood

On the basis of Erikson's writings, Orlofsky and his colleagues have identified six distinct statuses associated with intimacy issues during early adulthood (Orlofsky, 1976; Orlofsky, Marcia, & Lesser, 1973). Individuals are interviewed and their responses classified according to three criteria: (1) the presence or absence of relationships with same- and other-sex friends; (2) the presence or absence of enduring, committed sexual-love relationships; and (3) the depth (emotional closeness) or superficiality of their relationships. **Intimate individuals** have deep relationships with male and female friends and are involved in enduring, committed heterosexual relationships. **Preintimate individuals** also have close emotional ties to others, but are ambivalent about committing themselves to enduring love relationships. **Stereotyped individuals** have many relationships, but they are superficial and utilitarian and lacking in closeness and commitment. **Pseudointimate individuals,** like stereotyped people, form relationships that lack depth; unlike stereotyped people, however, they have entered into enduring heterosexual commitments. **Isolated individuals** are completely, or nearly completely, withdrawn from social situations and relationships with peers (Orlofsky, Marcia, & Lesser, 1973, p. 213). **Merger individuals** are those who have committed themselves to enduring relationships or those who are uncommitted but are seeking committed relationships. Merger individuals in committed relationships have become absorbed in their relationships at the expense of their own autonomy and sense of self. Such relationships are characterized by excessive dependency and **enmeshment**. Merger individuals in uncommitted relationships are insecure and tend to seek out dependency relationships (Levitz-Jones & Orlofsky, 1985, p. 158; Orlofsky, 1993, pp. 127–128).

Research has shown that intimates work at developing mutual personal relationships and have several close friends with whom they discuss personal matters (Orlofsky, Marcia, & Lesser, 1973, p. 213). Although they will disclose personal information to their close friends, they will not discuss personal matters with casual acquaintances. Thus, they are selectively self-revealing, in contrast to individuals in the lower intimacy statuses (Prager, 1986, p. 91). Intimates are warm, candid people who have a genuine interest in and concern for others. Their sexual relationships are mutually satisfactory, and they are able to make lasting commitments without overly compromising their own independence (Orlofsky, Marcia, & Lesser, 1973, p. 213; Orlofsky, 1978, p. 436). According to Prager (1986, p. 96), they also have a strong internal locus of control over their lives. In other research, Prager (1989, p. 448) found that unmarried and married couples who had attained intimacy status had a history of greater self-disclosure over a broad range of topics with their partners than did pseudointimate-status couples. Intimacy-status couples also reported the highest levels of satisfaction with their relationships.

Preintimates have had some dating experience, but are in conflict regarding commitment and are ambivalent about the risk of failure involved in intimate sexuality. Their values, however, are similar to those held by intimates—namely, respect for the integrity of others, openness, a sense of responsibility, and mutuality—and it is possible that they can resolve their ambivalence and move into the highest intimacy status.

Stereotyped individuals have superficial relationships. They date regularly and will sometimes see the other person for months, but do not become further involved. They enjoy sex and tend to be continually searching for new conquests. They treat others as sexual objects and are only interested in satisfying their own needs. They tend to be shallow and exploitative, and have limited self-awareness.

Pseudointimates resemble stereotyped individuals, with one major exception: they have made a lasting commitment to one person. In this sense, they resemble intimate individuals, but they are self-absorbed and not genuinely concerned about others.

Isolates are characterized by the absence of any enduring relationships. They rarely initiate social contacts and date very rarely. The anxiety that accompanies close personal contacts forces them to withdraw from others. Isolates are nonassertive and lack social skills. They may present themselves as bitter and mistrustful or as smug and self-satisfied. Their interpersonal difficulties may be traced to a lack of trust in themselves and others (Orlofsky, Marcia, & Lesser, 1973, p. 213).

Orlofsky's research has shown further that high-intimacy men are almost invariably identity achievers; preintimates are most frequently in the moratorium status; stereotyped and pseudointimate men tend to be foreclosures; and isolates tend toward identity diffusion (Orlofsky, Marcia, & Lesser, 1973, p. 217).

Research on the newest status, mergers, shows that women in this group are excessively dependent on their male partners. To achieve their goals, such women may employ subtle manipulation such as acting seductively, using flattery, or dropping hints, while their male partners rely on domineering and bullying tactics such as threatening, ridiculing, and insulting their partners (Howard, Blumstein, & Schwartz, 1986, p. 107). In such relationships, the woman loses her own sense of autonomy and fails to see her partner as a separate individual. The result is excessive possessiveness, jealousy, and a belief that she is unable to get along or find any happiness without her partner. Merger women frequently disclosed that they bickered continually with their boyfriends as a means of delineating a sense of separateness. One merger woman said, "I broke up with my boyfriend because he won't argue with me and I *need* someone to argue with" (Levitz-Jones & Orlofsky, 1985, p. 167). Although these couples cling to each other, they are actually low in mutuality, trust, and openness and, therefore, low in intimacy. One outcome is that, as compared with high-intimacy women, merger women are more likely to become depressed.

Generativity in Middle Adulthood

Van de Water and McAdams (1989) tested several of Erikson's ideas about generativity. Generativity was assessed by asking subjects to identify three creative products or projects in which they were currently involved. They were told that creativity was broadly defined and included such activities as making *things* (such as building a model airplane or making a delicious dinner), coming up with good *ideas* (providing useful advice, telling a good story), or doing things for *people* (raising children, teaching students, serving as an example to others). Finally, they were asked to give their reasons for getting involved in the activities. Judges rated the subjects' descriptions in terms of their degree of generativity. In the judges' opinion, the first of the following examples of the subjects' responses shows no generativity, while the second shows considerable generativity.

[Subject 1] Made several dresses for myself recently. I think sewing saves me money (which makes me feel good) and . . . results in a wardrobe that looks and fits better than store-bought clothing. It is basically a self-satisfying endeavor. (Van de Water & McAdams, 1989, p. 440)

[Subject 2] Successful business career. Attained management objective. [I am a] good example for women to follow. [I helped to] expand [the] role of women in free enterprise. (Van de Water & McAdams, 1989, p. 441)

Following this assessment of the subjects' level of generativity, all subjects filled out a series of self-report scales designed to assess their belief in the species, their trust in human beings, and their tendencies toward nurturance or self-absorption. In line with Erikson's ideas, generative subjects exhibited a basic belief in the goodness and worthwhileness of human life. They trusted in the future advancement of human life, even in the face of compelling evidence of human destructiveness, and were more committed to helping others reach their goals than were individuals suffering from stagnation in their lives. Generative subjects were not self-absorbed, but oriented toward helping others (Van de Water & McAdams, 1989, pp. 437–438). Not surprisingly, subjects high in generativity report greater happiness and satisfaction with their lives than do subjects low in generativity (McAdams, de St. Aubin, & Logan, 1993, p. 225).

A recent investigation by Snarey (1993) showed that good fathers—those who were caring and active in their children's physical, social, and intellectual development—were also happier in their marriages than were uninvolved fathers. Also, contrary to speculation in the print media that greater involvement in family life would hinder men's careers, their more active participation with their families was associated with greater occupational success (Snarey, 1993, pp. 349–353).

Other research by Snarey and his colleagues has focused on the relationship between male infertility in early adulthood and its implications for the subsequent attainment of generativity in middle adulthood (Snarey, Son, Kuehne, Hauser, & Vaillant, 1987). Although there are many possible ways to achieve generativity, a primary way for many males is to guide the development of their biological offspring. Thus, men who learn that they are infertile are likely to experience a sense of shock, disbelief, and helplessness, a feeling that their ability to choose their destiny has been denied. There are various styles of coping with this difficulty, and the investigators sought to determine which were most successful in helping such men resolve their anxieties and move toward the attainment of a sense of generativity in middle adulthood.

The study found that men who used parent-like substitute activities, by encouraging the development of other people's children (for example, by leading a youth group, teaching Sunday school, or becoming a Big Brother to a neighborhood boy), were the most likely to adopt a child and the least likely to divorce. They were also the most likely to experience a strong sense of generativity in middle adulthood. Conversely, men who exhibited self-centered substitute behavior were least likely to adopt a child, most likely to divorce, and least likely to achieve generativity in later life. Self-centered substitution styles included treating themselves as if they were their only child, becoming preoccupied with body building and health foods, and treating nonhuman objects (such as pets or cars) as if they were their babies.

In summary, this study showed clearly that generativity is not tied exclusively to the biological act of becoming a father. It can also be achieved through the substitution of altruistic, parent-like activities with other children or the adoption of children (Snarey, Son, Kuehne, Hauser, & Vaillant, 1987, pp. 593–603).

Ego Integrity in Late Adulthood

Focusing on the crisis experienced by individuals during the final stage of life, Walaskay, Whitbourne, and Nehrke (1983/1984) used an interview procedure to classify elderly men and women (of average age 75) as characterized by ego integrity or despair. Following the interview, all of the subjects responded to several personality questionnaires designed to assess their anxieties about death, their memories of earlier life stages, and their current levels of psychological well-being. As expected on the basis of Erikson's theory, the investigators found that despairing individuals had more negative memories, experienced greater death anxiety, and were more dissatisfied and maladjusted as compared to individuals high in ego integrity. In a subsequent study by Taft and Nehrke (1990, pp. 191–193), elderly people with a strong sense of ego integrity reported that they had reminisced about their past in order to resolve troubling experiences and arrive at a better understanding of their lives, whereas individuals filled with despair had not engaged in such life reviews. Furthermore, research by Santor and Zuroff (1994) shows that elderly people with a strong sense of ego integrity who accepted their past—including the facts that they could have worked harder and preferred that certain events had not occurred—experienced fewer feelings of hostility, resentment, and depression than did those who were less accepting. In brief, elderly individuals who accepted their past were more psychologically healthy than were those who did not (Santor & Zuroff, 1994, pp. 297–309).

Although research on the crises during middle and late adulthood is still relatively sparse, the available evidence shows consistent support for Erikson's ideas. Moreover, it rests on a much more substantial base of evidence in support of Erikson's theorizing about ego identity and intimacy in adolescence and early adulthood.

ASSESSMENT TECHNIQUES

Erikson always identified himself as a psychoanalyst and paid homage to Freud's insights and techniques. At the same time, he extended and modified many of Freud's concepts and methods and forged new ones of his own.

One basic difference in technique involves Erikson's view of the relationship between therapist and patient. He adopted a more egalitarian and personal stance toward his patients than did Freud. Whereas Freud tried to foster an impersonal, objective atmosphere by requiring his patients to recline on a couch while he remained seated in a chair out of sight, Erikson asked many of his patients to sit across from him in an easy chair. Freud was guided by his view of the consulting room as primarily a scientific laboratory, and only secondarily as a healing sanctuary. Erikson, however, believed that such neutrality on the part of the therapist can prove harmful to patients, because it may induce fears of losing their identity. In his view, patients can be helped only to the extent that the therapist becomes actual or real to them (Roazen, 1976, pp. 67–69). Thus, Erikson advocated a stance of "disciplined subjectivity," in which the therapist seeks to analyze and understand the patient's problems through empathy, as well as by examining historical events that have affected the patient's life.

Erikson used the Freudian concepts and procedures of transference, free association, and dream analysis in his work, but his usage differs in a number of respects from his mentor's. Especially different is his view of dreams and their meanings. Whereas Freud interpreted dreams as wish fulfillment of sexual needs, Erikson typically interpreted them in psychosocial terms as attempts to preserve and enhance identity. He agreed with Freud that dreams can be indicators of people's struggles to understand prior developmental crises; in Erikson's view, however, they are more likely to revolve around questions of identity than of sexuality. Erikson also differed from Freud in that he attached considerable importance to understanding the manifest content of dreams, rather than delving into the depths of dreamers' psyches to get at latent contents and their meanings. In Erikson's view, a dream's manifest content can reveal important information about current life problems and about the dreamer's view of his or her relationship with the therapist. Although Erikson acknowledged that analysis of latent content can lead to the discovery of important information about the sources of prior conflicts, he believed that dreams also have a healing function; they provide suggestions about how to cope with the future as well as the past (Roazen, 1976, p. 56).

Freud worked primarily with neurotic adults; Erikson was essentially a child analyst and, as such, he had to use techniques appropriate to that age group. Thus, Erikson utilized a variety of play-therapy techniques to increase his understanding of the unique problems of his young patients (Erikson, 1977). For example, he encouraged his patients to use toys to construct exciting scenes from their own imaginations. He found that these play constructions provide important clues to the sources of the child's problems. They also provide an opportunity for the child to create ideal situations and to master reality through experiment and planning (Erikson, 1963, p. 222). Thus, play enables youngsters to relive their past, to redeem their failures, and to strengthen their hopes for the future. It is not a recreational activity, but a work activity designed to enhance mastery.

Finally, Erikson was a pioneer in the use of **psychohistorical analysis** to increase our understanding of the lives of important historical figures. Erikson developed the procedure because he was interested in building a bridge between psychoanalysis and history. All too often, he maintained, historians have ignored the role of individual development in their attempts to explain historical events, while analysts have focused too narrowly on early personal development and have deemphasized the role of broader historical processes in their efforts to explain the behavior of individuals. Psychohistorical analysis was Erikson's attempt to overcome such myopia by applying his theory of ego development and its various crises throughout the life cycle to the biographies of prominent individuals, including Thomas Jefferson, Maxim Gorky, George Bernard Shaw, Martin Luther, Mahatma Gandhi, and Adolf Hitler. At the same time, the analyst seeks to understand their lives by judging them in terms of the unique historical periods in which they lived and wrote. Psychohistorical analysis takes a broad perspective that includes an appreciation of the tremendous impact of political, economic, social, and cultural forces on the development and personalities of historical figures. It also seeks to recognize and take into account the subtle ways in which the analysts' own values and experiences, and their own historical period, guide their interpretations of these people's lives (Erikson, 1974, pp. 14–15).

THEORY'S IMPLICATIONS FOR THERAPY

For Erikson, neurotics and psychotics are people with confused identities who lack a sense of mastery over their experiences. Their egos are fragmented and weak, and they are unable to relate well to others or to take their place in society. These difficulties are an outgrowth of their failure to resolve successfully one or more of the crises inherent in their life cycles.

Failure to develop a sense of basic trust in the first stage of life, Erikson believed, can lead to serious pathology in later life, including schizophrenia. In this case, failure to establish trust in others eventually leads the person to break with external reality. To help such a person, Erikson maintained, the therapist must teach the patient to trust the world again (Evans, 1967, p. 55).

In the case of paranoia, Erikson saw a fixation in development "somewhere between the hope and will state" (Evans, 1967, p. 56). Paranoids are unable to overcome the suspicion that the adults who tried to train their will during the anal stage were really trying to break it. If confronted later in life with restricted opportunities (such as not being able to find a job), they are likely to believe that others are out to get them—to stop them from demonstrating their ability to succeed independently (Evans, 1967, pp. 56–57).

Erikson believed that obsessive-compulsive neuroses also result from fixations at the anal stage, which stem from parental over-harshness in their training procedures. Obsessive-compulsives are given to stubbornness, procrastination, and ritualistic repetitions as means of regaining control of their lives (Erikson, 1968b, p. 111). Treatment requires not only identification of the sources of the conflict with parents, but also encouragement by the therapist of the patient's own capabilities and freedom to exercise will without feelings of shame and doubt (Evans, 1967, p. 58).

Major adjustment problems in adolescence typically center on the lack of clear occupational goals. This difficulty may be traced, in part, to a failure to develop a sense of self-control over one's choices or to a lack of imagination and direction concerning one's ideals and goals during the muscular-anal and locomotor-genital stages. These problems may be compounded by a strong sense of inferiority about one's competence to perform tasks well, as a result of failure to grow during the latency period. Under these circumstances, confused adolescents faced with the tremendous pressures of making a decision may react badly. They may drop out of school, leave jobs, stay out all night, turn to destructive acts such as vandalism and robbery, or withdraw into bizarre and horrible moods.

Erikson believed that adolescents' only salvation in this situation is for friends, family, therapist, and judiciary personnel to avoid typing them with diagnostic labels, such as borderline psychotic or schizoid, and to accept the fact that there are special social and cultural conditions that trigger such behavior (Erikson, 1968b, p. 132). The use of labels may force young people to embrace a negative identity more strongly, thereby exacerbating their problems; what they need from the therapist is sympathetic treatment and encouragement. At the core of therapeutic treatment is the patient's need to rebuild a personal identity. This is an extremely difficult task and, because it is so painful, patients typically engage in resistive behavior; usually, they try to convince the therapist that their negative identities are real and necessary. Erikson believed that the therapist should acknowledge the validity of this contention, but not let the patient conclude that this negative identity is "all there is to me." The therapist should treat such patients with understanding and affection, but not permissively; it is important to point out firmly the patients' strengths and to indicate directions for positive growth (Erikson, 1968b, pp. 212–216). The therapist should encourage patients to develop their talents through social experimentation; such activities typically result in increased ego strength.

A major contributing factor to the development of neurosis in young adults is their failure to relate intimately to others. Neurotics are often lonely, isolated people who have been unable to accept the risks and responsibilities associated with the establishment of truly intimate relationships. They lack the ability to love and to establish deep, enduring friendships. Because sexual relations are part of the expression of mature love, we might expect such individuals to experience difficulties in the form of impotence, premature ejaculation, or frigidity. These problems can be overcome only when these disturbed and distressed individuals have undergone therapeutic experiences that strengthen their sense of identity. Erikson believed that only people with strong egos are capable of coping with the disappointments, hurts, and possibilities of rejection associated with opening oneself up to another.

Neurosis during middle adulthood is associated with an inability to experience satisfaction in guiding and helping the next generation. Such self-absorbed individuals feel strongly that life should have greater meaning and joy, yet they experience boredom and stagnation. Treatment of these individuals focuses on the early-childhood origins of their excessive self-love and lack of trust, which now prevent them from extending themselves to others.

Finally, pathology in late adulthood is correlated with fragmentation of the ego. Elderly neurotics are still unable to adapt themselves to earlier defeats and to integrate these experiences into their self-concepts. They are likely to feel that they have not accomplished all their goals and that there is not enough time to rectify the situation. They fear death. Treatment is aimed at helping the patient see that each life cycle is unique, that it permits no substitutions, and that death is an inevitable part of it (Erikson, 1968b, p. 139).

EVALUATIVE COMMENTS

We now examine the scientific worth of Erikson's theory.

Comprehensiveness An imaginative and original thinker, Erikson created a theory that is indeed comprehensive. It addresses itself to a wide variety of phenomena, both normal and abnormal, and seeks to account for the biological, social, cultural, and historical factors that jointly determine personality development and functioning. The range of phenomena explored includes race relations, mythology, national identity, play activities, marriage, divorce, incest, sexual relations, occupational choice, academic success and failure, love, womanhood, and cross-cultural rituals. In addition to its focus on different types of psychopathology, it also makes an effort to describe and explain healthy personality functioning.

Precision and testability   Erikson's theory fails to meet the criterion of precision and testability. It is populated by highly abstract concepts that have few clear referents. The identity concept is particularly nebulous. At one point, Erikson described it as "wholeheartedness, wholemindedness, wholesomeness, and the like. As a Gestalt, then, wholeness emphasizes a sound, organic, progressive mutuality between diversified functions and parts within an entirety, the boundaries of which are open and fluent" (Erikson, 1964, p. 92). At another, he defined it as "the capacity of the ego to sustain sameness and continuity in the face of changing fate" (Erikson, 1964, p. 96). In another context, it refers to the "things which we want to become, and we know we are supposed to be, and which . . . we can fulfill" (Evans, 1967, p. 32). Evidently, the concept is extremely complex and does not lend itself readily to precise measurement. As a result, the theory is difficult to test.

Difficulties in testing also arise because the theory's general propositions and the specific hypotheses associated with them are often stated rather vaguely. For example, Erikson maintained that fixations that occur during specific stages influence later character development in specific ways. This would suggest a number of distinct character types, each with a unique set of personality characteristics or traits, but nowhere has Erikson had much to say about these implications of his theorizing. In fairness to Erikson, however, he tackled an enormously difficult task—namely, the description and explanation of the eight stages of ego development as they are influenced by complicated biological, social, cultural, and historical forces. Nor does the ambiguity of his concepts mean that they are useless. We have seen, for example, how his ideas about ego identity in adolescence and about intimacy in young adulthood have been refined and utilized successfully in testing aspects of the theory.

Parsimony   Although we can admire the scope of Erikson's theory, its explanatory base is rather limited. Most phenomena are explained in terms of identity formation, disintegration, or integration, often in post hoc fashion. The identity concept seems to carry too heavy a burden, and thus the theory is not parsimonious.

Empirical validity   Not enough research has been conducted to test the richness of Erikson's theorizing. There are several reasons for this. First, Erikson's formulations are highly abstract, and it is difficult to convert them into testable terms. Second, it is difficult and costly to conduct the longitudinal studies necessary to validate his theorizing about the developmental process. Third, psychologists tend to use readily available populations for their research; as a result, most of the tests of Erikson's theory have focused on adolescents and young adults rather than middle-aged adults and the elderly. Empirical research on the crises of adolescence and young adulthood, however, has produced findings that are highly consistent with Erikson's theory. In addition, researchers have begun to address Erikson's ideas about middle and late adulthood, and the preliminary evidence is supportive.

Heuristic value   Erikson's theory has had strong heuristic value; it has generated interest among scholars in many disciplines. His ethical concerns, expressed in his discussions of the various virtues associated with development, have stimulated thinking among theologians and moral philosophers. His extensive analysis of the meaning of rituals in various societies has influenced cultural anthropologists. His use of psychohistorical analysis to study political, religious, and literary figures has had a considerable impact on historians. Within psychology, Erikson's work has also contributed greatly to lifespan psychology and the development of adult psychology. Perhaps the most significant impact of his ego psychology is that it has served to broaden the theoretical base of psychoanalysis and has influenced the thinking of colleagues within the psychoanalytic community.

Applied value   Erikson's work has had tremendous practical impact in the areas of child psychology and psychiatry, vocational counseling, marriage counseling, education, social work, and business. His ideas about the stages of ego development and their inherent conflicts have stimulated clinicians to develop treatment programs for children, adolescents, and older adults. Vocational counselors make use of Erikson's provocative thinking in advising young people about occupational goals. Mental health consultants conduct workshops with business employees to discuss ways of overcoming the sense of stagnation that many of them experience midway through their careers, and use Erikson's ideas to help them achieve increased feelings of generativity.

Erikson's work has also been popular with students and other members of the general public; it helps to increase their understanding of the kinds of stresses they are likely to experience at a given stage in their lives and provides recommendations for alleviating these stresses so that positive growth can be achieved.

DISCUSSION QUESTIONS

1. What is an identity crisis? Is it a typical experience for adolescents, as Erikson claimed?
2. Do you agree with Erikson that women have innate maternal feelings that, if repressed, could produce feelings of anxiety and dissatisfaction?
3. Erikson emphasized the role of the mother in creating a sense of basic trust or mistrust in children. What is the role of the father in child care? Is it as important as the mother's? Is it different? In what ways?
4. In Erikson's view, the ability to love someone presupposes a strong identity; since many adolescents have confused identities, they cannot truly love anyone. Do you agree or disagree with this conclusion? Why?
5. If Erikson took the position that healthy, intimate relationships involve a mutuality of orgasm with a loved partner of the opposite sex, what was his view of homosexual relationships?
6. In your opinion, does organized religion exploit the masses in order to achieve its own selfish ends? Cite reasons for your answer.
7. Do you agree with Erikson's belief that the most disturbing part of adolescence centers on the inability to decide on an occupational identity? Is this a major problem for you or any of your friends?
8. In what ways are adolescents with weak egos remarkably clannish, intolerant, and cruel in their exclusion of people who are different?
9. Which one of Marcia's identity statuses, if any, characterizes you or your friends? Do you agree that foreclosures are closest to their parents?
10. Why is Erikson's theory of ego development and functioning more optimistic in its view of human beings than is Freud's position? Do you think that Erikson's optimism is warranted?

GLOSSARY

autonomy Sense of independence that individuals experience if they successfully resolve conflicts during the second stage of life.

basic mistrust Belief that others cannot be trusted; it results from the mother's failure to act in a consistent and affectionate manner toward her infant.

basic trust Belief that others are reliable; it stems from the receipt of consistent and affectionate treatment by mothers during the first stage of development.

care Virtue in healthy middle-aged people that leads them to feel a concern for the welfare of the younger generation.

competence Strength in healthy children involving the ability to make things and complete tasks.

crisis Turning point in individual development in which conflicts can be resolved positively, thereby strengthening the ego, or negatively, thereby weakening it.

despair Negative outcome in the last stage of life for individuals who have been unable to resolve their conflicts constructively; it includes the fear of death and the belief that their lives have been failures and that they are unable to rectify the situation.

ego integrity Feeling by the elderly that, on balance, their lives have had positive meaning and have been worth living.

ego psychology Theory that the ego is not always controlled by id impulses, but often functions independently of these urges, thereby providing the individual with an opportunity for creative action and positive growth.

enmeshment Fusion with another person, in which one's own sense of self and identity is lost.

epigenetic principle Principle that there is a genetically determined sequence to human growth and that each stage in the sequence unfolds in an invariant order.

fidelity Sense of loyalty and commitment to friends and coworkers and to a value system; fidelity results from the positive resolution of conflicts during adolescence.

foreclosure Identity status within adolescence in which individuals who have never experienced a crisis concerning their goals have nevertheless made firm commitments concerning them.

generativity The productivity of middle-aged adults, including the production of children and guidance of the younger generation and also the production of ideas, art, books, and so forth, with the implication that this legacy will live on and benefit the next generation.

guilt Feeling of wrongdoing experienced by youngsters when they show inappropriate behavior and are punished for it.

hope Optimistic belief that persistent wishes and goals can be attained.

identity Multifaceted concept that involves knowing who you are and where you are going, as well as what you are not and do not want to be; the unified sense of self as uniquely different from others.

identity achievement Identity status within adolescence in which individuals have undergone a period of crisis and, as a result, have developed firm commitments concerning their life goals.

identity crisis A developmental turning point, associated primarily with adolescence, in which basic choices need to be made by the person in various life areas. For example, primary decisions and commitments need to be made about a career, a mate, and an ideology to live by.

identity diffusion Identity status within adolescence in which individuals are not actively in crisis about their life goals and have not made any commitments concerning them.

industry Sense of satisfaction that accrues to children as a result of being actively engaged in learning new skills and completing tasks.

inferiority Negative outcome of the fourth stage of development; in this state, children feel that they are incompetent failures.

initiative Feeling that one has control over one's outcomes and can therefore be the source of ideas and action.

intimacy Ability of people with mature egos to become one with their partners without losing their separate sense of identity.

intimate individuals Individuals whose relationships are characterized by depth and commitment.

isolated individuals Individuals who have withdrawn from social relationships.

isolation Inability to take chances with one's identity by sharing true intimacy.

love Ability to trust and share one's experiences and identity with a partner so that both parties are enhanced.

merger individuals People who have lost their sense of identity and who live through their partners.

moratorium Time of exploration during adolescence in which individuals are experiencing a crisis concerning their life goals and are actively considering alternatives in an attempt to arrive at decisions.

negative identity   Commitment to values and roles that are unacceptable to society.

preintimate individuals   Individuals who have deep relationships, but are reluctant to commit themselves to enduring relationships.

pseudointimate individuals   People who have enduring relationships, but whose relationships lack depth.

psychohistorical analysis   Erikson's technique for analyzing the lives of historical figures on the basis of his theory of ego development.

purpose   Virtue that emerges when parents guide their children into socially desirable activities and, as a result, the children set (in a preliminary fashion) life goals.

role confusion   State in adolescence in which young people cannot decide on their proper life roles.

shame and doubt   Negative state in which youngsters feel unable to make their own judgments or to exercise control over their lives, as a result of faulty parenting in the anal stage.

stagnation   Feeling of being unproductive and useless that stems from an inability to care for something or someone.

stereotyped individuals   Individuals whose relationships are shallow and exploitative.

totalism   Premature, unquestioning commitment by adolescents to simplistic ideologies and ideas as a means of reducing their own painful feelings of confusion.

virtue   Strengthening of the ego that emerges following the successful resolution of a crisis associated with one of the developmental stages.

will   Virtue that involves youngsters' determination to exercise free choice in making decisions and not be controlled by others.

wisdom   Virtue that emerges following successful resolution of the crisis of old age; the ability to put one's life experiences into a life-cycle perspective, to accept that one's life, in general, had unity and meaning and that it was worth living.

SUGGESTED READINGS

Erikson, E. H. (1963). *Childhood and society* (2nd ed.). New York: Norton.
Erikson, E. H. (1964). *Insight and responsibility*. New York: Norton.
Erikson, E. H. (1968). *Identity: Youth and crisis*. New York: Norton.

Evans, R. (1967). *Dialogue with Erik Erikson*. New York: Harper & Row.

Marcia, J. E., Waterman, A. S., Matteson, D. R., Archer, S. L., & Orlofsky, J. L. (Eds.) (1993). *Ego identity: A handbook for psychosocial research*. New York: Springer-Verlag.

REFERENCES

Adams, G. R., & Fitch, S. A. (1982). Ego stage and identity status development: A cross-sequential analysis. *Journal of Personality and Social Psychology, 43,* 574–583.

Adams, G. R., & Fitch, S. A. (1983). Psychological environments of university departments: Effects on college students' identity status and ego stage development. *Journal of Personality and Social Psychology, 44,* 1266–1275.

Archer, S. L. (1989). Gender differences in identity development: Issues of process, domain and timing. *Journal of Adolescence, 12,* 117–138.

Berzonsky, M. D. (1992). Identity style and coping strategies. *Journal of Personality, 60,* 771–788.

Berzonsky, M. D., & Neimeyer, G. J. (1988). Identity status and personal construct systems. *Journal of Adolescence, 11,* 195–204.

Blustein, D. L., & Phillips, S. D. (1990). Relation between ego identity statuses and decision-making styles. *Journal of Counseling Psychology, 37,* 160–168.

Bourne, E. (1978). The state of research on ego identity: A review and appraisal: Part 1. *Journal of Youth and Adolescence, 7,* 223–251.

Coles, R. (1970). *Erik H. Erikson: The growth of his work*. Boston: Little, Brown.

Cote, J. E., & Levine, C. (1983). Marcia and Erikson: The relationships among ego identity status, neuroticism, dogmatism, and purpose in life. *Journal of Youth and Adolescence, 12,* 43–53.

Erikson, E. H. (1963). *Childhood and society* (2nd ed.). New York: Norton.

Erikson, E. H. (1964). *Insight and responsibility*. New York: Norton.

Erikson, E. H. (1968a). Identity and identity diffusion. In C. Gordon & K. J. Gergen (Eds.), *The self in social interaction* (pp. 197–205). New York: Wiley.

Erikson, E. H. (1968b). *Identity: Youth and crisis*. New York: Norton.

Erikson, E. H. (1974). *Dimensions of a new identity: The 1973 Jefferson lectures in the humanities*. New York: Norton.

Erikson, E. H. (1975). *Life history and the historical moment*. New York: Norton.

Erikson, E. H. (1977). *Toys and reasons: Stages in the ritualization of experience*. New York: Norton.

Evans, R. (1967). *Dialogue with Erik Erikson*. New York: Harper & Row.

Howard, J. A., Blumstein, P., & Schwartz, P. (1986). Sex, power, and influence tactics in intimate relationships. *Journal of Personality and Social Psychology, 51,* 102–109.

Kowaz, A. M., & Marcia, J. E. (1991). Development and validation of a measure of Eriksonian industry. *Journal of Personality and Social Psychology, 60,* 390–397.

Kroger, J. (1989). *Identity in adolescence: The balance between self and other.* London: Routledge.

Levitz-Jones, E. M., & Orlofsky, J. L. (1985). Separation-individuation and intimacy capacity in college women. *Journal of Personality and Social Psychology, 49,* 156–169.

Marcia, J. E. (1966). Development and validation of ego-identity status. *Journal of Personality and Social Psychology, 3,* 551–558.

Marcia, J. E. (1967). Ego identity status: Relationship to change in self-esteem, "general maladjustment" and authoritarianism. *Journal of Personality, 35,* 118–133.

Marcia, J. E. (1993). The status of the statuses: Research review. In J. E. Marcia, A. S. Waterman, D. R. Matteson, S. L. Archer, & J. L. Orlofsky (Eds.), *Ego identity: A handbook for psychosocial research* (pp. 22–41). New York: Springer-Verlag.

Marcia, J. E. (1994). Ego identity and object relations. In J. M. Masling and R. F. Bornstein (Eds.), *Empirical perspectives on object relations theory* (pp. 59–103). Washington, DC: American Psychological Association.

Marcia, J. E., & Friedman, M. L. (1970). Ego identity status in college women. *Journal of Personality, 38,* 249–263.

McAdams, D. P., de St. Aubin, E., & Logan, R. L. (1993). Generativity among young, midlife, and older adults. *Psychology and Aging, 8,* 221–230.

O'Connell, A. N. (1976). The relationship between life style and identity synthesis and resynthesis in traditional, neotraditional, and nontraditional women. *Journal of Personality, 44,* 675–688.

Orlofsky, J. L. (1976). Intimacy status: Relationship to interpersonal perception. *Journal of Youth and Adolescence, 5,* 73–88.

Orlofsky, J. L. (1978). The relationship between intimacy and antecedent personality components. *Adolescence, 8,* 420–441.

Orlofsky, J. L. (1993). Intimacy status: Theory and research. In J. E. Marcia, A. S. Waterman, D. R. Matteson, S. L. Archer, & J. L. Orlofsky (Eds.), *Ego identity: A handbook for psychosocial research* (pp. 111–133). New York: Springer-Verlag.

Orlofsky, J. L., Marcia, J. E., & Lesser, I. (1973). Ego identity status and the intimacy versus isolation crisis of young adulthood. *Journal of Personality and Social Psychology, 27,* 211–219.

Prager, K. J. (1986). Intimacy status: Its relationship to locus of control, self-disclosure, and anxiety in adults. *Personality and Social Psychology Bulletin, 12,* 91–109.

Prager, K. J. (1989). Intimacy status and couple communication. *Journal of Social and Personal Relationships, 6,* 435–449.

Pulkkinen, L., & Ronka, A. (1994). Personal control over development, identity formation, and future orientation as components of life orientation: A developmental approach. *Developmental Psychology, 30,* 260–271.

Read, D., Adams, G. R., & Dobson, W. R. (1984). Ego identity, personality, and social influence style. *Journal of Personality and Social Psychology, 46,* 169–177.

Roazen, P. (1976). *Erik H. Erikson: The power and limits of a vision.* New York: Free Press.

Rosenthal, D. A., Gurney, R. M., & Moore, S. M. (1981). From trust to intimacy: A new inventory for examining Erikson's stages of psychosocial development. *Journal of Youth and Adolescence, 9,* 87–99.

Rowe, I., & Marcia, J. E. (1980). Ego identity status, formal operations, and moral development. *Journal of Youth and Adolescence, 9,* 87–99.

Santor, D. A., & Zuroff, D. C. (1994). Depressive symptoms: Effects of negative affectivity and failing to accept the past. *Journal of Personality Assessment, 63,* 294–312.

Schenkel, S., & Marcia, J. E. (1972). Attitudes toward premarital intercourse in determining ego identity status in college women. *Journal of Personality, 40,* 472–482.

Slugoski, B. R., Marcia, J. E., & Koopman, R. F. (1984). Cognitive and social interactional characteristics of ego identity statuses in college. *Journal of Personality and Social Psychology, 47,* 646–661.

Snarey, J. (1993). *How fathers care for the next generation: A four-decade study.* Cambridge, MA: Harvard University Press.

Snarey, J., Son, L., Kuehne, V. S., Hauser, S., & Vaillant, G. (1987). The role of parenting in men's psychosocial development: A longitudinal study of early adulthood infertility and midlife generativity. *Developmental Psychology, 23,* 593–603.

Taft, L. B., & Nehrke, M. F. (1990). Reminiscence, life review, and ego integrity in nursing home residents. *International Journal of Aging and Human Development, 30,* 189–196.

Van de Water, D. A., & McAdams, D. P. (1989). Generativity and Erikson's "Belief in the species." *Journal of Research in Personality, 23,* 435–449.

Violato, C., & Holden, W. B. (1988). A confirmatory factor analysis of a four-factor model of adolescent concerns. *Journal of Youth and Adolescence, 17,* 101–113.

Walaskay, M., Whitbourne, S. K., & Nehrke, M. F. (1983/1984). Construction and validation of an ego integrity interview. *International Journal of Aging and Human Development, 18,* 61–72.

Wallerstein, R. S. (1995). Obituary: Erik Erikson (1902–1994). *International Journal of Psychoanalysis, 76,* 173–175.

Waterman, A. S. (1982). Identity development from adolescence to adulthood: An extension of theory and a review of research. *Developmental Psychology, 18,* 341–358.

Waterman, A. S. (1985). Identity in the context of adolescent psychology. In

A. S. Waterman (Ed.), *Identity in adolescence: Processes and contents* (pp. 5–24). San Francisco: Jossey-Bass.

Waterman, A. S. (1993). Developmental perspectives on identity formation: From adolescence to adulthood. In J. E. Marcia, A. S. Waterman, D. R. Matteson, S. L. Archer, & J. L. Orlofsky (Eds.), *Ego identity: A handbook for psychosocial research* (pp. 42–68). New York: Springer-Verlag.

Waterman, A. S., Geary, P. S., & Waterman, C. K. (1974). Longitudinal study of changes in ego identity status from the freshman to the senior year at college. *Developmental Psychology, 10,* 387–392.

Waterman, A. S., & Waterman, C. K. (1970). The relationship between ego identity status and satisfaction with college. *The Journal of Education Research, 64,* 165–168.

Weisstein, N. (1975). Psychology constructs the female, or the fantasy life of the male psychologist (with some attention to the fantasies of his friends, the male biologist and the male anthropologist). In I. Cohen (Ed.), *Perspectives on psychology* (pp. 318–331). New York: Praeger.

Kohut's Self Psychology

BIOGRAPHICAL SKETCH

Heinz Kohut was born in Vienna, Austria on May 3, 1913. His father, Felix, was a highly successful businessman and a very cultured person. A gifted pianist, Felix was heading for a career in music when World War I broke out and he had to enter the military. As a result of his service obligation, Kohut's father was absent much of the time starting when Heinz was 1 year old and lasting until he was 5. Even after Felix returned home from the war, he remained a rather distant figure in his son's life, and Heinz had ambivalent feelings about him. Heinz also had very ambivalent feelings toward his mother, Else Lampl. An only child, Heinz felt that his mother was oppressively close at times, but distant at others.

Kohut's education was remarkable. As a member of one of Vienna's elite families, Heinz was provided with an education in the classics while he was in high school. He studied French and then, as a young man, spent a full year in Paris perfecting his skills. He was also exposed to eight years of Latin and six of Greek. He spent time studying literature, music, art, and history. From the time he was 8 until he was 14, his parents hired a tutor to stimulate him intellectually. Heinz and the tutor would go to the opera and to art museums; they also talked and played intellectual games as they strolled the streets of beautiful Vienna. At the time of his graduation from high school, Heinz was at or near the top of his class academically and was also active in athletics; he was good at track and he boxed well.

At 19, Kohut entered the University of Vienna and eventually earned an M.D. degree in 1938; he received his principal training in neurology. He also became highly interested in psychoanalysis during this period. Kohut never knew or met Freud, but he admired him tremendously and consciously tried to model himself after his idol. In fact, Kohut showed up at the train station in Vienna when Freud and his family began their journey to England to escape the Nazis, in 1938. Kohut fondly recalled, in later years, that Freud looked out of the train window and saw Kohut and a friend standing on the platform. Kohut tipped his hat, and Freud tipped his hat in return as the train rolled out of the station. Already, it was clear that Kohut was on a mission to follow in Freud's footsteps and to promote psychoanalysis as a science and therapy.

In 1940, Kohut left Vienna and came to the United States. He settled in Chicago, grew to love the city with its rich and diverse cultural life, and lived there until his death. He was a lecturer in the Department of Psychiatry at the University of Chicago, and a faculty member and training and supervising analyst at the Chicago Institute for Psychoanalysis. During his professional life, he worked tirelessly as an administrator promoting psychoanalysis, had a full clinical practice, and taught classes in psychoanalytic theory. In the classroom, Dr. Kohut made an indelible impact on his students. He was a brilliant teacher and could weave an entire lecture from just about any comment or question. Taking every question seriously, he tried to put himself in the questioner's shoes.

Eventually, Kohut decided to publish his ideas. They were the product of his intense, lifelong concern with the task of understanding another human being. His major theoretical works, *The Analysis of the Self* (1971) and *The Restoration of the Self* (1977), emphasize his new perspective on narcissism and emphasize the importance of the role of an empathic environment on personality development and mental health. Published posthumously, *How Does Analysis Cure?* (1984) presents an elaboration of his ideas about the nature of psychoanalytic cure, a further elaboration of the concept of empathy, a clarification of the status and meaning of the Oedipal complex within self psychology, a presentation of his ideas on the nature of defenses and resistances, and a revision of his ideas about the alterego transference. Finally, *Self Psychology and the Humanities* (1985) details how the humanities—particularly history, literature, and art—inspired and provided affirmation of his neoanalytic views.

Kohut received many honors and awards in his life, from being elected as President of the American Psychoanalytic Association to being awarded the Heinz Hartmann prize of the New York Psychoanalytic Association. As he grew older, he turned down many other awards and ceremonies, so that he could devote all of his energies to his work. He had a single-minded purpose—to advance psychoanalysis as a science and as a therapy through the addition of his ideas on the self. His single-mindedness often led to conflicts with some of his colleagues, who accused him of failing to recognize the contributions of his peers in the discipline and sometimes even appropriating and publishing others' ideas as his own. His original ideas were also highly controversial, however, and he faced an unrelenting barrage of criticism from within the analytic community. Many analysts, especially those with orthodox orientations, rejected his views. He lost many of his valued colleagues and friends, primarily because he dared to express ideas that deviated from the classical psychoanalytic position. Kohut died on October 8, 1981 (Goldberg, 1982, pp. 257–258; Strozier, 1985, pp. 3–12).

CONCEPTS AND PRINCIPLES

Self Psychology: The Newest Development in Classical Psychoanalysis

Kohut's **self psychology** focuses primarily on understanding and explaining the development of the self and its impact on the person's mental health within a context of human interaction. Kohut strongly criticized classical psychoanalytic theory in many respects and saw his own work as more accurately recognizing the role of narcissism in normal adult psychology. As Kohut's ideas developed, they involved reinterpretations of many of the phenomena originally examined by Freud. For example, Kohut criticized Freud's libido theory, which maintained that individuals are driven by sexual and aggressive instincts to gratify their urges on various targets, usually other people. In Kohut's theory, individuals do not seek relationships with other people primarily to gratify these instinctual needs. Instead, satisfaction of sexual and aggressive needs is secondary to people's basic needs for human relatedness. Whereas Freud believed that the frustration and repression of sexual and aggressive instincts caused pathological behavior, Kohut believed that it was threats and damage to the self that produced aberrant sexual and aggressive behavior.

Kohut also thought that Freud's preoccupation with instinctual needs in personality development caused him to obscure the needs that all individuals have for contact and affiliation with others. Indeed, there is scientific evidence that the development of affectional bonds between parents and their children is not usually an outgrowth of libidinal aims, but rather is a critical, independent aspect of development that expresses biological propensities to establish links to people (Eagle, 1984, pp. 15–16).

Kohut believed that his theory modifies and extends not only classical psychoanalytic theory, but also important aspects of **ego psychology.** You may recall that Erikson's psychology focuses on the emergence of a strong ego identity as individuals resolve the crises inherent in the developmental process. For Erikson, the ego was the key theoretical concept. It acts, when healthy, to unify and direct personality functioning. In Kohut's theory, this unifying and directing role is attributed to the self and not to the ego. But aren't these two concepts interchangeable synonyms? In Kohut's opinion, the answer is no. He believed that there are important distinctions between the self and the ego, and that the self is the more fundamental concept. In this view, it might be said that the id, ego, and superego are all facets and agencies of an underlying self; their actions are controlled and directed by the self when it is functioning in a healthy way. Coherent functioning of the self structure leads to feelings of well-being and also secondarily to an increase in the strength and dominance of the ego. The ego then provides the individual with the means to solve his or her problems realistically and creatively. When the self is damaged psychologically, it becomes fragmented and enfeebled, the ego fails to function properly, and the individual is unable to cope with his or her problems in an adaptive and satisfying way (Kohut, 1971, p. 119). Thus, Kohut postulated that many of the insights achieved by an ego psychology like Erikson's complement his own theory (Kohut, 1984, p. 65).

Self Psychology as Object-Relations Theory

Psychoanalytic models of personality development may be divided into several categories. One kind is called **object-relations theory.** A fundamental premise of object-relations models is that **object relations** are central to psychoanalytic thinking and treatment. However, the meanings associated with the term *object relations* vary considerably from theory to theory. It is important to clarify these meanings so that we can better understand the various models. For example, in classical psychoanalysis, an object refers to a target of the instincts, that is, of sexual or aggressive drives. Thus, in the Freudian sense, an object could be another person (for example, one's husband or wife), a part or parts of the person (for example, breasts or a penis), or a thing (for example, in the discharge of aggressive impulses by destroying a chair).

For object-relations theorists like Kohut, however, objects are defined as other people. These people may be internal or external to the individual and may be real or imagined. External objects are real people. Internal objects are mental representations of people or things that exist within the self. They are called **self-objects** because the individual experiences them as an integral part of the self. Self-objects generally denote psychologically important people who support the cohesion of the self. They help individuals regulate tensions and stresses that confront them and that they are incapable of handling. For infants, these self-objects are the parents, who minister to their infants' needs by feeding, bathing, clothing, and comforting them. By doing so, the parents are able to reduce the infants' tensions and stresses. Later in childhood, as children actively interact with relatives, siblings, friends, teachers, and so forth, these individuals have the potential to become self-objects. In adulthood, the range of potential self-objects is expanded even further and may include boyfriends or girlfriends, spouses, and political, religious, military, and academic leaders. Thus, Kohut maintained that the need for self-objects does not fade with maturity. Self-objects are required throughout the lifespan to help us cope with the particular problems and issues that confront us (Leider, 1995, pp. 26–27). While self-objects are required to help us cope with our own difficulties, we need to transform them gradually and integrate them into our personalities so that we can act in psychologically healthy ways.

PERSONALITY DEVELOPMENT

Pre-Oedipal Development of the Nuclear Self

Kohut maintained that, strictly speaking, the neonate has no self (Kohut & Wolf, 1978, p. 416). However, the social environment into which the child is born also includes the primary caregivers, who treat the child as if he or she had a self, by giving the child a name and by taking care of his or her bodily needs. Through those interactions, a rudimentary self begins to crystallize. As reliably as they can, the parents care for the child's needs, laugh and talk to the child, play with the child, and comfort and console the child when he or she is distressed. Thus, there is often an immediate and strong bond between the child and his or her parents. Without their general care, support, and love, the infant would soon perish. This positive interactive process between the child and the parents contributes to the development of a core or **nuclear self** within the first two or three years of life.

More specifically, the mother is usually the primary self-object, the one who ministers to the infant's needs, although Kohut pointed out that the father and other adults can respond adequately to the baby's needs (Kohut, 1985, p. 167). Initially the infant exists in a state of **primary narcissism**—in a state of self-love that is perfect and blissful; all of the child's needs are fulfilled by the mother. Inevitably, however, the equilibrium of this primary narcissism is disturbed by the unavoidable delays and shortcomings of the mother's care (Kohut, 1971, p. 64). For example, she may not always respond to the infant's cries for food or drink immediately because of an emergency elsewhere in the home, or she may not always return the infant's smile because she is tired at the end of a long day of household chores. She may neglect to comfort the child when in distress, to put the appropriate winter clothing on the child for an outing on a snowy, windy day, and so forth. Kohut maintained that, under these conditions, the infant tries to remove the disequilibrium, but this requires the responsiveness of the self-object. If the mother is not sufficiently responsive, a traumatic state ensues; the infant then tries to restore the original state of perfection by the establishment of a **grandiose self.**

The grandiose self involves the unconscious belief of the child that he or she is great and perfect. The child also has a **need to be mirrored,** that is, a yearning to be admired and to have an impact on others. According to Kohut, it is usually the mother who does the mirroring for both sexes. She mirrors the child by reflecting, echoing, approving, and confirming his or her innate sense of greatness (Kohut & Wolf, 1978, p. 414). By her mirroring and empathizing, she makes it possible for the child to internalize others' approval and admiration. The child now feels worthwhile. This process is facilitated by the mother's **empathy.** She must be able to put herself in the child's place, to recognize and understand the child's exhibitionistic needs to be admired, and to try to meet them. Such mirroring is necessary if the child is going to start developing in a healthy way.

However, continued healthy development also depends on the mother's efforts to support realistic change in the child's grandiose self by setting limits on the expressions of his or her strongly unrealistic exhibitionistic needs and by helping the child to accept the realistic limits of his or her actual abilities and talents. Kohut said that such discipline involves **optimal frustration,** which means that the mother handles the immature, exhibitionistic needs of her child by adopting a calming, soothing, and loving attitude as she makes clear the unrealistic nature of the child's strivings rather than by acting aggressively toward the child (Kohut & Seitz, 1963, pp. 138–139). In other words, the child's unrealistic grandiosity and exhibitionism must be modified by gradual frustrations accompanied by loving support (Kohut, 1966, p. 253). As a result of these phase-appropriate optimal frustrations, the child undergoes **transmuting internalization,** which means that he or she can now decathect (disengage) some of the primitive narcissistic libido from the grandiose self and invest it in an emerging new psychic structure—a more realistic and independent nuclear self. In other words, optimal frustrations in parental responsiveness can facilitate maturation because, when self-object support is phase-appropriate and gradually limited, the child can learn to do without assistance what previously had been done for him or her by the parents (Watson, Biderman, & Sawrie, 1994, p. 701). For example, consider a boy with the grandiose belief that he is so special that his parents should only pay attention to him and should cater to his every need and demand. Such a boy could demand that his parents wash, feed, and dress him each morning. While such a grandiose wish and related parental behavior is developmentally appropriate during infancy, it is clearly inappropriate once the boy is 2 or 3 years old. At this point, the parents would have to begin gently frustrating him by firmly insisting that he learn how to wash, feed, and dress himself. If their encouragement and insistence is successful, the boy will eventually begin to learn a set of skills that allow him to see himself more realistically as an initiator of action and as competent.

Failure of the mother to empathize with her child and her inability to appropriately mirror the child because of her own pathology produces a lowering of his or her self-esteem; then, in a defensive attempt to ward off feelings of inadequacy, the child fixates on the grandiose self and, as a result, behaviors associated with an unbridled, primitive, grandiose, exhibitionistic self are enhanced and displayed. Consider the inadequate boy who protects himself by acting as though everyone is his slave and under his control. He may become bossy, throw frequent temper tantrums when he doesn't get his way, and even hit his parents or others when they oppose him. A mother with strong dependency needs of her own may fail to point out to him, in a loving and yet firm way, that his behavior is wrong and will not be permitted. Instead, she may overindulge him. She may laugh and comply with his demands when he becomes bossy, consider his temper tantrums cute, and ignore his hitting behavior because of her fear of losing his approval or love. Given her own pathological needs, she doesn't dare to frustrate him and so he fails to recognize and learn that there are limits on his behavior. The formation of a more realistic nuclear self is precluded, and consequently his narcissistic libido remains invested in a primitive, unmodified grandiose and exhibitionistic self.

Or consider the case of a girl who does not receive appropriate mirroring from her mother. She may fantasize in a grandiose way that she is precious. She may insist that her parents buy her the most fashionable clothes and jewelry, no matter what the financial income of the family. Instead of calmly pointing out to her that she cannot have her own way all the time and refusing her unreasonable demands, the mother may simply comply. Later, the girl may become almost totally self-absorbed and concerned with clothes and her physical appearance. As a result, she may be unable to maintain relationships with other females, because she sees herself as superior to them. Her male admirers may also grow tired of worshipping at her feet and suffering her demands for continual praise.

The nuclear self is based on interactions not only with the mother, but importantly with the father as well. When unavoidable shortcomings in parenting disturb the balanced state of primary narcissism, the child unconsciously attempts to restore equilibrium by identifying and associating with an admired, omnipotent, self-object—the **idealized parent imago.** This idealization occurs because the child has an innate **need to idealize.** According to Kohut, it is principally the father who is idealized by the male. For the female, it is usually the mother who is idealized (Kohut, 1977, p. 185). The infant now cathects (invests or attaches) his or her libido (for example, love, affection, admiration) to this idealized structure. This idealized parent imago involves an unconscious merger with those people that the child can admire with those who present an image of calmness, infallibility, and omnipotence (Kohut & Wolf, 1978, p. 414). Initially, these positive feelings toward the revered parent accompany the relief of the infant's distress on being picked up, soothed, and rocked in the powerful embrace of the parent. Later, in early childhood, children often express unbridled admiration for a parent because they are cognitively immature and unable to make appropriate discriminations. They often imitate the parent's mannerisms, speech, and activities; because they have a massive narcissistic investment in the parent, they experience tremendous gratification through such imitative expressions (Kohut, 1971, p. 139). In such situations, children are not separate initially from their parents but are simply merged with them. They are living through their parents and are highly dependent on them.

Kohut believed that such unrealistic idealization is necessary initially, if children are to begin growing in a healthy way. Thus, empathic parents allow their children to glorify them initially, so that their children can vicariously experience feelings of being worthwhile (Kohut, 1971, p. 139). However, Kohut maintained that, soon afterward, these parents must gradually support the process of taming this unabashed admiration through the effective use of optimal frustrations; that is, they must teach them about the realistic imperfections and limitations of the idealized parent imago. For example, the father may allow his son to learn that he is not invincible, that there are times when others beat him fairly in athletic or business competitions. Or the mother may allow her daughter to learn that she sometimes feels resentful and hostile and acts harshly toward others when they fail to agree with her viewpoint. The healthy parent is one who is optimally failing. An effective father must not lose all credibility by complaining constantly to his son that he is an abject failure totally unworthy of admiration, nor should the father pose as a superman without faults or flaws. Instead, the father must gradually reveal some of his limitations to his son when he considers it helpful to the son's personal growth.

This new learning process enables the children to see their parents more realistically and to engage in the transmuting internalizations that result in the consolidation of a cohesive self structure—that is, in the formation of the nuclear self. If the parents fail to empathize properly with their children, the idealized parent imago remains primitive and largely unrealistic. In a clinical case cited by Kohut, a patient's attempt to idealize his father was rejected; the father responded by criticizing and belittling his son. Analysis revealed that the father was unable to accept this idealizing role because he had low self-esteem. As a result, the son tried to enhance his self-esteem by reinstating the old grandiosity and exhibitionism that had been fostered by his mother (Kohut, 1971, pp. 139–140).

In summary, the nuclear self evolves during the first two or three years of life and is therefore pre-Oedipal (Okun, 1992, p. 32). It is also bipolar, because it represents the outgrowth of efforts to recognize and to come to grips with the imperfections and limitations of two poles of the self: the grandiose self and the idealizing self (as represented mentally by the idealized parent imago). As a result of these efforts, the domain and power of the child's infantile fantasies are diminished, and a core or nuclear self encompassing a rudimentary and more realistic set of skills and talents is established. This nuclear self then serves as a solid foundation upon which a more organized and integrated **cohesive self** can be built. Formation of the cohesive self is not distinct from the formation of the nuclear self. Rather, the cohesive self is simply a quality of the nuclear self; specifically, it refers to the degree of integration, coherence, and vitality of the nuclear self (Tolpin, 1980, p. 310). If the cohesive self is developing properly, it helps the individual make even more progress toward the attainment of optimal mental health.

Pre-Oedipal Development: The Oral and Anal Stages

Kohut did not abandon Freud's theory of psychosexual development completely. He agreed with Freud that the child may develop oral or anal fixations during this early period, but he explained their etiology differently than did Freud. In general, Kohut saw these fixations as the result of the child's defensive efforts to cope with damage to the nuclear self that has been caused by unempathic caretaking and not as the result of frustration of the child's sexual aims.

Oral stage For Freud, the focus during this stage is on the feeding process itself and on frustrations experienced when the mother either underindulges the child by premature weaning or overindulges the child, who consequently feels frustrated at finally having to give up the breast or bottle. The result is oral fixations that have a negative impact on later personality functioning. Thus, for Freud, frustration of the child's pleasure-seeking (sexual) needs leads to disordered functioning.

In contrast, Kohut believed that, during this period, the child demands an emotionally supportive, food-giving self-object (the mother) to empathically minister to his or her needs. If the mother is unempathic—for example, indifferent or rejecting—there is damage to the child's self-esteem. The self then fragments; the child regresses to pleasure-seeking (sexual) oral stimulation and becomes orally fixated. Thus, it is damage to the self that produces pleasure-seeking, sexualized drive fixations (Kohut, 1977, p. 81).

Anal stage   Freud claimed that the child may become anally fixated in response to frustration of the pleasure-seeking impulses associated with the retention or expulsion of feces. The anal retentive individual may be characterized later in life as obstinate and stingy, whereas the anal expulsive individual may become very messy or, through reaction formation, a person with compulsive needs for orderliness and cleanliness.

Kohut, on the other hand, believed that the mother is not only responding to the child's pleasure-seeking (libidinal) impulses, but also to the child's self-object needs. Again, her attitude plays a critical role in the child's development. More specifically, she can respond to her child's giving and offering feces by mirroring her approval, thereby confirming the child's self. The child would then feel pride. Conversely, if she rejects the gift of the feces, she is rejecting a self that is just beginning to assert itself as a center of creative-productive initiative. In reaction, the child could easily become preoccupied with his or her feces and the pleasures associated with their retention. In brief, the child would experience a fragmentation of the self, that is, excessive concern with a body part (Kohut, 1977, pp. 75–76).

Oedipal Development: The Phallic Stage

In Kohut's view, the Oedipal complex is a basic and important phenomenon discovered by Freud. However, Kohut believed that Freud's explanation of its operation is limited and needs amplification (Kohut, 1977, p. 223).

Phallic stage   You may recall Freud's description of the Oedipal process in 4- and 5-year-old boys and girls. Boys, according to Freud, develop a longing for sexual contact with the mother, but fear that they will be punished by their fathers for their desires. They experience castration anxiety, and identify with their fathers to alleviate it. The resolution of their conflict is accompanied by the formation of the superego, as boys take on the values and ideals of their fathers. In girls, the process is considerably different. Upon discovery that they lack a penis, they experience penis envy. According to Freud, they resent the mother for bringing them into the world without a penis and begin to love their father because he has the desired object. They then identify with the mother as a means of vicariously obtaining it. Their fantasies revolve around the wish to have sexual intercourse with the father and to have his baby. Specifically, they long for a male baby who will bring the longed-for penis with him.

Kohut reinterpreted the Freudian explanation of the Oedipal process. He believed that the only children able to adequately resolve Oedipal conflicts are those with cohesive nuclear selves, formed during the pre-Oedipal years by associations with empathic parents. Unless they see themselves as independent centers of initiative, they are unable to experience the instinctual desires for the parent of the opposite sex that initiate the Oedipal conflicts and their eventual resolution (Kohut, 1977, p. 227). For example, if the mother's responses to her son during the pre-Oedipal period were grossly unempathic and unreliable, he would be very likely to cling to an infantile grandiose self. As a result, he would be unable to engage in the transmuting internalizations that are necessary for the establishment of a stable and clear nuclear self separate from his mother. Thus, the Oedipal conflict would remain unresolved, because his libidinal energies would remain focused on his grandiose self rather than on the mother (Kohut, 1971, pp. 64–65).

Kohut's interpretation of an unresolved Oedipal conflict in girls is also very different from Freud's. He described his analysis of an artist in her forties who was experiencing low self-esteem and feelings of hopelessness. She had previously been to another analyst, who had interpreted her difficulties in classical psychoanalytic terms. The analyst had pointed out to her that her present depressive feelings stemmed from her inability to accept her femaleness; that is, her problems were the result of penis envy. Kohut noted that the woman did have bathroom dreams about wanting to have a penis and to urinate standing up like a man. She had also dreamed that, as a little girl, she had yearned to see her father's body, especially his genitals. Kohut reassured her that these dreams were not primarily related to sexual matters. Instead they were based on her need to extricate herself from her relationship with her emotionally shallow and unempathic mother and to turn toward her emotionally more responsive (empathic) and loving father. He arrived at this insight when the patient reported the memory that her mother had repeatedly and harshly warned her never to sit down on a toilet outside their own house because the seats were contaminated with dirt, bacteria, infections, and so forth. This fear was inculcated in the daughter because of the mother's own hidden paranoid outlook on the world. And the daughter's healthy attempts to move toward the world were made impossible by the infiltration of the mother's paranoid beliefs into the child's psyche. Her wish to see the father's penis was her sexualized attempt to turn toward him for a positive, healthy, nonparanoid view of the world. She needed his support to overcome her mother's influence over her, so that she could, metaphorically, sit down on the toilet; that is, she needed to gain his support in order to rebuild her weakened self, so that she could be joyful and alive in her sexual and nonsexual experiences, not empty and suspicious like her mother (Kohut, 1977, pp. 221–222).

In conclusion, Kohut believed that a successful resolution of the Oedipal conflict takes place only when the child already possesses a firm nuclear self. The successful resolution of the conflict makes the person more definitely a male or female self on moving into the latency period (Kohut, 1977, pp. 239–240).

Post-Oedipal Development: The Latency and Genital Stages

Latency stage   For Freud, the sexual instinct lies dormant during the latency stage, from about the sixth year to puberty. He believed that the fundamental personality was established during the first five years of life and drastic changes were extremely difficult, if not impossible, to make thereafter. Freud also thought that, during this period, children turned to the world of school and peers and became motivated to learn a variety of physical, social, and academic skills that would increase their sense of competence and ability to function more effectively in their daily living.

Kohut, in contrast, believed that the person's personality is still subject to considerable changes after age five. He asserted, for example, that the superego is fragile, and subject to change, not only during the latency period but in adolescence as well. Under the impact of a traumatic experience, such as his father's decision to sever all ties with the family following divorce, an adolescent boy may reject the uncertain superego, which was based largely on the internalization of his father's values, and seek another external object to idealize. In that search, the boy may attach his narcissistic libido to an antisocial group, for example, a teenage gang or an extremist religious cult. In Kohut's view, gradual disappointments in the father that lead to a more realistic view of him have healthy repercussions for the child's development, whereas severely negative experiences such as abandonment by the father are likely to do lasting damage to the nuclear self (Kohut, 1971, pp. 44–48).

Genital stage   With puberty, sexual tension in the adolescent increases greatly. The reproductive organs have matured, and both sexes are now capable of reproduction. In the earlier stages, the aims of the sexual instincts have been predominantly autoerotic, but now the goal is to mate with a heterosexual object. In Freud's view, an adequate heterosexual adjustment depends on the amount of sexual energy or libido available to the person during this period. If the conflicts in the prior stages have been resolved adequately, so that there are no libidinal fixations on infantile objects, an adequate adjustment is possible. For Freud, when the person reaches adulthood, he or she typically marries and settles into family life. Careers are pursued to provide support for the family. Thus, normal development involves satisfactory adjustments in two areas—love and work. The normal or psychologically healthy person is called the genital character. Conversely, an inadequate adjustment in these areas because of libidinal fixations leads to the development of various character disorders.

Kohut's view of adolescence is much different. In discussing sexual fixations during this stage, he noted that they are almost always an outgrowth of damage to the self caused by unresponsive and unempathic parents. The parents' pathology causes the teenagers to feel unloved, alone, and vulnerable. To overcome these feelings, they may become intensely exhibitionistic, and commit destructive acts that win them the recognition, admiration, and approval of their peers—for example, stealing cars and taking their friends for a joyride; drinking excessively and damaging other people's private property while in a stupor; or attacking and beating the elderly. These acts are expressions of narcissistic rage and aggression; they temporarily relieve the adolescents' lethargy and depression resulting from the unavailability of a mirroring object and of an idealizable self-object (Kohut, 1977, p. 272).

Kohut believed that healthy development occurs when individuals have a firm and vigorous self and an accompanying strong ego that utilizes their skills and talents to love and work successfully (Kohut, 1977, p. 284). Healthy development is not achieved once and for all at a particular time in the lifespan. Rather, the individual continually attempts to strengthen his or her autonomous self by overcoming problems and conflicts that can occur at any time. Kohut asserted, for example, that people in late middle age (approximately

58–64) are especially prone to crisis. Such people are experiencing an "ultimate decline" and are wracked with anxiety and concern about whether they have lived up to their potentials. This is the time, according to Kohut, when many individuals who think they are failures feel completely hopeless and depressed. He believed that suicides committed in late middle age are a remedial act; they express a wish to wipe out the mortification and shame experienced by a fragmented and inadequate self (Kohut, 1977, p. 241). People in this age group can be helped to recover from their sense of shame and to reconcile themselves with impending death.

Disturbances to the Self

According to Kohut, disturbances to the self can be classified into several subgroups depending on the nature and severity of the problem. In many of these disturbances, parental pathology (for example, depression, paranoia) plays a major role in the etiology of disturbances to the self. He also thinks that some of these disturbances have a biological basis.

In the event of extremely serious permanent or protracted damage to the self, when few defense mechanisms are available to effectively cover the defect, the resulting pathological state is called a **psychosis.** In schizophrenia, for example, the nuclear self is disorganized and chaotic because of a confluence of biological and constitutional factors; a lack of joyful and empathic responses by the parents to the child's existence and assertiveness may also play a role. In addition, at a critical point, the child may have been deprived of an opportunity to merge with an idealized self-object (Kohut & Wolf, 1978, p. 415; Wolf, 1988, pp. 67–68). Kohut believed that, in such major disorders, the parents may fail to meet both needs—the need to be mirrored and the need to idealize the parents. The severe damage to the self results in a disorder characterized by delusions of greatness and disorganized speech and behavior (American Psychiatric Association, 1994, p. 285).

The second subgroup of important disorders consists of the **borderline states.** Here, too, the nuclear self is in a state of functional chaos, and the damage to the self is either permanent or protracted. The major difference between these disorders and the psychoses is that the people suffering from borderline states are able to cover the defects in the self by the use of complex defense mechanisms (Kohut & Wolf, 1978, p. 415; Wolf, 1988, pp. 68–69). Borderline states are psychotic-like conditions that typically do not collapse into the mass deterioration of a psychosis because the individual employs various protective defenses (Tolpin, 1980, p. 302; Leider, 1995, pp. 3–6).

Included among the borderline states we find the schizoid and paranoid personality disorders. Individuals with **schizoid personality disorders** achieve emotional distance from others by showing emotional coldness and flatness. This maneuver protects them from serious breakup or distortion of the self. Such individuals appear to lack a desire for intimacy, seem indifferent to opportunities to develop close relationships, and do not derive much satisfaction from being part of a family or other social group. They prefer being alone and engage most often in solitary activities or hobbies (American Psychiatric Association, 1994, p. 638).

Individuals suffering from **paranoid personality disorders,** in contrast, distance themselves from others by being hostile and suspicious. They assume that other people will exploit, harm, or deceive them, even if there is no evidence to support their belief. Such individuals are also reluctant to confide in others, or to become close to them, because they fear that any information they share will be used against them. Also, they read hidden meanings that are demeaning and threatening into innocuous remarks. For example, individuals with this disorder will see an honest mistake by a store clerk as an attempt to cheat them. They also tend to bear grudges and are unwilling to forgive any slights or insults they think they have received (American Psychiatric Association, 1994, p. 634).

The third subgroup consists of the narcissistic personality and behavior disorders. Kohut's term **narcissistic personality disorders** refers to individuals with grandiose styles of thinking, hypersensitivity to criticism, and overreactions to failure that interfere with effective interpersonal functioning, whereas his term **narcissistic behavior disorders** refers to individuals who act out their grandiose fantasies by engaging in perversions and delinquent behavior. In general, people with narcissistic disorders routinely have problems with self-esteem. They may overestimate their abilities and inflate their accomplishments, and will often appear boastful and pretentious. Alternately, they may be self-deprecating and minimize their abilities and accomplishments. They are often preoccupied with fantasies of unlimited success, power, brilliance, or beauty, or with fears of failure and deficiency. They may ruminate about long-overdue admiration and privilege and compare themselves favorably with famous people (American Psychiatric Association, 1994, p. 658). These disorders are pathological, but many of them are not necessarily severely pathological; that is, many of them operate within the normal range of thinking and behavior. Therefore, aspects of them are quite common among normal individuals.

Much of Kohut's personality theory is concerned with the impact of narcissistic disorders on human development and functioning. While the origins and course of development of these disorders are complex, Kohut offered a simpler typology of their operation in order to clarify our understanding of them.

Typology for Narcissistic Personality and Behavior Disorders

Narcissistic Personality Disorders

Kohut and his colleague Wolf listed four types of narcissistic personality disorders: the understimulated self, the fragmented self, the overstimulated self, and the overburdened self (Kohut & Wolf, 1978, pp. 118–122; Wolf, 1988, pp. 70–76).

The understimulated self   The first disordered type is the **understimulated self.** It results from prolonged lack of stimulating responsiveness on the part of the parents. Kohut saw this lack of parental responsiveness to the child's mirroring and idealizing needs as the most dangerous threat to the psychological survival of the individual in Western culture. He argued that many children today have fewer and fewer opportunities to participate emotionally in their parents' lives, given the high rates of divorce and separation and the need for both parents to work long hours at several jobs if the family is to survive economically. Although children may have an opportunity to participate with the parents in play and leisure activities, they do not usually have opportunities to get to know their parents more personally in their other life activities, particularly in regard to parental ambitions, ideals, and goals. Kohut believed that children should have an opportunity to learn not only about their parents' hopes and dreams, but also about their nontraumatic limitations, failures, and diappointments. Only through such revelations can children undergo the transmuting internalizations that are necessary for the establishment of independent nuclear selves (Kohut, 1977, pp. 269–270).

As a result of lack of parental stimulation, these individals experience themselves as boring and apathetic and will resort to any kind of stimulation in their attempts to ward off feelings of lethargy and deadness. According to Kohut, toddlers may try to alleviate apathy and lethargy by engaging in **head-banging**, older children by engaging in compulsive masturbation, and adolescents by engaging in various daredevil activities. Adults try to alleviate their boredom and deadness by engaging in promiscuous sexual activities and various perversions, gambling, drug and alcohol abuse, and hypersociability (Kohut & Wolf, 1978, p. 418; Wolf, 1988, pp. 70–71).

The fragmenting self   Kohut's second type of narcissistic personality disorder is the **fragmenting self.** It too results from a lack of parental responsiveness. But here the inability to respond adequately may focus on a single aspect of the child's total self. For example, consider a son whose mother is generally loving and empathic. One day he comes home from school and tells his mother exuberantly about the great grades he received on his report card. Suddenly, she remarks critically that he should stop waving his arms around when he's talking because everyone knows he's a klutz and he may hit her in the face or knock something over. This rejection of his emotional outpouring and his feelings of pride—his exhibitionism—may shift his attention to a part of his body (his wildly waving arms) just at the most vulnerable moment, when he was offering his total self to her for approval (Kohut, 1971, p. 121). Later in life, he may feel physically uncoordinated and inexplicably dejected after receiving recognition of his academic accomplishments from his teachers. Kohut would say there has been damage to the total self, so that the person feels fragmented whenever the traumatic experience is reactivated.

The overstimulated self   The third type of narcissistic personality disorder is the **overstimulated self.** It occurs as a result of excessive responsiveness to the child's grandiose and idealizing needs. The child's grandiose fantasies of greatness and unrealistic goals are constantly reinforced by the parents, who reward the exhibitionistic behavior with constant admiration, attention, and approval. Such parents do not provide the optimal frustration of the child's grandiose and idealizing fantasies; that is, they do not demonstrate the realistic limitations of the child's fantasies or of his or her talents and abilities and, as a result, the child does not begin to establish a strong nuclear self that is separate from the primitive grandiose self and its unrealistic counterpart, the primitive idealized parent imago. Such a child then moves into adulthood with only a weak separation between the fantasy selves and the realistic, but weak, nuclear self. Because the child is now subject to being flooded by unrealistic, archaic greatness fantasies, which produce painful tension and anxiety because they are at variance with his or her weak, realistic, nuclear self, the child may try to avoid becoming the center of attention. Thus, the child will shy away from creative and productive activities for fear of being overwhelmed by an uncontrollable grandiosity (Kohut & Wolf, 1978, p. 419; Wolf, 1988, pp. 71–72).

The overburdened self   The last type of narcissistic personality disorder is the **overburdened self.** People of this type view the world as hostile and dangerous. They quickly respond with irritability and hostility to even minor frustrations. However, these reactions rapidly subside once the frustrating event has passed. The disorder can be traced to early childhood and the lack of an opportunity for children to merge with the calmness of omnipotent self-objects (parents). In other words, idealized parents have failed to teach their children how to handle interference with their goals calmly and with composure. Consequently, they become quickly overburdened when threatened and react emotionally and irrationally.

Narcissistic Behavioral Disorders

Listed among the narcissistic behavioral disorders are mirror-hungry personalities, ideal-hungry personalities, alter-ego personalities, merger-hungry personalities, and contact-shunning personalities. While the first three disorders are relatively mild and occur within the normal range of functioning, the last two are much more severe types of psychopathology (Wolf, 1988, pp. 72–74).

Mirror-hungry personalities   **Mirror-hungry personalities** are continually searching for self-objects who will admire and nurture their famished selves. Such individuals typically were raised in families where the parents gave them insufficient mirroring attention. There are, however, mirror-hungry individuals who were given sufficient mirroring attention by their parents, usually their mother, but the attention focused not on meeting their needs but on the mother's needs. In other words, such a mother might continually praise her son's beautiful physical appearance, an area of intense concern to her, but not his physical strength, an area of strong concern to the son. Mirror-hungry individuals are impelled to display themselves, to show off, to evoke the attention of others as a means of counteracting their own lack of self-esteem. In adolescence, they may eventually find an admiring boyfriend or girlfriend who will fulfill their needs for a while, but most mirror-hungry personalities will soon become bored and seek new self-objects whose attention and recognition they hope to cultivate (Kohut & Wolf, 1978, p. 421; Wolf, 1988, p. 73).

Ideal-hungry personalities   **Ideal-hungry personalities** had their needs to idealize and admire various self-objects frustrated in childhood. As a result, they are continually searching for others whom they can admire for their intelligence, power, beauty, or moral stature. They experience themselves as worthwhile only for as long as they can continue their admiration of these idealized figures. Eventually, ideal-hungry people find defects in these figures, become disillusioned, and begin the search for the next great person to admire. They invest their libido in this figure until he or she disappoints them (Wolf, 1988, p. 73).

Alter-ego-hungry personalities   **Alter-ego-hungry personalities** can only experience themselves as real and worthwhile when they are in relationships with self-objects who will conform to their opinions, beliefs, values, and behavior. This disorder probably stems from severe frustration of their mirroring and idealizing needs during early childhood. Inevitably, such individuals discover that the other person is different from themselves and has his or her own separate and distinct personality. The estrangement that follows almost always leads to a breakup of the relationship. Like the mirror- and ideal-hungry personalities, alter-ego-hungry personalities are prone to look restlessly for one replacement after the other (Kohut & Wolf, 1978, p. 422; Wolf, 1988, p. 73).

Merger-hungry personalities   People with **merger-hungry personalities** have self structures that are seriously defective. According to Kohut, all children have a need to idealize. They attempt to fulfill this need by merging initially with an all-powerful and admired figure. However, if such a figure is not available in the family for any reason—for example, because of the early death of a parent or because of parental separation or divorce—merging is prevented. Consequently, under these conditions the idealizing needs of these children are not met. Also, they cannot learn about the limitations of the idealized figure through optimal frustration, nor can they develop an independent sense of self through transmuting internalizations. Merger-hungry personalities then continue to seek primitive self-objects to fulfill their desperate need for self structure. They incorporate such idealized figures and unfortunately blur the boundaries between themselves and the others. This blurring interferes with their ability to discriminate their own thoughts, feelings, wishes, and intentions from those of the idealized figures. One negative result of such blurring of boundaries is that merger-hungry personalities feel intolerant of the actual idealized figure's independence. They are very sensitive to separations from the self-object and demand his or her continual presence (Kohut & Wolf, 1978, p. 422; Wolf, 1988, p. 74).

Contact-shunning personalities   Contact-shunning personalities are also seriously disturbed individuals. They too were prevented from merging with admired figures in early childhood. As a result, they have a tremendous yearning for an all-encompassing union with idealized figures. However, unlike the merger-hungry individuals, the contact-shunning personalities avoid social contact and become isolated. They avoid others not because of disinterest, but because their need of them is so great. They fear rejection by the adored figures, and there is also the apprehension that their weakened self structure would be completely swallowed up by these figures if their union occurred (Kohut & Wolf, 1978, p. 422; Wolf, 1988, p. 74).

Development of the Healthy Self

In thinking about the role of narcissism in personality development, it would be easy to consider only the negative aspects of the construct. In popular usage of the term, people who are narcissistic are considered to be selfish and psychologically unhealthy. But Kohut maintained that narcissism has positive as well as negative implications for personality development. He believed that narcissism can contribute either to health or to mental illness, depending on the degree to which the two major narcissistic constellations or structures—the grandiose self and the idealized parent imago—can be transformed into more realistic structures. In families where parents are unempathic, the two major structures remain unrealistic and unchanged. The result is development of an unhealthy self. Threats to this damaged self often elicit narcissistic rage and pathological aggression. Where the parents are empathic and provide their children with adequate opportunity and encouragement to learn, however, the two structures—the grandiose self and the idealized parent imago—are modified and become more realistic. Out of this learning process, children invest their narcissism in a more independent core or nuclear self. This healthy narcissism serves as the mainspring in their struggle for human creativity and meaningful human exploration (C. Goldberg, 1980, p. 12). They can now transform innate aggressive tendencies into healthy, mature self-assertiveness. The nuclear self then exercises its assertiveness by initiating action and serves as the organizer of the ego's activities. This realistic and strong ego then works toward the attainment of the self's goals. In Kohut's view, the nuclear self aims at the unfolding of the person's intrinsic patterns for creative action, as expressed through the workings of its realistic ego. In short, an empathic and supportive family environment provides an opportunity for the establishment of a core nuclear self, its growth into a more cohesive self, and the movement of this more unified self toward the attainment of a cohesive and relatively **autonomous self.**

In Kohut's view, the autonomous self is the epitome of mental health. The development of this independent self does not mean that the individual has no further need of others. People are always with us; they listen to us, applaud us, challenge us, help us, or ignore us. Kohut believed that we all have a continuing need for relatedness to self-objects. But the person who has evolved into an autonomous self now has a less urgent need to follow the expectations and demands of others and a greater flexibility in their interactions with them (Goldberg, 1988, p. 72).

Also, as people move toward the attainment of this ideal state, they become increasingly liberated from unrealistic narcissistic needs, and experience instead the joy of creative maturity (Kohut, 1977, p. 285). The transformed narcissistic energies of mature people allow them to experience pleasure in living, to feel realistic pride in their accomplishments, to love others as well as themselves, and to be successful at their work. They are also able to accept the limitations of their physical, intellectual, and emotional powers and the inevitability of their death (Kohut, 1966, p. 268).

Research Support for the Theory of Self Development

There is ample longitudinal research showing that the quality of the interactions between infants and their caretakers has a decided impact on their cognitive and emotional development. Moreover, infants who are exposed to unempathic and unresponsive parents do tend to be at risk for the development of psychological disorders later in life

(Lichtenberg, 1991, p. 19). These findings are clearly consistent with Kohut's views. However, Kohut overemphasized the role of the mother in producing subsequent psychopathology in her child. Although Kohut recognized differences between infants in regard to their needs, drives, and anxiety tolerance, he nevertheless minimized the infants' influence on their environment (Silverman, 1986, p. 54). In fact, abundant research evidence shows that infants are very active in controlling interactions with their caregivers. For example, infants use gaze, smiling, crying, and head-turning to arouse maternal responsiveness. By virtue of their individual differences, some infants appear to enjoy cuddling and holding, whereas others react negatively, by kicking and thrashing (Lichtenberg, 1991, pp. 19–20). This limitation in Kohut's theorizing remains to be addressed by self psychology researchers.

There is greater difficulty in trying to validate Kohut's ideas about self-objects. He believed that infants use self-objects to regulate tensions but that eventually these self-objects must be transformed and gradually integrated into the personality, so that the individuals can act in psychologically healthy ways. Researchers are uncertain about when and how this modification process occurs (Lichtenberg, 1991, p. 31). Of course, the range of self-objects increases throughout childhood, as children establish relationships with relatives, friends, siblings, teachers, and others. In adulthood, the range of self-objects is expanded even further and may include romantic partners, spouses, and religious, military, and academic leaders. Kohut believed that self-objects are required throughout the lifespan. From a research standpoint, however, we know very little about how, when, and why certain self-objects are utilized and/or modified by individuals as they struggle toward self-realization. There is clearly a need for more research to determine whether Kohut's complicated theorizing has any validity and to assess longitudinal changes in self-objects as people proceed through the lifespan. Unfortunately, when we move beyond infancy research, we find that there are only a few longitudinal studies in existence, and those are based on adults' retrospective reports of their childhood experiences. Such reports must be viewed with caution because they are subject to memory bias and because it is impossible to establish cause-and-effect relationships among the variables. In addition, empirical validation of the theory is difficult, because many of the hypotheses are not clearly stated and many of the constructs are highly abstract and difficult to measure adequately. Despite these problems, investigators have begun to make some inroads in testing the theory, by developing reliable and valid measures of key constructs like empathy, narcissism, self-esteem, and mental health. Using these new measures, investigators have conducted important research testing certain aspects of Kohut's theorizing.

For example, several investigations have focused on Kohut's ideas concerning the relationships between empathy, narcissism, and mental health. This research provides consistent support for Kohut's theorizing. In one study, Gabriel, Critelli, and Ee (1994) showed that there are elements of grandiose thinking in highly narcissistic students. They found that male and female college students higher in narcissism had stronger tendencies to overestimate their physical attractiveness than did students lower in narcissism; that is, highly narcissistic students rated themselves as far more attractive than they were actually rated by a group of independent observers. The ratings of students low in narcissism did not differ from those provided by the observers. Also, in comparison to their actual performances on tests designed to measure their intelligence, students higher in narcissism more strongly overestimated their intelligence than did students lower in narcissism (Gabriel, Critelli, & Ee, 1994, pp. 151–153).

In another study involving college students, Zamostny, Slyter, and Rios (1993) found that male and female students who reported having had many narcissistic injuries in childhood were the ones who were most academically and socially maladjusted during their college careers. These traumatic experiences included parental loss, serious personal illness, physical and/or sexual abuse within the family, severe financial problems, and serious psychological disorders in parents.

Wink (1991; 1992) also examined the early life of college students. In particular, he examined reports by college female narcissists of their early childhood relations with parents. He found that the unhealthy narcissists—that is, those characterized by overt grandeur, exhibitionism, and poor impulse control—reported very negative and troubled relations with their parents, and especially their mother. Both parents were seen as cold and uncaring (unempathic), but only the mother was perceived as distrusted and disliked. These women also reported a lack of enjoyment of childhood activities. In contrast, healthy narcissists—that is, those characterized by an independent sense of self and high, but realistic, achievement aspirations—reported that their relations with parents were untroubled. They also stated that they had engaged in many positive activities during childhood, including writing poems and stories, painting, and going on hikes.

Wink also collected additional data on these college women approximately 20 years after their graduation, when they were in their early or mid-40s. These data showed that unhealthy narcissists were even more unempathic, irresponsible, and moody than they had been in college. Most importantly, there was a decrease in their feelings of well-being and a growing pessimism about their health and the future. Unhealthy narcissists also experienced less satisfaction in their marriages and in their occupations, and reported that they were unable to put their lives together effectively. In a related study, Wink (1991) found that these same women also reported drug use and conflicts in their friendships. Healthy narcissists, on the other hand, showed personal discomfort only in their 20s, when they were first trying to juggle the demands of family and career. By the time they reached their 40s, these problems were resolved. Healthy narcissists in their 40s showed a tremendous growth in self-confidence, social poise, understanding of self and others, an increased level of effective functioning, and a continued commitment to a high-status career. These women also reported less drug dependence, and had good marriages and careers. They were also satisfied with their roles as mothers (Wink, 1991, pp. 769–785; Wink, 1992, pp. 7–30).

Finally, some research focuses directly on the association between narcissism and self-esteem. Kohut maintained, for example, that the activation of the grandiose self reflects an attempt to ward off feelings of worthlessness and low self-esteem. According to him, such individuals are constantly seeking confirmation of their worth through unrealistic displays of grandiosity. Research by Raskin, Novacek, and Hogan (1991), using four different samples of college students, provides support for Kohut's theorizing. They found that unhealthy male and female narcissists in all four samples tried to bolster and enhance their feelings of self-esteem by engaging in grandiose and exhibitionistic behavior.

Kohut also believed that, if other people did not provide the needed confirmation of the individual's grandiose self, he or she would react with rage, anger, and hostility, and would then proceed to derogate them. Research by Morf and Rhodewalt (1993) provides confirmation for these ideas. They had subjects perform a competitive task that ostensibly measured their level of social sensitivity. They were then given feedback by the experimenter concerning the quality of their performance. In the high-threat condition, subjects were told that their opponents had much higher scores and thus were much more socially sensitive; in the low-threat condition, subjects were told that their opponents had about the same scores. Subjects were later given an opportunity to rate their opponents' personalities. The investigators found that subjects higher in narcissism gave a much more negative rating to their opponents than did subjects lower in narcissism, but only under the high-threat condition. Under the low-threat condition, high- and low-narcissistic subjects did not differ in their evaluations of their opponents' personalities (Morf & Rhodewalt, 1993, pp. 668–676).

ASSESSMENT TECHNIQUES

Kohut agreed with Freud that free association, dream analysis, and analyses of transference were techniques that could be used to probe the unconscious of patients, to help in understanding their problems, and to facilitate their cure. However, Kohut disagreed in many respects with Freud's interpretations of the psychological data gathered through the use of these techniques. In addition, Kohut elevated the concept of empathy to primary status as an assessment tool and believed that the other techniques were all auxiliaries of it.

Empathy as the Primary Data Collection Tool

Kohut defined psychoanalysis as the scientific study of complex mental states. In order to study these mental states, he thought, analysts must get as close to the immediate subjective experiences of their patients as they could. Consequently, Kohut advocated the use of empathy—or, as he sometimes called it, vicarious introspection—as the primary tool of inquiry. For him, empathy meant our ability to put ourselves in the place of others, to think about their experiences, and to feel them as though they were our own. Only then can we understand them.

> Let us consider a simple example. We see a person who is unusually tall. It is not to be disputed that this person's unusual size is an important fact for our psychological assessment—without introspection and empathy, however, his size remains simply a physical attribute. Only when we think ourselves into his place, only when we, by vicarious introspection, begin to feel his unusual size as if it were our own and thus revive inner experiences in which we had been unusual or conspicuous, only then do we begin to appreciate the meaning that the unusual size may have for this person and only then have we observed a psychological fact. (Kohut, 1959, p. 207)

Once therapists have collected these psychological facts or data, they could interpret their meanings for the patients. For Kohut, empathy was, in its essence, neutral and objective. It was a technique used by therapists to collect accurate, objective data about the inner subjective state of another person. This point, Kohut felt, was misunderstood by many professionals and laypersons, who confused empathy with either sympathy or compassion. But these terms are not equivalent. Rather, empathy serves as a prerequisite for our ability to experience compassion. Compassion, in other words, grows out of our ability to accurately assess another's needs. However, empathy can also be used in the service of people's destructive acts. In order to hurt our enemies, for example, we must have accurate knowledge of their weaknesses: our destructive actions are most effective when they are based on an empathic understanding of victims' sensitivities (Kohut, 1980, p. 483). Of course, analysts do view their patients with compassion, warmth, and sympathy, but that must be distinguished from the empathy used to collect accurate data about the patients' inner experience.

Free Association

Kohut maintained that the use of free association by patients facilitated therapists' ability to empathize with their patients' experiences. The patients' associations reveal areas of resistance that, once recognized, show the activities, vulnerabilities, and defenses of the archaic or immature self. This primitive self does not want to re-expose itself to the devastating, traumatizing narcissistic injury of finding that the parents do not respond to its basic mirroring and idealizing needs; that is, the resistances are a means of protecting patients from the anxiety associated with a disintegrating self (Kohut, 1977, p. 136). Freud, in contrast, believed that these resistances were attempts by his patients to protect themselves against the anxiety associated with early traumatic sexual or aggressive fantasies or experiences.

Dream Analysis

For Kohut, there are two types of dreams. The first follows Freud's analysis of the meaning of dreams very closely; that is, these dreams have both a manifest and latent content. The analyst's task is to interpret the associations to, and the symbols present in, the manifest content in an attempt to discover the latent meaning. Such dreams are unconscious attempts at wish fulfillment. The wishes are unacceptable to the person and are nearly always sexual in nature. The aim of the therapist is to follow the patient's free associations into the depths of the psyche until the unconscious meaning has been uncovered.

In the second type of dreams, free associations do not lead to unconscious hidden layers of the psyche. Instead, the free associations provide the therapist with further imagery on the same level as the manifest content. An examination of this content reveals that the healthy parts of the person's psyche are reacting to a disturbing change in the condition of the self. Kohut calls these dreams **self-state dreams.** Associations to these dreams do not lead to any deeper, underlying meaning (Kohut, 1977, pp. 109–110).

Kohut provides an interesting case study to illustrate the second type of dreams, that is, dreams in which the problem originates in a defect in the self. It involved a man whose mother provided him with grossly inadequate mirroring in his childhood and whose father provided a poor example of the needed, idealized father image. He recalled that, as a child, he drew people with large heads supported by bodies consisting of pencil-thin trunk and legs. Throughout his life, he had dreams in which he experienced himself as a brain at the top of a lifeless body. As the analysis progressed, he became able to describe the sexual fantasy he had whenever he became depressed, that is, whenever he experienced his self as empty and lifeless. In this fantasy, he imagined himself using his brains to subdue a powerful male figure; he then chained his adversary up to a wall, and performed oral sex on the male figure in order to deplete the giant's strength. In conjunction with these fantasies, he masturbated to orgasm. From early in his life, the patient had felt unreal: he experienced his body-self as fragmented and powerless, because of the lack of empathic responses from both of his parents. Only one fragment of his grandiose-exhibitionistic self had remained somewhat firm, namely, his thinking processes (his brains). His fantasy expressed the attempt to use the last remnant of his grandiose self (his omnipotent thought) in order to regain possession of the idealized omnipotent self-object (his father), that is, to exert absolute control over it and to internalize it via fellatio. Although the masturbatory act gave the patient a feeling of strength and increased self-esteem, it was unable to fill the structural defect in the self (absence of the idealized parent imago) and therefore had to be repeated again and again. In the course of therapy, the patient was able to fill the void by transmuting internalizations of idealized goals, which provided narcissistic sustenance to the self (Kohut, 1977, pp. 125–127).

Transference

In classical psychoanalysis, transference refers to the process in which the patient relives feelings, attitudes, desires, and fears from childhood in his relationships with people in the present. These feelings and attitudes almost always revolve around unresolved sexual and aggressive conflicts with the patient's parents. In treatment, these feelings are remobilized in relation to the therapist. The patient faces the traumatic memories again and reexperiences and slowly relinquishes the infantile wishes. This process is called *working through*. It has been compared with the work performed in the psyche of an individual who is in mourning. While the bereaved has to give up a love object of the present, the patient must give up the hope of fulfilling unmodified sexual wishes and must relinquish the objects of the past (Kohut & Seitz, 1963, p. 129).

Transference is also recognized in self psychology, but the disturbances that are relived are usually not sexual in nature. Instead, the disturbances are caused by damage to the self in early childhood. There has been developmental stunting of personal growth, because of the severe frustration of children's three basic needs. First, infants need to be mirrored, that is, to have their innate sense of greatness validated and approved. Later, as the grandiose self is modified, children's need to be mirrored is modified to a need to have their competent performances validated and approved. Second, infants need to idealize others, that is, to admire those who can protect them during times of stress that are beyond their competence to manage satisfactorily. At first, this admiration is unbridled, but later in childhood, as we mature and learn gradually about the imperfections in the admired figure, our admiration becomes more realistic and disillusionment less disturbing. Third, children need to be acknowledged by their kin as a fellow human being (for example, to feel a sense of acceptance and belonging). Initially, Kohut saw this last as a part of the mirroring process, but he later drew a distinction between the two needs (Kohut, 1984, pp. 192–194), on the grounds that there are situations in everyday life when the self is strengthened not because mirroring attests to the person's competence and achievement but because the person feels quietly sustained by another in whose presence he or she feels accepted (Basch, 1989, pp. 14–15).

The original childhood experiences that created these unmet needs can be reactivated in the therapeutic relationship if the analyst is able to respond properly, which requires that the analyst recognize and work through his or her own **countertransference** needs; that is, the analyst must recognize and work through his or her own unresolved narcissistic disturbances so as not to interfere with the developing transference. To accomplish this goal, the therapist must not become annoyed or irritated with the patient's attempts to glorify him or her. Second, the therapist must not respond to any of the patient's bizarre fantasies by becoming critical, moralistic, or judgmental. Third, the therapist must not deal with his or her own tensions or anxieties about the patient's experiences by responding with faulty interpretations or premature conclusions. Instead the therapist must adopt an attentive, but unobtrusive and noninterfering, attitude toward the patient. Under these circumstances, transference can take place, as the patient tentatively and gradually gives voice to the underlying fears and longings.

In **mirror transference,** patients relive early experiences in which their mother or father failed to mirror them and seek to be validated by the therapist's approval; in **idealizing transference,** patients relive early experiences in which their father or mother failed to fulfill their needs for a comforting protective figure and see the therapist as an admired and powerful figure who will protect and help them; and, in **alter-ego transference,** they seek from the therapist the comfort and acceptance that their own parents failed to provide (Basch, 1989, p. 14). If these transferences are successful, the therapist will be drawn into these narcissistically pathological situations, will gain better empathic understanding of the patients, and will be able to offer explanatory interpretations about the origin of the pathologies (Kohut, 1971, pp. 28–29; Kohut, 1984, pp. 104–108).

Finally, note that not all of the patient's self structure is defective. If it were, the patient would be psychotic and unanalyzable (Kohut, 1971, p. 31). Substantial portions of the self are healthy and cohesive and are utilized in the formation of a realistic bond and alliance between the patient and the therapist. On the basis of this realistic, trusting bond, the patient can now begin to work through the early, harmful experiences and to bring them under the increased control of his or her ego with the aid of the therapist's insight-providing interpretations.

THEORY'S IMPLICATIONS FOR THERAPY

The patient with a narcissistic personality disorder has suffered a stunting of personal growth because of disturbances in his or her relationships with parents during early childhood. The patient remains fixated on an archaic grandiose self and/or on an archaic idealized parent imago. These unrealistic structures were not modified and then integrated with the rest of the person's personality in the normal course of development. Thus, there is a defensive **splitting** between aspects of the deprived nuclear self and the two primitive, fixated self-structures. The person's ego is hampered in its attempts to function in a mature and realistic way (Kohut, 1971, p. 3). The goal of therapy, therefore, is to redirect narcissistic energies (libido) from these unrealistic structures to the nuclear self and its ego. The therapist uses the major psychoanalytic techniques to gather information about the defects in the patient's self and then provides understanding and interpretations that facilitate and make possible positive change. If these interpretations are accepted by the patient, transmuting internalizations (new learning) occur and lead to a revitalized nuclear self with an ego that is stronger, more cohesive, and more resilient. The person is now more free to continue moving toward the realization of his or her potentials (Paul, 1989, p. 126).

To understand this therapeutic process more fully, let us examine one of Kohut's case studies, involving a patient diagnosed with a narcissistic disorder (Kohut, 1977, pp. 6–54).

The patient was a professional writer in his early thirties when his wife left him, after six years of marriage. He sought help because he suffered from low self-esteem and a deep sense of inner emptiness. In other words, he manifested a primary structural defect in his self. His apathy and lack of initiative made him feel only half alive, and he attempted to overcome this sense of emptiness with the aid of emotionally highly charged sexual-aggressive fantasies. The fantasies involved exercising sadistic control over women by tying them up. He actually had acted out this fantasy with his wife, who regarded his behavior as sick. Kohut said these fantasies and enactments were attempts to cover a primary defect with the aid of defensive structures.

The man also complained about having a writing block and, though he still had a job, was not performing in a satisfactory way; that is, while writing, he often became tense and excited and then had to either suppress his imagination or stop writing.

Within a mirror transference, the therapist learned that the patient's difficulties were based partly on his mother's failure to mirror him appropriately when he was a child. Also, his idealizing transference revealed that his father had provided him with a poor idealized image. In regard to his mother, the patient recalled that he had experienced his mother's responsiveness to him as insufficient and faulty. He recalled how many times during his childhood he tried to look at her suddenly so that she could not have time to cover over her indifference to him by showing a falsely friendly and interested facial expression. He also remembered a situation when he had injured himself and some of his blood had stained his brother's clothes. His mother did not accurately discern that he was the injured party. Instead, she immediately grabbed his brother and rushed to the hospital; she left the patient at home.

One result of the mother's inadequate empathic responsiveness was a maldevelopment in the grandiose-exhibitionistic sector of the patient's personality. Because of her indifference, he did not learn that his real abilities might gain recognition. Thus, he was traumatically frustrated and remained fixated on archaic (primitive and unrealistic) forms of exhibitionism. This exhibitionism occasionally broke through in frantic activity and wild sexualized fantasies in which the mirroring object (always a woman) was under his complete, sadistically enforced control; she was a slave who had to comply with his every wish.

The patient's tenseness and feelings of fear when he was writing were due to deficiencies in the tension-regulating structures of his self, combined with fixations in his grandiose-exhibitionistic sector caused by his mother's failure to help him learn how to modulate his unrealistic feelings of grandiosity. Because he lacked sufficient self structure to curb and neutralize his grandiose and exhibitionistic impulses and to regulate tension, the activation of his imagination while writing resulted in extreme overstimulation; to defend himself against this terrifying experience, he stopped writing.

In part, the patient's writer's block could also be attributed to his father's lack of empathic responsiveness. To overcome the harm he had experienced as a result of his mother's chronic indifference, the patient turned toward his father for closeness, approval, and affirmation. The patient had tried to acquire and to integrate into his personality certain of his father's admired strengths and abilities; because his father loved language and writing, the patient throughout adolescence tried to come close to him through writing. The tragedy was that the father also failed him as the mother had before: the father could not allow himself to be idealized by his son; he did not foster, through the appropriate empathic responsiveness, the development of the idealizing relationship for which the son yearned. After his mother died, the patient tried, yet again, to lay claim to his father's attention. However, he was disappointed by his father's lack of interest in him and by his father's remarriage.

By reliving these painful experiences and working through them in many therapeutic sessions with the aid of the therapist, the patient began to make progress toward the development of a more realistic and cohesive self. He told the therapist that he had begun to formulate his own ideals and more healthy ways of gaining recognition from others. He said that he now realized that the possession of his own independent goals and ideals was essential to his emotional health. He returned to his writing and was no longer frightened when his imagination was activated. His writing resulted in some creative products and he found considerable satisfaction in his accomplishments. In addition, the patient came to realize that his sexual fantasies were mobilized in reaction to narcissistic injuries he had suffered. Some analytic gains were made in this area, but Kohut pointed out that more work remained to be done. As a result, the patient returned for further analysis in this area and eventually abandoned his fruitless attempts to strengthen his enfeebled self with the aid of sadistic sexual fantasies.

Finally, Kohut emphasized that successful analysis does not mean that patients who acquire a strong cohesive center to their personality will thereafter unfailingly be able to deal with others and their environment in accordance with their highest ideals. He maintained that patients who have undergone therapy will not undergo miraculous changes. Instead, when therapy is successful, individuals will show considerable improvement in various areas of their lives. On the whole, good analysis means that patients are able to experience the joy of existence more keenly and consider their life more worthwhile (Kohut, 1977, pp. 283–285; Kohut, 1984, p. 209).

EVALUATIVE COMMENTS

We turn now to an evaluation of the scientific worth of Kohut's theory.

Comprehensiveness   Kohut was a creative and controversial thinker who created a comprehensive theory of personality. His theory addresses both normal and abnormal phenomena, not only on the level of the individual but also on the group level. Kohut used his theoretical ideas to explain a variety of phenomena, including sex, aggression, dreams, fantasies, perversions, anxiety, vandalism, gambling, depression, hypochondriasis, masturbation, art, creativity, family development, independence, love, and group and political behavior. Not only did he focus on normal and abnormal behavior, but he made an effort to describe and explain states of optimal psychological health.

Precision and testability   Like classical psychoanalysis, Kohut's self psychology is dotted with imprecise concepts. The concept of the self-object, for example, is confusing. Self-objects are mental representations of external objects, such as our parents or other members of our family. They are conceptualized as a part of the self because functionally they fill in for deficient self structure. Sometimes they are merged with the individual's concept of himself; at other times, they are seen as having a separate existence within the self. If self-objects refer to other people, then why not simply talk about the person (self) and other people, each with their own separate existences? Although not all analysts would agree, a possible answer is that Kohut wanted to maintain the intrapsychic (within the person) orientation of psychoanalysis. Analysis is an in-depth exploration of the inner workings of a person's mind. It is not interpersonally oriented; it does not try to understand the interactions between two separate individuals. By discussing the self in terms of self-objects, Kohut is able to maintain the intrapsychic orientation characteristic of psychoanalytic theory. Nevertheless, some analysts still have difficulty understanding and accepting the concept (A. I. Goldberg, 1980, p. 2).

Narcissism, too, is a fuzzy concept for several reasons: first, because it is an abstract psychoanalytic concept; second, because, in the popular mind, it is tinged with negative connotations such as selfishness and excessive self-absorption. In fairness to Kohut, he noted this problem and made considerable efforts to inform people that narcissism can take many forms, some psychologically unhealthy and some healthy. Despite his efforts, it is not always clear which meaning of the term he has in mind when he discusses the role of narcissism in the person's development.

While it is easy to confuse the concept of empathy with sympathy and compassion, Kohut does take pains to give it a very precise meaning that distinguishes it from other emotional states. The problem here, therefore, is not with his conceptual definition but more with his ability to precisely measure it. Kohut claims that it is a neutral assessment tool whose use allows him to collect psychological data objectively. Here the analyst acts as the assessment instrument—that is, as a scientific observer who becomes immersed in the subjective experiences of the patient. If the analyst can adopt the perspective of the other without allowing his or her preconceptions and feelings to interfere with the process—that is, if the analyst can be neutral and objective—then he or she can gather psychological facts accurately. Of course, there is no direct proof possible that the analyst has indeed been able to become immersed in the experiences of the patient without distorting them via his or her own theoretical preconceptions, attitudes, biases, needs, and so forth. Thus, we are simply left with the analyst's word that he or she has tried to proceed in an objective way. Perhaps the analyst simply found what he or she was looking for (Akhtar, 1989, p. 353). Thus, there is a need to collect other corroborating data both inside and outside of the analytic setting before confidence in the therapist's findings can be established (Goldberg, 1988, p. 56).

Besides these problems, difficulties in testing also arise because many of the theory's hypotheses are stated vaguely. For example, Kohut maintains that children growing up with an unempathic mother will cling to a vaguely delimited image of absolute perfection and, as a consequence, will show a wide variety of pathological behaviors. These behaviors are dependent on the extent and severity of the mother's faulty response (Kohut, 1971, p. 65). Unfortunately, Kohut does not spell out very precisely what he means by a response that varies in extent and severity or what the specific behaviors might be.

Parsimony While Kohut's theory is complicated and comprehensive, it nevertheless has a restricted explanatory base. While, to a large extent, he does incorporate key Freudian concepts to explain a variety of phenomena, he still relegates many of these concepts to a secondary status. In much of his hypothesizing and theoretical explanations, he relies heavily on a few concepts, such as empathy, narcissism, and self-objects. Empathy, in particular, seems to be an overworked concept in his theory (Akhtar, 1989, p. 353). Failures in mental health are almost invariably attributed to the influence of unempathic parents. Yet it is clear that sometimes psychologically healthy people have grown up in relatively unempathic environments. Also, it is possible that pathological development may occur even where the child has had the benefits of empathic parenting (Goldberg, 1988, p. 112). Kohut's theory is too reductionistic and therefore fails to meet the parsimony criterion.

Empirical validity   Data collection within the therapeutic situation has not established much empirical support for Kohut's theory. Many psychoanalysts continue to endorse Freud's views that pathology is the result of unresolved conflicts of a sexual and aggressive nature, and reject Kohut's view that pathology stems from unresolved narcissistic disturbances and damage to the self. As a result, these analysts report that they see no disorders of the self in their therapy sessions with patients. Conversely, analysts who accept Kohut's view tend to overestimate the incidence of self psychopathology (Kohut, 1977, p. 278). Thus, these two opposing camps are collecting two different sets of psychological data. Adherents of the classical or orthodox analytic perspective find data supportive of Freud's theory, but not Kohut's; self psychologists find data more supportive of Kohut's theory than of Freud's classical theory.

There is also considerable controversy as to whether mirroring and idealizing transferences are necessary for a therapeutic cure.

Data collection outside of the therapeutic situation has yielded more evidence consistent with Kohut's theorizing. Unhealthy narcissism, for example, is associated with adjustment difficulties and low self-esteem. More research, however, is needed to demonstrate the role played by healthy narcissism in producing creative and positive mental health outcomes. Also, as yet, there is no research that examines the links between the level of transmuting internalizations experienced by individuals and their level of mental health. Finally, detailed study of the role played by self-objects in the mental health of individuals over the lifespan is sorely needed.

Heuristic value   Kohut's theory is highly heuristic. In place of the traditional psychoanalytic focus on instincts operating within a mental apparatus, Kohut introduced a concept of self that is inherently assertive and oriented toward development of its potentials. This dramatic shift in theoretical focus generated tremendous controversy and led to a reexamination of many of the concepts of classical psychoanalytic theory and therapy. Even today, debate continues to rage over a number of the changes advocated by Kohut. For example, there are still arguments between analysts concerning Kohut's assertion that damage to the self plays the key role in unhealthy personality development. Many analysts continue to argue that frustration of individuals' sexual and aggressive needs accounts for unhealthy development. Others disagree with Kohut's view that damage to the self due to faulty child-rearing practices can explain all kinds of psychopathology. Moreover, many analysts continue to maintain that narcissism is basically pathological (Akhtar, 1989, p. 349); they strongly reject Kohut's idea that narcissism can be associated positively with creativity and mental health. In the history of science, such conflicts between new theories and their predecessors are not unusual or necessarily destructive. In fact, they often result in scientific progress. Thus, these stimulating conflicts between advocates of classical psychoanalysis and self psychology may well eventually lead to an increased understanding of personality functioning (A. I. Goldberg, 1980, p. 2).

Finally, there is growing recognition that Kohut made substantial contributions to psychoanalysis, on both theoretical and therapeutic levels. He is credited with postulating a set of developmental needs in children—for example, needs to be mirrored, to idealize powerful figures, and to be accepted by others—that had been neglected by analysts in their clinical practices. He postulated that these needs, if unmet, result in pathology. He also broadened the concept of transference in original ways, by discussing how mirroring, idealizing, and alter-ego transferences help patients relive early experiences with significant self-objects in which these developmental needs were not met. Under empathic therapeutic conditions, therapists at different times serve as significant self-objects, so that patients can resume the thwarted developmental process, work through it, and experience a restoration of the self (Baker & Baker, 1987, p. 7).

Applied value   Kohut's writings and clinical observations of patients have stimulated considerable research on the narcissistic personality. His work on narcissism has also been at least partially responsible for increasing therapists' interest in understanding and trying to help patients suffering from narcissistic personality disorders. It also seems likely that, as a result of exposure to Kohut's ideas, many therapists are now more inclined to refocus their attention on the use of empathy and self-object transferences as therapeutic tools. Thus, Kohut's theory may have some applied value, although convincing demonstration of the usefulness of his views on therapy awaits the publication of more clinical data. Finally, there is a need to subject Kohut's hypotheses to experimental test.

DISCUSSION QUESTIONS

1. Why did Kohut think that it is necessary and healthy for the mother to mirror her child's grandiosity during infancy?

2. In what ways are children grandiose in their exhibitionism? How would a parent modify children's unrealistic beliefs and behavior as they grow older without permanently damaging their self views? Give some pertinent examples from your own upbringing.

3. Kohut said that idealized parents should be "optimal failures." What did he mean by that?

4. Why did Kohut think that empathy should not be confused with sympathy and compassion?

5. What are unempathic parents? List some behaviors of such parents and explain why you think they would have a negative effect on their children's development.

6. Do you agree with Kohut that the chief problem in today's society is that children grow up with understimulated selves? How do they cope with their feelings of emptiness and depression? What will you do to insure that your children do not develop along the same lines? If you have children, do they have understimulated selves or are they more vibrant, cohesive, and productive? What did you do to facilitate these outcomes?

7. Kohut said that late middle age is a very stressful time for most adults. Why? What could they possibly do to overcome the stresses of this time of their lives?

8. Is it all right to feel special or precious? Try to present pro and con arguments; utilize several of Kohut's concepts involving realistic and unrealistic self structures.

9. Do you think that Kohut's expanded treatment of the transference process in therapy is a significant contribution to psychoanalytic therapy? Give your reasoning.

10. Most of us think of narcissistic people as psychologically unhealthy. However, Kohut maintained that certain forms of narcissism are healthy. Can you think of any examples of your own narcissistically healthy behavior in personal relationships?

GLOSSARY

alter-ego-hungry personalities   Individuals who feel worthwhile only if they have a relationship with a self-object who looks and dresses like them and has similar opinions and values.

alter-ego transference   The process in which a patient whose needs for belonging as a member of the group have not been met by family members relives these experiences with an accepting therapist. This acceptance serves as a means of reassuring the patient that he or she shares a common humanity with others. The strengthening of the patient's self feeling does not derive from having his or her accomplishments mirrored, but from quietly being sustained by another in whose presence the patient feels accepted, irrespective of his or her level of accomplishment.

autonomous self   The self of an individual who has achieved optimal mental health and, with it, a freedom from inhibitions that interfere with his or her ability to act productively. The autonomous self is seen as the initiator of action and is able to avail itself of the talents and skills at its disposal; as a result, the person is able to love and work successfully.

borderline states   Primary disorders of the self in which damage to the self is permanent or protracted. In contrast to the psychoses, the central defect is better covered by major defenses.

cohesive self   A personality that is organized and resistant to fragmentation. It is healthy and functions effectively, because its narcissistic energies are primarily invested in the pursuit of realistic goals.

contact-shunning personalities   A common narcissistic character type. Because of their intense longing to merge with self-objects, such individuals are highly sensitive to rejection. To avoid this pain, they avoid social contact.

countertransference   The therapist's tendency to react to the patient on the basis of his or her own narcissistic needs and conflicts. Working through these conflicts can increase the therapist's self-understanding and facilitate movement toward the patient's cure.

ego psychology   Theory that postulates that the ego often operates independently of id impulses and, as a result, the individual has considerable opportunity for personal growth.

empathy   The ability to assume the perspective of another person, to know and understand his or her experiences.

fragmenting self   Pathological condition in which the person feels uncoordinated. In less severe cases, an individual may feel tired, mentally slow, and/or awkward following several minor experiences of failure. In more severe cases, a person may show hypochondriacal worry over his or her physical health.

grandiose self   A primitive view of oneself as great; this condition is expressed in unrealistic exhibitionism.

ideal-hungry personalities   Individuals who experience themselves as worthwhile as long as they can relate to people they can admire for reasons of intelligence, beauty, power, or moral stature.

idealized parent imago   Children's initial view of their parents as perfect, that is, as all-knowing and all-powerful.

idealizing transference   The process in which a patient whose needs to be protected by an admired, powerful parent in early childhood were frustrated relives these experiences. During this reliving, he or she is given an opportunity to work through these negative experiences with an idealized therapist in order to overcome the developmental defect.

merger-hungry personalities   Individuals who experience others as their own self. It does not matter to these individuals whether the merger is with mirroring, idealized, or alter-ego self-objects. The key to understanding them is to note that the self-objects are used as substitutes for their own self deficiencies and that the fluidity of the boundaries between them and others interferes with their ability to discriminate their own thoughts, feelings, wishes, and intentions from the self-objects'.

mirror-hungry personalities   Individuals who crave self-objects whose confirming and admiring responses will increase their feelings of self-worth.

mirror transference   A transference in which a person who had not been adequately mirrored—that is, confirmed and given approval—by his mother relives these experiences with the therapist. When such a transference develops, the patient has the opportunity to work through those negative experiences with the therapist and hence to overcome his or her feelings of worthlessness.

narcissistic behavior disorders   Self disorders characterized by individuals' attempts to shore up their fragile self-esteem by engaging in addictive, perverse, or delinquent behavior.

narcissistic personality disorders   Self disorders characterized by grandiose thinking, hypersensitivity to slights and perceived failures, inability to forgive, lack of zest, impaired personal relationships, and fragile self-esteem.

need to be mirrored   The grandiose self's fundamental, biologically based need for approval and validation.

need to idealize   A fundamental, biologically based need to seek protection and security by identifying with an all-powerful and all-knowing person, usually the parent (idealized parent imago).

nuclear self   The foundation of an individual's personality. It is established through a learning process initiated by parents, in which individuals modify their unrealistic beliefs about themselves and their caretakers. The result of this learning process is the firm establishment and comfortable utilization of skills and the ability to see oneself as a center of initiative and productivity.

object relations   Relationships between individuals and other people. In self psychology, object relations are usually discussed in terms of mental representations of real external people that exist within the individual or self.

object-relations theory   The theory that the course of human development depends on the quality of the relationships established between individuals, particularly between parents and their children.

optimal frustration   An ideal, nontraumatic, frustration of a person's needs that fosters new learning and personal growth. Parents who are too severe or too lenient with their children adversely affect their development.

overburdened self   Pathological condition in which the person has not had an opportunity to merge with the calmness of an omnipotent self-object, usually a parent. The result is lack of the self-soothing capacity that could have been learned through such contact. Thus, individuals without a capacity to soothe themselves in times of stress may overreact emotionally when confronted by threatening situations.

overstimulated self   Pathological condition in which individuals exposed to excessive stimulation in childhood, because their fantasies of greatness were continually reinforced by unempathic (nonunderstanding) caregivers, may later be frightened by their unmodified grandiose fantasies to the point of avoiding situations in which they are the center of attention.

paranoid personality disorders   Borderline states in which deficiencies in self structures are shielded against further damage by using hostility and suspicion to keep potentially injurious objects at a safe distance.

primary narcissism   An initial state of well-being and satisfaction in which all of the infant's needs are gratified and the infant feels an oceanic perfection and bliss.

psychosis   A primary disturbance of the self in which defenses do not cover major defects in the self.

schizoid personality disorders   Borderline states in which defective self structures are protected against further damage by aloofness and superficial involvement in relationships.

self-objects   Mental representations of other people, who function as tension-regulating structures of the self and who are experienced as if they are part of the self.

self psychology   Theory that the self (and its needs), and not the instincts, is the center of psychological motivation, organization, and change in personality. It also assumes that psychological damage to the self, not frustration of the sexual and aggressive instincts, produces psychopathology.

self-state dreams   Dreams that are not disguised attempts at wish fulfillment but rather straightforward depictions of the current state of the self. These dreams are analyzed for insight into the diffuse feelings of anxiety that the patient has about a fragmenting self. The analysis is in terms of the manifest content of the dreams. Attempts to find a latent content with underlying sexual meaning are believed to be unsuccessful.

splitting   A defense in which individuals disavow (split off) feelings of emptiness, depression, and deprivation in one sector of personality by acting out various grandiose ideas or by engaging in perverse, but exciting, activities under the control of another sector of the personality.

transmuting internalizations   The process whereby individuals learn more realistic and effective ways of thinking, feeling, and behaving as a consequence of interactions with empathic parents.

understimulated self   Pathological condition in which individuals feel empty, bored, and depressed because their parents have failed to respond empathically to their mirroring and idealizing needs. To overcome these aversive feelings, the individuals engage in various exciting but counterproductive activities, such as gambling, sexual perversions, excessive drinking, and drug abuse.

SUGGESTED READINGS

Kohut, H. (1971). *The analysis of the self*. New York: International Universities Press.

Kohut, H. (1977). *The restoration of the self*. New York: International Universities Press.

Kohut, H. (1984). *How does analysis cure?* Chicago: The University of Chicago Press.

Kohut, H., & Wolf, E. (1978). The disorders of the self and their treatment: An outline. *International Journal of Psychoanalysis, 59,* 413–426.

Leider, R. J. (1995). The psychology of the self. In E. Nersessian and R. Kopff (Eds.), *The textbook of psychoanalysis*. Washington, DC: American Psychiatric Association Press.

Wolf, E. S. (1988). *Treating the self*. New York: Guilford Press.

REFERENCES

Akhtar, S. (1989). Kohut and Kernberg: A critical comparison. In D. W. Detrick and S. P. Detrick (Eds.), *Self psychology: Comparisons and contrasts* (pp. 329–362). Hillsdale, NJ: Analytic Press.

American Psychiatric Association. (1994). *Diagnostic and statistical manual of mental disorders* (4th ed., rev.). Washington, DC: author.

Baker, H. S., & Baker, M. N. (1987). Heinz Kohut's self psychology: An overview. *American Journal of Psychiatry, 144,* 1–9.

Basch, M. F. (1989). A comparison of Freud and Kohut: Apostasy or synergy? In D. W. Detrick and S. P. Detrick (Eds.), *Self psychology: Comparisons and contrasts* (pp. 3–22). Hillsdale, NJ: Analytic Press.

Eagle, M. N. (1984). *Recent developments in psychoanalysis.* New York: McGraw-Hill.

Gabriel, M. T., Critelli, J. W., & Ee, J. S. (1994). Narcissistic illusions in self-evaluations of intelligence and attractiveness. *Journal of Personality, 62,* 143–155.

Goldberg, A. I. (1980). Introductory remarks. In A. Goldberg (Ed.), *Advances in self psychology* (pp. 1–21). New York: International Universities Press.

Goldberg, A. I. (1982). Obituary: Heinz Kohut (1913–1981). *International Journal of Psychoanalysis, 63,* 257–258.

Goldberg, A. I. (1988). *A fresh look at psychoanalysis: The view from self psychology.* Hillsdale, NJ: Analytic Press.

Goldberg, C. (1980). *In defense of narcissism.* New York: Gardner Press.

Kohut, H. (1959). Introspection, empathy and psychoanalysis. In P. Ornstein (Ed.), *The search for the self* (Vol. 1, pp. 205–232). New York: International Universities Press.

Kohut, H. (1966). Forms and transformations of narcissism. *Journal of the American Psychoanalytic Association, 14,* 243–272.

Kohut, H. (1971). *The analysis of the self.* New York: International Universities Press.

Kohut, H. (1977). *The restoration of the self.* New York: International Universities Press.

Kohut, H. (1980). Reflections on advances in self psychology. In A. Goldberg (Ed.), *Advances in self psychology* (pp. 473–554).

Kohut, H. (1984). *How does analysis cure?* Chicago: The University of Chicago Press.

Kohut, H. (1985). *Self psychology and the humanities: Reflections on a new psychoanalytic approach.* New York: W. W. Norton.

Kohut, H., & Seitz, P. F. D. (1963). Concepts and theories of psychoanalysis. In J. M. Wepman and R. W. Heine (Eds.), *Concepts of personality* (pp. 113–141). Chicago, IL: Aldine.

Kohut, H., & Wolf, E. (1978). The disorders of the self and their treatment: An outline. *International Journal of Psychoanalysis, 59,* 413–426.

Leider, R. J. (1995). The psychology of the self. In E. Nersessian and R. Kopff (Eds.), *The textbook of psychoanalysis*. Washington, DC: American Psychiatric Association Press.

Lichtenberg, J. D. (1991). *Psychoanalysis and infant research*. Hillsdale, NJ: Analytic Press.

Morf, C. C., & Rhodewalt, F. (1993). Narcissism and self-evaluation maintenance: Explorations in object relations. *Personality and Social Psychology Bulletin, 19,* 668–676.

Okun, B. F. (1992). Object relations and self psychology: Overview and feminist perspective. In L. S. Brown & M. Ballou (Eds.), *Personality and psychopathology: Feminist Reappraisals* (pp. 20–45). New York: Guilford Press.

Paul, H. A. (1989). Karen Horney's theory of self. In D. W. Detrick and S. P. Detrick (Eds.), *Self psychology: Comparisons and contrasts* (pp. 111–127). Hillsdale, NJ: Analytic Press.

Raskin, R., Novacek, J., & Hogan, R. (1991). Narcissism, self-esteem, and defensive self-enhancement. *Journal of Personality, 59,* 19–38.

Silverman, D. K. (1986). Some proposed modifications of psychoanalytic theories of early childhood development. In J. Masling (Ed.), *Empirical studies of psychoanalytic theories* (pp. 49–72). Hillsdale, NJ: Erlbaum.

Strozier, C. B. (1985). Glimpses of a life: Heinz Kohut (1913–1981). In A. Goldberg (Ed.). *Progress in self psychology* (Vol. 1, pp. 3–12). New York: Guilford Press.

Tolpin, P. (1980). The borderline personality: Its makeup and analyzability. In A. Goldberg (Ed.), *Advances in self psychology* (pp. 299–316). New York: International Universities Press.

Watson, P. J., Biderman, M. D., & Sawrie, S. M. (1994). Empathy, sex role orientation, and narcissism. *Sex Roles, 30,* 701–723.

Wink, P. (1991). Self- and object-directedness in adult women. *Journal of Personality, 59,* 769–785.

Wink, P. (1992). Three types of narcissism in women from college to mid-life. *Journal of Personality, 60,* 7–30.

Wolf, E. S. (1988). *Treating the self*. New York: Guilford Press.

Zamostny, K. P., Slyter, S. L., & Rios, P. (1993). Narcissistic injury and its relationship to early trauma, early resources, and adjustment to college. *Journal of Counseling Psychology, 40,* 501–510.

PART THREE

TRAIT PERSPECTIVES

The earliest attempts to explain human behavior involved the use of typologies, in which behavior was classified into discrete, all-or-nothing categories. For example, Hippocrates (and later Galen) classified individuals as melancholic, choleric, phlegmatic, or sanguine and explained the behavior of each of these mutually exclusive types by positing the operation of bodily humors, or internal fluids. Specifically, he proposed that a predominance of black bile caused people to be melancholic and depressed; an excess of yellow bile made them irritable and short-tempered; too much phlegm made them slow and lethargic; and disproportionate amounts of blood caused them to be hopeful and sanguine. Hippocrates also believed that body type was related to physical disease. On the basis of his many observations of patients, he concluded that people with short, thick bodies were prone to stroke (*habitus apoplecticus*), and those with tall, thin bodies to tuberculosis (*habitus phthisicus*).

The inadequacies of such typologies are painfully clear. They involve unsophisticated and oversimplified theoretical and empirical treatments of differences in behavior along with medical explanations that are obsolete in light of current knowledge. But useful vestiges of Hippocrates' legacy to the medical profession and to behavioral science can still be seen in research on hormonal therapy and the effects of various hormones on performance in humans and lower animals.

The assessment of personality traits based on facial features also had its origins in antiquity and, throughout history, has commanded the attention of theologians, poets, philosophers, artists, writers, and scientists. Before the 19th century, devotees of physiognomy tended to make their judgments about personality on artistic grounds; they offered lyrical descriptions of the beauties of various aspects of the face and sometimes presented their version of truth in aphorisms, such as:

> A beard on a woman is a sign of little honesty.
> Bright eyes are the sign of wantonness.
> The smallness of the forehead indicates a choleric man.
> Men with curved noses are magnanimous. (Mantegazza, 1899, p. 13)

Interest in the subject seems to have reached a peak in the late 19th century, but even today there are occasional books and studies on the topic.

The primary orientation of typological studies in the 19th century was scientific, with attempts to measure facial features and relate those measurements to psychological characteristics. Unfortunately, virtually all these findings are meaningless in a scientific sense, because they are based on the biased and subjective impressions of the investigators and on woefully inadequate methodologies. Yet, scientific research that examines the effects of physical attractiveness on behavior is extremely popular today. Cross-cultural evidence shows that standards of beauty vary from country to country, and most contemporary researchers in this area assume that standards of beauty are learned and not biologically based. Their work also shows that physically attractive people are better liked by others than are unattractive people. Among college students, the physically attractive are seen as possessing more socially desirable traits than unattractive people. Beautiful people are seen as more poised, interesting, sociable, independent, dominant, exciting, sexy, well adjusted, socially skilled, and successful than the unattractive (Baron & Byrne, 1994, p. 284). It does seem, then, that people who are seen as beautiful are also generally seen as good—a finding that was accurately predicted by a number of early physiognomists.

Phrenology was still another attempt to use physical traits to relate constitutional factors to individual differences in traits. This system purports to assess personality traits from the shape and contours of the skull. Popularly known as the study of bumps on the head, phrenology originated in the 19th century as a serious attempt to relate knowledge about brain structure and function to behavior

(Davies, 1955, p. 3). Its foremost proponent was Franz Gall (1758–1828), a German anatomist and physician who believed that the mind was composed of approximately 40 independent faculties. These faculties were catalogued by him, and later by various disciples, under such headings as combativeness, benevolence, amativeness, language, secretiveness, self-esteem, destructiveness, and hope (Davies, 1955, p. 6). Gall claimed that these faculties were located in various organs, or regions, of the brain and that the development or lack of development of these organs affected the size and shape of the skull. To judge a person's character or personality, therefore, he believed it was necessary only to study these contours. A person with a well-developed benevolence region, for example, would be judged as having a kindly character; one with an underdeveloped region would be characterized as cruel.

Gall had a single-minded passion for scientific inquiry about brain structure and function; his pupil and colleague Johann Spurzheim did not. Spurzheim's view of phrenology was based on religious and philosophical speculations as well as on scientific research. He sought to popularize phrenology and discussed, in public lectures, its applications to education, medicine, mental health, and penology (Davies, 1955, p. 8). These efforts and those by other disciples proved very successful, and phrenology flourished. During the last half of the 19th century, however, phrenology was attacked by numerous critics on religious and philosophical as well as scientific grounds (Davies, 1955, pp. 65–75).

Opponents attacked phrenology as atheistic and immoral, because it attributed behavior to natural, not divine, causes and because its acceptance implied an endorsement of fatalism. Fatalism, however, was not consistent with the aims of phrenology, whose proponents linked it directly to social reform. Phrenologists considered the diseased brains of the insane to have resulted from violations of natural laws. To overcome their deficiencies, these people should once again follow natural law; they should get plenty of fresh air and physical exercise, eat bland foods, and avoid liquor and tobacco. In the crudest sense, phrenologists were arguing for the establishment of a warm, supportive environment for the insane—an idea still acceptable to the contemporary mental health movement.

Despite the irrational nature of the attacks on phrenology, its critics were effective in damaging the movement. Scientific evidence also took its toll. Pierre Flourens demonstrated in his experiments with pigeon brains in 1845 that large portions of the brain could be destroyed without impairment of function. In 1861, Paul Broca showed conclusively that the faculty of speech was located not near the eyeballs, as Gall maintained, but in the temporal region (Davies, 1955, p. 142). Despite these overwhelming criticisms, phrenology is credited with having an important impact on the field of neurology, in that it directed the attention of researchers to cerebral structure and function. Sporadic interest in the topic still exists, not within the scientific community but among people who also embrace pseudosciences such as astrology and palmistry.

Although there have been numerous other investigators of the relationships between body build and behavior since Hippocrates, the leading researcher in this area in modern times is William Sheldon. Sheldon's typology links body type and personality traits by using a more sophisticated measurement system than his predecessors'. He and his associates examined the physiques of thousands of college students—by photographing them in the nude from the front, side, and rear—in an attempt to determine whether there were any basic regularities among them. After careful examination, Sheldon concluded that there were three extreme components of body builds: endomorphy, mesomorphy, and ectomorphy. Endomorphy is the relative predominance of soft roundness throughout the various regions of the body; mesomorphy is the relative predominance of muscle, bone, and connective tissue; ectomorphy is the relative predominance of linearity and fragility. Positing each of these as a continuous dimension that varied along a 7-point scale, he assigned each person a set of three numerals from 1 to 7. The resulting pattern was the person's somatotype. Thus, a 711 is an extreme endomorph, a 171 an extreme mesomorph, and a 117 an extreme ectomorph.

Sheldon maintained that the person's somatotype is genetically determined and causes people to develop and express personality traits consistent with their body builds. For example, he hypothesized that endomorphs (high in fatty tissue) would be sociable, complacent, and capable of easy communication of feelings. He thought mesomorphs (high in muscle tissue) would be adventurous, bold, competitive, aggressive, and energetic, whereas ectomorphs (low in fatty and muscle tissue) would be inhibited, introverted, hypersensitive to pain, and secretive. He tested these hypotheses by having observers rate individuals on these trait dimensions and found empirical support for his ideas (Sheldon, Hartl, & McDermott, 1949, pp. 26–27). Although this study has been strongly criticized on methodological grounds (Sheldon himself made both the physical and psychological ratings), more methodologically sound studies—in which investigator bias was minimized by having one investigator rate the somatotypes and having the subjects independently rate their own personality traits—have also produced supportive evidence for Sheldon's position (Child, 1950; Cortes & Gatti, 1965; Yates & Taylor, 1978). Despite these findings, however, there is no direct proof that the correlations were caused by biological factors. As an alternative to Sheldon's genetic position, social-learning theorists propose that the relation between body build and traits is the result of learning; that is, people have certain stereotypes about the kinds of traits that are associated with specific physiques—stereotypes that are perpetuated through books, films, magazines, and television, as well as through contact with other people. Adults often transmit these stereotypes to their children, who learn to incorporate the expected traits into their own body concepts, so that these traits eventually become a central part of their own self-concept.

Although Sheldon's measurement system is superior to his predecessors', it is still far too subjective and imprecise when compared to the procedures used by researchers such as Cattell and Eysenck to assess traits and types. Yet the fundamental ideas underlying the modern view of typologies, as exemplified by both Cattell and Eysenck, are found in Sheldon. Thus, these typologies do not classify behavior (from which traits are inferred) into discrete, mutually exclusive categories; instead, types are continuous, higher-order concepts that encompass a group of correlated traits. The difference between traits and types lies in the greater inclusiveness and abstractness of the type concept. Both traits and types, in the modern view, involve the use of graduated dimensions along which individual differences can be quantitatively arranged. For example, neuroticism is a major type, and people can and do differ in degree of neuroticism. Neuroticism, in turn, is the outgrowth of a number of traits that are correlated with each other, including (low) self-esteem, (high) depression, and (high) emotionality. Again, people can and do vary, from low to high, on each of these component traits.

In Part Three, we review and evaluate the positions of three of the most prominent trait theorists: Gordon Allport, Raymond Cattell, and Hans Eysenck. Gordon Allport, whose theory is discussed in Chapter 8, set out to correct Freud's pessimistic view of human nature by establishing the broad outlines of a humanistic psychology; he focused on the uniqueness of the individual and on the creative and rational aspirations of most people to realize their potentials. An important forerunner of the humanistic movement popular in psychology today, Allport and his work would fit quite readily in Part Five, where we discuss the humanistic/existential positions. Because he believed the trait concept to be central to an adequate theory of personality, however, Allport belongs firmly within the trait perspective framework.

After tracing Allport's humanistic roots, we detail his attempts to create an adequate definition of personality and outline his theory of traits. We review his theorizing about the developmental process of becoming, the role of traits in this emergent process, and his conception of the mature personality. According to Allport, the development of maturity takes considerable time, so that only adults are capable of coming close to self-actualization. Moreover, the process involves abrupt shifts, so that mature individuals are qualitatively different from abnormal or immature ones. Mature people have been able to free themselves from excessive reliance on the immediate gratification of basic impulses and drives; they are emotionally secure, self-accepting, and tolerant toward others. In Chapter 8, we also cover the many techniques Allport used to assess personality, the major differences between idiographic and nomothetic approaches to data collection, and the application of Allport's theory to the treatment of people with behavioral disorders.

In Chapter 9, we focus on Raymond Cattell, who believes that an adequate theory of personality must rest on solid measurement and statistical procedures, and provides an introduction to the complex factor-analytic methods he uses to identify the basic traits of personality. Originally, Cattell proposed 16 source traits that could be used to explain personality functioning. Through extensive research, however, he later discovered seven further factors. In addition, his Clinical Analysis Questionnaire (CAQ) can be used to measure 12 psychopathology factors. Cattell now believes that he has uncovered the major source traits found in normal and abnormal people.

In Chapter 9, we also present Cattell's econetic model, which describes the influence of the physical, social, and cultural environments on individuals and their subsequent behavior, and his specification equations, through which he seeks to combine traits and situations as a means of accurately predicting behavior. This multidimensional model includes a complex representation of how traits are dynamically interrelated and how they operate across a variety of situations. Next, we examine Cattell's views on the role of heredity and the role of learning in personality development, in which he goes beyond classical and instrumental conditioning to propose a more complex form of integration learning. We also discuss the use of precise measurement procedures in personality diagnosis, to identify disordered behavior and put the clinician in a better position to help clients. According to Cattell, the P technique, which involves testing the client repeatedly on a large number of personality dimensions over a long period of time, can provide an accurate assessment of changes occurring in the client during therapy. Finally, we present Cattell's ideas on the need for a new morality based on scientific data, a position he calls Beyondism.

In Chapter 10, we review the major contributions to personality theory and research of Hans Eysenck, who has made concerted efforts to gather factual support for his concepts through rigorous experimental research. We describe his typology, with its major dimensions of introversion/extraversion, stability/neuroticism, and impulse control/psychoticism, and the Eysenck Personality Questionnaire used to assess them. We review the limitations of his earlier inhibition theory and present his improved arousal theory, along with the latest evidence in its support. This theory seeks to explain behavioral differences among various types of individuals on the basis of an interaction between inherited arousal levels and levels of environmental stimulation. In discussing the development of personality types, Eysenck emphasizes their genetic basis and the implications for human functioning of genetic research on animals lower on the phylogenetic scale. We then discuss the socialization process and its impact on introverts, extraverts, neurotics, and psychotics, and outline Eysenck's use of numerous assessment techniques. Finally, we present Eysenck's views on the development and treatment of disordered behavior, with special attention to two major behavior-therapy techniques—flooding and systematic desensitization.

REFERENCES

Baron, R. A., & Byrne, D. (1994). *Social psychology: Understanding human interaction.* Boston: Allyn & Bacon.

Child, I. L. (1950). The relation of somatotype to self-ratings on Sheldon's temperamental traits. *Journal of Personality, 18,* 440–453.

Cortes, J. B., & Gatti, F. M. (1965). Physique and self-descriptions of temperament. *Journal of Consulting Psychology, 29,* 432–439.

Davies, J. D. (1955). *Psychology: Fad and science.* New Haven, CT: Yale University Press.

Mantegazza, P. (1899). *Physiognomy and expression.* New York: Scribner.

Sheldon, W. H., Hartl, E. M., & McDermott, E. (1949). *Varieties of delinquent youth: An introduction to constitutional psychiatry.* New York: Harper.

Yates, J., & Taylor, J. (1978). Stereotypes for somatotypes: Shared beliefs about Sheldon's physiques. *Psychological Reports, 43,* 777–778.

CHAPTER 8

Allport's Trait Theory

BIOGRAPHICAL SKETCH

Gordon Allport was born in 1897 in Montezuma, Indiana, the son of a country doctor and the youngest of four boys. He characterized his family life as marked by trust and affection, along with a strong emphasis on the virtue of hard work. Allport was scholarly from an early age; he was good with words but poor at sports. He did not get along very well with his peers. In a show of utter contempt, one of his classmates even said of the young scholar, "Aw, that guy swallowed a dictionary" (Allport, 1968, p. 378).

Although academically he finished second in his high school class of 100 students, Allport insisted that he was "a good routine student, but definitely uninspired . . . about anything beyond the usual adolescent concerns" (Allport, 1968, p. 379). Following his older brother Floyd, who had graduated from Harvard, Allport squeezed through the entrance tests and matriculated there in 1915. The years at Harvard were stimulating and enlightening, according to Allport. He was overwhelmed by the intellectual atmosphere and the strict adherence to the highest academic standards; it was a real intellectual awakening for the small-town boy from the Midwest. Allport followed the example of his older brother and majored in psychology. Besides enrolling in courses taught by prominent psychology professors, he also participated in a number of volunteer service projects (Allport, 1968, p. 381).

After receiving his baccalaureate in 1919, Allport took an opportunity to teach English and sociology at Robert College in Constantinople, Turkey. The following year he won a fellowship for graduate study at Harvard. Before returning to Cambridge, however, he decided to visit a brother who was working in Vienna at the time. He also decided to see if he could arrange a private meeting with Sigmund Freud. With the audacity of youth, he wrote a letter to Freud announcing that he was in Vienna and implying that Freud would no doubt be glad to meet him. To his great surprise, Freud replied in his own handwriting and invited Allport to visit him at his office.

When Allport arrived, Freud ushered him into his famous inner office and sat staring at him expectantly. Not expecting the silence and not knowing what to say, Allport thought fast and told him of an episode on a streetcar on his way to the office. He reported that he had seen a 4-year-old boy who displayed a conspicuous dirt phobia. The boy kept saying to his mother "I don't want to sit there . . . don't let that dirty man sit beside me." Since the mother was so clean and dominant looking, Allport assumed Freud would quickly see the point of the story—that the boy's abhorrence of dirt was a result of his mother's obsession with cleanliness. Instead, when he had finished the story, Freud hesitated and asked kindly, "And was that little boy you?" (Allport, 1968, p. 383). Allport, flabbergasted, realized that Freud was so accustomed to thinking in terms of neurotic defenses that Allport's manifest motivation had completely escaped him. Allport reported that the experience taught him that depth psychology often plunged too deeply into the psyche and that psychologists might understand people better if they paid more attention to their manifest, conscious motives before probing into their unconscious natures.

Allport entered graduate school in psychology and finished the work for his doctorate in two years. He received his Ph.D. in 1922, at the age of 24 (Allport, 1968, p. 384). He was interested in developing a psychology of personality, but practically no one else in academic life had similar interests; he reported that his thesis was perhaps the first one devoted to an examination of personality traits. Immediately after receiving the degree, Allport had a shattering experience that, he later claimed, was a turning point in his life and career. He was invited to attend a meeting of experimental psychologists at Clark University to discuss current problems and issues in sensory psychology. After two days of such discussions, the eminent psychologist Titchener allotted three minutes to each graduate student to describe his own investigations. Allport reported his work on personality traits and was punished by total silence and stares. Titchener strongly disapproved of his presentation and demanded of Allport's major professor, "Why did you let him work on that problem?" Allport was mortified, but later, when they had returned to Harvard, his professor consoled him by saying, "You don't care what Titchener thinks." And Allport found that in fact he did not (Allport, 1968, p. 385). The experience taught him another lesson—not to be unnecessarily bothered by rebukes or professional slights and to pursue his own interests. From that point on, Allport remained a maverick in psychology, a person who thought deeply and originally about issues and who stated his views candidly, no matter how controversial they were in the eyes of others.

Except for a brief stint at Dartmouth, Allport spent most of his professional life at Harvard. During this period, from 1930 to his death in 1967, he wrote many scholarly theoretical and research articles on topics that included prejudice, expressive movements, rumor, and attitudes and values. He also published a number of books, including *Personality: A Psychological Interpretation* (1937), *The Individual and His Religion: A Psychological Interpretation* (1950), *Becoming: Basic Considerations for a Psychology of Personality* (1955), *The Nature of Prejudice* (1958), and *Pattern and Growth in Personality* (1961). Fittingly, his work was recognized by his colleagues, and he was awarded many honors. He was elected president of the American Psychological Association in 1939 and received the Distinguished Scientific Contribution Award in 1964. He said, though, that he valued one honor above all others: at the 17th International Congress of Psychology in Washington, DC, in 1963, 55 of his former Ph.D. students presented him with two handsomely bound volumes of their own writings with the dedicatory inscription, "From his students—in appreciation of his respect for their individuality" (Allport, 1968, p. 407).

CONCEPTS AND PRINCIPLES

A Humanistic View of Personality

Allport, like many investigators in the discipline, commented on the virtual impossibility of defining personality in precise terms. After reviewing definitions offered by theologians, philosophers, lawyers, poets, sociologists, and psychologists, Allport proposed his own version in his first book. For him, personality was "what a man really is." But this definition was still too brief and vague; accordingly, he offered a more precise one: "Personality is the dynamic organization within the individual of those psychophysical systems that determine his characteristic behavior and thought" (Allport, 1961, p. 28).

Allport referred to personality as a dynamic organization because he believed that personality cannot usefully be regarded as a collection of fragmented components acting independently of one another. Allport saw personality as unified, as constantly evolving and changing, and as caused by forces within the person. Although situational influences have an effect, it is the individual's own perception of these influences that determines his or her behavior. Thus, in Allport's view, even behavior that seems to be controlled by external forces is really controlled by internal forces. For example, "if a child is a hellion at home, and an angel outside, he obviously has two contradictory tendencies in his nature or perhaps a deeper genotype that would explain the opposing phenotypes" (Allport, 1968, p. 46). A situationist would simply predict that the child would behave differently depending on which situation is salient. Allport contended that the differences in behavior are caused by opposing tendencies or traits in the person's nature—for example, by learned predispositions to act differently in two different situations.

Allport became more Freudian in his suggestion that a unifying **genotype** actually may be responsible for the two **phenotypes** (behaving like a hellion at home and an angel outside). For example, the underlying tendency, or genotype, might be expedience—the tendency to perform behaviors advantageous to oneself. Behaving like a hellion at home might maximize parental attention, whereas behaving like an angel outside might win the approval of teachers. As you can readily see, such trait explanations can be invoked on a post hoc basis and made to fit virtually any data. The point here is that, although situations play a role in behavior, Allport's primary focus is on traits and other internal characteristics as determinants of behavior. Moreover, he refers to these internal factors as **psychophysical systems**; this term implies that personality consists of both mind and body elements organized into a complex, inextricable unity.

Finally, Allport's definition of personality refers to the individual's characteristic, or unique, behavior and thought. Allport maintained that all the traits we apparently share with others are, at base, idiosyncratic. He acknowledged that this aspect of the definition is very broad, but he wanted to take into account the fact that we not only adjust to our environment by behaving in certain ways, but we also reflect on it. By so doing, we ensure not only survival but growth.

Allport's view of personality emphasizes the uniqueness of the individual and the internal cognitive and motivational processes that influence behavior. These internal processes and structures include the person's physique, intelligence, temperament, reflexes, drives, habits, skills, beliefs, intentions, attitudes, values, and traits. Allport sees personality as jointly determined by biology and the environment. The physique and intelligence level of the individual are largely inherited and set limits on the person's ability to adapt to his or her environment. Temperament, too, is inherited. It is the emotional facet of personality and is defined as "the characteristic phenomena of an individual's emotional nature, including his susceptibility to emotional stimulation, his customary strength and speed of response, the quality of his prevailing mood, and all [the] peculiarities of fluctuation and intensity in mood" (Allport, 1961, p. 34). These inherited structures and processes are shaped by the person's environmental experiences. For example, a child with an excitable and active nature may have it altered by a family environment where his parents are extraordinarily harsh and controlling (Allport, 1937, p. 125).

Allport believed that at birth the infant is almost entirely a creature of heredity. Yet not every inherited tendency is observable at birth; throughout life, there is a subtle biological influence upon development. As the person matures, however, changes also occur through interactions with the environment and the accompanying learning process. In general, Allport believed that, with growing maturity, we become increasingly active, creative, self-reliant, and characteristically rational, largely as a result of learning experiences. We become increasingly capable of making conscious and deliberate choices among alternative behaviors. Allport chose this positive and optimistic approach in reaction to the more pessimistic views current at the time, which he believed were too static, reductionistic, and mechanistic and placed too much emphasis on the unconscious and irrational side of human personality. Allport's **humanistic theory** was an attempt to provide a much-needed corrective for this one-sided view.

The Theory of Traits

The major concepts in Allport's **trait theory** revolve around the different kinds of traits in each of us and the different properties of the **proprium,** or self.

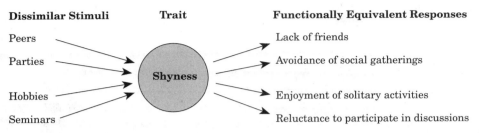

FIGURE 8.1   The trait in action. Dissimilar stimuli arouse the trait, which manifests itself in a variety of functionally equivalent responses.

What Is a Trait?

For Allport, a trait is "a generalized and focalized neuropsychic system (peculiar to the individual) with the capacity to render many stimuli functionally equivalent and to initiate and guide consistent (equivalent) forms of adaptive and expressive behavior" (Allport, 1937, p. 295). Thus, a trait is something that actually exists but is invisible. It is located in certain parts of the nervous system. Although we do not see it, we infer its existence by observing the consistencies in a person's behavior. Dissimilar stimuli are all capable of arousing a trait readiness within the person. The trait then manifests itself through a variety of responses. All these different responses are equivalent, however, in the sense that they serve the same function—that is, expression of the trait. Figure 8.1 illustrates the manner in which a trait operates. In this example, a college man's shyness is inferred from his inability to establish friendships with other students, his avoidance of social gatherings, his enjoyment of solitary recreational activities such as reading and stamp collecting, and his hesitancy in participating in seminar discussions.

Cardinal, Central, and Secondary Traits

Allport also made a number of distinctions among various kinds of traits. Characteristics that are pervasive and dominant in a person's life he called **cardinal traits.** These are master motives, ruling passions, eminent traits (Allport, 1961, p. 365). For example, a person may have an overwhelming need to be powerful, a need for power that can be inferred from virtually all his behavior. Such a person would not only strive to attain a position of power within society but would also interact with his golf partner, his mail carrier, his children, and his marriage partner in a similar fashion. He would try to dominate his spouse and would even try desperately to win a game of

Ping-Pong with his 5-year-old daughter. A casual conversation with an acquaintance might lead to a bitter struggle on his part to win on some trivial issue.

Characteristics that control less of a person's behavior but are nevertheless important are called **central traits.** Such traits are the ones people mention when asked to describe another person or to write a letter of recommendation. For example, we may say that someone is intelligent, sincere, kind, possessive, competitive, ambitious, funny, and honest. These are major characteristics that control the person's behavior in a variety of situations, but they do not possess the generality of a cardinal trait. Characteristics that are peripheral to the person—preferences, for example—are called **secondary traits.** A person might love banana cream pie or prefer to vacation in Maine or Nova Scotia. Such traits are generally less important, less conspicuous, less generalized, and less often called into play than central traits (Allport, 1937, p. 338).

Common Traits versus Personal Dispositions

Allport made yet another distinction among traits. **Common traits** are categories for classifying groups of people on a particular dimension (Allport, 1961, p. 349). We might say, for example, that some people are more dominant than others or that some people are more polite than others. Such generalized dispositions are, in Allport's view, of limited usefulness in a science of personality.

Much more to his liking is the concept of **personal dispositions.** In contrast to the common or generalized trait, the personal disposition is a unique characteristic of the person, a trait not shared with others (Allport, 1961, p. 358). Allport urged psychologists to stop paying so much attention to the role of common traits and focus instead on those characteristics unique to the individual. He believed that common traits were categories into which the individual is forced, whereas personal dispositions more accurately reflect the individual's own personality structure.

> By common trait methods, we find that Peter stands high in *aesthetic interest* and *anxiety,* but low in *leadership* and *need-achievement.* The truth is that all these common traits have a special coloring in his life, and—still more important—they interact with one another. Thus, it might be more accurate to say that his personal disposition is a kind of *artistic and self-sufficient solitude.* His separate scores on common traits do not fully reflect this pattern. (Allport, 1961, p. 359)

In Allport's view, only by focusing on the uniqueness of the individual can we hope to make substantial advances in our understanding of personality.

By and large, investigators have claimed that unique or individual constructs are impossible to imagine. If we used constructs that were unique to the individual, there would be no words in the language for them. We would continually have to invent new terms to describe each individual's motives and behavior—a hopeless undertaking. Of course, we can and do talk about the unique configurations or patterns of traits within an individual's personality, but even here critics have contended that a science focused on general differences between people can handle this problem; there is no need for Allport's highly personalized approach (Holt, 1962). In their zeal to prove him wrong, however, these critics may miss Allport's fundamental point about trying to focus more clearly on the uniqueness of the individual.

PERSONALITY DEVELOPMENT

In Allport's theory, personality development centers on the concept of the self. He acknowledged that this is a slippery concept and has been used by different investigators in different ways. It has also encountered vigorous opposition from many psychologists. Wundt, the eminent 19th-century structuralist, thought the concept of self or ego or soul was hindering progress in psychology and declared that he favored a "psychology without a soul" (Allport, 1955, p. 36). Wundt's objection, which was shared by many behaviorists who came after him, was that some investigators assign a primary role to the term *self* as a mysterious central agency that unifies our actions; that is, they tend to reify the term, to treat the self as though it actually exists and can direct behavior. An example of such reification might be: "Her strong sense of self caused her to give up smoking." Her behavior is explained in terms of her strong ego.

Allport agreed that such reification is damaging to psychology, but he thought we could avoid this pitfall and still make good use of the term. Indeed, he maintained that we *must* use the term, for two reasons. First, the one certain criterion we have of our identity and existence is our sense of self. It is a fundamental experience; if we discard it, we discard the essence of personality. Second, contemporary theories of learning, motivation, and development need some concept of self in order to account for differences in behavior produced by differences in individual experiences—that is, by their degree of relevance to the self. In other words, differences in learning and performance will occur as a function of the individual's ego involvement: a person who is very ego-involved or for whom the task has greater self-relevance may learn to master it more quickly.

At this point, behaviorists might argue that Allport comes very close to reifying the concept of self. Instead, they would simply translate self-relevance into reinforcement terms and predict differences in performance depending on the value or importance the person places on the outcomes of the performance. Thus, a person will work quickly to master a task that yields valuable reinforcers, but will not learn as efficiently a task in which the outcomes are relatively unimportant. (This issue is discussed in greater detail in Chapter 16.)

The Proprium, or Self

Substituting the term *proprium* for self, Allport used it to mean a sense of what is "peculiarly ours," including "all aspects of personality that make for inward unity" (Allport, 1955, p. 40). In his view, the proprium, or self, develops continuously from infancy to death and moves through a series of stages.

The bodily self   The first aspect of selfhood, the **bodily self,** becomes salient in infancy. As infants, we are continually receiving sensory information from our internal organs, muscles, joints, and tendons. These sensations become particularly acute when we are hungry, when we are frustrated, and when we bump into things. In such situations, we learn the limits of our own bodies. As we mature, these recurrent bodily sensations provide information that confirms our own existence. In Allport's view, these sensations provide an anchor for our self-awareness. When we are healthy, we hardly notice the sensations; when we are ill, we are keenly aware of our bodies (Allport, 1961, p. 114). How intimate these sensations are is suggested by Allport in an interesting example:

> Think first of swallowing the saliva in your mouth, or do so. Then imagine expectorating it into a tumbler and drinking it! What seemed natural and "mine" suddenly becomes disgusting and alien. Or picture yourself sucking blood from a prick in your finger; then imagine sucking blood from a bandage around your finger! What I perceive as belonging intimately to my body is warm and welcome; what I perceive as separate from my body becomes in the twinkling of an eye, cold and foreign. (Allport, 1955, p. 43)

Later in the developmental process, we experience sensations from our bodily growth. In adolescence, when these changes are abrupt, some people feel puny, ugly, and awkward; others feel strong, beautiful, and graceful. Some girls may test their ability to attract boys by accentuating female physical attributes. Some boys may test their prowess in physical games and exaggerate their sexual exploits. Allport believed strongly that this bodily sense forms the core of the self and remains an important aspect of selfhood throughout life.

Self-identity   The second aspect of the proprium, **self-identity,** also develops during the first 18 months of life. Despite the vast changes that occur in the course of our lives, there is a certain continuity and sameness in the way we perceive ourselves. "Today I remember some of my thoughts of yesterday; and tomorrow I shall remember some of my thoughts of both yesterday and today; and I am certain that they are the thoughts of the same person—of myself" (Allport, 1961, p. 114). Although this concept of self-identity may seem obvious and even trite, recall Erik Erikson's description of the crises faced by people, especially adolescents, who doubt or are confused about their identities.

Self-esteem   The third aspect of the proprium, which emerges during the second and third years of life, is **self-esteem.** At this point, children have become more familiar with their environment; they experience pride when they master available tasks and humiliation when they fail. One symptom of their growing self-awareness is the outpouring of opposition to virtually any suggestion from the parents. It is a time for testing the limits of the environment and for refusing to take orders from others. Children are typically very negativistic at this stage. These oppositional tendencies often reappear in adolescence, when the perceived enemies typically are parents and other authority figures.

Self-extension   From approximately 4 to 6 years of age, children are primarily concerned with possessions. At this age, children are typically very egocentric. Allport offers an amusing and informative example of egocentricity in a 5-year-old:

> Tommy . . . entered a church with his mother and noticed the cross upon the altar. "What's that?" he inquired. "A cross," whispered his mother. "Red Cross?" he asked. "No, just a cross." "Oh, I know," said the boy, "T for Tommy." It will be many years before Tommy will be capable of understanding the reverse interpretation of the symbol— that it represents "the I, crossed out." (Allport, 1950, p. 33)

As people mature, they extend their loyalties to family, church, nation, and career group. They no longer see these groups from a selfish perspective ("What can they do for me?"), but become more concerned with benefiting other people on the basis of moral principles and ideals (Allport, 1955, p. 45). Thus, **self-extension** in the earliest phases of development is selfish; in the later phases, it is unselfish.

Self-image   Along with self-extension, children begin to develop a **self-image.** According to Allport, the self-image has two components: (1) learned expectations of the roles we are required to enact; and (2) aspirations for the future we seek to attain (Allport, 1955, p. 47). The self-image evolves slowly in conjunction with the conscience. Children learn to do things that others expect of them and to avoid behaviors that will bring disapproval. They begin to formulate plans for the future and to make tentative decisions about careers and the values they will embrace.

The self-as-rational-coper   During the period between 6 and 12, children begin to engage in reflective thought. They devise strategies to cope with problems and delight in testing their skills, particularly intellectual ones. At the same time, they are capable of distortion and defense. Nevertheless, the thrust of Allport's argument is that children at this stage are beginning to sense their rational powers and to exercise them (Allport, 1955, p. 46). Allport calls this aspect of the proprium the **self-as-rational-coper,** or sometimes simply the rational agent.

Propriate striving   Finally, from age 12 on, people begin to develop the facet of the self that Allport called **propriate striving.** Allport distinguished between two kinds of motives: peripheral and propriate. Peripheral motives are impulses and drives—the striving toward the immediate gratification of needs and reduction of tension. We are hungry; we eat. We are thirsty; we drink. We are cold; we put on clothing. We are fatigued; we go to sleep. These are simple and automatic acts aimed at reducing tensions. Propriate motives, in contrast, involve the deliberate increase or maintenance of tensions in the service of important goals. We strive to attain a college degree, sometimes at tremendous personal cost; we try to become the best athlete in a given sport; we yearn to be a great artist or novelist. Propriate striving is ego-involved behavior, characterized by the unification of personality in pursuit of major life goals. To Allport, it is the highest form of selfhood. "The possession of long-range goals, regarded as central to one's personal existence, distinguishes the human being from the animal, the adult from the child, and in many cases the healthy from the sick" (Allport, 1955, p. 51).

The emergence of propriate striving is closely related to the development of conscience. In the child, the evolving conscience is a "must" conscience which is similar to Freud's conscience concept. It is a conscience based on fear of punishment. Children begin to internalize their parents' values and standards and feel guilty if they violate the rules. As people mature, however, there is a marked change in their perception of the world and other people. They begin to develop an "ought" conscience. At this stage, obedience to the external standards of authority gives way to internal, or self-generated, rules. Conduct is guided by the person's own values and self-image.

The shift from a "must" to an "ought" conscience is not automatic. Many chronological adults are still children in conduct. They continue to react in terms of parental prohibitions; they suffer from unresolved guilt feelings and rehash old conflicts with authority figures (Allport, 1955, p. 74). They have not learned to rely on their own judgment and to orient themselves toward the attainment of challenging goals.

Although the seven aspects of the proprium seem to emerge at different stages of life, in Allport's view they do not function separately. Several or even all of them can operate simultaneously:

Suppose that you are facing a difficult and critical examination. No doubt you are aware of the butterflies in your stomach (bodily self); also of the significance of the exam in terms of your past and future (self-identity); of your prideful involvement (self-esteem); of what success or failure may mean to your family (self-extension); of your hopes and aspirations (self-image); of your role as the solver of problems on the examination (rational agent); and of the relevance of the whole situation to your long-range goals (propriate striving). In actual life, then, a fusion of propriate states is the rule. (Allport, 1961, p. 137)

Development of the Mature Personality

Allport described the developmental process as one of **becoming.** The development of the mature personality takes time, he believed, so that only the adult is capable of coming close to self-realization. These shifts in development are not always smooth and even; they are, instead, often abrupt and discontinuous. The normal or mature person is qualitatively different from the abnormal or immature one.

> Initially, the infant is an unsocialized being: Even at the age of two the child is, when measured by standards applied to adults, an un-socialized horror. Picture, if you can, an adult who is extremely destructive of property, insistent and demanding that every desire be instantly gratified, helpless and dependent on others, unable to share his possessions, violent and uninhibited in the display of all his feelings. Such behavior, normal to a two year old, would be monstrous in a man. Unless these qualities are markedly altered in the process of becoming, we have on our hands an infantile and potentially evil personality. (Allport, 1955, pp. 28–29)

During this early stage of development, not only are children dependent on others, but most of their behavior is designed to help them survive. They perform those behaviors that will reduce hunger and thirst, for example. They also learn what Allport called our "tribal conformities"—for example, the wearing of clothes or brushing of teeth (Allport, 1955, p. 63).

As their propriums develop, children also learn to protect themselves against threats through the use of various defensive strategies. In this regard, Allport accepted the validity of Freud's ego defense mechanisms, but he held that excessive and indiscriminate use of these strategies is indicative of an abnormal or immature personality. The mature personality, in his view, is relatively free of these debilitating tactics. Granting that adult behavior is sometimes motivated by sexual and aggressive needs, Allport once again maintained that such motivations play a relatively small part in the functioning of the mature person, which is directed more by current motives and events. Thus, a student who eats too little, for example, may not be fixated at the oral stage but, rather, may have a contract to eat in the university dining hall, where the food is relatively unappetizing.

Functional Autonomy

The early development of the person, then, is characterized by the presence of peripheral motives. Later, as the proprium develops, there is a shift from this type of motivation and learning toward propriate strivings—the use of creative and spontaneous energies to move toward full maturity. The key question is how we free ourselves from our infantile motives so that we can function as mature adults.

The answer, according to Allport, is found in his general law of motivation called **functional autonomy.**

"Functional autonomy regards adult motives as varied and as self-sustaining, contemporary systems growing out of antecedent systems but functionally independent of them" (Allport, 1961, p. 227). As persons mature, their bonds with the past are broken. Mature individuals no longer depend on parents; their behavior is independent of their parents' wishes. Nor do they need to use defensive tactics to protect their self-esteem from attacks by others; they are now capable of judging their conduct by self-generated rules. A few examples may clarify the concept:

> An ex-sailor has a craving for the sea, a musician longs to return to his instrument after an enforced absence, a miser continues to build up his useless pile. Now the sailor may have first acquired his love for the sea as an incident in his struggle to earn a living. The sea was "secondary reinforcement" for his hunger drive. But now the ex-sailor is perhaps a wealthy banker; the original motive is destroyed and yet the hunger for the sea persists and even increases in intensity. The musician may first have been stung by a slur on his inferior performance into mastering his instrument; but now he is safely beyond these taunts, and finds that he loves his instrument more than anything else in the world. The miser perhaps learned his habit of thrift in dire necessity, but the miserliness persists and becomes stronger with the years even after the necessity has been relieved. (Allport, 1961, p. 227)

Thus, Allport's concept of functional autonomy serves as a bridge between the phase of development controlled by immature strivings and that characterized by mature motives. It should be noted that Allport's concept provides a description of shifts in the developmental process, not an explanation of *why* the shift occurs. Allport struggled mightily to provide an adequate explanation of the phenomenon. He saw its basic roots as biological, but concluded that we lack knowledge of the specific neurological mechanisms that may be involved (Allport, 1961, pp. 244–245). Speculating further, he proposed that each person has a creative energy level that must be satisfied. If it is not, then new interests and motives must develop. These new developments are qualitatively different from motives that operate simply to satisfy basic hunger, thirst, and sex needs. In Allport's view, people are innately curious; they seek to understand themselves, others, and their environments. They are continually trying to discover their place in the world, to establish their unique identities. This creative quest for growth, meaning, and selfhood is part of human nature

(Evans, 1970, p. 32). It underlies the phenomenon of functional autonomy and helps explain the radical shift in motives as people move toward maturity. To be sure, this creative urge for meaning is influenced and modified by experiences with others and the environment. For example, a person has no fully formed, innate need to be a physician, but acquires an interest in medicine through reading, friends, teachers, and parents. The creative urge simply provides the impetus to do something that is challenging and capable of fulfilling his or her potential.

Characteristics of Maturity

To Allport, then, mature individuals are those who are able to free themselves from excessive reliance on earlier motives. On this basis, he developed six criteria for judging whether or not a person is mature (Allport, 1961, p. 283).

Extension of the sense of self   Truly mature persons, according to Allport, are able to participate in activities that go beyond themselves. They are concerned not only about their own welfare but also about the welfare of others.

> True participation gives direction to life. Maturity advances in proportion as lives are decentered from the clamorous immediacy of the body and of ego-centeredness. Self-love is a prominent and inescapable factor in every life, but it need not dominate. Everyone has self-love, but only self-extension is the earmark of maturity. (Allport, 1961, p. 285)

Warm relatedness to others   The mature individual is also capable of relating warmly to others. Allport distinguished between two kinds of warmth. The first is intimacy—the capacity for love, whether of family or friends. The second kind is compassion. Allport believed that mature persons have a certain detachment in their dealings with others that allows them to be respectful and appreciative of individual differences in behavior and thought. Thus, they are not constantly complaining, criticizing, sarcastic, possessive, gossipy, or intrusive on the privacy or rights of others. In short, the mature person follows the rule, "Do not poison the air that other people have to breathe," and realizes

> that all mortals are in the same human situation: They did not ask to come into the world; they are saddled with an urge to survive and

are buffeted by drives and passions; they encounter failure, suffer, but somehow carry on. No one knows for sure the meaning of life; everyone is growing older as he sails to an unknown destination. (Allport, 1961, p. 285)

Self-acceptance   Mature persons are emotionally secure. They avoid overreacting in matters that are beyond their control. They have a high tolerance level for frustration because they have reached the point of **self-acceptance.** Immature persons, in contrast, tend to act impulsively and to blame others for their own mistakes. Unlike mature persons, they do not bide their time or make plans to circumvent obstacles in their path. In brief, they lack the kind of self-control that characterizes the mature person.

Realistic perception of reality   Mature persons are accurate in their perception of events. They do not continually distort reality. They have the knowledge and skills necessary for effective performance and living, and the capacity to lose themselves in their work. In short, they are problem-centered, not ego-centered.

Self-objectification   Mature persons know themselves. They are blessed with **self-objectification**—insight into their own abilities and limitations. Correlated with their insight is a sense of humor. Mature individuals have the ability to see the absurdity in life and not be overwhelmed by it. They can be amused by their own mistakes and not deceived by their own pretentiousness.

Unifying philosophy of life   Finally, mature individuals have developed "a clear comprehension of life's purpose in terms of an intelligible theory" (Allport, 1961, p. 294). They have a sense of directedness and a set of life goals. Although adolescents have ideals, they are typically vague. When young people seek to implement their ideals and fall short, they experience disappointment. In their late 20s, people begin to learn that they must compromise with reality. They find that their jobs are not as challenging or rewarding as they had hoped, that their marriages or living arrangements fall short of their desires, and that they have not been able to overcome some of their personal limitations (Allport, 1961, p. 295). They find that their goals and values are changing and a revised and clearer set of principles is beginning to emerge. Mature persons have a fairly clear self-image and a set of standards that guide their conduct.

We can only speculate concerning the relationship between traits and the proprium. Knowing that the proprium has its origins in infancy, whereas most of our complex traits are learned later in the developmental cycle, we might conclude that the proprium is the guiding force in our lives, and traits are an outgrowth of its functioning. Clearly some traits—the cardinal and central ones—are integral parts of ourselves, bound in important ways to proprium functioning. Finally, although the proprium guides our conduct, new experiences can also have an impact. For example, a person may be guided by a self-image that requires being kind to others, but both the self-image and the central trait of kindness may be modified as a result of experiences with a series of exploitative individuals.

ASSESSMENT TECHNIQUES

Idiographic versus Nomothetic Approach

Because Allport considered personality to be a dynamic and interrelated entity, he thought it pointless to focus on only one or two of its facets. Its complexity, he believed, meant that investigators must employ every "legitimate method" to study it (Allport, 1961, p. 395). By legitimate methods he meant reliable and valid assessment procedures based on objective and systematic observations of given phenomena. Illegitimate methods, according to Allport, include "gossip, prejudiced inference, the exaggerated single instance, unverified anecdote [and] 'character reading'" (Allport, 1961, pp. 395–396).

Among the legitimate methods used to study personality are (1) constitutional and physiological diagnosis; (2) studies of sociocultural membership, status, and roles; (3) personal documents and case studies; (4) self-appraisal techniques, such as self-ratings and Q-sorts (see Chapter 13); (5) conduct samplings, such as behavior assessments in everyday situations; (6) observer ratings; (7) personality tests and scales; (8) projective tests; (9) depth analysis, such as free association and dream analysis; (10) expressive behavior measures; and (11) synaptic procedures (Allport, 1961, p. 458). Synaptic procedures involve combining the outcomes of a variety of assessment techniques to produce a general picture or profile of the individual's personality (Allport, 1961, p. 445).

Although some of these techniques seek to define the typical case or average person, Allport's own focus was on the uniqueness of the individual. "Each person is an idiom unto himself, an apparent violation of the syntax of the species" (Allport, 1955, p. 19). Thus, he fought an uphill battle against the prevailing view in American psychology that a science of personality should seek to establish universal laws of human functioning—to understand the behavior and experience of people in general. Such an approach Allport labeled **nomothetic.** His own approach, in which the primary goal is to understand the functioning of a specific individual, he labeled **idiographic.**

These two views generate different kinds of information about people. The nomothetic approach relies heavily on the use of statistics in the analysis of human behavior. For example, it can tell us that, in comparison to Bill or Jane, John has a lower need for achievement because he scored only at the 10th percentile on a paper-and-pencil test designed to measure this characteristic, whereas the other two people scored well above the 95th percentile. Further testing could tell us that John is above average in intelligence as compared to other adolescents of the same age. Allport asserted that this sort of information about John, though useful, is limited, because it does not tell us anything about John's uniqueness. The idiographic approach, in contrast, would provide us with information about the ways in which these and many other characteristics interact within John's personality. It would give us a view of the dynamic and organized personality that is peculiar to John. Thus, Allport would seek to establish the lawfulness in John's behavior and experiences through the use of such techniques as personal records, pattern analysis of expressive movements, graphology, and case studies (Allport, 1937, pp. 369–399).

An Idiographic Analysis

A prime example of the use of personal documents to facilitate understanding of an individual's personality and life is Allport's pioneering analysis of the correspondence of Jenny Gove Masterson. Between the ages of 58 and 70, she wrote a series of 301 letters to two friends of her son, Ross, which provide insight into her personality and her strange, tempestuous relationship with Ross.

The Case of Jenny Gove Masterson

As a young woman, Jenny married a railway inspector named Henry Masterson. Before her marriage, she had earned her own living, and now she found it very irritating to remain at home idle all day. She complained often to her husband about her situation, but to no avail. Like most men in the early 1900s, he was vehemently opposed to his wife's seeking employment. Before the issue was resolved, her husband died. A month later, her son was born.

Shortly afterward, Jenny went to work as a telegrapher to support herself and her infant son. She did not complain about widowhood but was very happy to have a child to whom she could give her undivided attention. Jenny was so content with this arrangement that she rejected several desirable offers of marriage. She lavished affection on Ross and was his constant companion. Several of her relatives claimed that she spoiled him, but she replied that she would gladly scrub floors to buy him the things he said he wanted. After several quarrels with her relatives about her pampering of Ross, she severed her relationship with them for 25 years.

When Ross reached puberty, Jenny sent him to an expensive boarding school. In order to afford his educational expenses, she took a position as a librarian and lived chiefly on cereal and milk in a small, windowless room. For several years after, she remained Ross's closest companion. This overprotectiveness continued for several more years until finally he rebelled. He began to see other women, and quarrels with Jenny about them were frequent and very bitter. Eventually Ross married, but kept it a secret from his mother. She soon discovered the deception, however, and was furious. She drove him out of her home with violent denunciations and threatened to have him arrested if he tried to see her again. A few years later, she relented and began to see and correspond with him until his untimely death.

Let us now examine a sample of four letters that Jenny wrote to Ross's two friends, Glenn and Isabel, over this stormy period of more than a decade.

At the time the first letter was written, in 1928, Ross had abandoned his wife and had begun a relationship with another woman. Jenny was despondent and turned to his friends, Glenn and Isabel, for support; in the letter, she explained the reasons for her unhappiness with Ross and the antagonism between them.

> It isn't money that stands between Ross and me—not by any means—it's *women*—more women. (My writing is awful—I'm all nerves.) Sometimes I wonder if Ross is a trifle off balance—sex mad. At first he talked lovely about saving money, building up a character in business and that sort of thing, and I was in the 7th Heaven. He *has* saved money, it's in our joint names in a bank, several hundred dollars. That's why I skimped so. But all the time he was carrying on an affair with a woman, . . . a very bad affair, and before he got out

of it, he wasn't so far from the Pen. I helped him out of that—Now, it's Marie, the Butcher's daughter from Toledo . . . When Ross ditched his wife he wrote to Marie. [Now] Marie [speaks] of coming to N.Y. this winter and renting a room. Ross and I had a scrap—I refuse to do it. Marie will never enter any house that I am in . . . I did not intend to say so much, but I'm heartsore, and sick, and truly discouraged. Ross cares absolutely *nothing at all* for me—I am a great drawback and burden to him. (Allport, 1965, pp. 51–53)

In the second letter, written in 1929, Jenny mentions Ross's poor health. He suffered from an infected ear and, when they operated, the doctors found a large mastoid on the inner ear and an abscess on the outer covering of the brain. She also mentions her resentment of Ross's girlfriend, whom she calls a chip (whore).

Ross called to see me last week—he is still in the Dr.'s hands. He looks very poorly. I invited him to . . . have luncheon with me, and he did . . . It was a swell luncheon, and he seemed to enjoy it. You know . . . the way to bring Ross to his senses is to *give him what he wants* and then leave him alone. I wish now that I had left him last May when he moved the Chip to the Bronx. But even if he marries her now (she may force him into it) he will not remain with her long. And that is where I come in, and why I invited him to luncheon—so that he may not be *quite* alone until he finds a new chip. Right well I know that he hasn't a bit of use for me—is ashamed of me, and despises me, but still the tie of blood is there, and I cannot believe that he is altogether insensible to it. (Allport, 1965, p. 70)

Unfortunately, Ross did not recover from his illness and died shortly afterward. In the third letter, written at the end of 1929, Jenny's hostility toward Ross's girlfriend erupts, and she blames her for Ross's death.

My affairs. Oh, they are all in a turmoil. The chip lady [although] all dissolved in tears, and of course heartbroken, is not too liquid to forget that material things count in this mundane sphere, and lo! she claimed Ross's clothes, and Ross's car. [She claims to be Ross's closest relative.] If she is Ross's nearest relative it is she who will receive the [Veteran Administration's] compensation, and that would be tragic enough to make one die of laughter. She has only known him *6 months*. February was the beginning of their "Great Romance"—dirty and low as they are made—the low contemptible street dog. She killed Ross—morally and physically. (Allport, 1965, pp. 73–74)

Following Ross's death, Jenny entered into a series of legal entanglements with his girlfriend over his estate, from which Jenny emerged victorious. In the fourth letter, written in 1930, Jenny recalls the happy time she and Ross had shared on his last birthday.

> This month has been pretty hard on me—I had to move—it cost a lot—then came Ross's birthday, October 16. Last October 16 Ross spent with me—I watched for him all morning, my heart in my mouth. Then early in the afternoon he came, carrying a lovely bunch of red roses—my favorites—he always got red roses for me. I was in Heaven. He had not forgotten me—he chose to have dinner with me—not with the Chip. He took me to a nice place . . . on Broadway, and then to a show—a splendid show—he came to my room on the roof, and kissed [me] goodnight under the stars—how little we dreamed of what the next year would bring! I am always thinking of him—always wishing that I had done something I did not do—or left something undone, or unsaid, that I did do, and said. (Allport, 1965, p. 88)

In 1931 Jenny entered a home for women—she described it as similar to a good hotel—where she lived until her death in 1937. The superintendent of the home reported that she had become unbearably difficult during the year before her death. She had taken to sweeping her dinner onto the floor if it displeased her and had even attacked one of the other boarders; Jenny hit her over the head with a pail. The boarders were afraid of her, and the superintendent had been considering her removal to an institution for the insane just before her death.

Analyzing the Correspondence

Allport asked 36 judges to read Jenny's letters and then to characterize her in trait terms. The judges assigned a total of 198 trait names, which were subsequently reduced to eight major, central traits. In order of importance for understanding her personality, they were: quarrelsome/suspicious, self-centered, independent, dramatic, aesthetic/artistic, aggressive, cynical/morbid, and sentimental. Allport believed that these results provided some insights into Jenny's personality that went beyond a commonsense interpretation of the letters, but cautioned that the judges' assessments were nevertheless still primarily intuitive.

Allport then reported a follow-up study in which content analysis was used to assess the structure of Jenny's personality. Content analysis is a research technique for the objective, systematic, and quantitative description of communications (Allport, 1965, p. 197). First, the content of her letters was coded; that is, what she said was classified into a number of distinct categories, such as hostility, art appreciation, and affection. Then, for each category, a frequency count was recorded—for example, the number of times she made a hostile remark, mentioned her love of art, or commented on her affection for people. These data were then subjected to a complex statistical procedure called factor analysis (see Chapter 9) to discover the major traits of Jenny's personality. The results obtained by means of this relatively objective analysis were quite similar to the findings produced by the more intuitive judges' ratings.

Allport was careful to point out that, although these two approaches offer some valid insight into the uniqueness of Jenny's personality, they by no means provide all the answers about her.

THEORY'S IMPLICATIONS FOR THERAPY

For Allport, the healthy or mature person is continually in a state of becoming; the unhealthy or immature person is one whose growth has been stifled. He believed, like Freud, that development could be arrested as a result of faulty relationships with parents, especially the mother, in early childhood. Allport believed that people need to feel secure and protected and that deprivations of love and affection can have a lasting and harmful impact on growth.

> All in all a generous minimum of security seems required in early years for a start toward a productive lifestyle. Without it the individual develops a pathological craving for security, and is less able than others to tolerate setbacks in maturity. Through his insistent demanding, jealousy, depredation, and egoism he betrays the craving that still haunts him. By contrast, the child who receives adequate gratification of his infant needs is more likely to be prepared to give up his habits of demanding, and to learn tolerance for his later frustrations. Having completed successfully one stage of development he is free to abandon the habits appropriate to this stage and to enter the mature reaches of becoming. (Allport, 1955, p. 32)

To overcome these deprivations, Allport believed that the person must come to feel "accepted and wanted by therapist, family, and associates." The person must feel loved and must learn to love. "Love received and love given comprise the best form of therapy" (Allport, 1955, p. 33).

But this is only one side of the picture. Many people who have had secure and loving backgrounds later become neurotic. Although their secure backgrounds make them free to grow, other problems arise.

Society exerts pressures on individuals to adjust to its norms, and often these adjustments preclude positive growth.

> Society itself is sick. Why . . . make a patient content with its injustices, hypocrisies, and wars? And to what society shall we adjust the patient? To his social class, thus making him provincial and depriving him of aspiration? To his nation, thus giving him no vision of mankind as a whole? It is doubtful that we can accept society (any society) as a standard for a healthy personality. A head-hunter society demands well-adjusted head-hunters as citizens, but is the deviant in this group who questions the value of decapitation necessarily an immature human being? (Allport, 1961, p. 305)

Indiscriminate acceptance of society's demands restricts self-extension, distorts the self-image, produces a defensive self, and stunts propriate striving. Loyalties become restricted; correspondingly, there is a growing intolerance of other people and groups. People come to see themselves and their goals in terms of the values established by others. For example, a person may see himself as a lawyer and pursue that goal because his parents demand that he do so; in the process, important goals that he actually desires to pursue are shunted aside. As a result, the person experiences considerable conflict and uses defensive maneuvers to alleviate the suffering. Movement toward self-realization is hindered. The task of the therapist, in Allport's view, is to help such individuals become aware of the sources of their distorted goals and to assist them in the attainment of maturity and well-being.

EVALUATIVE COMMENTS

We now consider the scientific worth of Allport's theory.

Comprehensiveness Allport's theory is comprehensive in the sense that it is incredibly eclectic; it borrows concepts from learning theory, psychoanalysis, and existentialism. Its focus, however, is largely limited to healthy development. Moreover, it describes the developmental stages of the proprium only in general terms, with little attempt to specify precisely the variables that control the occurrence, maintenance, or modification of self phenomena. Finally, the theory is restricted in that, although it recognizes the influence of the environment, it does not specify in enough detail how the environment affects the development of personality.

Precision and testability   Allport's theory is populated with vague and ill-defined concepts and propositions. Terms such as *propriate striving* and the *self-as-rational-coper* do not lend themselves readily to operational definitions. Nor was Allport explicit in stating the relationship between his trait concepts and his theory of the development of the proprium. Given these problems, it would be difficult to design adequate tests of his theory.

Parsimony   Allport's theory fails to meet the parsimony criterion not because it is surfeited with excess concepts but because it has too few concepts to account for the phenomena within its domain. It is doubtful that the complexities of the developmental process can be described adequately in terms of his seven major aspects of the self.

Empirical validity   Very few attempts have been made to determine the validity of Allport's theory of traits and self-development, presumably because the theory is primarily descriptive and lacks specific propositions from which researchers might derive testable hypotheses. As a result, empirical support for his theory is weak.

Heuristic value   Although Allport's theory has not generated much research, his insistence on the role of individual traits (personal dispositions) in an adequate theory of personality remains highly relevant and provocative to the present day (Funder, 1991).

> Psychology is truly itself only when it can deal with individuality. It is vain to plead that other sciences do not do so, that they are allowed to brush off the bothersome issue of uniqueness. The truth is that psychology is *assigned* the task of being curious about human persons, and persons exist only in concrete and unique patterns. . . . We study the human person most fully when we take him as an individual. He is more than a bundle of habits, more than a point of intersection of abstract dimensions. He is more than a representative of his species, more than a citizen of the state, more than an incident in the movements of mankind. He transcends them all. The individual, striving ever for integrity and fulfillment, has existed under all forms of social lifeforms as varied as the nomadic and feudal, capitalist and communist. No society holds together for long without the respect man shows to man. The individual today struggles on even under oppression, always hoping and planning for a more perfect democracy where the dignity and growth of each personality will be prized above all else. (Allport, 1961, p. 573)

Thus, Allport remains the champion of the idiographic approach to the study of personality. Many investigators have been forced by Allport's clear voice to reconsider their acceptance of the tenets of a nomothetic science and to concede with him that any worthwhile theory of personality must take into account the uniqueness of the individual.

Applied value   Allport's theory has not had much impact on disciplines outside psychology. Within psychology, however, his theory of self-development has proved highly useful to clinical psychologists in their treatment of patients.

DISCUSSION QUESTIONS

1. What is a trait? What kinds of traits are there, according to Allport? Give concrete examples of each kind in people you know.
2. Is temperament an important part of personality? What is your temperament? How does it influence your behavior?
3. In what ways is Allport an important forerunner of the humanistic movement in psychology?
4. Is it always healthy to live by your own standards or values and not by the standards of others?
5. List the inadequacies of the concept of functional autonomy in explaining behavior.
6. Describe the criteria used by Allport to characterize the mature person. Can you think of any others?
7. Compare and contrast the nomothetic and idiographic approaches to the study of personality. What are the advantages and disadvantages of each view?
8. Is it truly possible to have traits that are unique to the individual?
9. Do you agree with Allport that young children are "unsocialized horrors"? What are the implications of his view for the disciplining of children?
10. What are some of the problems in utilizing trait concepts to explain behavior?

GLOSSARY

becoming   Developmental process involving movement toward self-realization.

bodily self   Feelings about oneself based on feedback from one's physical senses.

cardinal traits   Characteristics that serve as the motivating force for virtually all of an individual's behavior.

central traits   Characteristics that control an individual's behavior in many situations, but are less comprehensive than cardinal traits.

common traits   Dispositions shared with others.

functional autonomy   Process whereby a behavior that was once controlled by a basic motive comes to operate independently of that motive.

genotype   Inherited characteristic that may or may not be reflected in the phenotype, or outward appearance, of the individual.

humanistic theory   A theory that emphasizes the dignity and worth of the person. It optimistically assumes the creativity of the individual and movement toward psychological health.

idiographic   Scientific approach to the study of behavior that seeks to understand the uniqueness of a specific individual through intensive investigation.

nomothetic   Scientific approach to the study of behavior that seeks to establish laws by specifying the general relationships between variables.

personal dispositions   Traits unique to the individual.

phenotype   Outward appearance of a particular characteristic that may or may not reflect the underlying inherited genotype.

propriate striving   Motive that propels the individual toward the attainment of important, long-range goals. These drives involve an increase, rather than a decrease, in tension.

proprium   Term used by Allport to signify all the various aspects of the person that make him or her unique; the self.

psychophysical systems   Components of personality, as defined by Allport, on the basis of his belief that psychological concepts represent actual underlying states in the nervous system.

secondary traits   Peripheral characteristics, such as preferences, that exert little control over a person's behavior.

self-acceptance   Acknowledgement and understanding of one's own limitations, along with recognition of one's strengths.

self-as-rational-coper   Awareness of oneself as someone capable of rationally formulating and utilizing strategies in order to solve problems and attain personal goals.

self-esteem   Feelings about one's worth.

self-extension   Sense of identity with one's possessions, family, home, and country. In the immature person, self-extension involves egocentricity—a view of other objects, such as family or other people, only in terms of their contributions to one's own welfare and security. In the mature person, it involves the need to contribute to the well-being of individuals and groups that are central to one's existence.

self-identity The feeling that one is an established human being with a unique past that guides one's present and future judgments.

self-image Role played in order to win the approval of others; also, plans and behavioral strategies for the future that help people attain their goals.

self-objectification Ability to perceive accurately one's own abilities and limitations.

trait theory Conception of personality that postulates the existence of underlying dispositions or characteristics that direct behavior.

SUGGESTED READINGS

Allport, G. W. (1937). *Personality: A psychological interpretation*. New York: Holt.

Allport, G. W. (1955). *Becoming: Basic considerations for a psychology of personality*. New Haven, CT: Yale University Press.

Allport, G. W. (1961). *Pattern and growth in personality*. New York: Holt, Rinehart & Winston.

Allport, G. W. (1965). *Letters from Jenny*. New York: Harcourt, Brace & World.

REFERENCES

Allport, G. W. (1937). *Personality: A psychological interpretation*. New York: Holt.

Allport, G. W. (1950). *The individual and his religion: A psychological interpretation*. New York: Macmillan.

Allport, G. W. (1955). *Becoming: Basic considerations for a psychology of personality*. New Haven, CT: Yale University Press.

Allport, G. W. (1961). *Pattern and growth in personality*. New York: Holt, Rinehart & Winston.

Allport, G. W. (1965). *Letters from Jenny*. New York: Harcourt, Brace & World.

Allport, G. W. (1968). An autobiography. In G. W. Allport (Ed.), *The person in psychology: Selected essays*. Boston: Beacon Press.

Evans, R. I. (1970). *Gordon Allport: The man and his ideas*. New York: Dutton.

Funder, D. C. (1991). Global traits: A neo-Allportian approach to personality. *Psychological Science, 2,* 31–39.

Holt, R. R. (1962). Individuality and generalization in the psychology of personality. *Journal of Personality, 30,* 377–402.

Cattell's Structure-Based Systems Theory

BIOGRAPHICAL SKETCH

Raymond Bernard Cattell was born in Staffordshire, England, in 1905. He received a bachelor of science degree in chemistry from the University of London when he was 19 and his Ph.D. in psychology from the same institution in 1929. While at the university, he served as a research assistant to the famous psychologist/mathematician Charles Spearman, who was keenly interested in determining whether there was one general ability (intelligence) or many different, specific abilities. To answer that question, he administered a large series of tests, intercorrelated the scores, and came to the conclusion that there was, indeed, a single general-intelligence factor. Today, psychologists tend to focus more on people's specific abilities and to use particular skill measures to predict specific types of performance. However, in seeking to answer the question of general versus specific abilities, Spearman devised the method known as factor analysis. Cattell has relied heavily on this technique in developing his own theory of personality.

Through Spearman and his intellectual predecessors—British scientist Sir Francis Galton and statistician Karl Pearson—Cattell was introduced to the statistical study of personality and ability functioning. Galton, in his pioneering work on the origins of genius, used statistical analyses of biological data to show associations between phenomena. Pearson later developed a formal mathematical technique, known as the Pearson product-moment correlation coefficient, to measure the size and direction of the association between two events. This procedure was later used in the creation of the factor-analytic method.

Following his graduation, Cattell served as director of a psychology clinic in England, and then went to New York to become a research associate of learning theorist E. L. Thorndike at Columbia University. Following his brief stay at Columbia, he held positions at Clark University, Harvard, and Duke before accepting a post at the University of Illinois in 1944. He remained at Illinois until 1973, when he retired and left to establish the Institute for Research on Morality and Self-Realization in Boulder, Colorado. In 1977, Professor Cattell became affiliated with the department of psychology at the University of Hawaii at Manoa. He is now professor of psychology at the Forrest Institute of Professional Psychology in Honolulu, where he works to spread an appreciation of the principles of Beyondism (a new morality based on scientific research) among social scientists and educated laypeople.

Two other influences on Cattell's thinking should be mentioned. First, his clinical experience has led him to accept many of the psychoanalytic formulations, so that his theory is an interesting blend of rigorous experimental work and clinical observation. Second, Cattell has been greatly influenced by British social psychologist William McDougall, who espoused an instinct doctrine of social behavior. McDougall sought to explain social behavior by postulating seven basic instincts: repulsion, curiosity, flight, pugnacity, self-abasement, self-assertion, and parenting. Through extensive factor-analytic research, Cattell has identified ten **ergs** (innate motives that influence behavior): food seeking, mating, gregariousness, parental protectiveness, exploration, escape to security, self-assertion, narcissistic sex, pugnacity, and acquisitiveness. He has tentatively identified several others but wants to wait for more confirmatory research before assigning them independent status. As we shall see, Cattell also relies heavily on McDougall's concept of sentiment.

Over a period of 65 years, Cattell has published approximately 40 books and well over 400 research articles. He is also the author or coauthor of numerous personality tests, including the Culture Fair Intelligence Tests, the Eight State Questionnaire, the Motivation Analysis Test, the Object-Analytic (O-A) Personality Test Battery, the Institute for Personality and Ability Testing (IPAT) Anxiety Scale Questionnaire, the Clinical Analysis Questionnaire (CAQ), and the popular Sixteen Personality Factor Questionnaire (16 PF).

Among his more notable books, *Description and Measurement of Personality* (1946) is an early attempt to encourage good, solid, empirical research in the area of personality by presenting the basic concepts of his theory and attendant research findings. In *Personality: A Systematic Theoretical and Factual Study* (1950), he sought to build on this foundation and, in addition, to evaluate data and theories from other fields, including psychoanalysis, cultural and physical anthropology, and sociology. His next book, *Personality and Motivation: Structure and Measurement* (1957), offered the most comprehensive treatment of his position to date. In 1965, he published a popular version of his theory, *The Scientific Analysis of Personality* (updated with colleague P. Kline as *The Scientific Analysis of Personality and Motivation* in 1977). The *Handbook of Multivariate Experimental Psychology* (1966), edited by Cattell (and updated with colleague J. R. Nesselroade in 1988), includes some of his views on the multivariate approach to the study of personality. He coauthored (with D. Child) *Motivation and Dynamic Structure* (1975) and coedited (with R. M. Dreger) the *Handbook of Modern Personality Theory* (1977). Shortly thereafter, Cattell published *Personality and Learning Theory* in two volumes: Volume 1, *The Structure of Personality in Its Environment* (1979), and Volume 2, *A Systems Theory of Maturation and Structured Learning* (1980). This impressive work represents Cattell's monumental attempt to integrate his earlier theoretical and research efforts and to present an expanded theory of personality development that takes into account both biological and environmental influences. In 1982, he published *The Inheritance of Personality and Ability,* which seeks to demonstrate the importance of genetic factors in the determination of personality and features newer methodologies for assessing that role. Finally, Cattell has published two books in which he seeks to derive a code of ethics and spiritual values from science, *A New Morality from Science: Beyondism* (1972) and *Beyondism: Religion from Science* (1987).

CONCEPTS AND PRINCIPLES

Approach to Theory Building

Cattell's **structure-based systems theory** considers personality as a system in relation to the environment and seeks to explain the complicated transactions between them as they produce change and sometimes growth in the person. Structure-based learning implies that there are sets of traits within the person that can initiate and direct behavior. These traits are often genetically based but subject to modification by learning experiences. Cattell is convinced that an adequate theory of personality must examine and explain the goal-directed motivation of individuals, which goes beyond simple conditioning principles and involves individual cognitive activity. According to Cattell, we must focus on the complicated kinds of cognitive and motivational learning that guide people's actions. In addition, an adequate theory of personality must consider the ways in which the culture and various groups within it influence individuals and are, in turn, influenced by them.

To accomplish these goals, Cattell believes, the structure and process concepts (concepts that assess stability and change in personality functioning) of the theory must be grounded in multivariate research, analysis, and precise measurement. Disdaining "armchair speculation," Cattell believes strongly that all scientific advances depend on exact measurement (Cattell, 1950, p. 4). In his view, measurement provides the foundation from which theories spring, and not the reverse.

Cattell's approach to theory building is to begin with empirical observation and description and, on this basis, to generate a tentative rough hypothesis. From this hypothesis is derived an experiment for testing it empirically. The resulting observations, or experimental data, are used to generate a more precise hypothesis, from which the investigator deduces a new experiment to test it. New data are collected, and the process begins again. Cattell calls this process the **inductive-hypothetico-deductive spiral** (see Figure 9.1).

Cattell's inductive theory-building technique is in contrast to the hypothetico-deductive model presented in Chapter 1, in which the investigator begins with a set of general propositions, deduces a hypothesis, and then tests it through the collection of data. Although the hypothetico-deductive model is the one generally employed in the social sciences, Cattell criticizes it on several grounds. All too often, it demands that the investigator have a fully developed hypothesis before starting research. Thus, it fails to teach neophyte investigators about research as an exploratory process, and may lead them to believe that confirmation of the hypothesis rests on some single measurement difference. According to Cattell, this belief is particularly misleading because it encourages the researcher to conclude that the behavior under consideration was caused by a single event, when in fact it had multiple origins. Of course, Cattell may be knocking down

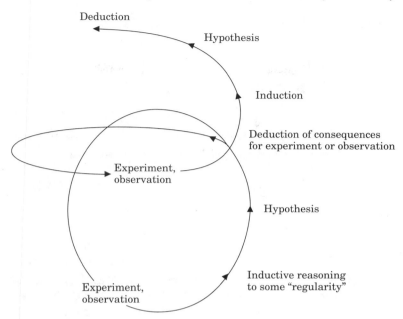

FIGURE 9.1   The inductive-hypothetico-deductive spiral. (Adapted from Nesselroade & Cattell, 1988, p. 17.)

a straw man: few investigators in contemporary psychology are naive enough to believe that behavior is usually caused by a single event. Cattell's point, however, is that excessive reliance on **bivariate experiments** can lead to oversimplified interpretations of the way events operate in reality and that only **multivariate experiments** allow investigators to analyze and interpret complex behavior adequately.

In making his case for the use of multivariate experiments in psychology, Cattell argues that the bivariate method—that is, manipulating an independent variable and assessing its impact on a dependent variable—artificially considers "bits" of human behavior and ignores the "total organism" (Cattell, 1965, p. 20). In contrast, the multivariate experimenter considers the "whole person" and the complexity of human behavior. The investigator "actually measures all the variables and . . . then set[s] an electronic computer to abstract the regularities which exist" (Cattell, 1965, p. 22). Cattell does not consider bivariate experimentation worthless. He simply believes that a far more rewarding and scientifically useful strategy is to utilize multivariate techniques in initial, exploratory research to identify key variables and generate hypotheses that can then be tested using bivariate and manipulative experimental designs (Cattell, 1979, p. 7).

Methodology: Factor Analysis

To study multiple-variable problems, Cattell relies heavily on **factor analysis**—a highly complicated statistical procedure used to isolate and identify a limited number of factors that underlie a larger group of observed, interrelated variables. Factor analysis has a number of forms, but most of Cattell's work relies on two of them: the R technique and the P technique.

R Technique

The most common form of factor analysis is the **R technique.** It usually involves giving large groups of subjects a variety of personality tests and then intercorrelating their scores. If, for example, we administered to a large introductory psychology class a series of tests measuring indecisiveness, tendency to brood, depression, aggressiveness, competitiveness, and conceit, scored each of them, and then intercorrelated all of the subjects' scores, we might obtain the series of correlations shown in Table 9.1. From these correlations, we can see that subjects who scored high in indecisiveness also had high scores on the brooding and depression tests; that is, these three tests are highly intercorrelated. The remaining three tests (aggressiveness, competitiveness, and conceit) are also highly intercorrelated, but are essentially unrelated (very low correlations) to the first three. High intercorrelations, or clustering, among variables suggest the presence of some underlying factor or factors that caused subjects to respond in the way they did on the tests that cluster together.

TABLE 9.1   Intercorrelations between six test variables

Test		A	B	C	D	E	F
A	Indecisiveness	—					
B	Brooding	.72	—				
C	Depression	.85	.67	—			
D	Aggressiveness	.02	.04	.07	—		
E	Competitiveness	.08	.18	.00	.83	—	
F	Conceit	.16	.04	.10	.92	.68	—

Thus, the investigator starts with a large number of surface variables (**surface traits**) and seeks to reduce them to a few common source factors (**source traits**) that can be used to predict the variation in the original surface-variable measures. Variables that are strongly intercorrelated are considered to be measuring, to a great extent, the same entity or factor. The problem facing investigators is that they must eventually label the underlying factors. Because these subjectively based interpretations have important implications for future theorizing and research, considerable skill and care must be exercised in the labeling process. Inaccurate interpretations can be costly.

Once the intercorrelations have been determined, further factor-analytic computations are employed to derive a factor matrix such as the one shown in Table 9.2. The degree of association between each surface variable and its underlying factor is called the **factor loading.** Loadings of .30 and above are usually considered substantial and significant. In Table 9.2 we can see that indecisiveness, brooding, and depression all load significantly on factor 1, which we can tentatively label "guilt-proneness." Aggressiveness, competitiveness, and conceit load significantly on factor 2, which we can tentatively label "dominance."

Once the factors have been tentatively identified, researchers usually seek to refine them using other samples and to cross-validate them by using subjects of different ages, ethnic and cultural backgrounds, and so forth. They may also throw more tests into the analysis in an effort to discover new variables that load significantly on the same factor. Finally, these **primary factors** may be further analyzed to yield what Cattell calls **second-order factors,** which control even more of the observed variation in test scores. For example, primary factors such as ego weakness, guilt-proneness, innate tension, and suspiciousness have all been found to load on a more general second-order factor—anxiety.

TABLE 9.2   Loading of six tests on two factors

Test		Guilt-proneness (factor 1)	Dominance (factor 2)
A	Indecisiveness	.68	.14
B	Brooding	.76	.08
C	Depression	.86	.04
D	Aggressiveness	.11	.88
E	Competitiveness	.03	.69
F	Conceit	.15	.52

P Technique

The R technique allows investigators to assess the existence of common traits in large populations; the **P technique** is designed to discover the unique trait structure of a single individual (Cattell, 1961, p. 415; 1965, p. 372). It involves testing the individual repeatedly over a period of time on a number of personality traits. Figure 9.2 shows the outcome of a P technique study of a 24-year-old graduate student in drama. This study measured eight traits in a series of 80 sessions over a 40-day period. During the same period, the student also kept a diary. The baseline in Figure 9.2 indicates a few of the major experiences he reported: rehearsals for a play in which he had a starring role; a cold he had during rehearsals; the play itself; an accident that happened to his father; reproach from an aunt for not

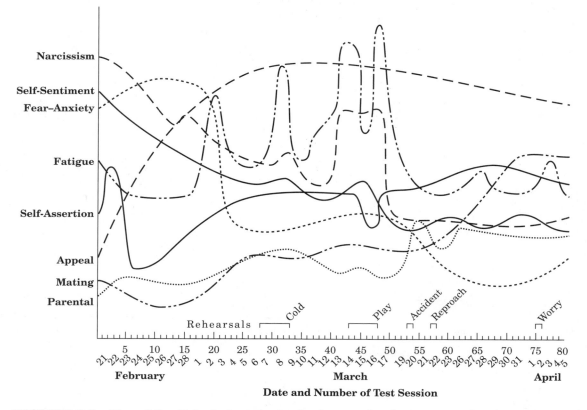

FIGURE 9.2   Use of the P technique to track changes in the intensity levels of various traits over time. (Adapted from Cattell, 1957.)

helping his family enough; and worry over apparent hostility from his academic advisor. Closer examination of the figure indicates that fatigue mounted continuously during the strenuous month before the play, and subsided somewhat afterward. His anxiety level was generally higher during the rehearsal period, when he reported falling further and further behind in his college work because of the time spent in rehearsals. His prayers to God to help him through this trying period (as seen in the activation of the appeal erg) also increased dramatically during the rehearsal period. His father's serious accident (fractured pelvis) on March 20th caused a sharp rise in his protective instinct toward his parent. There was also a rise in his sexual (mating) urges after the 57th session, which was connected with increased time spent in dating. On the crucial nights of the performance, there was a great temporary increase in his feelings of narcissism (self-absorption) and self-regard (self-sentiment), and a sharp relapse and recovery in self-assertion. Finally, his fear and anxiety levels started to rise as he worried about his advisor's apparent hostility because he was behind in his courses (Cattell, 1957, pp. 552–554). Using the P technique, Cattell can assess the process of change in an individual's motivation.

Defining Personality

Cattell defines personality as "that which tells what [a person] will do when placed in a given situation" (Cattell, 1965, pp. 117–118). Consistent with his mathematical analysis of personality, Cattell then presents the definition as a formula:

$$R = f(S, P)$$

In other words, the behavioral response (R) of a person is a function (f) of the situation (S) confronted and the individual's personality (P). Although most trait theorists deemphasize the role of situational parameters in influencing behavior, Cattell has expanded his theorizing to include the ways in which situations, in conjunction with personality traits, influence behavior (Cattell, 1979, 1980). To account for situational influences, he has constructed a model for classifying situations and assessing their impact on the individual. Before examining this model in more detail, however, we turn to Cattell's treatment of the major personality factors, including ergs, sentiments, attitudes, interests, emotional states, and especially traits.

Classifying Traits

According to Cattell, **traits** are relatively permanent and broad reaction tendencies and serve as the building blocks of personality. He distinguishes between constitutional and environmental-mold traits; ability, temperament, and dynamic traits; and surface and source traits. Let us consider each of these major distinctions in turn.

Constitutional Traits and Environmental-Mold Traits

Constitutional traits are determined by biology, whereas **environmental-mold** traits are determined by experience—that is, by interactions with the environment. In other words, some traits are determined by nature, whereas others are determined by nurture.

Cattell has created a complicated statistical procedure called **multiple abstract variance analysis** (MAVA) to assess the degree to which various traits are determined genetically or environmentally. The method is based upon complex comparisons among people of the same family who were raised together and those who were raised apart, as well as members of different families (that is, unrelated people) who were raised together and those who were raised apart. Specifically, a test designed to assess a particular trait is administered to identical twins raised together, identical twins raised apart, fraternal twins raised together, fraternal twins raised apart, siblings raised together, siblings raised apart, unrelated children raised together, and unrelated children raised apart (Cattell, 1982, p. 90). The degree of genetic similarity is, of course, greatest in identical twins and least in unrelated children. The test scores of the individuals in each of these groupings are then correlated with each other, through a technique known as intraclass correlations. Whereas ordinary correlations (see Chapter 1) are obtained by examining the same individual's scores on different tests, intraclass correlations result from comparing the scores of different individuals on the same test. By using a number of complex mathematical equations, researchers can then determine the relative contributions of genetic and environmental factors in the development of a particular trait.

For example, a researcher interested in determining the contributions of genetic and environmental factors to the development of intelligence would administer an intelligence test to members of the various groupings (or classes) just described. Because identical twins have the same genes, any differences in intelligence between them are presumably due (primarily) to differences in their environments.

Thus, the correlation between identical twins, even those raised in radically different environments, for a trait based entirely on heredity should theoretically be +1.00. (In reality, the correlation will be slightly lower, because of errors in measurement; the test will not be perfectly reliable.) In contrast, fraternal twins have only 50% of their genes in common; therefore, the correlation for a trait that is totally genetically determined would be lower for fraternal than for identical twins.

If the correlation between the scores on the intelligence test for identical twins raised together is +.86 and the correlation for identical twins raised apart is +.72, these results—correlations that are high and similar in magnitude—would suggest that intelligence is largely hereditary. However, if the correlation for identical twins raised together is +.86 and that for identical twins raised apart is only +.22, these radically different correlations would suggest that environment has a much greater impact than heredity.

Pursuing the same problem from another perspective, if the correlation is +.86 for identical twins raised together, +.60 for fraternal twins raised together, +.47 for siblings raised together, and +.32 for unrelated individuals raised together, these data would suggest that intelligence is largely hereditary. This conclusion is based on the principle that, for a genetically determined trait, the further away we get from genetic similarity, the smaller the correlations should be. As it happens, these decreasing correlations are based upon actual data and have led investigators to conclude that approximately 70% of the variation in intelligence among individuals is due to genetic factors and the remaining 30% to environmental factors and errors of measurement (McGee & Wilson, 1984, p. 320).

An important feature of MAVA is that it allows researchers to make more precise determinations of the contributions of genetic and environmental factors to the development of traits than do other methods. This information can then be used to help clinicians make decisions about the kinds of treatment that should be used to maximize the chances of patient recovery. Cattell points out that clinicians only ask for trouble if they try to change a largely genetic trait; instead, they should shrewdly use the trait as a fulcrum for levering some other trait that *is* susceptible to change—that is, an environmentally based trait. For example, a clinician who knows that a client has an IQ of 140 can use that fact to facilitate insights into the person's emotional problems. The same clinician would pursue a different strategy if the client's IQ were only 80 (Cattell, 1982, p. 396).

Ability Traits, Temperament Traits, and Dynamic Traits

Traits can be further subdivided into ability, temperament, and dynamic traits. **Ability traits** refer to the person's skill in dealing with the complexity of a given situation. Thus, intelligence is an ability trait in Cattell's scheme. **Temperament traits** refer to stylistic tendencies—being, for example, chronically irritable, excitable, moody, easygoing, or bold. **Dynamic traits** refer to the person's motivation and interests. An individual may be characterized, for example, as ambitious, power-seeking, or sports-oriented (Cattell, 1965, p. 28).

In addition to these distinctions, Cattell, like Allport, finds it useful to categorize traits as either common or unique. Common traits refer to characteristics shared by many people—for example, intelligence, confidence, powerlessness. Unique traits are those specific to one person; for example, Bill is the only person with an interest in collecting 1898 census records for the cities of Baltimore and Los Angeles. Virtually all of Cattell's work focuses on common traits, but his incorporation of the concept of unique traits enables him to emphasize that personalities are unique. The organization of common traits within a given personality, Cattell points out, is always unique.

Surface versus Source Traits

The distinction between surface and source traits is perhaps the most important that Cattell makes. Surface traits are "simply a collection of trait elements, of greater or lesser width of representation which obviously 'go together' in many different individuals and circumstances" (Cattell, 1950, p. 21). When intercorrelated, these variables cluster together to form surface traits. A source trait, in contrast, is the underlying factor that controls the variation in the surface cluster. Surface and source traits, as we have seen, are measured by the methods of factor analysis. Once we have accurately identified the major source traits controlling behavior, we should be in a better position to predict behavior accurately—on the assumption, of course, that we have sufficient information about the person's ways of reacting in a given situation.

Major Source Traits

According to Cattell, any attempt to discover the major source traits of personality must begin with an adequate inventory of all the personality traits that can be used to describe individuals. He calls this total domain of personality traits the **personality sphere** and suggests that the only practical source for such a listing is language. Cattell argues that, over the centuries, every aspect of behavior whereby one human being is likely to affect another has been assigned some verbal symbol—that is, a trait name (Cattell, 1957, p. 71). Therefore, Cattell began by examining the 4500 trait names found in the English language by Allport and Odbert (1936). By eliminating synonyms, he reduced the total to 171. Utilizing observer ratings of individuals on these traits, he then identified 36 clusters of correlations, or surface traits. Subsequently, he added ten more surface traits—a few from the psychiatric literature, and some that emerged in experiments over the years. These 46 surface traits, Cattell maintains, comprise the whole personality sphere (Cattell & Kline, 1977, pp. 30–31).

Later, Cattell and his coworkers constructed personality questionnaires on the basis of items that incorporated the surface traits, administered these questionnaires to subjects, scored them, and factor-analyzed the results to yield the underlying source traits of personality. Using these and other data collection techniques, they were able to identify 16 major source traits (Cattell, 1965, p. 64). These were initially labeled factors A, B, C, D, E, and so on, but later, as more and more supportive evidence accumulated, they were more clearly identified and given labels. (See Table 9.3.) These 16 basic traits were then used in the construction of the **Sixteen Personality**

TABLE 9.3   Major source traits on the Sixteen Personality Factor Test (16 PF)

Low score description	Factor versus Factor		High score description
Reserved (*schizothymia*)*	A–	A+	Outgoing (*affectothymia*)
Less intelligent (*low "8"*)	B–	B+	More intelligent (*high "8"*)
Emotional (*low ego strength*)	C–	C+	Stable (*high ego strength*)
Humble (*submissiveness*)	E–	E+	Assertive (*dominance*)
Sober (*desurgency*)	F–	F+	Happy-go-lucky (*surgency*)
Expedient (*low superego*)	G–	G+	Conscientious (*high superego*)
Shy (*threctia*)	H–	H+	Venturesome (*parmia*)
Tough-minded (*harria*)	I–	I+	Tender-minded (*premsia*)
Trusting (*alaxia*)	L–	L+	Suspicious (*protension*)
Practical (*praxernia*)	M–	M+	Imaginative (*autia*)
Forthright (*artlessness*)	N–	N+	Shrewd (*shrewdness*)
Placid (*assurance*)	O–	O+	Apprehensive (*guilt-proneness*)
Conservative (*conservatism*)	Q_1–	Q_1+	Experimenting (*radicalism*)
Group-tied (*group adherence*)	Q_2–	Q_2+	Self-sufficiency (*self-sufficiency*)
Casual (*low integration*)	Q_3–	Q_3+	Controlled (*high self-concept*)
Relaxed (*low ergic tension*)	Q_4–	Q_4+	Tense (*ergic tension*)

*Technical terms are in parentheses.
SOURCE: Adapted from Cattell, 1965, p. 365.

TABLE 9.4   Sample items on the 16 PF for factor A (reserved versus outgoing)

1. I would rather work as:
   a. an engineer.
   b. **a social science teacher.***
2. I could stand being a hermit.
   a. True
   b. **False**
3. I am careful to turn up when someone expects me.
   a. **True**
   b. False
4. I would prefer to marry someone who is:
   a. a thoughtful companion.
   b. **effective in a social group.**
5. I would prefer to read a book on:
   a. **national social service.**
   b. new scientific weapons.
6. I trust strangers.
   a. Sometimes
   b. **Practically always**

*A person who answers the items by choosing the boldfaced alternatives has an outgoing temperament.
SOURCE: Adapted from Cattell, 1965, p. 70.

Factor (16 PF) Questionnaire. The traits are listed in order of their importance in controlling variation in behavior, starting with factor A and ending with factor Q. For example, information about a person's intelligence (factor B) would enable an investigator to predict that person's performance on given tasks more effectively than would knowledge about the person's dominance (factor E).

To measure the traits, study participants are given hundreds, even thousands, of items; some sample items for factor A are given in Table 9.4. Then their scores are factor-analyzed. Once the factors begin to emerge, other items are added and given to additional large groups of normal study participants in order to refine the factors. The items that load most heavily on each factor are retained; the ones that do not are eliminated.

Factor A   The largest factor, factor A, turned out to be a dimension long recognized by psychiatrists as important in the differentiation of individuals who had been committed to mental hospitals. As Cattell notes, the German psychiatrist Kraepelin first defined schizophrenia in terms of withdrawal, and later the Swiss psychiatrist Bleuler devised a classification scheme in which "insane" people were categorized as either cyclic or schizophrenic types. In the 1920s, Kretschmer, a German psychiatrist who did pioneering research on the relationship between physique and psychopathology, proposed that the types recognized by Bleuler were also found in a less extreme form in normal individuals. Kretschmer showed that these types were associated with certain body builds: schizothymes (schizophrenics) tended to be tall and thin, whereas cyclothymes (manic-depressives) tended to be plump (Cattell, 1965, pp. 65–66). Thus, a long history of clinical observation and research findings supports the differentiation of individuals as either reserved or outgoing. Cattell's research shows that outgoing people tend to be warm-hearted, easygoing, good-natured, and trustful, whereas reserved people are aloof, critical, distrustful, and prone to sulk when they can't get their own way (Cattell, 1979, p. 61).

Factor B Clearly, one of the most important ability traits is intelligence (factor B). Cattell distinguishes between two kinds of intelligence: crystallized and fluid. **Crystallized intelligence** refers to "abilities [that are] distinct from fluid intelligence and considered [to be] due to investment of fluid intelligence in cultural learning" (Cattell, 1982, p. 432). **Fluid intelligence** is defined as abilities "which appear most purely in unlearned performances with new data" (Cattell, 1982, p. 432). In other words, fluid intelligence refers to innate abilities, whereas crystallized intelligence refers to abilities that are the product of cultural learning and schooling, based on the application of innate intelligence to problems.

Cattell believes that, too often, we equate intelligence with crystallized intelligence, which is what traditional IQ tests measure. To help overcome this simplistic view, Cattell has developed the **Culture Fair Intelligence Test,** which is designed to measure fluid or innate intelligence independent of cultural learning and training. See Figure 9.3 for some sample items from the test.

From a lifespan perspective, Cattell suggests that fluid intelligence increases from birth to about 18 years of age and then begins a slow decline to old age. Crystallized intelligence, representing an accumulation of learning *through* fluid intelligence, shows a slight, steady growth throughout life, despite the weakening of fluid intelligence (Cattell, 1987, p. 118).

Factor C Another main personality factor that emerged via statistical analysis is ego strength (factor C). People high on factor C tend to be emotionally mature, stable, and calm, whereas people low on this factor tend to become highly emotional when they are frustrated,

Sample

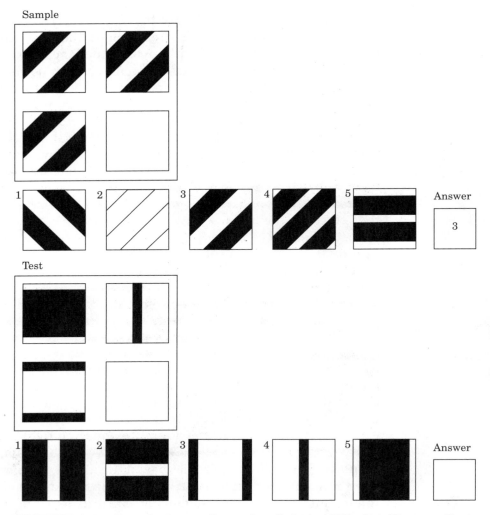

Test

FIGURE 9.3 Sample items from the Culture Fair Intelligence Test. (Adapted from Cattell, 1965, pp. 302–303.)

are easily perturbed, and often act irresponsibly (Cattell, 1979, p. 62). This source trait is very similar to the psychoanalytic concept of ego strength. Research in many different laboratories in North America and Great Britain shows that people who are neurotic or highly anxious also tend to have low ego strength. Cattell observes that alcoholics, narcotics addicts, juvenile delinquents, and school dropouts are abnormally low in ego strength. The essence of the factor is an inability to control one's impulses or to deal realistically with problems (Cattell, 1965, p. 73–74).

Factor E   Factor E is the bipolar source trait known as submissiveness/dominance. Dominant people (E+) are self-assertive, boastful, conceited, aggressive, vigorous, forceful, willful, and egotistical; submissive people (E−) tend to be unsure, modest, retiring, meek, quiet, and obedient. Note that almost all source traits have good and bad aspects at either pole; thus, a person whose scores load on the E+ pole may have both positive and negative characteristics, as may a person whose scores load on E− (Cattell, 1965, pp. 90–91). Dominance (E+) includes the positive characteristics of vigor and forcefulness and the negative characteristics of conceit and egotism; submissiveness (E−) carries the positive traits of modesty and quietness and the negative traits of uncertainty and excessive meekness.

Cattell mentions that men and boys score higher on dominance than women and girls; so do firefighters, Olympic champions, and pilots. Neurotics who are improving show increases in dominance. But dominance is also prevalent in psychopaths, including con artists and incorrigible criminals (Cattell, 1965, p. 92).

Factor F   Surgency/desurgency (factor F) is the largest single factor in children and is quite important in the personalities of adults. Cattell estimates that heredity determines 55% of the variation in this trait (Cattell, 1980, p. 58). High-surgency people are characterized as cheerful, joyous, sociable, responsive, energetic, witty, humorous, and talkative; those high in desurgency are characterized as depressed, pessimistic, seclusive, retiring, subdued, introspective, and worrying. Cattell poses the rhetorical question of why psychology creates so many neologisms such as *surgency*; his answer is that the popular counterparts of these terms are often misleading. Although *sociability* might seem adequate to describe surgency, for example, Cattell argues that surgency includes not only sociability, but other traits as well. In addition, the *quality* of the person's sociability will vary depending on whether we are talking about the test scores on factor A or factor F. The sociability incorporated in factor A refers to a warm, gentle, orientation of liking to be around people, whereas the sociability included in factor F refers to a person who is slightly exhibitionistic, the life of the party, with a practical-joker side that borders on crudeness (Cattell, 1965, pp. 92–93). It is for these reasons, then, that Cattell frequently invents terms.

Factor G   People high on factor G (superego strength) tend to be conscientious, persistent, emotionally disciplined, responsible, and concerned with moral rules and standards, whereas individuals low on this factor are self-indulgent, expedient, frivolous, undependable, and fickle. They show a disregard for rules and moral standards (Cattell, 1979, p. 64). The superego strength factor is similar in many respects to Freud's concept of the superego. People who are high in superego strength tend to be persistent in their pursuit of ideals and highly concerned with exercising self-control over their actions (Cattell, 1965, p. 94).

Factor H   Factor H carries the invented labels of parmia versus threctia. According to Cattell, "the H+ person is one in whom the normal parasympathetic performance predominance is not easily shaken by sympathetic system (threat) or other interrupting responses" (1957, p. 130). Thus, the word *parmia* is based on a shortening of the term *parasympathetic immunity,* and *threctia* is derived from the term *threat reactivity*. The parmic individual is characterized as bold, adventurous, gregarious, genial, and responsive; the threctic person tends to be shy, timid, aloof, and self-contained (Cattell, 1965, p. 95). This source trait has a moderate degree of inheritance—approximately 40%—according to the cumulative findings of several investigations that used a variety of statistical techniques to assess genetic and environmental contributions to trait development (Cattell, 1982, p. 341).

Factor I   Source trait I is labeled premsia (tender-mindedness) versus harria (tough-mindedness). Premsia is short for *protected emotional sensitivity;* harria comes from *hard realism*. According to Cattell, people learn to be either tender-minded or tough-minded. Tender-mindedness is associated with parental overprotection and indulgence, whereas tough-mindedness is related to strict parental disciplining. I+ individuals are impatient, demanding, immature, gentle, sentimental, imaginative, and anxious. I− people are mature, independent-minded, realistic, and self-sufficient. Cattell has also found that I+ people are more creative and more neurotic. In addition, he notes that older cultures tend to be more premsic, whereas pioneer cultures such as those of North America and Australia are more harric (Cattell, 1965, pp. 96–98).

Factor L   Factor L is labeled alaxia versus protension. Alaxia is apparently derived from *relaxation*, and protension from *projection* and *tension*. Protensives tend to be suspicious, jealous, and withdrawn; alaxics are trusting, understanding, and composed (Cattell, 1957, p. 143).

Factor M   Factor M is labeled praxernia versus autia. Autia (M+) is derived from *aut*istic and refers to people who are unconventional, fastidious, absorbed, highly imaginative, and intellectual. Praxernia is derived from *prac*tical and *concern*ed and refers to individuals who are conventional, practical, conscientious, logical, and worrying. M+ persons have a tendency to become completely absorbed in their own thoughts and to disregard practical planning; in other words, they tend to be removed, at times, from the demands of external reality. The M– person, in contrast, is very much concerned with the demands of the environment and tends to pay excessive attention to detail. Cattell believes that M– may be the basis for obsessive-compulsiveness (Cattell, 1957, pp. 147–149).

Factor N   Natural forthrightness (N–) characterizes people who are naive, unpretentious, and spontaneous, whereas shrewdness (N+) characterizes those who are worldly, astute, insightful, and smart (Cattell & Kline, 1977, p. 116). The N factor is probably acquired in childhood under conditions of intense competitiveness where children have to learn to fend for themselves (Cattell, 1979, p. 68).

Factor O   According to Cattell, guilt-proneness (O+) is a trait found in pathological individuals, including alcoholics, criminals, and patients with bipolar disorders. O+ people have few friends and are often critical of group life and standards. O– individuals are self-confident, resilient, and placid (Cattell & Kline, 1977, p. 116).

Factors Q_1–Q_4   The remaining factors account for a small proportion of the variation in behavior and have labels that are largely self-explanatory. One factor of considerable interest to the general public and scientific investigators alike is radicalism/conservatism (Q_1). Cattell found that radicals tend to believe in evolution rather than in judgments given by authority figures in the Old Testament. They also rely less on conventional rules than do conservatives; that is, they conform less to society's expectations of them. Other research has shown that radicals like to engage in self-analysis, prefer dealing with complicated problems, and enjoy discussing the serious questions of life with friends more than do conservatives (Cattell, 1957, p. 209).

In a more recent study, investigators hypothesized that conservatives have a generalized fear of uncertainty and, as a consequence, would be more likely than are liberals to express an aversion to complex and abstract works of art. They had college students express their feelings toward 20 paintings judged by an art expert to differ in terms of uncertainty. The paintings were categorized as simple representational, simple abstract, complex representational, and complex abstract. As expected, conservatives preferred paintings that were simple and representational (literal) in nature and strongly disliked paintings that were complex and abstract. Liberals, in contrast, tended to prefer the more complex and abstract paintings (Wilson, Ausman, & Mathews, 1973).

Research with the 16 PF

The 16 PF test has been used to good advantage by counselors to identify specific areas of conflict within marriages based on the personality characteristics of the partners. Cattell and Nesselroade (1967), for example, examined the relationship between marital stability and husbands' and wives' personalities. They first classified marriages as stable or unstable—operationally defined as "any known step being taken toward dissolution"—and then compared the personality traits of husbands and wives in both groups. In stable marriages they found similarities in the two partners' personality traits, whereas in unstable marriages they found dissimilar traits.

More recent research on married couples has indicated that in marriages where either partner is too high in Q_3 (too controlled) and low in F (very serious and silent), the partners are very dissatisfied with the relationship. Also, considerable dissatisfaction is experienced when either party is too easy-going (high on factor A) and casual (low on factor Q_3). Competitiveness and dominance (high on factor E) in either partner is also a major source of dissatisfaction with the relationship (Schuerger, 1992, p. 242).

Counselors have also made good use of the 16 PF test in the occupational realm. Individuals fill out the 16 PF test and then have the profile of their test scores—that is, their standing on the 16 source traits—compared with the personality profiles of large numbers of people who are in particular occupations and performing well. The major assumption of this matching procedure is that, the more similar a person is to others on a job, the more comfortable and satisfied the person would be once he begins employment in the job. People then can be counseled to seriously consider seeking a job that matches up well with their personality. People who do not match up well in a particular job can be encouraged to consider alternative jobs that might be more suitable and satisfying (Schuerger, 1992, p. 238).

FIGURE 9.4   College student profile on the 16 PF test.

Consider the case of Jill, a college student who was working part-time as a bookkeeper for a local small business while preparing for a career in accounting. She felt vaguely dissatisfied with her part-time job and began to question whether she actually wanted a career in accounting. Her test profile is presented in Figure 9.4, along with the profile of a typical accountant and social worker. It shows that Jill is very outgoing, bold, enthusiastic, assertive, and progressive (experimenting) in her thinking, but only moderately high in conscientiousness and self-control. Her test profile does not match up well with successful and satisfied accountants, who are more reserved, cautious, conscientious, and self-disciplined; it is much closer to the profile characteristic of social workers. On the basis of these results, Jill's advisor recommended that she seriously rethink her major career goal.

Additional Source Traits

Additions to the 16 PF   Beyond the 16 factors measured by his personality test, Cattell has proposed seven additional factors, on the basis of extensive subsequent research: excitability, zeppia versus coasthenia, boorishness versus mature socialization, sanguine casualness, group dedication with sensed inadequacy, and social panache versus explicit self-expression.

Excitability, a factor found in children, increases until early adolescence and then decreases through adulthood. Cattell stresses that this factor is not to be confused with emotionality and instability. Rather, it is a cognitive excitability—a restlessness in which people become hyperactive (Cattell & Kline, 1977, p. 113).

People with high scores on zeppia are zestful, enjoying attention and group action; coasthenics lack energy and are reflective and restrained in their behavior. People high in boorishness are ignorant of social requirements, awkward, and unconcerned about others; people characterized by mature socialization are self-disciplined, polished, and alert to their social responsibilities (Cattell, 1979, pp. 66–67). Sanguine casual individuals are unambitious, self-assured, modest, and casual. High scorers on group dedication with sensed inadequacy are devoted to groups but think that others do not see them as successful. People high in social panache feel persecuted by society, whereas people characterized by explicit self-expression like drama and the heady discourse of avant-garde ideas (Cattell & Kline, 1977, p. 119).

Abnormal traits   Although the source traits utilized in the 16 PF can distinguish between normals and neurotics, they do not measure all aspects of deviant behavior and do not assess the characteristics of psychotics. Applying factor analysis to surface traits in the normal and abnormal personality spheres, Cattell has derived 12 further factors that measure psychopathology. These 12 factors, listed in Table 9.5, have been combined with those previously included in the 16 PF in the construction of a new test, the **Clinical Analysis Questionnaire** (CAQ), which should be of considerable interest and use to clinical psychologists. Thus, Cattell believes that he has now identified the major source traits of both normal and abnormal personality.

TABLE 9.5 Major abnormal source traits assessed by the Clinical Analysis Questionnaire

Factor	Normal source trait	Abnormal source trait
D_1	**Low hypochondriasis** Is happy, mind works well, does not find ill health frightening	**High hypochondriasis** Shows overconcern with bodily functions, health, or disabilities
D_2	**Zestfulness** Is contented about life and surroundings, has no death wishes	**Suicidal disgust** Is disgusted with life, harbors thoughts or acts of self-destruction
D_3	**Low brooding discontent** Avoids dangerous and adventurous undertakings, has little need for excitement	**High brooding discontent** Seeks excitement, is restless, takes risks, tries new things
D_4	**Low anxious depression** Is calm in emergency, confident about surroundings, poised	**High anxious depression** Has disturbing dreams, is clumsy in handling things, tense, easily upset
D_5	**High energy euphoria** Shows enthusiasm for work, is energetic, sleeps soundly	**Low energy depression** Has feelings of weariness, worries, lacks energy to cope
D_6	**Low guilt and resentment** Is not troubled by guilt feelings, can sleep no matter what is left undone	**High guilt and resentment** Has feelings of guilt, blames self for everything that goes wrong, is critical of self
D_7	**Low bored depression** Is relaxed, considerate, cheerful with people	**High bored depression** Avoids contact and involvement with people, seeks isolation, shows discomfort with people
P_a	**Low paranoia** Is trusting, not bothered by jealousy or envy	**High paranoia** Believes he or she is being persecuted, poisoned, controlled, spied on, mistreated
P_p	**Low psychopathic deviation** Avoids engagement in illegal acts or breaking rules, sensitive	**High psychopathic deviation** Has complacent attitude towards own or others' antisocial behavior, is not hurt by criticism, likes crowds
S_c	**Low schizophrenia** Makes realistic appraisals of self and others, shows emotional harmony and absence of regressive behavior	**High schizophrenia** Hears voices or sounds without apparent source outside self, retreats from reality, has uncontrolled and sudden impulses
A_s	**Low psychasthenia** Is not bothered by unwelcome thoughts or ideas or compulsive habits	**High psychasthenia** Suffers insistent, repetitive ideas and impulses to perform certain acts
P_s	**Low general psychosis** Considers self as good, as dependable, and as smart as most others	**High general psychosis** Has feelings of inferiority and unworthiness, timid, loses control easily

SOURCE: Reproduced by special permission of the Institute for Personality and Ability Testing, Inc.

Dynamic Traits and the Dynamic Lattice

Cattell subdivides dynamic traits into attitudes, sentiments, and ergs. He defines attitudes as specific interests in particular courses of action toward certain objects in a given situation (Cattell, 1965, p. 175). Cattell views them as hypothetical constructs that intervene between environmental stimuli and eventual external responses. For example, a student might have the attitude, "I want very much to kiss this handsome guy the next time we go out together." The student shows an intense interest (I want very much) in a particular course of action (to kiss) toward a specific object (this handsome guy) in a given situation (the next time we go out together). Ergs and sentiments are inferred from the factor-analytic study of attitudes. For example, a man may have a timid disposition that is based on an underlying fear erg (Cattell, 1950, p. 84).

Sentiments are large, complex attitudes. They incorporate a host of interests, opinions, and minor attitudes. For instance, a man's sentiment about his home may be seen in his attitudes about his wife, his children, and marriage in general, as well as in his interests in home repairs, landscaping, and the like (Cattell, 1950, pp. 161–162). Such a sentiment would be learned over a long period of time. Cattell characterizes sentiments as environmental-mold traits—that is, traits learned through experience with people.

An *erg* is "an innate psychophysical disposition which permits its possessor to acquire reactivity (attention, recognition) to certain classes of objects more readily than others, to experience a specific emotion in regard to them, and to start on a course of action which ceases more completely at a certain specific goal activity than at any other" (Cattell, 1950, p. 199). In short, an erg is an innate drive triggered by stimuli in the environment that ceases when its goal is reached. For example, the parental erg is released by cries of distress from children and satisfied when they are out of danger. Other basic drives (see Biographical Sketch) include food seeking, mating, exploration, and acquisitiveness.

Why does Cattell think these drives are innate? He bases his judgment on both naturalistic and clinical studies. Naturalistic studies involve observation of behavior analogous to human behavior in mammals lower in the phylogenetic scale, as well as general observations of human behavior in a wide variety of situations and cultures (Cattell, 1979, p. 155). It is inconceivable to Cattell that human beings, who are clearly related structurally and functionally to primates and other mammals, could lack the instinctual equipment that those animals possess.

Cattell believes that we must seek not only to describe and measure a person's traits, but also to show how they are interconnected (Cattell, 1950, p. 156). Thus, he postulates that the dynamic traits are organized in complex ways within the cognitive and motivational structure of the organism, and form a **dynamic lattice.** To explain how the traits are intertwined, he relies heavily on the concept of **subsidiation**—the process whereby certain dynamic traits are subsidiary to (or dependent on) other traits. Thus, sentiments are dependent on ergs, and attitudes depend on sentiments. For example, a high school student may spend large amounts of time watching the stars (positive attitude or interest in such behavior) because of his great love of science (positive sentiment). His love of science is turn rests on the fact that involvement in science satisfies his strong curiosity about the ways in which the universe operates (positive erg satisfaction).

The dynamic lattice describes a complicated and often bewildering intertwining of interests, attitudes, sentiments, goals, and drives. Figure 9.5 presents only a fragment of a dynamic lattice for a hypothetical person, involving attitudes, sentiments, and innate goals. At the right of the diagram, we see the ergs; in the middle are the various sentiments; and at the left are a variety of attitudes. We can see that numerous ergs give expression to various sentiments, that the sentiments are related to one another, that several attitudes converge on the same sentiment, and that a few attitudes are common to different sentiments. We might speculate that this person's love for his wife is based on her satisfaction of his needs for sex, protection, and companionship. In addition, he knows that he must maintain a healthy bank account to ensure his security and to secure the material goods his wife needs to be happy. When all these facts are registered on a conscious level, the person may perceive a need to change his dynamic lattice. He may decide to discontinue his frequent recreational trips to New York for fear they will deplete his bank account and create unhappiness for himself. Alternatively, he may wish to talk to his business friend as a means of securing a higher income and thereby ensuring maximum satisfaction for both his wife and himself.

Changes in the dynamic lattice can also occur as a result of the person's mood or emotional state; that is, a person's traits, attitudes, sentiments, interests, and even goals can be modified by such states as fatigue, guilt, anxiety, depression, arousal, extraversion, stress, and regression. (For example, a person who feels confused may therefore act impulsively.) These states can be measured by the **Eight State Questionnaire** (Cattell & Kline, 1977, p. 22). Changes in the dynamic lattice can also be produced by changes in the person's envi-

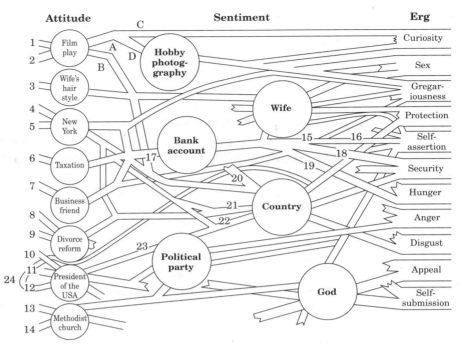

FIGURE 9.5 Fragment of a dynamic lattice, showing interrelationships among attitudes, sentiments, and ergic goals. (Adapted from Cattell, 1950, p. 158.)

ronment. (For example, a serious setback in business will force a drastic change in the person's lifestyle.)

Sentiments are less susceptible to change than are attitudes, according to Cattell, because sentiments are the deeper, underlying structures in personality. Occasionally, though, changes in personality can occur. A person may lose his family in a catastrophe, for instance, and this traumatic event will trigger major changes in personality functioning (Cattell, 1950, p. 160).

Finally, Cattell integrates all the attitudes, interests, ergs, and sentiments that continually interplay within the personality by postulating a master motive called the **self-sentiment.** The self-sentiment coordinates the various attitudes, sentiments, and interests of the person and also regulates expression of the ergs.

The Econetic Model

A major criticism of trait theories has been that they neglect the role of the environment in predicting behavior. The **econetic model** represents Cattell's efforts to remedy this deficiency. It postulates that human behavior is the result of a complex and subtle interplay between traits and situations. As a first step in trying to understand this complicated interaction, Cattell proposes the construction of a taxonomy of situations or environments. To map this vast **environmental sphere,** he began sampling situations mentioned on every tenth page of encyclopedias of a given culture. (This procedure is similar to his efforts to map the traits in the personality sphere.) This approach yielded some encouraging consistencies in the kinds of situations found, but so far investigators have not followed up on these pioneering efforts (Cattell, 1979, p. 218). Nevertheless, Cattell believes that econetics (the study of the ecology) is likely to develop rapidly in the future, with the cooperation of investigators from various disciplines in the social sciences, and that eventually a reliable and objective taxonomic scheme will be constructed.

The next step, according to Cattell, is to assess the impact of these situations on the individual. Some situations have relevance for the individual; others do not. Of the situations that do play a role in the person's life, some have tremendous impact; others have only minimal impact. Some objects in situations are accessible to the individual; others are not. What these situations mean to the individual also depends on the person's moods. In brief, once the classification task is complete, the unique psychological meaning of various situations for the individual must be established (Cattell, 1979, p. 220). Obviously, these assessments of environmental effects on the individual are complex. They involve measuring the effects of other people and of the physical, social, and cultural environments on the individual. Each of these components may be weighted differently and contribute differently to the modulation of the person's traits and subsequent behavior. Finally, the relative contributions of these factors change over time.

Dynamic Calculus

All these complexities, according to Cattell, can be integrated into the prediction of behavior by means of the **dynamic calculus.** It consists of a set of **specification equations** that take into account the multiple traits that influence behavior as well as the impact of the environment. They are called specification equations because they specify the ways in which traits and situations are to be combined to predict performance. In actuality, specification equations are highly complicated and take into account a number of factors not discussed in our treatment of Cattell's theory. (For a detailed discussion of the basic equations and their derivations, see Cattell, 1979, 1980.) The general form of the equation, however, is

$$R = (b_1 A_1 + b_2 A_2 \ldots + b_n A_n) + (b_1 B_1 + b_2 B_2 \ldots + b_n B_n) +$$
$$(b_1 C_1 + b_2 C_2 \ldots + b_n C_n) + (b_1 K_1 + b_2 K_2 \ldots + b_n K_n)$$

In this formula, R is the performance or response of the individual in a given situation. It is determined by a weighted combination of (1) the person's source traits (A_1, A_2, . . . , A_n); (2) the person's states and moods (B_1, B_2, . . . , B_n); and (3) the social and cultural meanings (C_1, C_2, . . . , C_n) of the situation for this person. It could also include the weighted combination of any other factors that have not yet been specified (K_1, K_2, . . . , K_n).

In the formula, b_1, b_2, . . . ,b_n are weights. They are unique to each factor and show the degree to which each is involved in the person's performance in the situation under consideration (Cattell, 1965, pp. 78–80). Weights for traits are generated by experiments in which the performances of large groups of comparable individuals are assessed and the relative importance of the traits is determined by factor analysis. These weights are then used in the general equation, along with the person's own scores, as a means of predicting performance. Other statistical procedures—for example, the P technique—are used to establish the weights for states and the unique meaning of the situation for the individual.

By way of example, suppose that we are interested in predicting a student's performance on a math test. Let us assume that we know that intelligence (A_1) is the most important source trait in predicting success on the test, followed by conscientiousness (A_2) and self-sufficiency (A_3). Let us also assume that we have been able to establish the weights for states (for example, anxiety and fatigue levels) and the unique meaning of the situation—that is, its relevance and importance—to this student.

If the weights on these factors can vary from .00 to 1.00 (with a weight of 1.00 signifying maximum loading, or highest importance), and if scores can vary between 0 and 100, then we might find a distribution of weights and scores as follows

$$R = [.8(90) + .6(80) + .3(30)] + [.6(90) + .8(100)] + [.9(70) + .8(100)]$$

In this equation, high scores of 100 indicate maximum intelligence, conscientiousness, and self-sufficiency; minimum anxiety and fatigue; and high relevance and importance of success on math tests. Working through the equation gives us an expected performance as follows

$$R = [.8(90) + .6(80) + .3(30)] + [.6(90) + .8(100)] + [.9(70) + .8(100)]$$
$$R = [72 + 48 + 9] + [54 + 80] + [63 + 80]$$
$$R = 129 + 134 + 143$$
$$R = 406$$

Maximum performance on the test would be predicted as follows

$$R = [.8(100) + .6(100) + .3(100)] + [.6(100) + .8(100)] + [.9(100) + .8(100)]$$
$$R = [80 + 60 + 30] + [60 + 80] + [90 + 80]$$
$$R = 170 + 140 + 170$$
$$R = 480$$

Thus, our hypothetical student scores 406, as compared to a maximum score of 480. Our prediction is that the student will perform well.

The combination model just presented is linear in nature. Cattell says that we should use it if it helps us predict behavior accurately, and we should modify or even abandon it if it does not. At this point, however, Cattell thinks that a linear model and not a curvilinear one is adequate for the prediction of much of our behavior (Cattell, 1965, p. 252). We could use it to predict academic performance or job success, for example. This multidimensional model includes a complex representation of the ways in which traits and situations are dynamically interrelated.

PERSONALITY DEVELOPMENT

The Role of Heredity and Environment

Unlike any of the other theorists reviewed in this text, Cattell discusses prenatal influences on personality in detail. It is known, for example, that children born with Down's syndrome, a chromosomal abnormality, have limited intelligence and severely restricted behavior patterns. Metabolic abnormalities can also lead to mental retardation. Injuries to the head at birth can produce deficiencies in intelligence and motor coordination, or even paralysis. Temperament, Cattell believes, is related to the mother's endocrine condition during the gestation period, although the nature of the relationship is unclear. Thus, the physiological condition of the mother affects the normal process of nervous-system maturation in utero (Cattell, 1950, pp. 557–559).

In addition to biological influences on personality, Cattell discusses the tremendous impact of the environment, especially at later stages of development. At first, biological and maturational influences are paramount. Research has shown that, in both motor and verbal learning, untaught twins achieve the same levels of performance as those who have been thoroughly trained (Cattell, 1950, p. 561); that is, untrained children learn certain skills very rapidly once they are mature enough to do so and quickly achieve levels of proficiency equal to those of their well-trained counterparts. As the person grows older, however, the environment has an increasing impact on personality formation.

The Role of Learning

Cattell distinguishes among three kinds of learning that are involved in personality formation: classical conditioning, instrumental conditioning (reward learning), and integration learning. **Classical conditioning** involves pairing a neutral stimulus with a stimulus that provokes a particular response until the presentation of the neutral stimulus itself is capable of evoking the response. A classical-conditioning interpretation has been used to account for the acquisition of many fears and phobias. Cattell believes that it plays a role in unconscious learning, in the formation of phobias, and in the acquisition of deep and powerful emotional attachments (Cattell, 1965, p. 268).

Much more of our personality learning, according to Cattell, occurs through reward learning, or **instrumental conditioning.** We perform a certain action in order to reach a goal. A rat in a Skinner box presses a bar and receives food pellets; it quickly learns to press the bar. Bar pressing is instrumental to the attainment of the goal. Under other conditions, the animal presses the bar and is shocked; it quickly learns to avoid pressing the bar. Similarly, a person learns to diet because weight loss will bring approval from his friends and from his doctor. Or a child takes a cookie without her parents' permission and is spanked. She rapidly learns not to take cookies from the cookie jar, at least not when her parents are in the vicinity.

Cattell believes that reward learning is paramount in the formation of dynamic lattices (Cattell, 1965, p. 269). A student may have a sentiment about her athletic prowess, for instance, and train hard and long. Such training may prove highly rewarding if she subsequently performs at a track meet and wins a race. As a consequence, her sentiment toward athletic prowess is satisfied, and so is her erg for self-assertion—that is, her innate need to feel proud. The formation and maintenance of the dynamic lattice depends on **confluence learning**—that is, the acquisition of behaviors and attitudes that simultaneously contribute to the satisfaction of two or more different goals (Cattell, 1965, p. 270). For example, the student athlete may develop a positive attitude toward dieting and physical exercise because they satisfy her need for pride (self-assertion erg) and her need to do something different (curiosity erg). Thus, learning may involve the satisfaction of a number of goals within the person's dynamic lattice. The sentiments themselves are learned via reward learning, as when the student's interest in proving her athletic prowess was reinforced by successful performance.

Cattell also postulates a complex form of learning called **integration learning.** It appears to be a form of cognitive and instrumental learning in which the developing person uses ego and superego processes to maximize long-term satisfactions. The person learns to seek realistic satisfactions (Cattell, 1965, p. 276). Cattell agrees with Freud that the development of the ego and superego occurs during the second through the fifth years of life, that this period is marked by conflicts, and that it is critical in the development of personality (Cattell, 1950, pp. 573–575).

Cattell sees ages 6 through 13 as a carefree period in which children continue to strengthen their egos and extend love beyond themselves and their parents to others. It is a period of consolidation. Adolescence brings rapid physical changes and increases in emotional instability, social awkwardness, and sex interests, along with augmented concerns about being altruistic and contributing to society. The primary sources of conflict during this period are: "(a) the task of gaining independence from the parents; (b) the task of gaining status in an occupation, preparing for that occupation, and achieving economic self-support; (c) achieving satisfactory sex expression by winning a mate; and (d) achieving a stable, integrated personality and satisfactory self-concept" (Cattell, 1950, p. 594). These conflicts are due, in Cattell's opinion, to both biological and environmental influences.

Maturity—the period from 25 to 55—is a time of little basic personality change. Although there is a slight decline in biological efficiency (for example, increased problems with hearing and vision and a slowing of metabolism), Cattell believes that, through learning and experience, increases in creativity are possible. Emotional stability increases for both sexes (Cattell, 1950, pp. 610–613). Maturity is also a period in which adjustments need to be made, as people discover that adolescent dreams and aspirations are, in many respects, unrealistic. Near the end of this period, increased leisure time brings a tendency to revive romantic interests. Cattell cites the finding in the Kinsey report that men at this age tend to show revived interest in extramarital affairs. In women, with the approach of the menopause, there is a wistful longing for romance (Cattell, 1950, p. 616).

Old age brings a more rapid decline in physical power. Performance on tasks demanding ingenuity suffers, whereas performance on tasks requiring experience remains steady or increases only slightly. Cattell thinks the following characteristics are typical of people in old age (Cattell, 1950, pp. 618–619): worry over finances; worry over health; feeling unwanted, isolated, or lonely; feeling suspicious; loss of memory; mental rigidity; hoarding (often of trivial things); feelings of inadequacy and, as a result, feelings of insecurity and anxiety; feelings of guilt; irritability; reduction of sexual activity but increased sexual interest, especially in the male; untidiness, uncleanliness; inability to adjust to changed conditions; and decreased social contacts.

Although it is true that decline in physical health and competence is associated with old age and that this deterioration may manifest itself in lessened performance, recent research casts doubt on the accuracy of the negative characteristics frequently attributed to the elderly (Field & Millsap, 1991). Older people do not necessarily lack confidence or feel powerless, and they are not necessarily wracked by guilt and anxiety. Indeed, many older people are highly competent, satisfied with their situations, and actively engaged in meaningful activities. Furthermore, recent research indicates that the elderly are generally less lonely than adolescents and young adults (Taylor, Peplau, & Sears, 1994, p. 303). Thus, it is time for a more realistic appraisal of both the strengths and deficiencies associated with old age. We need to move away from the concept of the elderly as doddering old codgers who cannot tie their shoelaces and also from the glorification of the period as the golden years when senior citizens flower and prosper without a care in the world.

Theory of Abnormal Development

Accepting the clinical notion that neurosis and psychosis are based on unresolved conflicts within the person, Cattell seeks to develop quantitative techniques to aid the therapist in diagnosis and treatment. He envisions the conflicts in Freudian terms—as involving struggles among id, ego, and superego—and calls for the development of a "quantitative psychoanalysis" (Cattell, 1965, p. 230). For example, a man's interest in marrying one of two women is based on the operation of a number of ergs and other personality factors. Cattell gives a simplified version of the formulas that could be used by a clinician to predict how the man might resolve his conflict

$$I_{\text{Jane}} = 0.6E_{\text{sex}} + 0.5E_{\text{greg}} + 0.3M_{\text{superego}}$$
$$I_{\text{Sally}} = 0.6E_{\text{sex}} + 0.3E_{\text{greg}} + 0.3M_{\text{superego}}$$

In this example, the man is in real conflict because the various ergs and the superego sentiment are approximately equal in strength. But because the gregariousness erg is slightly stronger for Jane, the decision will be in her favor. In ordinary language, the two women are approximately equal in their satisfaction of his sexual needs and their respectability in the eyes of others, but Jane is a more pleasing companion socially than Sally, so he decides to marry Jane (Cattell, 1965, p. 232). This example is only illustrative, of course, and deliberately oversimplifies the clinical situation.

Cattell also proposes that clinicians rely on diagnostic tools that have been empirically validated in trying to understand their clients' conflicts. These tools, including the 16 PF and the CAQ, provide a means of assessing the major factors in personality—not only the Freudian structures of id, ego, and superego, but also the attitudes, interests, and sentiments of the client (Cattell, 1961, chap. 14).

Neurosis

Neurosis, according to Cattell, is the "pattern of behavior shown by those individuals who come to a clinic for aid because they feel themselves to be in emotional difficulties (and who do not have that kind of disorder that a psychiatrist recognizes as psychosis)" (Cattell, 1965, p. 209). He uses such an operational definition because he is convinced that an understanding of neurosis must begin by identifying those measurements that differentiate this group from normal members of the general population. Using this initial criterion, he has found that neurotics do indeed differ from both psychotics and normals on a number of personality dimensions. Thus, neuroticism and psychoticism do not just differ in degree; they are different kinds of illness (Cattell, 1965, p. 210).

Antecedents of neurosis, according to Cattell, are a childhood family characterized by conflict, inconsistent discipline, and insufficient affection; parental demands to adhere to excessively high moral standards; and genetically based lower-than-average emotional stability (Cattell, 1950, p. 497).

Countless factor-analytic studies by Cattell and scores of other investigators have found neurotics to be low in ego strength or emotional stability, high on autia and premsia, and low on surgency and dominance. High autia means that neurotics tend to disregard externals and social necessities and refuse to change their ideas to bring them into line with acknowledged facts; high premsia means that they show extreme and indiscriminate emotional sensitivity to others and considerable capricious behavior. In addition, neurotics are shy and generally inhibited. Finally, their low ego strength means that they are easily overcome by their emotions, are subject to moods, and cannot adjust their behavior to the realities of a given situation (Cattell, 1965, pp. 211–212; Meyer, 1993, p. 96).

Above all, neurotics tend to be highly anxious (Meyer, 1993, p. 96). Cattell traces their anxiety to a number of sources. It may arise because the ergic tension of the person is unsatisfied. True to his Freudian roots, Cattell notes that ergic drives for sex and pugnacity (aggression) are more frequently punished in our society and, as a consequence, can give rise to high levels of anxiety. Also consistent with the orthodox Freudian position is Cattell's belief that anxiety can arise as a result of low ego strength and a highly punitive superego. In original fashion, however, Cattell suggests that high levels of anxiety may result in part from a constitutional proneness to threat reactivity; in other words, neurotics may be biologically more sensitive to threats than are normals. Another cause of high anxiety may be a very broad self-sentiment; that is, a person who is committed to a great variety of activities is more vulnerable to threats than is one who does not have such a broad range of pursuits. Finally, high levels of anxiety can arise if the individual is forced to deal with many trivial details in life in order to achieve ergic and self-sentiment satisfactions (Cattell, 1961, pp. 18–22).

Psychosis

Psychosis, according to Cattell, is "a form of mental disorder different from neurosis, in which the individual loses contact with reality and needs hospitalization for his own protection and that of others" (Cattell, 1965, p. 373). In contrast to neurotics, psychotics lack insight into their problems, are unable to take care of themselves, and may be a threat to others.

Bipolar disorder (formerly called manic-depressive psychosis) and schizophrenia are highly inheritable (Cattell, 1982, p. 28), but differences in family environments contribute to the onset of the two types of psychosis. Parents of bipolar disorder patients are warmer and much more overprotective of their children than are the parents of schizophrenics; parents of schizophrenics have been found to be much more ambivalent in their attitudes toward their children (Cattell, 1950, p. 542). Using the 16 PF, investigators have found that schizophrenics are lacking in ego strength, and are pessimistic, seclusive, retiring, subdued, shy, aloof, introverted and conceited, and motivated strongly by unresolved sexual and aggressive urges (high in drive tension) (Meyer, 1993, pp. 46–47). In the manic phase, patients with bipolar disorder tend to be highly energetic, talkative, extremely cheerful, joyous, and humorous, whereas in the depressive phase they tend to become absorbed in their own thoughts, are guilt-prone, and lack confidence (Meyer, 1993, pp. 77–80).

ASSESSMENT TECHNIQUES

Cattell rightfully can be called a "psychometrist of personality," because he places such heavy emphasis on the use of testing and statistical techniques. We have already seen how he uses factor analysis to derive personality traits. To apply the factor-analytic procedures, however, investigators must first collect masses of data from large numbers of people. Cattell relies on three major procedures to obtain such data: the L-data, Q-data, and T-data methods.

L-data, or life-record data, refers to the measurement of behavior in actual, everyday situations. Such data might include records that show the number of automobile accidents the person has had over the past 20 years, her marks in school, the number of civic organizations of which she is or has been a member, and so forth. Because some L-data might be very difficult to obtain, the investigator may be forced to take secondhand data, in the form of ratings by someone who knows the person well. Thus, different aspects of the person's behavior—such as her dependability on the job, her level of dissatisfaction with the job, her friendliness to coworkers—might be assessed by means of trait ratings (on 10-point scales, for example) by coworkers and friends.

The second source of information is called **Q-data,** or questionnaire data. Such information is often gathered in an interview situation, in which respondents fill out paper-and-pencil tests from which trait scores can be derived. The 16 PF is an excellent source of Q-data.

The third type of data, called **T-data,** is based on objective tests. Information is gathered by an observer in a standard test situation and is then scored. Whereas Q-data are based on self-reports that can be faked by the subject, T-data are essentially unfakeable. For example, if a person is asked on a questionnaire whether or not he ever cheats on examinations, he may report that he never does so, even though he does. If he is asked to respond to a Rorschach test, however, the inkblots are ambiguous and the subject does not know the dimensions on which his responses will eventually be scored (Cattell, 1965, pp. 60–62).

THEORY'S IMPLICATIONS FOR THERAPY

Skillful treatment of mental disorders, according to Cattell, depends on personality-factor assessments that provide not only a profile for diagnosis but also a statement about the kinds of constitutional factors that influence behavior (Cattell, 1965, p. 288). The availability of reliable and valid measuring instruments, moreover, can help the clinician make better judgments about the efficacy of treatment procedures; that is, the clinician can assess the client's personality before and after therapeutic intervention and note the changes in behavior (Cattell, 1961, p. 413). Cattell recommends the P technique—repeated testing over time on a number of personality dimensions—as the procedure best able to provide an accurate assessment of the complex changes occurring in clients as they move through therapy (Cattell, 1965, p. 372; 1961, p. 415).

Cattell believes that all therapy should rest on precise measurement, but that astute clinical observation also has merit and should be used in conjunction with testing procedures. In this regard, as in others, he is an eclectic. He appreciates and accepts many of Freud's clinical insights, but he maintains that a therapy built on pronouncements and not on measurement can, in the long run, do serious harm to society. In general, he is contemptuous of the "fanciful and presumptuous theorizing of premetric, preexperimental" theorists (Cattell, 1965, p. 333).

Cattell believes that a Freudian search for the causes of a disorder in early traumatic experiences may be beneficial to the client. By reliving the experiences, the client is in a better position to reevaluate his or her own emotional reactions and eventually to change destructive behavior. Some of these changes can be effected, in Cattell's view, through behavior therapy in which the person is taught new responses to threatening stimuli. Thus, to a limited degree, he accepts as valid therapeutic approaches that utilize historical analysis (for example, psychoanalysis) or a direct reconditioning approach (behavior therapy).

In the final analysis, however, Cattell opts for a view of therapy that recognizes that people with severe disorders are defective throughout their whole personality functioning (Cattell, 1965, p. 335). We cannot simply focus on traumatic experiences involving sex and aggression, nor can we focus only on certain limited and specific areas of behavior change. Rather, we must address ourselves to the full range of constitutional personality factors that set limits on the person's performance and to the complex interweaving of traits and sentiments that influence behavior patterns. In short, we need complex measurement procedures to assess complex underlying structures. On the basis of this assessment, we will be able to conclude that some kinds of therapy will prove more effective than others, depending on the kinds of factors that are causing the specific neurosis or psychosis. For example, in psychoses based largely on constitutional factors, therapy might involve the use of drugs, electric shock, or lobotomy (Cattell, 1950, p. 543). In certain neuroses, therapy might start with dream analysis and the reliving of traumatic experiences (Cattell, 1961, p. 415). Where the problem is of a minor and relatively restricted nature, in the sense that it does not involve deep-rooted trauma, behavior therapy might be effective. Thus, Cattell is eclectic in his attitude toward the kinds of treatment to be used in therapy, but he is single-minded in his determination that all therapy should be based on solid measurement procedures.

BEYONDISM: A NEW MORALITY BASED ON SCIENCE

Throughout his long scientific career, Cattell has written about the possibility of erecting ethical values on the firm foundation of science. Specifically, he thinks that only science can provide solutions to the problems that plague the various nations of the world. He has sought to convince the public that they should fund psychology more generously because he believes that advances in psychology are vital to humankind.

Cattell begins by arguing that scientific research and data should be used to identify the type of person who can help produce a more successfully surviving society (Cattell, 1972, p. 158). Such data could also be used to generate a moral code that will, when put into action, help solve the major problems that plague society. Cattell argues strongly that the survival of any society depends on sound ethical values and that, the more solid these values, the happier the future of the society (Cattell, 1987, p. 146).

For Cattell, the supreme value is survival of the group, not the individual. Whereas nonsurvival of a society is easy to document because it simply fails and ceases to exist, survival, in Cattell's view, is judged not simply by its continued existence, but rather in terms of graded levels of functioning along a dimension of success. Cattell uses several indices to identify more successfully surviving societies: (1) a population size per unit area that can be maintained at a standard of living adequate for effective citizenship; (2) a degree of control of the physical environment to protect the population against famine, volcanic eruptions, earthquakes, floods, and pollution; (3) creativity demonstrated by adaptability to even wider sections of the environment—for example, colonizing climatically difficult regions or exploring outer space; and (4) movement in a direction aimed at solving problems that historically have plagued, and continue to plague, society (Cattell, 1972, p. 115).

Cattell's examination of American society leads him to the pessimistic conclusion that it is declining and moving slowly toward extinction, because current values are not working. As evidence, he notes increases in drug abuse and crimes of violence, millions of people unemployed, high rates of divorce and out-of-wedlock births to teenagers (Vinovskis, 1988, pp. 28–30), decreases in the educational accomplishments of young people, overpopulation, poverty, and pollution of the environment. A new morality is needed, Cattell believes, because the current morality is not working.

Beyondism is Cattell's proposed system for discovering and clarifying ethical goals based on scientific knowledge and investigation (Cattell, 1987, p. 1). Beyondism refers not to an afterlife, such as that espoused by various religions, but to providing a better life for people by going beyond the present situation. According to Cattell, social-scientific research can generate knowledge that will enable us reach that goal by helping us adapt to evolutionary requirements.

Interestingly, Beyondism contains strong elements of faith, and thus can be characterized as a religion, even though it rests (or will rest eventually) on an empirical foundation. Its two major elements of faith are that the universe exists and that evolution exists within the universe (Cattell, 1987, p. 4). According to Cattell, the basic requirements of biological evolution are: (1) there must be natural variation; therefore, groups (nations) must agree to take separate paths, both culturally and racially; (2) individuals and groups must experience natural selection, under which some forms of life survive better than others through better adaptations to the environment (Cattell, 1987, pp. 5–8). Cattell maintains that natural selection occurs simultaneously between and within nations (Cattell, 1987, p. 6).

Cattell believes that, to ensure diversity in the human gene pool, nations should agree to compete against each other as they struggle to survive. In his view, increased interdependence tends to result in excessive imitation and uniformity; nations fail to branch out into more divergent cultural and genetic types (Cattell, 1972, p. 224). To make certain that nations develop separately, Cattell opposes immigration and the interbreeding of national groups. Critics point out that opposition to immigration in the belief that it would contaminate the genetic purity of the nation has served to justify bigotry in the past. The scientific IQ test was used early in the 20th century by U.S. citizens who felt threatened economically by the influx of immigrants. Their interpretation of the IQ test results was that members of immigrant groups (predominantly Italians, Russians, Poles, Slavs, and Jews) were genetically inferior and biologically prone to feeblemindedness. On the basis of this interpretation, the U.S. government severely restricted immigration by these groups (Duster, 1990, p. 11).

To Cattell, the evolutionary advantages of competition among nations outweigh the accompanying danger of war; to eliminate war by eliminating competition, he maintains, would be the supreme example of throwing the baby out with the bathwater (Cattell, 1972, p. 198). In Cattell's view, it would not work anyway, because a nation that lays down its arms would quickly be overthrown by another invading nation (Cattell, 1972, pp. 198–199); his solution is that each nation must create a defense so powerful that the costs of aggression would be prohibitive to other countries (Cattell, 1972, pp. 204–205). Critics might argue that such a strategy simply accelerates the arms race and thereby increases international tensions and the prospects of war.

Genetic diversity and group survival are also promoted by competition within nations, according to Cattell. To further the evolutionary process within nations, he maintains, we need to encourage development of a population with higher intelligence and emotional stability, because populations with these qualities are more likely to survive (Cattell, 1987, p. 213). Toward this end, Cattell favors implementation of a program with two aspects: restrictive eugenics and creative eugenics.

Restrictive eugenics is a policy aimed at reducing the number of mentally defective individuals through voluntary or forced sterilization (Cattell, 1972, p. 349). In nature, Cattell argues, defective individuals face early death; therefore, reducing the birth rate of such people would spare parents much pain and suffering. Thus, Cattell sees selection by birth rate as more humane than selection by death rate. He also points to new scientific techniques that can identify defects shortly after conception so that the embryo can be aborted (Cattell, 1972, p. 160). In a less controversial vein, Cattell foresees the use of genetic engineering to reduce the incidence of disabilities such as diabetes and phenylketonuria mental retardation (Cattell, 1972, p. 147).

Cattell's call for the sterilization of individuals viewed as mentally defective is essentially a replay of the views of a number of prominent biologists, mathematicians, psychologists, politicians, and writers associated with the eugenics movement early in the 20th century. These professionals recommended sterilization as a means of ridding society of heritable disorders. Critics argued that involuntary sterilization was an unconstitutional violation of people's rights. Although the U.S. Supreme Court agreed, several states still have sterilization laws (Duster, 1990, p. 30). Opponents also maintained that the eugenics movement consisted largely of middle- and upper-middle-class people, who used the results of flawed scientific research compatible with their own class bias to rationalize sterilization of lower-class individuals (Kevles, 1985, p. 167). The same class bias was also used to argue for reducing the birth rate among poor people and increasing it among the rich (Kevles, 1985, pp. 182–184).

Cattell argues not only for restricted eugenics, but also for a program of **creative eugenics.** This program, like its predecessors in the early 1900s, would encourage more intelligent people to have more children, while discouraging the less intelligent from reproducing. According to Cattell, there is a slight positive correlation between intelligence and socioeconomic status, as defined by education and income (Cattell, 1987, pp. 206–207). Although the correlation is not strong, Cattell thinks it offers the best available guide to a general policy aimed at producing the best (most intelligent) citizens. Specifically, he believes that socially successful individuals should be encouraged to have more children, and poorer people fewer. Toward this end, he advocates providing tax relief or cash to those with above-average incomes to encourage childbearing, while eliminating the current tax deductions for children in families earning less than the average income. Taxes paid by middle- and upper-class people legitimately can be given to poor people, in Cattell's view, only if they are capable of being reformed and rehabilitated (Cattell, 1972, p. 360). He considers such transfers illegitimate in the case of those who are, in his words, "inherently inadequate"—those marked by low intelligence (B–), emotional instability (C–), poor superego development (G–), self-absorption and a disregard for practical planning (M+), and conceit and egotism (E+) (Cattell, 1987, p. 57). Such people, according to Cattell, are highly irresponsible and deliberately evade their work responsibilities (Cattell, 1987, p. 57).

In Cattell's view, democracy offers the form of government best suited to implement Beyondism and bring about progress, because it provides a more favorable climate for scientific thought and research than other political systems. Above all, it is one of the few systems in which violent revolution is unnecessary for progress (Cattell, 1972, pp. 340–341).

Finally, Cattell believes that, if a government spends unrealistically on welfare for the poor and/or too little on defense, research, and education, it is likely to collapse economically or be defeated in war. Beyondists would establish national and international research centers to collect data relevant to evolutionary progress. They advocate a greatly increased commitment to education, with a focus on furthering the intellectual and moral growth of those born with higher intelligence (Cattell, 1987, p. 84). The chief challenge to education in the future, according to Cattell, is to teach students the fundamentals of genetics and social-scientific research, along with the art of analyzing arguments, so as to ensure that society will profit from their knowledge and expertise (Cattell, 1972, p. 380).

Cattell's ideas can be criticized on several grounds. Jahoda (1989), for example, suggests that Cattell's postulated link between higher intelligence and sound moral values is dubious. Leaders of organized crime or producers of pornography do not seem to suffer from below-average intelligence. Although Cattell maintains that Beyondism is rooted in science, most of the arguments he musters have little or no empirical basis; rather, they are based on his own value system and conservative philosophy.

Finally, Cattell's policy of providing higher education primarily for children from affluent families, on the grounds of their higher native intelligence, has little empirical support. Distributions of intelligence scores for richer and poorer people in fact show considerable overlap; many poor people can and do benefit from higher education. To limit their opportunities for advancement and a better standard of living by focusing our resources primarily on the children of the well-to-do seems shortsighted, uncaring, and contrary to the democratic ideal of equal opportunity.

EVALUATIVE COMMENTS

We turn now to an examination of the scientific worth of Cattell's theory.

Comprehensiveness   There is little doubt that Cattell has devised a comprehensive theory of personality. His theory addresses a wide range of diverse phenomena, both normal and abnormal, and seeks to account for both the biological and sociocultural factors that influence behavior. The range of his interests and efforts in pursuing this formidable task is indeed impressive.

Cattell fully recognizes the complexity of the motives that determine behavior and the need for measurement procedures equal to the task. It is from this perspective that he criticizes the overreliance of researchers on the bivariate experiment. However, he does not take an either/or position on the merits of the multivariate approach and the deficiencies of the controlled experiment, nor does he suggest that investigators abandon the bivariate approach altogether. Instead, he recognizes that both approaches have unique assets.

Thus, Cattell recognizes the complexity of personality; he has developed a theory that seeks to approximate that reality; and he seeks to utilize measurement procedures commensurate with the task.

Precision and testability   Of all the theorists in this text, Cattell has demonstrated the most concern with constructing a theory based on precise measurement. He has steadfastly worked to define and refine his concepts through the use of sophisticated and elaborate factor-analytic procedures. Despite this emphasis, critics have argued that his data are fraught with ambiguities and subjectivity. They maintain that he himself made the decision to include only certain traits in his factor analyses; therefore, it should not surprise anyone that he got out of the analyses the traits that he put in. In response, Cattell cites his painstaking efforts initially to include virtually all the traits known to human beings in his factor analyses.

Recall that his construction of the personality sphere was an attempt to examine all the traits that could be used to describe behavior. It is a good bet that he has covered most of them.

Another criticism of the factor-analytic approach concerns the subjectivity involved in labeling factors. Despite the emphasis on objectivity in his measurement procedures, Cattell must still use subjective judgment in interpreting the meaning of the factors and labeling them. Recognizing this problem, Cattell has proceeded cautiously and labeled factors only after several replications have provided supportive evidence. He has also sought cross-validation of factors through research with different populations. Through this continual process of refinement, the labeling of factors becomes more readily apparent, and less subjective.

Despite these criticisms and others, Cattell's theory appears to be a model of elegance and precision when compared to the various psychodynamic and humanistic-existential theories.

Parsimony   Cattell has attempted to construct a theory that is parsimonious by using factor-analytic techniques to uncover the major source traits of normal and abnormal behavior. He has also taken the person's abilities and mood fluctuations into account in creating his theory. In addition, his econetic model provides a number of concepts that help explain the impact of environment on behavior. Thus, Cattell's theory seems economical without being overly simplistic.

Empirical validity   Cattell has spent most of his research career establishing the reliability and validity of his trait concepts. Thus, there is considerable empirical support for these basic concepts, as well as some support for various hypotheses based on them. However, there is still only minimal support for his econetic model.

Heuristic value   Many psychologists agree that there is a great deal to admire about Cattell and his efforts as a scientific investigator. He is seen as a first-rate scholar with wide-ranging interests and expertise in many areas. There is little question that he has been incredibly productive as a researcher and prolific as a writer, and he has the kind of curiosity, intelligence, and boldness necessary in a pioneering investigator. Despite all this, the theory itself has generated relatively little research. Why? First, as with Jung, Cattell's work is difficult to understand. The language of the theory is often technical and forbidding, and his penchant for using neologisms is not designed to endear him to professionals. Second, although factor analysis is a relatively objective and precise statistical technique, some investigators believe that the investigator's own biases can influence the outcomes, and they look askance at the research results compiled by Cattell and his associates. Finally, and perhaps most importantly, for much of his career Cattell made little effort to expand his theory so as to include environmental factors in the prediction of behavior. To experimentalists wedded to a strong environmentalism, his emphasis on the primacy of inner traits was unappealing. It is possible that Cattell's later work on the econetic model will arouse investigators' interest in his theory and stimulate research.

While there has been little research on the theory itself, Cattell's pioneering ideas have stimulated new thinking and research in contemporary personality psychology. In particular, personality psychologists acknowledge Cattell's seminal contributions to behavior genetics, his creativity in devising new methods to study the complexity of traits, and the importance of his long-standing call for a new taxonomy of traits to focus research in their attempts to understand the influence of traits on behavior. (See Chapter 18 for more details.)

Finally, it should be noted that Cattell's philosophical views on the need for a new morality based on science (Beyondism) have not met with a positive reception from personality psychologists. Rather than criticize these speculations, his colleagues have tended to ignore them; it seems likely that his views will suffer the same ignominious fate as those of his predecessors in the 1920s and 1930s.

Applied value   Cattell's work has had considerable influence in the clinical diagnosis of psychopathology and in the assessment of therapeutic growth; it has had an even greater impact on occupational psychology. It has provided vocational counselors with reliable personality testing procedures that have been used to provide information to young people and adults concerning the kinds of occupations that might be compatible with their interests and abilities. Management supervisors in business and industry have also used Cattell's tests in making decisions about the placement of workers in jobs suited to their talents and personalities.

DISCUSSION QUESTIONS

1. What is the inductive-hypothetico-deductive spiral? How does this approach to the construction of personality theory differ from the hypothetico-deductive model used by most investigators?

2. What is factor analysis? What are some of its strengths and weaknesses as a personality assessment procedure?

3. What is a trait? What are the primary sources of traits in personality? Do you think Cattell has identified all of them? Which ones, if any, has he missed?

4. How do source traits differ from surface traits? What are the major source traits?

5. Why does Cattell consider it necessary to invent new terms, such as parmia and threctia, to describe personal dispositions?

6. What are Cattell's specification equations? Describe their use in the prediction of behavior.

7. What are the major aspects of the dynamic lattice?

8. List the three kinds of learning involved in the formation of personality. Give examples of each type.

9. Is there necessarily a decrease in physical and mental powers with the onset of old age? Are the elderly people you know powerless?

10. What kinds of family backgrounds are likely to give rise to neuroticism?

11. How do neurotics differ from psychotics? What are the major factors contributing to psychoticism, according to Cattell?

12. What is the P technique? How is it utilized in the treatment of people with behavioral disorders?

13. Are you a Beyondist? What are some of the strengths and limitations of Beyondism?

14. What primary source traits would you attribute to couples you know whose marriages are successful? What primary source traits characterize people you like or dislike?

15. How does Cattell define personality? What are some of the limitations of his definition?

GLOSSARY

ability traits   Skills that enable individuals to cope effectively with problems posed by the environment.

beyondism   A new morality Cattell claims is based on scientific research and data. He believes this new set of ethics will help society progress beyond the current state of instability, confusion, and crisis.

bivariate experiments   Investigations designed to assess the impact of one variable on another. Cattell thinks that such experiments are limited in their usefulness because they do not do justice to human behavior, which is typically determined by many variables.

classical conditioning   Type of learning in which a stimulus that is originally incapable of evoking a response becomes capable of evoking it after continued pairing of this stimulus with one that naturally produces the response.

Clinical Analysis Questionnaire   Personality test designed to measure normal and deviant personality traits. It includes the 16 PF traits and 12 other psychopathological traits.

confluence learning   Acquisition of attitudes and behaviors that contribute simultaneously to the satisfaction of two or more goals.

constitutional traits   Characteristics that are rooted in biology and are very resistant to change.

creative eugenics   A program advocated by Cattell to increase the birth rate of more intelligent people in the belief that such individuals will develop sounder ethical values and contribute more to society's well-being.

crystallized intelligence   Abilities that are the result of cultural learning—for example, verbal and mathematical skills.

Culture Fair Intelligence Test   Test developed by Cattell that assesses innate abilities, or fluid intelligence. It assesses abilities rooted in the genetic makeup of the person and independent of cultural learning.

dynamic calculus   A set of mathematical formulas (specification equations) that integrate traits, environment, and motivational factors in the prediction of behavior.

dynamic lattice   Complicated and organized system of traits within the human personality.

dynamic traits   Characteristics that embrace people's motives and interests.

econetic model   Model that postulates a complex interaction between traits and the physical, social, and cultural environments in the prediction of behavior.

Eight State Questionnaire   Personality test that measures basic moods and emotional states.

environmental-mold traits   Characteristics learned through experiences with the environment.

environmental sphere   Listing of all the terms used in a culture to designate situations or environments.

ergs   Innate drives that control behavior.

factor analysis   Statistical technique designed to simplify a complex set of data by accounting for them in terms of underlying factors, usually fewer in number than the original number of variables in the original data set.

factor loading The degree of association between a specific variable and a general factor.

fluid intelligence Abilities that are innately based.

inductive-hypothetico-deductive spiral Approach to theory construction and validation in which facts are collected first and then generalized into hypotheses, which lead to deductions that can be tested empirically.

instrumental conditioning Type of learning in which the presentation of a rewarding or punishing stimulus is made contingent on the occurrence of a response or behavior; also known as operant conditioning.

integration learning Type of learning proposed by Cattell in which people utilize their reasoning abilities and value systems to maximize the attainment of long-range goals.

L-data Information about a person's life based on the actual observance of the person's behavior or on records of the person's behavior. For example, a high school student's absences from class can actually be recorded by a truant officer who actually sits in the student's classes for a month; alternatively, finding this procedure too time-consuming, the truant officer may simply use the teacher's record of the student's class attendance.

multiple abstract variance analysis Statistical procedure used to determine the precise contributions of genetic and environmental factors to the development of traits.

multivariate experiments Investigations designed to assess the impact of several variables on a given behavior.

P technique Form of factor analysis that permits assessment of the unique trait structure of an individual.

personality sphere Listing of all the traits used to describe behavior in a culture.

primary factors Source factors or traits that emerge from an analysis of the correlations among a number of surface variables.

Q-data Information about a subject's behavior obtained through self-ratings on a questionnaire.

R technique Form of factor analysis used to infer underlying source traits in large subject populations.

restrictive eugenics A program to reduce the birth rate of the mentally handicapped; Cattell advocates this program in the belief that such individuals are a costly burden to society and slow its evolutionary growth.

second-order factors   Higher-order factors that emerge after an analysis of the associations among a number of primary factors or source traits.

self-sentiment   Master motive that integrates the various attitudes, sentiments, and interests of the person.

Sixteen Personality Factor (16 PF) Questionnaire   Factor-analytically derived questionnaire created by Cattell to measure the primary or basic underlying traits of personality.

source trait   An underlying characteristic inferred from the intercorrelations among a number of measured variables, or surface traits.

specification equations   Formulas that specify the ways in which traits are weighted in relation to given situations and then combined to predict behavior.

structure-based systems theory   Theory that seeks to explain the complicated, dynamic interactions between goal-oriented people and their environments.

subsidiation   Process involving the interrelatedness of traits within the dynamic lattice or organizational structure of personality. Attitudes are subsidiated to, or dependent on, sentiments; sentiments are dependent on ergs.

surface trait   An observable trait that is controlled by an underlying source trait.

T-data   Objective test information based on an observer's judgments of how a subject reacts to the environment; the data are collected in situations that do not permit the subject to know what aspect of his or her behavior is being evaluated.

temperament traits   Innate tendencies to react to the environment in particular ways. Temperament includes such variables as the person's moodiness, excitability, activity level, and speed of response to stimuli.

traits   Relatively permanent and broad reaction tendencies that serve as the building blocks of personality.

SUGGESTED READINGS

Cattell, R. B. (1965). *The scientific analysis of personality*. Baltimore, MD: Penguin.

Cattell, R. B. (1979/1980). *Personality and learning theory* (Vols. 1 and 2). New York: Springer.

Cattell, R. B. (1982). *The inheritance of personality and ability*. New York: Academic Press.

Cattell, R. B. (1987). *Beyondism: Religion from science*. New York: Praeger.

REFERENCES

Allport, G. W., & Odbert, H. S. (1936). Trait names: A psycholexical study. *Psychological Monographs, 47,* 171–220.

Cattell, R. B. (1950). *Personality: A systematic theoretical and factual study*. New York: McGraw-Hill.

Cattell, R. B. (1957). *Personality and motivation: Structure and measurement*. New York: Harcourt, Brace & World.

Cattell, R. B. (1961). *The meaning and measurement of neuroticism and anxiety*. New York: Ronald.

Cattell, R. B. (1965). *The scientific analysis of personality*. Baltimore, MD: Penguin.

Cattell, R. B. (1972). *A new morality from science: Beyondism*. New York: Pergamon Press.

Cattell, R. B. (1979). *Personality and learning theory: Vol. 1. The structure of personality in its environment*. New York: Springer.

Cattell, R. B. (1980). *Personality and learning theory: Vol. 2. A systems theory of maturation and structured learning*. New York: Springer.

Cattell, R. B. (1982). *The inheritance of personality and ability*. New York: Academic Press.

Cattell, R. B. (1987). *Beyondism: Religion from science*. New York: Praeger.

Cattell, R. B., & Kline, P. (1977). *The scientific analysis of personality and motivation*. New York: Academic Press.

Cattell, R. B., & Nesselroade, J. R. (1967). Likeness and completeness theories examined by sixteen personality factors measures by stably and unstably married couples. *Journal of Personality and Social Psychology, 7,* 351–361.

Duster, T. (1990). *Backdoor to eugenics*. New York: Routledge.

Field, D., & Millsap, R. E. (1991). Personality in advanced old age: Continuity or change? *Journal of Gerontology, 46,* 299–308.

Jahoda, M. (1989). A helping hand to evolution? *Contemporary Psychology, 34,* 816–817.

Kevles, D. J. (1985). *In the name of eugenics*. New York: Knopf.

McGee, M. G., & Wilson, D. W. (1984). *Psychology: Science and application*. New York: West.

Meyer, R. G. (1993). *The clinician's handbook* (3rd ed.). Boston, MA: Allyn and Bacon.

Nesselroade, J. R., & Cattell, R. B. (Eds.). (1988). *Handbook of multivariate experimental psychology* (2nd ed.). New York: Plenum.

Schuerger, J. M. (1992). The Sixteen Personality Factor Questionnaire and its junior versions. *Journal of Counseling and Development, 71,* 231–244.

Taylor, S. E., Peplau, L. A., & Sears, D. O. (1994). *Social psychology* (8th ed.). Englewood Cliffs, NJ: Prentice Hall.

Vinovskis, M. A. (1988). *An "epidemic" of adolescent pregnancy? Some historical and policy considerations.* New York: Oxford University Press.

Wilson, G. D., Ausman, J., & Mathews, T. R. (1973). Conservatism and art preferences. *Journal of Personality and Social Psychology, 25,* 286–288.

CHAPTER 10

Eysenck's Biological Typology

BIOGRAPHICAL SKETCH

Hans Eysenck was born in Berlin on March 4, 1916. His parents, both well-known actors, divorced when Eysenck was only 2 years old, and he went to live with his maternal grandmother. Like his parents, she had a deep fondness for the theater, but her own acting career had been cut short when she was crippled by a fall. Not surprisingly, Eysenck was also drawn to acting, and at the age of 5 or 6, he played in a film in which his mother was the star. His father wanted him to pursue a career in acting, but his mother, whom Eysenck calls the more sensible, opposed it, and he turned away from acting as a profession.

Eysenck's father was Catholic, his mother Protestant. Although he was christened and confirmed in the Lutheran faith, Eysenck was not particularly religious. In fact, he had to be bribed by the promise of a bicycle to attend the classes preparing him for confirmation.

Living in Germany between the wars, when economic and political turmoil culminated in the rise of Nazism, Eysenck took a great interest in politics and read widely. He embraced socialism, in which he saw the promise of a better world, free from war, prejudice, and poverty; as he matured, however, he began to see its problems and limitations. He summarizes this political maturation process as follows: one who is not a socialist in his or her youth has no heart; one who remains a socialist in middle age has no head. Although he is no longer a socialist, neither is he a conservative; he eschews all party labels and doctrines. Nevertheless, Eysenck has published numerous research papers on political matters, as well as two books: *The Psychology of Politics* (1954) and, with Glenn Wilson, *The Psychological Basis of Ideology* (1978).

In 1934, one year after Hitler assumed power, Eysenck left Germany; he had been told that he would not be allowed to enter the university unless he joined the SS (the Nazi secret police). His mother had married a Jewish film producer and moved to France, and they prevailed upon Eysenck to join them. He spent some time at the University of Dijon studying French literature and history, but eventually he settled in London. There, after studying for the matriculation examination for a year at Pitman's Commercial College, he enrolled at the University of London.

At the University of London, Eysenck had to select a major area for study. Although he had read widely in the classics of German, French, and English literature and loved music, painting, and poetry, he believed that the arts were primarily for fun and emotional experiences. He decided that his life's work would be in science, and declared physics as his major. However, university officials told him that he lacked the prerequisites to study physics and, rather than spend another year taking the required subjects, he asked if there was any science he could declare as a major. He was told, "There's always psychology." Eysenck asked, in ignorance, "What on earth is that?" "You'll like it," was the reply—and he became a psychology major!

Eysenck entered a department populated by a number of eminent faculty, including psychometricians Cyril Burt and Charles Spearman. He also studied genetics with J. B. S. Haldane and L. Penrose, and took a statistics course from Egon Pearson. His first research article appeared in 1939, just after he earned his B.A. degree, and he obtained a Ph.D. from the University of London in 1940.

By this time, Eysenck was married to Margaret Davies, a Canadian mathematician. The couple had one son, Michael, now a well-known psychologist in his own right. The marriage subsequently ended in divorce, and Eysenck later married Sybil Rostal, a psychologist and daughter of a famous violinist. Their marriage has produced three sons and a daughter.

With England at war with Nazi Germany, Eysenck tried to enlist in the Royal Air Force but he was turned down as an "enemy alien."

Employment opportunities were scarce for the same reason. Unable to secure a university position, Eysenck eventually obtained a research position at Mill Hill Emergency Hospital, where he began studies on suggestibility in hysterics. He also worked on such topics as parotid-gland secretion in affective mental disorders, screening tests for neurotics, memory tests, and the effects of motivation on intelligence. In addition, he completed a large-scale factor analysis of patients' symptoms, from which he derived the theory that there are two major personality factors: neuroticism and extraversion/introversion. These ideas led to the publication of his first book, *Dimensions of Personality* (1947). In his second book, *The Scientific Study of Personality* (1952), he added psychoticism as the third major dimension.

After the war, Eysenck began work at the Maudsley Hospital, the best-known psychiatric hospital and teaching unit in England. Appointed director of the psychology department, he was encouraged by officials to establish a training program for clinical psychologists. Toward this end, Eysenck traveled in 1949 to the United States to examine and evaluate clinical psychology programs at various universities.

On the basis of his trip to the United States, Eysenck came to three major conclusions about the shortcomings of clinical training and practice: first, clinical psychologists were subordinate to psychiatrists; second, many clinical psychologists slavishly utilized psychoanalytic concepts in their therapeutic work; third, clinicians depended too heavily on projective tests, even though they were unreliable and invalid. Eysenck resolved, upon his return to England, to forge an independent department of psychology, to move away from psychoanalysis, and to develop a program of study that was strongly scientific in orientation, with a focus on the interdependence of clinical and experimental work. To his credit, Eysenck has been able to create such a department, which is flourishing; his colleagues and students are carrying out research in behavior therapy (Eysenck, 1980, pp. 153–157).

A prolific writer, Eysenck has produced approximately 40 books, countless chapters in edited books, and approximately 600 research articles. Among his more notable books are *Uses and Abuses of Psychology* (1953), *The Dynamics of Anxiety and Hysteria* (1957), *Sense and Nonsense in Psychology* (1962), *Smoking, Health, and Personality* (1965), *The Causes and Cures of Neurosis* (with Stanley Rachman, 1965), *Personality Structure and Measurement* (with S. B. G.

Eysenck, 1969), *The Structure of Human Personality* (1970), *The IQ Argument* (1971), *The Experimental Study of Freudian Theories* (with Glenn Wilson, 1973), *The Inequality of Man* (1975), *Psychoticism as a Dimension of Personality* (1977), *The Intelligence Controversy* (with Leon Kamin, 1981), *Personality and Individual Differences: A Natural Science Approach* (with Michael Eysenck, 1985), *The Causes and Cures of Criminality* (with Gisli Gudjonsson, 1989), and *Genius: The Natural History of Creativity* (1995).

Hans Eysenck is currently professor emeritus at the Institute of Psychiatry and the University of London. He continues to write and participate actively in research.

CONCEPTS AND PRINCIPLES

Eysenck observes that psychology has two major orientations—personality psychology and experimental psychology—and that, unfortunately, theoreticians and researchers in the two areas tend to ignore each other's work; that is, experimental psychologists show little concern with individual differences, and personality theorists ignore the need for empirical evidence (Eysenck, 1967, p. 3). As a result of this mutual indifference, nonscientific or prescientific theorists and practitioners abound in the field of personality. We are left with dozens of theories of personality, but very little in the way of factual support for them (Eysenck, 1967, p. 27). To overcome this sad situation, Eysenck suggests, we must integrate the two approaches by: (1) identifying the main dimensions of personality; (2) devising means of measuring them; and (3) linking them with experimental, quantitative procedures (Eysenck, 1947, pp. 1–2). Only in this way, Eysenck believes, can we build a sound theory of personality.

Identifying and Measuring the Main Dimensions of Personality

Eysenck defines personality as

> a more or less stable and enduring organization of a person's character, temperament, intellect, and physique, which determines his unique adjustment to the environment. *Character* denotes a person's more or less stable and enduring system of conative behavior

(will); *temperament,* his more or less stable and enduring system of affective behavior *(emotion)*; *intellect,* his more or less stable and enduring system of cognitive behavior *(intelligence)*; *physique,* his more or less stable and enduring system of bodily configuration and neuroendocrine endowment. (Eysenck, 1970, p. 2)

Thus, his definition emphasizes traits (stable and enduring characteristics), which, when clustered together, are organized as types.

Eysenck's **typology** is hierarchically organized, and consists of types, traits, and habits. Types are most abstract, followed by traits, and then habits. Specifically, each of the type concepts is based on a set of observed intercorrelations among various traits. Each trait, in turn, is inferred from intercorrelations among habitual responses. Habitual responses, in turn, are based on specific observable responses. (See Figure 10.1.) For example, extraversion is based on observed intercorrelations among traits such as sociability, impulsivity, activity, liveliness, and excitability. Each of these traits is inferred from intercorrelated habitual responses such as going to parties, liking to talk to people, going to films on the spur of the moment, and so forth. These habits are themselves inferred from observable specific responses—actual occasions when the person went to a party, talked to people, and so forth.

On the basis of numerous factor analyses of personality data gathered from different subject populations all over the world, Eysenck derived two factors that could readily be labeled introversion/extraversion and stability/neuroticism. Later, on the basis of other statistical analyses, he postulated a third dimension, impulse control/psychoticism (Eysenck, 1982, p. 9). These three dimensions, according to Eysenck, are the major individual difference types most useful in describing personality functioning.

Once he had identified the three primary dimensions, Eysenck proceeded to construct a paper-and-pencil test to measure them. The most recent version of the test is the **Eysenck Personality Questionnaire** (EPQ) (Eysenck & Eysenck, 1975). Sample items for each dimension are listed in Table 10.1. It should be noted that subjects who score high in neuroticism or psychoticism are not necessarily neurotic or psychotic, but are at risk for developing the disorders.

Figures 10.2, 10.3, and 10.4 present the particular traits that define the type concepts, or primary dimensions, of extraversion, neuroticism, and psychoticism. **Extraverts** are sociable and impulsive individuals who like excitement and who are oriented toward external reality; **introverts** are quiet, introspective individuals who are

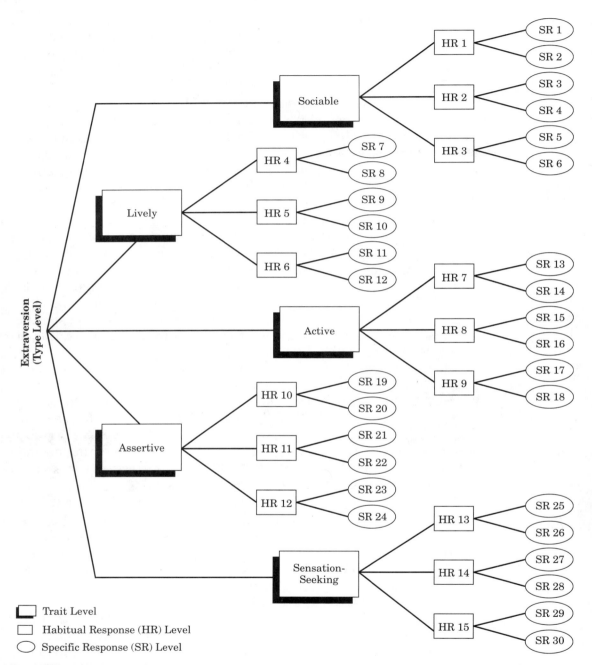

FIGURE 10.1 Hierarchical model of personality. (Adapted from *The Biological Basis of Personality,* by H. J. Eysenck, 1967, p. 36. Courtesy of Charles C Thomas, Publisher, Springfield, Illinois.)

TABLE 10.1   Sample items from the Eysenck
Personality Questionnaire*

Extraversion

1. Do you like mixing with people?
2. Do you like going out a lot?
3. Would you call yourself happy-go-lucky?

Neuroticism

1. Does your mood often go up and down?
2. Do you often feel "fed-up"?
3. Are you an irritable person?

Psychoticism

1. Do you enjoy cooperating with others?
2. Do you try not to be rude to people?
3. Do good manners and cleanliness matter to you?

*Yes responses to the extraversion and neuroticism items indicate extraverted and neurotic tendencies, respectively; *No* responses to the psychoticism items indicate a psychotic tendency. SOURCE: Adapted from Eysenck & Eysenck, 1975.

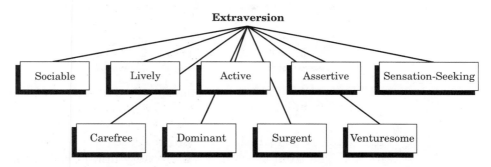

FIGURE 10.2   Traits making up the type concept of extraversion. (Adapted from Eysenck & Eysenck, 1985, p. 15.)

oriented toward inner reality and who prefer a well-ordered life. Although these definitions are similar to those used by Jung (see Chapter 3), Eysenck does not accept Jung's account of the origins of these attitudes nor the manner in which they operate in the subterranean psyche of the individual (Eysenck & Eysenck, 1985, p. 48).

Neurotics, in Eysenck's view, are emotionally unstable individuals. Some have unreasonable fears of certain objects, places, persons, animals, open spaces, or heights (Eysenck, 1965, p. 97); others may exhibit obsessional or impulsive symptoms. The hallmark of the disorder for most neurotics is an anxiety level disproportionate to the

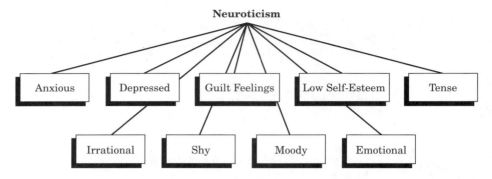

FIGURE 10.3   Traits making up the type concept of neuroticism. (Adapted from Eysenck & Eysenck, 1985, p. 15.)

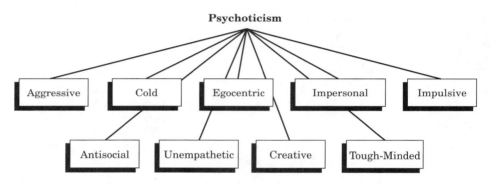

FIGURE 10.4   Traits making up the type concept of psychoticism. (Adapted from Eysenck & Eysenck, 1985, p. 14.)

realities of the situation (Eysenck, 1965, pp. 97–98). Yet some neurotics are free from the burden of anxiety and fear. In this grouping we find the psychopaths—individuals who seem unable to assess the consequences of their actions and who behave in an asocial or antisocial manner regardless of the punishment meted out by others (Eysenck, 1965, p. 100).

Psychotics differ from neurotics in the severity of their disorders. Showing the most severe type of **psychopathology,** psychotics may be insensitive to others, hostile, cruel, and inhumane, with a strong need to make fools of people and to upset them. Despite all these socially undesirable traits, however, Eysenck believes that psychotics tend to be creative (Eysenck & Eysenck, 1985, p. 14).

What is the basis for his contention? First, he points out that, throughout history, geniuses—that is, those who demonstrate supreme creative achievement—have tended to show various forms of psychopathological behavior. (See Table 10.2.) Thus, creativity is

TABLE 10.2   Eminent Personalities with Supposed Mental Illnesses

Schizophrenic disorders (and other cognitive psychoses):

Scientists: T. Brahe, Cantor, Copernicus, Descartes, Faraday, W. R. Hamilton, Kepler, Lagrange, Linnaeus, Newton, Pascal, Semmelweis, Weierstrass, H. Wells.
Thinkers: Kant, Nietzsche, Swedenborg.
Writers: Baudelaire, Lewis Carroll, Hawthorne, Hölderlin, S. Johnson, Pound, Rimbaud, Strindberg, Swift.
Artists: Bosch, Cellini, Dürer, Goya, El Greco, Kandinsky, Leonardo da Vinci, Rembrandt, Toulouse-Lautrec.
Composers: Donizetti, MacDowell, F. Mendelssohn, Rimsky-Korsakov, Saint-Saëns.
Others: M. Barrymore, de Sade, Goebbels, Herod the Great, Joan of Arc, Nero, Nijinsky, Shaka.

Affective disorders (depression, mania, or bipolar):

Scientists: Boltwood, Boltzmann, Carothers, C. Darwin, L. De Forest, J. F. W. Herschel, Julian Huxley, T. H. Huxley, Jung, Kammerer, J. R. von Mayer, V. Meyer, H. J. Muller, J. P. Müller, B. V. Schmidt, J. B. Watson.
Thinkers: W. James, J. S. Mill, Rousseau, Sabbatai Zevi, Schopenhauer.
Writers: Balzac, Barrie, Berryman, Blake, Boswell, V. W. Brooks, Byron, Chatterton, J. Clare, Coleridge, William Collins, Conrad, Cowper, H. Crane, Dickens, T. Dreiser, R. Fergusson, F. S. Fitzgerald, Frost, Goethe, G. Greene, Hemingway, Jarrell, Kafka, C. Lamb, J. London, R. Lowell, de Maupassant, E. O'Neill, Plath, Poe, Quiroga, Roethke, D. G. Rossetti, Saroyan, Schiller, Sexton, P. B. Shelley, C. Smart, T. Tasso, V. Woolf.
Artists: Michelangelo, Modigliani, Pollock, Raphael, Rothko, R. Soyer, Van Gogh.
Composers: Berlioz, Chopin, Elgar, Gershwin, Handel, Mahler, Rachmaninoff, Rossini, R. Schumann, Scriabin, Smetana, Tchaikovsky, Wolf.
Others: C. Borgia, Clive, O. Cromwell, A. Davis, J. Garland.

Personality disorders (including severe neuroses):

Scientists: Ampère, Cavendish, A. S. Couper, Diesel, Einstein, Frege, S. Freud, Galton, Heaviside, Huygens, Marconi, Mendel.
Thinkers: J. Austin, Beccaria, Comte, Descartes, Hegel, Hobbes, Hume, Kierkegaard, B. Russell, Spencer, Voltaire, Wittgenstein.
Writers: H. C. Andersen, E. B. Browning, R. Browning, Bunyan, Carlyle, Dickinson, Dostoevski, T. S. Eliot, Emerson, Flaubert, García Lorca, Gide, Allen Ginsberg, Gogol, Heine, G. M. Hopkins, A. Huxley, W. M. Inge, Melville, Pavese, Proust, S. Richardson, Rimbaud, Ruskin, Tennyson, de Tocqueville, Tolstoy, Verlaine, T. Williams, Zola.
Artists: Borromini, Bramante, Caravaggio, Cézanne, C. Chanel, Munch, Romney.
Composers: Beethoven, Bruckner, O. de Lasso, Schubert, Wagner.
Performers: S. Bernhardt, J. Dean, W. C. Fields, C. Gable, C. Grant, J. Joplin, M. Monroe, B. Powell.
Leaders: C. Barton, Bismarck, W. Churchill, M. B. Eddy, Göring, A. Gramsci, A. Hamilton, Hitler, H. Hughes, A. Krupp, H. Lee, R. E. Lee, Lincoln, Luther, Mussolini, Napoleon, Nightingale, Nixon, T. Roosevelt, W. Wilson, M. Wollstonecraft.

NOTE: Because almost all of these diagnoses are not based on objective clinical assessments, most are highly tentative.
SOURCE: From Simonton, 1994, p. 287.

linked directly to abnormality. Second, many of the traits associated with psychoticism are conducive to the pursuit of a creative career. Geniuses must buck tradition to strike out on their own. They cannot be concerned about pleasing others; instead they must be self-centered and persistent to overcome the many obstacles placed in their path (Simonton, 1994, p. 292).

Examples of the insensitivity, cruelty, and heartlessness of highly creative individuals abound. For instance, the mathematician Gauss was working on a particularly difficult problem when a servant came into his room to inform him that his sick wife was about to breathe her last. Gauss could only mutter, "Tell her to wait a moment till I'm through." Or there is the example of Cavendish, the notable physicist and chemist, who was so eccentric that, when he was about to be introduced to some scientific celebrities, he abandoned all amenities and ran down the hall, squealing like a bat. Cavendish ordinarily said no more than a few words to a man and refused to talk to any woman. At home, he communicated via written memos to his female servants, and fired instantly any servant who crossed his path (Simonton, 1994, p. 269).

Third, Eysenck notes that the hallmark of the creative genius is his or her ability to think in unusual, almost bizarre ways. Many psychotic individuals, especially those diagnosed with **schizophrenia,** also have concepts that are diffuse and overinclusive and, in consequence, are able to connect ideas that others would see as unrelated (Simonton, 1994, p. 292). Eysenck cites considerable evidence that schizophrenics perform very well on tests of creativity that require them to use **divergent thinking.** For example, an item on such a test might be: "How many uses can you think of for a brick?" Less creative people might reply that it can be used to build houses, to repair walkways, and to repair chimneys. A more creative person might give the same responses and quickly add the following: it could be used also as a doorstop, as a paperweight, as a thing to make water in a pond splash, as a weapon of aggression, as a walnut crusher, and as a substitute barbell to do bicep curls. As you can see, the more creative person gave more unusual responses and a greater number of responses, and thereby showed greater originality and fluency of ideas (Eysenck, 1995, pp. 236–245).

Eysenck claims that both geniuses and psychotics have a cognitive style that is overinclusive—that allows them to interpret all kinds of ideas as relevant to any problem under consideration. He thinks further that this overinclusiveness may be due to a failure of cognitive inhibition caused by an excess of **dopamine** and a lack of **serotonin** in the brain (Eysenck, 1995, pp. 264–265). Specifically,

Eysenck maintains that normal people process incoming information by narrowing it down—by deciding which information is relevant to the solution of a problem and which information is irrelevant. Normal individuals then include in their thinking the information that they consider will help them solve the problem and exclude the rest because of its perceived irrelevance. Eysenck argues that schizophrenics, in contrast, are characterized by a breakdown in this inhibitory process caused by very high levels of dopamine. Thus, the failure to inhibit ideas produces an overinclusiveness that is associated closely with creativity (Eysenck, 1995, pp. 249–279).

If psychotics and geniuses have the trait of creativity, why do geniuses produce outstanding works that contribute greatly to society, whereas most psychotics spend most of their lives in institutions and fail to achieve greatness? For the answer, Eysenck thinks we have to consider *combinations* of personality traits. Specifically, geniuses are generally characterized by high ego strength and confidence, extraordinarily high persistence motivation, and very high (although not extraordinarily high) intelligence. These traits interact with the trait of creativity to produce eminent men and women. These same qualities are not, however, typical in psychotics (Eysenck, 1995, pp. 114–123).

Finally, it must be acknowledged that many psychologists—most notably those in the humanistic tradition, as represented by Rogers and Maslow (see Chapters 12 and 13)—disagree vehemently with Eysenck. In stark contrast to him, they maintain that supreme creativity is associated with optimal psychological health (Simonton, 1994, p. 285). While Eysenck obviously doesn't agree with this viewpoint, he does say that we should be cautious in adopting his theory until much more validational research can be done (Eysenck, 1995, p. 246).

Inhibition Theory

Once Eysenck had described the major dimensions of personality to his satisfaction and devised a psychometrically sound test to measure them, it remained for him to develop a theory that would explain *why* people who differed along the dimensions should behave differently from one another. After developing such a theory, he needed to provide empirical evidence that different types of people did indeed differ in their actions. To achieve these goals, Eysenck began to construct a theory that had a strong physiological base, but did not ignore environmental influences.

Eysenck began by postulating that individual differences along the introversion/extraversion dimension are strongly determined by heredity and have their origins in the cerebral cortex of the central nervous system. Information from the environment is transmitted from the sense organs along neural pathways to the brain, where excitatory and inhibitory cortical processes result in either the facilitation or inhibition of behavioral and cognitive responses (Eysenck, 1965, p. 70). Drawing upon the work of Teplov (1964) and Pavlov (1927), Eysenck maintained that extraverts have relatively strong inhibitory processes and weak excitatory processes. In addition, their nervous systems are strong, which means that they have a large capacity to tolerate stimulation. Introverts, in contrast, have strong excitatory processes and weak inhibitory processes. Also, their nervous systems are weak, which means that they have only a small capacity to tolerate stimulation. Thus, the brains of extraverts react more slowly and weakly to stimuli, thereby creating a *stimulus hunger,* or desire for strong sensory stimulation, which causes them to seek excitement by approaching the environment, attending parties, making friends, taking risks, and so forth. Conversely, introverts are inherently more cortically aroused, have brains that react more quickly and strongly to stimuli, and can tolerate only relatively small amounts of stimulation. As a result, they tend to find strong stimulation from the environment aversive, and spend more time in contemplative activities such as reading, writing, and playing chess.

This **inhibition theory,** with its differential neurological underpinnings for introversion and extraversion, leads to a host of behavioral predictions that have generally received empirical confirmation. For example, in comparison to introverts, extraverts are fonder of loud music, bright colors, and jazz (perhaps because it is more complex and unusual, and therefore more interesting and stimulating). They are also more likely to use alcohol and other drugs, to smoke, and to engage in various types of sexual activity (Eysenck, 1965, pp. 84–85). More specifically, Eysenck's research has shown that, compared to introverts, extraverts have sexual intercourse at an earlier age, more frequently, with more partners, and in a wider range of positions (Eysenck & Eysenck, 1985, pp. 317–319). More recent research also indicates that extraverts are more likely than are introverts to seek help from others when they are undergoing life crises. The warm and happy outlooks of extraverts tend to attract and maintain networks of friends, and they are assertive enough to call upon these resources in times of trouble (Amirkhan, Risinger, & Swickert, 1995, p. 208).

Eysenck also conducted research in which introverts and extraverts were subjected to the same levels of strong, painful stimulation (electric shock) and asked to bear the pain as long as possible. He found that the pain tolerance of extraverts was much greater, presumably because their strong nervous systems were better able to inhibit the painful stimulation and thus the subjective experience of pain was less than it was for introverts (Eysenck, 1965, p. 83).

Still other studies have used sensory deprivation, an experimental condition in which subjects are placed alone for days in a small soundproof room, with their eyes blindfolded, their ears stuffed with cotton, and cardboard covers tied around their hands so that they cannot feel anything. A few studies have shown that extraverts, with their strong need for sensory stimulation, tolerate these conditions for a shorter period than do introverts, as would be expected on theoretical grounds (Eysenck, 1965, p. 84). In other studies, however, extraverts tolerated the situation longer than did introverts. Eysenck explains these anomalous results by suggesting that, because extraverts find the situation more aversive earlier in the process than introverts, they may devise means such as daydreaming or fidgeting to increase their level of arousal, thereby lasting longer. In other words, the total amount of deprivation time measured by the experimenter is not equal to the amount of actual deprivation experienced by the subject. Thus, Eysenck argues that the total amount of time for which subjects can endure the situation is not an adequate measure of deprivation tolerance.

Finally, Eysenck added the concept of **reactive inhibition** to his theorizing about introverts and extraverts. He borrowed the term from Hull's (1951) learning theory. Hull proposed that every repetition of an action creates reactive inhibition—a neural fatigue that builds to the point where the individual can no longer respond. Eysenck maintained that extraverts are more susceptible to reactive inhibition than are introverts and, as a result, are more likely to tire of a given activity sooner and turn to another. According to Eysenck, this changeableness of extraverts affects their behavior in many ways. They are more likely to change jobs or careers and to move from one company to another. They are also more likely to change boyfriends or girlfriends and to get divorced and change spouses (Eysenck, 1965, p. 81).

Arousal Theory

Although inhibition and excitation were useful concepts in helping to predict behavioral differences between introverts and extraverts, they were extremely difficult to measure. Eysenck turned to the concept of **cortical arousal** because it can be more precisely assessed and can generate predictions across a wider variety of tasks and in a wider range of situations. Finally, **arousal theory** has the advantage of identifying the physiological systems underlying individual differences in introversion/extraversion and stability/neuroticism, whereas the earlier inhibition theory was not able to identify precisely the physiological systems underlying inhibition (Eysenck & Eysenck, 1985, pp. 196–199).

Arousal Theory and Introversion/Extraversion

In the latest version of his theory, Eysenck traces the differences in behavior between introverts and extraverts to various parts of the **ascending reticular activating system** (ARAS). The ARAS is a network of fibers traveling upward from the lower brain stem to the thalamus and cortex. Stimulation of the ARAS results in increases in alertness and arousal of the cortex. Other fibers descend from the lower brain stem, and thereby influence bodily musculature and the **autonomic nervous system** (Cofer & Appley, 1964, pp. 399–400). At the same time, fibers descending from the cortex can modulate the activity of the brain stem. Thus, the relation between the ARAS and the cortex is reciprocal: the ARAS can activate the cortex, and the cortex in turn can influence the ARAS, either increasing its excitability or inhibiting it.

In Eysenck's theory, introverts are assumed to have innately higher levels of arousal than do extraverts and, consequently, to be more sensitive to stimulation. Eysenck explains the relation between arousal and sensitivity to stimulation as follows:

> If sensory stimulation is registered in the cortex to a degree which is a joint function of the objective level of intensity of the stimulation and of the arousal existing in the cortex at the time of arrival of the neural message, then identical intensities of input will be experienced as stronger by introverts than by extraverts. (Eysenck, 1976, p. 113)

Thus, any given level of incoming stimulation is amplified by the high cortical arousability of introverts. To date, however, research shows little support for the idea that introverts' levels of arousal are innately higher, although a good deal of scientific evidence indicates that introverts are indeed more sensitive to stimulation (Stelmack, 1990, p. 293).

Eysenck further assumes that very low and very high levels of stimulation produce negative **hedonic tone**—negative feelings and

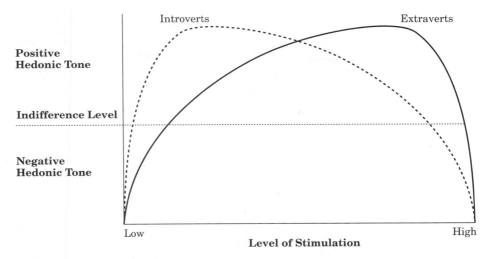

FIGURE 10.5   Theoretical relationship between level of stimulation and hedonic tone as a function of extraversion. (Adapted from Eysenck & Eysenck, 1985, p. 249.)

negative evaluation of the experience; whereas positive hedonic tone—positive feelings and positive evaluation of the experience—occurs only at intermediate levels of sensory stimulation. Thus, it follows that the preferred level of stimulation should be lower for introverts than for extraverts (Eysenck & Eysenck, 1985, p. 248). Figure 10.5 illustrates this relationship between levels of stimulation and hedonic tone for introverts and extraverts.

Using this new theoretical formulation, Eysenck could make and verify the same predictions concerning the behavior of introverts and extraverts in sensory-deprivation and pain-tolerance conditions that he had made using his earlier inhibition theory. In addition, the revised theory has been tested in several new and interesting areas, including students' study habits and their need for closure under time pressures. We now consider those findings.

Campbell and Hawley (1982) noted the study locations of students in the campus library and then obtained their consent for an interview about their study habits. They also asked students to fill out the Eysenck Personality Questionnaire (Eysenck & Eysenck, 1975). In the interview, subjects were asked to indicate, on a scale from 0 to 10, the number of times per hour that they took study breaks. They were also asked to indicate, on a scale from 1 (low) to 6 (high), what levels of noise, crowdedness, and socializing opportunities they preferred while they studied in the library. They were also asked to indicate, on a scale from 1 (not at all) to 6 (highly), how important socializing activities were to them in choosing a study location.

On the basis of Eysenck's theory, Campbell and Hawley predicted that introverts would prefer study locations that minimized intense external stimulation, such as individual study carrels where talking was not permitted, whereas extraverts would prefer seating arrangements that provided stimulation, such as a large reading area with sofas and lounge chairs, where socializing was permitted and where auditory and visual stimulation was high. This prediction was based on Eysenck's argument that introverts have a lower threshold for arousal of the reticular activating system than do extraverts. As a consequence, introverts should experience greater levels of arousal at lower intensities of stimulation. In addition, Eysenck's theory postulates that introverts would be more likely to experience negative hedonic tone and increased aversion to stimulation above an optimal level of stimulus intensity and that this optimal stimulus intensity would be lower for introverts than for extraverts. These predictions were strongly confirmed. Introverts tended to study in quiet areas and to use individual study carrels; extraverts studied in areas where they could socialize and where the level of auditory and visual stimulation was relatively high. Extraverts also reported that they preferred to study in noisier, more crowded areas, where they would have more opportunities to socialize. Such opportunities were highly important to them, and not as important to introverts.

Campbell and Hawley (1982) also predicted that extraverts would report taking more study breaks—looking around the room, walking around—than did introverts. Eysenck argues that, when performing long tasks, extraverts generate reactive inhibition (fatigue) more quickly and at greater levels than do introverts, and this rapid accumulation of reactive inhibition produces rest pauses. Since extraverts are more susceptible to inhibition, the monotony of studying should prompt extraverts to experience more rest pauses and consequently to take more study breaks. This prediction was also strongly confirmed. Furthermore, Davies and Parasuraman (1982) found that, on tasks that require vigilance, extraverts tire more easily than do introverts and are more likely to make errors. One practical implication of this finding for employers is to hire introverts rather than extraverts as air traffic controllers or quality-control workers.

Heaton and Kruglanski (1991) hypothesized that, under highly stressful conditions, introverts have a greater need for closure than do extraverts. The need for closure refers to a person's motivation to reduce high levels of aversive arousal by arriving at a definite answer to a problem without fully utilizing all the available information. The alternative—to remain open to all the incoming information—is confusing and aversively arousing. In comparison to extraverts, introverts find high levels of arousal more aversive, and hence, under highly stressful conditions, they should consider less of the available information and come to a decision more quickly than do extraverts.

To test this hypothesis, Heaton and Kruglanski asked introverts and extraverts to judge a male job candidate's likely success as a company president on the basis of information about the candidate's recent business experiences. When subjects were given only 30 seconds to reach their decision (high-pressure condition), introverts utilized less information than did extraverts in arriving at their judgment. When subjects were given all the time they needed to make their decision (low-pressure condition), both introverts and extraverts tended to utilize much of the available information. These results suggest that introverts' judgments may be ill-formed under certain conditions and may result in unfair decisions about job candidates. Other research shows that introverts are more likely than are extraverts to base their judgments of others on stereotypic information when pressured. These findings do not mean that introverts are less capable information processors than are extraverts. Under normal circumstances, they are as capable as are extraverts in their information processing abilities and, in fact, tend to exceed extraverts in academic performance (Heaton & Kruglanski, 1991, pp. 161–165).

Finally, Landrum (1992) has found that college extraverts tend to consume more chocolate, coffee, tea, and soft drinks like Coca-Cola and Dr. Pepper than do introverts. All of these contain caffeine, which has strong arousal effects. Many studies have shown that caffeine has a differential impact on the performances of introverts and extraverts—specifically, that increases in arousal induced by larger and larger doses of caffeine typically serve to improve extraverts' academic performance, whereas introverts' performance improves only to a point and then significantly declines at the highest doses (Bullock & Gilliland, 1993). In other words, the performance of both introverts and extraverts increases with moderate levels of caffeinated coffee drunk prior to the test (approximately one and one-half cups for a person weighing 150 pounds), but the performance of introverts declines considerably with higher levels of caffeinated coffee (three or more cups), whereas the performance of extraverts continues to improve.

Autonomic Activation and Neuroticism

In his arousal theory, Eysenck locates the seat of neuroticism in the **visceral brain,** or limbic system. The structures of the visceral brain—the hippocampus, amygdala, cingulum, septum, and hypothalamus—are involved in generating emotionality. The visceral brain and the ARAS are only partially independent of each other; thus, cortical and autonomic arousal can also be produced by activity in the visceral brain. In particular, such activity produces arousal of the sympathetic branch of the autonomic nervous system, thereby preparing individuals for fight (anger) or flight (fear). It stops digestion, makes the heart beat faster, and increases breathing rates. People high in neuroticism have lower thresholds for activity in the visceral brain and greater responsivity of the **sympathetic nervous system** (Eysenck & Eysenck, 1985, p. 206). Thus, neurotics are innately more reactive; they overreact to even mild forms of stimulation. Figure 10.6 illustrates the physiological systems involved in generating behavioral differences among individuals who vary along the stability/neuroticism and introversion/extraversion dimensions.

Eysenck proposed that the greater responsivity of the sympathetic nervous system in neurotics is most obvious under relatively stressful conditions (Eysenck & Eysenck, 1985, p. 206), when the emotional reaction engendered by stress may interfere with performance. Most researchers have not directly investigated the effects of neuroticism on performance but have opted to study the strongly related dimension of anxiety. (Subjects' anxiety scores typically correlate positively with their neuroticism scores in the +.60 to +.70 range.) Anxiety consists of two components: emotionality and worry. Emotionality refers to physiological changes and the accompanying unpleasant feelings of uneasiness, nervousness, and tension. Worry is the cognitive component of anxiety; it includes persistent concern about one's performance and its consequences, negative self-evaluations, and negative task expectations (Eysenck & Eysenck, 1985, p. 292).

According to Eysenck, the adverse effects of anxiety on performance are attributable to task-irrelevant processing activities such as worry. Students who report high levels of worry generally do poorly on exams and have lower grade-point averages (Eysenck & Eysenck, 1985, pp. 293–294). When highly anxious people do perform as well as those low in anxiety on certain tasks, they expend much more effort and experience much more distress. Thus, anxious people may perform as efficiently at times as nonanxious people, but at a

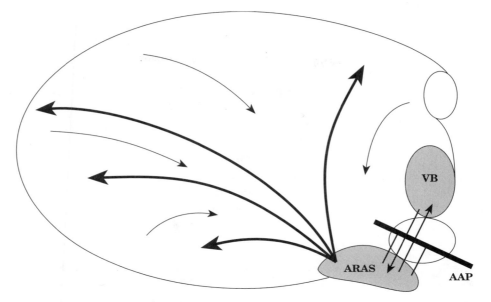

FIGURE 10.6   Diagrammatic representation of the mutual interactions among the reticular formation, visceral brain, and cortex. VB, visceral brain; ARAS, ascending reticular activating system; AAP, ascending afferent pathways. (Adapted from the *Biological Basis of Personality,* by H. J. Eysenck, 1967, p. 231. Courtesy of Charles C Thomas, Publisher, Springfield, Illinois.)

greater cost to their physical well-being (Eysenck & Eysenck, 1985, pp. 298–299).

Because neurotics possess labile and overactive autonomic nervous systems, they are very likely to experience high levels of fear and anxiety in stressful situations. Among such situations are those that involve intimacy between individuals; therefore, we would expect neurotics to attempt to reduce levels of intimacy. Research has shown that this is indeed the case. In a study by Campbell and Rushton (1978), for example, subjects high in neuroticism showed higher levels of gaze aversion than did subjects low in neuroticism when talking to an experimenter.

Hormones and Psychoticism

Eysenck's work on developing a causal theory of psychoticism remains at a rudimentary stage. However, a number of related facts—that males as a group invariably score much higher on the Psychoticism (*P*) scale of the EPQ than females, that criminals and psychopaths (with high P scores) tend to be male rather than female, and that women (at least premenopausal women) become schizophrenic less readily than do men—suggest to Eysenck that psychoticism is perhaps related to maleness. In particular, maleness is linked very closely to the secretion of **androgens** (Eysenck, 1982, p. 19). In addition, high P scorers, like schizophrenics, show a relative lack of serotonin and the presence of certain **antigens** in their bodies. This fact suggests a strong relation between P and schizophrenia and, according to Eysenck, may hold the key to a biological explanation of psychoticism (Eysenck, 1982, p. 20). At the present time, however, there is only rudimentary research evidence to support Eysenck's speculations about the association between hormones and psychoticism.

PERSONALITY DEVELOPMENT

In Eysenck's view, human beings are biosocial creatures; that is, people are born with certain innate predispositions to respond in particular ways to the environment, but these predispositions (or traits) can be altered to some extent by socialization demands. Thus, the environment and our genes interact to produce behavior; biological factors typically play the stronger role.

The Role of Heredity

Eysenck finds the strong genetic basis of the primary personality types confirmed in three ways: (1) the same three personality orientations are found universally, despite the unique social and cultural factors that pressure individuals in different national groups to behave in ways consistent with their national affiliations; (2) these traits show stability within given individuals over long periods of time, during which a variety of experiences occur without appreciably modifying basic responses; (3) the evidence provided by twin studies is consistent with the genetic hypothesis.

Carefully translated versions of the EPQ have been administered to large samples of people in a variety of nations and then factor-analyzed using a special method designed to show whether or not the same factors or different factors appear in all the cultures. If environment or culture played the major part in determining personality, we would expect to find different numbers and kinds of factors; if genetics played the major role, we would expect to find the same three factors despite cultural variations. Eysenck reports support for the genetic hypothesis: the same three factors emerge from the analysis despite cultural variations—or variations in age and sex, for that matter. These primary factors have been found in both males and females in 35 nations, including Greece, France, Spain, Hungary, Japan, Egypt, Iran, Iceland, Sri Lanka, Uganda, the Commonwealth of Independent States (formerly the Soviet Union), and the United States (Eysenck, 1990, pp. 245–246). Studies utilizing the **Junior Eysenck Personality Questionnaire** (S. B. G. Eysenck, 1965) to measure extraversion, neuroticism, and psychoticism in children within different cultures—including Hungary, Spain, Japan, Singapore, and Greece—have found results similar to those obtained with adults (Eysenck & Eysenck, 1985, pp. 102–107).

Other studies have found the same three dimensions—introversion/extraversion, stability/neuroticism, and impulse control/psychoticism—in children as well as adults (Rachman, 1969, pp. 253–254). Numerous longitudinal studies have shown, moreover, that these three traits are stable from childhood to adulthood. Individuals who are introverted in childhood, for example, tend to be introverted in adulthood (Eysenck & Eysenck, 1985, pp. 113–114). In other words, subjects respond consistently to the trait questionnaires, despite the many experiences that have occurred during the long intervals between testing.

Finally, Eysenck has reviewed a number of studies using identical and fraternal twins, raised together or apart, who were given the same tests to assess extraversion and neuroticism. These studies allow investigators to make relatively precise determinations of the contributions made by genetic and environmental factors to the development of these traits. (To review the logic and rationale of twin studies, see Chapter 9.) One study showed that, for extraversion, the intraclass correlation for **monozygotic twins** (MZ) brought up together was .42; for MZ twins raised apart, it was .61; and for **dizygotic twins** (DZ), it was –.17. Thus, MZ twins, whether raised apart or together, were more alike in extraversion than were DZ twins (Eysenck & Eysenck, 1985, pp. 93–95). For neuroticism, the corresponding correlations were .38, .53, and .11, respectively; these results again support the genetic hypothesis, even though the correlations for MZ twins raised apart are higher than the correlations for MZ twins raised together and seem counterintuitive. Furthermore, twin studies focusing on the biological basis of various psychoses, such as schizophrenia and manic-depression, also suggest that heredity plays an important part in the development of these disorders (Eysenck, 1967, p. 222).

The Role of Socialization

According to Eysenck, socialized conduct is mediated by conscience, which he defines as the sum total of an individual's learned or conditioned responses. Individuals learn behaviors that run counter to their own wishes in order to avoid being punished by authority figures such as parents, teachers, and clergy. For example, they must learn to be clean, not to defecate or urinate whenever and wherever they please, and to control their sexual and aggressive impulses. They also must learn not to lie, not to fight with others who disagree with them, and not to steal. Any performance of these behaviors meets with punishment. Eventually, the mere thought of performing the behavior produces an unpleasant emotional reaction, and the act is avoided. Later, these unpleasant emotional reactions occur in the presence of similar activities and lead to an avoidance of these secondary activities as well. For instance, a child may be punished severely for stealing from a particular playmate. Later he may experience unpleasant feelings if he even thinks about stealing from *any* of his peers. Thus, through conditioning, individuals learn to desist from performing behaviors that society deems harmful. The members of society also reward individuals for exhibiting certain behaviors, and thereby shape their behavior in ways that society considers acceptable.

Individuals differ in the degree to which they learn the rules of society. Specifically, Eysenck proposes that introverts learn the rules more quickly and efficiently than do extraverts. He believes that the basis for these differences is genetic: introverts have chronically higher cortical arousal than do extraverts; arousal tends to facilitate learning; therefore, introverts learn more readily than extraverts (Eysenck & Eysenck, 1985, p. 241). Because it is more difficult for extraverts to learn societal rules, they tend to be undersocialized, whereas extreme introverts tend to be oversocialized. Extraverts are less mature generally than introverts; that is, introverts learn how to behave appropriately (in line with societal demands) at a much earlier age. For extraverts to learn the appropriate behaviors, it takes many more instances of pairing the lying—or stealing or other behavior—with punishments before the lessons are learned. Thus, extraverts are older by the time they finally learn appropriate behaviors, if they ever learn them well.

Because they are less readily conditioned, extraverts experience less inhibition with respect to antisocial behavior. Thus, criminals tend to be extraverted. Extraversion in combination with neuroticism, Eysenck notes, facilitates the development of criminality, because neurotics are relatively anxious, and anxiety drives people who have acquired antisocial responses (extreme extraverts) to express those responses. Research has also shown that it is primarily the impulsivity rather than the sociability component that is related to criminality.

Introverts, in contrast, are characterized by an overreadiness to form very strong consciences; they tend to be wracked by guilt and anxiety whenever they think about violating the rules of society. As a result, they are unlikely to turn to crime. Eysenck believes that, under stressful conditions, extreme introversion may lead to obsessive-compulsive, phobic, or depressive behavior (Eysenck, 1965, p. 267). Eysenck also explains the shyness of neurotic introverts in terms of their innate arousal levels. Shyness is likely to occur in social situations characterized by stress, such as meeting new people or facing the possibility of criticism or disapproval by authority figures. Because introverts are chronically aroused, and neurotic people are innately more susceptible to stress, social situational stress is likely to produce withdrawal in people who combine these traits (Eysenck & Eysenck, 1985, pp. 316–317).

Psychoticism and intelligence level have also been linked to antisocial and criminal behavior (Eysenck & Eysenck, 1985, pp. 330–332; Eysenck & Gudjonsson, 1989, pp. 49–55). Criminals tend to have low IQs, according to Eysenck. One possible explanation, he suggests, is that people whose intelligence is low enough to prove a handicap in achieving educational success will find it difficult to earn a satisfactory living along conventional lines and, therefore, may turn to crime. Critics argue that it is not low intelligence that causes criminality, but rather the criminals' socioeconomic background. More specifically, they argue that the criminals' poverty deprives them of opportunities to increase their IQs through education, so that eventually they are motivated to engage in illegal activities. But Eysenck maintains that the scientific evidence shows that IQ has an effect on criminal behavior *independent* of social class (and race, for that matter). He admits that all the data used to reach this conclusion are based on offenders who have been caught, and the possibility exists that the more intelligent lawbreakers, whether violent or white-collar criminals, simply never get caught. But he maintains that the number of such criminals is relatively small and would not appreciably change his basic conclusion.

Despite the genetic basis of personality, Eysenck is most emphatic in pointing out that personality development can and does respond to socialization. He rejects the view that, if heredity is so important, modification of behavior is impossible. Predispositions for a person to behave in a certain manner are genetically determined, but these tendencies to respond can be modified by environmental influences (Eysenck, 1982, p. 29). For example, even though extraverts generally condition poorly, they can learn societal rules well if they are subjected to rigorous and prolonged training by parents and others, and so can be prevented from engaging in antisocial acts. Conversely, introverts may eventually engage in criminal acts if their parents neglect to provide them with appropriate training.

Intelligence, Heredity, and Social Policy

Although Eysenck does not formally incorporate intelligence into his tripartite typology, he does argue strongly that, as a major aspect of personality, intelligence must be considered in any discussion of the socialization process.

Eysenck believes that, as with the three primary types, intelligence has strong genetic roots, but its development can be altered by environmental influences. On the basis of considerable research, Eysenck concludes that approximately 80% of human intelligence is inherited, whereas 20% can be attributed to the influence of the environment (Eysenck, 1975, p. 244). Like Cattell, he uses research data based on twin studies as evidence of its strong biological base. (See Chapter 9.) Eysenck also cites IQ comparisons between various other blood relatives: generally speaking, the closer the degree of kinship between two individuals—that is, the more genes they share in common—the more similar are their IQs. For example, brothers resemble each other in IQ more than do first cousins (Eysenck & Kamin, 1981, p. 51).

To Eysenck, it is abundantly clear that human beings are genetically unequal in traits and intellectual abilities. Yet many modern sociologists and psychologists continue to insist that we are all genetically equal, out of a concern that recognition of genetic inequalities would lead to unequal treatment before the law, inequality of opportunity, and political inequality (Eysenck, 1975, p. 22). Eysenck readily acknowledges that their fears have a solid basis in fact, as evidenced by the crude eugenics programs advocated by proponents of the genetic position in the early 1900s (and today by Cattell); those programs gave rise to laws that restricted the immigration of groups considered inferior into the United States and provided for sterilization of all individuals labeled as feebleminded.

While sympathizing with the concerns of professionals who seek to protect the rights of all citizens, Eysenck strongly opposes the distortion or denial of scientific facts.

[What I am] trying to point out is that equality before the law, equality of opportunity, and equality as a citizen, are not dependent on *identity* of genetic endowment; *these are human rights, of universal validity, which are independent of biological findings*. Indeed, it would be extremely dangerous to argue . . . that people are universally entitled to these equal rights *because* they are genetically equal; if science should prove that such genetic equality was a myth . . . the whole case for equality as a human right would fall to the ground. . . . [S]cience does indeed show that genetic equality is a myth. [However], this does not in any way lead to an argument favoring inequality before the law, inequality of opportunity, or inequality of political rights. (Eysenck, 1975, p. 22)

Rejecting the crude eugenics position, Eysenck does favor a meritocracy. People with the highest ability levels should be selected for access to higher educational and career opportunities, without regard for their race, sex, age, religion, ethnic background, or social class. He notes that many people oppose a meritocracy on the grounds that it leads to elitism. However, Eysenck says that such people seldom consider the alternative—namely, allowing access to these positions to anyone, irrespective of ability levels. He asks, "If your child needed the services of a brain surgeon to remove a tumor to save his life, would you prefer a brain surgeon of the highest ability, or just any third-rate medical student?" Again, "If your plane had engines that began sputtering, would you prefer a pilot of the highest ability or would just anyone do?" (Eysenck, 1975, p. 222). For Eysenck, the answer is clear: a meritocracy is preferable to a "mediocracy" (Eysenck, 1975, p. 223).

Finally, Eysenck recognizes the difficulty of devising an IQ test free of social-class bias in order to make these selections fairly. There is reason to believe that traditional IQ tests discriminate against lower-class individuals by asking for information based on experiences to which they are unlikely to have been exposed. Thus, certain questions may have different meanings for middle-class and lower-class children and adults. One popular IQ test, for example, asks children: "What's the thing for you to do if another boy hits you without meaning to do it?" The correct answer is "Walk away." But for a ghetto child, whose survival depends on being tough, the logical answer is "Hit him back." This answer is considered incorrect and receives a score of zero on the test (Morris, 1982, p. 334).

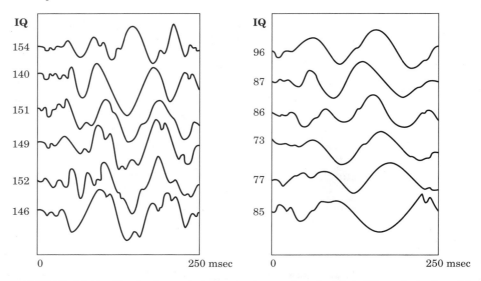

FIGURE 10.7 Evoked potential waveforms for six high-IQ and six low-IQ subjects: auditory stimulation. (Adapted from Eysenck & Eysenck, 1985, p. 170.)

Eysenck admits that no IQ test is ever completely culture-free or culture-fair. However, he argues that a revolution now occurring in the IQ testing area will solve the problem. Direct physiological measures of biologically based intelligence are now available. Electrodes placed on the skull measure changes in the electrical activity of the cerebral cortex. The resulting **electroencephalogram** (EEG) can be used to assess **evoked potentials.** If an experimenter presents a visual or auditory stimulus and records the subsequent activity in the brain, the stimulus evokes a series of waves. In highly intelligent people, the waves are complex; in less intelligent individuals, the waves are simpler. (See Figures 10.7 and 10.8.) The differences between high- and low-IQ individuals in the form of the evoked potentials are apparently related to the number of errors made in transmission of the incoming visual and auditory information. Low rates of error are associated with more complex evoked potentials, whereas high error rates are associated with simpler forms. Eysenck believes that the use of such procedures in the future will help ensure fairness in selection procedures (Eysenck & Eysenck, 1985, pp. 167–175). It should be noted, however, that one prominent critic, Leon Kamin, has called into question Eysenck's assertion that psychophysiological response measures are highly correlated with IQ. Kamin maintains that it has been impossible to replicate the results show-

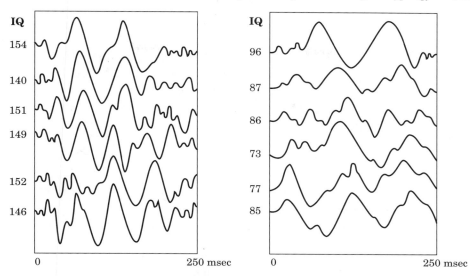

FIGURE 10.8   Evoked potential waveforms for six high-IQ and six low-IQ subjects: visual stimulation. (Adapted from Eysenck & Eysenck, 1985, p. 171.)

ing more highly complex waves in high-IQ people and simpler waves in low-IQ people (Eysenck & Kamin, 1981, pp. 180–181).

ASSESSMENT TECHNIQUES

Like Cattell, Eysenck can be considered a psychometrist of personality, because of his insistence on the need for rigorous measurement in studying personality structure and functioning. Seeking to develop reliable and valid measures to assess personality, Eysenck relied heavily on factor analysis and other statistical techniques. Having identified the major dimensions of personality through factor analysis, Eysenck constructed tests to assess them. He then administered the tests to identical and fraternal twins to assess the contribution of genetics to the major dimensions of personality. He has also sought to validate his theoretical ideas through a variety of experimental procedures.

To test his hypothesis that introverts condition more quickly and with fewer errors than do extraverts, for example, Eysenck has employed a host of experimental techniques, including eyeblink conditioning and vigilance tasks. In the eyeblink paradigm, a tone or other neutral stimulus is used as the conditioned stimulus, and a puff of air to the eye is the unconditioned stimulus. Conditioning occurs when the conditioned stimulus alone is sufficient to produce the eyeblink response. In general, introverts tend to learn the eyeblink response to the tone more quickly than do extraverts (Eysenck & Eysenck, 1985, pp. 241–248). A typical vigilance task requires subjects to detect sequences of three odd digits in a very long series of digits presented by tape recorder at a rate of one digit per second. For example, in the sequence 1, 4, 8, 2, 5, 4, 1, 3, 9, 4, 2, 6, subjects would have to pick out the sequence 1, 3, 9 (Eysenck, 1965, p. 42). Introverts are expected to perform better because they are more aroused, and in fact they generally do outperform extraverts on such tasks (Eysenck, 1965, p. 431).

In testing various aspects of his arousal theory, Eysenck relies on a variety of physiological measures to assess arousal, including heart rate, electroencephalogram (EEG), **electrodermal response,** and **pupillary response.** Although these physiological measures typically show only modest positive intercorrelations (the typical range is +.20 to +.30), it has been shown quite consistently that introverts manifest greater physiological responsiveness to stimulation than extraverts; the most consistent results are obtained on electrodermal measures (Eysenck & Eysenck, 1985, pp. 205–231). According to Eysenck, not only do introverts demonstrate greater emotional responsiveness, but they also exhibit higher chronic levels of arousal than do extraverts (Eysenck & Eysenck, 1985, pp. 223–224).

Finally, Eysenck uses research on lower animals to draw implications about the behavior of humans. For example, he reports exposing rats in a confined space to bright lights and loud noise and then recording their defecation and urination behavior. Animals that showed greater defecation and urination were assumed to be more emotional and reactive to stimuli than were those that showed less of these behaviors. Reactive, emotional rats were then bred with one another, and the nonreactive animals were also interbred. Over several generations, distinct reactive and nonreactive strains developed. Animals in both groups were trained to approach a goal box for food reward by running down an alleyway. Then, as they approached the goal box, all of them were shocked. The animals were then considered to be in conflict: they wanted to approach the goal box to obtain food but feared receiving shock if they did so. The hypothesis was that the reactive strain of animals, being more emotional than the nonreactive strain, would experience more stress in anticipating the electric shock, and correspondingly their goal-box approach responses would be slower. This hypothesis was supported. Eysenck sees clear implications for the behavior of neurotic (high innate emotionality) and nonneurotic (low innate emotionality) humans who are subjected to stress; that is, neurotics experience greater conflict under stress and perform less efficiently than nonneurotics (Eysenck & Eysenck, 1985, pp. 99–100).

THEORY'S IMPLICATIONS FOR THERAPY

In Eysenck's view, neurotic behavior is most likely to be learned under certain environmental conditions, especially in those individuals who have inherited labile autonomic nervous systems. The acquisition of disordered behavior by such individuals obeys the laws of learning, and these same conditioning principles can be used to eliminate the undesirable behaviors and to teach new, desirable ones. Eysenck calls the application of learning theory and principles to the treatment of disordered behavior **behavior therapy.**

Learning theory postulates that neurotic behavior is unadaptive behavior, harmful to the individual or others. People with an extreme dread of spiders, for example, are forced to live circumscribed lives. They may be unable to sleep at night for fear of being bitten. Their inability to sleep peacefully or for long periods of time may make them restless, irritable, and easily fatigued, and thus have a negative effect on their performance at home and their relationships with others. They may avoid social invitations to others' homes because of the possible presence of the feared creatures. They may avoid picnics outdoors, walks in the woods, and a variety of other recreational activities that might result in contact with spiders.

Acquisition of Neurotic Behavior through Classical Conditioning

In Pavlov's prototypical experiment on **classical conditioning,** a hungry dog who naturally salivated to the sight of food learned to associate a bell—originally a neutral stimulus that did not evoke salivation—with food, so that eventually, after several pairings, the sound of the bell alone acted as a conditioned stimulus to produce salivation. (See Figure 10.9.)

In the acquisition of neurotic behavior, Watson's famous (but, by current research standards, ethically questionable) experiment with

FIGURE 10.9   Classical conditioning procedure.

little Albert provides the classic illustration of the process. Albert was an infant of 11 months who was fond of white rats. He loved playing with them and showed no fear whatsoever. Using classical conditioning, Watson created a phobia for white rats in Albert. Watson stood behind Albert with an iron bar and hammer and, whenever the boy reached for the animal, made an extremely loud noise. In this experiment, the animal was the conditioned stimulus (CS), and the loud, fear-producing noise was the unconditioned stimulus (UCS). As expected, the unconditioned response (UCR), fear, became conditioned to the sight of the rat (the CS), and Albert developed an intense fear of the rat. He would whimper and cry and try to crawl away from it (Eysenck, 1982, pp. 125–126; Watson & Rayner, 1920). Figure 10.10 illustrates this process of phobic conditioning.

Elimination of Neurotic Behavior through Counterconditioning

Once neurotic behavior has been acquired, one major way to reduce or eliminate it, in Eysenck's view, is through **counterconditioning.** In counterconditioning, the person must learn to make a new response to a CS that elicits maladaptive behavior. The new response is one that is antagonistic to the old one. We know that the autonomic

Before Conditioning

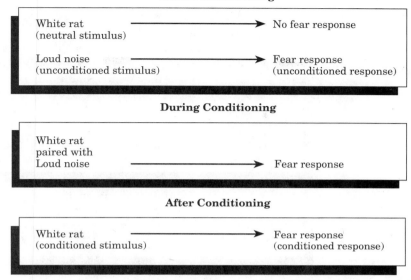

White rat
(neutral stimulus) ⟶ No fear response

Loud noise
(unconditioned stimulus) ⟶ Fear response
(unconditioned response)

During Conditioning

White rat
paired with
Loud noise ⟶ Fear response

After Conditioning

White rat
(conditioned stimulus) ⟶ Fear response
(conditioned response)

FIGURE 10.10   Phobia acquisition via classical conditioning.

nervous system, which mediates emotional reactions, is divided into two portions, sympathetic and parasympathetic. As we have seen, the sympathetic nervous system prepares the individual for fight (anger) or flight (fear) by slowing down the digestive process and increasing heart and breathing rates. The **parasympathetic nervous system** acts antagonistically: it speeds up the digestive process and slows heart and breathing rates when the person is relaxed.

Watson intended to eliminate the rat phobia in little Albert, but the boy's mother removed him from the hospital before the counterconditioning experiment could be started. Instead, Watson's associate, Mary Jones, conducted a related experiment in which she used counterconditioning to eliminate a fear of rabbits in Peter, a boy about the same age as Albert.

Jones began by offering Peter some chocolate when he was fairly hungry. As he began to eat, she brought the feared object into the room and placed it next to him. The basic idea was to eliminate Peter's phobia about rabbits by counterconditioning him to associate the sight of the rabbit not with fear, but with the pleasant sensations engendered by eating chocolate. A difficulty arose immediately, however, when the experimenter placed the rabbit next to the child. She found that the fear response was so strong that the boy cried despite the chocolate. The experimenter then moved the rabbit to a corner of

FIGURE 10.11 Reduction of phobia through counterconditioning.

the room 20 feet away, and the child stopped crying and resumed eating. Gradually, she brought the rabbit closer to Peter until the boy could play with it happily. The sympathetic conditioning of fear was completely eliminated by the parasympathetic conditioning of pleasantness associated with eating chocolate (Eysenck, 1965, pp. 132–135; Jones, 1924). This counterconditioning process is illustrated in Figure 10.11.

Use of Behavior Therapy to Eliminate Disorders

Eysenck advocates three major behavior techniques that have been used successfully to treat a variety of phobias—fears of the dark, heights, closed spaces, snakes, spiders, dogs, hospitals, and dentists—as well as enuresis (bedwetting), obsessions, compulsions, test anxiety, and public speaking anxiety. These three techniques are modeling, flooding, and systematic desensitization.

In **modeling,** phobic people watch nonphobics cope successfully with dreaded objects or situations. Clients later confronted with these objects show a reduction or elimination of their fears. (See Chapter 17 for a more detailed presentation of modeling techniques used to treat phobias by social cognitive theorist Albert Bandura.)

In **flooding,** clients are exposed to dreaded objects or situations for prolonged periods of time in order to extinguish their fear. Prolonged rather than brief exposure is generally more effective in reducing or eliminating fear (Hecker & Thorpe, 1987, p. 220). The rationale is that presentation of the feared stimulus initially elicits a strong, negative emotional reaction but that prolonged exposure results in a rapid decline in fearfulness (O'Leary & Wilson, 1987, pp. 166–167). Once the fear is reduced, the person can begin to reappraise the situation and learn that nothing dreadful will happen (Marshall, 1985, p. 132). To ensure full exposure to the dreaded object or situation, the client is prevented from making an avoidance or escape response.

A study by Marshall (1985) illustrates phobia reduction in people who are afraid of heights. Before therapy began, clients who reported a fear of heights were given a behavioral test requiring them to walk as far as they could up a flight of fire-escape stairs. The top step was approximately 30 feet above the ground. Clients generally became very upset when they were only 6.5 feet above the ground. At this point, they stopped and would go no further. They were then brought to the flat roof of a six-story building that was surrounded by a guard-rail 3 feet from the edge. The therapist instructed the clients to walk to the railing and look down at the street below. They were told to remain there, no matter how anxious they felt, until the therapist signaled the end of the session. Some of the clients were exposed only briefly (approximately 9 minutes) to the dreaded situation; others were exposed to it for a longer period (approximately 30 minutes). All clients were then retested by having them walk up the fire-escape stairs. Most of the clients who were exposed for long periods were able to walk up to the 20-foot level; a few walked up the entire 30 feet. Clients exposed for brief periods improved only slightly (walked up 7 or 8 feet), and a few actually worsened. A follow-up study one month later showed that the long-exposure clients maintained their gains, whereas the brief-exposure clients showed no improvement.

In contrast to flooding, **systematic desensitization** involves a gradual, client-controlled exposure to the anxiety-eliciting object or situation. Systematic desensitization involves counterconditioning by having the client make a response antagonistic to anxiety in the presence of the anxiety-evoking stimuli, so that the anxiety is suppressed. Typically, clients are trained in muscle relaxation, which results in lowered physiological arousal and feelings of calmness. The clients construct a hierarchy of anxiety-eliciting situations, ranging from mildly stressful to very stressful. Then, while deeply relaxed, clients are asked to imagine the mildest situation. If they experience great anxiety, they are instructed to stop visualizing the scene and to restore bodily relaxation. The scene is then repeated until they can visualize it without anxiety, and then the next item in the hierarchy is presented. Clients proceed through the hierarchy until they can be exposed to even the most threatening stimuli without distress. Then they are given a behavioral test to determine if the fear has been eliminated.

Systematic desensitization procedures can be used effectively in actual situations. For example, Redd (1980) reports that a cancer patient who had undergone successful gastrointestinal surgery for the removal of a tumor could not retain solid foods. Even though the cancer had been removed, the patient reported that, as she began to eat, she experienced discomfort, believed that it was caused by her cancer, became anxious, and vomited. As a result, she had lost 25 pounds and was readmitted to the hospital because of her weakened condition. The patient was trained to relax and then given small amounts of food while relaxed. She consumed a cup of soup without gagging or regurgitating. She was then given a spoonful of egg, gagged on it, and regurgitated the second spoonful. She began to cry and said she knew she would never be able to eat again. The therapist reassured her that she would. During the next session, she experienced some anxiety, but completed the relaxation exercises. She was then able to consume one egg. After 14 sessions, she was able to eat all the foods presented to her. During the next ten days the therapist met with her and praised her lavishly for her progress in putting on weight. When she regained her strength, she left the hospital and returned home. A nine-month follow-up showed no new problems or symptoms.

EVALUATIVE COMMENTS

We can now examine the scientific worth of Eysenck's theory.

Comprehensiveness   Eysenck's theory is clearly comprehensive; it addresses a broad range of normal and abnormal phenomena. Thus, Eysenck seeks to understand a wide variety of normal and abnormal behaviors, including student study behavior, coffee drinking, smoking, alcoholism and other drug use, sexual practices, phobias, criminal behavior, the creative behavior of normal people as well as geniuses and psychotics, physical diseases, and neurotic and psychotic behavior.

Precision and testability   Eysenck, like Cattell, has worked diligently to construct precise measures of his theoretical concepts. However, most of his efforts have centered on the construction of tests to assess the major dimensions of personality. There are measurement problems with the concept of arousal, as Eysenck acknowledges, but work to rectify these difficulties continues. In comparison to the Freudian viewpoint and its variants, Eysenck's theory is much more precisely stated and testable.

Parsimony   Eysenck's theory fails to meet the parsimony criterion. For example, he himself acknowledges that the three major types—extraversion, neuroticism, and psychoticism—cannot adequately describe personality functioning. Some of the traits that make up the types appear to describe aspects of personality functioning independently of the three types. According to Eysenck, however, these traits cannot be measured as reliably as the three types, nor can they be linked as easily to other physiological measures and other types of laboratory measures. Thus, Eysenck advocates focusing first on the three types before utilizing the more specific traits (Eysenck & Eysenck, 1985, p. 74). In this respect, he clearly differs from Cattell, who now conducts research with approximately 35 normal and abnormal primary traits. As a result, Eysenck's theory appears to be too economical, although one can appreciate the rationale for his decision.

The fact that Eysenck's theory lacks an explicit and independent situational taxonomy also makes it simplistic. He focuses primarily on the biological end of personality, and does not fully address the differential impact of various situations on people. Instead of extending the theory to include an independent assessment of the impact of these situational influences, Eysenck argues that his type and trait approach implicitly acknowledges the role of the situation. He maintains that people with particular personality traits *choose* the situations in which they find themselves: an interest in books takes the introverted person to the library and bookstores; an interest in sports takes the athletic person to the athletic field and the gym, and so forth. Eysenck maintains, therefore, that the kind of situations in which these people operate is not primary; instead, it is the kinds of previously existing systems of likes and dislikes—that is, traits—that rule their behavior (Eysenck & Eysenck, 1985, p. 35).

Although Eysenck's contention has some validity, it does not address the many involuntary situations that do have an independent and differential impact on specific kinds of people. The athlete finds herself in academic situations like classes on astronomy or physics;

the bookworm finds himself assigned by the campus administration to a small room with two other roommates even though he prefers living in a room by himself; or the extraverted student who prefers a large triple is assigned to a single room. This problem is not addressed by Eysenck.

Eysenck also argues that the names of given traits usually imply the situations in which they can be demonstrated and measured. Thus, he maintains, a trait theory indirectly implies a taxonomy of situations (Eysenck & Eysenck, 1985, pp. 38–39). For example, the trait of sociability can only refer to situations involving relatively free interactions between people; the trait of athleticism implies situations where one can test one's athletic skills. Yet Eysenck seems to be treating the concept of situations much too globally. Situations involving sociability, for example, can be distinguished one from another—office parties, business meetings, home parties, receiving lines at the opera, or dorm parties—and it is doubtful that these specific kinds of situations would all have the same impact on the sociable person.

Empirical validity   There is considerable empirical support for Eysenck's arousal theory, especially as it applies to the differential behaviors of introverts and extraverts. However, much more research is required to test Eysenck's ideas about the differential behavior of neurotics and psychotics. Also, Eysenck's interesting and provocative theory of genius, which shows its links to biology and psychopathology, needs much research (Eysenck, 1995, p. 9).

Heuristic value   There is much to be admired in Eysenck's prodigious efforts as a scientist. He is seen by many psychologists as an excellent scholar, highly creative, and incredibly productive. Although much of his influence has been in Great Britain, many American psychologists are familiar with his work. Because the language of Eysenck's theory is less forbidding, it is more appealing to researchers than is Cattell's approach. In fact, the popularity of Eysenck's theory is growing rapidly in the United States and is likely to increase even more as Eysenck and his colleagues continue to refine and extend it.

Applied value   Eysenck was one of the pioneers in creating the behavior-therapy movement. His views on the acquisition and elimination of behavioral disorders has had a positive impact on behavior therapists. Thus, his theory has strong applied value in helping people with a variety of behavioral disorders.

DISCUSSION QUESTIONS

1. Do you think that Eysenck's use of only three types to describe personality functioning is an oversimplification?
2. Why are extraverts likely to engage in a wider variety of sexual activities than are introverts?
3. Are you primarily introverted or extraverted? How does your personality orientation influence your study behavior?
4. What are the limitations of Eysenck's argument that the three major dimensions of personality are universal?
5. What techniques does Eysenck use to show that there is a large genetic component in neuroticism?
6. Who would tend to make better pilots, introverts or extraverts? Why?
7. Do you see any problems with Eysenck's proposed meritocracy in selecting individuals for higher educational opportunities? How would you ensure fair treatment for everyone?
8. What principles of learning do behavior therapists rely on to eliminate phobias? Are the procedures they use to eliminate fears effective, in your opinion?
9. What is flooding? Under what conditions does it work to eliminate fear in phobics?
10. Do you have any ethical concerns about the use of flooding as a therapeutic technique?

GLOSSARY

androgens   Male sex hormones; in mammals, the principal one is testosterone.

antigens   Protein or carbohydrate substances (such as toxins or enzymes) that, when introduced into the body, stimulate the production of antibodies.

arousal theory   Explanation of behavioral differences in terms of the interactions between inherited levels of nervous system arousal and levels of environmental stimulation.

ascending reticular activating system (ARAS)   The part of the central nervous system located in the lower brain stem; it is involved in the arousal of the cerebral cortex.

autonomic nervous system   The part of the peripheral nervous system—usually not under the individual's voluntary control—that regulates the operation of internal organs and glands; it consists of sympathetic and parasympathetic subsystems.

behavior therapy   Multifaceted approach to the treatment of disorders based on the principles of conditioning, counterconditioning, extinction, and reinforcement.

classical conditioning   Association learning whereby a neutral stimulus is paired with an unconditioned stimulus (UCS) that naturally evokes an unconditioned response (UCR). Through pairing with the UCS, the neutral stimulus becomes a conditioned stimulus (CS), which, when presented in the absence of the UCS, evokes a conditioned response (CR) that is similar to the UCR.

cortical arousal   State of the cortex during periods of perceptual or cognitive activity.

counterconditioning   Procedure often utilized for therapeutic purposes, in which a conditioned response (CR) is weakened by associating the stimulus (CS) that evokes it with a new response that is antagonistic (incompatible) with the CR.

divergent thinking   The ability to think along many different paths, to consider alternatives not ordinarily considered in trying to solve problems.

dizygotic twins   Twins that develop simultaneously from two separate fertilized eggs (also called fraternal twins).

dopamine   A neurotransmitter or chemical in the brain that, in excessive amounts, can reduce cognitive inhibitions.

electrodermal response   Changes in the electrical conductance of the skin that are associated with arousal.

electroencephalogram (EEG)   Recording of electrical activity in the cerebral cortex obtained by means of electrodes placed on the skull.

evoked potentials   Patterns of waves that occur in the brain following its stimulation.

extraverts   Individuals who have an outgoing and sociable approach to life.

Eysenck Personality Questionnaire (EPQ)   An inventory designed to measure the major personality types in adults.

flooding   Form of behavior therapy in which the client is exposed to the most intense stimuli that evoke fear, typically for prolonged periods of time, in an effort to extinguish it.

hedonic tone   Positive or negative feelings and evaluations associated with various levels of arousal.

inhibition theory   Explanation of behavioral differences on the basis of inhibitory cortical processes that hinder nervous-system arousal.

introverts   Individuals who have a shy and retiring approach to life.

Junior Eysenck Personality Questionnaire   Inventory designed to measure the major personality types in children.

modeling   Demonstration of behavior by one person so that another person can imitate it.

monozygotic twins   Twins who develop from the splitting of a single fertilized egg (also called identical twins).

neurotics   Individuals who are emotionally unstable and overly reactive to stimuli.

parasympathetic nervous system   Division of the autonomic nervous system that conserves bodily energies by slowing heart and breathing rates.

psychopathology   Various forms of disordered behavior that vary in terms of the severity of impairment.

psychotics   Individuals who are aloof, inhumane, aggressive, and insensitive to the needs of others, but also creative.

pupillary response   Changes in dilation of the pupils of the eyes associated with arousal.

reactive inhibition   Each time a person responds, a small increment of neural fatigue is built up. Over many responses, fatigue builds to the point where the person stops responding.

schizophrenia   Severe psychotic disorder characterized by flat or inappropriate emotion and by withdrawal from external reality and other people. Schizophrenics are also characterized by thought disorder. While their lack of cognitive inhibition may sometimes result in creative test performances because it allows them to think in unusual ways, sometimes their inability to control the running together of ideas produces gibberish.

serotonin   A chemical neurotransmitter in the brain believed to be associated with psychoticism and schizophrenic thinking.

sympathetic nervous system   Division of the autonomic nervous system that mobilizes the body's resources for action, speeding up heart and breathing rates and slowing the digestive process.

systematic desensitization   Behavior therapy designed to reduce the strong anxieties associated with various stimuli; the client is gradually exposed to them and, at each level in the anxiety hierarchy, learns new responses through counterconditioning.

typology   A means of classifying behavior through the use of continuous, highly abstract concepts (types) that encompass clusters of correlated traits.

visceral brain   Parts of the brain that underlie emotional feelings and expression; also known as the limbic system.

SUGGESTED READINGS

Eysenck, H. J. (1967). *The biological basis of personality*. Springfield, IL: Charles C Thomas.

Eysenck, H. J. (1970). *The structure of human personality* (3rd ed.). London: Methuen.

Eysenck, H. J. (1995). *Genius: The natural history of creativity*. New York: Cambridge University Press.

Eysenck, H. J., & Eysenck, M. W. (1985). *Personality and individual differences: A natural science approach*. New York: Plenum Press.

REFERENCES

Amirkhan, J. H., Risinger, R. T., & Swickert, R. J. (1995). Extraversion: A "hidden" personality factor in coping. *Journal of Personality, 63,* 189–212.

Bullock, W. A., & Gilliland, K. (1993). Eysenck's arousal theory of introversion-extraversion: A converging measures investigation. *Journal of Personality and Social Psychology, 64,* 113–123.

Campbell, A., & Rushton, J. P. (1978). Bodily communication and personality. *British Journal of Social and Clinical Psychology, 17,* 31–36.

Campbell, J. B., & Hawley, C. W. (1982). Study habits and Eysenck's theory of extraversion-introversion. *Journal of Research in Personality, 16,* 139–146.

Cofer, C. N., & Appley, M. H. (1964). *Motivation: Theory and research*. New York: Wiley.

Davies, D. R., & Parasuraman, R. (1982). *The psychology of vigilance*. London: Academic Press.

Eysenck, H. J. (1947). *Dimensions of personality*. London: Routledge & Kegan Paul.

Eysenck, H. J. (1965). *Fact and fiction in psychology*. Baltimore, MD: Penguin Books.

Eysenck, H. J. (1967). *The biological basis of personality*. Springfield, IL: Charles C Thomas.

Eysenck, H. J. (1970). *The structure of human personality* (3rd ed.). London: Methuen.

Eysenck, H. J. (1975). *The inequality of man*. San Diego: EdITS.

Eysenck, H. J. (1976). *The measurement of personality*. Lancaster: Medical & Technical Publishers.

Eysenck, H. J. (1980). Hans Jurgen Eysenck. In G. Lindzey (Ed.), *A history of psychology in autobiography* (Vol. 7, pp. 153–187). San Francisco: W. H. Freeman.

Eysenck, H. J. (1982). Development of a theory. In H. J. Eysenck (Ed.), *Per-*

sonality, genetics, and behavior: Selected papers (pp. 1–48). New York: Praeger.

Eysenck, H. J. (1990). Biological dimensions of personality. In L. A. Pervin (Ed.), *Handbook of personality: Theory and research* (pp. 244–276). New York: Guilford Press.

Eysenck, H. J. (1995). *Genius: The natural history of creativity.* New York: Cambridge University Press.

Eysenck, H. J., & Eysenck, M. W. (1985). *Personality and individual differences: A natural science approach.* New York: Plenum Press.

Eysenck, H. J., & Eysenck, S. B. G. (1975). *Manual of the Eysenck Personality Questionnaire.* San Diego: EdITS.

Eysenck, H. J., & Gudjonsson, G. H. (1989). *The causes and cures of criminality.* New York: Plenum Press.

Eysenck, H. J., & Kamin, L. (1981). *The intelligence controversy: H. J. Eysenck versus Kamin.* New York: John Wiley.

Eysenck, S. B. G. (1965). *Manual of the Junior Eysenck Personality Inventory.* London: Hodder & Stoughton.

Heaton, A. W., & Kruglanski, A. W. (1991). Person perception by introverts and extraverts under time pressure: Effects of need for closure. *Personality and Social Psychology Bulletin, 17,* 161–165.

Hecker, J. E., & Thorpe, G. L. (1987). Fear reduction processes in imaginal and in vivo flooding: A comment on James' review. *Behavioural Psychotherapy, 15,* 215–223.

Hull, C. L. (1951). *Essentials of behavior.* New Haven, CT: Yale University Press.

Jones, M. C. (1924). A laboratory study of fear: The case of Peter. *Pedagogical Seminar, 31,* 308–315.

Landrum, R. E. (1992). College students' use of caffeine and its relationship to personality. *College Student Journal, 26,* 151–155.

Marshall, W. L. (1985). The effects of variable exposure in flooding therapy. *Behavior Therapy, 16,* 117–135.

Morris, C. G. (1982). *Psychology: An introduction* (4th ed.). Englewood Cliffs, NJ: Prentice-Hall.

O'Leary, K. D., & Wilson, G. T. (1987). *Behavior therapy: Application and outcome* (2nd ed.). Englewood Cliffs, NJ: Prentice-Hall.

Pavlov, I. P. (1927). *Conditioned reflexes: An investigation into the physiological activity of the cortex.* New York: Dover.

Rachman, S. (1969). Extraversion and neuroticism in childhood. In H. J. Eysenck & S. B. G. Eysenck (Eds.), *Personality structure and measurement* (pp. 253–264). London: Routledge & Kegan Paul.

Redd, W. H. (1980). In vivo desensitization in the treatment of chronic emesis following gastrointestinal surgery. *Behavior Therapy, 11,* 421–427.

Simonton, D. K. (1994). *Greatness: Who makes history and why.* New York: Guilford Press.

Stelmack, R. M. (1990). Biological bases of extraversion: Psychophysiological evidence. *Journal of Personality, 58,* 293–311.

Teplov, B. M. (1964). The historical development of Pavlov's theory of typological differences in the dog. In J. A. Gray (Ed.), *Pavlov's typology* (pp. 3–153). New York: Macmillan.

Watson, J. B., & Rayner, R. (1920). Conditioned emotional reactions. *Journal of Experimental Psychology, 3,* 1–14.

PART FOUR

COGNITIVE PERSPECTIVES

To understand the role of cognition in current theories of personality, we must first examine the meaning of the term. In ordinary language, *cognition* refers to the thoughts or ideas we have about the world around us. Thus, in the broadest sense, we are talking about symbols that occur inside us and that help us make sense of the world. Technically, theories of cognition are concerned with how we gather information about events and how we process this information in order to act on the environment.

If cognition involves internal ideas or thoughts, it could be argued that the various psychodynamic and trait theories considered so far are all cognitive. After all, Freud's concept of the ego deals, in large measure, with our attempts to understand external reality and to perform those behaviors that will maximize our pleasure. The conflicts between id and superego also involve the use of internalized rules to restrict the expression of inappropriate id impulses. These rules, which we use frequently in decision making, can be construed as primarily cognitive in nature.

The trait concept employed by Allport, Cattell, and Eysenck to account for personality functioning is also a cognitive construct. Traits are beliefs assumed to guide behaviors and influence judgments about the environment. Allport goes beyond Cattell in postulating a developmental process of becoming that is largely cognitive: for Allport, the mature person is one who is capable of making use of information in a rational way. The self-actualization theories created by Maslow and Rogers can also be construed as cognitive, as we shall see in Part Five; so can the work of some of the social-learning theorists reviewed in Part Six. These positions incorporate cognitive constructs such as expectancy, imitation, verbal and pictorial imagery, and memory.

Why, then, is this section of the text limited to Kelly's theory? The answer is that, although many other theories have elements of cognition, Kelly's stands alone as a comprehensive and pure cognitive theory of personality, focused solely on the ways in which we process information as a means of increasing our understanding of the world. His is a largely intellectualized view of personality that sees all of us acting as scientists in order to predict and control events. In Kelly's view, we are all continually trying to make sense of our world by forming hypotheses about how it works, testing them in the real world, and then revising them if they do not fit or work. Our aim, according to him, is to maximize our predictive accuracy about the ways in which the world operates.

To present this view, Kelly built a theory with a brand new terminology and changed or did away with many of the traditional concepts used in psychology to explain the actions of individuals. For example, Kelly did away with the concept of need as it was used by traditional learning theorists. In their view, individuals in a quiescent state start to experience bodily needs for food, water, and sex. These needs then motivate them to seek objects that reduce their tensions so that they can once again exist in a homeostatic state. Kelly also did away with the concept of incentive, whereby people are motivated to work toward the attainment of certain goals for reinforcement. Kelly did not like the conceptualization of human beings as inert objects who have to be prodded into action by internal needs or by external incentives and reinforcements. Instead, he postulated that human beings are born in process; they continually seek to predict accurately events in the world around them (Kelly, 1955, pp. 35–49). For Kelly, people are not passive pawns controlled by cyclic internal urges or external demands. Instead, they are very often active, curious, and creative beings who are continually seeking to increase their understanding of the world. Kelly clearly believed that human beings are motivated, but the focus is on cognitive motivation and not on biological drives rooted in tissue needs.

Kelly also had little use for the concept of reinforcement as it is traditionally used by learning theorists. For example, he rejected the empirical law of effect, which states that behavior is more likely to occur again if it has been followed by a positive reinforcer and less likely to occur again if it has been followed by a punishing stimulus, because this law suggests that our behavior is under the control of external influences. Instead, he believed that our actions are controlled more by cognitive processes: what is important is our anticipation of events and the subsequent validation of our predictions.

In Chapter 11, we take a close look at Kelly's unique and clearly stated theory. We begin by examining the fundamental assumption underlying the theory—the philosophical stance called *constructive alternativism*. After outlining the basic terms of the theory, we present the fundamental postulate and numerous corollaries of his personal-construct position. Next, we examine Kelly's Role Construct Repertory Test (RCRT), which is designed to measure individuals' personal-construct systems. We then discuss Kelly's view of psychotherapy and the roles of therapist and client. An actual case history illustrates how Kelly's theory is applied to psychopathology. Finally, a review of the research shows how investigators have used variants of Kelly's RCRT to study the cognitive functioning and behavior of schizophrenic patients.

REFERENCES

Kelly, G. A. (1955). *The psychology of personal constructs* (Vol. 1). New York: Norton.

CHAPTER 11

Kelly's Theory of Personal Constructs

George Alexander Kelly was born in a small town in Kansas in 1905, the only child of a Presbyterian minister and his wife. He attended high school in Wichita, Kansas, and then Friends University, where he enrolled in courses in music and public debating. He graduated from Park College in 1926 with a degree in mathematics and physics. He flirted with the idea of becoming an aeronautical engineer but eventually committed himself to education. He held a variety of jobs; for instance, he taught speech-making to students in a labor college and taught an Americanization class for recent immigrants.

In 1929 he was awarded an exchange scholarship and spent a year at the University of Edinburgh, where he earned a bachelor's degree in education. He returned to the United States with a developing interest in psychology and entered the graduate program in that field at the University of Iowa. In 1931 he was awarded his Ph.D. for a dissertation in the area of speech and reading disabilities.

Kelly's professional career in psychology began with his acceptance of a position at Fort Hays State College in Kansas. Soon afterward, he began developing psychological services for the State of Kansas; he established a network of traveling clinics throughout the state. It was during this period that Kelly largely abandoned the psychoanalytic approach to human personality. He reported that his clinical experiences had taught him that people in the Midwest were paralyzed by prolonged drought, dust storms, and economic concerns, rather than by overflowing libidinal forces. He began to develop his own theory, which he based partly on his observation of a friend who took a part in a dramatic production in college, lived it for the two or three weeks the play was in rehearsal, and was profoundly influenced by it. Kelly noted that, although many people would dismiss his friend's efforts as sheer affectation, in fact his behavior was not false or without substance. It eventually expressed his real self. This experience led Kelly to formulate a fixed-role-therapy technique designed to help people overcome their own limitations.

The crux of Kelly's theory of personal **constructs** arose from his observation that "people tended to have the symptoms they had read about or had seen in other people" (Kelly, 1955, Vol. 1, p. 366). When the terms, or constructs, *inferiority complex* and *anxiety* were popular in the 1920s and 1930s, people began to describe themselves as having inferiority complexes or anxieties. These self-descriptions were subsequently used in their interpretations of reality. Kelly's preoccupation with the structure of language and the impact of language and roles on behavior led him to read the works of the eminent linguist Korzybski and the role-playing theorist Jacob Moreno; on the basis of his reading, he was able to refine his theory (Kelly, 1955, Vol. 1, pp. 360–366).

After a stint in the navy as an aviation psychologist during World War II, Kelly was appointed associate professor at the University of Maryland. He left Maryland in 1946 to become professor of psychology and director of clinical psychology at Ohio State University. During the following two decades, he completed his major theoretical work, *The Psychology of Personal Constructs* (1955). He also traveled widely and lectured at many universities throughout the world. In 1965, he accepted the Riklis Chair of Behavioral Science at Brandeis University. He died in 1967.

CONCEPTS AND PRINCIPLES

Constructive Alternativism

The concept of **constructive alternativism** underlies Kelly's theory of cognition. Quite simply, it is the assumption that all of us are capable of changing or replacing our present interpretation of events

(Kelly, 1955, Vol. 1, p. 15). In colloquial terms, we can always change our minds. The assumption also implies that our behavior is never completely determined; we are always free to some extent to reinterpret our experiences. Thus, Kelly believed in the primacy of individuals as responsible agents who make their own choices and decisions. We don't just react to our experiences; we act upon them by interpreting and reinterpreting them in our own idiosyncratic ways (Fransella & Dalton, 1990, p. 1). Yet Kelly also believed that some of our thoughts and behavior are determined by other phenomena. In other words, his theory is constructed on a joint base of freedom and determinism. "Determinism and freedom are inseparable, for that which determines another is, by the same token, free of the other" (Kelly, 1955, Vol. 1, p. 21).

Thus, if a student decides that the attainment of a college degree summa cum laude is important to her, this subjective fact will then determine certain other behaviors: for example, she will curtail her social activities and spend more time studying in the library or her dormitory room. In brief, she was free to choose her goal but, once chosen, the goal determines certain related behaviors. Translating this example into Kelly's terminology, we can say that the **superordinate construct**—attainment of the college degree—was freely chosen. It then acted to control other **subordinate constructs**—the number of social activities and the number of hours spent studying.

> The relation established by a construct or a construction system over its subordinate elements is deterministic. In this sense the tendency to subordinate constitutes determinism. The natural events themselves do not subordinate our constructions of them, we can look at them in any way we like. . . . The structure we erect is what rules us. (Kelly, 1955, Vol. 1, p. 20)

Theorists who adopt a behavioral stance, in contrast, maintain that all behavior is determined. They disagree with Kelly on the free choice of goals, which, they argue, are also determined by prior experiences.

Every Person as Scientist

Kelly believed that each of us, like the scientist, attempts to predict and control events. We are continually in the process of evaluating and reevaluating our experiences and trying to use our interpretations to understand and control the world around us. We have our own theories about human behavior. We test hypotheses based on the theories, and we weigh the experimental evidence (Kelly, 1955, Vol. 1, p. 5). On the basis of this evidence, the world becomes more predictable, or we come to understand that we must change our concepts or constructs about it if we are to function effectively.

As scientists in this sense, we use our own highly personalized view of reality in making judgments, which are rarely open to the scrutiny of others. Our constructs are not as objectively defined as those used by research scientists, and our theories rarely meet the rigorous criteria set by conventional science. In short, we have rather commonsense views of ourselves and reality, and the possibilities for distortion and error are great. Moreover, many of us continually shift our view of reality to fit the data. No matter how distorted our views of reality are, however, they are still real to us, and we operate accordingly. "A person may misrepresent a real phenomenon, such as his income or his ills, and yet his misrepresentation will itself be entirely real. This applies even to the badly deluded patient: what he perceives may not exist, but his perception does" (Kelly, 1955, Vol. 1, p. 8).

Thus, Kelly embraced the phenomenologist position of the humanist theorists reviewed in Part Five. Like the humanists, Kelly believed we are not passive organisms; we relate actively to the environment, often in creative ways.

The Nature of Constructs and Construing

In building our systems of personal constructs, we place interpretations on events; that is, we construe them. We construe the meaning of events for ourselves through an abstraction process, by placing constructions upon our experiences (Kelly, 1955, Vol. 1, p. 50). We then utilize our constructions to deal with new information from the environment. These interpretations are reality for us and determine how we act. They are also highly personalized: we may have the same experiences as others do, but we often interpret them differently.

The constructs that we form and then use to deal with new experiences are based on our previous experiences. For Kelly, constructs are ways of organizing experiences in terms of similarities and contrasts: "In its minimum context, a construct is a way in which at least two elements are similar and contrast with a third" (Kelly, 1955, Vol. 1, p. 61). Thus, constructs must contain at least three elements and may contain many more. At the same time, they are bipolar; they involve contrasts as well as similarities. To say that an object is a chair implies that it is not also a table. To say that bearded men tend to be virile is to imply that clean-shaven men are impotent. To say that Beth and Marie are intelligent is to imply that someone else, perhaps Jane, is stupid.

Because constructs are personal, people may apply different labels to the same experiences. For example, an individual may believe that she is being "pleasant" in interpersonal relationships, while others may see her willingness to yield indiscriminately to their wishes as "excessive dependence." Even when two people label an experience similarly, the contrast end of the dimension may differ. For example, Bill and Jim may both label certain behaviors as "sincere." However, Bill may see behavior at the opposite end of the spectrum as "insincere," whereas Jim may label it "morally degenerate." Thus, Bill might react to these contrast behaviors with mild disapproval, whereas Jim would probably become angry and upset under the same circumstances. Their subsequent behavior toward the person exhibiting the contrast behavior may also differ. Bill might try to reason with the insincere person; Jim might attack or avoid the moral degenerate.

Finally, Kelly believed that constructs are not identical to the verbal labels used to express them. Constructs are actual discriminations people make on an experiential level between varieties of experiences (Bannister, 1977, p. 33). Sometimes people formulate constructs before they can verbalize them. This is particularly true of children, who, for example, may be capable of showing affection toward loved ones but incapable of verbalizing their feelings. People who are disturbed often repress or distort certain experiences and are unable or unwilling to deal with them on a verbal level; therapy with an expert may help them deal with the limitations inherent in their construct systems.

Additional Characteristics of Constructs

Kelly refers to constructs that are highly important in people's lives as **core constructs.** These are beliefs that reflect their personal identity, structures that help maintain their existence. Core constructs are very resistant to change, whereas **peripheral constructs** are relatively easy to change. For many people, a belief in God is a core construct central to their existence. For these same people, their belief that baseball great Ted Williams hit .401 during the 1941 season is a peripheral belief, which would change readily should they learn that Williams actually hit .406 during the 1941 season. Peripheral constructs, according to Kelly, can be altered without serious modifications in the core structure. In the previous example, changes in the individuals' beliefs about Williams's batting average would not produce any modification in their beliefs about God (Kelly, 1955, Vol. 1, pp. 482–483).

Constructs are arranged hierarchically within a particular person's cognitive world; that is, one construct may subsume one or more other constructs (Kelly, 1955, Vol. 1, p. 57). For example, a person seen by others as a moralizer may actually use a superordinate construct of good versus bad to control many other concepts: a good person might be intelligent, cooperative, kind, ambitious, and sincere; a bad person might be stupid, competitive, cruel, unambitious, and insincere.

Constructs also vary in their **range of convenience**—the number of other constructs to which they are related; that is, a given construct has relevance for some constructs but not for others (Kelly, 1955, Vol. 1, p. 68). The good/bad dichotomy probably has a wide range of convenience for many people, although they still would not apply it to every construct. Other constructs—fat/thin, for example—are much more limited. We may think of fat people versus thin people, or fat lions versus thin lions, but we do not ordinarily think of fat weather versus thin weather, or fat crying versus thin crying.

Related to a construct's range of convenience is its **permeability.** A construct is considered permeable if it will allow new elements—that is, constructs currently excluded from its range of convenience—to be construed within its framework (Kelly, 1955, Vol. 1, p. 79). For instance, the construct of right versus wrong may allow people to include new ideas and behavior as right or wrong. They may be prepared to make a judgment concerning the moral validity of euthanasia, for example, a topic about which they had previously been ignorant. If the construct were impermeable, they would be incapable of making such a moral evaluation. Of course, it is rare that a construct is completely impermeable; usually, there are varying degrees of permeability. By introducing the notion of permeability, Kelly made allowances for change in the system. Other ways of talking about change would include growth, personal development, and realization of the self.

In short, Kelly has posited a complicated, hierarchical system of cognition populated by personal constructs derived from experience that now control or determine the ways in which the person will react to incoming stimuli or information. Although much of the person's behavior is determined by such constructs, there is also room within the system for change because the superordinate concepts are free and often permeable. Change in these permeable constructs would then produce changes in the subordinate construct system.

In addition, Kelly proposed that constructs could be characterized as preemptive, constellatory, and propositional. A construct that includes only its own elements and precludes these elements from being part of other constructs is called a **preemptive construct.** For instance, a person may argue that "anything which is a ball can be nothing but a ball"; thus, balls cannot be "pellets," "spheres," or "shots" (Kelly, 1955, Vol. 1, p. 153). Such black-or-white thinking sometimes characterizes interpersonal relationships as well, as when someone argues that "capitalism is nothing but exploitation of the masses by big business," or "the women's movement is nothing but an attempt by a few frustrated and ugly hags to castrate men."

A **constellatory construct** "permits its elements to belong to other realms concurrently, but fixes their realm memberships" (Kelly, 1955, Vol. 1, p. 155). Stereotypes belong to this category; that is, once we identify persons or objects as members of a given category, we then attribute to them a cluster, or constellation, of other characteristics or traits. Although we are fully aware that we tend to stereotype people in terms of ethnic and cultural backgrounds, we also have reliable stereotypes of people (that may have harmful consequences) on the basis of other, seemingly insignificant characteristics, such as hair color. For example, Lawson (1971) asked college men and women to rate fictitious people with different hair colors on a variety of personality characteristics. He found that men tended to see blonde women as more beautiful, delicate, and feminine than either brunettes or redheads. Both men and women rated brunette women most favorably, and artificial or bleached blondes most unfavorably. Brunettes were seen as intelligent, ambitious, sincere, strong, safe, valuable, and effective. Both men and women also gave their highest rating to dark-haired men, who were seen as more handsome, intelligent, ambitious, sincere, strong, rugged, valuable, effective, and masculine than were men with blond or red hair. Men with blond hair were generally rated more favorably than were redheads. Thus, people with certain genetic traits may become victims of other people's constellatory constructs, or stereotypes.

Finally, a construct whose elements are open to construction in every respect is called a **propositional construct.** "Any round object can be considered, among other things, to be a ball." Under this construct, a ball can also be elliptical, worn, or small. Propositional thinking is flexible thinking. The person is continuously open to new experience and is capable of modifying existing constructs. In Kelly's view, the person best equipped to deal with the environment is one who knows the circumstances under which propositional or preemptive thinking is appropriate. If we relied exclusively on propositional thinking, we would be immobilized; because we were continually re-evaluating and reconstruing our experiences, we would be unable to act. A star receiver on a professional football team, for instance, needs to consider the object being hurled at him as a football and nothing else; in this case, preemptive thinking is appropriate and effective. But sole reliance on preemptive thinking leads people to make dogmatic and unyielding judgments, often to their own detriment.

The Fundamental Postulate and Its Corollaries

The basic assumption underlying Kelly's theory is that "a person's processes are psychologically channelized by the ways in which he anticipates events" (Kelly, 1955, Vol. 1, p. 46). Kelly believed that people are behaving, changing organisms who operate in terms of their expectations about events. In short, expectations direct actions. They provide the motivation for behavior. In terms of Kelly's scientist analogy, people seek to predict and verify their views of events. They generate a construct system by construing events, and then act on the basis of those constructs. From this basic postulate, Kelly derived a number of corollaries or propositions.

Individuality corollary   People anticipate events in different ways. According to Kelly, this **individuality corollary** lays the groundwork for the study of individual differences. People differ because they have had different experiences and also because they take different approaches to anticipation of the same event (Kelly, 1955, Vol. 1, p. 55). Thus, the construct systems people generate are idiosyncratic in many respects. But there are also commonalities among people in the way they construe events; people can and do interpret experiences in the same ways.

Organization corollary   Kelly's **organization corollary** proposes that "each person characteristically evolves, for his convenience in anticipating events, a construction system embracing ordinal relationships between constructs" (Kelly, 1955, Vol. 1, p. 56). People differ not only in their constructs but also in the way in which they organize them. Organization of constructs also serves to reduce conflict for the person. If a married man knows that his wife and family come first, even before his mother, then potential conflicts can be minimized. Doubt as to which construct is superordinate can be painful, as many husbands have learned.

Choice corollary   Kelly assumed that all of us are continually making choices between the poles of our constructs. In proposing the **choice corollary,** he assumed further that we tend to make choices that will allow us to deal most effectively with ensuing events. Should we be cautious or risk-taking in a given situation? Should we marry or not marry? Should we pursue a college degree or drop out? Kelly maintained that people tend, in general, to make choices that define and elaborate the system; that is, we choose alternatives designed to increase our confidence in our interpretations of the world, as well as alternatives that increase our understanding of it through personal growth. Kelly believed that we are biologically predisposed to make the elaborative choice; that is, we are predisposed to take risk, to try out new constructs, so that we can increase our understanding of more and more of our worlds.

Fragmentation corollary   According to Kelly, our construct systems are in a continual state of flux. Within these systems, we may successively use a variety of subsystems that are inferentially incompatible with one another (Kelly, 1955, Vol. 1, p. 104). In other words, our construct subsystems are not always mutually consistent, and we may sometimes show behaviors that are inconsistent with our most recent experiences. Kelly calls this the **fragmentation corollary.**

Suppose, for example, that a young woman decides that she loves a man and declares to friends that she has agreed to marry him. The following day, however, instead of showing affection toward him, she begins to revile him in front of friends and to point out his limitations, and she declares that the marriage is off. Kelly might explain the inconsistency in her behavior by pointing out that, although she loves him, she also knows that he is selfish and inconsiderate and will eventually hurt her. Thus, the construct "fiance" subsumes the construct "love" and also the construct "despising his personal characteristics." Such fragmented and inconsistent construct systems can exist side by side within a person's cognitive world and show up in successive behaviors when other constructs in the larger system trigger them. In this case, the incompatible systems may have been triggered by the superordinate construct "mother" if it was her mother who brought the man's shortcomings to her attention.

In trying to predict behavior, according to Kelly, we have to discover such ruling constructs and show how, in the final analysis, they control the person's behavior. Kelly is taking issue here with some of the early learning theorists, who held that behavior is determined by its immediate antecedents. What Kelly is saying is that the prediction of behavior is much more complicated, that it involves an assessment of the meanderings of the individual's cognitive world, and that this world is not always composed of logical and consistent subsystems.

Commonality corollary   Kelly's individuality corollary states that people who differ in their construction of events will behave differently; his **commonality corollary** states that those who interpret events similarly will behave alike. The underlying assumption is that "to the extent that one person employs a construction of experience which is similar to that employed by another, his psychological processes are similar to those of the other person" (Kelly, 1955, Vol. 1, p. 90). Thus, if their constructs are similar, people may act alike, even though they have been exposed to different stimuli. For example, two students may enroll in the same philosophy course on existentialism even if one has previously attended a philosophy course on formal logic and the other has attended one on the philosophy of art. Even though they have been exposed to different stimuli (the materials on formal logic, in one case, and the materials on the philosophy of art, in the other), they may act alike (enroll in the course on existentialism) if they construe their experiences in these two courses similarly, that is, if they both conclude that courses in philosophy are good. If courses in philosophy are good, then it is likely that the course in existentialism will be good, and therefore they will enroll in it.

Sociality corollary   Finally, Kelly proposed that, "to the extent that one person construes the construction processes of another, he may play a role in a social process involving the other person" (Kelly, 1955, Vol. 1, p. 95). In other words, insofar as we can understand another person's construct system, we can predict accurately what the other person will do and adjust our behavior accordingly. Much of our behavior, Kelly maintained, consists of such mutual adjustment. In this way, the **sociality corollary** enables us to function effectively in society and in our interpersonal relationships.

In healthy marriages, for example, there is a mutual understanding of the roles each partner is seeking to enact; each partner validates the image the other person is trying to project (Neimeyer & Hall, 1988, p. 297). Kelly referred to these images as **core role constructs**—the important, ongoing pattern of behaviors that follow from each partner's understanding of how the other person thinks

(Kelly, 1955, Vol. 1, pp. 97–98). In unhealthy marriages, the partners repeatedly invalidate each other's images. The role relationships become strained, because each partner can no longer predict with accuracy what the other person is going to do. For example, if a woman believes that a loving relationship between husband and wife is characterized by kindness and affection, insensitive or abusive behavior on the part of her husband is likely to weaken her beliefs about the relationship, thereby reducing the predictive power of her construct system, until she experiences chaos in the relationship (Kelly, 1955, Vol. 1, p. 501; Neimeyer & Hall, 1988, p. 298).

PERSONALITY DEVELOPMENT

Kelly assumed that the development of each person revolves around attempts to maximize understanding of the world through the continuing definition and elaboration of his or her construct system. Like other major humanistic psychologists, Kelly simply assumed that this tendency was innate. Certainly he did not believe it was learned, although he assumed that the person's interaction with the environment plays the major role in helping to move the individual toward personal growth. He rejected outright the mechanistic learning view that behavior was determined solely by the operation of environmental events. Individuals do not simply react to the environment. Instead, they actively, uniquely, and systematically construe it and then utilize these constructions to anticipate events. They use previous experiences to create hypotheses about possible new outcomes. In Kelly's view, people do not respond to the environment in order to maximize pleasure and avoid pain, as reinforcement theorists assume. Instead, they actively seek to maximize the accuracy of their views.

Kelly developed several models of the ways in which the individual utilizes information from the environment in deciding on a course of action. One of the more important ones he termed the circumspection-preemption-control (C-P-C) cycle. The cycle begins, according to Kelly, when the person circumspects by considering all the possible ways of construing a given situation; that is, the person considers a series of propositional constructs that might help in dealing with the situation at hand. Next comes the preemption phase, when the person reduces the number of available constructs and seriously considers only those that will help solve the problem. Finally, in the control phase, the person decides on a course of action by choosing the single construct that he or she believes to be most useful in solving the problem (Kelly, 1955, Vol. 1, pp. 516–517). As an illustration, consider the case of a young woman who wants to become a world-renowned violinist. She could construe herself in many different ways—as a future tennis great, a lazy person, or a popular local actress. Until she rejects these self-constructs and settles on one that paints her as a dedicated student of music, she is unlikely ever to become successful and to realize her ambition. By making that choice, she exercises control over her behavior and anticipates the extension of her construct system.

In Kelly's view, people are continually acting in this way; that is, they consider the alternatives in a given situation, reduce the possibilities to those that they think will work, and then act in accordance with their choices. Thus, he saw the developmental process as a creative and dynamic interchange between individual and environment, with constructions and reconstructions in the light of new experiences. Its aim is to maximize the person's understanding and, therefore, his or her control over the environment. The healthy person, then, is one who has an accurate and valid construct system and a flexible view of the world.

ASSESSMENT TECHNIQUES

Kelly used many different techniques to assess personality and promote positive growth in his clients. Some of these procedures he devised himself; others he borrowed and adapted from the works of other major personality theorists.

Kelly noted two general approaches to the appraisal of clients' experiences—one focusing on the past, and the other tending to deemphasize the past and to concentrate instead on the present. Kelly agreed that therapists should not dwell exclusively on the past, but he did think clinicians should make use of case histories. As he saw it, the past is important because its

> events are the validational evidence against which [the client] won and lost his wagers, against which he tested his personal constructs. They are the checkpoints he had to use in charting the course of his life. To understand what they actually were is to get some notion of the ranges of convenience of the client's constructs, what the system was designed to deal with, one way or another. Moreover, many of

these events will have to be given some stabilizing interpretation in the new construct system produced under therapeutic intervention. (Kelly, 1955, Vol. 2, p. 688)

Moreover, case histories provide evidence of how people's culture affects their lives. Kelly believed that the culture provides people with evidence of what is true or false in life. To assess the effects of culture, Kelly turned to his own form of personality testing.

Although Kelly made considerable use of personality testing as an aid in diagnosing problems and in assessing therapy effectiveness, he stressed that it should not be used to classify or pigeonhole the individual in any fixed way. Nor should it interfere with the ongoing therapeutic process. Thus, testing should occur early in the process—not after several months of therapy, when it might lead clients to believe the therapist was uncertain about their progress. Clients should be assured that there are no right or wrong answers to the questions and that the therapist will continue to see them as worthwhile individuals no matter what the test results show. Testing should be seen simply as a way of providing helpful information to the therapist—information that will guide the therapy in a positive direction.

The Role Construct Repertory Test

One test that proved extremely useful to Kelly in his therapeutic work was the **Role Construct Repertory Test** (RCRT), which he devised as the major diagnostic tool for assessing the personal construct systems of people in clinical settings. Clients are first asked to list the names of the important people in their social environments across the top of a matrix, or grid. (See Table 11.1.) They are then asked to sort these people by successively considering three of them at a time, making circles under their names, and marking down, in a space to the right of each row in the grid, the way in which two of them are alike but different from the third. When they have decided on the two people and the important way in which they are alike, they are asked to put an X in the two circles corresponding to the ones who are alike. This identifies the similarity part of the construct. Next they are asked to write in a space to the right the way in which the third person is different from the other two. This is the contrast part of the construct.

Clients are then asked to consider all the other people listed in the grid and to place a checkmark (✔) under each person to whom the similarity of the first two people also applies. If the space is left

TABLE 11.1　Client's repertory grid

#	Self	Mother	Father	Brother	Sister	Spouse	Ex-girlfriend	Friend	Ex-friend	Rejected person	Pitied person	Threatening person	Attractive person	Accepted teacher	Rejected teacher	Boss	Successful person	Happy person	Ethical person	Similarity pole	Contrast pole
1	✓				✓		✓			✓		✓					⊗	⊗	○	Don't believe in God	Very religious
2			✓	✓	✓			✓		⊗	○	✓		⊗	⊗	○	✓			Same sort of education	Completely different education
3		⊗	⊗	○		✓	⊗		✓				⊗				✓			Not athletic	Athletic
4	✓	✓		✓	✓	⊗		○										✓	✓	Both girls	A boy
5	✓	⊗		✓	○	✓		✓						✓	✓	✓	✓	⊗		Parents	Ideas different
6		⊗		✓	✓			✓						⊗	✓					Understand me better	Don't understand me at all
7		✓	○		✓				○					⊗	✓	✓		✓	✓	Teach the right way	Teach the wrong way
8		✓	✓	✓			✓							✓		⊗	⊗		✓	Achieved a lot	Hasn't achieved a lot
9	✓			⊗		✓	⊗	✓		○	○	✓		✓	⊗	✓	✓			Higher education	No education
10	✓			⊗			○			⊗		⊗	✓		○					Don't like other people	Like other people
11	✓	✓	✓	⊗				✓	○		✓	⊗		✓	✓		✓	✓	⊗	More religious	Not religious
12	✓	✓	✓	⊗	✓		✓	✓			✓			✓	✓		✓	✓	✓	Believe in higher education	Don't believe in much education
13		✓				○												⊗		More sociable	Not sociable
14		○		✓	○	⊗	⊗	✓				✓	⊗	✓	✓	✓	✓		✓	Both girls	Not girls
15	✓	✓	✓		✓		○	⊗	○			✓		⊗	⊗	✓	✓	✓	✓	More understanding	Less understanding
16	✓	✓		⊗	○			✓					✓	✓	✓			✓	✓	Both have high morals	Low morals
17	⊗	✓		✓	✓	✓								✓	✓		⊗	✓	✓	Think alike	Think differently
18				✓			⊗	✓	✓	✓	○					⊗		✓	○	Same age	Different ages
19	⊗			✓	○	⊗	⊗		✓	✓										Both friends	Not friends
20	⊗			✓		✓						✓			✓		✓		✓	Both appreciate music	Don't understand music

⊗ and ✓ indicate similarity; ○ and blanks indicate contrast.
SOURCE:　Adapted from Kelly, 1955, Vol. 1, p. 270.

blank, it means that the contrast part of the construct applies. Clients then proceed to sort all these people again on new dimensions. The number of constructs utilized varies from client to client: some will be able to sort people on only a few dimensions or constructs; others will sort them on a great many dimensions.

Table 11.1 shows the cognitive matrix of one of Kelly's clients. The columns list the important individuals in this person's life; the rows represent the constructs used by the client to construe them. Construct 2, for example, can be termed an education construct. The client sees both a teacher he accepts ($\otimes$) and one he rejects ($\otimes$) as similar in terms of educational level. He sees his boss, in contrast, as having a different educational background ($\bigcirc$). His brother ($\checkmark$), sister ($\checkmark$), friend ($\checkmark$), and a successful person he knows ($\checkmark$) are all similar to his teachers in educational background. The remaining figures (blanks)—himself, mother, father, spouse, ex-girlfriend, ex-friend, a rejected person, a pitied person, a threatening person, an attractive person, a happy person, and an ethical person—all have an educational background that is different from his teachers'.

Once the grid has been completed, it can be scored in a variety of ways. One simple way used by psychologist James Bieri (1955) is to compare the check patterns across the various rows. Similar patterns suggest a lack of differentiation in the person's perception of others (cognitive simplicity); highly dissimilar patterns suggest a highly differentiated view of others (cognitive complexity). In a clinical setting, the therapist can use cognitive complexity, along with other testing information, to illuminate the client's problems.

Other, more detailed interpretations can be derived from the RCRT as the therapist seeks to understand a specific client's construct system. By way of illustration, look at the client matrix shown in Table 11.1. If we look at column 1 (self) and simply note the incidents ($\otimes$ and $\checkmark$) and voids (blanks and empty circles), we can get some idea of how this person sees himself. Remember that the incidents refer to the similarity poles, and the blanks and empty circles to the contrast poles of the constructs. The client describes himself as similar to his parents in a few respects, including being very religious. He claims that he does not understand himself; nor do his parents, wife, or ex-girlfriend understand him. He is not friends with his parents or his sister. He sees his brother as one of the few people who understand him. Although he sees his brother as having accomplished a great deal in his lifetime, the client does not think of himself as very successful. Although the client seems to admire his brother very much, he does not consider him a friend, or perhaps his brother does not see him as a friend. He sees his ex-girlfriend and his wife as friends (see construct 19) but, ironically, the person he calls his friend is not someone he regards as a real friend.

We might tentatively interpret his construct system to mean that the client sees himself as alone and isolated, even among people who are supposed to be close to him. He is convinced that his parents do not understand him. Although he believes his brother and his friend understand him, he does not really see them as his friends. The client also describes himself as not sociable. We have, then, a clinical picture of a young man who may be lonely either because his family and friends have failed to communicate with him or because he is unsociable and withdrawn. Of course, it is possible that his feelings of isolation are being produced by other factors, but his responses on the RCRT provide the clinician with clues that can be supplemented by other techniques.

Research Applications of the RCRT

Bieri (1955) sought to test the validity of Kelly's RCRT using college students. He began by classifying students as either cognitively complex or cognitively simple on the basis of their scores on the RCRT. Using Kelly's assumptions that a basic characteristic of human beings is to move toward greater predictability of their environments and that each person has a set of constructs to use in making those predictions, Bieri hypothesized that people who are cognitively complex would be better able to predict the behavior of others than would those who are cognitively simple. His reasoning was that those who can differentiate among many different events in the environment would be more capable of making discerning and accurate judgments than would those who see many events as similar and who apply the same labels to them.

To test this hypothesis, Bieri had cognitively complex and cognitively simple subjects respond to a questionnaire depicting 12 social situations with four alternative behaviors, as in the following sample item:

> You are working intently to finish a paper in the library when two people sit down across from you and distract you with their continual loud talking. Would you most likely:
>
> a. Move to another seat?
> b. Let them know how you feel by your facial expression?
> c. Try to finish up in spite of their talking?
> d. Ask them to stop talking?

After subjects had completed the questionnaire, they were asked to guess how two of their classmates would respond in the same situations. The subjects' predictive accuracy was assessed by noting the number of times their predictions matched the actual responses of their classmates. As expected, the cognitively complex students were much more accurate in their predictions than were the cognitively simple ones. It was also found that the cognitively simple, or undifferentiated, subjects were more likely than were the complex subjects to perceive inaccurate similarities between themselves and others; that is, they tended to assume that the predictions they made for themselves would also apply to others. In brief, cognitively simple subjects tended to be egocentric. Bieri's study is only one of many based on Kelly's theorizing; in general, the findings tend to support his formulations (Bonarius, 1965).

Another interesting use of the RCRT can be seen in the area of trying to map out individuals' construct systems as they relate to work and to show how these systems of personal meaning guide people in making effective vocational choices. One interesting early finding in this research literature shows that people with less differentiated construct systems about work tended to make less realistic choices in their selection of an occupation than did those with more differentiated systems. An undifferentiated system would include only a few constructs (for example, high/low salary, easy/hard), whereas a more differentiated system would include many constructs (for example, high/low salary, easy/hard work, pleasant/unpleasant work, stimulating/boring work, upward mobility/downward mobility, high/low status, good/poor retirement plan, good/poor coworkers). The realism of the person's vocational choices was assessed by examining their aptitudes and abilities to do the job. Thus, subjects with relatively simple cognitive systems who considered only the salary associated with the job and its degree of difficulty chose jobs for which they were unsuited, whereas subjects with more complex systems who considered a larger number of factors made choices that were consistent with their actual skill levels and interests.

More recent research in this area shows that it is not only the level of differentiation that is important in making realistic vocational choices but also the degree of integration of the person's construct system. System integration is determined by the intercorrelations among the constructs. Systems that are integrated show high intercorrelations; systems that are fragmented show little or no correlations among the constructs. A person with a fragmented system, for example, would think of the salary and the difficulty of the work separately. Thinking about salary level would not trigger a thought about the difficulty of the job and vice versa. On the other hand, a person with an integrated or organized system would see the interconnections between the salary level of the job, its degree of difficulty, its level of stimulation or challenge, its associations with promotion and upward mobility, and other factors. People with more differentiated and integrated systems are better able to make more realistic and ultimately satisfying vocational choices (Neimeyer, 1992, pp. 93–97).

THEORY'S IMPLICATIONS FOR THERAPY

The Role of the Therapist

In Kelly's view, the sick person is one who continues to use constructs that are invalid. Thus, the basic aim of psychotherapy is to help clients form new constructs or revise old ones so that they can deal more effectively with their environment. Therapy is concerned primarily with opening up the possibility of continual change in the client's construct system. The therapist's job is to diagnose the illness and to throw light on the paths by which clients can become well (Kelly, 1955, Vol. 2, p. 582).

The therapeutic process begins as both parties try to define their roles. Clinicians, Kelly believed, should conceptualize their role quite broadly. If a client sees therapy as involving only minor adjustments, the therapist must begin with this limited view but help the client see the need for more drastic change; the therapist listens closely to the client's complaints and uses a variety of techniques to produce change.

Techniques that produce minor change include threat, invalidation, and exhortation (Kelly, 1955, Vol. 2, pp. 583–587). By threat, Kelly meant clients' awareness of the possibility of imminent change in their construct structures. Under such conditions, Kelly believed, the therapist can take advantage of the situation by pointing out new ways for clients to construe their experiences in order to facilitate constructive growth. Change can also be produced if the therapist invalidates clients' constructs, by showing them why and how their constructs do not work. Finally, the therapist can produce minor change by admonishing clients and exhorting them to behave differently and more effectively.

For major change to occur, clients must be convinced that the therapist accepts them and is willing to help them think through their problems. Kelly's view of acceptance differs from that of other nondirective therapists, however. In the traditional view, the therapist assumes that everyone has the right to choose to become anything she or he desires. In Kelly's view, acceptance does not necessarily imply approval of the clients' characteristics, but rather a readiness to understand clients' construct systems and to use their own systems to help them get well. One implication of this stance is that therapists must have a clear and firm understanding of their own construct systems. They must be able to empathize with clients without surrendering their own viewpoint. Toward this end, therapists should try to subsume much of the client's system into their own (Kelly, 1955, Vol. 2, pp. 585–587).

Controlled elaboration is Kelly's term for the therapist-assisted process of thinking through. Its aim is to make the client's construct system internally consistent and communicable so that it can eventually be validated or invalidated by new experiences. The therapist takes an active role in this process, by suggesting that new elements be added to old constructs (for example, "Your view of your brother should also include the fact that he is highly considerate of your friends") or helping the person formulate new constructs (for example, "Your minister is a person who might help you to better understand why you doubt the existence of God"). These suggestions create anxiety in clients, because the new elements lie mostly outside the range of convenience of their construct system. This anxiety is necessary, however, as a precondition to making changes in the construct system (Kelly, 1955, Vol. 1, p. 498). In challenging the client's system in these and other ways, however, the therapist tries to avoid precipitating a catastrophe (Kelly, 1955, Vol. 2, pp. 589–590).

Another aspect of the therapist's role is to help clients use current constructs to deal with problems experienced in childhood. All too often, in Kelly's view, therapists allow their clients to dwell on the past and to recount their experiences in childish terms. Revision of these constructs, he believed, can happen only if client and therapist are willing to apply new, adult thinking to the old experiences. The therapist also helps clients to design new experiments, to test hypotheses with courage, and to weigh the evidence critically. Thus, the role of the therapist is similar to that of an experienced scientific investigator helping to initiate a beginner into the realm of science. The therapist also acts as a validator of the evidence the client accumulates.

> It is . . . important that the therapist play his role, not only with an acceptance and a generosity possibly rare in the client's interpersonal world but always with a kind of naturalness and faithfulness to reality which will not mislead the client who uses him as a

validator. In a sense, the therapist must play a part as a reasonably faithful example of natural human reactions, rather than one which is superhuman or divested of all human spontaneity. In a sense, the therapist takes the best to be found in human nature and portrays it in such a way as to enable the client to validate his constructs against it. Having identified the therapist's generalization of the acceptable values in human nature, the client may seek them out among his companions. (Kelly, 1955, Vol. 2, p. 593)

In summary, therapists must have a clear idea of their own construct systems, and must be alert and sensitive to a variety of cues emanating from their clients. As scientists, they must display propositional thinking and a willingness to change their views on the basis of the evidence. They must, in brief, be flexible. They must also be courageous, according to Kelly, because psychotherapy is often a distressing experience for them as well as for their clients. Finally, therapists must be verbally skilled, creative, and energetic (Kelly, 1955, Vol. 2, pp. 595–605).

The Therapeutic Conference and Role Playing

One of Kelly's principal methods is the interview or conference. In a series of therapeutic conferences, therapists attempt not only to assess the realities of their clients' lives but also to point out directions in which they can proceed toward solution of their problems (Kelly, 1955, Vol. 2, pp. 774–775). During these sessions, therapists encourage clients to discuss their problems by acting in a supportive, reassuring, and accepting manner. Acceptance does not mean approval of the clients' construct systems nor their views of themselves (Kelly, 1955, Vol. 2, p. 587); instead, it means that therapists are capable of understanding their clients and of anticipating events in the way that the clients anticipate them. In this nonthreatening environment, clients should feel free to experiment with new ideas or beliefs and to revise or discard existing ones without fear of suffering devastating consequences if their experiments go awry (Kelly, 1955, Vol. 2, p. 581).

A large part of this experimentation involves role playing. Role enactment provides clients with insights into their maladaptive behavior and gives them new and more satisfying ways of behaving; thus, it enables them to change their invalid construct systems. Clients are typically assigned roles by their therapists, who often engage in complementary role playing to clarify their clients' feelings about themselves and to provide them with an opportunity for self-insight. Clients are not passive, however. They may also cast their therapists into a variety of roles—for example, parent, teacher, or child. This process is similar to Freudian transference, in that clients may act toward their therapists as though they were significant authority figures from their past. Through this intellectual and emotional process, they may achieve needed insight into their own problems. However, the emphasis in Kelly's therapy is not on reliving the past; rather, the therapy aims to provide clients with new roles that will promote growth and allow them to participate more fully and effectively in current life situations.

Kelly viewed therapy as a creative process, and role playing as the major technique enabling clients to act creatively. Although playing new roles seems artificial and stultifying at first, this feeling soon dissipates and clients become more spontaneous. Role playing makes them more susceptible to change. Loosening of constructs can also be achieved, in Kelly's judgment, by use of relaxation techniques, free association, and dream analysis.

Self-Characterization Sketches and Fixed-Role Therapy

As part of the therapeutic process, the clinician may ask the client to write a **self-characterization sketch.** This technique reflects Kelly's belief in the direct approach: "If you do not know what is wrong with a person, ask him; he may tell you" (Kelly, 1955, Vol. 1, pp. 322–323). Clients are asked to imagine themselves as the principal character in a play written by a friend who knows them intimately and sympathetically. This other-person format is designed to make the task as nonthreatening as possible.

After the client writes the sketch, the therapist interprets it and then uses the interpretation to write a fixed-role sketch, which the client is asked to enact. The sketch is designed to contrast sharply with the client's current self-perception, as revealed in the self-characterization sketch, and thus to produce major changes in the client (Kelly, 1955, Vol. 1, p. 370). At the same time, the fixed-role sketch is designed to protect the client by encouraging the belief that he or she is simply playing a fictitious character. Kelly found that, with this disclaimer, clients were willing to try out the new role and that later they began to see its implications for them and to act accordingly.

Kelly provided a clear example of how the self-characterization and **fixed-role therapy** techniques worked in the case of an actual client he called Ronald Barrett. Ronald's self-characterization sketch revealed a compulsive individual who believed dogmatically that there was a reason behind all existence and that the only way to understand the causes of his existence (that is, the causes of his behaviors and the behaviors of others) was to rely on rational thought and logic. Thus, the only way for Ronald to solve problems was to maintain control over his feelings and to rely solely on reason. Despite his attempt at maintaining strict control, however, Ronald saw himself "ready to explode" on many occasions; these feelings disturbed him, because he believed they would bring disapproval from others. Although he had no warm and friendly relationships with people, he thought that he must have their approval and that it could be gained only by keeping his emotions in check and appearing calm and restrained. His concern with restraining his feelings even extended to his relationships with women. He wrote in his self-characterization sketch:

> He [Ronald] has some ideas concerning girls that seem odd or just plain crazy to most people. He completely refrains from calling a girl "beautiful." She may be cute, pretty, attractive, or some other adjective in his mind, but he uses the word "beautiful" only [to] describe material things that have no "feeling" as humans have. Although he listens attentively to stories or general discussions about sex, he rarely enters into the conversation. One may say that he puts too much meaning and thought into kissing a girl. If he has gone out with a girl a couple of times, or even once, and doesn't continue to go out with her or to call her, he is very hesitant about asking her for a date again, say two or three months later. He is usually lost for conversation when meeting someone new, or seeing a girl he knows, but if he once "breaks the ice," he can usually talk freely. However, when he calls a girl on the telephone, no matter how well he knows her, he hates to have anyone around him or even within hearing distance. Furthermore, he doesn't like to practice anything, such as a musical instrument, any place where he can be seen or heard. (Kelly, 1955, Vol. 1, p. 328)

Kelly noted that Ronald was himself disturbed by some of his ideas about women. Pointing out that Ronald attributed feeling to women, but not to beautiful ones, Kelly drew the inference that Ronald saw women, like all feeling things, as imperfect. As a consequence, he was continually hesitant and awkward in his relationships with women.

To help Ronald overcome his problems, Kelly wrote a fixed-role sketch for him to enact in his daily life. The sketch was about a man called Kenneth Norton.

> Kenneth Norton is the kind of man who, after a few minutes of conversation, somehow makes you feel that he must have known you intimately for a long time. This comes about not by any particular questions that he asks but by the understanding way in which he listens. It is as if he had a knack of seeing the world through your eyes. The things which you have come to see as being important he, too, soon seems to sense as similarly important. Thus, he catches not only your words but the punctuations of feeling with which they are formed and the little accents of meaning with which they are chosen. . . .
>
> Girls he finds attractive for many reasons, not the least of which is the exciting opportunity they provide for his understanding the feminine point of view. Unlike some men, he does not "throw the ladies a line," but, so skillful a listener is he, soon has them throwing him one—and he is thoroughly enjoying it.
>
> With his own parents and in his own home he is somewhat more expressive of his own ideas and feelings. Thus, his parents are given an opportunity to share and supplement his new enthusiasms and accomplishments. (Kelly, 1955, Vol. 1, pp. 374–375)

According to Kelly, the sketch centered on a simple theme—namely, seeking answers in the feelings of other people rather than in argument with them (Kelly, 1955, Vol. 1, p. 375). He asked Ronald to become Kenneth Norton for two weeks. First, however, Kelly let Ronald rehearse in his office a number of times until he was thoroughly familiar with the sketch (Kelly, 1955, Vol. 1, p. 387). Of course, Kelly insisted on addressing the client as Kenneth throughout the rehearsal and enactment period. Kelly also held therapy sessions during the enactment period to assess Ronald's progress or lack of progress. Progress was uncertain at first but, by the 12th interview, Ronald reported feeling much less insecure in social situations and more willing to express his feelings. Shortly afterward, the therapist broke the client's Kenneth Norton role and told him that Kenneth Norton was, in a sense, supposed to be Ronald Barrett. Ronald accepted this view after some discussion and then thanked the therapist for all his help. Ronald returned to his everyday situation with a changed set of constructs and a more realistic assessment of his own behavior and the behavior of others (Kelly, 1955, Vol. 1, pp. 394–395).

Assessment and Treatment of Schizophrenics

Much of the research utilizing Kelly's theory has employed variants of his RCRT to study psychiatric patients who have been diagnosed as schizophrenic. Kelly (1955) originally proposed that the thinking of schizophrenics involves the use of **loose constructions**—weak and unstable ideas and networks of ideas that lead to varying predictions.

To test the assertion that schizophrenia is associated with disordered thinking, Bannister and Fransella (1966) measured the thinking of schizophrenics and compared it with the thinking of depressives, neurotics, patients with mild forms of brain damage (organics), and normal individuals. A variant of the RCRT served as the instrument to measure disordered thinking. All subjects were tested individually. Each person studied eight photos of strangers, one at a time, and then rank-ordered the photos according to how kind the person in the photo appeared to be, from 1 (most) to 8 (least). Then the eight photos were reshuffled and each subject was asked to rank-order them again along a dimension of stupidity. The photos were again reshuffled and then rank-ordered along a dimension of selfishness. This same rating procedure was used again to elicit judgments of the degree of sincerity, meanness, and honesty of the people in the photos.

After completing this task (administration 1), subjects were given the same set of photos and were asked to repeat the entire procedure (administration 2); that is, subjects were asked to rank-order the same eight people on the same six personality dimensions.

Correlational analyses were then conducted between the ratings of the photos on the six dimensions for each group of subjects for administration 1 and 2. Separate correlations were computed for each group—schizophrenics, depressives, neurotics, organics, and normals—to determine the extent to which the various groups were consistent in their rankings from one administration to the next. Ranking a given person as most kind the first time and as most kind the second time would be consistent; ranking a person most honest the first time but low on honesty the second time would be inconsistent. The results were as follows: for normals, $r = +.80$; for depressives, $r = +.75$; for neurotics, $r = +.74$; for organics, $r = +.73$; and for schizophrenics, $r = +.18$. The high correlations for the first four groups indicate highly consistent rankings, whereas the low correlation for schizophrenics indicates a lack of consistency, even though the second set of rankings was made *immediately* after completion of the first set. These results do suggest a problem in thinking for schizophrenics. Bannister, Fransella, and Agnew (1971) showed further that not only is the structure (organization and consistency) of thinking poor in schizophrenics, but the content of their thinking (the kind of beliefs they hold) is bizarre; that is, much of their thinking is characterized by paranoid delusions and by illogical connections between constructs.

In comparison to normal individuals, schizophrenics also have been found to have very weak and simplistic perceptions of themselves; that is, they use very few traits to describe themselves. In addition, schizophrenics are not very accurate in their descriptions of other people; that is, they have stereotypic views of others (Gara, Rosenberg, & Mueller, 1989, pp. 265–266; Rosenberg, 1993, p. 231).

Schizophrenics also have difficulty categorizing people in terms of their personal qualities (abilities, motives, traits). When investigators asked schizophrenics to look at photos of people and react to them, their comments were impersonal: they observed, for example, whether the person was standing or sitting, or that there was a book in the photo. Normals, in contrast, made many more personal judgments: they reported, for example, that the person looked kind, sincere, or competitive (McPherson, Armstrong, & Heather, 1978; McPherson, Buckley, & Draffan, 1971).

Bannister, Adams-Webber, Penn, and Radley (1975) have attempted to explain the origins of loose constructions in schizophrenics. They propose that schizophrenics, like normals, utilize constructs to make predictions about how the world operates, but that their predictions do not work very well; that is, they are invalid. The consequence of being wrong is to receive punishment from others. To avoid more punishment, schizophrenics weaken the constructs themselves and the associations between them; as a consequence, they begin to live subjectively in a highly fluid and largely meaningless (for them) universe. Specifically, as children, schizophrenics may have lived in a family situation riddled with inconsistencies, in which they were treated sometimes with kindness and at other times with cruelty. For example, their parents may have rewarded them for a particular behavior at times and punished them for the same behavior at other times. Perhaps their parents also ridiculed them unexpectedly in front of peers and arbitrarily reneged on promises. As a consequence of severe and erratic treatment, schizophrenics develop highly fluid constructs about their parents and an inability or unwillingness to make definite predictions about how their parents—or people in general—will behave toward them.

On the basis of this analysis, Bannister and associates reasoned that the process of thought disorder in schizophrenics can be reversed by providing them with new experiences that are consistently accurate. If thought disorder is the long-term consequence of repeated failures to predict accurately the behavior of others and themselves, then implementing therapeutic procedures in which patients are provided with evidence that they *can* accurately predict their own behavior and the behavior of others should result in an improvement in their health and functioning. Accordingly, they recruited therapists to help schizophrenic patients, over a two-year period, identify beliefs that were weak and then strengthen them. For instance, if a patient very tentatively believed that loud-mouthed people were mean, the therapist would enlist the support of the staff (psychologists and nurses) to present themselves in a loud-mouthed way to the patient whenever she requested cigarettes or candy and to refuse to give them to her. Similarly, if a patient believed that it was manly to be aggressive, the therapist would work to convince him that this belief was faulty and that it was manly to act like a gentleman. The therapist then arranged situations in which staff members would praise the patient and call him a fine gentleman for acting in a cooperative and nonaggressive way. Although the results of this long-term project were not completely positive, they were generally supportive of the investigators' theorizing, and there was evidence of some improvement in the thinking and psychological health of the patients.

EVALUATIVE COMMENTS

We now examine the scientific worth of Kelly's theory.

Comprehensiveness Kelly's theory is not very comprehensive, but it has the potential to handle far more phenomena than it does currently. Its perspective has focused largely on psychopathological behavior, for example, schizophrenia, depression, eating disorders, and dysfunctional families. However, there have been attempts to redress this imbalance by focusing on more normal behaviors, such as occupational choice and decision making, and on the development of healthy personal relationships. Expansion of the scope of the theory is increasingly likely as interest in Kelly's theory among investigators grows (Neimeyer, 1992).

Precision and testability In comparison to most of the theories reviewed in this text, Kelly's position is unusually clear and testable. The theory is housed within an explicitly stated framework, so that hypotheses can be derived and tested. In addition, the RCRT provides a precise and reliable way of measuring many of the basic ideas in the theory.

Parsimony   Kelly's position seems too economical. It has too few concepts to account for personality functioning. There are relatively few concepts used to describe the developmental process, and an independent assessment of the impact of various situations on the person's behavior is not emphasized.

Empirical validity   The experimental evidence in support of certain aspects of Kelly's theory is strong. Much of this research has been concerned with establishing the reliability and validity of the RCRT and with testing some of the basic propositions of the theory. In the clinical area, research has centered mainly on Kelly's seminal ideas about thought disorder in schizophrenia, and has provided general support for Kelly's theorizing (Pierce, Sewell, & Cromwell, 1992).

Two points should be made about this empirical support, however. First, the evidence is largely correlational and paper-and-pencil in nature. There is a definite need for more sophisticated experimental work that uses behavioral criterion measures and assesses interaction effects between the individual's cognitive functioning in specific situations. There is also a need to move beyond the laboratory to test the theory in natural settings. Despite the provocative nature of Kelly's formulations, research efforts have remained at a fairly unsophisticated level. Perhaps investigators will remedy this problem in the near future, so that the worth of Kelly's theory can be assessed more adequately. Second, it should be pointed out that the RCRT is primarily a descriptive device; that is, it describes the constructs the client claims to use in articulating and ordering experiences. Interpretation of the meanings of the constructs, however, rests on the clinician's skills and sensitivity. Kelly contends that the measure can be used to help clients improve their behavior, but the evidence he offers is based on the therapist's subjective judgment that the client has improved. In this respect, Kelly's claim that his case-history materials prove the validity of his views on psychotherapy cannot be totally convincing.

Heuristic value   Kelly's theory has proven very interesting and challenging to British psychologists, who have been most active in testing various aspects of it. Some contributions to personal construct theory have also been made by researchers in the Netherlands, Canada, and Israel. Yet, given the originality and provocative nature of much of Kelly's thinking, research by U.S. psychologists has been remarkably sparse (Jankowicz, 1987, p. 481). Perhaps part of the difficulty is that the theory is sharply different from other existing positions in U.S. psychology. Nor is it clear to many U.S. psychologists that the elimination of important traditional concepts, such as motivation and reinforcement, is a move in the right direction. Advocates of personal-construct theory increasingly recognize their isolation from the mainstream of U.S. psychological thought. They think that the tendency of personal-construct researchers to disaffiliate themselves from more traditional lines of thought has resulted in an ingrown pattern of communication, thereby hindering the development of the theory (Neimeyer, 1985, pp. 111–112). In addition, some U.S. psychologists believe that the theory is too cognitive and presents a view of personality that is too one-sided and simplistic, although one prominent British advocate of the theory has sought to convince psychologists that such a view is erroneous (Bannister, 1977).

Applied value   Until recently, Kelly's theory had little effect on disciplines outside of psychology. Today, however, Kelly's ideas and measurement techniques are being utilized successfully by business managers and occupational counselors. For example, business measurement specialists have used variations of the RCRT to assess consumers' views of a variety of products. The test provides a systematic basis for discovering the criteria that consumers use in making their purchasing decisions and is helpful to business owners and managers in their efforts to make certain that their products meet the needs of their customers. In the employment counseling field, counselors have used the RCRT to help people seeking work to identify occupations they view as similar, to determine which occupations they identify as ideal, and to become aware of the implications of their thoughts (constructs) about employment (Jankowicz, 1987). Thus, although the theory is currently in its initial stages of verification, it is beginning to have a positive impact on the solution of social problems.

DISCUSSION QUESTIONS

1. Why do many people want to believe that their behavior is free and not determined?
2. In what ways do we act as scientists in the prediction of our behavior? Cite limitations to the use of this analogy as an aid in understanding our behavior.

3. What is a personal construct? Why must constructs contain at least three elements? Can you think of constructs that contain only two elements?

4. How do propositional and constellatory constructs differ? Give examples of each type of construct.

5. Make up a repertory grid that describes your own constructs in relation to the important people in your life. When you are finished, report whether the exercise provided you with any insights into your personality.

6. What are some of the strengths and weaknesses of using Kelly's Role Construct Repertory Test (RCRT) to assess personality?

7. What are some potentially harmful consequences to other people of using stereotypes about hair color?

8. Are the traits associated with stereotypes always negative? Can you think of sex-role traits that are positive, for example? Why do people rely on stereotypes to guide their behavior?

9. What are some of your superordinate constructs? In your view, is your social success superordinate to academic success or vice versa? Why?

10. Do you agree with Kelly that people are generally rational in their behavior?

GLOSSARY

choice corollary   The proposition that people select between alternatives in dichotomized constructs in making their judgments about reality.

commonality corollary   The proposition that similar construct systems in different individuals lead to similarities in their behavior.

constellatory construct   Type of construct that allows its elements to belong to other constructs concurrently; however, once identified in a particular way, these elements are fixed. For example, an individual may have a stereotypic construct of a fat person as lazy, dirty, and slovenly. These elements or traits could also belong to some of the individual's other constructs—for example, homeless person, coal miner; that is, the individual might also see a homeless person and a coal miner as lazy, dirty, and slovenly. However, once the individual applies the fat-person construct to a person in a particular situation, the traits (or elements) lazy, dirty, and slovenly are automatically and inflexibly attributed to that person.

constructive alternativism   Fundamental assumption that human beings are capable of changing their interpretations of events.

constructs   Ways of representing our experiences; they are abstractions that are defined in terms of the similarities and contrasts of their poles.

controlled elaboration   Therapeutic technique in which clients are encouraged to clarify and think through their problems in consultation with the therapist; this process enables them to revise or discard old constructs and to formulate new and more effective ones.

core constructs   Important beliefs that are part of the individual's personal identity.

core role constructs   Set of beliefs associated with important role relationships that constitute the person's social identity.

fixed-role therapy   Therapeutic procedure used by Kelly to produce personality changes in clients by constructing roles for them that help them overcome their weaknesses and, in the process, enable them to reconstrue themselves and their life situations.

fragmentation corollary   The proposition that an individual's personal construct subsystems may be disjointed and mutually incompatible and that the person is often unaware of the inconsistency.

individuality corollary   The proposition that people differ in their constructions of reality.

loose constructions   Beliefs that are unstable, weak, and poorly defined and that lead to erratic and often invalid predictions about how the world operates.

organization corollary   The proposition that the individual's constructs are arranged in particular ways within his or her personal system.

peripheral constructs   Beliefs that are relatively unimportant to the person and that can be changed rather easily.

permeability   The degree to which new elements will be admitted within the boundaries of a construct.

preemptive construct   Type of construct that includes only its own elements and maintains that these elements cannot apply to other constructs.

propositional construct   Type of construct that leaves all of its elements open to modification.

range of convenience   The scope of a construct; the number of other constructs to which it is related.

Role Construct Repertory Test (RCRT)   Test devised by Kelly to assess an individual's personal construct system; also known as the REP test.

self-characterization sketch   Initial step in fixed-role therapy, in which clients are asked to write a brief character outline of themselves as it might be written by an intimate and sympathetic friend.

sociality corollary   The proposition that constructive interpersonal relationships depend on mutual understanding of each other's construct systems.

subordinate constructs   Constructs that are controlled by other constructs.

superordinate construct   Construct that controls many other constructs.

SUGGESTED READINGS

Fransella, F., & Thomas, L. (Eds.). (1988). *Experimenting with personal construct theory*. London: Routledge & Kegan Paul.

Kelly, G. A. (1955). *The psychology of personal constructs* (Vols. 1 & 2). New York: Norton.

Neimeyer, R. A., & Neimeyer, G. J. (Eds.) (1992). *Advances in personal construct psychology* (Vol. 2). Greenwich, CT: JAI Press.

REFERENCES

Bannister, D. (Ed.). (1977). *New perspectives in personal construct theory*. New York: Academic Press.

Bannister, D., Adams-Webber, J. R., Penn, W. L., & Radley, A. R. (1975). Reversing the process of thought disorder: A serial validation experiment. *British Journal of Social and Clinical Psychology, 14,* 169–180.

Bannister, D., & Fransella, F. (1966). A grid test of schizophrenic thought disorder. *British Journal of Social and Clinical Psychology, 5,* 95–102.

Bannister, D., Fransella, F., & Agnew, J. (1971). Characteristics and validity of the grid test of thought disorder. *British Journal of Social and Clinical Psychology, 10,* 144–151.

Bieri, J. (1955). Cognitive complexity-simplicity and predictive behavior. *Journal of Abnormal and Social Psychology, 51,* 263–268.

Bonarius, J. (1965). Research in the personal construct theory of George A. Kelly: Role Construct Repertory Test and basic theory. In B. Maher

(Ed.), *Progress in experimental personality research* (pp. 1–46). New York: Academic Press.

Fransella, F., & Dalton, P. (1990). *Personal construct counseling in action.* Newbury Park, CA: Sage.

Gara, M. A., Rosenberg, S., & Mueller, D. R. (1989). Perception of self and other in schizophrenia. *International Journal of Personal Construct Psychology, 2,* 253–270.

Jankowicz, A. D. (1987). Whatever became of George Kelly? *American Psychologist, 42,* 481–487.

Kelly, G. A. (1955). *The psychology of personal constructs* (Vols. 1 & 2). New York: Norton.

Lawson, E. D. (1971). Hair color, personality and the observer. *Psychological Reports, 28,* 311–322.

McPherson, F. M., Armstrong, J., & Heather, B. B. (1978). Psychological construing and thought disorder: Another test of the "difficulty" hypothesis. *British Journal of Medical Psychology, 51,* 319–324.

McPherson, F. M., Buckley, F., & Draffan, J. (1971). "Psychological" constructs and delusions of persecution and "nonintegration" in schizophrenia. *British Journal of Medical Psychology, 44,* 277–280.

Neimeyer, G. J. (1992). Personal constructs and vocational structure. In R. A. Neimeyer and G. J. Neimeyer (Eds.), *Advances in personal construct psychology* (Vol. 2, pp. 91–120). Greenwich, CT: JAI Press.

Neimeyer, G. J., & Hall, A. G. (1988). Personal identity in disturbed marital relationships. In F. Fransella & L. Thomas (Eds.), *Experimenting with personal construct theory* (pp. 297–307). London: Routledge & Kegan Paul.

Neimeyer, R. A. (1985). *The development of personal construct psychology.* Lincoln: University of Nebraska Press.

Pierce, D. L., Sewell, K. W., & Cromwell, R. L. (1992). Schizophrenia and depression: Construing and constructing empirical research. In R. A. Neimeyer and G. J. Neimeyer (Eds.), *Advances in personal construct psychology* (Vol. 2, pp. 151–184). Greenwich, CT: JAI Press.

Rosenberg, S. (1993). Social self and the schizophrenic process: Theory and research. In R. L. Cromwell and C. R. Snyder (Eds.), *Schizophrenia: Origins, processes, treatment, and outcome* (pp. 223–240). New York: Oxford University Press.

PART FIVE

HUMANISTIC/EXISTENTIAL PERSPECTIVES

The theories considered this section of the text are part of the third-force movement in contemporary psychology. (The other two movements are psychoanalysis and behaviorism.) The term was coined by Abraham Maslow (Chapter 12) to describe a position that focuses on the creative potentialities inherent in human beings and that seeks ways to help them realize their highest and most important goals. Virtually all of the humanistic theories postulate the existence of an innate growth mechanism within individuals that will move them toward realization of their potentialities if environmental conditions are right. This growth process has been variously labeled by its numerous proponents as the drive toward self-actualization, self-realization, or selfhood.

The roots of the humanistic movement can be found in the writings of Jung, Adler, Horney, Kohut, Allport, Maslow, Rogers, May, and others. These theorists all emphasize the uniqueness of individuals and believe they should be free to make their own choices about the direction they want to take in their own lives. People should be allowed to organize and control their own behavior; they should not be controlled by society. Society is generally seen as the "bad guy"—the enforcer of rules and regulations that stifle personal growth. According to the humanists, a benevolent, helpful attitude toward people allows them to grow and prosper. Most societies, they believe, attempt to coerce individuals into behaving appropriately—that is, normally. The result is rather dull, conventional people who usually obey, without much question, the moral prescriptions of the majority. In other words, the result is the average, law-abiding man or woman.

The humanistic psychologists argue, instead, for allowing individuals to develop to their fullest potential. They see people as naturally striving to be creative and happy rather than mediocre and conventional. Of course, the assumption that what is conventional is mediocre is open to question, especially in a society that encourages people to strive for excellence in their pursuits. Another assumption underlying many of the humanist positions is that it is possible to specify a universal set of values that will provide people with a moral anchor so that they will be able to decide what is right or wrong and good or bad. Such a set of values, rooted in biology, would allow people to make moral decisions by looking inside themselves, instead of relying on the judgments of society. Yet there has never been clear-cut agreement among philosophers or psychologists on a universal set of values, although numerous attempts to devise such a list have been made. Also the question of who will decide which values are universally valid has never been resolved. Is it the philosophers? The psychologists? The politicians? The artists? The theologians? As we will see in Chapter 15, Skinner thinks that behavioral psychologists can best make this decision, but surely not everyone will agree with him. Finally, despite the claims of the humanists, there is little scientific evidence for the existence of an innate mechanism that would allow us to make morally correct decisions.

Instead of rejecting this aspect of the humanistic psychologists' position, however, we ought to give it a fair hearing. First, the fact that there is no agreement on a universal set of values does not mean that such a value system can never be devised. Second, although there is currently no evidence for the existence of an internal, biologically based mechanism to guide moral behavior, such evidence may be found in the future. Even if it is not found, this does not mean there is nothing of merit in the humanistic position. By raising significant questions and challenging the tenets of orthodox psychology, humanistic psychologists have forced more traditional psychologists to reconsider the directions and value of their work. In this author's view, the overall impact of the humanists has been most beneficial, although some of the more rigorous experimental psychologists would certainly disagree. After we review the two major challenges hurled by the humanists at orthodox psychology, you can make your own judgment.

The first challenge is the assertion that contemporary psychologies, including psychoanalysis and behaviorism, provide only a partial and limited view of human functioning, which is in need of drastic revision. Allport put the matter succinctly and picturesquely:

> It is especially in relation to the formation and development of human *personality* that we need to open doors. For it is precisely here that our ignorance and uncertainty are greatest. Our methods, however well suited to the study of sensory processes, animal research, and pathology, are not fully adequate; and interpretations arising from the exclusive use of these methods are stultifying. Some theories . . . are based largely upon the behavior of sick and anxious people or upon the antics of captive and desperate rats. Fewer theories have derived from the study of healthy beings, those who strive not so much to preserve life as to make it worth living. Thus we find today many studies of criminals, few of law-abiders; many of fear, few of courage; more on hostility than on affiliation; much on the blindness in man, little on his vision; much on his past, little on his outreaching into the future. (Allport, 1955, p. 18)

In building his theory of self-actualization, Maslow also pointed out the limitations of the Freudian conception of personality. Freud devoted most of his attention to understanding the unconscious forces that determine behavior and neglected the rational, conscious forces. The Freudian world is one in which neurotic people are continually struggling to adjust to the environment and to gain a feeling of security. Maslow, in contrast, posited that human beings have a need hierarchy consisting of basic and growth urges. The need for security is one of the lower, basic needs; if gratified, it frees the individual to pursue higher goals. Most of Maslow's attention was directed to establishing a psychology of personal growth and creative striving. He set out to study the behavior of psychologically healthy people in order to learn more about the growth process. In Chapter 12, we outline his efforts and provide a review of the major characteristics of self-actualizing individuals.

In summary, the first challenge posed by Maslow and other humanistic psychologists is the need for a drastic revision of contemporary psychology so that primary attention can be paid to topics that have been relatively ignored by existing theories—among others, love, affiliation, creativity, spontaneity, joy, courage, humor, independence, and personal growth. Focusing on these should teach us about the good side of human nature and serve as a corrective to the more limited and pessimistic picture projected by Freudians and behaviorists.

The second challenge is to the prevailing view that psychology is a natural science and must therefore employ methods of study consistent with those used in physics, chemistry, physiology, and biology. The humanists claim that this attitude has led to a psychology that does not do justice to the full range of human experience and behavior. To understand the arguments of the humanists more fully, let us look briefly at the history of psychology and the reasons for its initial alliance with the natural sciences.

Psychology as a science began in 1879, when Wundt established his experimental laboratory in Leipzig, Germany. Psychologists had originally been linked with speculative philosophers, but dissatisfaction with this relationship and the desire to establish an independent, more empirically oriented discipline led them toward the natural sciences and the scientific method. The benefits of this move would be twofold: first, psychologists would have a ready-made approach to the study of behavior acceptable to members of the scientific community; second, psychology would gain status and respectability. So appealing was this prospect that psychologists adopted rather uncritically the scientific method used in the natural sciences.

The natural-science approach focuses on the accumulation of facts by means of objective and reliable measurement procedures. It avoids speculation and deduction and relies instead on induction. This tough-minded empiricism can be seen most clearly in the work of Watson and Skinner. Because of their concern with objective and precise measurement, advocates of this approach have focused only on those problems that can meet their criteria; as a result, phenomena such as jealousy, hatred of a parent, and love between mature adults have been excluded from consideration.

The natural-science approach also insists that investigators be objective in their study of problems. It tends to see the investigator as a potential source of bias, whose influence on the inquiry process must be neutralized and controlled. The implication is that science is a value-free enterprise and that the investigator should study phenomena dispassionately as well as objectively. It is this depersonalized view of science that has been rejected by the humanistic psychologists. Rogers, for example, argued that

> science exists only in people. Each scientific project has its creative inception, its process, and its tentative conclusion, in a person or persons. Knowledge—even scientific knowledge—is that which is subjectively acceptable. Scientific knowledge can be communicated only to those who are subjectively ready to receive its communication. The utilization of science also occurs only through people who are in pursuit of values which have meaning for them. (Rogers, 1965, p. 164)

Rogers wanted psychologists to develop a science of psychology that has its primary focus within the person. In Chapter 13, we review Carl Rogers's reasons for the establishment of such a science and his theory of personality. Rogers's approach is based on personal growth and respect for the worth of the individual and his or her innate potential.

Rollo May (Chapter 14) developed an orientation similar to Rogers's. In his view, we should regard science as a human endeavor and begin our inquiry by asking, "What is it in human nature that leads to the emergence of a scientific attitude?" We should not begin with an established methodology and try to fit human problems into that mold; instead, we should start with our own experiences and formulations of problems and use procedures that will allow us to obtain answers. This orientation would mean emphasizing the problem rather than the use of elegant measurement techniques and equipment for the sake of being scientific. It would make psychology a human science, rather than a natural science.

The humanists do not think the natural-science approach is meaningless; their point is that psychology should adopt an expanded set of methods to help us better understand reality. We now begin our examination of theories in the humanistic/existential tradition that reflect these hopes for change.

REFERENCES

Allport, G. W. (1955). *Becoming*. New Haven, CT: Yale University Press.

Rogers, C. R. (1965). Persons or science? In F. T. Severin (Ed.), *Humanistic viewpoints in psychology* (pp. 163–170). New York: McGraw-Hill.

CHAPTER 12

Maslow's Self-Actualization Position

BIOGRAPHICAL SKETCH

Abraham Maslow was born in Brooklyn, New York, in 1908; he was the eldest of seven children. His parents were Russian Jews who had emigrated to the United States. At 18, he entered City College of New York to study law but, despite his high IQ, he did poorly in some of his courses. He had chosen to study law only to satisfy his father's wishes and had little interest in becoming a lawyer; he found the course materials dry and boring. Even more disheartening to Maslow was the nearly total absence of moral considerations in the class discussions of legal cases, which seemed to him "to deal only with evil men, and with the sins of [humankind]" (Hoffman, 1988, p. 23). During the second semester of his first year, he quit school.

Maslow later transferred to Cornell, which he hoped would offer greater academic stimulation. While there, he enrolled in the introductory psychology course, but his high expectations for the class were quickly crushed. As he put it, the subject matter was "awful and bloodless and had nothing to do with people, so I shuddered and turned away from it" (Hoffman, 1988, p. 26). Disappointed academically, he then left Cornell and returned to his parents' home in Brooklyn—and to his friend and cousin, Bertha Goodman, who still lived in the Bronx.

Maslow was enormously attracted to Bertha and was determined to be with her; but he was also very shy with women. For several weeks, he visited Bertha at her home, but said nothing about his affection for her. Then, one day, he sat down beside her on a couch.

> They exchanged warm glances. As the silence grew, she gazed at him demurely and moved a bit closer. Timid and yet wanting desperately to touch her, Maslow sat there, hesitating. Bertha's sister, Anna, older and more experienced in affairs of the heart, intervened in this slow-motion romance. Shoving him toward Bertha by the scruff of his neck, she exclaimed, "For the love of Pete, kiss her, will ya!" Startled, and almost intimidated by Anna's shove, Maslow did so. Bertha "didn't protest or fight back," he recalled. "She kissed back and then life began." (Hoffman, 1988, p. 29)

Maslow always regarded that first kiss as one of the greatest moments of his life—a true peak experience.

Eventually, he matriculated at the University of Wisconsin, but his longing for Bertha continued. Although his parents opposed the marriage and all of his friends and professors at the university discouraged him because he had no money to support a family, Maslow sent Bertha a telegram announcing that they would marry over the Christmas break. He felt so certain of his decision that he did not even bother to ask Bertha for her consent. But she loved him equally and immediately agreed. They were married on December 31, 1928, and returned to Wisconsin together. They remained happily married until his death (Hoffman, 1988, pp. 36–37).

At the University of Wisconsin, he was first exposed to the scientific psychology of the Wundt/Titchener structuralism school. Advocates of the structuralist position sought to demonstrate that "mental life" could be studied in the same way as phenomena in chemistry—that is, by analyzing the various "elements" of sensation and perception and the ways in which they combined to affect behavior. Maslow found this approach boring, but his interest was piqued by the behaviorist approach being promulgated by John B. Watson. It is difficult to imagine that Maslow could be stimulated by Watson's crude stimulus-response (S-R) treatment of human behavior; later in his career, in fact, he rejected that approach. While Maslow was a student, however, Watson's method did interest him, because it seemed to imply that people could be understood and improved scientifically, a belief directly in line with Maslow's interest in helping people realize their potential.

During his Wisconsin days, Maslow worked with Harry Harlow, who later became famous for his work on curiosity and affectional motives in monkeys. Maslow was interested in the fact that monkeys would work to solve problems for long periods of time, even when they were not hungry. He observed similar behavior in pigs. The stronger and healthier pigs would explore their surroundings much more than did the weaker ones. Maslow was also aware of an early experiment showing that, if chickens are allowed to choose their own diets, some will select a healthy diet and others will not. These results suggested to Maslow that there is a fundamental drive toward health in animals. Eventually, he came to believe that a similar drive toward knowledge, power, and insight also exists in humans. Thus, his initial work in animal biology provided the groundwork for his theory of self-actualization.

Maslow received his doctorate from Wisconsin in 1934, and then worked for 18 months at Columbia University with eminent learning theorist E. L. Thorndike. As Thorndike's assistant, Maslow was required to do research designed to discover the percentage of human behavior determined by genes and the percentage controlled by culture. Maslow found the project silly because he believed that behavior was determined by both. He made his views known to Thorndike and, much to his surprise, Thorndike gave him permission to pursue his own research on dominance and sexuality in monkeys and humans. Out of this work emerged Maslow's ideas about the hierarchy of needs in human beings. His classic paper was published in *Psychological Review* in 1943, after he had left Columbia and begun teaching at Brooklyn College. During Maslow's 14 years at Brooklyn College, he had an opportunity to meet and be exposed to the ideas of such prominent psychologists, psychoanalysts, and cultural anthropologists as Max Wertheimer, Karen Horney, Alfred Adler, Erich Fromm, and Ruth Benedict. The exposure had a considerable influence on his thinking, and it was at this point that he rejected the oversimplified S-R view of human behavior and embraced instead a more holistic and dynamic view of personality functioning.

In 1951, Maslow moved to Brandeis University, where he served as department chair for many years. While at Brandeis, he produced two of his most creative works, *Motivation and Personality* (1954) and *Toward a Psychology of Being* (1962). In 1967, he was elected president of the American Psychological Association. That same year, he accepted a fellowship at the Laughlin Foundation in Menlo Park, California, to devote all his time to writing. Unfortunately, he died of a heart attack one year later, at the age of 62 (Wilson, 1972, pp. 129–202).

CONCEPTS AND PRINCIPLES

Humanistic Biology and Self-Actualization

Maslow laid the groundwork for his theory of **self-actualization** by making the assumption that each of us has an intrinsic nature that is good or, at the very least, neutral (Maslow, 1962, p. 3). Because this inner nature is good or neutral, he argued, it is best to encourage its development. Healthy development is likely, however, only in a society that "offers all [the] necessary raw materials and then gets out of the way and stands aside to let the . . . organism itself utter its wishes and demands and make its choices" (Maslow, 1970a, p. 277). If the environment is restrictive and minimizes personal choice, the individual is likely to develop in neurotic ways, because this inner nature is weak and subject to control by environmental forces. Maslow believed that this inner tendency, though weak, remains and continuously presses toward actualization (Maslow, 1962, pp. 3–4).

The objective of Maslow's **humanistic biology** was to establish a "scientific ethics, a natural value system, a court of ultimate appeal for the determination of good and bad, of right and wrong" (Maslow, 1962, p. 4). Such an ethic would overcome the relativism inherent in traditional appeals to moral authority and provide a set of ideals to serve as guides for human conduct. If our inner natures, for example, told us that aggression against others is wrong, then no amount of preaching or exhortation by authorities that it is justified under certain circumstances would dissuade us from our inner conviction. Presumably, we would be able to cast out this evil in ourselves. Because the evidence for a natural ethic is unconvincing, however, we are left with only the word of a moral authority—Maslow—that such a set of values indeed exists.

The Hierarchy of Human Needs

According to Maslow, human beings have two basic sets of needs that are rooted in their biology: **deficiency** (or basic) **needs,** and **growth** (or meta) **needs.** The basic needs are more urgent than the growth needs and are arranged in a hierarchical order. Maslow acknowledged that there may be exceptions to this hierarchical arrangement. For example, he maintained that there are creative people whose drive to create is more important than any other need. There are also people whose values and ideals are so strong that they will die rather than renounce them. The meta needs, in contrast, are not arranged hierarchically. In general, they are equally powerful and can be easily substituted one for another. When any of these needs is not fulfilled, the person becomes sick. Just as we need adequate amounts of vitamin C to remain healthy, so we need love from others in sufficient quantities to function properly (Maslow, 1962, p. 21). In order to move toward self-actualization, we must have sufficiently gratified our basic needs, so that we are free to pursue fulfillment of the higher, transcending, meta needs (Maslow, 1962, p. 23).

Basic Needs

From most to least powerful, the basic needs are the physiological drives, safety needs, belongingness and love needs, and esteem needs. (See Figure 12.1.) The preconditions necessary for the satisfaction of these needs include the "freedom to speak, freedom to do what one wishes so long as no harm is done to others, freedom to express oneself, freedom to investigate and seek for information, freedom to defend oneself, justice, fairness, honesty, orderliness in the group" (Maslow, 1970a, p. 47). Without these freedoms, satisfaction of the basic needs is virtually impossible.

The physiological needs include, among others, hunger, thirst, and sex. People deprived of food for long periods of time, for example,

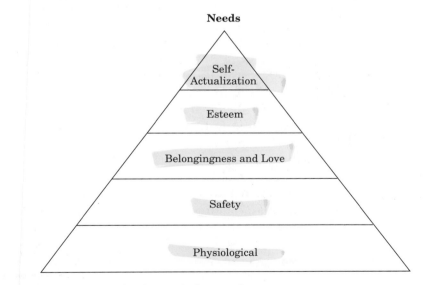

FIGURE 12.1   Maslow's needs hierarchy.

would begin to focus more and more of their attention on that deficiency. They would start to think and dream about food in an obsessive way. They would become less and less concerned with other activities, such as fixing the roof, buying a car, or taking the children on camping and fishing trips. They would also become less interested in what other people thought of them and in trying to help others. In short, when hunger is not satisfied, people are less concerned with safety needs, love and belongingness, esteem needs, and movement toward self-actualization. Thus, one implication of Maslow's scheme is that few poor people are involved in the quest for self-actualization. The poor use all their energies in finding enough work to feed themselves and their families.

Once people's physiological needs are relatively well satisfied, however, a set of safety needs is presumed to emerge. This set includes needs for security, protection, structure, law, order, limits, and freedom from fear, anxiety, and chaos (Maslow, 1970a, p. 39). In Maslow's view, the need for security manifests itself in infants and children when their environment is disturbed. For example, they may feel threatened by loud noises, flashing lights, rough handling, and inadequate support (Maslow, 1970a, p. 39). Needs for safety may also be reflected in their preference for an environment in which reinforcers are dispensed in a systematic and consistent manner; erratic behavior on the part of parents can be especially debilitating. Children also need limits on their behavior, according to Maslow. Without such limits, they function poorly. Maslow maintained that the typical child will often react with panic in unfamiliar and unmanageable situations. For example, a mother may be surprised to find her young son crying and clinging to the handrail of a stairway that leads to his classroom a few minutes after he had given her repeated assurances that he knew how to get there.

Like children, adults also have definite needs for safety, but they are more subtle and difficult to detect. A stable society frees adults from worry about adequate food supplies and housing, about being assaulted on the streets or in their homes, about military coups or civilian takeovers of the government, and the like. In a more moderate way, people act to secure tenure in their jobs and to receive old-age pensions and medical coverage in case of illness or accidents.

The needs for belongingness and love tend to emerge once the physiological and safety needs are routinely met. Maslow argued that all of us need to feel wanted and accepted by others. Some of us find gratification of these needs through our friends, others through family life, and still others through membership in groups and organizations. Without such ties, we would feel rootless and lonely. Of course, loneliness need not always be harmful to personal development; it can provide the basis for creativity and self-insight in some people. Often, however, loneliness is an unwanted and painful experience. Maslow believed that the emphasis on sensitivity and encounter groups in American culture in the 1960s was evidence of a strong need for contact and affection. He observed that increased mobility, the breakdown of the traditional family, and depersonalization resulting from increased urbanization had led to greater personal loneliness and alienation (Maslow, 1970a, p. 44).

The basic, or deficiency, need for love is a selfish concern with seeking love from others; Maslow termed it **D-love** (deficiency-love). Once this need is relatively gratified, however, we become capable of loving others. Maslow called this **B-love** (being-love), to distinguish it from the lower need to be loved. B-love, or mature love, becomes possible in Maslow's system only when the basic needs have been sufficiently gratified and the person is moving toward self-actualization.

Research by Dietch (1978) provides support for some of Maslow's ideas about mature love. He found that college men and women with higher scores on a test of self-actualization were more likely to have been truly in love with at least one person during the past three years than were students with lower scores. The implication is that students who were higher in self-actualization were more capable of giving affection and of intimately relating to others than those who were lower in the actualization hierarchy. Dietch also found a positive correlation between capacity for mature love and self-actualization in this sample of students. Among students who reported that their relationships had broken up, moreover, those who were higher in self-actualization were less resentful toward their former lovers than were those who were less actualizing. In accordance with Maslow's theory, this finding suggests that students higher in actualization were more mature and could accept the ending of an important relationship with more grace and understanding than did those who were lower in the hierarchy.

Esteem needs are the last of the basic urges to emerge. Maslow maintained that individuals become sick when these needs are thwarted. He divided them into two sets: esteem based on respect for our own competence, independence, and accomplishments, and esteem based on others' evaluations. Esteem needs of the second type are best seen in the striving for recognition from others and in attempts to secure status, fame, dominance, importance, and appreciation (Maslow, 1970a, p. 45). He also believed that we should base our self-esteem on actual competence and adequacy at the task rather than on praise or criticism from others. Surely there is little question that acceptance of undeserved praise from others may eventually have harmful consequences for personal development. A young woman who has been continually praised by her high school teachers and her parents for academic prowess that she does not really possess, and who consequently believes that she will excel at college, may find her first year at the university traumatic. Conversely, undeserved criticism may hinder functioning. A creative young man who writes marvelous poems may never share them with others, because of excessive reliance on the opinion of family members who continually derogate his efforts. Eventually, he might even give up poetry completely.

In these extreme cases, individuals would do better to rely on themselves and not others in making their judgments. In many instances, however, people lack the competence to make correct judgments and need to rely on the advice of others. For example, children on a picnic might do well to heed their parents' advice to avoid swimming in certain areas. Similarly, self-diagnosis and treatment of illness can have serious consequences; listening to the advice of a competent doctor may be wiser. Thus, Maslow's general prescription that we rely on ourselves and not on others in making decisions is questionable. We do not exist in a social vacuum, and we do not always know what actions are in our best interest. We cannot always rely on that "which comes naturally and easily out of one's own true inner nature, one's constitution, one's biological fate or destiny" (Maslow, 1970a, p. 46). Such a biologically based individualism can deteriorate into a kind of idiosyncratic subjectivism that assumes that each person's comprehension of reality is just as accurate as any other person's.

Meta Needs

Once the basic needs in Maslow's hierarchy have been sufficiently gratified, the needs for self-actualization and cognitive understanding become salient. People seek to gratify their innate curiosity about themselves and the workings of the environment, to know and understand phenomena that go beyond the gratification of basic needs, to move toward realization of their own unique potentialities. But movement in this positive direction is not automatic. Maslow believed that we often fear "our best side, . . . our talents, . . . our finest impulses, . . . our creativeness" (Maslow, 1962, p. 58). Discovery of our abilities brings happiness, but it also brings fear of new responsibilities and duties, fear of the unknown. Maslow called this fear the **Jonah complex.**

For women, Maslow argued, this fear takes the form of reluctance to make full use of their intellectual abilities, because achievement is considered unfeminine and they fear social rejection. However, while Maslow's argument may apply to some women, such fear of success is not present in *all* women: Piedmont (1988) found differences among women in terms of their fear of success. In comparison to women with a high fear of success, women with a low fear of success performed well on a masculine-oriented task.

For men, the motives underlying fear of success are different, because success is considered gender-appropriate behavior for males, and does not bring with it a loss in masculinity or social rejection. Instead, fear of success in men may reflect a wish to avoid the responsibilities that continued success brings, a feeling that material success somehow will not bring emotional well-being or spiritual fulfillment, or a belief that success will not bring them enough social recognition (Hoffman, 1974, p. 356).

Crawford and Marecek (1989) have criticized the concept of fear of success in females because it implies that females have a problem; that is, fear of success is used to explain deficiencies in females' achievement strivings and performances. Females are seen as acting against their own best interest when they fail to perform as well as they can on male-oriented tasks. Thus, females are being judged in relation to male norms and values, which assume that it is good to compete against others and to strive for success (Crawford & Marecek, 1989, pp. 151–153).

As an alternative to this deficiency view, Hyland (1989) proposes that success-avoiding behavior in females occurs not because they are motivated to avoid success but because success avoidance is a compromise reflecting the desire for some other goal(s). For example, some females may avoid getting ahead so that they can get on and make friends (Hyland, 1989, p. 668). In Hyland's view, avoiding success is not always an irrational or self-destructive behavior, but may reflect a rational choice to sacrifice success for more important goals (Hyland, 1989, p. 674).

In reality, however, people do not always sacrifice one goal for another; often they have a variety of goals that they value highly and pursue simultaneously. It does not seem rational for females (or males) to enroll in college with the goal of earning good grades and achieving success by graduating, and then to jeopardize the attainment of this goal by performing poorly because they wish to avoid rejection by their peers. A more rational strategy would be to pursue academic excellence, while at the same time making and keeping close friends. The goals are not mutually exclusive. Why should females or males waste thousands of dollars in tuition and fees and all that time and effort (and pain from poor performance) to pursue only the fulfillment of their affiliative needs?

To the extent that our socialization practices teach one sex or the other values that restrict individual growth, people will have difficulty moving toward self-actualization, according to Maslow. The fears that some females have of appearing unfeminine because they are pursuing traditionally masculine goals are being reduced gradually, as their roles evolve and become less restrictive. Males, too, have been subjected to socialization practices that restrict their personal growth. As their roles evolve, men are learning that the expression of emotion and feelings of tenderness toward others makes them more fully human.

In Maslow's view, poor socialization practices also contribute to a **desacralizing attitude** among young people that hinders movement toward self-actualization. Maslow believed this attitude emerges because many adolescents have parents whom they do not respect, parents who are confused about their own values. They never punish their children or stop them from doing things that are wrong. They are terrified of their children and let them do whatever they want. As a result, the children despise them, often with good reason. Concluding that all grown-ups are like their parents, they lose their respect for adults. As adolescents, they are cynical and mistrustful of all grown-ups. Maslow believed that movement toward self-actualization is possible for such people only when they learn to resacralize their lives—that is, when they give up their cynicism and mistrust and begin to see not only the weaknesses in adults but also their virtues and strengths (Maslow, 1971, pp. 49–50).

In summary, movement toward actualization depends upon good environmental conditions (Maslow, 1970a, p. 99), including a socialization process that fosters equality and trust between people, along with respect and support of the individual's right to make his or her own decisions.

B-Cognition and Actualization

Assuming that good conditions are present and that people are willing and able to take risks, positive growth will occur. Individuals begin more and more to exist in a **B-cognition** state. In Maslow's scheme, **D-cognition** experiences involve judging, condemning, and approving and disapproving of ourselves and others; B-cognition experiences are nonjudgmental, self-validating, nonstriving, and temporary (Maslow, 1962, p. 68). In such states of **peak experience,** people experience phenomena in their simplicity, "oughtness," beauty, goodness, and completeness. There is a lack of strain, an effortlessness, a spontaneity about the experience that is almost overwhelming (Maslow, 1962, p. 73). Typically, the person has no consciousness of space and time and feels intense emotions such as wonder, awe, and reverence. During these intense experiences, individuals transcend their own selfishness, and perceive events and objects as they truly are, without distorting them to meet their own needs or wishes (Maslow, 1970b, pp. 59–68). As examples, Maslow (1962, p. 79) cites "perceiving the beautiful person or the beautiful painting, experiencing perfect sex and/or perfect love, insight, creativeness." College students cite watching the beauties of nature, moments of quiet reflection, and listening to music, among other experiences, as triggers to peak experiences. (See Table 12.1.) In addition, recent research found that Canadian campers who had a greater appreciation of the uniqueness and beauty of the wilderness and a greater approval of its preservation were more self-actualizing

TABLE 12.1   Triggers to peak experiences among college students

Events	Percentage of students endorsing an event*
1. Looking at the beauties of nature	45%
2. Moments of quiet reflection	42%
3. Listening to music	32%
4. Drugs	22%
5. Physical exercise	21%
6. Watching little children	19%
7. Reading a poem or novel	18%
8. Your own creative work	18%
9. Prayer	16%
10. Sexual love making	14%
11. Looking at a painting	10%
12. Being alone in church	8%
13. Attending church service	7%
14. Reading the Bible	7%
15. Others (meditation, theater, writing, my own poetry, dreaming, etc.)	33%

*Students could endorse as many or as few of the 15 events on the list as they wished.
SOURCE: Adapted from Keutzer, 1978, p. 78.

than were those who were less appreciative of wilderness (Shin, 1993, p. 252).

B-cognition is not a perfect state in which people live happily forever after. Although self-actualizing people are more capable than ordinary people of B-cognizing, they do not live in this state continuously (Maslow, 1962, pp. 109–110). Continual existence in such a passive and noninterfering state would prove fatal, because survival often demands action. The person who appreciates the beauty of the tiger without taking safety precautions may not survive the experience. As Maslow put it, "The demands of self-actualization may necessitate killing the tiger, even though B-cognition of the tiger is against killing the tiger" (1962, p. 111). In this example, self-actualization demands D-cognition, or the arousal of safety needs, as well as B-cognition. In a broader sense, the actualization process involves conflict, struggle, uncertainty, guilt, and regret, as well as bliss and pleasure (Maslow, 1962, p. 111).

Another danger associated with B-cognizing is indiscriminate acceptance of others, "because every person, seen from the viewpoint of his own Being exclusively, is seen as perfect in his own kind. Evaluation, condemnation, . . . criticism, comparison [with others] are all then inapplicable and beside the point" (Maslow, 1962, p. 115). Yet there are times when people can be too tolerant of others. In Maslow's view, people must also accept responsibility for fostering growth in others by setting limits for them, by disciplining them, and by deliberately being the frustrater. Parents and teachers are confronted continuously by this painful dilemma (Maslow, 1962, p. 112). A related danger is that people may misinterpret the B-cognizer's failure to evaluate and criticize as a lack of love, concern, and compassion. If, as a consequence, they come to perceive others as bad, or less deserving of their trust and respect, their growth may be retarded (Maslow, 1962, p. 113).

Peak Experiences and the Concept of Flow

There is a close correspondence between Maslow's peak experience and Csikszentmihalyi's idea of **flow.** Flow refers to optimal experiences of creativity and joy in which the person is so totally absorbed that nothing else seems to matter. People in such a state are so involved in what they are doing that it becomes spontaneous, almost automatic; they stop being aware of themselves as entities separate from the actions they are performing (Csikszentmihalyi, 1990, pp. 3–

6). To capture the essence of the flow experience, Csikszentmihalyi (1990, p. 53) offers several descriptions of it—by a dancer, a rock climber, and a mother sharing a reading experience with her daughter.

> [Dancer] Your concentration is very complete. Your mind isn't wandering, you are not thinking of something else; you are totally involved in what you are doing . . . Your energy is flowing very smoothly. You feel relaxed, comfortable, and energetic.
>
> [Rock climber] You are so involved in what you are doing [that] you aren't thinking of yourself as separate from the immediate activity.
>
> [Mother] Her reading is the one thing that she's really into, and we read together. She reads to me, and I read to her, and that's a time when I sort of lose touch with the rest of the world.

Maslow described individuals in peak experience similarly, as totally absorbed and experiencing a loss of self-consciousness (Maslow, 1962, pp. 70–71).

To attain the highest levels of the flow experience requires maximum mental and physical discipline. The piano virtuoso must undergo years of training to be able to master the intricacies of, say, Chopin. The winner of a marathon must train rigorously for a long period of time to perform her best in the race. According to Csikszentmihalyi, such performers have invariably set clear goals for themselves and work extremely hard to attain them. Flow occurs when their evolving skills finally match the ideal ones embedded in their goals. The result is a graceful, coordinated, effortless performance that is highly enjoyable. Echoing Csikszentmihalyi's view, Maslow maintained that peak experiences usually require tremendous discipline to attain, and that individuals in peak experience feel themselves to be at the zenith of their powers, to be using all of their abilities to the maximum (Maslow, 1962, pp. 77, 99).

Csikszentmihalyi has some interesting ideas about the kind of family life that facilitates movement toward flow experiences in adolescents. He thinks that young people in these special families know what their parents expect of them. In other words, communication between them and their parents is very clear. Thus, the teenagers do not waste their energies on continual arguments over what rules of conduct govern family life; instead, they are free to concentrate their energies on the development and pursuit of their goals. These adolescents also perceive that their parents are truly interested in their present activities; the parents are not unduly preoccupied with whether their offspring will be able to secure well-paying jobs following graduation. Because these young people do not have to worry about meeting parents' success-oriented expectations or demands, they are free to strive for their own goals. These adolescents also know that they have choices, including breaking parental rules, as long as they are prepared to face the consequences. Because they feel that their parents trust them, they can become unselfconsciously involved in a variety of activities that interest them. Finally, their parents are dedicated to providing challenging and increasingly complex opportunities for growth (Csikszentmihalyi, 1990, pp. 88–89).

Maslow espoused a similar view. He believed that personal growth occurs in families in which parents provide a safe, nonthreatening environment and children are encouraged, but not pushed, to try new and challenging activities. He maintained that, ultimately, it is the children themselves who must set their own goals and make their own choices (Maslow, 1962, p. 47).

Finally, Csikszentmihalyi provides some recommendations to help people overcome the anxieties, depression, and boredom often experienced in this culture. He suggests that individuals have to become more independent of their social environments (other people) by learning to provide rewards for themselves. They need to develop the ability to find enjoyment and purpose in life, regardless of external circumstances. These recommendations are admittedly difficult to implement because they require discipline and drastic changes in people's orientations toward society (Csikszentmihalyi, 1990, p. 16).

According to Csikszentmihalyi, the essence of socialization is to make people dependent on rules, so that society can function and survive. It teaches people to work hard in order to secure good jobs in the future and reap the benefits from them. As key authority figures within society, parents assure their children that, if they develop good habits now, they will be better off as adults. Company presidents tell their employees to have patience and work diligently, and one of these days they will be promoted to the executive ranks. In order to survive in a complex society, it is necessary to delay gratifications to some extent and to work for goals set by society. But, Csikszentmihalyi maintains, people do not have to be puppets jerked about by society. They can learn to be freer of societal constraints and to substitute goals that provide satisfactions and rewards that are under their own control (Csikszentmihalyi, 1990, pp. 16–18).

In Csikszentmihalyi's view, we should concentrate on living fully in the present moment. Maslow agreed that such an orientation is psychologically most healthy (Maslow, 1962, p. 102). We should try to make our lives as enjoyable as we can by establishing clear and increasingly challenging goals for ourselves. For example, to keep a marriage from becoming boring and frustrating, couples can establish both short- and long-range goals. Short-range goals might be taking dance lessons together, planning for a vacation, going on a picnic, or becoming bird-watchers. Long-range goals might include planning to build an ideal home or determining how to provide the best education possible for their children (Csikszentmihalyi, 1990, p. 180). If the workplace is boring, individuals can restructure their environments. For example, a clerk in a hardware store may find it highly monotonous to ring up sales hour after hour. But he can reduce the boredom by making an effort to get to know his customers as individuals, instead of thinking only about the mechanics of the sale. Whether a job provides enjoyment or not depends, in Csikszentmihalyi's view, more on a person's approach to it than on the actual working conditions (Csikszentmihalyi, 1990, p. 161).

Finally, Csikszentmihalyi thinks that people who have frequent flow experiences are more likely to be psychologically healthy. Similarly, Maslow believed that individuals who have frequent peak experiences are more likely to be self-actualizing.

Characteristics of Self-Actualizing People

To discover the distinguishing characteristics of **self-actualizers,** Maslow selected the best specimens of humanity he could find from among his friends and acquaintances and from among various public and historical figures—including Abraham Lincoln in his later years, Thomas Jefferson, Albert Einstein, Eleanor Roosevelt, Jane Addams, William James, Albert Schweitzer, Aldous Huxley, and Spinoza. He selected these individuals for intensive study because they all showed an absence of neurosis, psychopathic personality, or psychosis and the presence of self-actualization tendencies. He admitted that his data were impressionistic and did not meet conventional scientific reliability, validity, and sampling standards, but he felt the problem of psychological health was so important that he was compelled to present this evidence for its heuristic value (Maslow, 1970a, pp. 149–152).

After extensive analysis of these individuals' lives, Maslow concluded that actualizers have a more efficient perception of reality than do nonactualizers. They are more capable than are nonactualizers of perceiving the truth in many different situations and of detecting dishonesty and fakery in others, and they are less guided in their judgments by stereotypes and prejudices (Maslow, 1970a, pp. 153–154). Actualizers show a greater acceptance of themselves, others, and nature than do nonactualizers. They recognize their own and others' shortcomings, but they do not feel excessively guilty or anxious about them. Instead, they tend to deal with them stoically, in the same way that we accept the workings of nature. Maslow also found that actualizers tend to be hearty in their appetites and to enjoy themselves without regret, shame, or apology (Maslow, 1970a, p. 156). They sleep well and enjoy sex without unnecessary inhibitions. They are not ashamed of their biological functioning—urination, defecation, menstruation, pregnancy, and growing older—which they accept as part of reality (Maslow, 1970a, p. 156).

Actualizing people are more problem-centered than are nonactualizers, more concerned with undertaking tasks that will benefit others, less introspective, and more task-oriented. Nonactualizers tend to be very concerned with themselves and are characterized by feelings of inferiority (Maslow, 1970a, pp. 159–160). Actualizers tend to resist enculturation, to be "ruled by the laws of their own character rather than by the rules of society" (Maslow, 1970a, p. 174). They show neither excessive rejection nor uncritical acceptance of society's rules, but tend to be detached from the culture. They can yield to folkways perceived by them as harmless, yet react strongly against injustices. In general, they "show what might be called a calm, long-time concern with culture improvement that seems . . . to imply an acceptance to slowness of change along with the unquestioned desirability and necessity of such change" (Maslow, 1970a, p. 172).

Actualizers, according to Maslow, possess a democratic character structure. Compared to nonactualizers, they are less likely to focus attention on race, creed, sex, religious affiliation, educational level, or social class. Although they tend to be more creative than their more average counterparts, they do not consider themselves superior in all respects. They acknowledge their own limitations and can ask for help in areas in which they lack expertise. They honestly respect others and can be genuinely humble before people who can teach them something they do not know. Although they tend to select elite individuals for their friends, that choice is made on the basis of talent and ability, not birth, race, sex, family, age, fame, or power (Maslow, 1970a, pp. 167–168).

Actualizers do have their weaknesses. They "can be boring, stubborn, [and] irritating. They are by no means free from . . . superficial vanity, pride, partiality to their own productions, family, friends, and children. Temper outbursts are not rare" (Maslow, 1970a, p. 175). They can also show extraordinary ruthlessness; for example, they may reject a friend totally and irrevocably if they find he or she has been dishonest with them. They may show behavior and use language that is shocking and insulting. In brief, they are as capable as any other human being of displaying injurious and primitive behavior on occasion.

PERSONALITY DEVELOPMENT

Maslow posited a universal stage-emergent theory of personal development, in which the individual must satisfy, at least to a certain extent, the lower needs before higher ones can become operative. The emergence or nonemergence of the stages depends to a considerable degree on the environment. Environments that threaten the individual and do not allow for the satisfaction of basic needs are detrimental to growth, whereas environments that are supportive and provide for the gratification of these needs promote growth toward self-actualization. In Maslow's view, environment is crucial in the early stages of development when people are struggling to gratify basic needs. The needs for safety, love, and belongingness all depend on the cooperation of other people for gratification. Later on, as the higher needs emerge, people become less dependent on the environment and on rewards or approval from others. They rely increasingly on their own inner experiences to guide behavior—their inner nature, capacities, potentialities, talents, and creative impulses (Maslow, 1962, p. 32). In support for Maslow's view, Bordages (1989) has shown that self-actualizing individuals behave independently of the expectations and demands of others. They rely heavily on their own abilities and judgments in solving problems.

> The techniques of repeatedly acquiring from the outside world satisfactions of motivational deficiencies are much less needed. Associative learning [or simple conditioning] . . . give[s] way more to perceptual learning, to the increase of insight and understanding, to knowledge of self and to the steady growth of personality. . . . Change becomes much less an acquisition of habits or associations one by one, and much more a total change of the total person. . . . This kind of character-change learning means changing a very complex, highly integrated, holistic organism, which in turn means that many impacts will make no change at all because more and more such impacts will be rejected as the person becomes more stable and more autonomous. (Maslow, 1962, p. 36)

With the advent of persistent perceptual learning, people are free to make their own spontaneous choices—not by relying on the values and expectations of others, but by listening to their inner nature.

ASSESSMENT TECHNIQUES

Identifying Self-Actualizers

Maslow utilized a variety of research techniques in an attempt to identify self-actualizing individuals. He began by employing a selection technique called *iteration* (Maslow, 1970a, p. 151). Starting with his general belief concerning the meaning of self-actualization, he collated it with other, popularly used definitions and, by the systematic elimination of logical inconsistencies among them, arrived at a common definition. He then used this definition to divide a group of 3000 college students into actualizers and nonactualizers. The same students were then examined in case-study fashion—using the Rorschach Test, Murray's Thematic Apperception Test, free association, and in-depth interviews—to determine whether they possessed the characteristics of actualizers.

In an ongoing effort to validate the concept of self-actualization empirically, the definition was then changed and corrected, as necessary, in light of the findings. Then the original subject pool was reselected on the basis of the new definition, and the retainees were restudied using the same clinical procedures. On the basis of these new data, the self-actualization definition was again revised, and the new definition was used to reselect subjects from the remaining subject pool for further clinical study, and so on, until a precise identification of actualizers and nonactualizers was obtained. As you might expect, this iterative procedure greatly reduced the number of individuals who met the stringent definition of self-actualization within the original sample of 3000. Maslow concluded that perhaps young people had not had sufficient time and experience to develop the characteristics associated with actualization, and that it might be more useful to study middle-aged and older people.

As his next pool of potential actualizers, Maslow used his personal friends and acquaintances and a number of public and historical figures—among them, Lincoln, Jefferson, Eleanor Roosevelt, Einstein, Schweitzer, Spinoza, G. W. Carver, Eugene V. Debs, Pablo

Casals, Adlai Stevenson, George Washington, Robert Benchley, and Camille Pissarro. Maslow turned to historical figures because he found that biographical sources provided sufficient information about them to permit meaningful conclusions, whereas it was nearly impossible to obtain such information about living figures, many of whom, when informed of the purpose of his research, "became self-conscious, froze up, laughed off the whole effort, or broke off the relationship" (Maslow, 1970a, p. 151). The results of his investigations revealed that, although more older people than college students were self-actualized, the numbers remained very small.

Maslow's assessment procedures are fraught with ambiguities and imprecisions. We are not certain, for example, how the various tests used in the interviews were administered or scored, what kinds of free associations led Maslow to conclude that his subjects were or were not actualized, or how he decided that some of his historical figures were self-actualized and others were not. Most important, since Maslow chose for study people he greatly admired, it is distinctly possible that his definition of self-actualization was simply a reflection of his own personal value system.

The Personal Orientation Inventory

Although Maslow's theory was initially plagued by methodological problems that prevented adequate research, investigation of certain aspects of the theory has been facilitated by the construction of a more reliable and valid measure of self-actualization called the **Personal Orientation Inventory (POI)** (Shostrom, 1963). The POI is a self-report questionnaire consisting of 150 forced-choice items that purportedly reflect the values and behavior of major importance in the development of a self-actualizing person. Subjects are asked to select the one statement in each of the 150 pairs that is most true of themselves. These responses are then scored on two major scales—time competence (effective use of time) and inner direction (the extent to which individuals depend on themselves or on others in making judgments)—and ten subscales. The subscales are: self-actualizing values, existentiality, feeling reactivity, spontaneity, self-regard, self-acceptance, nature of man, synergy, acceptance of aggression, and capacity for intimate contact. Sample items and scoring for the two major scales and ten subsidiary scales are presented in Table 12.2.

TABLE 12.2 Sample items from Shostrom's Personal Orientation Inventory*

Time competence

1. a. I strive always to predict what will happen in the future.
   b. **I do not feel it necessary always to predict what will happen in the future.**
2. a. I prefer to save good things for future use.
   b. **I prefer to use good things now.**
3. a. I worry about the future.
   b. **I do not worry about the future.**
4. a. **It is important to me how I live in the here and now.**
   b. It is of little importance to me how I live in the here and now.

Inner direction

1. a. My moral values are dictated by society.
   b. **My moral values are self-determined.**
2. a. I feel guilty when I am selfish.
   b. **I don't feel guilty when I am selfish.**
3. a. I am bound by the principle of fairness.
   b. **I am not absolutely bound by the principle of fairness.**

Self-actualizing values

1. a. **I often make my decisions spontaneously.**
   b. I seldom make my decisions spontaneously.
2. a. **It is possible to live life in terms of what I want to do.**
   b. It is not possible to live life in terms of what I want to do.

Existentiality

1. a. I feel I must always tell the truth.
   b. **I do not always tell the truth.**

Feeling reactivity

1. a. I live by values which are in agreement with others.
   b. **I live by values which are primarily based on my own feelings.**

Spontaneity

1. a. I must justify my actions in the pursuit of my own interests.
   b. **I need not justify my actions in the pursuit of my own interests.**

Self-regard

1. a. It is important that others accept my point of view.
   b. **It is not necessary for others to accept my point of view.**

Self-acceptance

1. a. **I try to be sincere but I sometimes fail.**
   b. I try to be sincere and I am sincere.

TABLE 12.2   (continued)

Nature of man

1. **a. I believe that man is essentially good and can be trusted.**
    b. I believe that man is essentially evil and cannot be trusted.

Synergy

1. **a. For me, work and play are the same.**
    b. For me, work and play are opposites.

Acceptance of aggression

1. **a. I find some people who are stupid and uninteresting.**
    b. I never find any people who are stupid and uninteresting.

Capacity for intimate contact

1. a. I am afraid to be tender.
    b. I am not afraid to be tender.

*A person who answers the items by choosing the bold-faced alternatives is more self-actualizing than is a person who does not.
SOURCE: Adapted from Shostrom, 1963.

High scores on the time-competence scale indicate that the respondents are living in the present. Self-actualizing individuals are considered to live most fully in the here and now and to relate the past and future to current experience in a meaningful way. They do not dwell on the past or the future, but use the past to illuminate current problems and future aspirations and to help make decisions. On the second major scale, self-actualizing respondents are essentially inner-directed, but they recognize to a certain degree the need to be sensitive to other people's approval and affection. High scores for self-actualizing values suggest that respondents hold and practice the values of self-actualizing people. High scores on existentiality indicate an ability to hold and practice self-actualizing values flexibly; low scores indicate that respondents hold their values rigidly and compulsively. High scores on the remaining dimensions indicate that respondents are sensitive to their own needs, act spontaneously, consider themselves worthwhile, accept their weaknesses and like themselves in spite of these deficiencies, believe that human beings are essentially good, can see that the opposites of life are related, can accept their feelings of anger as natural, and can develop meaningful relationships with other human beings.

Much of the early work with the POI was concerned with establishing its reliability and validity as a research instrument. Test/

retest reliabilities for various samples are satisfactory, although the coefficients for certain subscales have been low to moderate in certain studies (Ilardi & May, 1968).

In terms of validity, a number of studies show that the measure can be used to distinguish between groups in society that we would ordinarily consider to differ in their actualization levels. For example, two studies have shown that groups of psychiatric patients scored lower (were less self-actualized) on virtually all the POI scales than were groups of people judged by experienced clinical psychologists to be self-actualized (Fox, Knapp, & Michael, 1968). In another study, all scales of the POI discriminated among groups of alcoholic wives, nonalcoholic wives, and clinically judged self-actualizers in the expected way. A group of normal subjects also scored higher on many of the POI scales than did the alcoholic wives (Zaccaria & Weir, 1967). In general, these studies and others indicate that POI is a valid discriminator between normal and abnormal groups.

A large number of studies indicate that the POI can be utilized effectively to measure changes in self-actualization following sensitivity training and encounter-group experiences. Dosamantes-Alperson and Merrill (1980), for example, administered the POI to groups of people before and after they participated in a number of group-therapy sessions. Control groups (a ballet class and a waiting-list group drawn from the same population as the therapy groups) also filled out the POI at the same time, but received no therapeutic experiences. The results indicated that, in comparison to the controls, participants in the therapy sessions became more self-actualizing; that is, they became more inner-directed, spontaneous, and self-accepting. Another investigation also found changes in POI scores on the two major scales and most of the subscales in the direction of greater self-actualization following counseling that emphasized expression of feelings and the need to be sensitive to the desires of others, as compared to a variety of control groups who received no counseling (Pearson, 1966).

Despite these generally positive results, the POI does have methodological flaws. A primary, recurring problem is that subjects can deliberately fake their responses in ways designed to elicit positive impressions from others. That is, subjects who are familiar with the **humanistic psychology** literature can deliberately present themselves as actualized when in fact they are not. Even though the POI has a built-in lie-detection scale to uncover such dissimulation, its usefulness as a research instrument would be weakened if it could be shown that sizable numbers of subjects do indeed fake their responses. The percentage of such subjects in various populations has yet to be determined, but a reasonable conclusion would be that the instrument can be used primarily with naive populations.

Another problem is that subjects generally dislike responding to forced-choice questionnaires, because such instruments do not allow them to present their feelings and opinions fully and accurately. As with most measures of personality, moreover, the POI cannot assess people's traits in interaction with specific situations. One POI item, for example, is:

a. I can cope with the ups and downs of life.
b. I cannot cope with the ups and downs of life.

Perhaps the subject can cope with the downs (or failures) in life when they involve schoolwork but not when they involve the loss of a close friend. Maybe the person copes well with success in school but reacts poorly to praise from teachers or friends. The point is that a number of questions on the POI do not assess people's reactions in specific situations.

Although the many investigations based on the POI have established its reliability and validity (Knapp, 1976), attempts to extend and refine concepts of actualization have led to development of the **Personal Orientation Dimensions** (POD) (Shostrom, 1975; 1977). Many of the scales in this new measure are conceptually similar to those in the POI, although a few are not. Unfortunately, research with the POD shows that it is psychometrically inferior to the POI (Forest & Sciz, 1981; Hattie, Hancock, & Brereton, 1984). Deficiencies of the POD cited in this research include: (1) its development without a theoretical rationale for the addition of new scales to assess self-actualization; (2) the fact that it has 260 items, which makes it lengthier and more difficult to administer than the POI; and (3) its lack of a strong research base. Thus, it appears that researchers will continue to use the POI until they are convinced by subsequent research that the POD has more adequate psychometric properties.

THEORY'S IMPLICATIONS FOR THERAPY

In Maslow's view, neurotics are people who have been prevented and who have prevented themselves from attaining gratification of their basic needs, and thus have been precluded from moving toward the ultimate goal of self-actualization. They feel threatened and insecure and have little self-respect or self-esteem. Because gratification of these basic needs can occur only through contact with other people, it follows that therapy must be interpersonal in nature (Maslow, 1970a, p. 242).

Maslow likened the psychotherapeutic relationship between therapist and client to a relationship between friends. The therapy situation must involve mutual frankness, trust, honesty, and lack of defensiveness. It should also allow for the expression of a healthy amount of childishness and silliness (Maslow, 1970a, p. 249). This is only possible when the relationship is nonthreatening and supportive. In such a democratic context, the therapist should provide the client with the respect, love, and feelings of belongingness he or she must have in order to grow. In other words, the therapist must act to gratify the client's basic need deficiencies. But effective therapy must go beyond this point. The therapeutic relationship should encourage not only the therapist's giving of love to the client but also the client's expression of love and affection toward the therapist and others (Maslow, 1970a, p. 250). More generally, the client should be encouraged to display those values associated with positive growth—to open up to the world and learn to understand more about its complex nature.

Maslow realized that a warm, supportive therapeutic approach was unworkable with some clients, particularly those with chronic, stabilized neuroses that involve deep mistrust and hostility toward others (Maslow, 1970a, p. 251). He believed that, under those conditions, a depth analysis in the Freudian tradition might be more useful. In such an analysis, clients would work through their problems both cognitively *and* emotionally, as a means of achieving change and self-improvement.

EVALUATIVE COMMENTS

We now evaluate the scientific worth of Maslow's position in terms of our six criteria.

Comprehensiveness   Maslow's theory is a pioneering and creative effort aimed at moving personality psychology away from an exclusive concern with psychopathology and toward a more positive and optimistic view of people and their potential creativeness. His theory can be considered comprehensive in the sense that it incorporates much of the Freudian model of pathology and, in addition, addresses itself to the issue of positive growth; but, technically speaking, its focus is primarily and explicitly on the latter rather than the former. In this sense, the theory is not quite as comprehensive as it appears at first. Thus, Maslow's theory is somewhat limited both in the range and diversity of phenomena it explicitly encompasses and in the explanatory system it uses to account for these events.

Precision and testability   Maslow's theory is not very precise and, as a result, is difficult to test properly. Take, for example, his hierarchical scheme of human motivation, in which the emergence of basic needs from most to least potent is presumed to follow their successive gratification. Yet some people are willing to suffer hunger and thirst, and eventually even to die, for values Maslow assumed to be less potent than physiological needs. Although he recognized this problem, his theory does not account for the exceptions.

The theory also lacks precision regarding the amount of gratification the individual must experience before the next higher need will emerge. Maslow maintained that most people's basic needs are partially satisfied and partially dissatisfied at the same time. Thus, a given need will not be completely gratified before the next one emerges. Instead, Maslow posited a gradual emergence of higher needs as lower needs become increasingly gratified. For example, if a lower need is 10% gratified, the next higher need may not emerge. But if the lower need is 25% gratified, then the higher need may emerge at 5% of potency; if the lower need is 50% gratified, there may be a 25% emergence; and so on (Maslow, 1970a, pp. 53–54).

Adequate definition of self-actualization and a number of other terms (purposefulness, inner requiredness, and good and bad situations) remains a major problem with the theory.

Parsimony   Maslow's theory fails to meet the parsimony criterion. The motivational deficiency scheme he used to account for various behaviors is too simplistic to account adequately for the phenomena within its domain. Moreover, it does not spell out precisely the situational variables that control the occurrence, maintenance, and modification of self-actualization phenomena (Lethbridge, 1986, p. 90).

Empirical validity   Without adequate measures of the major constructs in Maslow's theory, tests of its empirical validity are impossible. As we have seen, researchers have constructed an adequate measure of actualization but, when it has been used to test the theory, the research results have not been consistently supportive. For example, Mathes (1978) found no evidence for Maslow's hypothesis that self-actualizers are more creative than nonactualizers. Similarly, Ryckman, Robbins, Thornton, Gold, and Kuehnel (1985), using two independent samples of college undergraduates, could find no support for his hypothesis that actualizers tend to be physically strong, fit people. Despite these negative findings, research interest in Maslow's theory continues to grow, as evidenced by the construction of new individual-difference measures of peak experiences (Mathes & Zevon, 1982) and basic needs (Haymes & Green, 1982).

Heuristic value   Despite its many limitations, Maslow's theory has been provocative and has stimulated the thinking of many investigators in a variety of disciplines. Not only has he encouraged theorists and researchers to consider the healthy side of human nature, but he has also forced some of them to reconsider their own myopic view of science and its limitations for understanding human functioning. Specifically, he castigated them for their "inevitable stress on elegance, polish, technique, and apparatus [that] has, as a frequent consequence, a playing down of meaningfulness, vitality, and significance of a problem and of creativeness in general" (Maslow, 1970a, p. 11). As a result, he has persuaded some of them to think of science as an enterprise in which people ask significant questions and then adopt techniques to help answer them, rather than an enterprise in which they use sophisticated techniques to study relatively unimportant problems.

Applied value   Maslow's theory is also very strong in the applied area. His formulations have had a decided impact on pastoral and educational counseling programs. In addition, many business managers have embraced Maslow's idea that humane, enlightened companies have a responsibility to help their employees move toward self-actualization and that helping them reach that goal will also prove financially profitable. As a result, they have endorsed and implemented programs of shared decision making, mutual trust, caring, and cooperation among people at all levels of the company (Maslow, 1987, p. 257).

DISCUSSION QUESTIONS

1. What are the implications for personality development of Maslow's assumption that human nature is good or, at the very least, neutral?

2. Is it possible, in your opinion, to discover a universal set of ethical principles? What principles guide your behavior? Where did they originate?
3. What are some of the limitations of Maslow's proposed hierarchy of needs?
4. Do you agree with Maslow that children need limits on their behavior? Why?
5. Have you experienced B-love? How could you be certain?
6. What is the need for cognitive understanding? In what ways can this need be satisfied?
7. Maslow maintained that we not only fear failure but often are afraid to be successful. Why did he hold such a belief? What great work are you planning in your own life? Are you satisfied with your progress toward your goals?
8. What are some of the dangers associated with B-cognition states?
9. In terms of the self-actualization hierarchy, how would you characterize yourself?
10. List and discuss the strengths and weaknesses of self-actualizing people.

GLOSSARY

B-cognition   State of experiencing that is nonjudgmental and self-validating.

B-love   A mature form of love in which the person is more concerned with giving love to benefit others than in receiving love from others to gratify his or her needs; also known as being-love.

D-cognition   State of experiencing that involves judgments of approval and disapproval.

D-love   A selfish love in which the individual is more concerned with receiving love and gratifying his or her needs than with giving love to another; also known as deficiency-love.

deficiency needs   Basic needs that must be gratified to a large extent before an individual can progress toward self-actualization.

desacralizing attitude   Tendency to be disrespectful, cynical, and mistrustful; it causes the perceiver to overlook the virtues and strengths of the perceived.

flow   Totally absorbing experience of creativity and joy highly similar to a peak experience.

growth needs   Higher needs that may emerge once the basic needs have been satisfied; also known as meta needs.

humanistic biology View that the basic nature of human beings is potentially good and capable of pushing people in the direction of self-realization if the right social conditions prevail.

humanistic psychology Approach to psychology that is primarily concerned with helping individuals to reach their maximum and that emphasizes, and tries to foster, the dignity and worth of each human being.

Jonah complex Fear that exercising our abilities to the maximum will bring with it responsibilities and duties that we will be unable to handle; an unwillingness to sacrifice current safety and security for the unknown.

peak experience Intense, mystical experience in which an individual exists in a temporary state of joy and wonderment.

Personal Orientation Dimensions (POD) Test designed to measure self-actualization in adolescents and adults in a more reliable and valid way than the earlier Personal Orientation Inventory.

Personal Orientation Inventory (POI) Test designed to measure an individual's self-actualizing tendencies.

self-actualization Process whereby the healthy development of people's abilities enables them to fulfill their own true natures.

self-actualizers Individuals who have gratified their basic needs and developed their potentialities to the point that they can be considered healthy, fully functioning human beings.

SUGGESTED READINGS

Goble, F. (1970). *The third force: The psychology of Abraham Maslow*. New York: Pocket Books.

Maslow, A. H. (1943). A theory of human motivation. *Psychological Review, 50,* 370–396.

Maslow, A. H. (1962). *Toward a psychology of being*. New York: Van Nostrand.

Maslow, A. H. (1971). *The farther reaches of human nature*. New York: Viking Press.

Maslow, A. H. (1987). *Motivation and personality* (3rd ed.). New York: Harper & Row.

REFERENCES

Bordages, J. W. (1989). Self-actualization and personal autonomy. *Psychological Reports, 64,* 1263–1266.

Crawford, M., & Marecek, J. (1989). Psychology reconstructs the female: 1968–1988. *Psychology of Women Quarterly, 13,* 147–165.

Csikszentmihalyi, M. (1990). *Flow: The psychology of optimal experience.* New York: Harper & Row.

Dietch, J. (1978). Love, sex roles, and psychological health. *Journal of Personality Assessment, 42,* 626–634.

Dosamantes-Alperson, E., & Merrill, N. (1980). Growth effects of experiential movement psychotherapy. *Psychotherapy: Theory, Research and Practice, 17,* 63–68.

Forest, J., & Sciz, G. (1981). A review of the Personal Orientation Dimension Inventory. *Journal of Personality Assessment, 45,* 433–435.

Fox, J., Knapp, R. R., & Michael, W. B. (1968). Assessment of self-actualization of psychiatric patients: Validity of the Personal Orientation Inventory. *Educational and Psychological Measurement, 28,* 565–569.

Hattie, J., Hancock, P., & Brereton, K. (1984). The relationship between two measures of self-actualization. *Journal of Personality Assessment, 48,* 17–25.

Haymes, M., & Green, L. (1982). The assessment of motivation within Maslow's framework. *Journal of Research in Personality, 16,* 179–192.

Hoffman, E. (1988). *The right to be human: A biography of Abraham Maslow.* New York: St. Martin's Press.

Hoffman, L. W. (1974). Fear of success in males and females: 1965–1971. *Journal of Consulting and Clinical Psychology, 24,* 353–358.

Hyland, M. E. (1989). There is no motive to avoid success: The compromise explanation for success-avoiding behavior. *Journal of Personality, 57,* 665–693.

Ilardi, R. L., & May, W. T. (1968). A reliability study of Shostrom's Personal Orientation Inventory. *Journal of Humanistic Psychology, 8,* 68–72.

Keutzer, C. S. (1978). Whatever turns you on: Triggers to transcendent experiences. *Journal of Humanistic Psychology, 18,* 77–80.

Knapp, R. R. (1976). *Handbook for the Personal Orientation Inventory.* San Diego: EdITS/Educational and Industrial Testing Service.

Lethbridge, D. (1986). A Marxist theory of self-actualization. *Journal of Humanistic Psychology, 26,* 84–153.

Maslow, A. H. (1962). *Toward a psychology of being.* New York: Van Nostrand.

Maslow, A. H. (1970a). *Motivation and personality* (2nd ed.). New York: Harper & Row.

Maslow, A. H. (1970b). *Religions, values, and peak-experiences.* New York: Viking Press.

Maslow, A. H. (1971). *The farther reaches of human nature.* New York: Viking Press.

Maslow, A. H. (1987). *Motivation and personality* (3rd ed.). New York: Harper & Row.

Mathes, E. W. (1978). Self-actualization, metavalues, and creativity. *Psychological Reports, 43,* 215–222.

Mathes, E. W., & Zevon, M. A. (1982). Peak experience tendencies: Scale development and theory testing. *Journal of Humanistic Psychology, 22,* 92–108.

Pearson, O. (1966). *Effects of group guidance upon college adjustment.* Unpublished doctoral dissertation, University of Kentucky, Lexington.

Piedmont, R. L. (1988). An interactional model of achievement motivation and fear of success. *Sex Roles, 19,* 467–490.

Ryckman, R. M., Robbins, M. A., Thornton, B., Gold, J. A., & Kuehnel, R. H. (1985). Physical self-efficacy and actualization. *Journal of Research in Personality, 19,* 288–298.

Shin, W. S. (1993). Self-actualization and wilderness attitudes: A replication. *Journal of Social Behavior and Personality, 8,* 241–256.

Shostrom, E. L. (1963). *Personal Orientation Inventory.* San Diego: EdITS/Educational and Industrial Testing Service.

Shostrom, E. L. (1975). *Personal Orientation Dimensions.* San Diego: EdITS/Educational and Industrial Testing Service.

Shostrom, E. L. (1977). *Manual for the Personal Orientation Dimensions.* San Diego: EdITS/Educational and Industrial Testing Service.

Wilson, C. (1972). *New pathways in psychology.* London: Gollancz.

Zaccaria, J. S., & Weir, W. R. (1967). A comparison of alcoholics and selected samples of nonalcoholics in terms of a positive concept of mental health. *Journal of Social Psychology, 71,* 151–157.

CHAPTER 13

Rogers's Person-Centered Theory

BIOGRAPHICAL SKETCH

Carl Ransom Rogers was born in 1902 in Oak Park, Illinois, a suburb of Chicago; he was the fourth in a family of six children. His father was a successful civil engineer and contractor. Rogers was raised in a home marked by close, warm family relationships but also by strict and uncompromising religious principles. His parents controlled his behavior and would allow no alcoholic beverages, no dancing, no card playing or theatergoing, and very little contact with other people. They extolled the virtues of the Protestant ethic: hard work, responsibility for one's actions, and the importance of personal success. Rogers reported that "even carbonated beverages had a faintly sinful aroma, and I remember my slight feeling of wickedness when I had my first bottle of 'pop'" (Rogers, 1961, p. 5). His wife, who was his childhood sweetheart, remembers him as a "shy, sensitive, and unsocial boy who preferred to live in his books and his dream world rather than encounter the rough [and] tumble of the play yard or enter into competitive sports" (H. E. Rogers, 1965, p. 94).

When he was 12, his parents bought a farm a short distance from Chicago, and Rogers spent his adolescence there. His father encouraged his sons to raise animals for profit, and Rogers reared chickens, lambs, pigs, and calves. The venture aroused an interest in scientific agriculture and the application of scientific methods to farming. In retrospect, Rogers concluded that the experience had taught him a healthy respect for science as a means of solving problems. He entered the University of Wisconsin and chose scientific agriculture as his field of study. Shortly afterward, his professional goals shifted dramatically, as a result of some emotion-laden experiences at a student religious conference. Specifically, Rogers was chosen as one of only a dozen students from the United States to attend a World Student Christian Federation conference in Peking, China. On the trip, he was forced to modify drastically his thinking about his strict, family-based religious beliefs, because of his associations with this small group of highly intelligent and creative young people. Rogers came to recognize that it was possible for other sincere and honest people to have religious beliefs that differed from his own. He wrote to his parents about his new feelings and ideas, and these letters undoubtedly deeply distressed and even scandalized them. Also, during this trip, Rogers corresponded with his childhood sweetheart, Helen, and the relationship became increasingly intimate. Upon his return to Wisconsin, Rogers bought his first car and frequently drove 25 miles over rough roads in order to see her. In time, his feelings toward her were reciprocated. Finally, the day arrived when, in his own words, "the most wonderful miracle in the world took place," when she told him she loved him too. They were married two months after his graduation from the University of Wisconsin. They piled all of their worldly possessions into a used car that Rogers bought for $450 and set out for New York City, where he had enrolled in the Union Theological Seminary (Thorne, 1992, pp. 4–6).

At the seminary, he and a group of other students decided they were being unilaterally presented with ideas by their instructors and were not being given an opportunity to explore their own personal doubts and questions. Accordingly, they petitioned the administration for a seminar without a formal instructor. To their surprise, the request was granted. Rogers found the seminar most gratifying; he later said that, as a result of the experience, he thought himself right out of religious work.

Rogers had taken some courses in psychology and enjoyed them, and he decided to enter that field. He began his studies at Columbia University, across the street from the seminary. At the end of his clinical internship, even though he had not completed his doctorate, Rogers felt he had to have a job to support his growing family. He took a position as a psychologist in the Child Study Department of the Society for the Prevention of Cruelty to Children in Rochester,

New York, and completed his doctorate in 1928. For Rogers, the 12 years spent at Rochester were valuable ones. During most of that time, he was immersed in practical work—the diagnosis and treatment of delinquent and disadvantaged children. His unique non-directive, or client-centered, approach to therapy evolved during this period, which culminated in a book entitled *The Clinical Treatment of the Problem Child* (1939). In 1940, he accepted an academic position as a full professor at Ohio State University, where he began to attract capable students, to conduct research on his theory, and to achieve international recognition. *Counseling and Psychotherapy* (1942), a book designed to provide therapists with procedures he felt would engender constructive changes in their clients, was written during this time.

In 1944, Rogers was given an opportunity to establish a counseling center at the University of Chicago. He then wrote *Client-Centered Therapy* (1951), in which he laid out the theory that underlies his approach to understanding human relationships. A decade later he published *On Becoming a Person* (1961), a collection of papers on a variety of issues related to this basic approach to understanding personal growth.

In 1957, Rogers returned to the University of Wisconsin. He recalls that his experiences there were generally unpleasant, as he became aware of the restrictions under which graduate students were forced to work. Rogers called for massive reform in the graduate program; he argued that students have within themselves the potential for learning and development but that this potential can be realized only when they are provided with freedom and a supportive environment (Rogers, 1968). Shortly after he released the reasons for his disagreement with current educational policies, he resigned from the department.

In 1963, Rogers became a member of the Western Behavioral Sciences Institute in La Jolla, California. In 1968, he left the institute to help form the Center for the Studies of the Person in La Jolla.

In 1967, he wrote *Person to Person: The Problem of Being Human* in collaboration with Barry Stevens. This book was followed by *Freedom to Learn* (1969), *Carl Rogers on Encounter Groups* (1970), *Becoming Partners: Marriage and Its Alternatives* (1972), *Carl Rogers on Personal Power* (1977), *A Way of Being* (1980), and *Freedom to Learn for the 80s* (1983). In the book on personal power, Rogers attempted to illustrate the revolutionary impact of his person-centered approach on psychotherapy, family life, education, administration, and politics. He also discussed the implications of his approach for the emergence of a new type of self-empowered person, who would spearhead the revolution in human relationships that Rogers saw occurring.

Rogers received many honors and awards from his professional colleagues. He served as president of the American Psychological Association in 1946–1947. In 1956, he received the first Distinguished Scientific Contribution Award presented by the American Psychological Association, which also honored him with its Distinguished Professional Contribution Award in 1972.

Carl Rogers died of a heart attack in La Jolla on February 4, 1987, at the age of 85. His last few years were spent productively: he attended numerous international workshops, at which he demonstrated to psychologists and other mental health workers, educators, and politicians how various concepts and propositions from his person-centered approach could be utilized to ease world tensions and promote peace.

CONCEPTS AND PRINCIPLES

The Fundamental Perspective: The Person's Experiences as the Ultimate Authority

Rogers's psychology starts and ends with the subjective experiences of the individual. In his view, the subjective experiencing of reality serves as the basis for all the individual's judgments and behavior. It is this phenomenological, inner reality, rather than external, objective reality, that plays the key role in determining the person's behavior.

Inner experience includes everything that is occurring within the organism at a particular moment. All this experience, conscious and unconscious, is said to comprise the person's phenomenal field. Conscious experience, or awareness, is the aspect of the phenomenal field that can be symbolized—that is, verbalized or imagined. Unconscious experience, in contrast, is experience that cannot be verbalized or imagined by the person. Healthy individuals, in Rogers's view, are those who can symbolize their experiences accurately and completely; unhealthy people distort or repress their experiences and are unable to symbolize them accurately and sense them fully.

The Master Motive: Self-Actualizing Tendency

Within each of us, according to Rogers, is an innate motivation called the self-actualizing tendency—an active, controlling drive toward fulfillment of our potentials that enables us to maintain and enhance ourselves.

Rogers based this concept primarily on his varied and prolonged experience with troubled individuals in therapy. He noticed in them

> a growth tendency, a drive toward self-actualization. . . . It is the urge which is evident in all organic and human life—to expand, extend, become autonomous, develop, mature. . . . This tendency may become deeply buried under layer after layer of encrusted psychological defenses . . . but it is my belief that it exists in every individual, and awaits only the proper conditions to be released and expressed. (Rogers, 1961, p. 35)

In support of this concept, he cited experiments showing that even rats prefer an environment offering more complex stimuli over one offering less complex stimuli. Human beings similarly seek new experiences and avoid environments that are lacking in stimulation. Experiments have shown that, when people are suspended weightless in a soundproof tank of water, they soon experience aversive hallucinations. To Rogers, these studies, together with his clinical experience, suggested that there is a directional tendency in each of us to grow, to seek new and varied experiences.

The actualizing tendency has both a biological and a psychological aspect. The biological aspect includes drives aimed at the satisfaction of basic survival needs—the need for water, food, and air. The psychological aspect involves the development of potentials that make us more worthwhile human beings. In Rogers's judgment, we are all basically good. The actualizing tendency is, thus, selective and directional; it is a constructive tendency. Organisms do not, according to Rogers, develop their capacity for nausea or self-destruction except under the most perverse circumstances (Rogers, 1977, p. 242). Instead, they develop their innate goodness, but only if society acts toward them in a helpful, encouraging way. Although Rogers was clearly optimistic about human nature, he was nevertheless keenly aware that human beings are sometimes immature and antisocial and that they sometimes act out of fear, ignorance, and defensiveness. Such behavior, however, is not in accordance with their basic natures, according to Rogers, but is the result of faulty socialization practices. Thus, society can facilitate or hinder movement toward self-actualization.

PERSONALITY DEVELOPMENT

The Valuing Process in Infants

Rogers maintained that infants perceive their experiences as reality. They operate from an internal frame of reference, unencumbered by the evaluations of others. He also believed that infants interact with their reality in terms of their basic actualizing tendency (Rogers, 1959, p. 222); their behavior is directed toward the goal of satisfying their need for self-actualization as they perceive it. Thus, infants engage in an **organismic valuing process,** in which they use their actualization tendency as a criterion in making judgments about the worth of a given experience. Experiences that help promote actualization are good, or positively valued; experiences that hinder actualization are bad, or negatively valued. In support of this view, Rogers cited the example of an infant who values food when hungry but rejects it when satiated. According to Rogers, infants have a built-in mechanism that allows them to select the diet that, in the long run, enhances their development (Rogers, 1959, p. 210; Rogers & Stevens, 1967, p. 6); in other words, infants know instinctively which foods and experiences are good for them and which are bad.

The investigation most cited by Rogers, Maslow, and others who have attempted to build a psychology on the notion that people instinctively know what is best for them is the Davis (1928) study of infant feeding behavior. Three infants ranging in age from 8 to 10 months were given thorough physical examinations by a medical doctor—including a blood count, urinalysis, and skeletal X-rays—and then given the opportunity to select their own diets from saucers holding a variety of foods and glasses holding a variety of liquids. The choices for a typical meal are shown in Table 13.1. Nurses were present at each feeding but did not offer any food to the infants. If the infants reached or pointed to a food, the nurses were allowed to offer them a spoonful. Two infants remained on such a diet for six months, and the third for one year. At the end of this period, the infants were again given complete physical examinations. The results showed that, in general, the diets selected were optimal and the infants were healthy.

TABLE 13.1   Typical meal served to test for adequacy of self-selection diet

Milk, grade A	Lamb, cooked	Cauliflower, cooked
Milk, lactic	Chicken, cooked	Cabbage, raw
Sea salt	Lettuce, raw	Cabbage, cooked
Rye-Krisp	Potatoes, cooked	Spinach, cooked
Bone marrow, raw	Beets, cooked	Peas, cooked
Bone marrow, cooked	Carrots, raw	Peas, raw
Beef, raw	Carrots, cooked	Cornmeal, cooked
Beef, cooked	Turnips, cooked	

SOURCE: Adapted from Davis, 1928, p. 659.

What is wrong with this study? One possible source of error is the role of the nurses, who could have misjudged random arm waving and reaching as signs of the infants' wanting a particular food. Because the experiment lasted a relatively short time, the long-range impact on development is impossible to assess. It should also be noted that none of the foods offered to the infants was lacking in nutritive value; arguably, the available choices could only promote health. Of course, it would have been unethical to provide infants with nonnutritive food choices, but this does not negate the theoretical shortcoming. Finally, only three infants participated in the study, and so it is clearly unwarranted to generalize these results to all infants in the culture.

A recent review of the research literature with lower animals does not support the notion of specific hungers—that is, the notion that animals tend to select those foods that enable them to compensate for specific nutritional deficiencies (Galef, 1991). Moreover, some studies have shown that animals can be easily trained to eat sweet foods with no nutritional value and to bypass nonsweetened foods with nutritional value (Garcia, Kimeldurf, & Hunt, 1961). Thus, if we could generalize the results of the study by Garcia and his colleagues conducted on rats to the behavior of human beings, we might conclude that humans would have an extremely difficult time getting in touch with their organismic wisdom mechanism (assuming that one existed) in order to make good decisions, because of interference from their learning experiences. Rogers hinted at this problem when he stated that the drive toward self-actualization may be "deeply buried under layer after layer of encrusted psychological defenses" (Rogers, 1961, p. 35). At the very least, then, the process of getting in touch with our innermost feelings would be difficult.

The Valuing Process in Adults

In adults, the valuing process is much more complex than it is in infants. At this point in the developmental process, the adult is making much more complicated judgments about a variety of experiences relating to issues in art, politics, career, ethics, personal relationships, and so forth. Value judgments in these areas often change. A painting we found satisfying last year may be abhorrent to us now. Judgments about friends, acquaintances, politicians, doctors, teachers, clergy, parents, and others do not remain constant. In addition, adults, unlike infants, are exposed to a variety of opinions and come to incorporate them into their value systems. Yet, in Rogers's view, adults, after listening to what others think, must ultimately trust the wisdom of their own bodies if they are to grow constructively. If they can trust themselves fully, he maintained, their feelings and intuitions may be wiser than their thinking or what they have learned from others (Rogers & Stevens, 1967, pp. 15–16).

The Fully Functioning Person

If people are able to utilize their organismic valuing processes fully, they will inevitably begin to experience personal growth and movement toward realization of their potentials. In Rogers's terminology, they will be moving toward becoming **fully functioning persons.** Such individuals have the following characteristics, according to Rogers:

1. *They are open to experience.* Fully functioning people are nondefensive individuals who are open to all their feelings—fear, discouragement, pain, tenderness, courage, and awe. They are fully aware of their experiences and accept them, rather than shutting them out.

2. *They are characterized by existential living.* Fully functioning people live their experiences as they occur in the present, without trying to superimpose preconceived meaning on them. They are open and flexible, deal with the experience as it is, and discover its meaning for themselves.

3. *They trust their organisms.* Fully functioning people do what feels right. This does not mean they are inevitably right in their choices, but rather that they make their own choices, experience the consequences, and correct them if they are less than satisfying.

4. *They are creative.* Creative products and creative living emerge when individuals are open to new experiences, able to trust their own

judgments, and willing to take risks if they feel good about a new venture.

5. *They live richer lives than do other people.* They live the good life, not in the sense of happiness, contentment, security, and bliss—although fully functioning people experience each of these feelings at appropriate times—but a life that is exciting, challenging, meaning-ful, and rewarding. Not a life for the fainthearted, it involves taking risks, experiencing pain occasionally, and facing challenges coura-geously (Rogers, 1961, pp. 187–196).

In his later writings, Rogers (1977) extended and amplified his view of the fully functioning person and applied it to what he called **emerging persons**: corporate executives who have given up the rat race to live a simpler life; young people who have defied many of the current cultural values and formed a counterculture; priests and nuns who have rejected the dogma of their churches to live more meaningful lives; African Americans, Chicanos, women, and others outside of the dominant culture who have shed their passivity and begun to live more assertive and positive lives (Rogers, 1977, p. 264). He described them as having the following characteristics:

1. *They are honest and open.* They reject the sham and hypocrisy of government, Madison Avenue, parents, teachers, and clergy. They are open about their sexual relationships and open in their dealing with others. These humanistically oriented people are opposed to highly structured, inflexible bureaucracies. They believe that institu-tions exist for human beings and not vice versa.

2. *They are indifferent to material comforts and rewards.* Blue jeans replace expensive clothes; sleeping bags replace Holiday Inns; and natural foods replace fine cuisine. Emerging people are not power-hungry or achievement-hungry. They are not concerned with status but prefer to relate to people in informal, egalitarian ways.

3. *They are caring persons.* They have a deep desire to help oth-ers, to contribute to society. They are suspicious of people in the help-ing professions—therapists, social workers, and drug counselors, for example—who earn their livelihood by offering help for pay and very frequently hide behind a professional facade. Instead, emerging peo-ple voluntarily help others in crisis. They share food and lodging without question. Their caring is gentle, subtle, and nonmoralistic. When they help others down from a bad drug trip, for example, they do not preach to them.

4. *They have a deep distrust of cognitively based science and a tech-nology that uses that science to exploit and harm nature and people.* Emerging people have an intuitive belief that significant discoveries

involve feelings. They also respect the environment and do not want to see technology used to destroy it. For example, they oppose nuclear arms and the profound disregard for human life of political leaders who continue to advocate the construction of increasingly destructive weapons (Rogers, 1982). Emerging persons can support the use of technology, but only when it is used wisely to promote human welfare.

5. *They have a trust in their own experience and a profound distrust of all external authority.* Neither the Pope nor the President nor intellectuals can convince emerging persons of anything that is not borne out by personal experience. They do not obey laws just for the sake of obeying; they obey when it feels right for them to do so. They will deliberately disobey the law and accept the consequences when the law seems unjust or immoral.

6. *They are always in process.* These new people expect to change unjust political and social situations. They are not afraid of change but are fully aware that change is the one constant in life (Rogers, 1977, pp. 255–274).

Rogers recognized that emerging persons are a small minority of the total population. However, he believed that they are having an impact on society out of proportion to their numbers and will continue to exert significant influence in the future.

The Social Self and the True Self

The **social self** is the organized set of characteristics that the individual perceives as being peculiar to himself or herself. The social self is primarily acquired through contact with others. Rogers believed that when we interact with significant people in our environment— parents, brothers, sisters, friends, teachers—we begin to develop a concept of self that is largely based on the evaluations of others; that is, we come to evaluate ourselves in terms of what others think and not in terms of what we actually feel.

The reason we rely so heavily on the evaluation of others, according to Rogers, is that we have a strong **need for positive regard.** Rogers was uncertain whether this need is innate or learned, but maintained that its origins are less important than its impact on the individual. When we satisfy another's needs, we experience satisfaction of our own need for positive regard (Rogers, 1959, p. 223). As a consequence, the desire for positive regard from others may become more compelling than our own organismic valuing process (Rogers, 1959, p. 224). If, for example, we feel that aggression against others is wrong, but significant others place a positive value on it, we may ignore the validity of the feelings of our **true self** and act in terms of their expectations as a means of gaining their approval.

This need to seek approval and avoid disapproval leads to a social self-concept that is conditional on the performance of certain kinds of behavior (Rogers, 1959, p. 209). Such a self-concept carries with it **conditions of worth.** We perceive experiences and behaviors as acceptable only if they meet with approval from others; experiences and behaviors that meet with disapproval we perceive as unacceptable.

The ideal condition for development of a healthy self-concept and movement toward becoming fully functioning, in Rogers's view, is **unconditional positive regard**—a deep and genuine caring by others, uncontaminated by judgments or evaluations of our thoughts, feelings, or behaviors (Rogers & Sanford, 1984, p. 1379). With unconditional positive regard, the self-concept carries no conditions of worth, there is a **congruence** between the true self and experience, and the person is psychologically healthy.

In real life, we all have conditions of worth placed on our behavior. We all learn in the course of socialization that some of our feelings and behaviors are appropriate and others are inappropriate. When these normative rules are congruent with our organismic evaluations, we can get in touch with our true self and continue our movement toward self-actualization. In such cases, our social selves and our true selves are in harmony. Rogers believed that parents and others can establish creativity-fostering environments, with rules that encourage children to be curious, self-reliant, and respectful of themselves and others. Research by Harrington, Block, and Block (1987) has shown that children raised in such environments are more creative later in life than are children raised in environments with overly controlling, critical parents who did not give them freedom to grow and make their own decisions.

However, when we are guided by the expectations of others that run counter to our innate evaluations, problems occur. In this case, our social selves prevent our getting in touch with our true selves and actual feelings, and movement toward actualization is hindered. Congruence between the true self and organismic experiencing leads to accurate symbolization of experiences and positive growth; incongruence leads to inaccurate or distorted symbolization, psychological maladjustment, and vulnerability. Under such incongruent conditions, the person may experience a vague sense that something is wrong. The threat, in Rogers's view, may be "subceived" before it is clearly perceived; that is, the person may experience an increase in heartbeat and breathing rate and a sense of anxiety without being able to identify accurately the source of the difficulty. This anxiety triggers defense mechanisms to cope with the threat. If the incongruence between the true self and organismic experiencing is too great, the defense may be unsuccessful; the result is a profound state of disorganization that may be labeled psychotic.

Empirical Support for the Self Theory

If Rogers's theorizing about the relationship between the self and organismic experiencing is correct, we would expect persons who deny threats to their self-picture—that is, persons who are defensive—to be more maladjusted than those who are less defensive. Chodorkoff (1954) hypothesized that, the greater the agreement between a person's self-description and a description of the person by others, the less perceptual defense the person will show. This hypothesis was based on the assumption that nondefensive people are open to all their experiences, threatening or otherwise; they should be able to assimilate them into their self-concept, as long as they are organismically valid. Chodorkoff's second hypothesis was that, the greater the agreement between the personal and objective descriptions, the greater would be the individual's personal adjustment.

To test these hypotheses, clinical judges provided descriptions based on biographical information and on the results of two projective tests—the Rorschach and the Thematic Apperception Test. (The assumption was that diagnostic tests accurately reflect the individual's own assessment at an organismic level—an assumption that Rogers himself repeatedly challenged.) Scores based on the degree of agreement between the two sets of ratings were then correlated with the person's perceptual defense score, as measured by the time it took the subject to react to tachistoscopic presentations of threatening words (for example, bitch and whore) compared with time latencies for nonthreatening words (for example, chair and table). Personal adjustment was measured by having the judges check on a list of adjectives—such as kind, confident, well-liked—all those they thought described the subject; the more adjectives they checked, the higher the personal adjustment score. Perceptual agreement scores were found to be related to defense and adjustment scores as predicted, and the hypotheses were confirmed.

Rogers's self theory also predicts that persons who are nondefensive (self-accepting) should also be more accepting of the behavior of others. "When the individual perceives and accepts into one consistent and integrated system all his sensory and visceral experiences, then he is necessarily more understanding of others and is more accepting of others as separate individuals" (Rogers, 1951, p. 520). A study by Phillips (1951), using groups of high school and college students, found positive correlations ranging from +.51 to +.74 between self-acceptance and acceptance of others. Similar studies using introductory psychology students have found correlations of +.35 and +.57 (Suinn & Geiger, 1965; Suinn & Hill, 1964). Thus, the data for this aspect of the theory are largely supportive, although Wylie (1979) suggests some unresolved problems with the kinds of self-report measures used to assess acceptance of self and others.

ASSESSMENT TECHNIQUES

Rogers believed that assessment of the individual's personality must be based on an exploration of the person's feelings and attitudes toward himself or herself and others. It is the client who subjectively interprets experiences and who provides the therapist with valid information about his or her functioning. Rogers recognized that this phenomenological extremism has its limitations. The therapist can gain only that experiential information about the client that the client is able or willing to articulate. Moreover, clients may purposely distort reports to the therapist to win approval. Despite these limitations, Rogers believed that his person-centered approach provides a meaningful way to understand the individual's personality. When the therapist provides a supportive and nonthreatening milieu for the client, distortions and evasions are minimized. The therapist also actively tries not to prejudge the client by fitting him or her into a preconceived theoretical structure. Under these conditions, the therapist can gain an accurate understanding of the unique strengths and weaknesses of the client, with the goal of enabling the client to move toward self-realization.

Although Rogers argued against the clinical use of formal assessment techniques, he was forced to rely on measurement procedures to test his theory. In the Chodorkoff study, for example, judges' ratings were used to assess the person's organismic experiencing. Rogers was also a pioneer in developing a technique for assessing the nature of the interactions between client and therapist and in showing how these data are related to the therapeutic outcome. The technique involves the use of video and audio tape recordings of the therapeutic process. These tapes provide a more accurate, comprehensive, and available set of data for analysis and interpretation than do written records of therapy sessions made by the therapist from memory.

Rogers also conducted research on the impact of person-centered therapy using the **Q-sort,** an assessment procedure pioneered by Stephenson (1953). According to Rogers, a person's self-concept should change over the course of therapy. He believed that the initial discrepancies between the way in which clients actually view themselves and the way in which they would like to view themselves are reduced by effective counseling. The Q-sort is designed to measure these discrepancies between actual and ideal selves.

On entering therapy, clients are asked to sort (arrange) a large number of self-referent statements on a 7-point continuum ranging from "not like me" (1) to "like me" (7). The list might include statements such as "I am tolerant," "I am confident," "I am intelligent," and "I am emotionally mature." After sorting these statements (usually 100 or so), clients are asked to re-sort them in terms of their ideal selves, on a 7-point continuum ranging from "unlike my ideal" (1) to "like my ideal" (7). The two sets of scores are then correlated. Correlations for clients entering therapy are generally low; this suggests that clients see their actual selves as very different from their ideal (or wanted) selves. Following therapy, however, correlations tend to be high and positive; this suggests that clients see fewer discrepancies between their actual and their ideal selves.

In practice, then, Rogers utilized a variety of assessment procedures to ascertain the validity of his theory and the efficacy of his approach to therapy. His reliance on these measures may seem to be in direct contradiction to his statements opposing the use of such techniques in therapy. But a more reasonable interpretation might be that assessment procedures, although an inevitable and necessary part of the therapeutic process, should be deemphasized. They should not be allowed to become so important that they prevent the therapist from understanding the client's own experiencing.

THEORY'S IMPLICATIONS FOR THERAPY

Rogers not only created a theory of how the self evolves and is related to actualization; he also posited a theory of psychotherapy that focuses on the kind of relationship between the therapist and client that must be attained before positive growth is possible.

This theory had its roots in the soil of personal experience. When he first started practicing psychotherapy with children and adults at the guidance center in Rochester, he reported having very definite preconceptions about the nature of personality functioning, based on the center's Freudian orientation. In practice, however, Rogers found that the Freudian formulations were unworkable; they failed to produce constructive changes in his clients. As a consequence, he abandoned the Freudian view and adopted instead a more pragmatic orientation toward therapy. The only criterion he used to judge the validity of his work with patients was, "Does it work? Is it effective?" (Rogers, 1961, p. 10). Out of this inductive approach, Rogers established the therapeutic conditions necessary for positive growth.

Therapeutic Conditions That Facilitate Growth

In order to identify the conditions that promote growth, Rogers focused not only on his direct experiences with clients, but also on the history of attempts by counselors and others to change behavior. He noted that four major techniques had been used: (1) ordering and forbidding; (2) exhortation; (3) suggestion (which includes reassurance and encouragement); and (4) advice (Rogers, 1942, pp. 20–27). Since none of these techniques had been successful, Rogers thought it was time they were abandoned. But what is wrong, for example, with reassuring clients who are experiencing doubts about their personal worth? The problem, according to Rogers, is that counselors tend to use the technique indiscriminately. The consequence of telling clients repeatedly that they are improving is denial of their problems and failure to explore clients' feelings about the problems. Under these conditions, Rogers maintained, it is impossible for clients to improve.

In a broader sense, he held that all these techniques have directive aspects; that is, the therapist acts as an authority figure who understands the nature of the client's problems and the best way or ways to solve them. In terms of the therapeutic process, counselors perceive themselves as experts who discover, diagnose, and treat other people's problems. In Rogers's nondirective, person-centered approach, the focus is on the client. Instead of asking, "How can I treat and cure this person?" Rogers asked, "How can I provide a relationship which this person may use for his own personal growth?" (Rogers, 1961, p. 32).

Rogers believed that people have the capacity for change within themselves and will change in constructive ways if the therapist creates the appropriate conditions for growth. These conditions are:

1. The client and the therapist are in psychological contact; that is, each makes an impact on the phenomenological field of the other.
2. The client is in a state of incongruence and feels anxious about it.
3. The therapist is congruent in the relationship.
4. The therapist experiences unconditional positive regard for the client.
5. The therapist experiences an empathic understanding of the client's internal frame of reference.
6. The client perceives the therapist's unconditional positive regard and the therapist's empathic understanding (Rogers, 1959, p. 213).

For growth to occur, then, the therapist must be congruent—that is, genuine. The congruent therapist is not playing a role, but displays openly the feelings that are flowing within him or her at that moment. The therapist is aware of these feelings and able to communicate them to the client if it is appropriate to do so (Rogers & Stevens, 1967, p. 87). A therapist who feels bored with a client, for example, may choose not to report this feeling immediately; but if the client continues to be boring through many sessions, the therapist may then report his or her reaction in the hope of dealing with it openly and constructively. Thus, the therapist does not impulsively blurt out every passing feeling and accusation under the guise of being real and genuine. If and when the therapist does express negative feelings, however, they are presented as his or her own personal reaction, and not as an indication of some character flaw in the client (Rogers & Stevens, 1967, p. 88). Thus, the therapist might say, "I am feeling bored," but not "You are a boring person." The therapist is expressing an honest reaction, rather than passing judgment on the client.

The second essential ingredient in a facilitative therapeutic relationship is the therapist's empathic understanding of the client. The therapist should be able to sense accurately the client's inner world of private meanings (Rogers & Stevens, 1967, p. 89). The empathic therapist is able to sense the client's confusion, joy, anger, hostility, and tenderness and is able to communicate this information accurately. Under these conditions, the client will be more trusting and accepting of the therapist's communications even concerning experiences of which the therapist is scarcely aware (Rogers & Stevens, 1967, p. 89).

Finally, the facilitative therapist is one who feels unconditional positive regard for the client. This regard is "an outgoing, positive feeling without reservations and without evaluations. It means *not* making judgments" (Rogers & Stevens, 1967, p. 91). The therapist should not accept certain feelings in the client and reject others, but should prize the client in a total rather than in a conditional way. A possible exception involves working with schizophrenics. In such cases, Rogers noted, some therapists are more effective when they appear to be highly conditional—that is, when they do *not* accept some of the clients' bizarre, psychotic behavior (Rogers & Stevens, 1967, p. 94). At the very least, however, Rogers believed that all clients must be treated with respect and dignity and be given positive support by their therapists.

If the previously stated six conditions are operative, according to Rogers, the following changes will be observed in clients:

1. Clients will increasingly express their feelings about their lives and problems.
2. They will become increasingly accurate in their assessment of the meaning of their feelings.
3. They will begin to discern the incongruity between their self-concepts and their experiences.
4. They will feel threatened by the incongruity. The experience of threat is possible only because of the continued unconditional positive regard of the therapist.
5. They will then begin to experience fully, in awareness, feelings that have in the past been denied to awareness or distorted in awareness.
6. They will then become capable of reorganizing their self-concepts by assimilating these previously threatening experiences.
7. As therapy continues, their self-concepts will become increasingly congruent with their experiences. Their self-concepts will now include experiences that previously would have been too threatening to be in awareness. Defensiveness will be decreased.
8. They will become increasingly capable of experiencing the therapist's unconditional positive regard for them.
9. They will become increasingly positive in their regard for themselves.
10. They will come to evaluate their own experiences more in terms of their organismic valuing process and less in terms of the values endorsed by other people (Rogers, 1959, p. 216).

As a result of this process, Rogers believed, people will become what they organismically *are,* rather than what other people want them to be.

Empirical Support for the Theory of Therapy

To determine whether or not this theory of therapy had any validity, Rogers and his colleagues embarked on an ambitious research program. In one study, Butler and Haigh (1954) found that the average correlation between actual and ideal self for 25 clients before therapy was −.01; this indicates that there was no link between perceived actual and ideal selves. Following counseling, the correlation was +.34; this figure suggests that clients had changed their view of themselves by moving toward their ideal self-picture. A control group of 16 normal individuals who did not undergo therapy, but who did the Q-sorts in the same periods as the counseling group, had correlations of +.58 in the first test and +.59 in the second test. These correlations indicate that normals tend to see less discrepancy between their actual and ideal selves and that this relationship remains stable over time. Unfortunately, this study has a number of methodological flaws (Eysenck, 1961). For instance, the investigators failed to equate the control and treatment groups in terms of their initial psychological adjustment, and consequently it was impossible to assess the effectiveness of the person-centered therapy in producing changes in self-concept among the clients.

In a case study not subject to such methodological criticisms, Rogers (1954) analyzed the case of a patient known as Mrs. Oak, a dependent, inarticulate, passive person who had experienced rejection by others both at home and in social groups, as revealed by her self-sort responses before therapy. Repeated self-sorts during the course of therapy were correlated with this pretherapy baseline, with the following results: after the 7th therapeutic session, +.50; after the 25th session, +.42; at the end of therapy, +.39; and 12 months after therapy, +.30. These declining correlations indicate that during the course of therapy, and in the months thereafter, Mrs. Oak became increasingly unlike the person she described herself as being before therapy. Following therapy, she perceived herself to be much more secure, confident, emotionally mature, and expressive, warmer in relationships, and less afraid than she was before therapy began (Rogers, 1954, pp. 274–276). Although not every person who undergoes Rogerian therapy shows such improvement, Rogers concluded that her case did indicate that positive changes *can* be achieved when utilizing this type of psychotherapy (Rogers, 1954, p. 343).

If person-centered therapy is indeed effective in some cases, why does it work? The key, in Rogers's theory, is the facilitative therapist—one who is accurately empathic, genuine, respectful, and unconditionally supportive. Rogers believed that, if the therapist could create these facilitative conditions in therapy, constructive growth was inevitable. A host of research studies summarized by Sexton and Whiston (1994, pp. 11–15) indicate generally that these qualities are all helpful in promoting positive personality changes in clients and successful therapeutic outcomes. However, this research also shows that successful therapy is not inevitable just because the therapist believes that these facilitative conditions are present. Success also depends on the qualities that the clients bring to the therapeutic relationship. Clients have their own unique personalities, motives, symptoms, and backgrounds, and these factors all enter into the therapeutic process and influence the outcomes. For example, a recent study found that, in comparison to highly involved clients, those who were relatively uninvolved in the therapeutic process—for instance, clients who disclosed personal information at low and superficial levels—saw their therapists as less helpful if the therapists asked them many open-ended questions (for example, "Tell me more about your life"). Such questions tended to scare clients who were having difficulty talking about themselves, to make them feel inadequate, and to create the impression that the therapist was being unsupportive. Knowledge of client characteristics is considered crucial if therapists are going to be able to create the facilitating conditions that will help promote psychological health. Unfortunately, many Rogerian practitioners and also researchers tend to overemphasize the qualities of the therapist needed for therapeutic success, while deemphasizing the characteristics of clients (Gelso & Carter, 1985, pp. 155–243; Hill, Helms, Tichenor, Spiegel, O'Grady, & Perry, 1988, pp. 222–233).

While research generally suggests that facilitative therapists can promote some constructive growth in some clients, there are several problems associated with many of these investigations. In most of the studies, the measurement of successful therapeutic change is based only on clients' or therapists' verbalizations or clients' self-reports, and not on clients' actual *behavior*. There is also a lack of long-term follow-up studies; that is, most studies of treatment effectiveness assess only immediate changes in clients' functioning, without attempting to assess their permanence. Finally, there is a lack of agreement among researchers on the meaning of various key concepts. For example, Bachelor (1988) found that the term *empathy* has at least four separate meanings to people in therapy: first, it refers to the therapist's accurate, cognitive understanding of the client's subjective state at any particular time; second, it means that the therapist is experiencing the same feelings as the client; third, it refers to the client's feeling that he or she has experiences in common with the therapist; and, fourth, it refers to the therapist's nurturant attitude toward the client—that is, the therapist's supportive or totally attentive presence. Fuzzy concepts lead to the construction of inadequate measures and consequently to poor tests of the theory.

In conclusion, there is enough research support for Rogers's views on therapy to warrant further exploration and testing. Despite the complexity of the therapeutic process and the difficulty in measuring its various concepts, some progress has been made in the direction of increasing our understanding of the characteristics that therapists should possess if their efforts to promote the psychological growth of their clients are ever going to be successful.

THEORY'S IMPLICATIONS FOR EDUCATION

Rogers believed his theory to be applicable to many areas besides therapy, including family life, marriage, group leadership, politics, and education. We will look more closely at two of these areas: education and marriage.

In Rogers's view, current educational practices at the elementary, secondary, and college and university levels are basically authoritarian and coercive. Teachers are perceived as possessors of knowledge and students as its recipients, with lectures as the means of transmitting information from teachers to students. Rogers also believed that too much emphasis is placed on the acquisition of cognitive skills (the learning of facts and problem-solving skills) and not enough on the development of affective skills (learning how to be a sensitive and loving person). Moreover, too little attention is devoted to issues of importance to students—for example, sexual relationships and friendship. Educational settings are typically impersonal, with too much emphasis on performance and its evaluation through testing and grading.

According to Rogers, the educational establishment bases its program on a number of faulty assumptions (Rogers, 1968, 1969, 1983):

1. *Students cannot be trusted to pursue their own educational goals.* In Rogers' view, teachers exhibit their mistrust of students by constantly supervising and checking on them and their work. If students were allowed to make their own choices concerning their edu-

cational goals, he believed, there would be no need to monitor their behavior so closely because they would be positively motivated to study and learn. Surveillance is necessary to ensure compliance only when teachers set goals that are irrelevant or radically at variance with student concerns and interests.

Rogers maintained that students should be allowed to make their own educational choices and set their own goals, because they are the ones who know best what is right for them. This assumption seems dubious, in view of the continual shifting of goals experienced by many students in the course of their educational careers. However, even if they could choose the goals that are right for them, students exist in a society that may not recognize the worth and usefulness of their aims. People have the right to pursue whatever goals they wish, but society also has the right to express its priorities and reward those it considers worthy.

2. *Creative people develop from passive learners.* Rogers objected strongly to what he considered the primary emphasis in education—students as passive learners. University students, for example, are typically given information by professors and are expected to regurgitate that information on examinations. Rogers believed that such an emphasis stifles the development of original and creative ideas. Students are taught to conform, to defer coming to grips with their own ideas, and to accept unquestioningly the ideas of their professors. He argued that, in an atmosphere of trust, mutual respect, and freedom from constraints, students would be free to test their own ideas and become creative individuals.

Not everyone agrees with Rogers on this point. Brown and Tedeschi (1972) argued that many creative individuals throughout history have been impatient with the constraints of institutions but that their complaints "are interesting not because they tell us anything about the development of genius but because they tell us of [the geniuses'] reactions to the formalities of the learning environment" (p. 5). They observed that child prodigies such as John Stuart Mill, Charles Sanders Pierce, and Ludwig van Beethoven all learned under extremely demanding circumstances, yet their creative impulses were not stifled.

It is clear both from the evidence and from history that the mere absence of constraint or evaluation is not a necessary condition for the development of creative persons. Great ideas are not gathered while sitting under the banyan tree waiting for them to drop. Edison once said that creativity was 99% perspiration and 1% inspiration. What was meant is that the individual must gather a great deal of information that may be relevant for solving a problem. This assimilation process can be quite tedious and tests the motivational intensity of the individual's interest in the problem. Hence, there are times when the work takes on the form of sheer drudgery and there are times when the work is intensely exciting and exhilarating. (Brown & Tedeschi, 1972, p. 6)

By way of rebuttal, Rogers argued that self-discipline is one of the most demanding and fruitful of all constraints, and is present in almost every creative experience. Conformity, he maintained, does not breed self-discipline; to the contrary, it breeds undisciplined people dependent on the evaluations of others (Rogers, 1972b, pp. 17–18).

3. *Evaluation is education: education is evaluation.* Rogers argued forcefully that "examinations have become the beginning and the end of education" (Rogers, 1968, p. 691). Students face endless quizzes and final examinations in their courses. Such obstacles prevent them from doing the real independent learning necessary to a creative life. Thus, they are, in Rogers's view, stultifying to the student. Rogers's point is well taken that students would lack sufficient time to pursue their own interests under such grueling schedules. A more reasonable approach might be to ensure that students have the basic concepts that are a prerequisite of creative activity by testing them as early as possible in their courses and careers, and then to provide them with the latitude Rogers advocates.

In summary, Rogers believed that the educational system was in desperate need of reform. He saw it as too authoritarian and coercive and as not ministering to the needs of students. In his view, there is a need for more participation by students in the decisions that affect their academic and social development and a need for better communication and cooperation among faculty, students, and administrators. Students should be able to choose their own goals and to pursue them with the help and encouragement of faculty (Rogers, 1970, p. 154).

THEORY'S IMPLICATIONS FOR MARRIAGE

Rogers saw marriage as a failing institution. He attributed its decline to the fact that couples can now prevent conception, so that women need no longer be fully occupied with pregnancy, nursing, and child-rearing. They are now as free as men to explore relationships outside of marriage and to choose between family and career. For the first time in history, women are physically free agents, liberated from their subjugated role. The women's liberation movement has also played a part, by encouraging women to make their own choices and not to stay in unsatisfactory marriages that stifle their growth. Finally, increased life expectancies mean that flaws in a relationship that might have been endured in previous times, when life expectancies were lower, will no longer be tolerated in a relationship that is expected to endure for 50 years or more.

Rogers believed that people, especially young people, are searching for meaningful alternatives—hence the upsurge in cohabitation without legal ties, communal lifestyles, and the like. Another meaningful alternative, in Rogers's view, is a new kind of marriage that is radically different from the traditional version, in which the husband is the sole provider and the ultimate authority and the wife occupies a more subservient role. Rogers did not oppose marriage per se, but only the kind of marriage that is not egalitarian, enriching, satisfying, and a growth experience for both partners. He also opposed marriages that are consummated only to please parents or to resolve a crisis in the relationship—as when one person threatens to break up the relationship if the other does not agree to marry (Rogers, 1972a, p. 39). Rogers observed that marriages in which couples make the following kinds of statements may experience difficulties:

1. "I am more concerned for you than I am for myself." Although a loving relationship certainly involves a deep concern for the other person's welfare, an uncritical willingness to submerge one's own identity to please the other person can prove lethal to the relationship.

2. "We will work hard on our marriage." This statement is appropriate up to a point, but working hard to salvage a marriage that is persistently unsatisfying to the participants may be destructive.

3. "We pledge ourselves to each other until death do us part." Again, the sentiment is fine but, if the cost is too great, the parties are likely to demean or destroy themselves or each other or to break the bonds (Rogers, 1972a, p. 200).

As Rogers saw it, marriage is a free-flowing, changing process, rather than a contract with a list of unalterable stipulations. It does not involve a rigid commitment at any cost, but a dedication on the part of both people to try to enhance and enrich the relationship. An appropriate statement, in his view, would be: "We each commit ourselves to working together on the changing process of our present relationship, because that relationship is currently enriching our love and our life and we wish it to grow" (Rogers, 1972a, p. 201).

In such a relationship the following kinds of events are likely to occur:

1. *Difficulties always present in the partnership are brought into the open.* The parties are willing to take risks and explore the differences between them, thereby (usually) deepening the bonds of partnership.

2. *Communication is more open and more real, with mutual listening.* Trust is evident, and the parties are willing to listen to each other rather than attack and accuse.

3. *The partners will come to recognize the value of separateness.* The partners begin to recognize that each one has separate needs and desires and that they do not have to pursue the same activities and goals together to be happy.

4. *Women's growing independence is recognized as valuable in the relationship.* Wives are able to discuss their needs with their husbands, instead of submerging their resentments. As a result, husbands have more respect for their wives, and the relationship is more mutually satisfying.

5. *Roles and role expectations tend to drop away and are replaced by people choosing their own way of behaving.* The expectations inherent in the traditional marriage relationship are given up. Men no longer see themselves as superior to their wives and as controlling all activities, including sexual ones. Women no longer see themselves as subordinate and submissive to their husbands. The resulting role flexibility leads to behavior that is sometimes in line with role expectations, sometimes not. At no time, however, is behavior governed totally by the role the person is expected to play.

6. *Either partner may form satellite relationships, which will often cause great pain but enrich growth.* **Satellite relationships** are close secondary relationships outside the marriage that may or may not involve sexual intercourse but are valued for themselves. According to Rogers, when two people learn to see each other as separate persons, with separate as well as mutual needs and interests, they are likely to discover that outside relationships are among those needs. Thus, married people may feel the need to date or become sexually intimate with others.

Although Rogers saw satellite relationships as a legitimate part of healthy marriages, others would disagree strongly, and would condemn them as immoral, illegal, and grounds for divorce. They would say that such relationships are adulterous, plain and simple, and no fancy term can alter that fact. Rogers considered this view old-fashioned and ridiculous (Rogers, 1972a, p. 241); he argued that any partnership entered into by mutually consenting adults is legal, as long as it does no injury to others. Even if we accept his position on theoretical grounds (though, of course, many people would not), it seems to be a disaster in practice: partners who agree to such arrangements very often wind up in divorce court. Rogers's response was that in these cases, although both parties consented to the arrangement intellectually, emotionally they were not ready for it. As a result, they were jealous and hurt when their partner had a sexual relationship with someone else (Rogers, 1977, p. 53). It was his hope that couples of the future would be more sophisticated and able to accept these experiences both intellectually and emotionally. They would then be motivated to enhance each other and to promote mutually positive growth by allowing the other to satisfy his or her needs outside the relationship.

EVALUATIVE COMMENTS

Let us now examine Rogers's theory in terms of how well it meets the criteria outlined in Chapter 1 for acceptance of scientific theories.

Comprehensiveness   Initially, Rogers's theory was restricted in scope; it was concerned primarily with explaining the origins of pathological behavior and the means of treating it in therapy. Later he extended his theory to explain a number of other phenomena, including problems of marriage, family life, education, race relations, and politics, and to suggest ways of overcoming these difficulties. As a result, his theory is now much more comprehensive than it was originally.

Precision and testability   To Rogers's credit, he made a tremendous effort to construct a precise and testable theory. However, there are still serious problems associated with measuring key concepts such as empathy, genuineness, and unconditional positive regard. Nonetheless, Rogers did make significant strides toward the creation of a theory with explicitly stated concepts and hypotheses capable of being tested.

Parsimony   Rogers's theory fails to meet the parsimony criterion. Although the phenomena he chooses to examine are complex, he relied on only a few concepts and assumptions to account for them.

Thus, the explanatory base of Rogers's theory is restricted in scope and clearly reductionistic in nature.

For example, Rogers's proposed solutions to help minimize racial and international conflict, hostility, and aggression rely primarily on a *psychological analysis* of the problems and application of the same principles utilized in his work with troubled individuals in therapy. Thus, he proposed reducing these tensions by having the concerned parties communicate with each other under facilitative group conditions (Rogers, 1977). Although the proposal is provocative and would undoubtedly help promote better relations between antagonists, it ignores the complex set of historical, political, economic, and cultural factors that serve to preserve the status quo. A psychological analysis of such problems is useful but clearly limited if not coupled with social, economic, and political analyses.

Empirical validity   Numerous tests of Rogers's theory to date have produced generally positive results; this provides some encouragement for investigators to continue their explorations and testing.

Heuristic value   Rogers's views have been highly controversial and have provoked continued, vigorous debate. His strong stand on the sanctity of the person, however, has had a positive influence. His humanistic concern for the integrity and uniqueness of the individual has led many investigators to question views of human beings as automatons reacting uncritically to environmental forces. His theory has forced many people to reconsider the importance of the self-concept in their theorizing and research.

Applied value   Rogers's theory is also very strong in the applied area. Aspects of it have been applied fruitfully to such diverse areas as education, race relations, politics, family relationships, administration, leadership, and counseling. His views on therapy have had tremendous impact on the counseling and community mental health movement.

DISCUSSION QUESTIONS

1. Why did Rogers abandon the Freudian view of personality functioning?
2. In what ways is Rogers's position different from Freud's?
3. Discuss Rogers's concept of the organismic valuing process and

how it is related to the development of the person. What scientific evidence is there to support his hypothesis of organismic wisdom?

4. What are the consequences of an individual's need for positive regard?

5. What are some of the conditions of worth that you have placed on your parents? What conditions of worth have they attached to your behavior?

6. Why does Rogers feel that many educators are doing an ineffectual job in educating people? Do you agree with him? Can you cite additional problems with the current educational system? What are some of its strengths?

7. Do you believe it is possible to be creative without first learning the basic concepts in a discipline? Why?

8. What are some of the major problems of the Chodorkoff study cited in this chapter?

9. Do you think that cohabitation is a meaningful alternative to marriage?

10. What is your opinion about Rogers's view that sexual relationships outside marriage can be healthy if both partners agree?

GLOSSARY

conditions of worth   Stipulations upon which our sense of self-worth depends; they are associated with the belief that we are only worthwhile if we perform behaviors that others think are good and refrain from actions that others think are bad.

congruence   State of harmony that exists when there is no discrepancy between the person's experiencing and his or her self-concept.

emerging persons   People of the future whose interpersonal relationships are characterized by honesty, cooperation, and concern for others; who avoid sham, facades, and hypocrisy; and who welcome change and opt for growth even when it is painful to do so.

fully functioning persons   Individuals who are utilizing their potentials to the maximum degree. In other words, these individuals are engaged in self-realization or self-actualization.

need for positive regard   Learned or innate tendency to seek and need approval from others.

organismic valuing process   An innate bodily mechanism for evaluating which experiences are right or wrong for the person.

People experience satisfaction in those behaviors that maintain and enhance them and aversion to those behaviors that do not.

Q-sort   Self-report assessment procedure designed to measure the discrepancy between a person's actual and ideal selves.

satellite relationships   Relationships formed outside the marriage that may or may not involve sexual intimacy.

social self   A self-concept based largely on the expectations of others. It has a powerful influence on us because we want to please others and win their positive regard. When the social self is incongruent with the person's true self, we are likely to distort our true feelings by repressing, denying, or distorting them. Under these conditions, progress toward self-realization is hindered. However, when the social self is congruent with the true self, we have no need to repress, deny, or distort our actual feelings. Under such conditions, we can assimilate our actual experiences into the true self and move toward self-realization.

true self   A self-concept that is based on our actual feelings about our experiences. Under conditions of unconditional positive regard (or where the social self is congruent with the true self), we have no need to repress, deny, or distort our actual experiences. These experiences can be adequately symbolized (conceptualized or thought about) and assimilated into our true self. When this occurs, we make progress toward self-realization.

unconditional positive regard   A total caring or prizing of the person for what he or she is, without any reservations or conditions of worth; in therapy, the therapist's complete acceptance of the client's expression of negative as well as positive feelings.

SUGGESTED READINGS

Rogers, C. R. (1959). A theory of therapy, personality, and interpersonal relationships, as developed in the client-centered framework. In S. Koch (Ed.), *Psychology: A study of a science* (Vol. 3, pp. 184–256). New York: McGraw-Hill.

Rogers, C. R. (1961). *On becoming a person*. Boston: Houghton Mifflin.

Rogers, C. R. (1977). *Carl Rogers on personal power*. New York: Delacorte Press.

Rogers, C. R., & Stevens, B. (1967). *Person to person: The problem of being human*. New York: Simon & Schuster.

REFERENCES

Bachelor, A. (1988). How clients perceive therapist empathy: A content analysis of "received" empathy. *Psychotherapy, 25,* 227–240.

Brown, R. C., & Tedeschi, J. T. (1972). Graduate education and psychology: A comment on Rogers' passionate statement. *Journal of Humanistic Psychology, 12,* 1–15.

Butler, J. M., & Haigh, G. V. (1954). Changes in the relation between self-concepts and ideal concepts consequent upon client-centered counseling. In C. R. Rogers & R. F. Dymond (Eds.), *Psychotherapy and personality change* (pp. 55–75). Chicago: University of Chicago Press.

Chodorkoff, B. (1954). Self-perception, perceptual defense, and adjustment. *Journal of Abnormal and Social Psychology, 49,* 508–512.

Davis, C. M. (1928). Self-selection of diet by newly weaned infants. *American Journal of Diseases of Children, 36,* 651–679.

Eysenck, H. J. (1961). The effects of psychotherapy. In H. J. Eysenck (Ed.), *Handbook of abnormal psychology: An experimental approach* (pp. 697–725). New York: Basic Books.

Galef, Jr., B. G. (1991). A contrarian view of the wisdom of the body as it relates to dietary self-selection. *Psychological Review, 98,* 218–223.

Garcia, J., Kimeldurf, D. J., & Hunt, E. L. (1961). The use of ionizing radiation as a motivating stimulus. *Psychological Review, 68,* 383–395.

Gelso, C. J., & Carter, J. A. (1985). The relationship in counseling and psychotherapy: Components, consequences, and theoretical antecedents. *The Counseling Psychologist, 13,* 155–243.

Harrington, D. M., Block, J. H., & Block, J. (1987). Testing aspects of Carl Rogers's theory of creative environments: Child-rearing antecedents of creative potential in young adolescents. *Journal of Personality and Social Psychology, 52,* 851–856.

Hill, C. E., Helms, J. E., Tichenor, V., Spiegel, S. B., O'Grady, K. E., & Perry, E. S. (1988). Effects of therapist response modes in brief psychotherapy. *Journal of Counseling Psychology, 35,* 222–233.

Phillips, E. L. (1951). Attitudes toward self and others: A brief questionnaire report. *Journal of Consulting Psychology, 15,* 79–81.

Rogers, C. R. (1942). *Counseling and psychotherapy: Newer concepts in practice.* Boston: Houghton Mifflin.

Rogers, C. R. (1951). *Client-centered therapy: Its current practice, implications, and theory.* Boston: Houghton Mifflin.

Rogers, C. R. (1954). The case of Mrs. Oak: A research analysis. In C. R. Rogers & R. F. Dymond (Eds.), *Psychotherapy and personality change* (pp. 259–348). Chicago: University of Chicago Press.

Rogers, C. R. (1959). A theory of therapy, personality, and interpersonal relationships, as developed in the client-centered framework. In S. Koch

(Ed.), *Psychology: A study of a science* (Vol. 3, pp. 184–256). New York: McGraw-Hill.

Rogers, C. R. (1961). *On becoming a person*. Boston: Houghton Mifflin.

Rogers, C. R. (1968). Graduate education in psychology: A passionate statement. In W. G. Bennis, E. H. Schein, F. I. Steele, & D. E. Berlew (Eds.), *Interpersonal dynamics* (2nd ed., pp. 687–703). Homewood, IL: Dorsey Press.

Rogers, C. R. (1969). *Freedom to learn*. Columbus, OH: Merrill.

Rogers, C. R. (1970). *Carl Rogers on encounter groups*. New York: Harper & Row.

Rogers, C. R. (1972a). *Becoming partners: Marriage and its alternatives*. New York: Delacorte Press.

Rogers, C. R. (1972b). Comments on Brown and Tedeschi's article. *Journal of Humanistic Psychology, 12,* 16–21.

Rogers, C. R. (1977). *Carl Rogers on personal power*. New York: Delacorte Press.

Rogers, C. R. (1982). A psychologist looks at nuclear war: Its threat, its possible prevention. *Journal of Humanistic Psychology, 22,* 9–20.

Rogers, C. R. (1983). *Freedom to learn for the 80s*. Columbus, OH: Merrill.

Rogers, C. R., & Sanford, R. C. (1984). Client-centered psychotherapy. In H. I. Kaplan & B. J. Sadock (Eds.), *Comprehensive textbook of psychiatry* (Vol. 4, pp. 1374–1388). Baltimore: Williams & Wilkins.

Rogers, C. R., & Stevens, B. (1967). *Person to person: The problem of being human*. New York: Simon & Schuster.

Rogers, H. E. (1965). A wife's view of Carl Rogers. *Voices, 1,* 93–98.

Sexton, T. L., & Whiston, S. C. (1994). The status of the counseling relationship: An empirical review, theoretical implications, and research directions. *The Counseling Psychologist, 22,* 6–78.

Stephenson, W. (1953). *The study of behavior*. Chicago: University of Chicago Press.

Suinn, R. M., & Geiger, J. (1965). Stress and the stability of self- and other-attitudes. *Journal of General Psychology, 73,* 177–180.

Suinn, R. M., & Hill, H. (1964). Influence of anxiety on the relationship between self-acceptance and acceptance of others. *Journal of Consulting Psychology, 28,* 116–119.

Thorne, B. (1992). *Carl Rogers*. Newbury Park, CA: Sage Publications.

Wylie, R. C. (1979). *The self concept* (Vol. 2). Lincoln: University of Nebraska.

CHAPTER 14

May's Existential-Analytic Position

BIOGRAPHICAL SKETCH

Rollo May was born in Ada, Ohio, in 1909. He earned a bachelor of arts degree from Oberlin College in Ohio in 1930. After graduation, he pursued an early interest in art by touring Poland with a group of artists and painting pictures of its citizens (Reeves, 1977, p. 252). He then traveled extensively through Europe, taught at a college in Greece, and attended summer classes led by Alfred Adler.

When May returned to the United States in 1934, he served as an advisor to students at Michigan State University. Later he enrolled at Union Theological Seminary in New York, not to become a preacher but rather to ask fundamental questions about human existence (Reeves, 1977, p. 252). At the seminary he was exposed to the existentialism of Kierkegaard and Heidegger in classes led by theologian Paul Tillich, who greatly influenced his thinking. He earned his bachelor of divinity degree cum laude in 1938.

May served as a counselor to students at City College of New York and studied psychoanalysis at the William Alanson White Institute of Psychiatry, Psychoanalysis, and Psychology in New York. In 1946 he opened a private practice, and in 1948 he became a member of the faculty at the White Institute (Reeves, 1977, p. 256). In 1949 he submitted his dissertation on anxiety to Columbia University and was awarded the university's first Ph.D. in clinical psychology. The disser-

501

tation was published in modified form in 1950 as *The Meaning of Anxiety*.

During this period of his life, May contracted tuberculosis and lived for a few years at a sanitarium in upstate New York. This was a particularly terrifying and depressing time for May; several times he was close to death. During his illness, he studied Kierkegaard's and Freud's views on anxiety and came to the conclusion that, although Freud had brilliantly analyzed the reactions of the individual made anxious by threat, it was Kierkegaard who had seen most clearly that anxiety is ultimately the threat of becoming nothing (Reeves, 1977, p. 257).

Following his recovery, May continued to write, teach, and practice therapy. He has served as a faculty member at the New School for Social Research, New York University, Harvard, Yale, and Princeton. He has also published a number of books, including *Man's Search for Himself* (1953), *Psychology and the Human Dilemma* (1967), *Love and Will* (1969), *Power and Innocence* (1972), *Paulus: Reminiscences of a Friendship* (1973), *The Courage to Create* (1975), *Freedom and Destiny* (1981), *The Discovery of Being: Writings in Existential Psychology* (1983), *My Quest for Beauty* (1985), and *The Cry for Myth* (1991).

Professor May was honored with numerous awards for his outstanding achievements in psychology. He was a fellow of the American Psychological Association, emeritus fellow and faculty member at the White Institute, and a fellow of Brantford College, Yale University, and the National Council of Religion in Higher Education (Reeves, 1977, p. 263). He received the Dr. Martin Luther King Award from the New York Society of Clinical Psychology and the Psychological Professional Gold Medal from the American Psychological Association for his outstanding contributions to professional research.

In poor health for the last two years of his life, Professor May died from congestive heart failure on October 22, 1994, at his home in Tiburon, California.

CONCEPTS AND PRINCIPLES

What Is Existentialism?

The term **existentialism** has become popular in academic and literary circles and is used in so many different ways by philosophers, psychologists, theologians, novelists, actors, and others that it has almost lost its meaning. In the popular mind, it is often equated with gloom and despair, not to mention suicide and death. For some, it suggests that the world is an absurd place with no meaning, and they self-righteously invoke it when any misfortune befalls them. Because the concept is so central to an understanding of May's position, we will begin by tracing its use historically.

Existentialism has its roots in the 19th-century writings of Danish philosopher Soren Kierkegaard. In his attempts to understand human functioning, Kierkegaard rejected Hegel's monumental effort to comprehend reality by identifying it with abstract thought and logic (May, 1973, p. 263). Kierkegaard, and later Friedrich Nietzsche, sought to correct the one-sidedness of Hegel's arguments by starting with the basic realities of people's existence, or **Dasein.** Thus, existentialism is concerned with **ontology,** or the study of the nature of **being.** But what precisely did May mean by the term *being*? First, May said that existentialists' use of this term is unfortunate, because it connotes a substance that is static and unchanging; he preferred the term *becoming.* (Compare Allport's views, described in Chapter 8.) Being (becoming) is a process in which we ourselves are the source of change, as we struggle as individuals to realize our potential—that is, as we try to become what we truly are. Being (or becoming) is not given once and for all; it does not unfold automatically. Instead, we each must become aware of what our unique potentialities are and then take responsibility for realizing them (May, 1983, p. 97). To achieve self-realization, we must focus directly on our personal experiences and avoid analyzing our circumstances by means of logical systems of thought that are abstract and impersonal.

Proponents of this philosophy, and especially Kierkegaard, argued that truth cannot be regarded as something detached from human experience. According to Kierkegaard, truth can only be known by starting with the person's perception of it as it relates to natural phenomena. May argued that Kierkegaard's insight changed our way of thinking about truth, and his radical stance has had tremendous implications for all scientific endeavors, including psychology. Kierkegaard gave us the concept of relational truth, forerunner of the notion of relativity; he showed us that "the *subject,* man, can never be separated from the *object* which he observes" (May, 1958b, p. 26). May thus defines existentialism as "the endeavor to understand man by cutting below the cleavage between subject and object which has bedeviled Western thought and science since shortly after the Renaissance" (1958b, p. 11).

A major existentialist criticism of Western science is that it treats people as *objects.* Scientists tend to view human beings in an impersonal way and to restrict themselves to detached and objective measurement of human behavior. According to the existentialists, this value-free approach is incorrect; we are human beings first, and the scientific approach should emerge from that fundamental fact.

> Man may seek the meaning of science by approaching it as a typically human endeavor and asking: What is it in human nature that leads to the emergence of the scientific attitude? . . . Once I have the answer to this question . . . I may begin to grasp what science really means. From that moment on, I may be able to trace back to man's existence all forms, aims, and methods of science and to demonstrate that they are manifestations of his nature. (Van Kaam, 1969, p. 15)

What the existentialists are advocating, in effect, is that we bring the *subject*—our own inner world of experiences—into our view of science. Yet they do not dismiss the object side of the reality equation. Rather, they believe that we should focus first on our own subjective experiences in the formulation of problems and then proceed to study them as objectively as possible. Thus, scientists should adapt their methods of study to meaningful human problems and not tailor their problems to a restricted methodology borrowed from physics or physiology (Van Kaam, 1969, p. 26). May presented this view in the form of a parable:

> A psychologist—any psychologist, or all of us—arrives at the heavenly gates at the end of his long and productive life. He is brought up before St. Peter for the customary accounting. . . . An angel assistant in a white jacket drops a manila folder on the table which St. Peter opens and looks at, frowning. St. Peter's frown deepens. He drums with his fingers on the table and grunts a few nondirective "uhm-uhms" as he fixes the candidate with his Mosaic eyes.
>
> The silence is discomfiting. Finally, the psychologist opens his briefcase and cries, "Here! The reprints of my hundred and thirty-two papers."
>
> St. Peter slowly shakes his head. . . . At last [he] speaks, "I'm aware, my good man, [of] how industrious you were. It's not sloth you're accused of. . . . [Then he] slaps his hand resoundingly down on the table, and his tone is like Moses breaking the news of the ten commandments. "You are charged with *Nimis simplicandum* [oversimplifying]! You have spent your life making molehills out of mountains—that's what you're guilty of. When man was tragic, you made him trivial. . . . When he suffered passively, you described him as simpering; and when he drummed up enough courage to act, you called it stimulus and response. . . . You made man over into the image of your childhood Erector Set or Sunday School Maxims—both equally horrendous." (May, 1967, pp. 3–4)

In May's story, there is no ending. There is only the implication that eternal damnation awaits psychologists and others who continue to dissect the human experience and who, by so doing, tend to trivialize it. He also took issue with those who utilize only the subjective or objective view of reality in their formulations (May, 1967, pp. 15–20). As examples, he mentioned Rogers and Skinner. He criticized Rogers for overemphasizing the subjective side. Rogers was also guilty, in May's view, of assuming that people are "inherently good" and "exquisitely rational" and will always make the right choices if given an opportunity; Rogers ignored the evil and irrational side of human nature. May (1982) believed that all human beings have the capacity for both good and evil. Skinner, in contrast, placed too much emphasis on the objective side of human behavior. He was concerned almost exclusively with the ways in which the manipulation of precisely defined environmental variables determine behavior, and totally ignored the subjective side of human functioning.

May believed that both views of human nature are necessary for a science of psychology and for meaningful living, because we are all faced with the dilemma of living in both worlds at once. "The human dilemma is that which arises out of a man's capacity to experience himself as both subject and object at the same time" (May, 1967, p. 8). A major aspect of this dilemma is knowing that we are subject to illness, death, limitations of intelligence and experience, and other deterministic forces, but at the same time realizing that we have the subjective freedom to choose how we relate to these objective and deterministic forces. We alone can assign meaning to them; we are responsible for our own destinies. Of course, strict determinists such as Skinner would disagree; they maintain that all our behavior is determined, even our belief that we are free to make our own decisions, because we consider only those options determined by our past experiences and by current stimulation from the external environment.

Besides the subject/object dichotomy, a number of other interesting ideas have been put forth by prominent existentialists—among them, philosophers Martin Heidegger, Karl Jaspers, Maurice Merleau-Ponty, Paul Tillich, Albert Camus, and Jean-Paul Sartre and psychotherapists Ludwig Binswanger, Medard Boss, Viktor Frankl, and May. Although existentialism cannot be called a systematic and unified philosophy, its adherents do share certain views.

First, existentialists all take the *person* as the starting point in their analyses of human existence. They all ask fundamental questions about existence: Who am I? What is the meaning of life? Is there a meaning to life? Is life worth living? How do I realize my potentialities? How do I become an individual?

Second, they consider *free will* a central concept in understanding human functioning and development. To be human means to exercise free will, to consider goals, to make choices that we hope will promote our development. It is our freedom to make these choices that gives us a sense of significance and our feelings of dignity and worth (May, 1981, p. 9).

Third, in order to move toward answers, existentialists focus on our *immediate experience* as we exist from day to day—on what they often call our being-in-the-world. We view the world of natural phenomena from a subjective perspective. We face a world filled with uncertainties, a world that, in many respects, is absurd. The greatest absurdity from the existentialists' viewpoint is that we each realize we are finite and must die. Death is the great equalizer. All accomplishments, all hopes and dreams, will inevitably be blasted into oblivion at some point. The key question for the person under these circumstances is: What should I do? Should I retreat into nothingness or should I, in Tillich's words, have the courage to be? It is up to the person to make a choice and take action. As Kierkegaard said, "Truth exists only as the individual himself produces it in action" (May, 1958b, p. 12). Individuals must choose their own goals, and then commit themselves to pursue them.

Thus, the person assumes almost godlike status in the existential design. We must assign meaning to our existence and act in terms of that meaning. We must exercise our freedom and act authentically. We act inauthentically when we let other people define our goals and tell us how we should behave. To be authentic, we must be who we are.

The ultimate form of nothingness is suicide. But nothingness, or nonbeing, can be seen in less extreme forms. We may choose not to exercise our freedom to be; we may avoid commitment to goals and responsibilities; we may decide to follow the moral dictates of the crowd. Indeed, choosing these options is easier than facing our responsibilities. The exercise of freedom is costly. In many instances, it creates severe anxiety, and an immediate and easier way for us to cope is to lose ourselves by accepting the moral values dictated by society. Such acceptance of values at variance with our being leads to self-alienation, apathy, and despair. The similarity between the existentialists and Rogers and Maslow is apparent here. Human existence is seen as a continuous struggle, as we try to deal with the problems of life and to move toward the realization of our potentialities.

Existentialism and Psychoanalysis

The major applications of existentialism to personality and psychotherapy have come from the work of people trained in classical psychoanalysis. To better understand May's **existential-analytic perspective,** which is an integration of the Freudian and existentialist positions, let us look at some of the similarities and differences between these two approaches to the study of human behavior.

Both psychoanalysis and existentialism ask fundamental questions about human existence. Although Freud was distrustful of mere speculation unsubstantiated by data, he nevertheless frankly acknowledged at an early point in his career that he was vitally concerned with the great problems of human existence and with understanding human nature. (See Chapter 2.) Both positions also focus on the irrational as well as the rational side of our natures. The existentialists talk about the inevitability of death and nothingness and the varied ways in which we try to cope with it. Freud, too, recognized the overwhelming importance of death in the human psyche and incorporated it into his theory in terms of a self-destructive urge he called the death instinct. Freud was also rather pessimistic about our long-range chances for survival as a species, because he believed that we have within us the seeds for our own destruction.

Although the existentialists have generally been reproved for being overly concerned with death and unduly pessimistic, a careful reading of their work suggests that the criticism is not entirely justified. It is true that death is given a high priority in their formulations, but they would argue that in fact death touches us all. Their focus may be seen as morbid, because many of us have an unrealistic view of death and have been taught from a very early age to avoid thinking about it. Accordingly, they would argue that we are the ones with the unhealthy attitude, not they. As one existentialist has observed,

> throughout the ages men have shunned the sight of death and the mention of death, and they have devised innumerable ways of assuring themselves, when the reality of death inevitably confronts them, that death does not really change anything and that after death it will be business as usual. In contemporary America the attempts to deprive death of its reality are just as frantic at they ever were in any culture—the embalming of bodies, the expensive caskets designed to delay as long as possible decay and decomposition, soft music piped into tombs. Then there is the deep-freezing of bodies, in the hope that one day medicine will have discovered a cure for the victim's disease, and there can take place a joyous (?) resurrection.

It is, of course, natural to fear death or to be anxious in the face of death. But this is very different from constructing a vast cultural illusion (to say nothing of a highly profitable industry) to help us forget about death or to persuade ourselves that it is unreal. (Macquarrie, 1972, pp. 154–155)

Furthermore, not all existentialists treat death in the same way; some are more optimistic than others. For example, Sartre sees death as the final absurdity, but Heidegger maintains that an honest acceptance of death can help us to live more authentically and happily (Macquarrie, 1972, p. 155).

The next point of agreement between Freudians and existentialists lies in their concern with the alleviation of human suffering. Both positions address the ways in which conflict and anxiety disrupt functioning. Some existentialists focus on the positive features of anxiety, on anxiety as a prerequisite of self-affirmation. Both groups also assume that people often deal with severe anxiety by avoiding responsibilities. According to the existentialists, people deny what they really *are* (Boss, 1963, p. 68). Freudians talk about the avoidance of responsibility through the repression of impulses that are an integral part of human nature.

Both positions blame society, to a large extent, for not allowing people to be true to their natures. In the Freudian scheme, society works through superego mechanisms to restrain the expression of uncivilized impulses. In the existential design, society often waylays individuals by inducing them to behave in inauthentic and self-alienating ways. Advocates of both positions are deeply concerned with understanding human nature. Freud, like the existentialists, sought to free people from illusions about themselves and to get them to recognize who they really are (Boss, 1963, p. 62).

Despite these commonalities, there are a number of interesting and provocative differences between the two positions. As should be apparent from our discussion of the subject/object dichotomy, the existentialists disapprove strongly of Freud's attempts to fashion a science of human nature by relying on an abstract and logical system of thought. The existentialists want to avoid creating lofty theories removed from human experience. As Kierkegaard proclaimed, "away from Speculation, away from the System, and back to reality" (May, 1958b, p. 25). By reality, he meant experience as it is immediately given to us. This phenomenological stance, so characteristic of existential thought, is quite different from Freud's attempts to objectify experience, to measure and calculate it precisely.

In the existential view, Freudian theorizing also leads to a reductionism that violates the unity of experience. Reductionism means lessening an entity by changing it from one state to another. The existentialists accuse Freud of changing complex human experience into a few hypothetical components that he called id, ego, and super-ego. They accuse him of intellectualizing and analyzing the interplay of these three components in a structure he called the psyche. Such a reductionism, they contend, destroyed his primary understanding of our being-in-the-world.

Three Modes of Being-in-the-World

Existential analysts recognize three modes of being-in-the-world. There is the **Umwelt,** or biological environment. This is the natural environment for animals and humans. It is the world that includes biological needs, drives, and instincts—a world that would still exist if we had no self-consciousness. This is primarily what Freud investigated. But this is only one world, according to May, and to focus only on understanding this realm would be highly limiting.

The second mode of being-in-the-world is **Mitwelt.** This is the world of interrelationships. It includes the meanings of things that we share with others. Thus, love can never be totally understood by focusing only on its connections with the biological world of lust and sex. It also depends upon such Mitwelt factors as personal decision and commitment to the other person.

The final mode of being-in-the-world is **Eigenwelt,** our own world; it is the self in relation to itself. Eigenwelt involves self-awareness and self-relatedness. It occurs when I become aware of the impact that another person has on me, or aware of what a flower means to me. Without Eigenwelt, the world would be intellectually arid and impersonal.

According to May, human beings live in all three worlds simultaneously. Any complete understanding of the personality of the individual would have to examine all three modes of being-in-the-world (May, 1983, pp. 126–132). Existentialists seek to understand the unique problems of human beings without fragmenting their humanity (May, 1958b, p. 36).

The Disintegration of Values in Modern Society

May pointed out that we live in an age of transition, in which our values and goals are continually being called into question. A central value of the 19th century, he suggested, was a rugged individualism that consisted of self-reliance, competitiveness, and assertiveness. These qualities were healthy; they served to help clear the frontier, ensure economic growth, and maximize the prosperity of all. However, May believed that the basic flaw in rugged individualism is that it leaves us with no sense of community (May, 1991, p. 109). Today, he contended, we have adopted intensified versions of these qualities, and they are clearly unhealthy. For example, many of us have acquired an exploitative competitiveness that "makes every [person] the potential enemy of his neighbor, . . . generates much interpersonal hostility and resentment and increases our anxiety and isolation from each other" (May, 1953, p. 48). Our extreme self-reliance also serves to isolate us from others; it keeps us from asking for help and support when we need it most. Healthy assertiveness has been transformed into an aggressiveness and tendency toward violence that divides us even further.

Each of these unhealthy qualities is manifested in our behavior as we pursue personal success and material possessions. Making money is the highest goal for many people in our culture. Surveys have shown that many students are overwhelmingly materialistic, are cynical about societal institutions such as the church and government, and are so competitive that they condone cheating. Their aspirations are extremely individualistic and narcissistic rather than social and humanitarian (May, 1991, p. 56). And why shouldn't students have these attitudes, given the things they see around them? May contended that many parents provide poor examples for their children and are unworthy of emulation. Many parents make more money than they can possibly spend and yet give their children only 5% of their time (May, 1991, p. 60). Parents may justify their behavior by talking about quality time, but their children are not fooled. Other parents give little of their time because they are forced by circumstances to work in order to provide the economic basics of life. While such parents cannot be blamed, unfortunately the result is often the same. Specifically, their children grow up with little or no guidance, and turn to unhealthy alternatives like gangs, cults, and drugs. Students also have few heroes to imitate. Does contemporary society have figures of the stature of Martin Luther King, Albert Schweitzer, or Eleanor Roosevelt (May, 1991, p. 58)? Today, society gives us heroes in films who kill, athletes who are more interested in the almighty dollar than in the game or its fans, and celebrities who are glamorized by the media for their infidelities and excessive drinking and drug-taking. In the political realm, young people see corruption and scandals surrounding various politicians. In the religious area, they grow nauseous as they watch unctuous preachers exploit their congregations for their own personal ends (May, 1991, p. 56).

Besides losing a healthy individualism, May believed that we have lost another central value—that our belief in the efficacy of reason in solving problems has been seriously distorted (May, 1953, pp. 49–50). During the Enlightenment of the 18th century, this conviction led to magnificent advances in science and education. In the 19th century, however, the belief became corrupted. People began to separate reason from emotion: to reason was rational and good; to feel was irrational and bad. In the 20th century, reason was supposed to provide the answers to our problems, but it has not. This fragmentation of reason and emotion is also seen in the Freudian scheme of human nature, in which unacceptable instincts and emotions are repressed by ego and superego functions based, in part, on rational input from others in the environment. Such compartmentalization has led, in May's view, to a splitting of the personality and of the person so that we act inappropriately—that is, by applying either reason or emotion—in situations that call for unity in our experiencing.

A third value we have lost is our sense of self-worth and dignity (May, 1953, p. 55). In May's view, this loss is partially due to people's feeling that they are powerless to change the operations of government and business, which are seen as huge, impersonal enterprises unresponsive to the needs of society. Feelings of powerlessness accrue in a worsening economy in which inflation and recession operate simultaneously to raise the cost of living to unaffordable levels and to terminate the jobs of millions of workers with little or no warning. In such a threatening and uncertain world, people feel the situation is beyond their control—that they are pawns in a terrifying game, in which a few mediocre men make moves that affect their destinies.

Next, May contended that many of us have lost not only our sense of identity but also our sense of relatedness to nature (May, 1953, p. 68). In Western society, we have been too concerned with the development of techniques to master nature and not concerned enough with understanding our relationship to it. The romantic back-to-the-land movement in this country can be seen as a reaction to an indiscriminate emphasis on technology. Because of our anxiety and emptiness, we have lost our feelings for and sense of awe about nature (May, 1953, p. 69). Our task, as May saw it, is to fill the impersonality of nature with our own aliveness and awareness. We must confront the power and vastness of nature and relate to nature creatively (May, 1953, p. 75).

Finally, May (1969) maintained that many of us have lost our ability to relate to others in a mature, loving way. We have confused sex with love. The media have contributed to this confusion by glorifying sex and by suggesting that people who do not engage in continual sexual affairs are unhealthy. Thus, people are pressured to have innumerable temporary liaisons. In May's opinion, sex is used as a narcotic to dull the senses and to keep individuals from becoming fully aware of their essential separateness from others. Despite the AIDS threat, many people still regard the ability to perform the sexual act with many different partners as an indication of their worth and adequacy as human beings. Unfortunately, this production-line mentality is not ultimately satisfying, and people who are tied to it feel dissatisfied and lonely. In May's view, mature relationships are difficult to achieve and take time to develop. They involve a commitment to, and concern for, the welfare of the other person. Sex is the natural expression of affection and caring between people in an evolving, deepening relationship; it is not an experience that should be forced on individuals before they are ready for it. In a world fraught with troubles and anxiety, however, this lesson is difficult to learn, according to May. Although sex decreases anxiety, its effects are temporary. The eventual result is increased feelings of alienation and worthlessness (May, 1991, p. 214).

In conclusion, May maintained that our sense of worthlessness leads to a loss of the sense of the tragic significance of human life (May, 1953, p. 75). For May, tragedy is an integral part of the human experience. It implies the fall of someone who believes strongly in his or her dignity and worth. It also implies a final optimism, because it suggests that we take our freedom seriously and continue to struggle to achieve our potentialities.

Emptiness and Loneliness

The primary result of the confusion that comes from the disintegration of our values is that we feel empty inside and isolated from others. The vastness and complexity of the problems that confront us contribute to these feelings. According to May, however, feelings of emptiness should not be taken to mean that we are literally empty or without potential for feeling (May, 1953, p. 24). Instead, the experience of emptiness comes from feelings of powerlessness in which events seem beyond our control. We seem unable to direct our own lives, to influence others, or to change the world around us. As a result, we feel a deep sense of despair and futility. Eventually, if we see that our actions make no difference, we give up wanting and feeling; we become apathetic. In May's opinion, the greatest danger at this point is that the attempt to defend ourselves against despair will lead to painful anxiety. If the situation goes uncorrected, the result is the restriction of our potential to grow as human beings or our surrender to some destructive form of authoritarianism (May, 1953, pp. 25–26).

May believed that there is a close association between emptiness and loneliness. When we do not know what we want or feel and when we stand in the midst of a general upheaval and confusion about values in our society, we sense danger and turn to the people around us for answers (May, 1953, p. 27). We may turn to them because we have been taught by society to rely on others in times of crisis. Yet, paradoxically, the more we attempt to reach out to others to ease our feelings of loneliness, the more lonely and desperate we become. Many of us need to be in a relationship all the time in order to feel safe and secure. We tend to cling to partners we really do not like or respect. We are afraid that others will think less of us if we are single. As a result, we suffer in silence and try to make the best of a bad situation. We learn to adjust to the person and to stifle our own individuality in order to protect the status quo. We yearn for security and yet are constrained by it.

Part of the syndrome also involves seeking invitations to parties, dinners, or other outings with people. Often, we do not especially want to go but feel compelled to as a means of proving to ourselves that we are not alone and that we are acceptable to others. We know we have made it if we are continually sought after and if we are never alone. We do not even see the positive value of solitude (May, 1953, p. 26). We must be accepted in order to consider ourselves alive. This compulsive need for acceptance may manifest itself among college students in excessive partying, in the adoption of uniform clothing styles and uniform opinions, or in striving to be academically average. Many students try not to be different; they ridicule academic excellence and extol mediocrity. It feels safe to be average and anti-intellectual. But such conformity is illusory and, in the final analysis, harmful to human growth. It is temporarily comforting, but the eventual price is that we give up our separate identities. We avoid relying on ourselves and renounce the one thing that would help us overcome our loneliness in the long run—the development of our inner resources and values (May, 1953, p. 33).

The Emergence of Anxiety

According to May, feelings of anxiety stem from loneliness and emptiness. Like Freud, he believed that anxiety signals an internal conflict, but May's theorizing about the nature and source of the conflict differs from Freud's. For Freud, the conflict was nearly always sexual in nature; to reduce the unpleasant feelings that it generated, the person banned the conflict from consciousness. For May, anxiety is not simply an unpleasant feeling; it is "the human being's basic reaction to a danger to his existence, or to some value he identifies with his anxiety" (May, 1953, p. 40). Since ontological anxiety is a threat to values, no one can escape anxiety, for no values are unassailable (May, 1967, p. 79).

According to May, the conflict that generates ontological anxiety is between being and nonbeing. Anxiety occurs as the individual attempts to realize his or her potentialities. If, for example, a man's overtures at friendship have been rejected, he faces a fundamental conflict between being and nonbeing: he can try to understand the reasons for the rejection by questioning the other person, or he can avoid asking questions that may prove embarrassing. He is thus faced with a fundamental choice, a choice that generates anxiety. He has the freedom to move forward or backward, and it makes him anxious. Kierkegaard describes this feeling of anxiety as the "dizziness of freedom" (May, 1958a, p. 52). If the man decides to assume responsibility and question the other person, he is using the experience of ontological anxiety constructively. If he fails to ask the pertinent questions, he is denying his responsibility and blocking the realization of his potentialities. In this case, May would say he is guilty. Like anxiety, then, guilt is also an ontological characteristic of human existence (May, 1967, p. 52). But ontological guilt does not occur because the person fails to act in terms of cultural prohibitions, as Freud thought. It occurs because an individual who can choose fails to do so (May, 1958a, p. 55). Such a person fails to act in terms of his central need in life—the fulfillment of his potentialities (May, 1953, p. 93).

May clarified the meaning of ontological anxiety further by dividing it into two components: **normal anxiety** and **neurotic anxiety.** Normal anxiety is anxiety that is proportionate to the threat to our values. It does not involve repression and can be confronted constructively on the conscious level. Neurotic anxiety, in contrast, is a reaction that is disproportionate to the threat and involves repression. Neurotic anxiety develops when we are unable to address the normal anxiety arising at the time of the actual crisis in our growth and the threat to our values (May, 1967, p. 80). For example, normal anxiety occurs for many of us when we first move out of our parents' home. We experience a threat to our family security. Yet if we confront this threat directly we are usually able to live through it successfully and to emerge from the crisis as a more independent and self-reliant person. We experience a healthy transformation of values. In contrast, if we feel threatened when we first move away from home and repress our feelings of anxiety about it, we may find ourselves calling and writing home almost daily and rushing home during every school recess throughout our college career. Such behavior may keep us overly dependent on our parents for support, help, and advice, hinders formation of close friendships with other students, and prevents us from solving our own problems.

For May, the goal in helping people to maximize their mental health is not to free the person from all anxiety. It is rather to help free them from neurotic anxiety, so that they can confront normal anxiety constructively. Normal anxiety is an integral part of growth and creativity.

The Expansion of Consciousness

In May's theory, individuals cannot fulfill their potentialities if these capabilities are largely unconscious. The unconscious involves "those potentialities for knowing and experiencing which . . . individual[s] cannot or will not actualize" (May, 1983, p. 18). Thus, May believed that, the more conscious of our being we are, the more spontaneous and creative we will be, and the more capable we will be of choosing our plans and reaching our goals (May, 1953, pp. 94–104). Our objective, then, should clearly be an increase in consciousness. According to May, severe anxiety (neurotic anxiety) tends to restrict our consciousness, as we try to defend ourselves from pain through a variety of defense mechanisms, including those first postulated by Freud. These defenses help us avoid coping with our own being and are thus detrimental to growth.

In May's view, the sense of being that needs to be uncovered is the capacity to see ourselves as beings-in-the-world who can deal with the problems of our existence. This fundamental sense of being is not the same as the ego. The Freudian ego, according to May, is weak and passive, buffeted by id impulses and admonishments from the superego; it has little of the vitality and aliveness associated with a sense of being. Movement toward realization begins with awareness of our potentialities as we journey toward becoming fully human (May, 1958a, pp. 46–47). This awareness makes it possible for our potentialities to unfold; it also involves an increasing awareness of our links to others. By seeing that we are all mortal, on the planet for only small segments of time, and part of a world community where we depend on each other for survival, we all become brothers and sisters, in the same family at last (May, 1991, p. 302).

PERSONALITY DEVELOPMENT

May's discussion of the development process centers on the physical and psychological ties between us and our parents and parental substitutes—teachers, friends, clergy. He pointed out our physical dependence on our mothers, which begins when we are fed as fetuses through the umbilical cord. This tie is severed at birth, but physical dependency remains. As we grow older, physical dependence tends to subside, but psychological dependence often does not. This to May is a major problem, and the way in which we handle it will determine in large degree whether we will move toward maturity and personal growth. We must make a decision to assume responsibility for our actions or to let others make our decisions for us. Thus, "the conflict is between every human being's need to struggle toward enlarged self-awareness, maturity, freedom and responsibility, and his tendency to remain a child and cling to the protection of parents or parental substitutes" (May, 1953, p. 193).

This dependency struggle is May's reinterpretation of the classic Oedipal conflict postulated by Freud. Whereas Freud believed the conflict was sexual in nature, May sees it as a power confrontation. The struggle revolves around the attempt to establish autonomy and identity in our relationships with people who are very powerful. In this battle for freedom, we progress through several stages of consciousness (May, 1953, pp. 138–139). The first stage is simply our innocence as infants with no consciousness of self. The second stage is rebellion, whereby we seek to establish our inner strength. This struggle typically takes place at age 2 or 3 and again during adolescence. Although rebellion is a necessary step in the evolution of consciousness, it should not be confused with freedom. Rebellion is defiance, an active rejection of parental and societal rules. Such behavior is automatic, rigid, and reflexive. True freedom, in contrast, involves "*openness,* a readiness to grow; it means being flexible, ready to change for the sake of greater human values" (May, 1953, p. 159).

The third stage is ordinary consciousness of self. At this point, we are capable of understanding some of our errors and of recognizing some of our prejudices. We are also capable of learning from our mistakes and assuming responsibility for our actions. Many people identify this state of ordinary consciousness with being, maturity, and health. But, according to May, there is still another stage, a fourth stage of consciousness that, if attained, actually signifies maturity. He calls this stage the creative consciousness of self. Transcending the usual limits of consciousness, we are able to see the truth without distortion. These moments of insight are joyous ones and occur only occasionally. Note that May's concept of creative consciousness is closely akin to Maslow's peak experiences.

We attain maturity and move close to self-realization when we experience these joyous moments. We are able to make choices, confront our problems, and take responsibility for our actions. We are not pushed along by deterministic forces. We are not bound by the past, by our role training, or by the standards we have been taught by others. We are conscious of these forces, but are able to choose freely whether or not to act in accordance with them. "Consciousness of self gives us the power to stand outside the rigid chain of stimulus and response, to pause, and by this pause to throw some weight on either side, to cast some decision about what the response will be" (May, 1953, p. 161).

Critics might question whether our behavior can really be determined by something as vague as consciousness of self. But May's position is that, although behavior is often determined by other events, we still have the freedom to make choices. When our consciousness is restricted or stifled, we move away from self-realization and maturity. Such a lessening of consciousness results from threats to our sense of being. May saw neurosis and psychosis as attempts to adjust to these threats—ways of accepting nonbeing so that some aspect of being can be preserved (May, 1967, p. 117). To cope with the threats to our being, we repress or distort our experiences through defensive maneuvers. The overwhelming threats then recede into unconsciousness. But through these maneuvers we deny our own freedom to make choices. We shrink from our responsibilities and reject our own potentialities (May, 1958a).

ASSESSMENT TECHNIQUES

Like Rogers, May was not primarily concerned with technique in his attempts to understand human functioning. His main focus in the therapeutic relationship was on the dynamic encounter between the two participants. In fact, May believed that a premature emphasis on technique may actually hinder understanding:

> Existential analysis is a way of understanding human existence, and its representatives believe that one of the chief (if not *the* chief) blocks to the understanding of human beings in Western culture is precisely the overemphasis on technique, an overemphasis which goes along with the tendency to see the human being as an object to be calculated, managed, "analyzed." Our Western tendency has been to believe that *understanding follows technique*; if we get the right technique, then we can penetrate the riddle of the patient. . . . The existential approach holds the exact opposite; namely, that *technique follows understanding*. (May, 1958a, pp. 76–77)

May maintains that existential analysis is an *attitude* rather than a set of psychotherapeutic techniques. It involves a stress on understanding the special meanings of the person's existence. In the pursuit of this understanding, the therapist may derive new techniques or utilize existing ones. Thus, the therapist may employ dream analysis, free association, and transference, as do the Freudians, or personality measures, as do the Rogerians. But the therapist seeks to interpret dreams and symbols to ferret out their meaning for the patient's existence now and their implications for his or her future (May, 1958a, p. 77).

Thus, May's approach to understanding patients is characterized by flexibility and versatility; techniques vary from patient to patient and from time to time during the therapeutic process (May, 1958a, p. 78). His orientation is eclectic, but makes systematic use of each selected procedure to shed light on the person's unique potentialities and existence.

THEORY'S IMPLICATIONS FOR THERAPY

The Goal of Therapy

The primary task of the therapist, according to May, is to make empty and lonely people more aware of themselves and their potential for growth through the expansion of their consciousness and experience (May, 1967, p. 126). To accomplish these goals, the therapist must seek to understand patients as human beings and as beings-in-the-world (May, 1958a, p. 77). The focus is not on a detailed analysis of the patients' problems, but on how past experiences and aspirations shed light on where they are at the moment and where they are headed. "The context is the patient not as a set of psychic dynamisms or mechanisms but as a human being who is choosing, committing, and pointing himself toward something right now; the context is dynamic, immediately real, and present" (May, 1958a, p. 77). In short, the focus is on the ontological basis of the person's problems. These problems can be understood only when there is a real relationship between patient and therapist. The therapist, if he or she is to be successful, must relate to the person as "one existence communicating with another" (May, 1958a, p. 81).

Under such conditions, May believed, patients can experience their existence as real. They can become aware of their potentialities and develop the courage to act on the basis of them (May, 1958a, p. 45). The patients are cured, according to May, not when they come to accept the standards of the culture but when they become oriented toward the fulfillment of their own unique existence (May, 1958a, p. 87).

The Case of Mrs. Hutchens

May (1983) provided an actual case study to illustrate some of the assumptions and principles that guided him in therapy. The patient, known as Mrs. Hutchens, was a suburban woman in her mid-30s who suffered from a hysterical tenseness of the larynx, with the result that she spoke with a perpetual hoarseness.

As May's analysis revealed, the woman felt that, if she said what she really believed, especially to her parents, she would be rejected; therefore, she concluded, it was safer to be quiet. May believed that he understood the childhood origins of her problem—her need to protect herself against authoritarian criticism and belittling by her mother and grandmother—but to him this analysis and interpretation was not the most important part of the therapy. The most important part was the person now "existing, becoming, emerging . . . in the room with [him]" (May, 1983, p. 25). Focusing on his patient, May realized that this person, like every human being, was *centered* in herself; that is, she was attempting to preserve her existence by speaking in a hoarse voice. She also protected herself by being too controlled and proper in her behavior.

In the course of analysis, the patient revealed a dream in which she was searching room by room for a baby in an unfinished house near an airport. When she found the baby, she placed it in a pocket of her robe and then was seized by anxiety that it would be smothered. Much to her joy, she found that the baby was still alive. She then had a terrifying thought: "Shall I kill it?"

Analysis revealed that the airport was where, at age 20, she had learned to fly solo, an act that asserted her independence from her parents. The baby was her youngest son, whom she regularly identified with herself; the baby, therefore, was herself. The baby was also a symbol of her growing consciousness; in her dream, she considered killing that consciousness.

Approximately six years before entering therapy, Mrs. Hutchens had left her parents' religious faith and joined a church whose denomination she dared not tell her authoritarian parents. During therapy she considered telling them but, whenever May brought up the topic, she became faint. She would report feeling empty inside and would have to lie down on the couch for a few minutes. Finally, she wrote her parents informing them of her change in religious faith and telling them it would accomplish nothing if they tried to change her mind. In the next therapeutic session, she told May that she felt tremendous anxiety and wondered if she might become psychotic. May assured her that he thought this outcome was highly unlikely.

May interpreted her fainting and her anxiety attacks as attempts to kill her emerging consciousness. She was struggling to accept her hatred of her mother and her mother's hatred of her, to free herself from her mother's painful dominance, and to accept responsibility for her own actions and choices, even though they might not always have the best consequences. In brief, Mrs. Hutchens was actively confronting herself in these areas. The result was the opportunity for fuller independence, positive growth, and the development of a healthier lifestyle.

EVALUATIVE COMMENTS

We now evaluate May's theory in terms of our six criteria.

Comprehensiveness Like the other humanistic psychologists, May's primary concern was to develop a model of positive growth as a means of alleviating human suffering. Thus, he focused principally on understanding abnormal behavior and changing it. His position is more comprehensive than those of Rogers and Maslow, however, because he integrated psychoanalytic and existential principles more thoroughly into his theory and presented a more detailed treatment of the developmental process. In addition, May sought a compromise with American behaviorism and its assumptions. In some of his earlier work, he attempted to utilize learning principles and experiments to increase our understanding of the meaning of anxiety, although he saw this approach as limited. Thus, May's system is relatively comprehensive, especially when compared with the other major humanistic positions.

Precision and testability   May's theory is quite imprecise and difficult to test. Terms such as *being, potentiality,* and *ontological guilt* are vague and nearly impossible to define accurately. In addition, the theory consists of a series of disjointed and unconnected propositions that do not lend themselves readily to scientific inquiry.

May's position retains close ties to philosophy. This is not a weakness in itself, as some psychologists seem to think, but it does hinder any attempt to convince investigators of his theory's scientific status. At this point, because its deficiencies in terms of precision and testability are so apparent, May's theory will probably not even get a fair hearing from members of the scientific establishment. This is unfortunate, because it includes many interesting and provocative ideas, especially regarding the need for change in our ideas about science. At best, May will be seen as a philosophical gadfly to be endured, but the full impact of his message about the need for a humanistic science of psychology will go unheeded. It is a message that deserves a better fate.

Parsimony   While overall judgments about the parsimony of May's position are difficult to make, it does seem to have an excess of concepts. For example, there is considerable redundancy in the terms awareness, consciousness, self-awareness, self-consciousness, and self-relatedness (Reeves, 1977, p. 269). Also, he described the person who has achieved healthy self-expression as being spontaneous, original, and genuine, explaining each of these characteristics in the same way (Reeves, 1979, p. 36).

Empirical validity   Empirical support for the theory is limited. Much of the evidence is based on clinical observation in therapy sessions and is largely unsystematic and retrospective. Research on May's position is still in an exploratory stage.

Heuristic value   May's position has proved highly stimulating to investigators in the humanistic psychology movement and to members of the public but, for the most part, his efforts have been ignored by traditional investigators within psychology.

Applied value   May's theory has been fruitfully applied to problems in areas such as education, pastoral counseling, family life, and religion.

DISCUSSION QUESTIONS

1. How would you define existentialism?
2. Do you agree with May that many psychologists tend to study human behavior and experience in abstract and oversimplified terms? Give reasons for your judgment.
3. What does it mean to act authentically? Would you ever be willing to let others define your goals for you?
4. Compare and contrast psychoanalysis and existentialism.
5. Do you agree with May that we have lost our sense of values? Do you feel powerless to control your own destiny?
6. Has there been too much emphasis in our society on the development of new technology to help us master the environment? Do we have a good understanding of our relationship to the environment? Have you seen any progress in our attempts to preserve the environment in recent years?
7. How often do you feel empty, in the sense of being powerless to control your own outcomes? What are the causes of such feelings in you and others?
8. Do you agree with May that many people continue to endure basically unsatisfying relationships because they want to alleviate feelings of loneliness?
9. Do you think that many students yearn for uncritical acceptance from others? Do you believe that some students are anti-intellectual because it makes them more acceptable to others?
10. Do you think that many students are struggling to become independent of parental control? Do you agree with May that one of the basic struggles in life involves our attempts to accept ultimate responsibility for our actions? Is dependency always harmful to the person?

GLOSSARY

being   Developmental process whereby the individual seeks to realize his or her unique set of potentials.

dasein   A term derived from the German words *sein* (being) and *da* (there). Dasein indicates that a person exists in a particular place at a particular time. Thus, the individual can be conscious of, and responsible for, his or her existence, and can therefore choose the direction his or her life will take.

eigenwelt   The unique presence in human beings of self-awareness and self-relatedness.

existential-analytic perspective   Theoretical approach to understanding human personality that combines elements of existential philosophy with Freudian concepts. Both positions, for example, focus on how people cope with the anxieties that result from the inability to love others and the inevitability of death.

existentialism   Philosophy that focuses on people's attempts to make sense of their existence by assigning meaning to it and then taking responsibility for their own actions as they try to live in accordance with their chosen values and principles.

mitwelt   The world of interrelationships. The experiences and meanings we share with others through our relationships.

neurotic anxiety   Painful feeling that is produced by an excessive reaction to a threat to our values. It involves a failure to make a choice that could lead to further growth.

normal anxiety   Painful feeling that emanates from a realistic threat to our established values. It is healthy to confront this threat, by making choices that lead to further growth. A child decides to walk and leaves the security of his playpen; an adolescent decides to establish a romantic relationship with another person; an adult decides to marry and have children of her own.

ontology   Branch of philosophy that seeks to understand the nature of being.

umwelt   The biological or natural environment in which human beings exist. A world of biological needs and drives, it consists of natural cycles, of sleep and waking, of being born and dying, of desire and relief.

SUGGESTED READINGS

May, R. (1950). *The meaning of anxiety*. New York: Ronald Press.
May, R. (1953). *Man's search for himself*. New York: Norton.
May, R. (1969). *Love and will*. New York: Norton.
May, R. (1991). *The cry for myth*. New York: Norton.

REFERENCES

Boss, M. (1963). *Psychoanalysis and daseinanalysis*. New York: Basic Books.
Macquarrie, J. (1972). *Existentialism*. Baltimore: Penguin Books.
May, R. (1953). *Man's search for himself*. New York: Norton.
May, R. (1958a). Contributions of existential psychotherapy. In R. May, E. Angel, & H. F. Ellenberger (Eds.), *Existence: A new dimension in psychiatry and psychology* (pp. 37–91). New York: Basic Books.
May, R. (1958b). The origins and significance of the existential movement in psychology. In R. May, E. Angel, & H. F. Ellenberger (Eds.), *Existence: A new dimension in psychiatry and psychology* (pp. 3–36). New York: Basic Books.
May, R. (1967). *Psychology and the human dilemma*. New York: Van Nostrand.
May, R. (1969). *Love and will*. New York: Norton.
May, R. (1973). Existential psychology. In T. Millon (Ed.), *Theories of psychopathology and personality* (pp. 263–271). Philadelphia: Saunders.
May, R. (1981). *Freedom and destiny*. New York: Norton.
May, R. (1982). The problem of evil: An open letter to Carl Rogers. *Journal of Humanistic Psychology, 22,* 10–21.
May, R. (1983). *The discovery of being: Writings in existential psychology*. New York: Norton.
May, R. (1991). *The cry for myth*. New York: Norton.
Reeves, C. (1977). *The psychology of Rollo May*. San Francisco: Jossey-Bass.
Van Kaam, A. (1969). *Existential foundations of psychology*. Garden City, NY: Image Books.

PART SIX

SOCIAL-BEHAVIORISTIC PERSPECTIVES

Historically, two major lines of thought and investigation have shaped the course of personality psychology. One grew out of clinical practice, beginning with the work of the French physicians Charcot and Janet, and culminating in the efforts of Freud and his disciples. These investigators were medical practitioners concerned primarily with understanding the etiology of their patients' abnormal behavior in order to help them overcome their problems. Thus, they emphasized behavior change. They also focused on some of the most interesting, important, and complicated phenomena in human functioning: love, hate, death, sexual behavior, and aggressiveness.

In contrast to this medical orientation, the other major line of investigation had its roots in the experimental laboratory. Theorists in this tradition were primarily concerned with the scientific understanding of the learning process. They assumed that most of our behavior was acquired and that the task of the psychologist was to specify the environmental conditions responsible for producing behavior. Proponents of a simple stimulus-response (S-R) psychology, they sought to understand how given stimuli became linked to given responses.

The most important proponent of the S-R model in psychology was John B. Watson. Watson was originally educated at the University of Chicago as a functionalist. The functionalists explained behavior in terms of *mental functions*. Borrowing from Darwin's evolutionary theory, they maintained that human beings, like animals lower in the phylogenetic scale, were engaged in a constant struggle to survive. To survive, they had to learn to adjust their behavior. Such adjustment was possible because human beings possessed minds that encompassed the ability to reason and helped them solve problems presented by the environment.

Watson rejected this approach because, in his view, it did little to advance psychology as a science. He believed that terms such as mind, spirit, and soul were useless because the private events to which they referred could not be measured objectively and reliably. Psychology would advance only if it got rid of such mentalism and focused on public events that could be objectively validated. As a result, Watson proclaimed that psychology was the study of observable behavior and that references to all private events were unscientific and unworthy of scientific investigation.

Watson's pronouncements had a significant effect on psychology during his lifetime, and vestiges of his viewpoint can be seen in the work of the various contemporary social-behavioristic theorists discussed in this part of the text. Watson's influence is especially evident in the work of B. F. Skinner (Chapter 15), but it is also apparent to some extent in the positions taken by Julian Rotter and Albert Bandura (Chapters 16 and 17).

Like Watson, Skinner had a basic aversion to the study of private events. He concluded reluctantly that only those private events that could be measured objectively and reliably were worthy of scientific study. His primary focus was on observable behavior that could be recorded objectively. Like Watson, he was primarily concerned with trying to understand how environmental stimuli influence behavior, in the hope of generating fundamental laws. This goal could be achieved, Skinner believed, only through systematic observation and experimentation under controlled conditions. Such control could be exercised most readily in laboratory studies of animals lower in the evolutionary scale. Because the behaviors most amenable to control are simple ones, Skinner believed that the investigator should proceed from the simple to the complex.

Such a position means that his followers concern themselves primarily with a restricted set of phenomena and do not usually engage actively in attempts to explain phenomena such as love and hate. Skinner thought that his approach paid off handsomely, as principles of behavior painstakingly discovered in laboratory work with lower animals have been successfully applied to people in therapeutic and educational settings. In his later years, Skinner concentrated his attention directly on the study of human behavior; thus, he shifted from a simple behaviorism focused exclusively on lower animals to a more complex social behaviorism that addresses itself to important human issues and problems.

In Chapter 15, we review Skinner's arguments about the need for a scientific technology of behavior and the dangers of mentalistic explanations that seem to help us understand behavior but, in fact, impede our understanding. "He was kind to you because he has a pure soul," and "She scored an A on her chemistry exam because she has a good mind" are examples of mentalistic explanations that lack scientific explanatory power; they are invoked on a post hoc basis and are meaningless from a scientific standpoint. Skinner distinguished mentalism from cognition, which he considered a legitimate object of study. Although both terms refer to private events, *mentalism* describes events that cannot be studied scientifically, whereas *cognition* refers to events that can be objectively and reliably recorded and communicated clearly among scientists. Cognitive events are studied primarily by means of verbal reports, and Skinner accepted their use.

In Chapter 15, we also present the major terms and principles in Skinner's operant analysis of personality. Of particular importance is his study of various kinds of reinforcers and reinforcement schedules and their effects on the acquisition and modification of behavior. Skinner is frequently lambasted by critics as advocating the use of punishment to control behavior, but this accusation is simply not true. As we shall see, Skinner did not consider punishment an effective means of altering behavior. We also discuss the development of normal and abnormal personalities within Skinner's unique framework and the ways in which operant principles can be applied in therapeutic and educational settings.

The work of Rotter and Bandura also shares a number of features with the psychology advocated by Watson. Both Rotter and Bandura believe that most of our behavior is learned. They also believe that the advancement of psychology as a science depends on the establishment of precise measurement procedures and the systematic observation of behavior under controlled conditions. Yet their theories rely heavily on the use of cognitive constructs, in defiance of Watson's dictum that the study of such events has no place in psychology. Thus, their positions go far beyond Watson's simple, mechanistic model of human functioning. Whereas Watson leaned heavily on Pavlov's classical-conditioning paradigm to explain the acquisition of behavior, Rotter and Bandura expand this view by incorporating the role of organismic variables into their formulas. Their neobehavioristic position includes such cognitive constructs as expectancy, imitation, covert rehearsal of events, self-efficacy, value, memory, and habits. These stimulus-organism-response (S-O-R) models attempt to deal with more complex phenomena than those studied by Watson and, to a considerable extent, by Skinner. At the same time, however, Rotter and Bandura insist on accurate and objective measurement of these complex phenomena.

The positions of Rotter and Bandura are a more direct outgrowth of learning theories propounded after Watson. Rotter himself traces the origins of his position to the work of learning theorists Thorndike, Tolman, and Hull. From Thorndike, Rotter adopted the view that behavior is subject to modification by its consequences. In other words, Rotter, like Skinner, accepts the concept of instrumental or operant conditioning. From Tolman and Hull, Rotter borrowed the notion that behavior is purposive—that we are guided by our motives to attain certain goals. Rotter's thinking is particularly close to Hull's in this regard. To predict the probability that a behavior would occur, Hull proposed the formula

$$E = H \times D$$

where E refers to the excitatory potential (probability) of the behavior, H refers to habit strength, and D refers to drive strength. Thus, in Hull's formulation, the probability of a given response, or movement toward a goal, is a function of the animal's drive strength (motive) multiplied by its habit strength. In Rotter's scheme, excitatory potential becomes behavior potential; habit strength is roughly translated as expectancy of the occurrence of reinforcement; and drive strength is reinterpreted as the value of the reinforcement. Therefore, the probability that a given behavior will occur is a function of the expectancies or habits that a person has acquired—primarily as a result of previous experiences—and the importance of the reinforcer that will affect the person's drive level.

In Chapter 16, we review these and other concepts in Rotter's theory. We focus on one construct of particular importance in his social-learning position—internal/external control of reinforcement—and provide a sampling of recent research findings based on the measurement of individual differences in locus of control.

Bandura's work, like Rotter's, places heavy emphasis on the role played by cognition in the acquisition, retention, regulation, maintenance, and modification of behavior. He does not reject the concept of reinforcement; he simply utilizes it differently in his theorizing and research. Whereas Skinner believed that reinforcement automatically strengthens or weakens responses, Bandura's view is that reinforcement provides people with information—information concerning the kinds of behaviors they must perform in order to gain beneficial outcomes and avoid punishing ones. Within this framework, learning from response consequences is largely a cognitive process. According to Bandura, observational learning plays a primary role in the acquisition, maintenance, and modification of behavior.

As he rightly notes, the study of imitation learning has been relatively ignored by traditional learning theorists. Historically, the concept can be traced to the work of Lloyd Morgan in 1896, Gabriel Tarde in 1903, and William McDougall in 1908. All these theorists believed that imitation was an innate tendency in human beings. As the popularity of Watsonian behaviorism drove the instinct doctrine into disrepute, a few learning theorists, including Humphrey, Allport, and Holt, tried to account for imitation in terms of Pavlovian conditioning. According to this learning paradigm, imitative responses were the simple result of a person's matching his or her behavior to the behavior of another. In other terms, imitation involved contiguous associations between social stimuli. Soon, however, the behaviorist focus shifted from classical conditioning to instrumental, or operant, learning. This new view was advocated primarily by Miller and Dollard in their classic text *Social Learning and Imitation* (1941). In essence, their position was that imitation learning occurred when a motivated person was positively reinforced for matching the behavior of a model during a sequence of random trial-and-error responses.

Bandura's main objection to both the classical- and instrumental-conditioning explanations of imitation is that they fail to account for the acquisition of new responses through observation. Bandura believes that operant conditioning—the notion that the person makes a long series of random responses that are eventually shaped through reinforcement until they match the behavior of the model—is simply too cumbersome to account for the many responses we learn in the course of our lives. He suggests instead that imitative learning often occurs in the absence of external reinforcement. We acquire behavior without performing it overtly and without being reinforced for it. We simply watch the behavior of others, represent it cognitively (that is, symbolically), and then perform it under the appropriate conditions.

In Chapter 17, we discuss the major assumptions underlying Bandura's social-cognitive position and then present the basic concepts and principles of his theory. The focus is on the ways in which behavior is learned when the person is exposed to single and multiple models with varying personality characteristics. As we shall see, the impact of multiple models on children's behavior is often complicated and difficult to assess, because the models often show contradictory behaviors. We also discuss the role of self-control processes in the acquisition of behavior and examine some applications of modeling principles and research to two major social problems: violence in the media and problem behaviors, particularly phobias in children. In examining Bandura's treatment of the developmental process, we discuss his use of the concepts of imitation, successive approximation, and schedule of reinforcement. Finally, we present Bandura's more recent theorizing about self-efficacy and its role in the development and change of pathological behavior, along with supporting empirical evidence.

CHAPTER 15

Skinner's Operant Analysis

BIOGRAPHICAL SKETCH

Burrhus Frederick Skinner was born in Susquehanna, Pennsylvania, in 1904. In his autobiography (Skinner, 1976), he reported that his home life was warm and stable. He was never physically punished by his lawyer father and only once by his mother, when she washed his mouth with soap and water after he said a word that did not meet with her approval. He liked school and acquired a strong background in English, literature, mathematics, and the sciences from a few fine teachers. As a boy, he was always building and creating things. He built roller-skate scooters, wagons, sleds, seesaws, merry-go-rounds, slingshots, blowguns, kites, and model airplanes. This fascination with mechanical objects can be seen in his invention and use of various devices in his experimental work. These devices include the Skinner box, an apparatus designed to help investigators study the effects of different reinforcement schedules on animal behavior; the cumulative recorder, a device to assess the rate of responding of organisms; and the teaching machine, an instrument designed to facilitate learning in students.

Skinner enrolled at Hamilton College in New York State as an English major. He never really adjusted to student life, however. He joined a fraternity but knew little about fraternity life; he was inept at sports; and he complained bitterly about unnecessary curriculum requirements. By his senior year, he was in open revolt. He participated in activities to humiliate faculty members whom the students thought pompous and arrogant. One of these incidents is particularly noteworthy. In order to deflate a name-dropping English professor, Skinner and another student printed posters that read, in part: "Charles Chaplin, the famous cinema comedian, will deliver his lecture 'Moving Pictures as a Career' in the Hamilton College Chapel on Friday, October 9." The lecture was reported to be under the professor's auspices. After plastering posters all over town, they returned to the campus and went to bed. The next morning, the other student called the local newspaper and told reporters that the college president wanted the lecture publicly announced. By noon, the situation was completely out of hand. Swarms of children were taken by their parents to the railway station to greet the famous actor. In spite of police roadblocks, approximately 400 cars got through to the campus. Other escapades were followed by threats of expulsion, but Skinner was finally permitted to graduate.

After college, Skinner pursued a career as a writer. As a senior, he had met the famous poet Robert Frost, who requested that Skinner send him samples of his work. Skinner sent the poet three short stories and received encouraging comments in reply. He spent the next two years living in Greenwich Village in New York City and in Europe. Eventually he realized he would not be successful as a writer, presumably because he had nothing important to say. To explore his interest in human behavior, he then entered Harvard to study psychology.

Skinner found the intellectual atmosphere at Harvard stimulating and challenging. In order to improve his skills in a new field, he set up a rigorous study schedule and adhered to it for almost two years; he read nothing that did not pertain to psychology and physiology. Among his academic mentors were historian E. G. Boring, clinician Henry Murray, and physiologist W. J. Crozier. The writings of J. B. Watson, Ivan Pavlov, and E. L. Thorndike also had a considerable impact on the young psychologist. He was particularly impressed by Watson's concern with devising a technology of behavior. In one fell swoop, Watson had thrown out all mentalistic concepts, including mind, spirit, and consciousness, and proclaimed instead that psychology was the scientific study of observable behavior. Skinner, too, maintained that psychologists should focus on behavior that is observable and verifiable but, unlike Watson, he believed that psychologists must also account for internal or private events, as long as such events can be measured objectively and reliably.

Skinner was also greatly influenced by the work of the Russian physiologist Ivan Pavlov on the conditioned reflex. Pavlov was originally interested in the process of digestion in lower animals and the conditions under which digestive juices were secreted. In the course of his work, he discovered that animals salivated not only when food was actually in their mouths but also when it was shown to them by the experimenter. He called this phenomenon a "psychic secretion." His next step was to control the conditions under which such secretions occurred. As virtually every psychology student knows, Pavlov designed a room that minimized the intrusion of extraneous stimuli and was eventually able to demonstrate, through a precise series of maneuvers, that salivation could be brought under the control of specific stimuli such as a light or a bell. Previously neutral stimuli acquired the power to evoke responses originally evoked by other stimuli. The animals were classically conditioned. Besides the fact that such respondent conditioning can account for a variety of behaviors, Skinner was impressed by the procedure Pavlov used to bring the behavior under control. He reported that, then and throughout his career, he fully accepted Pavlov's dictum, "Control your conditions and you will see order."

Although some of our behavior is learned via classical conditioning, most of it is learned after we behave voluntarily and find that our actions are followed by positive or negative experiences. Skinner's interest in operant behavior—that is, behavior that operates on the environment—was piqued by animal experiments conducted by learning theorist E. L. Thorndike. Typically, cats were deprived of food, and then placed in problem boxes and left there until they accidentally moved a mechanism that opened a door and allowed them to escape. The animals usually made a variety of responses before making the correct one. Thorndike explained this trial-and-error learning by maintaining that an association was established between the animals' responses and the reinforcing consequences. Responses that resulted in pleasurable sensations Thorndike considered to be "stamped in," whereas he considered responses followed by an annoying state of affairs to be "stamped out." Skinner adopted a modification of this **law of effect** to explain the acquisition of behavior; he recast the law in terms of the changes in the probability of responding produced by the application of reinforcers or punishers.

After years of intensive study, Skinner received his Ph.D. from Harvard in 1931, and then spent five postdoctoral years working in Crozier's laboratory. In 1936, he accepted his first academic position, at the University of Minnesota; two years later, he wrote his first book, *The Behavior of Organisms,* which presented his initial formulations for an **operant analysis** of behavior. While at Minnesota, Skinner also found the time to begin a novel entitled *Walden Two,* a story about a miniature utopian society based on reinforcement principles. *Walden Two* was eventually published in 1948.

After a brief stint as chair of the psychology department at Indiana University, he returned to Harvard in 1948. Skinner was accorded many honors by his fellow psychologists, and was also one of the few behavioral scientists to win the President's Medal of Science. He was a prolific writer; his books include *Science and Human Behavior* (1953), *Verbal Behavior* (1957), *Schedules of Reinforcement* (with C. B. Ferster, 1957), *Cumulative Record* (1961), *The Technology of Teaching* (1968), *Contingencies of Reinforcement* (1969), *Beyond Freedom and Dignity* (1971), *About Behaviorism* (1974), *Particulars of My Life* (1976), *Reflections on Behaviorism and Society* (1978), *The Shaping of a Behaviorist* (1979), *A Matter of Consequences* (1983), *Enjoy Old Age* (with M. E. Vaughan, 1983), and *Upon Further Reflection* (1987). In his book on old age, Skinner offered advice to the elderly on how to manage their environments so as to maximize their enjoyment of old age despite declines in physical prowess and health (Skinner, 1970, pp. 1–21).

On August 10, 1990, Professor Skinner was awarded a Citation for Outstanding Lifetime Contribution to Psychology by the American Psychological Association. He died of complications from leukemia on August 18, 1990, in Cambridge, Massachusetts.

CONCEPTS AND PRINCIPLES

Scientific Behaviorism

Like virtually all of us, Skinner believed we are faced with problems that threaten our very existence. He argued that, although we often misuse the products of our technology, we can utilize the same technological prowess to solve our problems. We have even taken a few small steps in that direction—for example, in population control, pollution control, improved methods of crop production, and disease control (Skinner, 1971, p. 1). Yet in each of these areas we have only scratched the surface. Why is this so? In Skinner's view, it is because the solutions to these problems lie not in the application of our physical and biological knowledge but in an understanding of human behavior. Birth-control methods are useless if people do not use them; pollution-control devices accomplish nothing if people continue to ignore or resist them. Thus, what we need are drastic changes in our behavior (Skinner, 1971, p. 4).

Why, then, have we not made more progress in understanding human behavior? The answer, Skinner believed, lies in our refusal to give up mentalistic explanations of behavior that give the *appearance* of helping us understand our actions, but in fact hinder us in our quest.

> We are told that to control the number of people in the world we need to change *attitudes* toward children, overcome *pride* in size of family or in sexual potency, build some *sense of responsibility* toward offspring, and reduce the role played by a large family in allaying *concern* for old age. To work for peace we must deal with the *will to power* or the *paranoid delusions* of leaders; we must remember that wars begin in the *minds* of men, that there is something suicidal in man—a *death instinct* perhaps—which leads to war, and that man is aggressive by *nature*. To solve the problems of the poor we must inspire *self-respect,* encourage *initiative,* and reduce *frustration.* . . . This is staple fare. Almost no one questions it. Yet there is nothing like it in modern physics or most of biology, and that fact may well explain why a science and a technology of behavior have been so long delayed. (Skinner, 1971, pp. 9–10)

Such explanations are post hoc in nature, according to Skinner. They seem to provide answers to questions, but they do not. Further, such **mentalism** brings curiosity to an end (Skinner, 1971, p. 12). The problem seems to be solved, and we are lulled into a false sense of security. A scientific approach to the study of human behavior, Skinner maintained, must give up such nebulous inner explanations and search instead for the precise antecedent events that actually produce our behavior (Skinner, 1987, p. 785).

Skinner did not categorically reject the study of all private events. In his book *About Behaviorism,* he took pains to point out that Watson, in his zeal to establish psychology as a science, made an exaggerated and incorrect commitment to the elimination of the study of introspective life (Skinner, 1974, p. 5). Skinner believed, albeit halfheartedly, that psychologists must provide adequate explanations of private events. He insisted, however, that the events studied must be capable of being reliably and objectively recorded. Verbal reports could provide acceptable data for Skinner and his followers if scientific criteria were met (Skinner, 1974, p. 31). But because other people have difficulty teaching us the appropriate labels for our private experiences, we must be cautious in accepting such reports at face value. Thus, contrary to popular belief, Skinner did not simply accept Watson's simplistic stimulus-response formulation. Skinner maintained that such an approach was obsolete and claimed to recognize the complexity of human behavior. Those who continued to criticize him for treating human beings as robots, he suggested, should "stop beating a dead horse."

An example may help clarify what Skinner would find scientifically objectionable or acceptable. Imagine a person sitting down at a table in a restaurant and eating a meal consisting of fettuccini Alfredo, Beaujolais, spumoni, and coffee. Why did he eat? The typical answer is that he ate *because* he was hungry. Skinner would reject this explanation as mentalistic. The term *hunger* would have to be explained by linking it to antecedent events in the environment—for example, the number of hours since the previous meal. Hunger did not *cause* the person to eat; rather, food deprivation, along with a host of other environmental variables (the decor of the restaurant, the price and attractiveness of the food), contributed to the probability that he would eat that meal at that particular time.

A behaviorist analysis would force us to focus on those events in the environment—past or current—that help produce the behavior. This information—coupled with data about our genetic endowments, where it is pertinent to the explanation of a given behavior—helps us in prediction. For example, if the diner had been allergic to the starches in the fettuccini, he might have decided not to eat at all or to eat different food. Thus, inner events—that is, our prior histories, which are based on transactions with the environment, and our unique genetic heritages—contribute to the prediction of behavior. Although Skinner recognized the legitimacy of such inner events for a behavioral psychology, he nevertheless de-emphasized them in his own analysis. He accorded the same legitimacy to physiological events, but again paid little actual attention to them in experimental analysis. Besides the difficulty of reliable measurement, the scientist cannot systematically manipulate physiological events and observe their effects on behavior. Skinner believed that major advances will occur only when psychologists focus on the ways in which behavior and external environmental variables are causally related. What is needed, in brief, is a **functional analysis** of behavior.

Free Will versus Determinism

According to Skinner, this search for order among events is offensive to many people because, once these relationships are specified, scientists can begin to anticipate and determine our actions (Skinner,

1953, p. 6). They can start to exercise control over our behavior. Such an idea runs counter to a long tradition of viewing ourselves as free agents. We do not like to believe that our actions are the product of specifiable antecedent conditions; we prefer to believe we are free and capable of spontaneous inner change (Skinner, 1953, p. 7). As members of a democratically oriented society, we also resist anyone who says he or she wants to control our behavior. According to Skinner, this belief in our own autonomy has a number of unfortunate implications.

Acceptance of this belief may mean that we do not see the powerful role played by the environment in causing our behavior. Instead we believe that we alone are responsible for our own actions, and thus we should be rewarded for behaving well and punished when we behave badly. For example, some of us are convinced that people living in poverty are responsible for their own situation; they should show some initiative and work like we do. As to juvenile delinquents, "Well, they got themselves into it; let them get themselves out of it!" In making such judgments, we have lost sight of the part played by oppressive environments. The focus on the inner man or woman prevents us from seeing clearly the external factors that contribute to their behavior (Skinner, 1971, pp. 19–20). Interestingly, although Skinner's critics called him a fascist, a reactionary, and a Machiavellian because of his stand on determinism, in this regard he emerges as a superliberal.

A science of behavior that questions our autonomy threatens beliefs about personal worth and dignity. A scientific analysis shifts both the credit and the blame for our actions to the environment (Skinner, 1971, p. 21). We may not object to an analysis that absolves us of blame, but we do object to one that deprives us of a chance to be admired and loved (Skinner, 1971, p. 75). Typically, the amount of credit we give someone for a performance, Skinner observed, is inversely proportional to the conspicuousness of the causes of the behavior: "We stand in awe of the inexplicable, and it is therefore not surprising that we are likely to admire behavior more as we understand it less" (Skinner, 1971, p. 53). For example, we may be more impressed by the performance of a young figure skater if we do not know that she has practiced six hours a day every day for the past 11 years to attain her current level of skill. We are probably more impressed with a brilliant new novelist if we do not know that he began writing at age 10 and received 45 rejection slips from publishers before they decided to publish one of his manuscripts.

Denying that we are autonomous beings is also threatening because it implies that we are not free to do what we want (Carpenter,

1974, p. 87). But our wants, Skinner maintained, are conditioned by external events. For instance, if you buy a computer, it's not because you simply and freely want one; it's because your old one is broken down, or you see a new model advertised, or your friends or colleagues have been pressuring you to upgrade. Whatever the reason or reasons, your behavior is determined by events in the past or current environment.

Many of us have been taught to believe that all external control is bad (Carpenter, 1974, p. 89). But numerous instances in which our behavior is controlled are perfectly acceptable to us. Parents restrain small children from diving into the 12-foot end of the pool. Society controls driving behavior with elaborate rules and regulations. State governments require auto safety inspections. Compulsory vaccinations protect us against disease. Doctors exercise control when they operate on people. The list is endless. Skinner's critics continue to insist that a particular form of control—coercion—is bad because it involves the exploitation of one party by another. In fact, Skinner agreed wholeheartedly with them; he, too, opposed control of this sort.

What, then, are the objections to his position? There seem to be two main points: (1) that Skinner sought to manipulate people without their being aware of it; and (2) that Skinner sought to set himself up as the arbiter of good and evil (Carpenter, 1974, p. 90). Skinner answered by pointing out that all our behavior is determined, whether we are aware of it or not. As to good and bad, his position was that we already have a general consensus. Virtually everyone is against disease, poverty, war, and indiscriminate destruction of the environment. Nearly all of us prefer politeness to rudeness, generosity to greed, love to selfishness. Why quarrel over the obvious?

Despite the cogency of Skinner's arguments for a thoroughgoing determinism, the fact remains that the determinist viewpoint is an assumption on his part, even though there is considerable evidence to support it. Most of the evidence is based on studies with lower animals in which it is possible to control conditions and observe systematic changes in behavior. For human beings, the problem is much more complicated. The scientist usually does not have control over previous environments and thus, in contrast to experiments with lower animals, cannot observe changes in behavior as a function of the manipulation of events in the current environment. In short, there is too much noise in the human system for us to argue conclusively that determinism is scientifically proved. Nevertheless, it appears to be a reasonable working assumption; it continues to lead to the accumulation of data that advance our understanding of human behavior.

Personality from the Perspective of a Radical Behaviorist

Now that we have considered some of the major arguments underlying Skinner's scientific approach to behavior and some of its provocative philosophical implications, we come to an important question: What about the study of personality? Is it lost in Skinner's strict emphasis on a cause-and-effect analysis of behavior? Skinner considered the study of personality legitimate, but only if established scientific criteria are met. He would not, for example, accept the idea of a personality or self that guides or directs behavior. He regarded that as a vestige of animism, a doctrine that presupposed the existence of spirits as an animating force within the body (Skinner, 1974, p. 167). Nor, as we have seen, was he satisfied with dead-end mentalistic explanations of behavior.

Skinner believed that the study of personality involves a systematic examination of the idiosyncratic learning history and unique genetic background of the individual.

> In a behavioral analysis, a person is an organism . . . which has acquired a repertoire of behavior. [He] is not an originating agent; he is a locus, a point at which many genetic and environmental conditions come together in a joint effect. As such, he remains unquestionably unique. No one else (unless he has an identical twin) has his genetic endowment, and without exception no one else has his personal history. Hence no one else will behave in precisely the same way. (Skinner, 1974, pp. 167–168)

The study of personality, then, involves the discovery of the unique set of relationships between the behavior of an organism and its reinforcing or punishing consequences. Of course, such an analysis would have to be consistent with the organism's genetic capacity to respond to events in the environment.

Operant Conditioning

All behavior takes place in situations and produces outcomes. In terms of Skinner's system, we operate on the environment to generate consequences (Skinner, 1953, p. 65). Operant behavior includes talking to people, reading, walking, writing, kissing, dressing, singing a song, criticizing a teacher, hitting a friend, and countless other activities. If we are deprived of water and then drink, we are reinforced. If we physically assault another person, we are punished by the courts. Turning the house thermostat from 55 to 70 degrees on a winter morning is reinforcing. If, by accident, we turn the thermostat from 70 to 50 degrees that same morning, the consequences would be punishing. The establishment of an association between behavior and its consequences is called **operant conditioning.** Through operant conditioning, the occurrence of behavior is made more or less probable.

The Three-Term Contingency

A **contingency** is a rule stating that some event (B) will occur if and only if another event (A) occurs (Mazur, 1986, p. 131). For example, during an early afternoon play session at home, 6-year-old Matthew shares his toy truck (event A) with his 5-year-old brother, Leo, and receives a kiss (event B) from his mother for his cooperative behavior. After dinner, however, Matthew and Leo are watching television when Leo decides he does not like the program and arbitrarily changes the channel. Matthew becomes very upset and hits his brother (event A). Their mother then sends Matthew to bed early (event B) as punishment. Skinner would say that Matthew has learned that a kiss from his mother in a play situation is contingent, or dependent, on his cooperative behavior. The boy has also learned, in Skinner's view, that being sent to bed early when he is watching television is contingent on his aggressive behavior.

Thus, there are three important components in an operant-conditioning contingency: (1) the environmental or situational event in which a response or behavior occurs (that is, the event that precedes the behavior); (2) the behavior itself; and (3) the environmental stimuli (consequences) that follow the behavior (Skinner, 1953, pp. 108–109).

Discrimination

The stimuli preceding the behavior are important because they provide the occasion under which reinforcement is likely to occur if the behavior is performed. Thus, people learn a **discrimination.** They learn that, in the presence of certain stimuli (or in some situations), their behavior is likely to be reinforced, whereas the same behavior in the presence of other stimuli (or in other situations) is not likely to be reinforced. Or they learn the discrimination that their behavior is likely to be punished in certain situations, whereas the same behavior under different circumstances is unlikely to be punished. Traffic lights, for example, act as discriminative stimuli. We learn that a red light is a cue for us to bring our car to a halt, whereas a green light indicates that we can proceed. Failure to make this simple discrimination can lead to serious injury or death. Obviously, we do not have to learn this discrimination through direct experience. We can and do learn the appropriate behavior through oral or written instructions, through observation of what other drivers do in actual situations, or through films. Driver-education courses typically use films of accidents to show license applicants the tragic consequences of a failure to obey various traffic rules, including the failure to make an appropriate discrimination between green and red lights.

When our responses are differentially controlled by antecedent stimuli or situations, they are considered to be under **stimulus control.** Much of our behavior is under the control of stimuli. In social interactions, for example, we learn that we are likely to be reinforced when we approach people who are smiling, whereas we are likely to be punished when we approach people who are scowling. We also learn to be careful about the kinds of food we eat. The smells and colors of the foods influence our behavior. We quickly learn to avoid eating rancid meat, rotting tomatoes, and moldy bread. Instead, we purchase and eat fresh bread, firm tomatoes, and red meats. In our environmentally conscious society, we learn to react appropriately to various cues in our physical environment. For example, as we leave a classroom at the end of a session, we turn off the lights when we see instructions to "Please turn off the lights to conserve energy." We throw our litter into trash cans when we see instructions asking us to do so. We also avoid another person's property when we see ominous "No Trespassing" or "Beware of the Dog" signs.

Instructions, directions, examples, and models are all used to facilitate the development of responses. Such stimuli are called **prompts**—antecedent events that help initiate responses. Thus, if a parent tells a child to return home immediately after school and hugs and kisses her for complying, the prompt (instruction) becomes a discriminative stimulus. It signals the child that reinforcement is likely to follow when the behavior is performed. In general, when a prompt consistently precedes reinforcement of a behavior, it becomes a **discriminative stimulus** and can effectively control behavior. Prompts often take on the value of events (consequences) that follow them. Thus, the child is likely to look forward to hearing her parent instruct her to come home immediately after school.

Prompts can also become aversive if they are associated often enough with punishing consequences. If parents continually remind their son to clean his room or face a loss of privileges, it takes little time for such prompts to become aversive in their own right. The boy may try to terminate the aversive prompt by cleaning his room, leaving the house, or arguing with his parents (Kazdin, 1989, pp. 42–43).

Generalization

A response that is repeatedly reinforced in a particular situation is likely to be repeated in that situation. Situations, however, consist of complex sets of stimuli that often share common properties. In Skinner's view, the control exerted by a given stimulus is shared by other stimuli that are similar to it (Skinner, 1953, p. 132). **Stimulus generalization** occurs if a behavior that is reinforced in one situation also increases in other situations, even though it is not reinforced in those situations (Kazdin, 1989, p. 46).

Generalization is the opposite of discrimination. When people discriminate between two situations, it means that their response has failed to generalize from one situation to the other. When their response does generalize across two situations, it means that they have failed to discriminate between the two situations and make the same response in both situations. These two phenomena have highly important implications for the psychological health and well-being of humans. For example, if a man fails to discriminate between people who can be trusted and those who cannot be trusted, his generalized mistrust may result in his being highly suspicious of others and even paranoid. The teenager who is rewarded by her peers' smiles and laughter for swearing in a playground situation may face punishing consequences if she repeats the behavior in front of her date's parents and relatives at the dinner table in his home. Skinner would say that she failed to learn an appropriate discrimination. Stimulus generalization can operate in a beneficial way when the information learned in your college classes transfers to a job setting after you graduate.

Reinforcement

Behavior is controlled not only by antecedent stimuli, but also by its consequences. The principle of **positive reinforcement** refers to an increase in the frequency of a behavior when that behavior is followed by **positive reinforcers.** There are two types of positive reinforcers: **primary,** or unconditioned, **reinforcers** are automatically or naturally reinforcing—for example, food, water, and sex; **secondary,** or conditioned, **reinforcers** acquire their reinforcing properties through association with primary reinforcers or with other conditioned reinforcers. Examples of secondary reinforcers are praise, attention, money, and good grades. Giving a boy a candy bar for cleaning his room strengthens his room-cleaning behavior. Awarding an A to a student for writing a highly creative essay encourages this behavior.

Negative reinforcers are aversive stimuli, or punishers—for example, electric shock, loud noises, bright lights, and physical assault. The removal of an aversive stimulus (negative reinforcer) following a response increases the probability of that behavior occurring in the future under the same or similar circumstances. **Negative reinforcement** refers to the removal of an aversive stimulus following a response, thereby increasing the rate of occurrence of that response. Taking medicine that cures your stomachache is a good example of negative reinforcement. Medicine-taking behavior is strengthened when it is followed by the elimination of a punishing stimulus. Another example is the child who learns to apologize for undesirable behavior because it terminates parental criticism.

In summary, the principle of **reinforcement** is that a behavior will increase in frequency when it is followed either by the presentation of a positive reinforcer or by the removal of a punisher.

Punishment

The principle of **punishment** refers to a decrease in the frequency of a response when that response is followed immediately by certain consequences. Aversive events, or punishers, can be applied to behavior to make its occurrence less probable. This procedure is called **positive punishment. Primary,** or unconditioned, **punishers** are stimuli that are inherently aversive—for example, electric shock, loud noises, bright lights, and physical assault. **Secondary,** or conditioned, **punishers** acquire their aversive properties by being paired with primary punishers or other conditioned punishers. Examples of conditioned punishers are poor grades, criticism, ridicule, and sarcasm. Fining a person for speeding is intended to discourage the behavior. A teacher's reprimand to "Stop talking" is intended to decrease talking by students. The command "No" also serves as a conditioned punisher for many people. The word acquires its punitive value by being paired with physical pain or loss of privileges (for instance, taking the keys to the family car away from a teenager who loves to drive).

TABLE 15.1   Summary of operant conditioning principles

	Positive stimulus	Negative (aversive) stimulus
Presentation (contingent on response)	Positive reinforcement	Positive punishment
Removal (contingent on response)	Negative punishment	Negative reinforcement

negative

The removal of a positive stimulus (positive reinforcer) following a behavior also decreases its occurrence and is called **negative punishment.** Taking a toy away from a child for lying is a form of negative punishment called **response cost.** Response cost involves a penalty of some kind—for example, a fine for a traffic violation or fees for late filing of income tax or late registration for classes (Kazdin, 1989, p. 153). Another form of negative punishment is **time out from reinforcement**—the removal of all positive reinforcers for a certain period of time. Telling a child who misbehaves to stop watching television and go to his or her room is a good example of time out, if the child's room offers no opportunities for reinforcing activities such as playing music or reading comic books. Table 15.1 summarizes these operant principles, in terms of the various combinations of consequences that follow a response—presentation or removal of a positive or negative stimulus.

Skinner's View of Punishment

Skinner observed that punishment is the most common technique of control in modern life.

> If a man does not behave as you wish, knock him down; if a child misbehaves, spank him; if the people of a country misbehave, bomb them. Legal and police systems are based upon such punishments as fines . . . incarceration and hard labor. Religious control is exerted through penances, threats of excommunication, and consignment to hell-fire. Education has not wholly abandoned the birch rod. In everyday personal contact we control through censure, snubbing, disapproval, or banishment. . . . All of this is done with the intention of reducing tendencies to behave in certain ways. (Skinner, 1953, p. 182)

Why is punishment so pervasive? It is easy to apply, and it has immediate, observable, and satisfying effects for the punisher. In addition, the technique is easily learned, whereas alternative, positive techniques are more difficult to acquire. Punishment also has the ostensible support of history (Skinner, 1971, p. 80). For all these reasons, many of us resort to it.

Does punishment work? Certainly in the short run it seems to be effective: it stops the undesired behavior. Skinner maintained that this effect may be misleading, however, because the reduction in strength of the behavior may not be permanent (Skinner, 1953, p. 183). As evidence, he cited a study in which he trained rats of the same sex, age, and genetic strain to press a lever in a Skinner box as a means of obtaining food pellets (Skinner, 1938, pp. 151–160). After establishing the bar-pressing response, Skinner withheld the reinforcers from these animals in order to bring about **extinction** of the behavior. Skinner let some of the animals in a control group continue to press the bar without punishment until they stopped responding completely. In the experimental group, each time the animals pressed the lever, they were punished by a mechanically administered slap on the paws. This punishment continued for the first ten minutes of the extinction period and then was terminated. Skinner found an initial decrease in the rate of response for the animals while they were being punished. When the punishment was ended, however, the experimental group began to respond again. Eventually, this group produced as many responses as the controls. Skinner concluded that punishment temporarily suppresses behavior, but the behavior is likely to reappear when the punishing contingencies are withdrawn. More recent studies, it should be noted, have produced impressive evidence that punishment can effectively stop undesired behavior when it is properly applied (Walters & Grusec, 1977; Kazdin, 1989).

Punishment, according to Skinner, has two other undesirable effects. First, it may give rise to emotional responses that are incompatible with appropriate behavior (Skinner, 1953, pp. 186–187). For example, a man who, as an adolescent, is severely punished for masturbating while looking at pictures of naked women may later experience strong feelings of guilt in a situation where sexual behavior is appropriate. Or a child who has been beaten by her parents for reading poorly may later experience considerable resentment toward teachers who are trying to help her improve her reading skills; as a result, she may refuse to read and perpetuate her reading difficulties.

Second, punishment may create strong conflict in people (Skinner, 1953, p. 190). In Skinnerian terms, such conflict would not be an inner struggle, but rather an incompatibility between responses, one of which is positively reinforcing and the other potentially punishing.

The male student who has been rejected by a number of female students but who continues to seek relationships with women on campus would be a pertinent example. In traditional personality terms, such a person might be labeled as awkward, indecisive, and timid.

For all these reasons, Skinner believed we should shun the use of punishment to control behavior, but should focus instead on the use of positive reinforcers. (The use of positive reinforcers in education will be discussed later in this chapter.)

Operant Extinction

As we saw in Skinner's rat study, failure to reinforce a response reduces the probability that the response will occur. In traditional terms

> [a] person is . . . said to suffer a loss of confidence, certainty, or sense of power. [He] is said to be unable to go to work because he is discouraged or depressed, although his not going, together with what he feels [discouragement and depression], is due to a lack of reinforcement—either in his work or in some other part of his life. (Skinner, 1974, p. 58)

We control the behavior of others by withholding reinforcement. To eliminate behavior we consider undesirable, for example, we ignore it. If our roommate acts in obnoxious ways, we may simply pay no attention to him. If a child has a temper tantrum, her parents may ignore her by reading the newspaper or turning on the television set. Such a procedure seems to make sense, but unfortunately is often unworkable in practice. If the undesirable behavior has been reinforced many times in the past, it is highly resistant to extinction. The mother who tries to eliminate temper tantrums by ignoring her child's behavior is likely to give in eventually by listening to her child, comforting her, and giving her what she wants. These actions positively reinforce the child's behavior and ensure that it will continue. An alternate strategy in this situation might be to send the child to her room for a brief period (time out) until she stops whining and complaining, and then to show her a more constructive way of solving her problem and to reinforce her for using it.

Shaping

Sometimes it is impossible to develop new behavior by reinforcing the response when it occurs. The target behavior may not be in the repertoire of the individual because it is too complex. For example, the use of language in children is a complicated activity that can be developed only slowly, with the help of a shaping procedure. **Shaping** means teaching a new behavior by reinforcing responses that approximate it. **Successive approximations**—behaviors increasingly similar to the final goal—are reinforced, until eventually the goal is achieved. For example, when parents want to teach their child to say *mommy* and *daddy*, they first reinforce sounds like *ma* and *da* by giving effusive praise when the child utters them. At the same time, they ignore other sounds (*bo, go*) that do not resemble the terminal words. Over time they continue to reinforce sounds that come closer to the words *mommy* and *daddy* until eventually the child says them and receives strong reinforcement from the elated parents (Kazdin, 1989, p. 38).

Schedules of Reinforcement

All of us are exposed to different environments and to different schedules or arrangements of reinforcement in our daily lives. Some parents, for example, consistently reinforce their children's behavior; others supply only intermittent reinforcers. These schedules have a tremendous impact on our responses. Numerous studies with lower animals, for example, have shown that behavior learned on a **continuous reinforcement** schedule—that is, a schedule in which each performance is followed by a reinforcer—produces higher rates of response than behavior reinforced only intermittently. Behavior learned on a schedule of **intermittent** (or partial) **reinforcement,** however, is much more resistant to extinction than behavior acquired on a continuous schedule (Skinner, 1953, p. 99). Animals trained on a continuous reinforcement schedule also show greater signs of emotional reaction or low frustration tolerance when their behaviors are subjected to extinction than do animals trained on intermittent schedules.

The implications for human functioning are quite straightforward. Affluent parents who raise their children on continuous reinforcement schedules should not be surprised that their offspring do not show behaviors that could be labeled persistent, hardworking, ambitious, and competitive. These behaviors are more likely to be found in children who have been subjected to partial or intermittent schedules of reinforcement (Carpenter, 1974, pp. 27–28).

Intermittent reinforcement can take many forms. Two of the most common are the fixed-ratio schedule and the fixed-interval schedule. In a **fixed-ratio schedule,** an absolute number of behaviors is required before reinforcement is applied (Ferster & Perrott, 1968, p. 525). For example, a student may have to complete two class projects before receiving a grade in the course. Or a worker may be placed on a fixed-ratio schedule, commonly known as piecework pay. In a **fixed-interval schedule,** the first performance that occurs after an absolute amount of time has elapsed is reinforced (Ferster & Perrott, 1968, p. 526). There are many examples of the operation of such schedules in our daily lives. We eat at certain times of the day; we go to bed and get up at a regular time. Sometimes we get paid by the hour. An interesting feature of behavior regulated on fixed-interval schedules is that the rate of responding tends to be low just after reinforcement but increases rapidly as the time for reinforcement approaches.

Self-Control Processes

Skinner was interested not only in the ways in which schedules of reinforcement determine behavior but also in the role of **self-control processes.** For him, studying self-control involves an analysis of "how the individual acts to alter the variables of which other parts of his behavior are functions" (Skinner, 1953, p. 229). Individuals are said to exercise self-control when they actively change those variables or factors that determine their behavior. For example, we may find that we cannot study when there is a stereo blaring music. We get up and shut it off. We have actively changed the nature of the variable (loud music) that affected our behavior. Another example might be an obese person who exercises control over his behavior by buying and eating only low-calorie foods. He can also politely refuse to eat high-calorie foods when they are offered to him by others.

Skinner outlined a number of the techniques that we use to control our behavior (Skinner, 1953, pp. 231–241); many of these have subsequently been studied by social-learning theorists interested in modeling and behavior modification. (See Chapter 17.)

Physical restraints   Sometimes we control our behavior through the use of physical restraints. For instance, some of us clap our hands over our mouths to avoid laughing at someone else's mistakes. Others put their hands in their pockets to keep from biting their fingernails. In unusual cases, people who feel strongly tempted to commit criminal or psychotic acts may present themselves at the door of an institution for incarceration.

Another form of physical restraint is simply to move out of situations in which the behavior to be controlled takes place. We walk away from someone who has insulted us, lest we lose control and physically attack him. Parents often prevent the occurrence of undesirable behavior (for example, fights, ridicule, criticism, or taunts) between their children by physically separating them. They may order one child to go outside to play and the other to stay inside and watch television.

Physical aids   Physical aids can also be used to control behavior. Some truckers take stimulants to avoid falling asleep at the wheel. Students often drink large amounts of coffee after all-night study sessions in an effort to remain alert during early morning exams.

Physical aids can also be used to facilitate certain behavior, as when people with vision problems put on eyeglasses or the hearing impaired make use of hearing aids.

Changing the stimulus conditions   Another technique we use to control our behavior is to change the stimuli responsible for it. Overweight people put a box of candy out of sight so that they can restrain themselves. Some alcoholics avoid temptation by giving their liquor supply away. Some student athletes put their athletic equipment out of sight when they sit down to study. Other students draw the curtains in their rooms to avoid being lured out of doors on a bright spring day.

Smokers sometimes try to reduce their smoking behavior by destroying their cigarettes. Other smokers adopt more moderate strategies (Williams & Long, 1979, p. 117). If they ordinarily carry their pack of cigarettes in their right-hand shirt pocket, they shift it to their left-hand pocket or to their coat so that it is more difficult to find. Sometimes they deliberately neglect to carry matches or a lighter; as a result, they must ask someone for a light each time they want to smoke. The object of these strategies, of course, is to disrupt the smokers' habits and consequently to limit the unhealthy behavior.

Another way to reduce smoking frequency is to reduce the range of stimuli associated with it. Smokers typically have favorite times and situations in which they smoke—for example, while studying, working, eating, partying, or watching television. Various studies have shown that, if they can break these associations, they can reduce their smoking drastically (Williams & Long, 1979, p. 118).

In each of these examples, people are removing a discriminative stimulus that induces unwanted behavior. Not only do we remove certain stimuli in given situations, however, we also present stimuli in order to make certain behaviors more probable. For example, we may use a mirror to master a difficult dance step or listen to our voice on tape in an attempt to improve our diction. We enter dates and times in an appointment book to remind ourselves of our responsibilities.

Manipulating emotional conditions   We sometimes induce emotional changes in ourselves for purposes of control. Some people employ meditation techniques to alleviate stress. Similarly, we may work ourselves into a good mood before a stressful meeting in order to increase our likelihood of performing well. When athletes psych themselves up before an important game, they are using this method of control.

Performing alternative responses   We often keep ourselves from engaging in behavior that leads to punishment by energetically engaging in something else. The overweight person may turn to an intensive jogging regimen to burn off excess calories and to keep from excessive eating. The recently bereaved may be advised by friends to keep very busy as a means of avoiding depressing thoughts. To keep from verbally or physically attacking people we dislike intensely, we may find ourselves thinking thoughts and performing actions unrelated to our opinions of them. To avoid talking about taboo topics—for example, telling nuns about a woman's right to abortion—we may talk about the less threatening subject of how to play a good game of bridge.

Positive self-reinforcement   We also control behavior by positive self-reinforcement: we reward ourselves for commendable behavior. A student may reward himself for studying hard and doing well on an exam by going to the movies. An athlete may promise herself an expensive meal at a favorite restaurant if she surpasses her old record in the 100-meter dash.

Self-punishment   Individuals also punish themselves for failure to reach self-generated goals. As punishment for failing to do well on an exam, a student may give away valuable concert tickets. College football players often voluntarily jog extra laps around the track Monday morning as punishment for failure to perform adequately during a game on Saturday afternoon.

PERSONALITY DEVELOPMENT

A Schedule-of-Reinforcement Approach

In seeking to explain changes in the individual's personality over time, Skinner looked to unique environmental schedules of reinforcement rather than the emergence of maturational stages. Although he acknowledged some predictive value in theories such as Freud's and Piaget's, Skinner generally opposed them because they do not allow for the control or manipulation of events, a procedure he considered crucial for a science of behavior (Skinner, 1974, p. 12). Such theories tend to be descriptive rather than explanatory and, as Skinner saw it, the primary goal of science is the prediction and control of events (Skinner, 1953, p. 6).

In Piaget's stage theory, for example, children in stage 1 (from birth to about 3 years of age) are observed to play games without any attempt to adapt to social rules. In stage 2, children between the ages of 3 and 5 imitate the rule-regulated behavior of adults and regard the rules of a game as sacred and immutable. In stage 3, children who range in age from 7 to adolescence play games with a mutually agreed upon set of rules, but understand that the rules can always be changed with the approval of the other players (Flavell, 1963, pp. 291–292). With these descriptions of behavior at the various age levels, we can predict the kind of behavior children will exhibit if we know their age. But we do not have an adequate explanation for their behavior; that is, we do not know *why* they behave as they do. We have descriptive information of limited usefulness, not causal information. To ascertain why children behave as they do, we must be able to control and manipulate events that have an effect on their game-playing behavior.

For these reasons, Skinner preferred to study personality by focusing on the learning of a multitude of behaviors that allow the individual to survive and prosper in his or her transactions with the environment. In rough terms, people learn throughout life which contingencies provide satisfaction and which produce pain in given situations. The child learns to discriminate between stimuli or situations that are occasions for the reinforcement of specific behaviors and those that do not lead to reinforcement of the same behaviors. These learned behaviors are said to be under stimulus control. A child, for example, may learn to cry in public and not at home because crying in public usually brings immediate attention and comfort from the mother, whereas crying at home is generally ignored. Or a student may quickly learn that studying in a library and not in a noisy dormitory leads to passing grades. Simple skills are learned at first; later on, more and more complex behaviors are acquired and utilized. But Skinner did not see people as passive organisms who simply respond automatically to reinforcement cues. Instead, they exercise self-control over their environments by actively selecting and changing environmental variables in order to satisfy their own needs.

The Development of Normal and Abnormal Personalities

Some people have had a unique set of transactions with the environment that results in the acquisition of a **repertoire** we might label normal. Others have had a set of experiences that result in the acquisition of unique response patterns we might label abnormal. In Skinner's view, there is no qualitative difference between so-called normal and abnormal individuals; the same set of reinforcement principles can account for the behavior of all individuals, irrespective of the labels we might use in describing their actions. According to him, we should focus more on the environmental determinants of behavior than on inner determinants. He would eliminate all references to a mental apparatus such as Freud employed. Such theorizing, in his view, is imprecise and ambiguous, and leads to pseudoexplanations of behavior.

Skinner believed, however, that Freud contributed much to our understanding of behavior and that many of his ideas can profitably be translated into terms amenable to scientific inquiry. For example, the various ego defense mechanisms Freud postulated can be examined in terms of people's attempts to avoid or escape punishment. In Skinner's view, punishment makes the stimuli associated with punished behavior aversive. As a consequence, any behavior that reduces or eliminates that stimulation becomes positively reinforcing. In repression, therefore, behavior which is punished becomes aversive, and by not engaging in it or by not 'seeing' it, a person avoids conditioned aversive stimulation" (Skinner, 1974, p. 155). There is no need to postulate an inner process in which id impulses incapable of fulfillment are kept lurking in the unconscious. Another example is sublimation. In Freudian terms, sublimation is the "discharge of instinctual energy and especially that associated with pregenital impulses through socially approved activities" (Skinner, 1974, p. 156). In Skinnerian terms, if two forms of behavior are positively reinforcing, but one of them is punished, the other is more likely to occur. Again, for Freud, conversion is "the transformation of an unconscious conflict into a symbolically equivalent somatic symptom" (Skinner, 1974, p. 156). Such mental events are presumed to have the power to produce physical illness. Inner-directed rage, for example, is said to produce ulcers. Skinner maintained that "the condition felt as rage is medically related to the ulcer, and that a complex social situation causes both" (Skinner, 1974, pp. 156–157). Of course, the complex social situation would have to be precisely and adequately defined. Hypothetically, however, it might include a punishing boss, a nagging spouse, whiny kids, loss of a loved one, and so on. Skinner's central point is that many traditional clinical concepts can be translated into terms that make them amenable to scientific investigation.

ASSESSMENT TECHNIQUES

Skinner was primarily interested in the experimental analysis of behavior. He sought to identify those environmental variables that control the emission of behavior—namely, situational factors and reinforcement schedules. As the functional analysis of behavior is a complicated matter that involves the interplay of a multitude of variables, Skinner proceeded by focusing on specific behaviors and those environmental events considered to be controlling influences. In short, Skinner sought to discover a cause-and-effect relationship between events. To accomplish this goal, Skinner first focused on simple, observable behaviors that could be readily and reliably quantified and on those environmental stimuli thought to control the emission of these behaviors. Other variables thought to be irrelevant he eliminated or held constant.

Skinner believed that his approach could be implemented best by focusing on the behavior of nonhuman species, because their environments are relatively easy to control and many of their behaviors are simple and readily quantifiable. The environment usually used for study purposes is the so-called Skinner box—a small, soundproof chamber usually containing a lever or bar that an animal such as a rat can depress to obtain food reinforcers. For work with pigeons, translucent disks are used: when the pigeon pecks at the right disk— that is, a disk of a particular color chosen by the experimenter as correct—food is delivered via a feeding disk. Behavior is quantified through the use of a cumulative recorder wired to the apparatus, which precisely and automatically records the frequency of response and displays it by means of a stylus or pen that moves along paper attached to a revolving drum.

Skinner maintained that the use of lower animals, such as rats and pigeons, to establish the principles of behavior is a good strategy and that these principles are generalizable to the behavior of human beings. In his view, a single set of principles can account for much, though not all, of the behavior of both nonhuman and human organisms.

THEORY'S IMPLICATIONS FOR THERAPY

Psychopathology and Behavior Modification

Behavior modification is an attempt to change undesirable behavior by the application of learning principles derived primarily from laboratory experiments (Krasner, 1970, p. 89). These principles are based on research in classical conditioning and observational learning as well as in operant conditioning. Because Skinner's work focused mainly on operant conditioning, however, we will examine the use of operant conditioning principles to reduce or eliminate a variety of problem behaviors. Specifically, investigators have demonstrated that, by employing a variety of therapeutic procedures, it is possible to increase the social skills of those with mental retardation, to develop appropriate speech in such individuals, to lessen the amount of aggressive and disruptive behavior of youngsters and delinquents, to reduce echolalia in autistic individuals, to enable obese individuals to lose weight, to curtail smoking in cigarette smokers, to reduce stuttering in children and adults, and to control the undesirable behavior of people experiencing difficulties in their lives.

Discrimination Training

Many obese individuals report that their eating occurs in a wide variety of situations and at many different times of the day. They may eat snacks while reading a book or magazine, talking on the phone, watching television, or arguing with their families, for example. These situations exert control over the person's behavior and act as cues that facilitate the occurrence of the eating behavior. A classic study by Penick, Filion, Fox, and Stunkard (1971) demonstrated that it is possible to encourage such overweight individuals to make appropriate discriminations by teaching them to confine their eating to one place only—namely, a dining-room table with a distinctively colored place mat and napkin. In this study, patients were asked to keep written accounts of the amount, time, and situations in which they ate food over a three-month period. This record-keeping device helped make patients aware of the situations that stimulated their eating, so that it became easier to dissociate the situations from their eating of food. If they behaved appropriately—that is, if they ate only at the dining-room table—patients were awarded points that could subsequently be exchanged for money. They lost points (and therefore money) for failure to exercise control over their behavior—that is, for eating while reading or watching television. Patients also received points for decreasing the speed of their eating, chewing their food slowly, and counting each mouthful of food eaten, and lost points for failure to perform these behaviors.

The amount of weight loss achieved by patients using these behavior-modification techniques (approximately 18 pounds) exceeded the amount lost by a control group who received traditional counseling to encourage weight loss (approximately 14 pounds). What the authors found even more significant was the difference in the percentage of patients who lost 40 pounds or more in the course of treatment. Of the patients in the behavior-modification program, 27% achieved this level of weight loss, whereas only 12% of the control patients did so. It should be noted that the number of patients in the study was very small (15 in the behavior-modification program and 17 in the control program), so that the results are unlikely to be highly reliable. More recent research, however, indicates that even larger losses in weight can be achieved by establishing programs that last more than three months and by coupling these longer programs with exercise.

After leaving the program, most people regain some, if not all, of the weight they have lost. To deal with this problem, leading researchers are now suggesting that therapists reconceptualize the problem of obesity, and regard it as a chronic condition, similar to hypertension or diabetes, rather than an acute condition. As such, it requires long-term treatment. In such a program, eating and exercise behavior would be monitored on an ongoing basis. Threshold levels would be set for weight gain or relapse. When these thresholds were exceeded, treatment would emphasize identifying likely situations in which relapses occur (for example, the loss of a boyfriend/girlfriend), so that preventive action (for example, development of new hobbies, interests, or friends) could be taken (Brownell & Jeffery, 1987).

Time Out from Reinforcement

According to Porterfield, Herbert-Jackson, and Risley (1976), a major problem in day-care programs for young children (1–2 years of age) is the child's immaturity in the development of appropriate play behavior. Some children engage in behavior that disrupts the activities of others, including aggressive behavior (hitting, pushing, biting, kicking), destructive use of toys (pounding a toy against the wall or on a piece of furniture), creating a situation dangerous to themselves or others (standing on a bench, throwing hard toys), or having temper tantrums. Parents and teachers are often counseled by media experts to respond to such behavior by describing its inappropriateness to the child and then redirecting him or her to an alternative toy or activity. If a child took a toy from another child, for example, the caregiver would say, "No, don't take toys. Come over here and listen to a story." Unfortunately, this **redirection procedure** is not very effective in reducing disruptive behavior, because young children learn that, if they behave inappropriately, they will be reinforced with an attractive toy or a pleasurable alternative activity. Another technique, time out by seclusion (isolating the child), is considered too harsh a penalty for disruptive behavior and does not allow the child to observe appropriate social behavior.

Porterfield and associates conducted a study in a toddler day-care program in which they tested a different technique. Caregivers used each instance of disruptive behavior to instruct the child in appropriate alternative behavior, and then had the child sit on the periphery of the group and observe the appropriate social behavior of the other children. After a sit and watch period (usually less than a minute), the child was asked whether he or she understood how to play appropriately and, after a positive response, was invited to return to the group. For example, if a child took a toy from another child, the caregiver would say, "No, don't take toys from other children. Ask me for the toy you want." The caregiver then moved the child to the periphery of the group, sat him or her on the floor without play materials, and said, "Sit here and watch how the other children ask for the toys they want." When the child had watched quietly for a brief period of time, the caregiver would inquire, "Do you know how to ask for the toys you want?" Upon indicating—by a nod or a word—that he or she was ready to rejoin the group, the child was allowed to do so. If the child did not respond or responded negatively, the caregiver said, "Sit here and watch the children until you think you can ask for the toy you want." When the child finally expressed readiness to rejoin the group (usually 30 seconds to 1 minute), he or she was allowed to do so. When the child returned to the group, the caregiver took the first opportunity that presented itself to give positive reinforcement for the correct behavior by saying, "Good! You asked for the toy you wanted." This **contingent observation procedure** was highly effective in reducing disruptive behavior in the group, as compared to the redirection procedure described earlier. Furthermore, the investigators reported that caregivers and parents found this observational time out method easy to administer, effective, and humane (Porter-field, Herbert-Jackson, & Risley, 1976).

Response-Cost Procedure

Hyperactive children are known for their impulsivity, attentional problems, and poor classroom performance. The most common form of treatment is the prescription of medication, usually methylpheni-date (Ritalin). Rapport, Murphy, and Bailey (1982) conducted a study in which they demonstrated that the use of a response-cost procedure was more effective than Ritalin in reducing the attentional problems of two hyperactive boys, ages 7 and 8.

The two children were required to solve various problems in arithmetic and reading. Two observers recorded the amount of time they spent on task (paying attention to the materials and solving the problems) and off task (not paying attention to the materials) during two daily sessions of 20 minutes each. Baseline data were collected for one week before any treatment procedures were implemented. Then the boys were given Ritalin for several weeks. Finally, the medi-cation was discontinued and the experimental response-cost proce-dure was implemented. The boys were told they could earn points by paying attention and working hard on the problems and could subse-quently exchange these points for up to 20 minutes of free time (for play). They were also told that failure to pay attention would cost them points. Although the use of Ritalin resulted in some improve-ment in comparison to the baseline, the data showed clearly that the greatest improvement in on-task behavior and academic perfor-mance occurred during the days when the response-cost procedure was used.

Habit Reversal

Behavioral therapists have created a very simple yet highly useful procedure to reduce stuttering. Oral and laryngeal muscle tension increases during a stuttering episode. As stutterers start to speak, the tension in their vocal musculature leads to airflow problems. This tension is reduced by stuttering. The therapy involves training cli-ents to make a response that is incompatible with stuttering behav-ior. One obvious incompatible reaction to stuttering is to discontinue speaking. Since speaking requires exhalation of air and inhalation is incompatible with speaking, children with stuttering difficulties were trained to stop speaking following the anticipation or start of a stuttered word, to take a deep diaphragmatic breath by exhaling the remaining air in their lungs and then inhaling slowly to consciously relax their chest and throat muscles. As they inhaled, they were asked to formulate mentally the words to be spoken, to start speaking shortly after they began exhaling, and to exhale slowly and smoothly. As they spoke, they were to emphasize the initial part of a statement, and to speak for short durations. As their speech became more fluent, they gradually increased the duration of speech. This regulated breathing procedure was practiced during a two-hour counseling session. The therapist modeled the procedure for each client by placing his or her fingertips in front of the therapist's mouth to demonstrate what a slight exhalation of air felt like. Clients then practiced the procedure by placing their fingers in front of their mouths until they could speak without stuttering. This training dramatically reduced stuttering in the clients (Wagaman, Miltenberger, & Arndorfer, 1993, p. 53). Moreover, a follow-up study conducted three and one-half years later showed that none of the clients who continued using the procedure had any problem with stuttering. The two clients who reported not using the procedure during the follow-up period reverted to high levels of stuttering (Wagaman, Miltenberger, & Woods, 1995, pp. 233–234).

The Token Economy

To alter the behavior of psychotics within institutions, investigators have designed special environments in which patients can earn tokens for performing socially appropriate tasks and then exchange them for goods and activities that are positively reinforcing. Such an incentive system is commonly known as a **token economy.**

Ayllon and Azrin (1965) conducted the classical attempt to design such an environment within a mental hospital as a means of strengthening key desirable behaviors in psychotics. They pointed out that the most important limitation in trying to develop a technology of behavior is lack of standardization in observing and recording behavior and in administering reinforcers. Different attendants may define the target behaviors differently; for example, they may be stricter or more lenient in their assessment of good grooming. In addition, it is difficult to record and reinforce desired behaviors on a ward of approximately 45 patients, all of whom engage in a variety of activities at the same time. Research has shown that reinforcers are most effective if they are applied immediately following the desired response. If different attendants reinforce patients at varying time intervals following responses, the impact on behavior will be lessened or even nonexistent. In short, if the attendants do not know which behaviors to reinforce, how much to reinforce, or when to reinforce, it seems unlikely that there will be much improvement. Accordingly, the investigators spent 18 months developing their program in order to eliminate these and other problems. The final program included a standard list of behaviors to be changed, as well as a list of reinforcers. The behaviors to be strengthened differed from patient to patient, but included: helping serve meals to the other patients; washing dishes; cleaning tables; typing letters; answering the telephone and calling hospital personnel to the phone; washing sheets, pillow cases, and towels in the laundry; and so on. A list of the reinforcers to be given in exchange for tokens is shown in Table 15.2.

In general, the results of the program showed significant improvement in patient behaviors over a 42-day period. In another experiment within the same program, the investigators found that, when the tokens were withdrawn, the behavior of the patients deteriorated. When the system was reinstated, performance levels rose again. This shift in performance shows the powerful impact of the tokens in changing behavior.

This study and other experiments with token economies, though generally successful (Kazdin, 1989), have raised a number of questions. First, what is so wonderful about getting patients to comb their hair or wash some dishes? The answer is that, although major problem behaviors remain untouched, the behaviors that were strengthened represent a significant shift in functioning for these patients. At the beginning of the experiments, some patients refused to wash or groom themselves. A few of them lay in their own excrement. Some refused to utter a word. The application of operant techniques changed this state of affairs and was the first step toward recovery. It also increased the patients' freedom, in the sense that it provided them with an opportunity to perform a variety of activities for positive payoffs rather than simply sitting all day doing nothing. The changes in appearance are also beneficial because staff members tend to treat patients better. "If you can't tell the patient from the staff without a score card, you will most likely react to him (or her) as if he (or she) were normal just like you" (Krasner, 1970, p. 97). The effort to implement some method of treatment is monumentally preferable to providing no treatment at all, which is the alternative all

TABLE 15.2   List of reinforcers available to patients for tokens

Reinforcer	Number of tokens daily
I. Privacy	
Selection of room 1	0
Selection of room 2	4
Selection of room 3	8
Selection of room 4	15
Selection of room 5	30
Personal chair	1
Screen (room divider)	1
Choice of bedspreads	1
Coat rack	1
II. Leave from the ward	
Twenty-minute walk on hospital grounds (with escort)	2
Thirty-minute grounds pass	10
Trip to town (with escort)	100
III. Social interaction with staff	
Private audience with ward psychologist	20
Private audience with social worker	100
IV. Devotional opportunities	
Extra religious services on ward	1
Extra religious services off ward	10
V. Recreational opportunities	
Movie on ward	1
Exclusive use of a radio	1
Television (choice of program)	3
VI. Commissary items	
Candy, milk, cigarettes, coffee, and sandwich	1–5
Toilet articles such as toothpaste, comb, lipstick, and talcum powder	1–10
Clothing such as gloves, scarf, and skirt	12–400
Reading and writing materials such as pen, greeting card, newspaper, and magazine	2–5
Miscellaneous items such as ashtray, potted plant, picture holder, and stuffed animals	1–50

SOURCE: Adapted from Ayllon & Azrin, 1965, p. 360.

too often adopted in mental institutions. Behavior modification is not the only therapeutic method that can be employed to overcome this impasse, but it does work.

Second, do the new behaviors learned in the token-economy program generalize to other settings once the patients leave the institution? In fact, removal of the contingencies learned in the program usually results in a decline in performance of the behaviors in other settings. In the past several years, however, tremendous progress has been made in elaborating the principles whereby the behaviors will transfer to new settings. One obvious procedure for ensuring that the behaviors will be maintained is to bring them under the control of consequences that ordinarily occur in the new settings. For example, the treatment of a withdrawn patient in a hospital setting might involve having staff members give attention and an expression of interest whenever the patient socializes with them or with other patients. Later, in a home setting, the patient's parents and relatives can continue to reinforce the person's social interactions through the use of praise, smiles, displays of affection, and expressions of interest. However, researchers have found that, in the home setting, family members do not necessarily use the required reinforcers; in other words, some people do not ordinarily give much praise and attention to others. Instead, they tend to ignore attempts at showing social behaviors, or to reinforce the wrong behaviors. This problem can usually be overcome by training family members to reinforce appropriate behaviors (Kazdin, 1989, pp. 264–269).

Aversive Techniques

Behavior modification also raises some serious ethical questions, especially with regard to aversive techniques. Is it morally acceptable to use punishment, for example, to change behavior? Experts in the area of behavior modification agree that the use of physical punishment should generally be avoided, because it has undesirable side effects and interferes with the learning of socially appropriate behavior. However, it can be used to stop extremely undesirable behavior if other procedures based on positive reinforcement have been tried and failed (Kazdin, 1989, pp. 142–148).

Let us examine an actual case history in which aversive control techniques were used, so that you can decide for yourself whether or not the use of punishment can be justified under certain circumstances. The case involved self-destructive behavior in a severely retarded 7-year-old boy who was nonverbal and who functioned like a 2-year-old (Kushner, 1970, pp. 42–44). The self-destructive behavior consisted of hand-biting severe enough to cause bleeding and infection. Hospital personnel tried to prevent the behavior by placing boxing gloves on the boy's hands but, when they were removed, he simply went back to biting his hands. The child also tried to prevent the behavior by sitting on his hands or by holding onto his nurse's hand. This strategy worked only temporarily, and he continued to bite his hands when they were free. Observation by the investigator indicated that the nurses' reaction to his crying following the hand-biting was to become very solicitous, to pick him up, and to give him a great deal of attention and affection. Discussion with the nurses about the reinforcing properties of their behavior met with great resistance. It was obvious that the nurses could not be convinced of the necessity to ignore the behavior and, in any case, the extinction process would be so slow that much more damage would be inflicted. Therefore, the investigator decided to use electric shock to prevent the behavior. Electrodes were placed on the child's thigh and shock was administered following any hand-biting behavior. After the initial application of shock, the mother was brought into the room and was asked to say "No" at the same time that the shock was being administered. The decline in hand-biting was rapid and dramatic. Later the nurses were instructed to say "No" whenever the child moved his hand to his mouth and to say "Good boy" when he moved his hand away. Other behavioral methods were then applied to maintain the low rate of hand-biting.

Would you condone the use of punishment in this case? It is a very difficult judgment to make. If all other possibilities have been tried and found wanting, perhaps aversive control can be justified in certain instances. There are no easy answers in this situation, but no progress in helping people is made by denying the efficacy of punishment in producing behavioral change.

In the past, there have been abuses of patients' rights in programs using behavior-modification techniques. Occasionally, investigators have administered cruel and unusual punishment; in one study, for example, patients were shocked without their consent and deprived of meals for a number of days. Even in the Ayllon and Azrin (1965) study reviewed in this chapter, there is a question of the abuse of patients' rights. A reexamination of Table 15.2, which shows the kinds of reinforcers that could be bought with earned tokens, indicates that, theoretically at least, attendance at extra religious services could be prohibited by the investigators if the patient had not earned any tokens. This kind of prohibition comes very close to an abridgment of the patient's constitutional rights concerning freedom of religion. This is not to say, however, that denial of patient rights or the administration of cruel and unusual punishment is pervasive and, therefore, that behavior modification procedures should be abandoned. Abuses are relatively few, and the benefits to thousands and thousands of people have been tremendous. Instead, investigators must work to eliminate abusive practices and uphold, to the best of their abilities, the ethical ideals of the profession.

Shaping

Jackson and Wallace (1974) used shaping to develop appropriate speech in a 15-year-old girl named Alice who was diagnosed as "severely disturbed, withdrawn, and mildly retarded" by the school diagnostician. Her teacher reported that Alice participated only rarely in group activities and almost never spoke at an audible level. The goal was to shape the loudness of her voice until it reached a normal level.

Wearing a microphone to detect the volume of her speech, Alice sat in a private booth, and read to the experimenter single words taken from her classroom reading books. When her voice achieved a specified volume, a token was automatically delivered. At first, only slight increases in volume were required for the delivery of a token. Eventually, however, Alice had to speak louder to activate the relay attached to the microphone sound system that triggered delivery of the tokens. Alice underwent 20 shaping sessions. After each session, she was required to read from a book to the experimenter for ten minutes. The tokens Alice earned could be exchanged for several items she wanted, including books, beauty aids, and a photo album.

Once Alice spoke at a normal level, the experimenter attempted to generalize Alice's new behavior to her classroom. To promote generalization, the experimenter rearranged the laboratory setting so that it resembled her actual classroom and continued her training. For example, the side of Alice's booth was swung out at a 45-degree angle, greatly reducing her privacy. Five students and her teacher conducted a study period in the room during the shaping period. Eventually, following intense training, Alice was returned to her regular classroom, where she began to behave in a more appropriate way. Her teacher reported that, although she was a long way from being a typical teenager, she had made considerable improvement both in voice loudness and in other social behaviors such as smiling, playing with others, and initiating verbal interactions with her peers.

THEORY'S IMPLICATIONS FOR EDUCATION

According to Skinner, teachers and administrators in this country and in many others tend to rely on aversive practices to control the behavior of students. Fifty years ago, children learned the prescribed materials to escape the cane or birch rod. Today the rod is seldom used, but Skinner (1969, p. 149) maintained that we have merely shifted from one kind of aversive control to another. In the lower grades, the child fills in a workbook to avoid the teacher's displeasure or criticism and the ridicule of classmates. Not infrequently, a child with low marks must stay after school, is sent to the principal's office, or is admonished or spanked by parents. Homework is imposed by the teacher and is sometimes used as punishment for troublemaking. Many of the same practices occur at the college and university level; in place of the principal, students face the college dean. The competition for marks in higher education is especially keen, and high marks for one student often mean low marks for another, because many teachers continue to grade in terms of the traditional bell curve.

These and many other practices are painful for large numbers of students and generate many unwanted by-products (Skinner, 1968, p. 97). The student may try to escape from the punishing situation by being tardy, or may eventually drop out of school altogether. Students who commit suicide are often those who have experienced difficulties in school. Subtler forms of escape include chronic daydreaming and restlessness. A student who cannot sit still for a few minutes in class can spend hours playing in the neighborhood park or watching television. Another serious result of aversive control, in Skinner's view, is that students may attempt to attack their controllers, by becoming defiant, rude, or impudent, using obscene language, and even physically assaulting their teachers. For Skinner, vandalism is another indirect manifestation of students' attempts to weaken the control of powerful others.

The detrimental nature of aversive practices has prompted many well-intentioned and concerned teachers to seek alternatives. According to Skinner, one major alternative to punishment accepted by educators in practice, if not in theory, is permissiveness. Permissiveness has a number of seeming advantages; one of these is that the practitioners are spared the labor of supervision and the enforcement of standards. But "permissiveness is not . . . a policy; it is the abandonment of policy; and its apparent advantages are illusory. To refuse to control is to leave control not to the person himself but to other parts of the social and nonsocial environments" (Skinner, 1968, p. 84).

Another major alternative, related in many respects to permissiveness, is guidance. Its effects on the educational process are usually described with a horticultural metaphor: students are said to grow like a flower or tree if their experiences occur in the right soil; behavior can be cultivated but only under the right conditions; behavior is developed until maturity (Skinner, 1968, p. 87). In Chapters 12 and 13 on Maslow and Rogers, we saw good examples of the guidance position. Skinner notes some convenient advantages for its practitioners:

> One who merely guides a natural development cannot easily be accused of trying to control it. Growth remains an achievement of the individual, testifying to his freedom and worth, his "hidden propensities," and as the gardener is not responsible for the ultimate form of what he grows, so one who merely guides is exonerated when things go wrong. (Skinner, 1968, pp. 87–88)

In Skinner's view, the primary disadvantage of this position is that it obscures the reinforcements actually responsible for the changes in behavior by attributing them to "the unfolding of some predetermined pattern" (Skinner, 1968, p. 88).

Skinner himself opted for a detailed examination of the environmental determinants of behavior. In his view, education involves "the arrangement of [the] contingencies of reinforcement under which students learn" (Skinner, 1968, p. 64). These contingencies can be effectively arranged through the use of teaching machines, computer-assisted instruction, and other programmed techniques. Complex subject matter is presented to the student in a series of small, easy-to-learn steps. In one form of programmed learning, a question is presented and the students write their answer in a space provided by the program. Then they lift a lever that moves the answer under a transparent cover and simultaneously exposes the correct answer. If the two answers match, the students punch a hole in the paper near their response to indicate that they have answered correctly. This procedure instructs the machine to allow the next question to appear. Following the same procedure, the students answer all the questions. They then start the series again and attempt to answer correctly those questions they answered incorrectly at first. The process is repeated until they have mastered the program materials (Skinner, 1968, p. 162).

Skinner maintained that such a format has many advantages over the traditional system. It is more efficient than traditional instructional procedures. It is a labor-saving device, because it can bring many students into contact with one programmer (Skinner, 1968, p. 162). Although programming may suggest mass production to some people, in reality it acts almost like a private tutor for the student. Unlike lectures and films, there is a continual interplay between the student and the materials. Programming does not eliminate the need for the teacher. The teacher is the key person who arranges the contingencies of reinforcement for the student, but now he or she can make these arrangements pay off in effective learning. In addition, the teacher still has the tremendous responsibility of weaning students from the machine and showing them how the facts and principles they have learned can be related to other areas of life.

The teaching machine is programmed to ensure that the student thoroughly understands a point before he or she can proceed. One of the tragedies of traditional educational practices is that, all too often, the teacher is faced with the task of educating large numbers of students simultaneously. Under such conditions, it is impossible for even the best teacher to give each student the amount of attention he or she needs to learn the materials well. Still another advantage is that the machine reinforces the student sufficiently for each response and does it immediately (Skinner, 1968, p. 39). Very often, the teacher in the traditional setting knows the value of immediate and adequate reinforcement but cannot provide it. Finally, the programmed-learning approach recognizes the importance of individual differences. Skinner (1968, p. 242) maintained that failure to account for these differences is the greatest single inefficiency in education today.

For all these reasons, Skinner strongly advocated the adoption of his programmed-learning approach. But, although he was hopeful of eventual change in our educational system, he realized that his innovations might be resisted by educators.

> Many of these charged with the improvement of education are unaware that . . . technical help is available, and many are afraid of it when it is pointed out. They resist any new practice which does not have the familiar and reassuring character of day-to-day communication. They continue to discuss learning and teaching in the language of the layman. (Skinner, 1968, p. 259)

Thus, Skinner recommended the application of a scientific analysis of behavior to educational practices. It seems that his approach is gaining some support among educators, as evidenced by the large number of academic institutions that now use the programmed-learning format to help educate students.

THEORY'S IMPLICATIONS FOR SOCIETY

In his book *Walden Two,* Skinner (1948) makes an effort to apply operant principles not only to education and psychopathology but to the extremely complicated problem of creating an ideal society. Skinner envisages Walden Two as this behaviorally engineered utopia. It is portrayed as a rural community with cooperative housing and dining systems for its nearly 1000 members. Such a communal arrangement avoids the unnecessary duplication of facilities and the great expense associated with building separate houses. Because of the relatively small size of the living quarters, it is possible to interconnect all of the bedrooms with common lounge areas, dining rooms, a theater, and a library. Thus, for the most part, members can avoid going out in bad weather. These protected arrangements are consistent with Skinner's emphasis on changing the environment to meet individual needs; they permit more control of undesirable weather conditions, so that community members are masters of their own situation rather than the victims of it.

An additional benefit of living in such a small, largely self-contained community is that there is no long-distance commuting to work along congested and polluted highways, a nerve-wracking practice that continues to plague many contemporary workers (Freedman, 1972, chap. 2, p. 3). A few trucks simply ferry some of the workers back and forth over the short distance from the living quarters to the workshops (where, for example, furniture is made and repaired), gardens, and livestock areas.

Skinner insisted that his utopia was not founded on the simplistic and romanticized return-to-the-farm philosophy of the 1800s, nor did it spring from a rejection of modern life. For example, the farming to meet food and clothing needs relies on the best equipment available, bought from the larger, outside community. Also, the power to run these machines (including the trucks) is supplied by the larger community. The emphasis in Walden Two is on minimizing uncreative and uninteresting work for its members. This orientation demands the best that technology can offer.

Although necessary at times for transactions with the larger community, money is not needed or used within Walden Two. Money earned by members as a result of work done for outsiders is placed in a community fund to be used for future purchases from outsiders. Within Walden Two, food, clothing, shelter, recreation, and medical services are provided, and so there is no need for money. To keep the system operating, however, members are required to contribute 1200 labor credits a year (or four credits for each of 300 workdays) in return for the goods and services provided to them. In general, one credit is given for each hour of work; thus, the average workday lasts four hours, so that residents have ample time for recreational activities and other diversions (for instance, games, theatrical plays, reading, writing, art, science, hobbies). To ensure that unpleasant jobs get done and to avoid resentment over aversive types of work, the apportionment of the labor credits is adjusted to make all kinds of work equally attractive. For example, cleaning sewers earns 1.5 credits per hour, whereas working in the community flower garden earns only 0.7 or 0.8 credits per hour (Skinner, 1948, p. 52). Even though each member works an average of only 20 hours per week, such an economy is viable, for several reasons. Thus, there is little unnecessary duplication of goods; for example, there are community automobiles but not everyone owns one. Unnecessary services are eliminated; for instance, there are no bars or taverns, because Skinner believed that the satisfied people of his utopia would have no need to drink (Freedman, 1972, chap. 2, p. 3). Because community members are not bombarded daily by fashion advertisers, clothing styles change more slowly in Walden Two, and members do not throw away clothes in good condition (Skinner, 1948, p. 35). And because there is no unemployment, the bureaucratic burden and cost of administering benefits to the unemployed are eliminated.

Walden Two also makes efficient use of all of its citizens, including women. Skinner was unequivocally egalitarian in his views on the relationships and roles of men and women; he predated the current women's liberation movement by approximately 20 years. There is no sexual division of labor in Walden Two. Because all community members, irrespective of gender, share the labor of preparing and serving food, cleaning the living quarters, and educating the young, women are able to participate equally with men in every area of communal life. Child care is also shared by members of the community of both sexes.

Child care was of particular concern to Skinner, and he devoted considerable attention to it. Children in Walden Two do not live with their natural parents, nor are they raised by them. Instead, group members share the responsibility of raising children. In the nursery, infants are raised by community experts, both male and female. They live in a controlled environment so that they never know fear, frustration, or anxiety. After the first year of life, they are placed in dormitory quarters, and annoyances are introduced on a gradual basis in order to develop tolerance for a certain degree of frustration. For example, Skinner describes a situation in which, tired and hungry, a group of children come home after a long walk. Instead of being allowed to eat immediately, they must stand for five minutes in front of steaming bowls of soup (Skinner, 1948, p. 109). Children are encouraged to have a sense of humor and not to take annoyances too seriously. These lessons in self-control are taught so that children can handle any unhappiness they might experience later in life. Whereas in our culture children may meet with uncontrolled frustration and subsequent defeat, in Walden Two the degree of frustration is carefully controlled so that success can be assured (Freedman, 1972, chap. 3, p. 3).

Group care of children weakens the relationship between parent and child; this state of affairs is encouraged in Walden Two. Skinner believed that, in the typical home, parents do not know how to raise their children properly. This job is best left in the hands of experts. Children regard all adult members of Walden Two as their parents, which provides several benefits. Children are discouraged from being too dependent on their biological parents. Foster children and stepchildren are loved as dearly as one's own. If the biological parents divorce, children are not embarrassed by severe changes in their lifestyles. It is also easier to discourage people who are unfit or unwell from seeking parenthood, because no stigma attaches to being childless and the childless have others to love. Finally, children grow up more secure, because they receive affection and help from hundreds of adults (Skinner, 1948, pp. 142–145).

Walden Two is governed by a board of six planners, three of whom are usually women. The planners are chosen by the board members themselves, from names supplied by the managers. Planners may serve for a period of up to ten years but no more. They are responsible for policy making and for the supervision of the managers.

The managers are responsible for providing adequate goods and services to community members; for example, there are managers of food, health, dentistry, play, arts, nursery school, and dairy. They are specialists who have been carefully trained and selected for the job through apprenticeship procedures (Skinner, 1948, p. 55).

The only other group besides the workers, managers, and planners is the scientists. The community supports research aimed at the improvement of the economy and the psychological well-being of its members. Experiments are often done in plant and animal breeding to improve the economy, and psychological experiments are performed to increase knowledge of the impact of the environment on behavior, so that the environment can be effectively manipulated to increase community members' happiness.

In Walden Two, the workers do not elect the planners, managers, or scientists. Skinner maintained that the average citizen (worker) is unable to make such selections intelligently (Skinner, 1948, p. 267). These decisions are best left in the hands of specialists, who, he believed, would wield their power for the good of others. Should they take any steps that reduced the total happiness of the community, they would begin to experience a reduction in their power. Skinner was convinced that this potential reduction in power would serve as a check against misuse of authority (Skinner, 1948, p. 264).

It could be argued that Skinner's view is naive and that concentration of power in the hands of a few people is likely to lead to misuse of that power, irrespective of the level of unhappiness of community members. This criticism assumes that power is a means to personal gain: dictators exploit citizens to enhance their own feelings of esteem and to accrue wealth and possessions. In Skinner's utopia, however, a person's self-esteem is based on contributing to the betterment of the community and not on personal gain. Possessions and wealth are shared, and so there is no incentive to accumulate goods. A loss in power would signify to leaders that community members are less accepting of their efforts to help them; consequently, the leaders would be unhappy. Also, the socialization process in Walden Two ensures that members do not see punishment as a primary means of controlling behavior; rather, the emphasis is on positive reinforcement and cooperative behavior (Skinner, 1948, p. 272). Finally, if the planners did abuse their authority, they could be replaced, under the code adopted by community members to govern behavior. Despite all these assurances, Walden Two is clearly a dictatorship, albeit a benevolent one, and as such is unsettling to most democratically oriented Americans.

Even more unsettling is Skinner's harsh indictment of democracy. He argued that democracy is really despotism, because the minority is at the mercy of the majority (Freedman, 1972, chap. 3, p. 7). Skinner saw little point in national elections, especially presidential elections; with so little difference between the parties and their political platforms, the election of either candidate makes no appreciable difference in the lives of the electorate. Instead of striving to improve democracy, he would simply abandon it (Freedman, 1972, chap. 3, p. 7).

In Skinner's version of the ideal society, people would be in a position to tell the experts (planners, managers, and scientists) directly what they like or dislike about the life they are leading. Thus, protests would be legitimate and would be taken "as seriously as the pilot of an airplane takes a sputtering engine" (Skinner, 1948, p. 269). If current practices were unsatisfactory, they would be changed, because Skinner's utopia is an experimenting society, where the aim is maximization of the happiness of every community member.

EVALUATIVE COMMENTS

An evaluation of the scientific worth of Skinner's theory in terms of our six criteria is now in order.

Comprehensiveness   Skinner constructed a theory of behavior that initially focused almost exclusively on the functioning of lower animals. His primary concern was to generate a set of learning principles for certain types of simple, nonsocial performance. Thus, the range of topics actually covered by Skinner in his initial theorizing was highly limited, and he was severely criticized for this narrow focus. His principal rebuttal was that, in all sciences, advances occur as investigators focus first on the simple and then progress to the more complex. The focus on simple behaviors allows scientists to control current situational conditions better, to record behavior over longer periods of time, and to control genetic and environmental-history variables (Skinner, 1953, p. 38). Once the basic processes are understood in lower animals, this information can be utilized in the study of the more diverse and complicated behavior of human beings.

This research strategy has had considerable payoff value in terms of the important findings about behavior it has generated. Yet there is a kind of conservatism about it that may seem unnecessarily stultifying to investigators of human behavior. Science is a human enterprise and should, at least occasionally, be fun. Part of the enjoyment is based on taking risks—on testing hunches that are not firmly grounded in data. Nonetheless, Skinner's allegiance to the strict simple-to-complex principle is generally cogent.

In his later writings, Skinner argued that the imbalance in his work had been corrected, because much of the current work in behavior modification focuses exclusively on human behavior. On this basis, Skinner's theory can now be considered comprehensive.

Precision and testability   The terms of Skinner's theory are precisely defined, and the various relational statements are capable of experimental verification. The concern with rigor and precision in the study of behavioral phenomena is one of the impressive strengths of the work of Skinner and his operant colleagues.

Parsimony   Skinner's theory is relatively economical, especially when compared with some of the psychodynamic positions. It is not burdened by excess concepts and assumptions. In fact, it can be argued that the theory lacks a number of concepts that could help to explain various social-learning phenomena. Skinner himself recognized that additional concepts may be needed in a theory that attempts to account for complex and cognitively based human learning.

Empirical validity   Skinner's position, in sharp contrast to the psychodynamic positions, is firmly grounded in laboratory data. Despite strong empirical support for many aspects of his learning theory, however, critics argue that Skinner's claim to a technology of behavior that can solve complex social problems is unsupported—that he made sweeping and unwarranted generalizations on the basis of limited empirical evidence (Black, 1973, p. 129). Skinner acknowledged that he was indeed offering interpretations about the functioning of society from limited data, but argued that this is perfectly legitimate and is done by scientists in other fields without attracting much attention. He maintained that "when phenomena are out of reach in time or space, or too large or small to be directly manipulated, we must talk about them with less than a complete account of relevant conditions" (Skinner, 1973, p. 261). This is true, but it is also easy to confuse speculation with fact, and Skinner's arguments about the efficacy of his approach in solving major social problems like poverty and overpopulation are as yet unproven.

Heuristic value   Skinner's theory has had tremendous impact on the thinking and research activities of investigators in many disciplines. He was a controversial figure, whose position has been severely criticized by a variety of critics, including humanistic psychologists, psychiatrists, politicians, philosophers, theologians, biologists, novelists, and journalists. Some people have taken these attacks as proof that Skinner was a revolutionary thinker whose position will eventually force a major shift in the way we view ourselves and others (Platt, 1973, p. 23). Be that as it may, it is clear that Skinner's theory ranks high in heuristic value.

Applied value   Skinner's position has far-reaching implications for the functioning of society. Beginning with experiments on the behavior of lower animals, he derived, over approximately a 60-year period, a set of simple and precise reinforcement principles that have been applied to a number of significant problems faced by human beings. The theory's applied value can perhaps be seen most clearly in the areas of psychopathology and education.

DISCUSSION QUESTIONS

1. Why does Skinner think there is a need for a scientific technology of behavior? Do you agree or disagree with him?
2. Do you ever use mentalistic explanations to account for behavior? If so, cite some recent instances and try to reanalyze them in terms of possible environmental variables salient at the time.
3. How might the stereotypic belief that individuals are solely responsible for their behavior result in the continuation of racial discrimination?
4. Is all control of behavior bad? In what ways does control yield positive or negative outcomes for people? Why do many people dislike those who control the outcomes of others?
5. What is operant conditioning? How does it differ from classical conditioning?
6. Do you agree with Skinner that punishment is the most common technique of control in modern life? What are the limitations of punishment as a control technique? Is its use ever effective and desirable? Discuss the implications of the use of failing grades as a punishment technique. Can you propose alternative, more effective, and rewarding ways of evaluating students' performance that provide them with accurate feedback regarding their progress (or lack of it) in a course?
7. What is extinction? Have you ever tried to extinguish someone's obnoxious behavior by ignoring it? What happened? What are some of the limitations of the technique?
8. Describe the various types of reinforcement schedules. Cite some examples in your everyday routine in which your behavior is controlled by the different schedule types.

9. What is behavior modification? What are its strengths and weaknesses? Do you think that token economies are useless, sterile, and unethical ways of changing undesirable behavior? Who decides which behaviors are undesirable? Who should decide?
10. Do you agree with Skinner's application of behavioral technology to education? What are the strengths and deficiencies of his arguments for reforming the educational system?

GLOSSARY

behavior modification   Series of procedures that seek to change behavior through reliance on reinforcement principles or, less often, by reliance on punishment principles.

contingency   Relationship between a behavior and its consequences. In some cases, events that precede the behavior are also specified by a contingency.

contingent observation procedure   Technique in which children who have behaved disruptively in a play situation are required to sit on the periphery of the group and watch the other children playing appropriately. A return to the group is dependent on the child's acknowledgment that he or she understands the correct behavior to be exhibited in the play situation.

continuous reinforcement   Schedule of reinforcement in which each response is followed by a reinforcer.

discrimination   Responding differently in the presence of different situational events.

discriminative stimulus   Stimulus whose presence signals an individual to respond because he or she has learned previously that its presence leads to reinforcing consequences.

extinction   Reduction in behavior that occurs as a result of the failure to reinforce previously reinforced behavior.

fixed-interval schedule   Schedule of reinforcement in which the first response that occurs after a fixed amount of time has elapsed is reinforced.

fixed-ratio schedule   Schedule of reinforcement in which a fixed number of responses is required before a reinforcer is applied.

functional analysis   Attempt to understand behavior by identifying the environmental conditions that determine its occurrence or nonoccurrence. A functional analysis says that behavior is caused by the operation of environmental factors.

intermittent reinforcement   Schedule of reinforcement in which responses produce reinforcers only occasionally or intermittently.

law of effect   For Thorndike, the principle that behavior is determined by its consequences. In his view, behavior followed by reward was "stamped in," whereas behavior followed by punishment was "stamped out." In current operant-conditioning theory, the principle is that a behavior becomes more probable when it is followed by a positive reinforcer and less probable when it is followed by a punisher.

mentalism   Pejorative term used by some learning theorists to indicate their dissatisfaction with the use of concepts that cannot be objectively assessed or validated as explanatory devices in attempts to account for behavior. These concepts are supposed to have explanatory power, but in reality do not.

negative punishment   Removal of a positive reinforcer following a response, with the result that the rate of that response decreases.

negative reinforcement   The removal of an aversive stimulus following a response, with the result that the rate of that response increases.

negative reinforcers   Aversive stimuli whose removal following a response strengthens the occurrence of that response.

operant analysis   Study of the ways in which behavior is acquired, maintained, or modified by its reinforcing or punishing consequences.

operant conditioning   Establishment of the linkage or association between a behavior and its consequences.

positive punishment   Presentation of an aversive stimulus following a response, with the result that the rate of that response decreases.

positive reinforcement   The presentation of a positive reinforcer following a response, with the result that the rate of that response increases.

positive reinforcers   Stimuli that, when they follow behavior, increase the frequency of the behavior.

primary punishers   Stimuli that are innately aversive. They do not need to be paired with other aversive stimuli to achieve their aversive properties.

primary reinforcers   Stimuli that are innately reinforcing. They do not depend on learning to achieve their reinforcing properties.

prompts   Antecedent stimuli that help initiate behaviors.

punishment   Presentation of an aversive stimulus or removal of a positive reinforcer following a behavior, with the result that the performance of that behavior decreases.

redirection procedure   A technique in which children who are acting inappropriately are removed from the situation and their attention is directed to an alternative activity.

reinforcement   Presentation of a positive reinforcer or removal of a punisher following a behavior, with the result that the frequency of that behavior increases.

repertoire   Unique set of acquired behavior patterns.

response cost   A punishment procedure in which, contingent on undesirable behavior, a positive reinforcer is removed or lost.

secondary punishers   Stimuli that become aversive by being paired with other stimuli (primary or conditioned) that are already punishing.

secondary reinforcers   Stimuli that become reinforcing by being paired with other stimuli (primary or conditioned) that are already reinforcing.

self-control processes   Actions instigated by a person to alter the conditions that influence his or her behavior.

shaping   Teaching a new behavior by reinforcing responses that successively approximate it.

stimulus control   The process in which a person's response is determined by particular stimuli. If a person has been reinforced for a given behavior in the presence of certain stimuli and not in the presence of others, he or she learns to respond only in the presence of those stimuli that provide the opportunity for reinforcement. Behavior is then said to be under the control of those stimuli.

stimulus generalization   The process by which responses made in the presence of a particular stimulus come to be made in the presence of other, similar stimuli.

successive approximations   A procedure whereby responses that more and more closely resemble a terminal response are reinforced.

time out from reinforcement   A punishment procedure in which, contingent on undesirable behavior, access to positive reinforcers is withdrawn for a brief period.

token economy   A behavior modification procedure in which patients earn tokens (or chips or points) for performing behaviors that the hospital staff judges are necessary if the patients are to live effectively. The tokens are conditioned reinforcers that can be exchanged for experiences and/or goods desired by the patients.

SUGGESTED READINGS

Skinner, B. F. (1948). *Walden Two*. New York: Macmillan.

Skinner, B. F. (1953). *Science and human behavior*. New York: Macmillan.

Skinner, B. F. (1971). *Beyond freedom and dignity*. New York: Knopf.

Skinner, B. F. (1974). *About behaviorism*. New York: Knopf.

Skinner, B. F. (1978). *Reflections on behaviorism and society*. Englewood Cliffs, NJ: Prentice-Hall.

Skinner, B. F., & Vaughan, M. E. (1983). *Enjoy old age*. New York: Norton.

REFERENCES

Ayllon, T., & Azrin, N. H. (1965). The measurement and reinforcement of behavior of psychotics. *Journal of the Experimental Analysis of Behavior, 8,* 357–383.

Black, M. (1973). Some aversive responses to a would-be reinforcer. In H. Wheeler (Ed.), *Beyond the punitive society* (pp. 125–134). San Francisco: W. H. Freeman.

Brownell, K. D., & Jeffery, R. W. (1987). Improving long-term weight loss: Pushing the limits of treatment. *Behavior Therapy, 18,* 353–374.

Carpenter, F. (1974). *The Skinner primer*. New York: Free Press.

Ferster, C. B., & Perrott, M. C. (1968). *Behavior principles*. New York: Appleton-Century-Crofts.

Flavell, J. H. (1963). *The developmental psychology of Jean Piaget*. New York: Van Nostrand.

Freedman, A. E. (1972). *The planned society: An analysis of Skinner's proposals*. Kalamazoo, MI: Behaviordelia.

Jackson, D. A., & Wallace, R. F. (1974). The modification and generalization of voice loudness in a fifteen-year-old retarded girl. *Journal of Applied Behavior Analysis, 7,* 461–471.

Kazdin, A. E. (1989). *Behavior modification in applied settings* (4th ed.). Pacific Grove, CA: Brooks/Cole.

Krasner, L. (1970). Behavior modification, token economies, and training in clinical psychology. In C. Neuringer & J. L. Michael (Eds.), *Behavior modification in clinical psychology* (pp. 86–104). New York: Appleton-Century-Crofts.

Kushner, M. (1970). Faradic aversive controls in clinical practice. In C. Neuringer & J. L. Michael (Eds.), *Behavior modification in clinical psychology* (pp. 26–51). New York: Appleton-Century-Crofts.

Mazur, J. E. (1986). *Learning and behavior*. Englewood Cliffs, NJ: Prentice-Hall.

Penick, S. B., Filion, R., Fox, S., & Stunkard, A. J. (1971). Behavior modification in the treatment of obesity. *Psychosomatic Medicine, 33,* 49–55.

578   Part Six   Social-Behavioristic Perspectives

Platt, J. R. (1973). The Skinnerian revolution. In H. Wheeler (Ed.), *Beyond the punitive society* (pp. 22–56). San Francisco: W. H. Freeman.

Porterfield, J. K., Herbert-Jackson, E., & Risley, T. R. (1976). Contingent observation: An effective and acceptable procedure for reducing disruptive behavior of young children in a group setting. *Journal of Applied Behavior Analysis, 9,* 55–64.

Rapport, M. D., Murphy, H. A., & Bailey, J. S. (1982). Ritalin vs. response cost in the control of hyperactive children: A within-subject comparison. *Journal of Applied Behavior Analysis, 15,* 205–216.

Skinner, B. F. (1938). *The behavior of organisms.* New York: Appleton-Century-Crofts.

Skinner, B. F. (1948). *Walden Two.* New York: Macmillan.

Skinner, B. F. (1953). *Science and human behavior.* New York: Macmillan.

Skinner, B. F. (1968). *The technology of teaching.* New York: Appleton-Century-Crofts.

Skinner, B. F. (1969). *Contingencies of reinforcement.* New York: Appleton-Century-Crofts.

Skinner, B. F. (1970). An autobiography. In P. B. Dews (Ed.), *Festschrift for B. F. Skinner* (pp. 1–21). New York: Appleton-Century-Crofts.

Skinner, B. F. (1971). *Beyond freedom and dignity.* New York: Knopf.

Skinner, B. F. (1973). Answers for my critics. In H. Wheeler (Ed.), *Beyond the punitive society* (pp. 256–266). San Francisco: W. H. Freeman.

Skinner, B. F. (1974). *About behaviorism.* New York: Knopf.

Skinner, B. F. (1976). *Particulars of my life.* New York: Knopf.

Skinner, B. F. (1987). Whatever happened to psychology as the science of behavior? *American Psychologist, 42,* 780–786.

Wagaman, J. R., Miltenberger, R. G., & Arndorfer, R. E. (1993). Analysis of a simplified treatment for stuttering in children. *Journal of Applied Behavior Analysis, 26,* 53–61.

Wagaman, J. R., Miltenberger, R. G., & Woods, D. (1995). Long-term follow-up of a behavioral treatment for stuttering in children. *Journal of Applied Behavior Analysis, 28,* 233–234.

Walters, G. C., & Grusec, J. E. (1977). *Punishment.* San Francisco: W. H. Freeman.

Williams, R. L., & Long, J. D. (1979). *Toward a self-managed life style.* Boston: Houghton Mifflin.

CHAPTER 16

Rotter's Expectancy-Reinforcement Value Model

BIOGRAPHICAL SKETCH

Julian Rotter was born in Brooklyn, New York, in 1916. He received his B.A. from Brooklyn College in 1937, his M.A. from the University of Iowa in 1938, and his Ph.D. in psychology from Indiana University in 1941. During his undergraduate and graduate days he was greatly influenced by neoanalyst Alfred Adler and by Kurt Lewin, a prominent social psychologist. Rotter attended a series of Adler's clinics, demonstrations, and university seminars and also met informally with Adler at his home (Mosher, 1968). He credits Adler with focusing his attention on the goal-directedness of behavior and on the unity of personality. Many of the concepts in Rotter's position, as we shall see, can be traced directly to Adler's influence.

Rotter was also influenced by Lewin's field-theory approach, which emphasizes the interrelatedness of behavior and postulates that multiple factors are responsible for the occurrence of any behavior. Rotter accepted these assumptions, as well as the view that behavior must be described from the perspective of the person whose behavior is under scrutiny (Rotter & Hochreich, 1975, p. 97). In addition to Adler and Lewin, Rotter reports being influenced by the writings of a number of learning theorists, including Thorndike, Tolman, and Hull. In general terms, his social-learning position is an attempt to integrate two major trends embodied in the work of these theorists: a reinforcement approach and cognitive or **field theory** (Rotter, Chance, & Phares, 1972, p. 1).

After serving as a psychologist and personnel consultant to the U.S. Army during World War II, Rotter accepted a position at Ohio State University, where he eventually became director of the psychological clinic. During his stay at Ohio State, he published *Social Learning and Clinical Psychology* (1954), in which he presented an extended treatment of his social-learning theory of personality. He also attracted a number of capable students, who worked with him to test various predictions derived from the theory. Some of these students have since become leading proponents of the social-learning view in contemporary psychology.

In 1963, Rotter left Ohio State and accepted a position as a full professor in the department of psychology at the University of Connecticut, where he also served as director of the clinical-psychology training program. Rotter is a diplomate in clinical psychology of the American Board of Examiners in Professional Psychology. He coauthored *Applications of a Social Learning Theory of Personality* (1972) with two former students, J. E. Chance and E. J. Phares, and *Personality* (1975) with colleague Dorothy Hochreich. In 1982, Rotter published *The Development and Application of Social Learning Theory,* a compilation of his most important theoretical and research papers. In 1976–1977 he served as president of the Eastern Psychological Association, and in 1988 the American Psychological Association honored him with an award for Distinguished Scientific Contributions to Psychology. Although Professor Rotter retired in 1987, he continues to be actively engaged in writing and research work in the social-learning area.

CONCEPTS AND PRINCIPLES

Rotter has constructed a theory of personality based on learning concepts and principles. The basic assumptions are that most of our behavior is learned and that it is acquired through our experiences with other people (Rotter, Chance, & Phares, 1972, p. 4). Such a social-learning view also makes use of a historical approach to the study of personality, in which the antecedent events in people's lives are investigated to understand their present behavior. Unlike the Freudians, however, Rotter does not believe it necessary to probe the individual's past experiences in great depth in order to predict behavior adequately. Instead, he argues that we should focus on past events only to the extent that they help us to meet our predictive goals (Rotter, Chance, & Phares, 1972, p. 5). For example, there may be no need to inquire into a student's traumatic experiences during the oral stage of infancy in order to predict his failure to attain a college degree; an examination of his relatively poor high school grades and low college-board scores may be sufficient.

Rotter emphasizes the unity or interdependence of personality (Rotter, Chance, & Phares, 1972, p. 7), in which a person's experiences and interactions continually influence one another. Past experiences influence current experiences, and current experiences change the things learned in the past. For example, a student may reject potentially helpful advice from her college counselor because she has consistently been given poor advice by other counselors in the past. If she can be induced to accept the advice of this counselor, however, and it proves helpful, her general attitude toward counselors may become more positive. Thus, personality is seen as both changing, because the individual is continuously exposed to new experiences, and stable, because previous experiences affect new learning (Rotter & Hochreich, 1975, p. 94).

Another aspect of unity or interdependence is that different behaviors are functionally related (Katkovsky, 1968, p. 215). For example, you may succeed in having your name added to the class list for a popular course by getting up very early and being first in line, by asking a friend to register for you, by speaking directly to the instructor, by getting approval from the college dean, and so on. Each of these behaviors is functionally related; that is, they all operate to secure the same outcome. Reinforcements can also become functionally related (Rotter, Chance, & Phares, 1972, p. 19). For example, a star hockey player may learn that leading his team to the coveted Stanley Cup means not only a healthy increase in his annual salary but praise from teammates, the coach, and members of the media and also lucrative advertising contracts with major manufacturers.

Motivation

Rotter assumes that much of our behavior is goal-directed. This directionality is inferred from the effect of reinforcing conditions (Rotter, Chance, & Phares, 1972, p. 8). In other words, Rotter considers human behavior to be motivated. People strive to maximize rewards and to minimize or avoid punishment. Thus Rotter, like Skinner, endorses the empirical law of effect. In his formulation, "any stimulus complex has reinforcing properties to the extent that it influences movement toward or away from a goal" (Rotter, Chance, & Phares, 1972, p. 9). Some investigators have objected to this principle, because it seems circular: there is no attempt to define a reinforcer independently of behavior. Rotter argues that this criticism might be valid if we were unable to identify reinforcers until after they had occurred, but that in fact it is possible to identify reinforcing events that have known effects both for groups and for individuals (Rotter, Chance, & Phares, 1972, p. 9). This knowledge can then be used to make predictions about behavior.

Two other aspects of motivation should be mentioned at this point. First, when investigators using social-learning theory focus on the environmental conditions that determine the direction of behavior, they speak in terms of goals or reinforcements; when they focus on the person determining the direction of behavior, they speak of needs. For Rotter, the distinction between needs and goals is a semantic one used merely for convenience (Rotter, Chance, & Phares, 1972, p. 10).

Second, social-learning theory assumes that early goals are learned within a family setting. We are born with certain physiological needs that are satisfied by parents and parent surrogates. Our association of our parents with the satisfaction or frustration of our basic, unlearned needs provides the basis, in Rotter's judgment, for our later reliance on them and others for affection, love, praise, recognition, status, and dependency (Rotter, Chance, & Phares, 1972, p. 10).

This view, however, creates theoretical difficulties. It assumes that all reinforcers are reinforcing because they have become associated with drive reduction. For example, a mother's praise of her son's performance in school is positively reinforcing to him because it is associated with earlier feeding experiences that reduced his hunger drive. Such a drive-reduction view of reinforcement may be adequate when we are dealing with simple behaviors, but it becomes difficult to defend when we begin to consider complex social behavior (Rotter, Chance, & Phares, 1972, p. 9). For example, how can we show that an athlete with a high need for achievement has experienced reduction of an unlearned drive (such as hunger) by winning the mile run in a track meet? To overcome this difficulty, social-learning theory relies instead on an empirical law of effect: reinforcement is judged to have occurred if changes in behavior are observed following the introduction or removal of stimulating events. Thus, social-learning theory assumes that the initial learning of goals occurs within a drive-reduction framework, but that the later acquisition of highly complex behaviors is better explained by using a reinforcement concept based on the empirical law of effect.

Social-Learning Concepts

The social-learning approach is based on four major concepts: behavior potential, expectancy, reinforcement value, and the psychological situation. In its simplest form, the formula for behavior is that "the potential for a behavior to occur in any specific situation is a function of the expectancy that the behavior will lead to a particular reinforcement in that situation and the value of that reinforcement" (Rotter, 1975, p. 57). Let us examine each of these concepts in turn.

Behavior potential   In Rotter's formulation, **behavior potential** is "the potentiality of any behavior's occurring in any situation or situations as calculated in relation to any single reinforcement or set of reinforcements" (Rotter, Chance, & Phares, 1972, p. 12). Like Skinner, Rotter is talking about the probability of the individual's responding when certain environmental conditions are present. Rotter's view, however, places more emphasis on the role of cognitive factors than does Skinner's, because Rotter makes active use of people's subjective interpretations of the events that confront them. For example, he assumes that the potential for behavior is affected by people's perception of the other behaviors available to them in a given situation. Thus, a complex set of internal, or cognitive, factors is typically involved in the prediction of behavior. Finally, it should be noted that Rotter's definition of behavior is quite broad:

> Behavior may be that which is directly observed but also that which is indirect or implicit. This notion includes a broad spectrum of possibilities—swearing, running, crying, fighting, smiling, choosing, and so on are all included. These are all observable behaviors, but implicit behavior that can only be measured indirectly, such as rationalizing, repressing, considering alternatives, planning, and reclassifying, would also be included. The objective study of cognitive activity is a difficult but important aspect of social learning theory. Principles governing the occurrence of such cognitive activities are not considered different from those that might apply to any observable behavior. (Rotter, Chance, & Phares, 1972, p. 12)

Expectancy   Rotter defines **expectancy** as a cognition or belief about the property of some object or event (Rotter, 1982, p. 13). Expectancies can vary in magnitude from 0% to 100% and are subject to modification by experience. For example, a person might believe initially that a woman could never be elected President of the United States (an expectancy of 0%) but, as a result of the women's liberation movement and media coverage of the number of women who have entered politics and been elected, this expectancy could change radically and even approach absolute certainty (100%).

Social-learning theory postulates three different kinds of expectancy (Rotter, 1982, p. 4): (1) simple cognitions or labeling of stimuli ("I think that is a painting by Picasso"); (2) expectancies for behavior-reinforcement outcomes ("If I wear my three-piece Pierre Cardin suit, my employees will compliment me"); and (3) expectancies for reinforcement sequences ("If I graduate from college, I will probably get a high-paying job and become wealthy and respected").

In social-learning theory, any behavior that has been associated with a reinforcement gives rise to an expectancy. Thus, each expectancy is based on past experience (Rotter & Hochreich, 1975, p. 96). According to Rotter, simply knowing how important a goal or reinforcement is to a person is no guarantee that we can predict the person's behavior. A student may want to obtain an A in a history course very badly, but his previous experiences in other courses lead him to expect that he will fail no matter how much effort he expends. It is virtually certain he will not study and will, as a consequence, fail.

Expectancies vary in terms of their generality; that is, we may acquire generalized expectancies or expectancies specific to a given situation (Rotter & Hochreich, 1975, p. 97). Generalized expectancies operate across a variety of situations. For example, a student may acquire a generalized expectancy for academic success: having obtained As in a variety of courses or situations, she always expects to do well. Another student may have learned a specific expectancy in his academic career: having earned As in mathematics but struggled for Cs in literature and philosophy, he expects to do well only in mathematics courses.

Later in this chapter, we will focus on another generalized expectancy called internal/external control of reinforcement, a construct that has generated a considerable amount of interesting research.

Reinforcement value   Rotter defines **reinforcement value** as "the degree of preference for any one of a group of reinforcements to occur, if the probabilities of all occurring were equal" (Rotter, Chance,

& Phares, 1972, p. 21). In the simplest terms, reinforcement value refers to the importance we attach to different activities. For some of us, attending a symphony concert is highly rewarding; others would find it dreadfully dull. Some of us like to play tennis; others do not. In addition to these differences among people, we can arrange our own activities in order of preference. Given the option, we may attach more importance to reading a novel by Dostoevsky than to playing a game of basketball or riding a bicycle. Like expectancies, the values associated with different reinforcers are based on our past experiences.

Psychological situation   The fourth major concept utilized in the prediction of behavior is the **psychological situation**—that is, the situation as it is defined from the individual's personal perspective. In Rotter's view, this concept plays an extremely important part in the determination of behavior. Traditional theories tend to focus almost exclusively on an inner core of personality, within which certain motives or traits are considered to control behavior, irrespective of the operation of situational demands (Rotter, Chance, & Phares, 1972, p. 37). For example, a man may be seized periodically by uncontrollable sexual impulses, as manifested in his spouting obscenities in a wide variety of situations. In terms of trait theory, a person may have a strong need for aggression that erupts into fighting, irrespective of the situation. At the other end of the spectrum, approaches such as Skinner's emphasize the importance of situational influences and minimize, at least in research practice, individual differences based on idiosyncratic learning histories. Social-learning theory recognizes the importance of *both* dispositional and situational influences. In other words, it pays attention to the ways in which behavior is influenced by the unique past experiences of the person *and* by current situational cues. For example, a person who has strong aggressive tendencies based on a learning experience may not act aggressively in a given situation if such behavior is likely to lead to punishment by others.

Rotter believes that, on the basis of the complex cues in a particular situation, the person develops expectancies for behavior-reinforcement outcomes and also for reinforcement-reinforcement sequences (Rotter, 1981, p. 3). For example, a college student about to give a speech to her interpersonal communications class might believe that she will do poorly and will therefore receive a low grade from her instructor and ridicule from her classmates. As a result, we might expect her to drop the course or to take other action designed to prevent the anticipated humiliating outcome.

Freedom of movement and minimal goal   Two other concepts, freedom of movement and minimal goal, play a lesser but nevertheless important role in Rotter's theory.

Freedom of movement is defined as the "mean expectancy of obtaining positive satisfactions as a result of a set of related behaviors directed toward obtaining a group of functionally related reinforcements" (Rotter, Chance, & Phares, 1972, p. 34). For example, students usually acquire general expectancies as to how well they will do in various academic courses and situations. Some students have high general expectations for success; others have very low ones. Thus, we could say that the former students have high freedom of movement, whereas the latter are hindered by low freedom of movement.

Minimal goal is defined as "the lowest goal in a continuum of potential reinforcements for some life situation or situations which will be perceived as a satisfaction" (Rotter, 1954, p. 213). In other words, a minimal goal is the dividing point, on some dimension, between those outcomes that are positively reinforcing and those that are punishing. If we consider course grades on a continuum, one student may find a grade of B punishing, whereas another would be happy with it. The first student would be said to have a higher minimal goal than the second.

These concepts can be combined and used in the prediction of behavior. Thus, students who are adjusted in terms of academic achievement are those who have high freedom of movement in their academic expectations and who do not set exceedingly high minimal goals for themselves in that area. On the basis of many successful experiences in a variety of courses, they have come to expect success; at the same time, they do not set their goals for positive reinforcement so high that they are bound to experience disappointment. Thus, they do not set a minimal goal of A in every course. Such indiscriminate goal striving is unrealistic for most people. Conversely, students can be considered maladjusted if they have low freedom of movement in terms of academic achievement but continue to set high minimal goals for themselves. If, on the basis of past experiences, they expect to fail in virtually all their courses, yet feel they must attain all As, they are engaging in unproductive behavior. A study by Catanzaro (1991, pp. 243–261) provides empirical support for these ideas.

Finally, Rotter's conception of the maladjusted person who sets unattainable minimal goals is clearly reminiscent of Adler's conception of the neurotic person who sets fictional goals that cannot be attained; similarly, Rotter's low freedom of movement echoes Adler's feelings of inferiority.

PERSONALITY DEVELOPMENT

Rotter believes that personality development hinges largely on the range, diversity, and quality of the individual's experiences with other people. Early in life, these important figures are usually, and quite obviously, our parents. The individual's early goals arise out of certain physiological needs that are then satisfied by the parents or parent substitutes. As a result of their association with need reduction, parents become reinforcing stimuli in their own right. The child comes to rely on them for affection, love, praise, recognition, and other reinforcers. Rotter assumes that **stimulus generalization** occurs, so that other people who resemble the parents are perceived and evaluated in the same or similar ways. Rotter assumes that, once parents and others (teachers, clergy, other adults) acquire value as conditioned reinforcers, the child will work to secure their approval and avoid their disapproval, irrespective of whether their behavior toward the child results in primary-drive reduction.

In Rotter's view, language acquisition also plays a critical role in the child's development. Words serve as cues in directing people's behavior. Parents issue instructions that often help children solve problems in a few trials rather than the hundreds of trials it would take by unassisted trial and error. Parents thus direct their children to the relevant cues in given situations and show them how to avoid the irrelevant ones. Parents also use words as verbal reinforcers—in statements of recognition, love, rejection, and shame—to shape their children's behavior (Rotter, 1954, p. 218). In this way, children learn different expectancies for success and failure in many different situations.

These expectancies are also subject to modification through the use of verbalizations. People can build up or tear down children's expectancies—and the value of their reinforcers, for that matter—by directing their attention to new and previously neglected consequences of performing given behaviors. Or parents can change their children's expectancies by analyzing the children's previous experiences and showing them how they are responding to the wrong cues and how to rectify the situation (Rotter, 1954, pp. 219–220). Language can be used not only to help children make appropriate discriminations between events, but also to increase generalization.

> Since the effect of language is to classify, to categorize, or to abstract similarity in events, it serves, therefore, to determine and enhance the nature of generalization. If an event is symbolized, it will increase generalization to other events that are similarly abstracted. Not only does language determine generalization . . . on the basis of the subject's implicit categorizing, . . . the language of others may be used by the observer as a stimulus to determine, control, or enhance generalization. (Rotter, 1954, p. 220)

Thus, the developmental process involves the acquisition and modification of expectancies and reinforcement values through contact with various socialization agents. These socialization agents include not only adult authority figures but also peers (Rotter, 1954, p. 414). Rotter believes that development is contingent on the standards, mores, goals, and techniques communicated to children by classmates as well as by parents. Next to the home, the school has the greatest influence on development, according to Rotter (1954, p. 416). He contends that the origins of healthy or unhealthy behavior are in the home, and later transfer to the school situation. Health is promoted by parents who encourage the development and maintenance of behavior that leads to acceptance, love, and identification with others. Such behavior is most likely to occur in homes in which the parents themselves show affection and concern for the welfare and development of their offspring. In homes where parents do not provide such reinforcement, children are unlikely to learn the kinds of behaviors that will permit them to adjust to the larger society (Rotter, 1954, pp. 406–407). Such individuals are likely to develop in an antisocial way and to show selfish behaviors that produce hostility in others.

Not only do neglect and rejection lead to maladjustment, Rotter believes, but overindulgence and overprotection can create problems, too. For overindulged children, school may be a traumatic experience. In contrast to the home, school may seem to be a place where they are unwanted, unloved, and unprotected (Rotter, 1954, p. 418). Generally speaking, the rejected child is likely to enter school with low expectations for success, whereas the overindulged one will likely have expectations that are too high. Both attitudes are unrealistic. According to Rotter, the main role of the school is to correct these views and help children achieve a feeling of security and a realistic set of expectations for success that will serve them well when they assume adult responsibilities (Rotter, 1954, p. 419). To help children grow into effective citizens, then, Rotter believes that parents, teachers, and others should be warm, accepting, good-natured, democratic, and consistent in their disciplinary practices.

ASSESSMENT TECHNIQUES

Rotter relies on a variety of measurement procedures in his attempts to assess personality. In his early efforts to test hypotheses derived from social-learning theory, he utilized the experimental method to good advantage. His central question was whether people learn tasks and perform differently in situations in which they perceive reinforcing outcomes to be related or unrelated to their behavior. In other words, he wanted to determine whether learning and performance were different for people under skill and chance conditions. After a series of experimental studies, he concluded that there were significant differences in behavior in the two situations. People who perceived a task as controlled by chance relied less on past experiences in guiding current behavior, learned less, and performed less well than did people who perceived the task as skill-determined (Rotter, 1966). These results suggested that reinforcement effects do not have a direct impact on behavior but are mediated by the person's perception of the relationship (or lack of it) between behavior and application of the reinforcer.

Rotter notes the potential usefulness of five major techniques for the clinical measurement of personality: (1) the interview, (2) projective tests, (3) controlled behavioral tests, (4) behavioral observation methods, and (5) the questionnaire (Rotter, 1954, p. 250). Each of these techniques has limitations as well as strengths.

The interview is useful for the assessment of personality traits and for counseling and therapeutic purposes. In terms of social-learning theory, it can be used to assess an individual's need potentials, freedom of movement, and need value (Rotter, 1954, p. 252).

Projective tests such as the Rorschach, Thematic Apperception Test (TAT), and his own Incomplete Sentences Blank, Rotter believes, can be used to advantage in clinical diagnostic work. While he finds the Rorschach of relatively little use in measuring social-learning concepts (Rotter, 1954, p. 289), the TAT can be used to advantage, because the social-learning position is concerned with the individual's reactions to stimuli such as mother and father. The incomplete-sentences method can also be used to measure freedom of movement. In this technique, people are asked to finish sentences after the investigator provides the first few words—for example, "I like . . .," "I suffer . . .," "I wish . . .," "My father . . .," "Sometimes I feel . . ." Responses are assumed to indicate underlying conflicts that determine expectancy levels of failure in given situations (Rotter, 1954, pp. 302–304).

In controlled behavioral tests, people are placed in actual situations and their behavior is assessed in reaction to stimulus changes engineered by the investigator (Rotter, 1954, p. 311). For example, suppose that a clinician wants to know how clients react to stress. Instead of simply asking the clients to report how they might behave, the clinician can place them under actual conditions of stress and watch their reactions. Such measures have been used to test hypotheses derived from social-learning theory, most notably in the area of expectancy changes following experiences of success or failure. The behavioral-observation technique, in contrast to the controlled behavioral test, involves the relatively informal assessment of behavior by observers in natural settings (Rotter, 1954, p. 326). This technique, Rotter believes, should be used to assess the generality of experimental findings to real-life situations.

Finally, Rotter believes that questionnaires can be employed to test social-learning hypotheses. Rotter's own I-E Scale is one such questionnaire; we turn now to a consideration of this test and some of its personality and behavioral correlates.

Internal/External Control and the I-E Scale

One of the key constructs in social-learning theory is called **internal/ external control of reinforcement.** According to Rotter, people acquire generalized expectancies to perceive reinforcing events either as dependent on their own behavior or as beyond their control (Rotter, 1966, p. 1). Internally oriented people tend to believe that reinforcers are subject to their own control and occur when they display their skills. Externals, in contrast, see little or no connection between their behavior and various reinforcers; they perceive the occurrence of the reinforcers as determined primarily by fate, luck, or powerful others. Constructs such as competence, powerlessness, helplessness, hopelessness, mastery, and alienation have been used by other investigators in psychology and sociology to describe the degree to which

TABLE 16.1   Sample items from Rotter's I-E Scale

1. a. I have often found that what is going to happen will happen. (E)
   b. Trusting to fate has never turned out as well for me as making a decision to take a definite course of action. (I)
2. a. Becoming a success is a matter of hard work; luck has little or nothing to do with it. (I)
   b. Getting a good job depends mainly on being in the right place at the right time. (E)
3. a. In the long run, people get the respect they deserve in this world. (I)
   b. Unfortunately, an individual's worth often passes unrecognized no matter how hard he tries. (E)

SOURCE: Adapted from Rotter, 1966, p. 11.

people feel they can control important events in their lives. Rotter's construct of internal/external control, however, has the advantage of being an integral part of a formal theory from which relatively precise predictions can be made.

Although there are many different measures of control orientation for use with children and adults, the **I-E Scale** constructed by Rotter has most often been used by investigators in the area. It is a forced-choice scale consisting of 23 items. (See Table 16.1 for some examples.) Scores are obtained by assigning one point for each external alternative endorsed by the subject and summing across all items. Thus, scores can range from 0 to 23; higher scores indicate greater externality. In research using the measure, the distribution of scores is usually divided at the median or mean, the subjects are classified correspondingly as either internals or externals, and then these test responses are correlated with other personality variables and behavior. This split into two categories is not meant to imply a typology, but is done for research convenience. Rotter conceptualized people as being more or less internal or external, but not as falling into one category or the other (Rotter, 1975, p. 57).

Research on I-E

Origins of I-E Orientations

The bulk of the research literature indicates that children in families where parents are consistent in their disciplinary practices develop a belief in internal control. In other words, parents of internally oriented children consistently reward appropriate behavior and punish inappropriate behavior. They do not change the rules continually or administer punishments that are much more severe than the offense. Such parents are also warm and supportive of their children, praise them for their accomplishments, and do not try to exercise excessive control over them. Under such conditions, the children learn to accept blame for failure as well as credit for success.

During the late childhood of internal children, the family atmosphere tends to change from one of support and involvement to one of more parental detachment. At this stage, both parents—but especially the mothers—encourage their children to be independent. They show less involvement and less contact with their offspring. As a result, the children have more opportunity to observe the effects of their own behavior and the contingencies between their own actions and ensuing events (Crandall, 1973, p. 13; Carton & Nowicki, 1994, pp. 38–40).

In contrast, parents of external children tend to be inconsistent in their disciplinary practices. They continually change the rules and administer punishment that is excessive. Such parents also tend to be overprotective and overly controlling. Research indicates further that families characterized by continual conflict tend to have children who are externally controlled. Also, families where the father is absent due to divorce or death have children who are more externally controlled. Furthermore, college students who reported that their parents had divorced when they were very young were more externally controlled than were their peers from intact families (Carton & Nowicki, 1994, p. 41).

Changes in I-E over the Lifespan

Several investigations show that people tend to become more internally oriented as they grow older (Lefcourt, 1982, pp. 150–151). But what about **locus of control** in the elderly? Aren't the elderly very externally oriented? Research by Rhee and Gatz (1993) indicates that many college students think so. However, the matter is not so straightforward. A study by Mirowsky (1995) suggests that it depends on the educational level of the elderly. He maintains that education develops people's abilities to be flexible and to solve a wide variety of problems, and these abilities increase control over events and outcomes in life. He collected data from a large national sample of elderly ranging in ages from 65 through their 80s and found that, whereas uneducated elderly are externally oriented, more highly educated elderly are quite internally oriented, despite physical impairments that include trouble in seeing, hearing, walking, lifting, and climbing stairs. Moreover, a study by Brandtstadter and Rothermund

(1994) indicates that many highly educated elderly people maintain their internal orientations by being flexible; that is, they change the value that they assign to goals that they can no longer attain. For example, elderly people whose physical health has become impaired might adapt to their new health status by reducing the importance of their goal of excelling in competitive sports; they adjust their goal to make it commensurate with the reality of their physical situation. For example, if their physician diagnoses severe arthritis in their hands, they may give up competitive tennis or racquetball and turn to power walking or jogging to keep physically fit. Elderly who are characterized by even greater physical impairments, such as severe lung disease, may give virtually no importance to the attainment of physical sports goals and may begin instead to place more value on goals of intellectual competence and to pursue these with greater intensity. In this way, elderly individuals can maintain, or perhaps even enhance, general perceptions of personal control over their lives and outcomes.

I-E and Performance Task Skills

Various studies have shown that internals not only believe they have the power to affect their outcomes, but actually perform more effectively in both laboratory and academic situations. In a review of the literature, Findley and Cooper (1983) found very strong evidence that internality is associated positively with superior performance on a variety of standard achievement tests. Internals also receive higher course grades than do externals (Bar-Tal & Bar-Zohar, 1977). Mooney, Sherman, and Lo Presto (1991) showed further that internal task skills are associated positively with personal, social, and academic adjustment in college.

There are several explanations for these general findings. As compared to externals, internals are more focused on the task, persistent, cognitively active and flexible, and efficient in learning the rules necessary for problem solving. They have also been found to gather more information about their situations, which helps them to cope with and control outcomes (Ryckman, 1979).

I-E and Social Skills

Internals not only have more information about their situations and greater problem-solving ability than externals; they are also more socially adept. A series of studies by Lefcourt and his colleagues demonstrates this point convincingly. Subjects in one study were videotaped as they listened to same-sex peers describe what characteristics they wished to change about themselves. In comparison to externals, internals were found to nod more often while listening to their partners. Although the amount of gaze behavior did not differ for internals and externals, speakers did talk for longer periods to internal partners. In addition, speakers rated internal listeners as more interested in and accepting of them than external listeners. In another study, internals held up their side of the conversation more than externals; that is, when their partners stopped speaking, internals filled the gap by responding with utterances that facilitated continuation of the conversation. Externals, in contrast, often issued brief, conversation-stopping utterances. If successful social interactions are free-flowing information-sharing experiences, it is clear that internals act in a more socially skillful manner by responding appropriately (Lefcourt, Martin, Fick, & Saleh, 1985).

I-E and Attribution of Responsibility

Thus far, we have painted a general picture of internals as competent and socially skilled people who, in comparison to externals, generally perform more effectively on a variety of skill-determined tasks. It should be clear that a person's willingness to strive for excellence in performance is clearly related to how the person accounts for success and failure. A great variety of studies, with only a few exceptions, have shown that, in contrast to externals, internals tend to attribute success to internal factors (ability and effort) rather than to external factors (luck or task difficulty). In other words, internals attribute their success to ability and hard work, whereas externals attribute it to good luck or an easy task. Thus, internals experience more pride in their achievements and a greater willingness to persist at tasks than do externals.

Research has also shown that internals attribute their failures internally, that is, to a lack of ability and/or effort. Thus, when they suffer defeat, internals experience more shame and guilt than do externals. Externals rely more on external attributions in trying to explain their failures. They may claim, for example, that the test was too difficult or that they simply had bad luck (Phares, 1976, pp. 113–115). Moreover, Basgall and Snyder (1988, pp. 656–657) found that externals were more likely to use the following excuses to justify their poor performances on a test: 1) "It doesn't matter how I did on this test because I am doing very well in my other classes"; and 2) "I just had a bad day." The implication in this second excuse is that on some other day the excuse maker's performance would have been better.

Externals also tend to use other excuses for failure. Thus, they devalue tests that they fail, in a classic example of sour grapes. After failing tests that they strongly wanted to pass, externals claimed that success on these tests was not so important (Phares, 1971, 1979).

Phares and Lamiell (1974) found that externals employ defensive strategies *prior* to task performance as well as after it. These investigators gave internals and externals the choice of taking one of four tests. Two of the tests contained built-in rationalizations for subsequent failure; for example, on the task instructions for one test, the experimenter wrote, "Some of the symbols . . . on this sheet did not print out very well. . . . I hope it won't affect your performance too much, but there is always that possibility." The other two did not contain such rationalizations. Externals, more than internals, chose to take the tests that contained the excuses for failure already built in.

Research indicates that internals not only take responsibility for their own actions but also assume that others are responsible for theirs. Externals, in contrast, assume that others' behavior as well as their own is controlled by outside forces (Phares, 1976, pp. 102–104). Given the opportunity, internals are thus more likely than externals to mete out more severe punishment to rule violators in a variety of situations. Thus, they may be more punitive and less sympathetic than are externals in their judgments and behavior toward wrongdoers (Kauffman & Ryckman, 1979).

I-E and Career Development and Status

Internals show a stronger tendency to take responsibility for their own actions and to work hard to achieve long-range goals. In the area of career development, for example, Luzzo and Ward (1995) found that internal students were more likely than were external students to take the time and effort necessary to obtain part-time employment experiences that were congruent with their career aspirations. Some examples include: (1) internal students with career interests in business obtained part-time jobs in retail sales rather than as mechanics; (2) internals with interests in public administration and city management secured part-time jobs in municipal government rather than as housepainters; and (3) internal students with interests in athletic careers secured part-time jobs in the athletic programs of local YMCAs rather than as bartenders. Employment in congruent part-time jobs may help to facilitate career development and eventual occupational success. Luzzo (1993) also found that internal students were more task-oriented and serious in their attitudes toward work and their careers.

Considerable research has shown that internally oriented people have the characteristics that help promote and maintain occupational success. In comparison to externals, internals are assertive, independent, dominant, efficient, competent, and confident; they also tend to be more satisfied with their jobs, to report less stress, and to perceive themselves as having more autonomy and control on the job. Internals also report being on the job longer without thinking of quitting (Spector, 1988). As a result, they are highly successful in a variety of high-status occupations that demand strong leadership qualities (Kapalka & Lachenmeyer, 1988, pp. 418–419).

I-E and Romantic Relationships

Some interesting research has shown that internal and external students differ in the number and kinds of heterosexual romantic experiences they have (Dion & Dion, 1973). Internals were found to have proportionally fewer romantic attachments than did externals. They also reported experiencing romantic love as less mysterious and volatile than externals. In addition, internals were more opposed to an idealistic view of romantic love than were externals. In comparison with externals, they disagreed more with these statements: (1) there is only one real love for a person; (2) true love lasts forever; (3) true love leads to almost perfect happiness.

Why do internals and externals differ in their orientations toward romantic love? The investigators who conducted the study suggest a number of reasons, all of which are compatible with previous research findings. Romantic love implies that both parties give themselves up to their partners—that is, become vulnerable and pliable to each other's wishes. However, as we have seen, internals do not like to be influenced by others. In addition, internals like to manipulate others, and it is difficult to assume a calculating, manipulative attitude toward someone you love. For these reasons, then, it is perhaps not surprising that many internal students do not become as involved in romantic liaisons as do externals.

I-E and Physical Health

Considerable research evidence indicates that internally oriented individuals are physically healthier than are externally oriented individuals (Ryckman, Robbins, Thornton, & Cantrell, 1982; Strickland,

1979; Wallston & Wallston, 1981). One major explanation for this reliable finding is based on the early family experiences of internals and externals. Lau (1982) found that, in comparison to external children, internal children were more likely to have been encouraged by their parents to follow a good diet, to get enough exercise, to brush their teeth properly, and to have regular dental and medical checkups. As a consequence of these early experiences, internals have learned to see themselves as responsible for their own physical health. Thus, we would expect to find that internals know more about the conditions that cause poor health and are more likely to take steps to improve or maintain their own health.

Although the data are not completely consistent (Wallston & Wallston, 1982), the majority of studies do support these expectations. One early study of the relationship between locus of control and information-seeking behavior in tuberculosis patients found that internal patients knew more about their particular medical problems and sought more information from their physicians than did external patients (Seeman & Evans, 1962). A more recent study showed that college students with an internal orientation had more knowledge about proper nutrition and diet, the need for exercise to maintain or enhance health, and the hazards of smoking and excessive drinking than did external students (Quadrel & Lau, 1989, p. 1505). Other research has shown that internals take more precautionary measures to protect their health than do externals. Internal high school students report greater use of seat belts when driving than do externals. They also report going to the dentist for checkups and maintenance more often than do externals, even when their teeth or gums are not sore or hurting. Several studies have shown that internals are also more likely than are externals to reduce or quit smoking (Strickland, 1978, pp. 1193–1194; Wallston & Wallston, 1982, p. 78). Of those individuals who quit smoking, internals are less likely to begin smoking again (Segall & Wynd, 1990). Studies also show that internals have more positive attitudes than do externals toward physical exercise and cardiovascular fitness (Strickland, 1979, pp. 223–224). Thus, an internal locus of control is associated generally with good health, preventive health care, and more adequate coping with illness when it does occur.

I-E and Psychological Health

Most of the research investigating the association between I-E and mental health indicates that internals are psychologically healthier than externals. Several studies have shown that depressives, schizophrenics, and neurotics are more likely to be external than internal. Externals are also more likely to be Machiavellian; that is, they are more likely to lie, cheat, and manipulate others to get what they want. They are also dogmatic and low in self-esteem, and have high levels of debilitating anxiety (Holder & Levi, 1988; Keltikangas-Jarvinen & Raikkonen, 1990; Lefcourt, 1982, pp. 119–124; Mudrack, 1990, pp. 125–126; Phares, 1976, pp. 121–126; Schmitt & Kurdek, 1984). Debilitating anxiety is reflected in items on the I-E scale such as: "During exams, I block on questions to which I know the answers, even though I might remember them as soon as the exam is over" and "I am so tired from worrying about an exam that I find I almost don't care how well I do by the time I start the test." Conversely, internals tend to have more facilitating anxiety than do externals; they endorse items such as: "I work most effectively under pressure, as when the task is very important"; and "Nervousness while taking a test helps me do well" (Lefcourt, 1982, p. 122).

Finally, considerable research has indicated that internals are better able to cope successfully with stress associated with divorce and bereavement than are externals. For example, Barnet (1990) found that, while internal divorced women reported experiencing more predecision stress than did externals, they experienced far less stress during the divorce proper, less postdivorce stress, and less social maladjustment following the divorce (Barnet, 1990, p. 107). Investigators have found that, in coping with stress following the death of their spouse, internal Israeli widows were more able to cope with monetary, house maintenance, and transportation concerns and to engage in meaningful social activities than were externals; that is, internally oriented widows were more likely to ask their parents, grown-up children, relatives, and friends for help in solving these problems than were externally oriented widows (Lowenstein & Rosen, 1995, pp. 114–115).

Despite the consistency of these findings, some studies suggest that certain internals may have psychological difficulties. For example, compulsive individuals, with their excessive concern for order and control, are likely to score high on internal locus of control (Smith, Magaro, & Pederson, 1983, p. 499). Similarly, Berrenberg (1987, p. 199) found that internals have an exaggerated need to control their outcomes. As mentioned earlier, several studies also suggest that, as compared to externals, internals may experience more guilt and shame when they fail (Phares, 1976, pp. 113–115).

The composite picture of internals and externals formed by integrating study findings is complicated and intriguing. Although internals are better adjusted than externals in many respects, they also have their limitations. In fact, recent theory and research developments with the I-E construct suggest that extreme internals (those who score very low on the Rotter scale) may be maladjusted controllers, who seek to exert total control over their own and others' outcomes by acting in aggressive, obtrusive, and domineering ways. They may experience considerable frustration and anxiety when placed in a subservient role or in a situation in which the attainment of their goals is in fact beyond their control. Moderate internals (those who score in the middle range of Rotter's scale) may be more flexible than the controllers and less controlling and domineering; they may show greater adjustment in various situations (Wong & Sproule, 1984). Thus, extreme and indiscriminate reliance on either internal or external factors to account for one's experiences may be unhealthy.

In conclusion, research with the I-E construct has proven highly informative, and there is little doubt that it will continue to be a popular area of investigation for personality psychologists.

THEORY'S IMPLICATIONS FOR THERAPY

In Rotter's view, psychotherapy is a learning process. Thus, the same learning principles applied to change the behavior of people in everyday situations can also be utilized to advantage in a therapeutic setting (Rotter, 1954, p. 335). Rotter sees the problems of maladjusted people as originating not in their heads but in their relationships with other people (Rotter & Hochreich, 1975, p. 109). In general, adjusted individuals experience satisfactions growing out of the performance of behaviors that are seen as constructive by society; maladjusted people, in contrast, are perpetually dissatisfied with themselves and behave in ways that precipitate punishing responses from society. Furthermore, Rotter believes that maladjusted people are often characterized by low freedom of movement and high need value (Rotter & Hochreich, 1975, p. 106). Such individuals are convinced that they are unable to obtain the gratification they desire. As a result, instead of learning how to achieve their goals, they learn how to avoid or defend themselves against actual or anticipated failure.

Rotter and other social-learning theorists accept the defense mechanisms postulated by Freud but reconceptualize them as avoidance or escape behaviors. Projection, for example, involves blaming others for one's own mistakes in order to avoid anticipated punishment. Rationalization is the construction of elaborate excuses for one's own inadequate behavior in an effort to stave off punishment. One of the unfortunate results of such maneuvering is that maladjusted people fail to learn new behaviors. They simply continue to gain temporary relief by avoiding the punishment, criticism, failure, or rejection they believe will follow if they attempt to perform behaviors for which they have low expectations for success. In the long run, however, such defensive maneuvers are maladaptive.

Maladjusted people often inappropriately apply their low expectations for success in one area (for example, the workplace) to other areas (for example, home life), so that they come to perceive themselves as generally worthless. Clinicians have found that maladjusted people also tend to place too much importance on the gratification of one need (Katkovsky, 1968, p. 228). For example, people with a strong need to dominate others may distort what others say in order to act in an aggressive manner when it is totally inappropriate (Katkovsky, 1968, p. 228). Such individuals will often be dissatisfied, because their need to dominate will bring them into repeated conflicts with others.

Maladjusted individuals tend to engage in behaviors that lead to immediate rewards but are punishing in the long run (Katkovsky, 1968, pp. 229–230). Compulsive gamblers find gambling exciting but usually learn that their behavior has severe negative consequences for themselves and their families. In order to pursue their passion, they may cut into the food budget, sell household property, and even steal from other family members. Maladjusted people not only engage in behavior that others consider undesirable; they often also fail to show behaviors that others consider desirable (Katkovsky, 1968, p. 230). Society encourages its members to communicate with one another, for example, but maladjusted people lack the necessary verbal and social skills.

In order to change the behavior of such individuals, Rotter believes, therapists need to be flexible. Because clients come into the therapeutic setting with different problems arising from unique life experiences and motives, the environmental conditions that promote optimal change will vary from person to person. In some cases, treatment strategies may include recommendations for changes in the client's job, academic situation, or home life. For other clients, various behavior therapies, direct or indirect suggestions, or support and reassurance may be appropriate. All these procedures and others can be used singly or in combination to help clients (Rotter & Hochreich, 1975, p. 109).

In general, Rotter believes that therapy should be an evolving relationship between client and therapist in which clients are helped to discover how their present needs, attitudes, and behaviors developed, which ones are appropriate or inappropriate for effective living, and what alternatives are available. Clients must take responsibility for change, be motivated to change, and be willing to try out new behaviors (Rotter, 1954, p. 353). Therapeutic goals may include teaching clients to discriminate between situations in which behaviors are likely to lead to failure and those likely to produce success, helping them to lower unrealistically high expectations for punishment, and encouraging them to assess the importance of their goals more critically and appropriately.

In order to encourage discrimination between situations, the therapist may analyze and contrast a client's past life situation with his present situation and show him that his previous experiences of failure are unlikely to transfer into the present. For example, the therapist might encourage a first-year student to minimize past experiences of failure in elementary school and to believe instead that he can and will be successful in college on the basis of outstanding aptitude test scores. In this case, the therapist's job is to teach the person to differentiate between two situations and to raise his expectations for success on the basis of solid evidence. Another client may have inordinately high expectations for success that need lowering. We all know of people who brag about abilities they do not in fact possess. This bragging may bring temporary gratification and a bolstering of self-esteem, but the long-range consequences of such behavior are likely to be punishing. Therapy in such a case may call for a lowering of the person's expectations.

Therapy may also require changes in the importance a person attaches to certain goals. For example, a woman who has learned to value winning above everything else because it brought acceptance and love from her parents may be encouraged to de-emphasize that goal. The therapist might point out that her indiscriminate attempts to prove herself better than others, even in a friendly game of Ping-Pong, serve only to alienate people. She could be shown that her feeling of being disliked by everyone stems from indiscriminate pursuit of her goal and that a change in behavior is therefore necessary.

Rotter advocates a therapy that focuses not only on the elimination of undesirable and inadequate behaviors but also on the acquisition of desirable ones. The person is taught methods of analyzing problems as a means of finding better solutions and encouraged to try out new behaviors. It is not enough, in Rotter's view, for therapists to help clients understand the sources of their problems; clients must be shown how to perform new behaviors designed to overcome them (Rotter, 1954, p. 398).

EVALUATIVE COMMENTS

We now examine the scientific worth of Rotter's theory in terms of our six criteria.

Comprehensiveness   Rotter's theory has its roots in both the clinical setting and the experimental laboratory. It covers a wide range of phenomena, including parental attitudes and behaviors, academic achievement, defensive behavior, interpersonal trust, social activism, alcoholism, maladjustment, mental retardation, and a host of psychopathological behaviors. As such, it is quite comprehensive.

Precision and testability   Compared to most of the other theories covered in the text, Rotter's is characterized by concepts that are well-defined and hypotheses that are capable of being tested.

Parsimony   Rotter's position seems fairly parsimonious, at least in its attempts to account for individual performance phenomena. The picture is unsettled, however, when we consider the theory's treatment of abnormal and therapeutic phenomena. Rotter seems undecided about whether to retain, modify, or reject some of the psychoanalytic concepts, for example. As a result, it is difficult to assess the parsimony of his views on abnormal phenomena.

Empirical validity   Most of the research based on Rotter's theory has focused on his I-E concept. Empirical support for this aspect of the theory is very strong. However, this work has not been balanced by research on the rest of Rotter's theory, which, unfortunately, remains largely fallow.

Heuristic value   The I-E concept has stimulated research in many areas, including learning theory, psychopathology, psychotherapy, personality development, and social psychology. Also, whereas Rotter's scale assesses the tendency for people to be more internal or external across a variety of situations, a more recent development has been the creation of a number of situation-specific scales (for example, the Work Locus of Control Scale, the Drinking-Related Locus of Control Scale, and the Health Locus of Control Scale). Researchers working in particular areas often prefer these scales because they typically lead to more accurate predictions of behaviors than is the case when a generalized I-E scale is used. The use of these situation-specific scales has sparked considerable research and increased our understanding of personality functioning in the diverse areas of work, problem drinking, and physical health.

Specifically, research with the Work Locus of Control Scale has shown that, in comparison to externals, internals tend to be more satisfied with their jobs, to report less stress, and to perceive themselves as having more autonomy and control on the job. As we noted earlier, they also report being on the job longer without thinking of quitting (Spector, 1988). Research using the Drinking-Related Locus of Control Scale has found that externals tend to have higher levels of anxiety, lower ego strength (lower self-confidence), greater dependence and depression, and more suicide ideation than do those who score on the internal end of the scale (Donovan & O'Leary, 1978). Finally, research using the Health Locus of Control Scale found that internals tended to seek out more information about a particular illness (hypertension) than did externals (Wallston, Wallston, Kaplan, & Maides, 1976). However, only those internals who valued their health highly—that is, those for whom good health had high reinforcement value—sought out this information; there was no relation between information seeking and locus of control for those who did not value their health highly. This study lends support to Rotter's theory that behavior is predicted most accurately when there is an assessment not only of the individual's expectancies but also of the value of the reinforcer. According to Rotter (1975, p. 59), the most frequent conceptual problem on the part of many investigators is the failure to treat reinforcement value as a separate variable in their research.

Thus, the heuristic value of Rotter's ideas regarding I-E differences is clear.

Applied value   Rotter's theory has strong applied value. It has been used, for example, by clinical psychologists in their diagnoses of the origins of a variety of deviant behaviors, including alcoholism, depression, anxiety reaction, and shyness. The theory has also proved useful to clinical psychologists in their efforts to devise effective strategies for treating different types of patients. Abramowitz, Abramowitz, Roback, and Jackson (1974), for example, have shown that therapists who use treatment strategies that are congruent with their patients' control expectancies are likely to be more successful in helping their patients than are therapists who use procedures that are incongruent with their patients' expectancies. Specifically, they found that nondirective therapies work better with internals, whereas more directive techniques work better with externals. In the area of physical health, treatments tailored to patients' control expectancies have proved useful in maximizing weight loss in the obese and in reducing cigarette smoking in smokers (Strickland, 1978, 1979).

DISCUSSION QUESTIONS

1. Describe the four basic concepts of Rotter's social-learning theory of personality. Give some personal examples of how the concepts could be combined to predict the behavior of one of your friends.
2. What is a minimal goal? What is your minimal goal for academic grades? Do you think it is realistic in terms of your abilities and motivation as a student? What is your minimal goal for establishing a friendship with someone?
3. Describe the behavior of a maladjusted person using the terminology of Rotter's social-learning position.
4. What is meant by internal/external control of reinforcement? How much of your own behavior is determined by forces beyond your control? Are you an internal (or an external) in every situation? Is it healthy to be externally oriented in some situations? If so, which ones?
5. What are some determinants of a person's locus of control? Are the elderly primarily external in their orientations?
6. Which concepts in Rotter's system bear striking resemblance to ones postulated by Adler?
7. Rotter maintained that detailed study of how people's early childhood experiences are related to their current behavior is usually unnecessary in order to predict such behavior. Do you agree?
8. What is the empirical law of effect? Is a concept of reinforcement always necessary to account for behavior adequately?

9. What are some of the strengths and weaknesses of the social-learning approach to the study of maladjusted behavior?
10. How do you attribute responsibility for your successes and failures in school? Why?

GLOSSARY

behavior potential   Probability that a particular behavior will occur, as a function of the person's unique expectancies and the perceived value of the reinforcer secured by the behavior in a given situation.

expectancy   A cognition or belief—held with a higher or lower degree of certainty—about the property of some object or event.

field theory   The idea that behavior is determined by a complex interplay between cognitive and environmental variables.

freedom of movement   The individual's expectancy that his or her behaviors will generally lead to success (high freedom of movement) or failure (low freedom of movement) in a given life area.

I-E scale   Test designed by Rotter to measure the individual's belief that forces are or are not beyond his or her control. Internals (Is) are people who believe that events are under their own control; externals (Es) are people who believe that outcomes are controlled by outside forces such as luck, fate, God, or powerful others.

internal/external control of reinforcement   The individual's belief that his or her behavior is self-determined (internal control) or determined by outside factors (external control).

locus of control   Term that refers to people's beliefs about the location (internal/external) of controlling forces in their lives.

minimal goal   Dividing point between those outcomes that produce feelings of satisfaction and those that produce dissatisfaction.

psychological situation   The meaning of the situation as it is defined by the person.

reinforcement value   The importance of a given reinforcer to an individual in relation to other reinforcers if the probabilities of attaining all of them are equal.

stimulus generalization   The process in which responses made in the presence of an original stimulus come to be made in the presence of other, similar stimuli.

SUGGESTED READINGS

Lefcourt, H. M. (Ed.). (1981). *Research with the locus of control construct: Vol. 1. Assessment methods.* New York: Academic Press.

Lefcourt, H. M. (1982). *Locus of control: Current trends in theory and research* (2nd ed.). Hillsdale, NJ: Erlbaum.

Lefcourt, H. M. (Ed.). (1983). *Research with the locus of control construct: Vol. 2. Developments and social problems.* New York: Academic Press.

Lefcourt, H. M. (Ed.). (1984). *Research with the locus of control construct: Vol. 3. Extensions and limitations.* New York: Academic Press.

Phares, E. J. (1976). *Locus of control in personality.* Morristown, NJ: General Learning Press.

Rotter, J. B. (1954). *Social learning and clinical psychology.* Englewood Cliffs, NJ: Prentice-Hall.

Rotter, J. B. (1966). Generalized expectancies for internal versus external control of reinforcement. *Psychological Monographs, 80* (Whole No. 609).

REFERENCES

Abramowitz, C. V., Abramowitz, S. I., Roback, H. B., & Jackson, C. (1974). Differential effectiveness of directive and nondirective group therapies as a function of client internal-external control. *Journal of Consulting and Clinical Psychology, 42,* 849–853.

Bar-Tal, D., & Bar-Zohar, Y. (1977). The relationship between perception of locus of control and academic achievement. *Contemporary Educational Psychology, 2,* 181–199.

Barnet, H. S. (1990). Divorce stress and adjustment model: Locus of control and demographic predictors. *Journal of Divorce, 13,* 93–109.

Basgall, J., & Snyder, C. R. (1988). Excuses in waiting: External locus of control and reactions to success-failure feedback. *Journal of Personality and Social Psychology, 54,* 656–662.

Berrenberg, J. L. (1987). A measure of God-mediated and exaggerated control. *Journal of Personality Assessment, 51,* 194–206.

Brandtstadter, J., & Rothermund, K. (1994). Self-percepts of control in middle and later adulthood: Buffering losses by rescaling goals. *Psychology and Aging, 9,* 265–273.

Carton, J. S., & Nowicki, Jr., S. (1994). Antecedents of individual differences in locus of control of reinforcement: A critical review. *Genetic, Social, and General Psychology Monographs, 120,* 33–81.

Catanzaro, S. J. (1991). Adjustment, depression, and minimal goal setting: The moderating effect of performance feedback. *Journal of Personality, 59,* 243–261.

Crandall, V. C. (1973). *Differences in parental antecedents of internal-*

external control in children and in young adulthood. Unpublished manuscript, Fels Research Institute, Dayton, Ohio.

Dion, K. L., & Dion, K. K. (1973). Correlates of romantic love. *Journal of Consulting and Clinical Psychology, 41,* 51–56.

Donovan, D. M., & O'Leary, M. R. (1978). The Drinking-Related Locus of Control Scale. *Journal of Studies on Alcohol, 39,* 759–784.

Findley, M. J., & Cooper, H. M. (1983). Locus of control and academic achievement: A literature review. *Journal of Personality and Social Psychology, 44,* 419–427.

Holder, E. E., & Levi, D. J. (1988). Mental health and locus of control: SCL-90-R and Levenson's IPC scales. *Journal of Clinical Psychology, 44,* 753–755.

Kapalka, G. M., & Lachenmeyer, J. R. (1988). Sex-role flexibility, locus of control, and occupational status. *Sex Roles, 19,* 417–427.

Katkovsky, W. (1968). Social-learning theory and maladjustment. In L. Gorlow & W. Katkovsky (Eds.), *Readings in the psychology of adjustment* (2nd ed.) (pp. 213–232). New York: McGraw-Hill.

Kauffman, R. A., & Ryckman, R. M. (1979). Effects of locus-of-control, outcome severity, and attitudinal similarity of defendant on attributions of criminal responsibility. *Personality and Social Psychology Bulletin, 5,* 340–343.

Keltikangas-Jarvinen, L., & Raikkonen, K. (1990). Healthy and maladjusted Type A behavior in adolescents. *Journal of Youth and Adolescence, 19,* 1–18.

Lau, R. A. (1982). Origins of health locus of control beliefs. *Journal of Personality and Social Psychology, 42,* 322–334.

Lefcourt, H. M. (1982). *Locus of control: Current trends in theory and research* (2nd ed.). Hillsdale, NJ: Erlbaum.

Lefcourt, H. M., Martin, R. A., Fick, C. M., & Saleh, W. E. (1985). Locus of control for affiliation and behavior in social interactions. *Journal of Personality and Social Psychology, 48,* 755–759.

Lowenstein, A., & Rosen, A. (1995). The relation of locus of control and social support to life-cycle related needs of widows. *International Journal of Aging and Human Development, 40,* 103–123.

Luzzo, D. A. (1993). Predicting the career maturity of undergraduates: A comparison of personal, educational, and psychological factors. *Journal of College Student Development, 34,* 271–275.

Luzzo, D. A., & Ward, B. E. (1995). The relative contributions of self-efficacy and locus of control to the prediction of vocational congruence. *Journal of Career Development, 21,* 307–317.

Mirowsky, J. (1995). Age and the sense of control. *Social Psychology Quarterly, 58,* 31–43.

Mooney, S. P., Sherman, M. F., & Lo Presto, C. T. (1991). Academic locus of control, self-esteem, and perceived distance from home as predictors of college adjustment. *Journal of Counseling & Development, 69,* 445–448.

Mosher, D. L. (1968). The influence of Adler on Rotter's social learning theory of personality. *Journal of Individual Psychology, 24,* 33–45.

Mudrack, P. E. (1990). Machiavellianism and locus of control: A meta-analytic review. *Journal of Social Psychology, 130,* 125–126.

Phares, E. J. (1971). Internal-external control and the reduction of reinforcement value after failure. *Journal of Consulting and Clinical Psychology, 37,* 386–390.

Phares, E. J. (1976). *Locus of control in personality.* Morristown, NJ: General Learning Press.

Phares, E. J. (1979). Defensiveness and perceived control. In L. C. Perlmutter & R. A. Monty (Eds.), *Choice and perceived control* (pp. 195–208). Hillsdale, NJ: Erlbaum.

Phares, E. J., & Lamiell, J. T. (1974). Relationship of internal-external control to defensive preferences. *Journal of Consulting and Clinical Psychology, 42,* 872–878.

Quadrel, M. J., & Lau, R. R. (1989). Health promotion, health locus of control, and health behavior: Two field experiments. *Journal of Applied Social Psychology, 19,* 1497–1521.

Rhee, C., & Gatz, M. (1993). Cross-generational attributions concerning locus of control beliefs. *International Journal of Aging and Human Development, 37,* 153–161.

Rotter, J. B. (1954). *Social learning and clinical psychology.* Englewood Cliffs, NJ: Prentice-Hall.

Rotter, J. B. (1966). Generalized expectancies for internal versus external control of reinforcement. *Psychological Monographs, 80* (Whole No. 609).

Rotter, J. B. (1975). Some problems and misconceptions related to the construct of internal versus external control of reinforcement. *Journal of Consulting and Clinical Psychology, 43,* 56–67.

Rotter, J. B. (1981). The psychological situation in social learning theory. In D. Magnusson (Ed.), *Toward a psychology of situations: An interactional perspective* (pp. 169–178). Hillsdale, NJ: Erlbaum.

Rotter, J. B. (1982). Social learning theory. In N. T. Feather (Ed.), *Expectations and actions: Expectancy-value models in psychology* (pp. 241–260). Hillsdale, NJ: Erlbaum.

Rotter, J. B., Chance, J. E., & Phares, E. J. (1972). *Applications of a social learning theory of personality.* New York: Holt, Rinehart & Winston.

Rotter, J. B., & Hochreich, D. J. (1975). *Personality.* Glenview, IL: Scott, Foresman.

Ryckman, R. M. (1979). Perceived locus of control and task performance. In L. C. Perlmutter and R. A. Monty (Eds.), *Choice and perceived control* (pp. 233–261). Hillsdale, NJ: Erlbaum.

Ryckman, R. M., Robbins, M. A., Thornton, B., & Cantrell, P. (1982). Development and validation of a physical self-efficacy scale. *Journal of Personality and Social Psychology, 42,* 891–900.

Schmitt, J. P., & Kurdek, L. A. (1984). Correlates of social anxiety in college students and homosexuals. *Journal of Personality Assessment, 48,* 403–409.

Seeman, M., & Evans, J. W. (1962). Alienation and learning in a hospital setting. *American Sociological Review, 27,* 772–783.

Segall, M. E., & Wynd, C. A. (1990). Health conception, health locus of control, and power as predictors of smoking behavior change. *American Journal of Health Promotion, 4,* 338–344.

Smith, P., Magaro, P., & Pederson, S. (1983). Clinical types in a normal population: Concurrent and construct validity. *Journal of Clinical Psychology, 39,* 498–506.

Spector, P. E. (1988). Development of the Work Locus of Control Scale. *Journal of Occupational Psychology, 61,* 335–340.

Strickland, B. R. (1978). Internal-external expectancies and health-related behaviors. *Journal of Consulting and Clinical Psychology, 46,* 1192–1211.

Strickland, B. R. (1979). Internal-external expectancies and cardiovascular functioning. In L. C. Perlmutter & R. A. Monty (Eds.), *Choice and perceived control* (pp. 221–231). Hillsdale, NJ: Erlbaum.

Wallston, B. S., Wallston, K. A., Kaplan, G. D., & Maides, S. A. (1976). Development and validation of the Health Locus of Control (HLC) Scale. *Journal of Consulting and Clinical Psychology, 44,* 580–585.

Wallston, K. A., & Wallston, B. S. (1981). Health locus of control scales. In H. M. Lefcourt (Ed.), *Research with the locus of control construct: Vol. 1. Assessment methods* (pp. 189–243). New York: Academic Press.

Wallston, K. A., & Wallston, B. S. (1982). Who is responsible for your health? The construct of health locus of control. In G. Sanders & J. Suls (Eds.), *Social psychology of health and illness* (pp. 65–95). Hillsdale, NJ: Erlbaum.

Wong, P. T. P., & Sproule, C. F. (1984). An attribution analysis of the locus of control construct and the Trent Attribution Profile. In H. M. Lefcourt (Ed.), *Research with the locus of control construct: Vol. 3. Extensions and limitations* (pp. 309–360). New York: Academic Press.

CHAPTER 17

Bandura's Social-Cognitive Theory

BIOGRAPHICAL SKETCH

Albert Bandura was born on December 4, 1925, to a family of wheat farmers of Polish heritage. He grew up in the small town of Mundare in northern Alberta, Canada, and attended a high school that had only two teachers and 20 students. Upon graduation from high school, Bandura spent the summer before entering college near Whitehorse, in the Yukon, filling holes in the Alaskan highway. He found himself in the midst of an unusual collection of characters, most of whom had fled creditors, alimony, or probation officers. This experience gave him an appreciation for the psychopathology of everyday life.

In search of an intellectually stimulating environment, Bandura enrolled in the University of British Columbia in Vancouver, where he graduated three years later, in 1949. He then earned an M.A. and Ph.D. in psychology from the University of Iowa in 1951 and 1952, respectively. After serving a year's clinical internship at the Wichita Guidance Center, he accepted a position in the department of psychology at Stanford University, where he has remained ever since. He became a full professor in 1964, and in 1974 was awarded an endowed chair, the David Starr Jordan Professor of Social Science in Psychology.

During his tenure at Stanford, Bandura has been actively engaged in the development of a social-cognitive approach to the understanding of human behavior. He has also been a highly productive scholar, publishing several influential books and countless research articles in scientific journals. His early books, *Adolescent Aggression* (1952) and *Social Learning and Personality Development* (1963), were written in collaboration with Richard H. Walters. His *Principles of Behavior Modification* (1969) is an extensive review and summary of the social-psychological principles that govern behavior; *Social Learning Theory* (1971) is an abbreviated treatment of these principles in pamphlet form. In 1973, he published *Aggression,* a review of current theory and research on the determinants of aggressive behavior. In 1977, Bandura greatly expanded his pamphlet coverage of the social-psychological principles that control behavior in his book, *Social Learning Theory. Social Foundations of Thought and Action* (1986) presents more recent theoretical and research developments in his position. In 1995, Bandura edited *Self-Efficacy in Changing Societies,* in which he and other colleagues examined the ways in which strong feelings of self-efficacy in people can help them to create beneficial familial, academic, occupational, and medical environments in a rapidly changing world. His most recent book, *Self-Efficacy: The Exercise of Control,* is about to be published.

In recognition of his contributions to psychology, Bandura has received numerous awards and honors. In 1969–1970, he was a fellow at the Center for Advanced Study in the Behavioral Sciences. In 1972, he received a Guggenheim Fellowship and was awarded the Distinguished Scientist Award in Clinical Psychology by the American Psychological Association. The California Psychological Association honored him with its Distinguished Scientific Achievement Award in 1973, and in 1974 he served as president of the American Psychological Association. He received the James McKeen Cattell Award in 1977 and an honorary Doctor of Science degree from the University of British Columbia in 1979. In 1980, he was honored with a Distinguished Contribution Award from the International Society for Research on Aggression, the Distinguished Scientific Contributions Award from the American Psychological Association, and election to fellow status in the American Academy of Arts and Sciences.

CONCEPTS AND PRINCIPLES

Assumptions of the Social-Cognitive Approach

According to Bandura, behavior is not caused solely by either inner forces or environmental influences. Like Rotter, Bandura believes that behavior occurs as a result of a complex interplay between inner processes and environmental influences (Bandura, 1971, p. 2). In his formulation, these internal processes, based largely on the previous experiences of the individual, are measurable and manipulable covert events. "These mediating events are extensively controlled by external stimulus events and in turn regulate overt responsiveness" (Bandura, 1969, p. 10). Unlike Skinner, who acknowledged that stimulus-response covariations are mediated by internal events but proceeded to neglect them in favor of causal explanations couched in terms of external manipulable events, Bandura places special emphasis on the role of the cognitive determinants of behavior (Bandura, 1969, p. 38). Thus, he sees cognitive events not as mere epiphenomena, but as actual causes of behavior.

Bandura postulates a **triadic reciprocal determinism,** in which cognitive and other personal factors, behavior, and environmental influences all operate interactively as determinants of one another (Bandura, 1986, pp. 23–24). Thus, people do not simply react to environmental events; they actively create their own environments and act to change them. Cognitive events determine which environmental events will be perceived and how they will be interpreted, organized, and acted on (Bandura, 1978, p. 345). Positive or negative feedback from behavior, in turn, influences people's thinking (cognitions) and the ways in which they act to change the environment (Bandura, 1986, p. 24).

Television viewing provides a good example of the interdependencies among cognition, behavior, and the environment. Personal preferences (in the form of thoughts or cognitions) influence when and which programs, from among available alternatives, individuals will choose to watch. Their actual viewing behavior then partly reshapes their preferences concerning which programs to watch in the future and determines to some extent the programming that television executives will provide. The kind of programming subsequently offered by the networks will then shape people's viewing behavior and their preferences for particular shows. Thus, all three factors—viewer preferences, viewing behavior, and televised offerings—mutually affect one another (Bandura, 1986, p. 24).

According to Bandura, we typically represent external events symbolically and later use both **verbal representation** and **imaginal representation** to guide our behavior. Thus, we can solve problems symbolically without having to resort to actual, overt trial-and-error behavior; we foresee the probable consequences of our behavior and modify our actions accordingly. The higher mental processes of human beings allow us to perform both insightful and foresightful behavior (Bandura, 1971, pp. 2–3).

Although Bandura places great emphasis on cognitive processes in his analysis of behavior, he does not ignore the effects of reinforcement. On the contrary, he assigns the reinforcement construct a major role in his theory, but its role is compatible with a cognitive orientation, and goes far beyond the view offered by many traditional learning theorists. Skinner, for example, focused on the changes in behavior that result from our direct experiences of the rewarding and punishing consequences of our actions: responses that are rewarded tend to be repeated; those that are punished tend to be inhibited. Bandura, in contrast, believes that reinforcers and punishers do not provide automatic strengthening or weakening of behavior, nor do they fully account for the ways in which our behavior is acquired, maintained, or altered (Bandura, 1971, p. 3).

In Bandura's view, most of our behavior is not controlled by immediate external reinforcement. As a result of earlier experiences, we tend to expect that certain kinds of behavior will have effects we desire, that others will produce unwanted outcomes, and that still others will have little significant impact. Our behavior is therefore regulated to a large extent by **anticipated outcomes** (Bandura, 1971, p. 3). For example, we do not wait until we have a car accident to buy insurance. Instead, in deciding to purchase it, we rely on information from others about the potentially disastrous consequences of not owning insurance. We do not wait until we are caught in a blinding snowstorm to decide what to wear in extremely cold weather; we can imagine the consequences of being poorly prepared and take the proper precautionary steps. In countless ways, we make decisions based on the anticipation of consequences. This notion of anticipation is similar to Rotter's concept of expectancy.

Bandura also maintains that behavior can be acquired without the administration of **external reinforcement.** We learn much of the behavior we eventually display by example: we simply watch what others do and then repeat their actions. Technically, we acquire the behavior through **observational learning.** According to Bandura, modeling plays a prominent role in our lives, for several reasons. Because the environment is loaded with potentially lethal consequences, trial-and-error behavior is too costly. We do not rely on trial and error in learning to swim, drive a car, or pilot an airplane; some explanation and instruction must be provided before the direct experience can be safely attempted. Furthermore, it would be too cumbersome to try to socialize people by selective reinforcement of their random activities. Imagine trying to teach children language and the many rules and customs of the culture in this way. The acquisition process can be shortened considerably through the use of appropriate models (Bandura, 1971, p. 5). Although the first cohort of learning theorists tended to neglect the role of observational learning in their attempts to understand human behavior, Bandura and other proponents of the social-cognitive approach have rectified this shortcoming and shed much more light on the ways in which we acquire, maintain, and modify our behavior through emulation of models.

Modeling Theory

At first glance, the modeling process seems simple and straightforward. We have an observer and a model, and the primary question is: Will the observer imitate the actions of the model? But the answer is far from simple, because it depends on a host of factors.

First, the personality characteristics of the observer play an important role. For example, whether the model's behavior is imitated may be determined, in part, by the gender of the observer and, correspondingly, by the gender of the model. An early study by Bandura and his colleagues showed that boys tend to show more aggressive behavior after watching an aggressive male model than a female one, whereas girls tend to imitate the aggressive actions of a female model more often than those of a male model (Bandura, Ross, & Ross, 1963a). Despite changes in the social roles and status of females over the next two decades, later research by Bussey and Bandura (1984) again showed that boys and girls tend to imitate models of the same gender. Other research has shown that people who lack self-esteem or are incompetent, as well as those who have been rewarded in the past for imitative behavior, are more likely than others to follow the behavior of a successful model (Bandura & Walters, 1963, p. 85).

Along with the characteristics and prior experiences of the observer, the characteristics of the model also play a significant role. Observers imitate the behavior of a competent model more rapidly than the behavior of an incompetent one (Rosenbaum & Tucker, 1952). Models who are similar in personal background and physical appearance to the observers tend to have a greater influence on them (Rosenkrans, 1967). Observers also tend to learn more of a model's behaviors when the model is highly nurturant or rewarding and when the model has control over the future resources of the observer (Grusec & Mischel, 1966).

Rewards and punishments associated with the model's behavior can also affect the imitative behavior of observers. We learn by observing the behavior of others and the occasions on which they are reinforced for their actions, and we alter our behavior accordingly. To test the effect of such **vicarious reinforcement,** Bandura exposed nursery school children to a five-minute film in which an adult model behaved aggressively toward a large plastic doll:

> The film began with a scene in which a model walked up to an adult-size plastic Bobo doll and ordered him to clear the way. After glaring for a moment at the noncompliant antagonist the model exhibited four novel aggressive responses each accompanied by a distinctive verbalization.
>
> First, the model laid the Bobo doll on its side, sat on it, and punched it in the nose while remarking, "Pow, right on the nose, boom, boom." The model then raised the doll and pommelled it on the head with a mallet. Each response was followed by the verbalization, "Sockeroo . . . stay down." Following the mallet aggression, the model kicked the doll about the room, and these responses were interspersed with the comment, "Fly away." Finally, the model threw rubber balls at the Bobo doll, each strike punctuated with "Bang." This sequence of physically and verbally aggressive behavior was repeated twice. (Bandura, 1965, pp. 590–591)

Children in the control condition saw only this film and observed no consequences to the model for his aggressive actions. Other children, however, saw a second film sequence in which the model was rewarded or punished for his behavior. In the reward condition, a second adult praised the model for his aggressive behavior and rewarded him with soda pop and candy. In the punishment condition, the second adult spoke disparagingly to the aggressive model, and accused him of being a coward and a bully. The punishing adult also spanked the model with a rolled-up newspaper and threatened him with a beating if he was caught being aggressive again.

The independent variable in this study was the nature of the reinforcement administered to the model for aggressive actions. The dependent measure was the amount of aggression exhibited by children in each of the three conditions when given an opportunity to display the behavior they had seen modeled. The children were escorted to a separate room that contained a Bobo doll, three balls, a mallet and pegboard, and an assortment of other toys. A wide variety of toys was presented so that the children had full opportunity to engage in either imitative or nonimitative behaviors. The experimenter left the room, presumably to fetch other toys, and the children were left alone to play. Observers then recorded the children's responses after watching their behavior through a one-way mirror. As expected, children exposed to the model who had been punished for his aggression showed significantly less aggression in the free-play situation than did children who observed the rewarded model or the one who had incurred no consequences for his behavior. Thus, the first phase of this study showed clearly that differential reinforcements administered to a model can indeed have a profound impact on the performance of observers.

But a question with practical social implications still remained. Although we know that the children in the various reinforcement conditions *performed* differently, did they all actually *acquire* the model's behavior? In other words, is it possible that all the children learned the model's behavior but that only those who saw him rewarded or go unpunished decided to imitate him? In the second phase of the study, Bandura showed that this was indeed the case. After their performances in phase one were measured, all the children were offered attractive prizes contingent on their reproducing the model's aggressive responses. The introduction of these attractive incentives completely washed out the previously observed differences in performance, and the researchers concluded that an equivalent amount of learning had taken place in the model-rewarded, model-punished, and no-consequences conditions. These findings suggest that people may *learn* a variety of behaviors but actively decide whether or not to *perform* them on the basis of their estimate of the consequences. Why is this acquisition/performance distinction so important? Bandura believes that it counters the argument that showing crime in the mass media is not harmful to young observers because the criminal is always punished. These results suggest that punishment of the model (the criminal) does not prevent the acquisition of immoral and illegal behaviors, which may surface later under the appropriate circumstances—for example, under conditions in which peers reward the person for such behaviors.

Modeling and Aggression

Bandura has conducted many other studies in which he applied modeling principles and research to the problem of violence in the media and its harmful effects on viewers. We now review his theorizing and some illustrative research in this important area.

Violence in the Mass Media and Imitative Behavior

As virtually all of us recognize, violence and aggressive acts permeate our society. We read in the newspapers every day about inhumane actions on the local, national, and international levels. We cannot help but notice the violence in the cartoons children watch on television. In the evenings, we watch the news and listen as commentators document for us the latest kill counts of faceless people who live in obscure foreign lands where political factions vie for power. On MTV, we watch videos in which rock stars senselessly break things, blow up their rivals and/or tall buildings, and commit acts of violence against women. On the law-and-order shows, the good guys and bad guys resolve their problems by systematically blowing holes in one another with a wide assortment of weapons. Many of the films we watch provide an even more gruesome catalogue of aggression. The old John Wayne shoot-'em-ups, though laden with aggression, are tame fare indeed in comparison to the films shown today.

Granted that we are exposed to a steady diet of violence in the media, does such exposure lead inevitably to aggression? Many people claim that any impact it may have is minimal and relatively innocuous. Bandura, however, believes that media portrayal of violence can have serious and harmful effects on behavior. While acknowledging that media portrayal of violence is neither a sufficient nor a necessary cause of aggression, he argues vigorously that such exposure can, under the right circumstances, facilitate aggression (Bandura, 1973, p. 267). As to the argument that the overall impact of media violence is minor, Bandura maintains that such a contention flies in the face of the evidence: "The same stimulus can have weak or powerful effects for different individuals and even for the same individual on different occasions, depending on the presence of other aggression inducements" (Bandura, 1973, p. 267).

Another argument used by critics is that exposure to violence only affects disturbed individuals. Bandura counters by pointing to research in which models were able to convince so-called normal people to act aggressively against others under the right circumstances (Milgram, 1963). By countering these and other arguments with an impressive mass of research evidence, Bandura has tried to make all of us aware of the potential danger inherent in the unabated portrayal of violence in the media. Let us examine some of these findings, to see how both personal and situational variables can act to facilitate or inhibit aggressive behavior.

Research Evidence

We have already learned that observers who watch models being punished for their actions tend not to repeat those actions, whereas observers who see models rewarded for certain behaviors tend to repeat them. We have also seen that, even though observers tend not to perform the actions of punished models, they have still learned the disapproved behaviors. Research has also shown that observers will imitate the aggressive behavior of filmed as well as live models.

Another study has shown that, even though young observers reported they disliked a model who had been rewarded for aggression, they still imitated him and reported wanting to be like him. It seems as though they knew aggression was wrong but also believed that it was fun. This finding suggested to the investigators an analogous situation in many television programs, in which the bad guy is rewarded throughout an episode for his wrongdoing and punished only at the very end (Bandura, Ross, & Ross, 1963b). Viewers may know he is guilty of wrongdoing and has been punished for it, but may admire him, nevertheless, for performing exciting and rewarding feats they themselves would love to perform. In other words, all the positive reinforcement he has received for his actions may easily override and outweigh the single punishment suffered at the end.

There is also a serious question about the advisability of using violence to punish wrongdoers. Although it is true that witnessing such punishment will inhibit imitative behavior, at least temporarily, we have already seen that viewers may learn the behavior anyway and show it under more favorable circumstances. More importantly, by giving viewers the impression that the use of violence is both justifiable and a ready solution for problems, this approach hinders their consideration of alternative, nonviolent strategies. An experiment by Berkowitz (1962) found that, when people view acts of violence that seem justified, their inhibitions are lowered and aggressive responding is facilitated; when they witness violence they consider inappropriate, their aggressive responding is inhibited. In a subsequent study, Meyer (1972) found that similar results are obtained whether the filmed violence represents nonfictional (real) or fictional events.

In the Meyer study, each college-student subject was paired with a partner, a confederate of the experimenter. The subjects were individually introduced to an experimenter, who informed each of them that the purpose of the study was to see how students react to grading another student's work. Grading, on a scale of 1 to 10, would be by means of electric shocks administered to the student whose paper was being graded—fewer shocks for a good paper, more shocks for a poor one. Each subject was then asked to write an essay on the importance of obtaining a college education, which was to be graded by the subject's partner. All subjects were then given eight shocks, regardless of what they wrote; naturally, this angered them.

Under the pretext of giving their partners enough time to write their essays, all the subjects were then asked to participate in a second experiment, in which they would see different films. Subjects were randomly assigned to eight different experimental conditions: (1) a real-violence segment; (2) an unjustified-real-violence segment; (3) a justified-real-violence segment; (4) a fictional-violence segment; (5) an unjustified-fictional-violence segment; (6) a justified-fictional-violence segment; (7) a nonviolent film; and (8) a control condition in which subjects were not exposed to a film. In the real-violence segment, taken from the "CBS Evening News with Walter Cronkite," South Vietnamese soldiers on patrol encountered the enemy and later executed a North Vietnamese prisoner by knifing him in the chest. Some subjects saw this film with no voice track; others heard a voice track that justified the execution, by saying that the enemy soldier had previously killed innocent women and children; a third group heard a voice track that said the killing was unjustified, because the enemy soldier was technically a prisoner of war and should have been turned over to South Vietnamese authorities. The fictional piece was a segment from the movie *From Here to Eternity* in which two soldiers engage in a knife fight and one of them stabs the other to death. Again, one group heard no voice track; another heard a sound track that said the victim's punishment was justified; and a third heard a sound track indicating that the attack was unjustified. The nonviolent-film group saw footage of a cowboy breaking in a wild horse, and the control group saw no film at all.

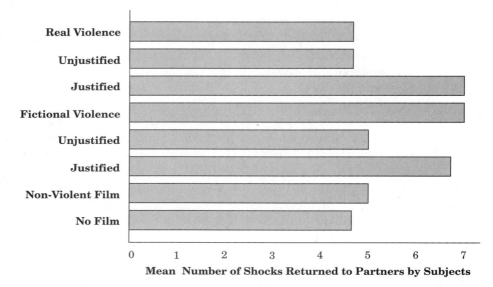

FIGURE 17.1 Comparison of the average number of shocks administered by subjects to partners in eight different filmed-violence and control conditions. (Adapted from Meyer, 1972, p. 26.)

Following this part of the experiment, all subjects were asked to grade their partners' essays. The results are depicted graphically in Figure 17.1. As you can see, subjects who viewed the films in which violence was justified showed more aggression toward their partners than did those who saw violent actions that were unjustified. Levels of aggression after viewing the real- and fictional-violence segments without sound tracks also differed, although such differences were not expected. These differences were obtained, the investigator discovered, because subjects who saw the fictional violence perceived it as justified, whereas those who saw the real violence perceived it as unjustified.

These findings suggest that typical film and television presentations in which the hero legitimately annihilates the villain by violent means may actually lead to an increase in aggressive behavior among viewers. The motto of such angry viewers may well be: "Give it to him! He deserves it!" This primitive eye-for-an-eye-and-tooth-for-a-tooth philosophy, which still governs the behavior of many people, seems to add to the problem of aggression in our culture.

Thus, a number of factors, both personal and situational, can serve to instigate and facilitate aggressive actions. In addition, research has shown that viewers are more apt to behave aggressively if they identify with the victor, as in the case of moviegoers who imagine themselves to be the winners of fights in the films that they see (Turner & Berkowitz, 1972). Observers are also more apt to be aggressive if they find themselves in the presence of stimuli previously associated with violence—for example, in the presence of guns and knives (Berkowitz & LePage, 1967).

Recommendations

In light of the possibility that media violence can have harmful effects on viewers under certain circumstances, Bandura (1973, pp. 276–281) has suggested a number of steps that people can take to modify and control media representations of aggressive behavior. One popular procedure is to petition government agencies to control the commercial marketing of violence. According to Bandura, this procedure is largely ineffective, because the Constitution guarantees free communication and restricts government tampering with program content and, furthermore, we have a strong tradition of opposing government control over what we watch. Some representatives of the broadcasting industry exploit our fear of government regulation and censorship by likening such controls to the practices of military dictatorships. Yet, Bandura points out, most countries have adopted some regulations without jeopardizing their democratic institutions. He suggests that the public may eventually gain some control over program content through concerted legal action.

A second step is to have members of the public protest strongly to government officials about the amount of violence shown in the media. Although such protests cannot be ignored, Bandura feels they are again relatively ineffective, because usually congressional committees will simply issue threats to the broadcasting industry to stop their unsavory practices and will not follow through to verify compliance. A third procedure is to allow broadcasters to regulate themselves. According to Bandura, this method is unworkable because, no matter how well-intentioned media people may be, content is dictated by profit. A fourth procedure is to create a public violence-monitoring system, funded by private sources, that would exercise control by publicly assessing violence levels in the media. Scientific surveys could be published in a variety of sources, including TV guides, popular magazines, PTA pamphlets, and newspapers. Bandura feels that this approach might be effective, because media advertisers are conscious of their public images and would change policies that are detrimental to their companies and stockholders.

Bandura also cites a fifth procedure, which is to reward desirable practices by members of the media rather than to focus solely on the curtailment of undesirable practices. Creating shows that are interesting, informative, and nonviolent would probably lead to greater progress than condemning shows that are saturated with violence. One example is the children's show "Sesame Street," which was designed with the help of psychologists. It is informative and entertaining and has demonstrated that it can attract large audiences of children. In contrast to many of the morning cartoon shows, "Sesame Street" does not rely on violence, but it has proved highly successful.

In addition, Bandura urges parents to limit their children's exposure to media violence by monitoring the content of programs in advance, modeling nonaggressive behavior for their children, and rewarding nonviolent behavior.

> Like so many other problems confronting man, there is no single grand design for lowering the level of destructiveness within a society. It requires both individual corrective effort and group action aimed at changing the practices of social systems. Since aggression is not an inevitable or unchangeable aspect of man but a product of aggression-promoting conditions operating within a society, man has the power to reduce his level of aggressiveness. Whether this capability is used wisely or destructively is another matter. (Bandura, 1973, p. 323)

Efficacy Expectations

Bandura has come to place the cognitive mechanism of self-efficacy in a primary position in his theory as he tries to account for personality functioning and change. Modeling, while still retaining an important role in the theory, is now seen more as a procedure that can help instill in people the level of self-efficacy necessary for effective behavior (Bandura, 1977, 1982b, 1986). In Bandura's view, people who perform effectively have acquired high (but realistic) efficacy expectations that guide their actions, whereas people who are unable to perform adequately in a variety of situations typically have acquired low and often unrealistic expectations that adversely influence their performances. **Efficacy expectations** are beliefs or convictions on the part of individuals that they can produce certain outcomes or effects. They are not to be equated with people's actual skills. Bandura points out that individuals who know what to do in a situation and have the skills required to do it will not necessarily perform well, if they have serious self-doubts about their capabilities. Thus, different people with the same skills, or the same person on different occasions, may perform poorly, adequately, or extraordinarily. Competent functioning requires not only skills but the judgments of self-efficacy to permit their effective use. Furthermore, even when people possess the needed skills and a strong sense of efficacy, they may not choose to perform the activities if they have no incentive to do so (Bandura, 1986, p. 391).

According to Bandura, efficacy expectations influence people's choices of activities and environmental settings. Judgments of self-efficacy also determine how much effort people will expend on activities and how long they will persist on challenging tasks and in the face of aversive experiences.

People with low efficacy expectations are likely to avoid threatening situations that they believe to exceed their coping skills. If, for some reason, they have to perform in threatening situations, their low efficacy expectations lead them to expend little effort and give up after a short time. As a result, they are unlikely to gain corrective experiences that would enhance their sense of efficacy, and they remain defensive and fearful. Thus, for example, shy people may avoid social situations. If they must attend social functions, they will expend little effort in trying to meet and converse with people; they usually end up as wallflowers. Such people are wracked by self-doubts and persistently engage in debilitating self-criticism about their incompetence, which, in turn, leads to poor performances in a variety of social situations. These poor performances serve to reinforce low expectations of efficacy and to prevent the learning of new, assertive behaviors.

People with high efficacy expectations, in contrast, opt for challenging tasks where they have an opportunity to develop new skills. In such challenging situations, they are likely to expend maximum effort, to persist in the pursuit of their goals despite obstacles, and to engage in a minimum of debilitating self-criticism; as a result, they increase the probability of eventual success. This probability can be further enhanced by the setting of proximal goals—subgoals that can be attained along the way to final, distal goals. Proximal goals help focus people's attention and provide them with feedback that sustains efforts. Breaking a task into a number of small steps also increases their initial perceptions of self-efficacy by making the task seem more manageable. Subgoal attainment then provides an indicator of progress that is likely to further boost perceptions of self-efficacy and to enhance their chances of attaining the final goal

(Stock & Cervone, 1990). In one study, for example, obese individuals who adopted daily subgoal limits for how much they ate achieved substantial continuing reductions in their weight. In contrast, individuals who pursued distal weekly goals rarely attained them and shed no weight (Bandura, 1986, p. 474).

According to Bandura (1977, 1986), the acquisition of high or low efficacy expectations has four major sources: performance accomplishments, vicarious experiences, verbal persuasion, and states of physiological (emotional) arousal.

Performance accomplishments   Bandura believes that efficacy expectations are rooted primarily in personal mastery experiences. Success experiences tend to create high expectations, whereas failure experiences tend to generate low expectations. Once strong high-efficacy expectations have been created, however, occasional failures are unlikely to have much impact on people's judgments of their capabilities. Conversely, once low expectations have been instilled by repeated failure, occasional successes are not very effective in changing people's judgments of their capabilities. However, low expectations can be changed by repeated and frequent successes fueled by determined effort on the part of individuals. Through such efforts, people can eventually overcome and master the most difficult obstacles (Bandura, 1981, p. 203).

Vicarious experiences   Performance accomplishments are the most influential source of efficacy expectations, because they are based on actual mastery experiences, but vicarious experiences can also influence the acquisition of efficacy expectations. In other words, seeing or visualizing other people performing successfully can instill high self-perceptions of efficacy in observers, who come to believe that they too possess the capabilities to master comparable activities (Bandura, 1982a, p. 27). Watching others of similar competence fail despite high efforts, conversely, lowers observers' judgments of their own capabilities and undermines their efforts.

Verbal persuasion   Verbal persuasion is used very often to convince people that they have the necessary capabilities to accomplish their goals. Many parents, for example, encourage their children to believe that they can succeed in different life spheres. To the extent that such encouragement persuades the children to try hard enough to succeed, it may promote development of skills and a sense of personal efficacy. This encouragement must be kept within realistic bounds, however, because unsuccessful attempts to accomplish goals following persuasion are likely to create low efficacy expectations and lessen the credibility of the source (Bandura, 1977, p. 198). Conversely, parents who continually discourage mastery attempts by their children through ridicule, criticism, and belittling are likely to generate low efficacy expectations in their offspring.

Emotional arousal   Stressful and difficult situations tend to generate high states of arousal in most individuals, and they use this arousal information to judge their capabilities. Because high arousal usually debilitates performance, individuals are more likely to expect failure—that is, to experience low efficacy expectations—when they feel that they are tense and physiologically aroused. Conversely, they are more likely to expect success—to experience high efficacy expectations—when they perceive that they are relaxed and not highly aroused in the face of challenge or obstacles.

Research on Self-Efficacy

The study of individual differences in self-efficacy as they relate to performances in clinical and nonclinical areas has mushroomed since Bandura first introduced the concept into his theory. Numerous studies have indicated that people with higher self-efficacy expectations are more likely to seek early treatment for various physical and mental health problems than are those with lower efficacy expectations. Furthermore, in contrast to low self-efficacy people, individuals with high efficacy expectations are more likely to control a harmful behavior (for example, to control their obesity through diet and exercise), to stop a self-destructive behavior (for example, to give up smoking or excessive drinking), or to increase a desirable behavior (for example, to have safer sex by using condoms). Other investigations have shown that after self-efficacy expectations are strengthened—for example, through graded mastery experiences, verbal persuasion, or vicarious modeling experiences—people can manage their physical or mental problems more effectively. For example, such procedures have been utilized to help reduce depression and phobias in people who initially lacked confidence in their abilities to overcome these disorders (Grembowski et al., 1993; O'Leary, 1992).

The self-efficacy concept has also been used to increase our understanding of career-relevant behaviors, such as vocational choice and satisfaction and performance on the job. For example, Betz and

Hackett (1981) found that male and female college students differed in their beliefs about whether they could successfully complete the educational or training requirements for various occupations. In general, men perceived themselves as efficacious in preparing for traditionally masculine occupations (accountant, engineer, highway patrol officer, mathematician) and, to some extent, for traditionally feminine occupations (art teacher, medical technician, social worker, X-ray technician). Females, in contrast, perceived themselves as much more efficacious in preparing for traditionally feminine than for traditionally masculine occupations, with two exceptions (physician and lawyer). Perhaps the women's movement has helped increase women's confidence concerning these two occupations. In any event, females who believed that they could not successfully complete the required training or education in the traditionally masculine occupations also reported that they were unwilling to consider careers in those areas. These results were obtained even though both the male and female subjects had the same levels of verbal and mathematical skills. More recently, Bonett (1994) obtained similar results. Thus, low self-efficacy perceptions may be an important factor in females' decisions to eliminate certain career choices. Lent, Brown, and Larkin (1986) showed further that female subjects with lower perceived self-efficacy in completing the training requirements for traditionally masculine occupations in the sciences received lower grades in science and technical courses than did students with higher levels of perceived self-efficacy. Betz and Hackett (1981, p. 409) concluded that therapeutic interventions (modeling, persuasion, and counseling) based on Bandura's theory should be directed at increasing females' perceptions of self-efficacy. Such interventions could well broaden career options for females and improve their grades.

Finally, Saks (1995, p. 216) examined employees' levels of satisfaction and performance on their jobs following training by company managers. He found increases in self-efficacy among accountants in several large and medium-sized accounting firms who reported that, on being hired, they had received training in audit procedures and in how to interact and work with clients. These increases in self-efficacy, in turn, were related to increased ability to cope with job-related problems and were also linked directly to greater job satisfaction and performance effectiveness. Accountants who had not received any training on entering the firm showed lower levels of self-efficacy, less satisfaction with the job, and poorer job performances.

PERSONALITY DEVELOPMENT

In Bandura's theory, social-cognitive experiences play a crucial role in the development and modification of behavior. New behaviors are acquired as children watch the behavior of their caretakers. Imitation of parents' behaviors often meets with reward but sometimes with punishment. Rewarded behavior tends to be repeated and, when performed in the presence of other people, is reinforced positively. As a result, children learn at an early age to match the behavior of successful models. They also learn to avoid imitating the behavior of unsuccessful ones. The acquisition of complex forms of behavior is not always so simple and direct, however. Children are often exposed to multiple models, who present conflicting behaviors. One parent might reward them for speaking in the presence of guests, for example, whereas the other might punish them for the same behavior. Even when both parents are in agreement, teachers or other social agents may disagree and communicate that information to the children. Peers may try to indoctrinate the children in still other ways. Thus, the reinforcers for given behaviors are not always applied consistently.

Another complication is that behavior is not always imitated accurately or completely and must be shaped by the socializing agents through the application of the successive-approximation principles pioneered by Skinner. The establishment of proper table manners in children provides a clear example of the need to apply reinforcers in a subtle manner to a variety of behaviors that initially bear little resemblance to the complicated set of behaviors that eventually emerges.

In addition to imitation and successive approximation, Bandura believes, the maintenance and extinction of behaviors in the person's repertoire depends on the application of various schedules of reinforcement. In particular, he proposes that behavior is maintained through the application of combined schedules. He cites, as a prime example, attention-seeking behavior in children.

> In the training of children, the use of combined schedules certainly predominates. Let us take the example of attention-seeking behavior. Most young children attempt many times in the day to elicit a nurturant response from their mothers. Sometimes the mother will respond immediately, but more often she is busy. At varying intervals she will reward the child with interest and attention. Many mothers are inclined to ignore mild forms of attention-seeking be-

havior and to respond only when this behavior is frequent or intense. It can be predicted, on the basis of laboratory studies . . . , that these mothers should have children who show persistent attention-seeking behavior occurring at the rates and intensities that have previously brought reward. One may suspect that most "troublesome" behavior has been rewarded on a combined schedule by which undesirable responses of high magnitude and frequency are unwittingly reinforced. The behavior is thus persistent, difficult to extinguish, and baffling for the parents. Perhaps the genesis of much aggressive behavior is to be found in the use of schedules which reward *only* responses of high magnitude; these could be attention-seeking, food-seeking, and other so-called "dependency" responses, as well as responses of the kind more usually regarded as "aggressive." (Bandura & Walters, 1963, p. 7)

Thus, reinforcers appear to be dispensed in complicated ways by various socializing agents. Also, most importantly, children learn in the course of their development to apply reinforcers to their own behavior. Standards for self-reward and self-punishment can be acquired in a variety of ways. Children may be taught rules of behavior by their parents and others and be rewarded for following them and punished for violating them. Children may also learn these standards through exposure to books, newspapers, films, television, and radio. And, as you might expect, they may also learn them through modeling procedures.

In one study, two groups of children participated in a miniature bowling game with adult models (Bandura & Kupers, 1964). In one condition, the children watched a model reward himself with candies only for excellent performances. In another condition, they watched a model reward himself even for poor performances. After exposure to the models, the children were left alone to play the game with no models present. The results indicated that the children tended to match the behavior of the model to whom they had been exposed. Although both groups of children had access to a generous supply of candy, those who were exposed to a high-performance standard rewarded themselves sparingly and only when they had matched or exceeded the criterion, whereas those who were exposed to the low-standard model rewarded themselves quite often, even for poor performances.

In an extension of this work, two investigators sought to determine **multiple modeling effects** on imitative behavior (McMains & Liebert, 1968). Using the bowling game just described, adults in phase one imposed either a stringent criterion for self-reward (that is, they rewarded themselves only for attaining a certain score and told the children to do likewise) or a lenient standard for self-reward (that is, they rewarded themselves for attaining either of two scores). In phase two of the investigation, the children who had seen the model impose a stringent standard were introduced to a second adult model, who either adhered to the stringent criterion set by the first model or violated it by rewarding himself for attaining the lenient standard. The investigators found that children who had initially been trained on the stringent criterion and then saw the second model adhere to the same standard deviated very little from the standard; that is, they rewarded themselves only when they met the stringent criterion. Children who had been trained on the stringent standard but then saw a second adult violate that standard were the least likely to hold to the stringent standard in the absence of the models; they rewarded themselves for attaining a variety of scores. These findings suggest that parents and others who impose severe restrictions on children but do not follow through by example are likely to be quite ineffective in training children to adopt their rules. It is not adequate, it seems, to use the old saw, "Do as I say, not as I do," to instill desired behaviors in children. Rather, the motto should probably be, "Do as I say *and* do."

One speculation associated with this study concerns the relationship between the learning of standards and feelings of well-being. If people learn to accept standards that are too high or that can be attained only rarely, they may experience stress. As a result, they may feel anxious, guilty, and depressed. Part of the tragedy here is that many people who adopt such standards are relatively competent, but live in continual agony because they rarely consider their best efforts to be good enough. Approval—the application of rewards and praise—by others may not be acceptable to such people; that is, external reinforcement may have little impact on their behavior. This notion of self-reward contingent on the attainment of extremely high standards is similar to Rotter's concept of high minimal goals and Adler's concept of the unrealistic pursuit of fictional goals. Thus, Bandura clearly recognizes the need to account for the impact of self-determined reinforcement, as well as external reinforcement, on behavior (Bandura, 1969, p. 39).

Although Bandura places great emphasis on observational and instrumental learning and on self-reinforcement, he does not pay similar attention to the biological determinants of behavior. He does recognize, however, that constitutional factors inevitably influence the nature of the individual's social-learning history.

Social manipulations can have relatively little influence on some biologically determined characteristics, such as the body type or facial features of an individual. Yet within a society that sets high value on the possession of certain physical attributes, the frequency with which social reinforcers are dispensed is partly dependent on the extent to which these cultural ideals are met. In North American society, where prestige and social rewards are bestowed for athletic ability and physique, boys who are small, lack muscular strength or dexterity, or who are obese and possess feminine-like physiques, are relatively unsuccessful in obtaining positive reinforcement from peers. Similarly, a female who does not match the standards of beauty within her society evokes far fewer positive responses, especially from males, than one who possesses these socially esteemed characteristics. The slender, petite female has been highly admired in North American culture; she may, however, be the recipient of relatively few positive reinforcers and considerable aversive treatment in cultures lacking in labor-saving devices. (Bandura & Walters, 1963, pp. 26–27)

Not only constitutional factors but also biochemical factors exert an indirect influence on development. Despite his recognition of the role of biology in personality development, however, Bandura de-emphasizes it in his theory. Because there is currently little knowledge of the specific ways in which biology operates to control behavior, he feels there is more to be gained by studying the role of social-learning variables in personality development.

ASSESSMENT TECHNIQUES

Bandura does not use dream analysis, free association, transference, or any of the other techniques utilized by practitioners in the psychodynamic tradition. Nor does he seem particularly interested in using personality questionnaires as assessment devices, although his position does not preclude the use of reliable and valid questionnaires, such as Rotter's I-E Scale, when they are helpful in understanding behavior.

For the most part, Bandura relies on experimental methods to assess personality functioning and change. He believes that the most stringent tests of a theory are provided by anchoring a hypothesized mediator (for example, a cognitive event) in an independently measurable indicant and then confirming that external factors are linked to the indicant and that the indicant is linked to overt behavior

(Bandura, 1982b, p. 123). In other words, Bandura is interested in demonstrating that experimental manipulations of antecedent events influence cognitive functioning, which, in turn, influences subsequent responses. If the problem area is complex and uncharted, however, Bandura thinks it is advantageous to begin by conducting field studies that are essentially correlational in nature (Bandura & Walters, 1963, p. 391).

THEORY'S IMPLICATIONS FOR THERAPY

Modeling as a Therapeutic Technique

Modeling has been employed successfully in the treatment of language deficiencies in autistic children (Lovaas, 1967). Such children are typically not very responsive to environmental influences; before employing modeling procedures, the therapist must first gain their attention. To accomplish this goal, the therapist sits directly in front of the children, so that they cannot ignore him or her. The therapist also rewards them for maintaining eye contact and physically restrains any effort by the children to move away. Having established attentional control, the therapist proceeds to model sounds, words, and phrases of speech and to administer rewards for appropriate responding. Under such training procedures, it has been possible to develop some language skills in autistic children. Modeling has also been used to increase communication skills in asocial psychiatric patients (Gutride, Goldstein, & Hunter, 1973).

Modeling has been used to reduce a variety of fears in children. In one particularly interesting study, Bandura and Menlove (1968) showed that avoidance behaviors could be eliminated through observation of modeled approach responses. Specifically, the investigators were able to eliminate a fear of dogs in nursery school children by having them watch another person approach, pet, and handle the animals without being bitten. Bandura and Menlove began by administering a standardized test of avoidance behavior in order to identify those children who were fearful of dogs. The test consisted of a graded series of 14 tasks, in which the children were required to participate in increasingly intimate interactions with a dog. The tasks included: walking up to a playpen containing a dog and looking down at it; touching and petting it; opening the enclosure; walking the dog; and eventually getting into the playpen with the dog and petting it. Following the identification procedure, the dog-phobic children were assigned randomly to one of three conditions. In one condition, children observed a single model who displayed progressively bolder approach responses to a cocker spaniel. In a second, multiple-model condition, other children observed the same sequence of events and, in addition, watched other models of various ages playing with a wide variety of dogs, both small and large. In the control condition, still other children saw movies of Disneyland and Marineland but no modeled interactions with dogs. Following the administration of these procedures, all the children were retested using the same standardized test. Approximately one month after the posttest, they were tested again, to determine the stability of the modeling effects. The results (Figure 17.2) showed clearly that the modeling procedures were instrumental in reducing and sustaining a reduction in the children's fears. Similar modeling procedures have been used to reduce fear of snakes in adolescents and adults (Bandura, Blanchard, & Ritter, 1969).

Research has shown that test-anxious college students tend to perform poorly because they spend much of their time paying attention to irrelevant cues. Such students tend to be self-centered and overly concerned with questions about their intellectual competence and the reaction of others to their performances. Sarason (1975) conducted an investigation to determine whether models' disclosures about their own anxieties in evaluation situations and the strategies they had devised to cope with these interfering cues could improve

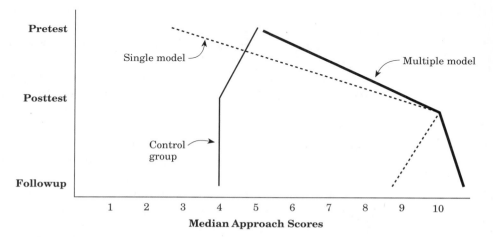

FIGURE 17.2 Median approach scores obtained by children under the various conditions of the experiment. (Adapted from Bandura & Menlove, 1968, p. 102.)

the task performances of highly anxious students. All study participants filled out a personality questionnaire to determine their characteristic levels of test anxiety. Then groups of subjects who were
classified as either high or low in test anxiety were exposed to a variety of models. In one condition, they were exposed to an anxious coping model, who mentioned that she became anxious during testing
situations and that she attempted to cope with her anxiety by (1)
reminding herself periodically to stop thinking about herself and to
concentrate on the task; (2) thinking about interesting aspects of the
task; (3) not allowing herself to get flustered by errors; and (4) forcing
herself not to think about the reactions of other people. In the second
condition, a noncoping anxious model simply mentioned that she became very anxious during testing, had difficulty concentrating on the
task, and was continually worried about what others would think of
her if she failed. In a third condition, a neutral model did not mention
testing or grading and talked instead about activities, programs, and
issues on the campus.

All subjects then performed a task that involved learning a series
of nonsense syllables. As expected, the model who not only mentioned
that testing situations caused her anxiety but provided information
on how she coped with it had the greatest positive impact on the
students with high test anxiety. (See Figure 17.3.) Apparently, the

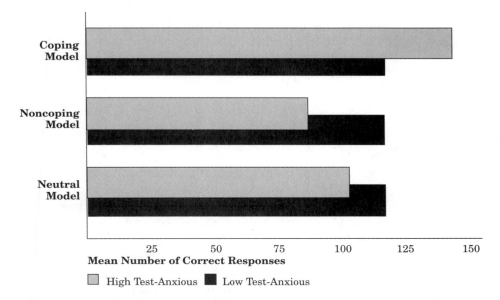

FIGURE 17.3   Mean number of correct responses on serial learning task
for students with low and high test anxiety under different modeling conditions. (Adapted from Sarason, 1975, p. 150.)

self-disclosures provided them with modeled information about ways to improve their performances, and they utilized it.

Finally, an intriguing study by Downs, Rosenthal, and Lichstein (1988) demonstrated the powerful therapeutic effects of modeling in changing the undesirable behavior of elderly (average age 75) residents of a care facility. Many of these elderly patients are required by their physicians to take whirlpool baths, as a means of promoting healthy skin tissue and relieving pain associated with arthritis, bursitis, or limb amputation. The bath-time procedure is very stressful for these patients. They cannot enter or depart the bath independently, because the tub walls are approximately three feet high. Instead, the patient is strapped into a chair, which is then raised by a mechanical lift over the edge of the tub and then lowered into the water up to the patient's waist. After the bath, the lifting procedure is reversed. Even though you might expect bath-time to be a refreshing highlight of the patient's routine, many dislike it and resist strongly. Some patients resist entering the bathroom or sitting down in the chair. Some express fear and aggravation, shout verbal insults or obscenities at the staff, or struggle to avoid being strapped into the chair.

In this study, patients who were highly avoidant of bathing were randomly assigned to one of three conditions. In the in vivo (actual situation) **guided participation modeling** condition, a therapist model guided patients through the bath-time procedure by modeling the desired behavior and then showing them how to perform the activity themselves; the therapist also provided physical support and verbal encouragement. In the filmed modeling condition, patients watched two peers who were initially afraid of the bath-time procedure successfully cope with their fears after being guided through the activity by a therapist. In the third condition, a control group received no exposure to models.

Initially, the results in the in vivo guided participation modeling condition were not in accordance with what the investigators expected on the basis of Bandura's modeling theory; that is, very few of the patients made any positive progress in overcoming their fears. The reason, however, was obvious. When the therapist was modeling the bathing procedure for a group of four patients, one became extremely anxious and disruptive; the other patients then became very afraid and were unable to make much progress during subsequent sessions. In a second experiment, this problem was corrected by having patients undergo treatment by the therapist individually. Under these conditions, the patients showed substantial progress. After several training sessions, they were much more comfortable in the bath situation, showed little resistance, and successfully completed the bathing activity. Almost as much progress was made in the filmed modeling condition; and both groups performed better than the control subjects, who continued to be disruptive and avoidant in the bath situation. On the basis of these findings, the investigators recommended that the modeling film be used to introduce new patients to the bathing situation, and then followed up with in vivo modeling by a therapist to ensure that patients would be comfortable with the bathing procedure.

These studies and countless others demonstrate quite conclusively the positive impact that modeling can have in changing undesirable behavior. Modeling is thus a viable alternative to traditional psychodynamic approaches that seek to give people insights into their behavior through protracted and costly analysis but provide little guidance as to specific courses of action they can take to help themselves. Its continued usage as an aid in therapeutic settings seems assured.

Efficacy Expectations and Phobia Reduction

Most of Bandura's recent research focuses on attempts to eliminate a variety of phobias in clients by raising efficacy expectations. In effect, the factors that contribute to the acquisition of efficacy expectations can be manipulated experimentally to reduce pathological behavior by raising clients' perceptions of their own efficacy.

In a variety of studies, Bandura (1986) has employed clinical treatments involving performance accomplishments to reduce and eliminate snake phobias. Snake phobics are guided by models to engage in progressively more threatening interactions with boa constrictors or corn snakes, including: (1) approaching a glass cage containing the snake; (2) looking down at it; (3) holding it with gloved and bare hands; (4) letting it loose in the room and returning it to the cage; (5) holding it within 12 centimeters of their faces; and (6) tolerating the snake crawling in their laps while they held their hands passively at their sides. Bandura found that, before the guided modeling occurred, the phobics' efficacy expectations for completing these tasks was very low, but after the treatment achievement of mastery was high, and so were the phobics' efficacy expectations. Control subjects who did not receive the guided participation modeling had lower levels of expectations throughout the experiment and did not achieve mastery.

In other experiments, Bandura has demonstrated that vicarious-experience treatments—in which snake phobics simply watch models successfully engage in the increasingly threatening activities (without guided participation) and then independently try to imitate the behavior of the models—result in higher efficacy expectations, lower physiological arousal (that is, reductions in heart rate and blood pressure), and more effective performances than are found in phobic subjects not exposed to models at all (Bandura, 1977, p. 206; Bandura, Reese, & Adams, 1982, pp. 14–21). It should be noted, however, that exposure to models under vicarious conditions is not as effective in reducing phobics' fearful behavior as having the phobics engage directly in mastery experiences under guided participation conditions.

Finally, Bandura and his colleagues have demonstrated that these therapeutic treatments work not only with subjects who are immobilized by fears of animals but also with people who are afraid of public places (agoraphobics) (Bandura, Adams, Hardy, & Howells, 1980). Many agoraphobics cannot shop in stores and supermarkets, because they find the crowds and checkout lines too threatening. Similarly, theaters, restaurants, buses, subways, and even riding as a passenger in cars arouse highly negative emotions in many of them. If untreated, most of these individuals are eventually unable to venture out at all into public settings and become virtual prisoners in their own homes.

To help these clients, Bandura and his associates utilized a number of therapeutic treatments simultaneously. They began with group sessions in which clients were taught how to identify the situations that aroused varying levels of fear. They also learned how to identify self-debilitating thoughts and how to cope with them through the use of body relaxation procedures and through the substitution of more positive, emboldening thoughts. But the primary treatment consisted of experiences of mastery in the field. The emphasis in this treatment was on successful experiences with the feared objects and settings, because successes tend to raise mastery expectations. Exposure to these highly intimidating situations was undertaken gradually, by using graded subtasks and by carefully and slowly lengthening the time spent in the settings. For example, agoraphobics who feared automobile travel first rode in residential areas, then on busier streets, and eventually on freeways. Clients who shunned supermarkets and department stores made shopping trips first to small, uncrowded stores and then to progressively larger stores. Those who feared restaurants gradually extended the amount of time they spent in them.

These performance accomplishments were generally aided by treatments that employed modeling by therapists and by ex-agoraphobics using guided performance and encouragement. Whenever clients became unduly distressed, they were encouraged to retreat momentarily and then to move forward again with proper guidance and support. As clients developed their ability to cope, however, the field therapists gradually reduced their support and their guided participation. Clients were assigned progressively more challenging tasks to perform alone while the therapists remained in the vicinity. Using these multiple techniques, Bandura and his associates were able to reduce substantially the fears of these clients and to restore mastery behavior.

EVALUATIVE COMMENTS

We now evaluate the scientific worth of Bandura's theory in terms of our six criteria.

Comprehensiveness   In comparison to Freudian theory, for example, Bandura's position is somewhat limited in the diversity of phenomena it covers. However, it does provide a relatively thorough analysis of the social-cognitive variables responsible for the acquisition, maintenance, and modification of disordered behavior, thereby contributing to our understanding of alcoholism, academic anxieties, frigidity, impotence, exhibitionism, insomnia, nightmares, obsessive-compulsive problems, and phobias. In addition, Bandura and his associates have focused a great deal of attention on the variables responsible for the acquisition and modification of aggressive behavior. More generally, social-cognitive research has increased our knowledge of the ways in which childhood training practices influence personality development, how language is acquired and honed, and how self-reinforcement can be utilized in the acquisition, maintenance, and modification of behavior. This last area seems especially promising and exciting to investigators, as evidenced by the amount of research conducted on such phenomena in recent years.

Precision and testability   Many of the cognitive variables in Bandura's theory are complex and difficult to define precisely, but Bandura has made strong efforts to define and measure them objectively and reliably. To a substantial degree, these efforts have been successful, and he has been able to incorporate the cognitive variables into experimental tests of his theory and to enhance its predictive accuracy.

Parsimony   Social-cognitive theory is based on relatively few assumptions, but those it does make are broadly stated and designed to encourage investigation of the ways in which social and cultural phenomena affect behavior and thought. The theory encompasses not only the concepts traditionally associated with learning positions (reinforcement, discrimination, generalization, extinction) but also a variety of new and different cognitive concepts. Although Skinner believed that Bandura invented needless constructs to account for behavior, it is this author's judgment that these constructs are necessary for the development of an adequate theory of personality and that Bandura's theory is, in most respects, commensurate with the complexity of the phenomena it seeks to explain. Thus, it is a parsimonious theory.

Empirical validity   The evidence in support of Bandura's position is impressive. There have been countless empirical tests of the theory, and the results to date have been highly encouraging. For example, studies of observational learning have yielded evidence showing the importance of modeling in helping to mold, maintain, and vary behavior. Although much of this research has focused on the use of modeling to eliminate fears, anxieties, and disordered behaviors, modeling principles have been applied to the study of nonneurotic behaviors as well. In general, then, Bandura's position has a high degree of empirical validity.

Heuristic value   Although Bandura's position has had considerable impact on the work of psychologists, especially in the clinical and social-psychology areas, it has only recently begun to influence the work of professionals in other disciplines. Certainly it has not had the interdisciplinary impact of Freud's theory. Still, its promise remains strong, and in the future we should see an increase in its heuristic value for professionals in other disciplines.

Applied value   The applied value of social-learning theory is very high in the area of psychopathology. A variety of behavioral therapy techniques derived from social-cognitive theory have been successfully utilized in the treatment of an assortment of phobias and other problems. In addition, Bandura's pioneering research in the area of aggression has increased our understanding of the origins of such behavior and has provided insights into the ways it can be modified and controlled. Although his work on aggression has not achieved its potential in helping to eliminate violence in our culture, its applied value should become increasingly apparent in the future.

DISCUSSION QUESTIONS

1. Is it possible for a person to survive by relying solely on the trial-and-error method of learning? Cite reasons for your position.
2. According to a study cited in this chapter, girls more readily imitate female models, whereas boys will mimic male authority figures. Do you agree? Cite reasons for your answer.
3. Why is the distinction between acquisition and performance so important in the argument over the effects of television violence on children's behavior? Do you agree with Bandura on this point?
4. If positive reinforcers are such a potent determinant of behavior, why don't we praise and reinforce each other more often?
5. Do you believe that violence in the media has had an adverse effect on your behavior and that of your friends and relatives? Why or why not?
6. What are some of the primary personal and situational determinants of aggressive behavior?
7. What suggestions do you have for decreasing aggressive behavior in our culture?
8. Design an experiment that would utilize modeling procedures to eradicate a child's fear of bugs.
9. How anxious do you and your friends become before taking an examination? Does this anxiety interfere with your performance? If so, how would you rearrange environmental conditions to minimize anxiety?
10. Bandura maintains that one source of efficacy expectations is verbal persuasion. What are some of the limitations of using verbal persuasion to convince individuals that they have the abilities necessary to accomplish their goals?

GLOSSARY

anticipated outcomes   A person's expectancy that the performance of certain behaviors will secure certain reinforcers.

efficacy expectations   Individuals' convictions or beliefs that they can execute the behaviors required to produce certain response consequences.

external reinforcement   A reinforcing environmental stimulus that controls the occurrence of behavior; it might be food, money, praise, approval from others, a pat on the back, or a smile.

guided participation modeling   Phobia-reduction procedure in which models first show subjects how to successfully tolerate increasingly threatening interactions with dreaded objects, and then guide the subjects through these threatening activities until they are finally able to master their fears.

imaginal representation   An image called up by a person that resembles an object in the environment. For example, the person can picture, or imagine, a professor who exists in the environment.

multiple modeling effects   Impact on a person's imitative behavior of being exposed to a variety of models.

observational learning   Type of learning in which new responses are made as a result of watching the performance of others; also called imitative learning.

triadic reciprocal determinism   The belief that cognition, behavior, and the environment operate interactively as determinants of one another.

verbal representation   A word that signifies an object in the environment. For example, the word *dog* is a verbal representation of a barking quadruped that exists in the environment.

vicarious reinforcement   Willingness to imitate the behavior of a model after observing that the model was reinforced for the behavior.

SUGGESTED READINGS

Bandura, A. (1969). *Principles of behavior modification.* New York: Holt, Rinehart & Winston.

Bandura, A. (1973). *Aggression: A social learning analysis.* Englewood Cliffs, NJ: Prentice-Hall.

Bandura, A. (1986). *Social foundations of thought and action: A social cognitive theory.* Englewood Cliffs, NJ: Prentice-Hall.

Bandura, A. (1995). *Self-efficacy in changing societies.* New York: Cambridge University Press.

REFERENCES

Bandura, A. (1965). Influence of models' reinforcement contingencies on the acquisition of imitative responses. *Journal of Personality and Social Psychology, 1,* 589–595.

Bandura, A. (1969). *Principles of behavior modification.* New York: Holt, Rinehart & Winston.

Bandura, A. (1971). *Social learning theory.* Morristown, NJ: General Learning Press.

Bandura, A. (1973). *Aggression: A social learning analysis.* Englewood Cliffs, NJ: Prentice-Hall.

Bandura, A. (1977). Self-efficacy: Toward a unifying theory of behavioral change. *Psychological Review, 84,* 191–215.

Bandura, A. (1978). The self system in reciprocal determinism. *American Psychologist, 33,* 344–358.

Bandura, A. (1981). Self-referent thought: A developmental analysis of self-efficacy. In J. H. Flavell & L. Ross (Eds.), *Social cognitive development: Frontiers and possible futures* (pp. 200–239). Cambridge, England: Cambridge University Press.

Bandura, A. (1982a). The self and mechanisms of agency. In J. Suls (Ed.), *Psychological perspectives on the self* (Vol. 1, pp. 3–39). Hillsdale, NJ: Erlbaum.

Bandura, A. (1982b). Self-efficacy mechanism in human agency. *American Psychologist, 37,* 122–147.

Bandura, A. (1986). *Social foundations of thought and action: A social cognitive theory.* Englewood Cliffs, NJ: Prentice-Hall.

Bandura, A., Adams, N. E., Hardy, A. B., & Howells, G. N. (1980). Tests of the generality of self-efficacy theory. *Cognitive Therapy and Research, 4,* 39–66.

Bandura, A., Blanchard, B., & Ritter, B. (1969). Relative efficiency of desensitization and modeling approaches for inducing behavioral, affective, and attitudinal changes. *Journal of Personality and Social Psychology, 13,* 173–199.

Bandura, A., & Kupers, C. J. (1964). The transmission of patterns of self-reinforcement through modeling. *Journal of Abnormal and Social Psychology, 69,* 1–9.

Bandura, A., & Menlove, F. L. (1968). Factors determining vicarious extinction of avoidance behavior through symbolic modeling. *Journal of Personality and Social Psychology, 8,* 99–108.

Bandura, A., Reese, L., & Adams, N. E. (1982). Microanalysis of action and fear arousal as a function of differential levels of perceived self-efficacy. *Journal of Personality and Social Psychology, 43,* 5–21.

Bandura, A., Ross, D., & Ross, S. A. (1963a). Imitation of film-mediated aggressive models. *Journal of Abnormal and Social Psychology, 66,* 3–11.

Bandura, A., Ross, D., & Ross, S. A. (1963b). Vicarious reinforcement and imitative learning. *Journal of Abnormal and Social Psychology, 67,* 601–607.

Bandura, A., & Walters, R. H. (1963). *Social learning and personality development.* New York: Holt, Rinehart & Winston.

Berkowitz, L. (1962). *Aggression: A social psychological analysis.* New York: McGraw-Hill.

Berkowitz, L., & LePage, A. (1967). Weapons as aggression-eliciting stimuli. *Journal of Personality and Social Psychology, 7,* 202–207.

Betz, N. E., & Hackett, G. (1981). The relationship of career-related self-efficacy expectations to perceived career options in women and men. *Journal of Counseling Psychology, 28,* 399–410.

Bonett, R. M. (1994). Marital status and sex: Impact on career self-efficacy. *Journal of Counseling and Development, 73,* 187–190.

Bussey, K., & Bandura, A. (1984). Gender constancy, social power, and sex-linked modeling. *Journal of Personality and Social Psychology, 47,* 1292–1302.

Downs, A. F. D., Rosenthal, T. L., & Lichstein, K. L. (1988). Modeling therapies reduce avoidance of bath-time by the institutionalized elderly. *Behavior Therapy, 19,* 359–368.

Grembowski, D., Patrick, D., Diehr, P., Durham, M., Beresford, S., Kay, E., & Hecht, J. (1993). Self-efficacy and health behavior among older adults. *Journal of Health and Social Behavior, 34,* 89–104.

Grusec, J., & Mischel, W. (1966). Model's characteristics as determinants of social learning. *Journal of Personality and Social Psychology, 4,* 211–215.

Gutride, M. E., Goldstein, A. P., & Hunter, G. F. (1973). The use of modeling to increase social interaction among asocial psychiatric patients. *Journal of Consulting and Clinical Psychology, 40,* 408–415.

Lent, R. W., Brown, S. D., & Larkin, K. C. (1986). Self-efficacy in the prediction of academic performance and perceived career options. *Journal of Counseling Psychology, 33,* 265–269.

Lovaas, O. I. (1967). A behavior therapy approach to the treatment of childhood schizophrenia. In J. P. Hill (Ed.), *Minnesota symposia on child psychology* (Vol. 1., pp. 108–159). Minneapolis: University of Minnesota Press.

McMains, M. J., & Liebert, R. M. (1968). The influence of discrepancies between successively modeled self-reward criteria on the adoption of a self-imposed standard. *Journal of Personality and Social Psychology, 8,* 166–171.

Meyer, T. P. (1972). Effects of viewing justified and unjustified real film violence on aggressive behavior. *Journal of Personality and Social Psychology, 23,* 21–29.

Milgram, S. (1963). Behavioral study of obedience. *Journal of Abnormal and Social Psychology, 67,* 371–378.

O'Leary, A. (1992). Self-efficacy and health: Behavioral and stress-physiological mediation. *Cognitive Therapy and Research, 16,* 229–245.

Rosenbaum, M. E., & Tucker, I. F. (1952). Competence of the model and the learning of imitation and nonimitation. *Journal of Experimental Psychology, 63,* 183–190.

Rosenkrans, M. A. (1967). Imitation in children as a function of perceived similarity to a social model and vicarious reinforcement. *Journal of Personality and Social Psychology, 7,* 307–355.

Saks, A. M. (1995). Longitudinal field investigation of the moderating and mediating effects of self-efficacy on the relationship between training and newcomer adjustment. *Journal of Applied Psychology, 80,* 211–225.

Sarason, I. G. (1975). Test anxiety and the self-disclosing coping model. *Journal of Consulting and Clinical Psychology, 43,* 148–153.

Stock, J., & Cervone, D. (1990). Proximal goal-setting and self-regulatory processes. *Cognitive Therapy and Research, 14,* 483–489.

Turner, C., & Berkowitz, L. (1972). Identification with film aggression (covert role taking) and reactions to film violence. *Journal of Personality and Social Psychology, 21,* 256–264.

PART SEVEN

THE ROLE OF PERSONALITY THEORIES IN CONTEMPORARY PERSONALITY PSYCHOLOGY

Some personality psychologists have claimed that the grand theories of personality covered in this text are populated by old ideas that are informative primarily in a historical sense (Singer & Kolligan, 1987; Mendelsohn, 1993). Although it is true that many investigators prominent in personality psychology today are currently using more circumscribed theoretical models that focus on fewer phenomena in their research programs, this does not mean that the grand theories are lying dormant and untested. To the contrary, many of these more comprehensive theories are being actively tested by researchers. For example, consider the wealth of data currently being gathered to test the validity of different aspects of the theories of Freud, Kohut, Erikson, Kelly, Eysenck, Skinner, Rotter, and Bandura. Thus, in terms of their current status, most of these theories are alive and well. Besides generating new data, many of the theories continue to serve a vital heuristic function in the discipline, as they inspire personality psychologists who are pursuing their own theoretical and research interests. In the last chapter of this book, we highlight the critical importance of the theories as sources of inspiration to personality psychologists in their own scholarly work; we end by discussing some of the new developments in the discipline.

REFERENCES

Mendelsohn, G. A. (1993). It's time to put theories of personality in their place, or, Allport and Stagner got it right, why can't we? In K. H. Craik, R. Hogan, and R. N. Wolfe (Eds.), *Fifty years of personality psychology* (pp. 103–115). New York: Plenum Press.

Singer, J. L., & Kolligan, J., Jr. (1987). Developments in the study of private experience. *Annual Review of Psychology, 38,* 533–574.

Contributions of Personality Theories to the Discipline

We have now completed a long and complicated—yet hopefully interesting and enlightening—journey through the major theoretical perspectives on human personality. It should be apparent that none of these theories ranks at the highest level on all the criteria used by investigators in judging the scientific worth of a theory. Thus, some theories excel in organizing a mass of facts into a coherent framework. A few are superior in terms of parsimony, internal consistency, and precision, so that they are more likely to generate clear, testable predictions. Some are more comprehensive in the number and variety of phenomena they treat; others are more limited. Some are highly stimulating and provocative; others are less broadly influential. Some of the theories are strongly supported by data; others have less empirical validity. Some have considerable applied value; they help investigators to solve human problems. Overall, some theories have yielded greater insights than others, but all of them have contributed to our understanding of personality functioning.

In the discipline itself, most of the theories continue under active investigation, despite erroneous claims by critics that such **grand theories of personality** are mere historical curiosities. It is true, however, that these theories could contribute even more to our understanding of personality if they were placed in more active competition with one another in the marketplace of ideas, through investigations that compared and contrasted them empirically (Feshbach, 1984, p. 448). The conceptual diversity of the field means that universal acceptance of a single, integrated theory of personality is extremely unlikely. However, competition among the theories would eventually allow theorists to discard less valid positions in favor of those that are more scientifically useful.

Nevertheless, active competition among the theories will not, by itself, determine which theories will continue to have importance in the 1990s and which will fade from the scene. As the Zeitgeist of the culture changes, certain positions will recede in prominence, only to be replaced by those more in tune with the current intellectual, moral, political, social, and cultural climate. Still others will be revised and made more precise and testable, so that their validity can be more adequately assessed, and some will be extended, so that they are capable of explaining more phenomena.

Unfortunately, it also appears likely that some of the concepts embedded in the current personality theories will be discovered anew by investigators with rather limited knowledge of the content of the theories, who will present them as original and place new labels on them. Thus, much time, energy, and effort will be wasted in research that generates knowledge we already possess. We can also expect that some investigators will dismiss other theorists and their theories as they single-mindedly pursue their own views. As Allport noted many years ago, such intolerance is harmful to the advancement of the discipline. "Our censure should be reserved for those who would close all doors but one. The surest way to lose truth is to pretend that one already wholly possesses it. Dogmatism makes for scientific anemia" (Allport, 1955, p. 17).

Finally, some researchers will opt to investigate specific topics or concepts without much thought about the need for a theoretical framework. In the long run, such mindless empiricism is likely to lead to a confusing and wasteful dead-end. Without a guiding theoretical framework, investigators are unlikely to achieve substantial understanding of the phenomena they are studying. Progress is most likely when researchers pursue possibilities suggested by existing theories and knowledge (Maddi, 1993).

HEURISTIC VALUE OF THE THEORIES

Stimulated by the current theories, members of the discipline have reached a consensus and some substantive conclusions about human personality and how to study it.

Conclusion 1: An adequate view of personality must incorporate biological factors

Various personality theorists—especially Freud, Cattell, and Eysenck—have sought to explain personality development largely in biological terms. Yet, until recently, personality psychologists did not pay much attention to genetic explanations; they favored environmental explanations instead. Major advances in **behavior genetics**—procedures used to assess the relative contributions of both genetic and environmental influences to personality functioning—have redressed the imbalance. Behavior geneticists have developed new assessment procedures based on the pioneering work of Cattell and Eysenck. For example, they credit Cattell with development of a multimethod approach, multiple abstract variance analysis (MAVA), that is highly useful in assessing the relative contributions of genes and environmental influences to personality functioning (Plomin, Chipuer, & Loehlin, 1990, p. 234). MAVA allows behavior geneticists to assess family, twin, and adoption data from several studies in the same analysis. (See Chapter 9.) With the development of these new procedures, personality psychology has begun to shift away from a simple-minded environmentalism (Plomin, Chipuer, & Loehlin, 1990, p. 225).

One outgrowth of the increased interest in genetic contributions to personality is the development of various forms of **evolutionary theory** (Buss, 1988). Evolutionary theory points out that humans are mammals—specifically, primates—and, as such, are biologically similar to the three great apes: orangutans, gorillas, and chimpanzees. Although it is clear that we differ from the great apes in important ways—for instance, our language, imagery, and thought processes are far more advanced than theirs—we do share the same sense organs, many ways of perceiving and learning, many facial expressions, and various behaviors.

Like other primates, we follow a circadian rhythm of activity, which typically reaches a low point at night and peaks during the day, especially before feeding; we also exhibit intense bursts of energy in aggressive, escape, and sexual behavior, or in rollicking play. We are curious and move around to investigate our environments, just as they do. In the process we (and they) may meet strangers and become wary and shy. Thus, shyness may be one component of fear. Despite differences in the way in which we and the other primates express fear, activation of the sympathetic nervous system triggers a common set of reactions, including an increased rate of breathing, higher blood pressure, and the shunting of blood from the digestive system to the skeletal muscles in preparation for fight or flight (Buss, 1988, pp. 1–4). According to A. H. Buss (1988, p. 10; 1995, p. 50), these diverse behaviors are expressions of underlying, broad-based temperaments that we share with other primates. The definitions of these traits are as follows:

1. *Emotionality* refers to high physiological arousal and generalized negative affect. It is the tendency to become aroused easily and intensely, to become easily frustrated and distressed.
2. *Fearfulness* involves the tendency to be wary, run away, or cower, as well as the accompanying physiological arousal.
3. *Activity* refers to total energy output, as expressed in vigor or tempo.
4. *Nurturance* is the tendency to help others; it includes altruism.
5. *Sociability* is a preference for being with others rather than remaining alone.
6. *Impulsivity* is the tendency to act on the spur of the moment without pause or reflection.
7. *Aggressiveness* consists of attacking or threatening.
8. *Dominance* refers to seeking and maintaining superior status over others.

Each of these traits has a genetic component. They have evolved because they have adaptive value; that is, they help ensure survival and reproduction. A closer examination suggests that moderate levels of these traits are more likely to be adaptive than extreme levels (Zuckerman, 1990, p. 315). For example, extreme fearfulness and a complete lack of activity would probably result in severe injury or death.

Although these traits have a biological basis, it is clear that the environment also plays a determining role in each of them (Buss, 1988, p. 20). Evolutionary theorists assume that both biology and environment influence behavior. They endorse an **interactional temperament model,** which states that environment and temperament traits mutually influence each other. Let us examine how several of these traits interact with environments to influence the expression of an individual's behavior.

1. *Emotionality:* People differ considerably in the degree of distress they show in various situations. Some people are more easily upset, more excitable, and restless than others. If a mother and her child are both low in emotionality, their relationship should be relatively tranquil. If the child is emotional and the mother is not, there

will be upheavals; the child will sometimes become very angry, and the mother will try to calm the child down. If the child is not emotional and the mother is, she offers an emotional role model that the child may copy. In a marriage, if both partners are highly emotional, the relationship is likely to be filled with conflict and may not endure. If there is a mismatch, with one emotional partner and one unemotional partner, the calm one may be able to soothe the upset one. Where both partners are unemotional, temperament should pose no problem to the relationship (Buss, 1995, pp. 50–52).

2. *Activity:* Some people speak rapidly and loudly, walk and run quickly, and gesticulate frequently and emphatically; others speak deliberately and softly, stroll when they walk, and, in general, maintain a slow pace of life. More active individuals should perform more effectively in jobs where their schedule is completely filled with tasks; they would be frustrated in a job that consisted only of one or two simple tasks. Lethargic people, in contrast, are more likely to become frustrated in high-stress, fast-paced jobs that demand large amounts of energy. If a mother and her child are low in the trait of activity, the mother should be more understanding and could perhaps even reinforce slow-paced behavior. If the mother is relatively inactive and her child is highly active, the mother may experience great stress. The child may refuse to sit quietly, continually insist on being taken places, and resist going to sleep at regular times. The relationship is likely to be filled with conflicts and to be very wearing on the mother. Even if the mother is highly active, her superenergetic child may still create problems in the relationship. If the mother is highly active and the child relatively inactive, the mother will serve as a role model and possibly modify the inherited disposition (Buss, 1995, pp. 62–68). Outside the home, highly active children may have their behavior curtailed, at least temporarily, by the teacher in a highly structured classroom environment. On the other hand, they can sometimes arrange their environment so that they can keep busy by scheduling a huge list of tasks (Buss & Plomin, 1975, pp. 3–4).

3. *Sociability:* Some people have a very strong need to be with others. Why? According to Buss, they (1) think that others can help them with tasks that need to be completed; (2) believe that they can barter with others for goods and services; and (3) believe that they can better defend themselves in a group. In a father-child relationship, if both are highly sociable, the father should be receptive to the child's demands for shared activities and attention. Being sociable himself, he would understand and expect his child to place such demands on him. If both the father and his child are low in sociability,

the father will also understand his child's weak needs for attention and responsivity. Thus, matches between the father and his child (both are high or both are low in sociability) should promote harmony. In a relationship where the father is highly sociable and the child is not, we would expect problems. The father is likely to be annoyed that his child likes playing alone and does not want to participate in various activities with him. In contrast, a father who is low in sociability will tend to see his highly sociable child as too demanding and clinging. In marriage, if both partners are high in sociability, there will be no problem; both will enjoy seeking out others. If both partners are unsociable, one can spend time alone without the other being offended. Difficulties in the marriage are more likely to occur in mismatched situations, where one partner is low in sociability and the other is high in sociability. If the wife is sociable and wants to attend a party but the husband prefers to watch his favorite television program, sparks could fly (Buss, 1995, pp. 73–83).

4. *Impulsivity:* People high in impulsivity are quick to act without thinking about the consequences. In contrast, people low in impulsivity are more reflective and weigh all the alternatives before acting. When a mother and her child are both low in impulsivity, there is very little conflict. Parental modeling and training in delay of gratification tend to reinforce tendencies already present in the child. When both a mother and her child are impulsive, conflicts abound. Both parties have difficulty in controlling their emotions. In a situation where the child is highly impulsive and the mother is not, there are likely to be severe problems. It would be very difficult for the mother to live with a child who has an uncontrollable temper and an inability to resist temptation; she may have little empathy for the child's behavior. If the mother is high in impulsivity and the child is not, she may not understand her child's deliberate and reflective ways. She may see the child as too serious and not fun-loving enough. In a marriage where both partners are impulsive, severe problems are likely. Both parties may go on spending sprees continually, and run up huge debts. Lack of planning may also result in a chaotic household. In a marriage where one party is impulsive and the other is not, the patience and planning of the partner low in impulsivity can be quickly undone by the highly impulsive partner. One solution suggested by Buss is for the partners to reach an agreement that the more reflective partner should be the decision maker and that the more impulsive partner consent to abide by this agreement. Where both partners are low in impulsivity, the marriage will be more stable (Buss, 1995, pp. 85–96).

A. H. Buss also believes that we inherit broad temperament traits, which become more differentiated into specific components as we mature. Aggressiveness, for example, may become differentiated as physical aggression, verbal aggression, irritability, and passive aggression. Passive-aggressive people try to hurt or get back at their antagonists by indirect means: for example, they may give their antagonists the silent treatment, respond excruciatingly slowly to requests from others, or do the opposite of what they are asked to do (Buss, 1988, pp. 177–178). An individual may use one or more of these forms of aggression.

The temperament traits can also combine together to produce unique behaviors. For example, people who are sociable *and* dominant tend to seek social status through sharing and working with others. In contrast, people who are low in sociability *and* high in dominance are likely to seek social status through aggression. Sociable people who are altruistic will feel empathy for others and try to be helpful not only to friends and relatives but also to strangers in distress. Unsociable people who are altruistic will tend to help others, not out of empathy, but because of a moral code or a sense of responsibility (Buss, 1995, pp. 174–175).

Finally, evolutionary theorists argue that there are biologically rooted sex differences in humans and in other primates for most of these traits. Primate males tend to be larger and stronger than are females, which may account for males' more aggressive and dominant behavior. Primate males also have more testosterone than females, and this hormone has been implicated in the aggressiveness and dominance of mammalian males. Primate males are more active than are females and tend to explore their environments more. In contrast, females tend to be more fearful, more sociable, and more nurturant than are males. The male-oriented traits all emphasize moving out into the environment with great energy. The female-oriented traits emphasize safety. In brief, primate males tend to poke, pry, and stir things up, whereas females tend to act as a conservative, quieting, and nurturant force in primate groups (Buss, 1988, pp. 24–25).

Evolutionary theorists also maintain that primate males are more likely to compete amongst themselves for access to females, whereas females are more likely to exercise selectivity in their choice of mates. This difference is explained in terms of a **differential parental investment hypothesis** (Buss & Schmitt, 1993, p. 206); that is, females are thought to make a greater investment in each offspring because they carry the fetus, nurse the infant, and, in contrast to the male, are limited in the number of offspring they can produce.

Because of their different levels of investment in each offspring, males and females are likely to engage in different mating strategies. Specifically, females will be attracted to males who show characteristics associated with dominance, including an ability to provide the resources necessary for the survival of females and their offspring. Thus, females also generally prefer to mate with males who are a few years older than themselves, because the male's age provides an important cue to their access to resources; that is, income usually increases with age in many cultures. Females also believe that older males are likely to be more mature, more stable, and more reliable in their provision of support (Buss, 1994, p. 28).

Males, on the other hand, will be more concerned with the female's physical attractiveness. In evolutionary history, males who preferred to mate with females marked by physical signs of old age and disease (wrinkled skin, gray hair, open sores) produced few or no children. In contrast, males who preferred to mate with females possessing physical cues linked to youth and health (smooth, clear skin, lustrous hair, full lips, absence of lesions) experienced greater reproductive success. Because females' reproductive capacity is strongly correlated with age, and because physical appearance historically provided the most reliable cues to age, males have evolved powerful mate preferences for females who are young and physically attractive (Buss & Dedden, 1990, pp. 399–400). Also, considerable research has shown that males gain in social status by their associations with attractive females. Unattractive males are thought to have high status if they can interest stunning females, presumably because attractive females are known to have high value as mates and therefore to be able usually to get what they want in a mate (Buss, 1994, pp. 59–60).

Research on humans based on these speculations has been consistently supportive. A study of university students found that, in comparison to males, females were much more concerned with a possible mate's earning capacity, wealth, and social status. Females, more than males, also wanted their mates to be powerful, ambitious, and intelligent. In couples who were dating exclusively, females were more concerned that their partners wanted children following marriage, whereas males were more concerned that their prospective marriage partners be physically attractive (Kenrick, Sadalla, Groth, & Trost, 1990). D. M. Buss (1989) has reported confirmatory findings in 37 cultures.

Although these results are supportive of the evolutionary perspective, they are also consistent with a social-learning or socialization approach to sex differences; that is, it can be argued that these differences between the sexes are learned in the course of the socialization process. Traditionally, males have been expected to pursue careers that will eventually provide them with social status and the resources necessary to support and protect their mates and offspring. Females, in contrast, are trained traditionally to believe that their physical attractiveness is their chief marketable asset and that it can and should be used to entice males into long-term relationships. Thus, the evolutionary and socialization views are compatible, even though the etiology of the viewpoints differs.

The evolutionary position, however, cannot explain why many females today are independent, assertive, and ambitious and are directed toward high-prestige careers. In some cases, they are the primary providers in their households, while their mates assume a more submissive and nurturant orientation. Gender-role socialization theory readily explains such differences in terms of the socialization to nontraditional roles that has occurred in recent years. Theorists who adopt an evolutionary perspective, however, do not see the biological and socialization explanations as mutually exclusive. Instead, they suggest that socialization can modify the impact of biologically based sex differences under certain circumstances. Because of the women's movement, these theorists acknowledge, many females today are more active (girls and women engage in more energetic sports), less fearful (women are being taught to defend themselves against physical attack), and more dominant (women are being encouraged to be more competitive and to struggle for leadership positions). These changes in socialization will likely continue into the future and may reduce sex differences even more (Buss, 1988, pp. 243–244).

Conclusion 2: An adequate taxonomy of personality traits is needed

Allport's provocative theory of traits raises an important question about the number of traits required to describe human personality adequately. Within personality, traits are arranged hierarchically; those higher in the hierarchy are broader and more abstract than those lower in the hierarchy. Knowledge of the broad traits, or factors, higher in the hierarchy would help us define, organize, and understand the narrower sets of traits lower in the hierarchy that are associated with each broad factor. Such a taxonomy (structural framework) would help reduce the current confusion generated by simply compiling long lists of traits on an intuitive and unsystematic basis. It would also reduce the redundancy that results from measuring the same construct under different names (McCrae & John, 1992, p. 177). Furthermore, a generally accepted taxonomy would promote cooperative research and facilitate the communication of empirical findings among investigators by providing a standard set of trait terms (John, 1990, p. 66). Finally, a comprehensive taxonomy would assure personality psychologists that they had not inadvertently omitted consideration of an important trait in their study of some problem (McCrae & Costa, 1990, p. 32).

In their early, provocative research, Allport and Odbert (1936) took the natural language of personality description as the starting point for construction of this taxonomy. They made the reasonable assumption that the most important individual differences in human transactions will come to be encoded as single trait terms in language. Accordingly, they began by extracting all personality-relevant terms from an unabridged dictionary. The final list totaled nearly 18,000 words, of which approximately 4500 described personality traits.

Cattell (1943) later utilized this list in his own pioneering work and eventually reduced it to 35 variables, by developing bipolar clusters of related traits. Stimulated by his innovative work, other researchers examined simplified descriptions of these traits with a variety of populations and ultimately were able to derive five relatively strong factors (Borgatta, 1964; Digman & Takemoto-Chock, 1981; Goldberg, 1981, 1990; Norman, 1963, 1967; Tupes & Christal, 1961). In the most recent of these studies, Goldberg (1990) administered a list of 339 trait adjectives to university students and asked them to describe themselves on each trait in terms of a 9-point scale, where 1 denoted "extremely inaccurate as a self-description," 5 denoted "I'm uncertain" or "the meaning of the term is unclear," and 9 denoted "extremely accurate as a self-description." The data were then factor-analyzed, and five factors emerged. These **Big Five factors,** with some of their representative traits, are listed in Table 18.1.

Do these five factors—Surgency, Agreeableness, Conscientiousness, Emotional Stability, and Intellect—represent a comprehensive taxonomy of personality traits? Unfortunately not. The basic criticisms are two-fold. First, the factor analyses in the various studies designed to discover the underlying broad factors have not been based on a comprehensive list of personality traits. Goldberg acknowledges that the list used in his analysis, though more comprehensive than any previously employed, is still not quite complete (Goldberg, 1990, pp. 1217, 1223). Second, researchers do not agree on the factor labels (Briggs, 1989, p. 248; John, 1989, p. 262). For exam-

TABLE 18.1 The Big Five factors and their associated traits

Factor I: Surgency

Positive Factor Pole/Cluster	**Trait Terms Included**
Gregariousness	Extraverted, gregarious, sociable
Expressiveness	Communicative, expressive, verbal
Spontaneity	Carefree, happy-go-lucky, spontaneous
Energy level	Active, energetic, vigorous
Talkativeness	Talkative, verbose, wordy
Negative Factor Pole/Cluster	
Aloofness	Seclusive, unsociable, withdrawn
Silence	Quiet, silent, untalkative
Reserve	Detached, reserved, secretive
Shyness	Bashful, shy, timid
Inhibition	Inhibited, restrained

Factor II: Agreeableness

Positive Factor Pole	
Cooperation	Accommodating, agreeable, cooperative, helpful, patient, peaceful, reasonable
Amiability	Amiable, cordial, friendly, genial, pleasant
Empathy	Considerate, kind, sympathetic, trustful, understanding
Leniency	Lenient, uncritical, undemanding
Courtesy	Courteous, diplomatic, polite, respectful, tactful
Negative Factor Pole	
Belligerence	Antagonistic, argumentative, combative, quarrelsome
Overcriticalness	Faultfinding, harsh, unforgiving, unsympathetic
Bossiness	Bossy, demanding, domineering, manipulative
Rudeness	Abusive, disrespectful, impolite, impudent, rude, scornful
Cruelty	Cruel, ruthless, vindictive

Factor III: Conscientiousness

Positive Factor Pole	
Organization	Orderly, organized, systematic
Efficiency	Concise, exacting, efficient, fastidious, self-disciplined
Dependability	Dependable, reliable, responsible
Precision	Meticulous, perfectionist, precise
Persistence	Industrious, persistent, tenacious, thorough
Negative Factor Pole	
Disorganization	Disorganized, haphazard, inefficient, scatterbrained, sloppy, unsystematic
Negligence	Careless, negligent, undependable, unconscientious, unreliable
Inconsistency	Erratic, inconsistent, unpredictable
Forgetfulness	Forgetful, absentminded
Recklessness	Foolhardy, rash, reckless

(continued)

TABLE 18.1 (continued)

Factor IV: Emotional Stability

Positive Factor Pole
Placidity	Passionless, unexcitable, unemotional
Independence	Autonomous, independent, individualistic

Negative Factor Pole
Insecurity	Defensive, fretful, insecure, negativistic, self-critical, self-pitying
Fear	Anxious, fearful, nervous
Instability	Temperamental, touchy, unstable
Emotionality	Emotional, excitable
Envy	Envious, jealous

Factor V: Intellect

Positive Factor Pole
Intellectuality	Contemplative, intellectual, introspective, meditative, philosophical
Depth	Complex, deep
Insight	Foresighted, insightful, perceptive
Intelligence	Bright, intelligent, smart
Creativity	Artistic, creative, imaginative, innovative, inventive

Negative Factor Pole
Shallowness	Shallow, unintellectual, unreflective
Unimaginativeness	Uncreative, unimaginative
Imperceptiveness	Imperceptive, unobservant
Stupidity	Dull, ignorant, unintelligent

SOURCE: Adapted from Goldberg, 1990, pp. 1224–1225.

ple, some researchers label Factor I Extraversion rather than Surgency. A perusal of the traits associated with Factor I in Table 18.1 show clearly that some of these traits (extraverted, gregarious, sociable) are associated with extraversion, whereas others (active, energetic, vigorous) are more clearly linked to surgency. Factor II, Agreeableness, is ambiguous because it refers both to a person's being pleasing (genial, pleasant, friendly) to others and to the tendency to agree with others (accommodating, cooperative). Factor III, Conscientiousness, has been interpreted variously as Dependability, Conformity, Prudence, Task Interest, and the Will to Achieve. Factor IV, Emotional Stability (versus Neuroticism on the negative pole) has almost universal acceptance. Finally, Factor V, Intellect, has also been labeled Culture and Openness to Experience (John, 1990, p. 95). Openness to experience refers to a person's receptiveness to new ideas, approaches, and experiences. People who are closed to experience are not necessarily defensive, nor are they necessarily narrow-minded in the sense of being intolerant and judgmental. Rather, they are characterized by a preference for the familiar, practical, and concrete, and show a lack of interest in experience for its own sake (McCrae & Costa, 1990, pp. 41–42).

Not only is the interpretation of the factors still subject to debate, but other investigators have suggested that there are probably other basic personality dimensions beyond those summarized in the Big Five factors. Advocates of the five-factor model concede that this might be the case, but they maintain that some version of the Big Five factors is at least *necessary* for an adequate description of personality (McCrae & John, 1992, p. 177). Research to clarify the meaning of the five factors and to determine whether or not five factors are sufficient to describe personality is currently under way. In the meantime, convinced that, even with its limitations, the current five-factor model is an important breakthrough in the study of personality, researchers have proceeded to generate some interesting research utilizing the five basic dimensions of personality, which they label as Extraversion (or Surgency), Agreeableness, Conscientiousness, Neuroticism, and Openness to Experience.

For example, a recent study of these five factors in relation to juvenile delinquency and school performance in adolescent males (John, Caspi, Robins, Moffitt, & Stouthamer-Loeber, 1994) found that males who had committed severe kinds of delinquent behavior (for example, firesetting with major damage, theft of a car, selling of drugs, gang fighting, and breaking and entering) were lower in Agreeableness, Conscientiousness, and Openness to Experience and higher in Extraversion than were adolescents who had committed no delinquent acts. There were no differences between delinquents and nondelinquents in Neuroticism. The lower scores in Agreeableness mean that delinquents are more stubborn and bossy, selfish, antagonistic, inconsiderate of the feelings of others, and manipulative. Lower scores on the Conscientiousness dimension mean that delinquents set lower standards for themselves, are not motivated to get things done, are unreliable, and do not think of the consequences before they act. Lower scores in Openness to Experience mean that delinquents are not very curious, creative, imaginative, or intelligent. Higher scores on the Extraversion dimension suggest that delinquents show openly how they feel, irrespective of whether it's good or bad, are fast-paced (move and react quickly), and enjoy being with others. In terms of Neuroticism, delinquents and nondelinquents did not differ in their levels of worry, fear, or ability to bounce back from stressful and threatening situations.

Delinquents also performed less well in school than did nondelinquents. This finding is not surprising, because research by Graziano and Ward (1992) had already shown that the primary and most important predictors of students' healthy adjustment to school were high levels of Conscientiousness and Openness to Experience, two traits that were low in juvenile delinquents. Graziano and Ward also found that Extraversion was correlated positively with school adjustment, but that possession of this trait was not a very strong predictor of students' adjustment. Thus, even though delinquents are high in this trait, their very low levels of Conscientiousness and Openness to Experience would probably override this one positive quality.

While the preceding work concentrated on the application of the five-factor model to adolescents in a school context, research by D. M. Buss (1992) sought to show how the five basic personality traits in married couples were linked to various manipulation tactics used by each partner to get his or her own way when there was a dispute. Buss found that men high in Surgency (those who were very active, energetic, talkative, wordy, extraverted) used coercion tactics to get their own way during an argument; that is, such men made demands and criticized and yelled at their wives to get them to comply. Wives did not use such tactics. Both husband and wives low in Surgency (those who were quiet, withdrawn, and shy) tended to use debasement tactics to get their own way. Specifically, such spouses reported that they lowered or devalued themselves by saying that they were not as competent or intelligent as their partner.

Buss reported further that both spouses high on Agreeableness (those who are cooperative, helpful, friendly, respectful and considerate) or on Openness to Experience (those who are creative, imaginative, and intelligent) used two kinds of tactics: pleasure induction and reason. In other words, these spouses tried to convince their partners that they would have fun if they engaged in the contested behavior. For example, a husband might try to convince his wife to take a ride on his motorcycle by telling her that she would enjoy herself immensely. A wife might try to convince her husband to take dance lessons by telling him how much fun he would have. Spouses high in Agreeableness and in Openness to Experience and also those high in Conscientiousness (those who are self-disciplined, dependable, and responsible) also tried to use reason to get their partners to do something. They would explain to their partners why they should do it and point out all the good things that would come from it. Those spouses low in Agreeableness (those who were antagonistic, argumentative, faultfinding, domineering, and disrespectful) tended to use coercion tactics and the silent treatment; in other words, they would ignore the spouse until she or he agreed to do it.

Buss also found that spouses high in Neuroticism (those who are fearful, anxious, touchy, and unstable) used the tactics of regression and hardball. Regression tactics—sulking, pouting, and whining—were used primarily by wives. Hardball, which was used primarily by husbands, involved hitting the spouse or threatening to leave if she didn't comply.

Finally, Buss pointed out the implications of these findings for people planning to marry. Marrying someone low in Agreeableness might subject the partner to yelling, demanding, and criticizing (that is, coercion tactics), whereas marrying someone high in Neuroticism might subject the partner not only to coercion, but to pouting, sulking, and whining (that is, regression tactics). Those seeking to marry spouses who are likely to use reason tactics might do well to select mates who are high in Agreeableness, Conscientious, and Openness to Experience (Buss, 1992, pp. 477–499).

In conclusion, it is clear that the general consensus on a taxonomy within the discipline has already begun to bear fruit. However, the five-factor model is useful primarily for descriptive and general predictive purposes; ties to explanatory theoretical frameworks are needed. A good start has been made in this direction, because two of the three dimensions used by Eysenck in his powerful explanatory biological theory of personality—Extraversion and Neuroticism—are inherent in the five-factor model.

Conclusion 3: There is a need to assess the dynamic organization of traits within persons and their interactive impact on behavior

Many personality psychologists consider the trait concept to be of primary importance for understanding and predicting behavior. Thus, the ideas about traits expressed by Allport, Cattell, and Eysenck continue to serve as a source of inspiration for many contemporary researchers (Funder, 1991).

For example, Allport pointed out that learning a trait is a complex process; it is far more than a simple matter of reward and punishment. Because they develop as the result of complex patterns of experience, traits are interrelated in complicated ways. In Allport's view, every behavior is the product of multiple traits. These views have long been echoed by Cattell (1950, 1965), who has incorporated them into his multivariate approach to the study of personality (Cattell,

1979, 1980). Recall, for example, Cattell's concept of the dynamic lattice. It involves the complex organization of dynamic traits (attitudes, sentiments, and ergs) within the individual's cognitive and motivational structure. Cattell uses the 16 PF test and other personality inventories to assess this dynamic organization of traits and then shows through the use of multivariate statistical techniques how these traits combine to influence behavior. (See Chapter 9.)

According to Funder (1991, p. 33), the views of Allport and Cattell have at least two important implications for modern research on traits. First, contemporary researchers should conduct a renewed examination of how traits combine in the determination of behavior; that is, moving beyond the traditional research question of how single traits affect single behaviors, they should examine how multiple traits interact within the person. Second, researchers need to develop statistical and methodological models to take this complexity more fully into account (Bowers, 1987). Although some progress has been made in this area, there is a great distance yet to be traveled (West, 1986).

Allport's ideas about personality assessment also have relevance for modern researchers. For example, Allport suggested more than 70 years ago that peer reports about a person's personality characteristics may provide a very accurate means of assessing the person's traits (Allport & Allport, 1921; Funder, 1991, 1993). In Funder's view, self-reports about personality characteristics will agree to a large extent with peer judgments, but not always; sometimes peer reports are decidedly superior. People may not always be aware of some of their own traits, or their reports may be distorted by faulty memories. They may also distort their self-views because of a desire to portray themselves in the most favorable light. Peer reports are not subject to these kinds of problems. For all these reasons, Funder believes, peer reports about the person's characteristics should be used to complement self-reports.

Conclusion 4: Personality is usually understood best by analyzing the operation of traits within situational contexts

Approximately 30 years ago, psychologist Walter Mischel (1968) sparked a debate in personality psychology that raged throughout the 1970s and much of the 1980s. This **person/situation debate** revolved around two fundamental questions: (1) To what extent does behavior change as a result of situational changes? (2) To what extent does behavior remain the same despite situational changes? Mischel maintained that most current personality theories are inadequate because they assume that people's behavior remains the same despite changes in the situation; that is, most of the current theories address the second question, but ignore or de-emphasize the first. These theories rely almost exclusively on **person variables** (traits, motives, needs, cognitions). They downplay or ignore the role played by **situation variables** in determining the person's unique behavior. Person variables, according to Mischel, are cognitive and motivational structures that direct people's behavior; these variables cause individuals to act in consistent ways across a number of situations. Situation variables refer to the environmental conditions that confront individuals as they proceed through various activities.

This one-sided emphasis on person variables, Mischel maintained, can be seen clearly in the conflict theories of Freud and Jung and in the works of prominent trait theorists such as Allport and Eysenck. Although both these trait theorists acknowledge the interaction between person and situation, most of their attention has been focused on person variables (Mischel, 1968, p. 281). Eysenck, for example, favors person variables (genetic and temperamental factors) because he is primarily concerned with understanding how biology determines behavior. Consequently, he pays less attention to the role of the environment. Eysenck, you may recall, considers it unnecessary to assess the impact of situations on people's behavior, on the grounds that situations are implicitly embedded in traits.

Mischel's most controversial contention was that these person-oriented approaches have little predictive utility. Behavior, according to Mischel, is controlled primarily by situational demands. Person variables do have an impact on behavior, but not to the same extent as situations. Mischel concluded that a new theoretical model was needed, one that incorporated *both* person and situation variables. This **interactional model of personality,** he believed, would most adequately account for personality functioning.

Mischel's critics disagreed with his view that the traditional, cross-situational trait concept was untenable and could not be used to predict behavior accurately. After much debate and research, they were able to show rather convincingly that such broad dispositions (traits) exist and can be utilized to predict behavior accurately across situations, if precautions are taken to measure the constructs precisely and to ensure that they are highly reliable (Epstein, 1983a; Moskowitz, 1982; Small, Zeldin, Savin-Williams, 1983).

Thus, even Mischel has been forced to acknowledge that broad, cross-situational traits do exist (Mischel, 1983). At the same time, however, leading personality psychologists recognize that the strategy of using broad, stable dispositions or traits to predict behavior in specific situations is not very useful because it typically yields poor predictive outcomes (Epstein, 1983a, 1983b; Mischel & Peake, 1983). Thanks to this debate, a consensus now exists within the discipline that the lives of individuals show substantial coherence and stability, but that there is also substantial discrimination in behavior patterning from situation to situation and even within situations over time (Mischel, 1983, p. 600). In other words, individual behavior is sometimes cross-situationally consistent, and sometimes situationally specific. The best way to understand personality functioning is to account for both stability and change. Thus, research should focus more on person-by-situation interactions.

While personality psychologists now generally agree that research should focus more on person-by-situation interactions, they are not saying that only the study of person-situation interactions is important. There are times when these interactions are critical, but there are other times when person variables are most important, and still other times when situation factors account for most of the variation in particular behaviors. Thus, the question "Which is most important in the prediction of behavior—person, situation, or person/situation interactions?" is a pseudo-issue because research conditions can be (and have been) constructed that demonstrate the superiority of each of the three factors (see, for example, Alker, 1977; Epstein, 1977; Olweus, 1977).

To illustrate the point, Epstein (1977) offered the nonresearch example of predicting the outcome of races. By selecting races (situations) that vary little in distance—say, 50, 100, and 200 meters—and runners who vary greatly in speed (large person-variable differences), we can show that person variables account for almost all the variation in outcomes. If, however, we allow only runners of highly similar ability to run and we vary the race distances (situations) considerably—say, 50, 1500, 3000 meters—we would expect situation variables (distance) to account for outcomes. Finally, if we select races of different types—say, dashes and hurdle races—and runners who excel in one type and not in the other, it can be shown that person-situation interactions account for most of the variation in outcomes. Hurdle specialists would do well in hurdle races but not in dashes, whereas dash specialists would perform well in dashes but not in hurdle races. Thus, the study of person-situation interactions is sometimes, though not always, of central importance for the accurate prediction of behavior.

With these caveats in mind, Mischel and his colleague, Jack Wright, have proceeded to create a theoretical model to help us understand complicated person-by-situation interactions better, given the relative lack of such models in contemporary personality psychology (Wright & Mischel, 1987, 1988). In this **conditional approach to dispositions,** traits are viewed as clusters of condition/behavior contingencies—sets of if-then propositions that link situations and behavior. For example, a dispositional attribution that a child is aggressive refers to a cluster of condition-behavior contingencies such as: if threatened or subjected to high levels of stress, the child is likely to act aggressively by yelling at or hitting others; if not subjected to stress or threat by the situation, the child is unlikely to act aggressively. In effect, Mischel is saying that there are certain types of situations that foster high trait-behavior correlations and others that do not (Mischel, 1977, p. 347). That is, high-stress situations tend to foster hitting and yelling behavior in children who (on the basis of their past history) are highly disposed to be aggressive; low-stress situations are very unlikely to produce the same behavior in the same children.

A key task in the use of this model is to specify *in advance* the specific types of situations that are likely to foster certain kinds of behavior in certain types of people and those that are not (Wright & Mischel, 1987, p. 1162). Mischel much prefers this more circumscribed situational approach to the attempts by researchers to find broad traits that predict behavior well across many situations (Wright & Mischel, 1987, p. 1175).

To demonstrate the validity of the conditional approach, Wright and Mischel (1987) studied the behavior of different types of children in various situations in a summer camp. The children differed in their levels of dispositional aggressiveness, and the situations varied in terms of the levels of stress they created in the children. Low-stress situations included art lessons, fishing, playing on the trampoline, physical movement exercises, and waterfront games. High-stress situations included academic tutoring, cabin meetings, wood working, crafts, and learning time.

Wright and Mischel predicted that trait-behavior correlations would be higher in high-stress situations than in low-stress situations. Specifically, they expected children who had been assessed as more aggressive by adult observers earlier in the summer to behave more aggressively (than those assessed as less aggressive) in those situations that had been identified in advance as highly stressful. In other words, Wright and Mischel thought that knowledge of the children's level of dispositional aggressiveness would permit them to predict the children's subsequent behavior in certain situations—that is, situations that were highly stressful. Conversely, they predicted lower trait-behavior correlations in the low-stress situations; that is, knowledge of the children's level of dispositional aggressiveness would not permit accurate prediction of their behavior in these situations.

Wright and Mischel found strong support for their predictions. In the high-stress situations, children with strong aggressive tendencies proved less able to cope with task requirements and acted more aggressively—by hitting, yelling, pushing, threatening, or bullying their peers—than did those children who were low in dispositional aggressiveness. In the low-stress situations, in contrast, there was very little aggressive behavior from any children, irrespective of their level of dispositional aggressiveness. Thus, cross-situational stability was evident in the behavior of aggression-prone children under stressful conditions, but their behavior changed (that is, they showed no aggressiveness) under low-stress conditions (Wright & Mischel, 1987). A focus on the interaction between person and situational variables allowed the investigators to predict both stability *and* change in the children's behavior very precisely. The use of this conditional approach promises to increase our understanding of the personality functioning of individuals, by enabling us to take into account not only their personality characteristics but also the role played by situations.

Conclusion 5: We need to incorporate concepts related to individuals' search for meaning into our theorizing and research on personality

Many of the personality theorists reviewed in this text—Jung, Adler, Kohut, Horney, Allport, Kelly, Maslow, Rogers, May, Rotter, and Bandura—have argued strongly that human beings have **purposive orientations.** They assume that all of us try to give our lives meaning by adopting certain goals and values and a philosophy of life. Contemporary personality psychologists have been influenced by these theorists. Baumeister (1989), for example, maintains that people try to make sense out of their lives by creating goals based on their values. In pursuing these goals, he believes, people seek to feel competent and worthwhile through the exercise of control over their outcomes and through the achievement of success on self-generated tasks. At the same time, they are also striving to demonstrate to themselves and others that they are good and worthy of respect and recognition, in an effort to maintain or enhance their self-esteem.

To understand how this search for meaning shapes personal growth, personality psychologists are conducting research on the kinds of goals that people generate at particular times in their lives, how they pursue them, and the consequences of attaining or not attaining them. Having established goals, individuals devise strategies (based on their dispositions) to attain them. They select situations to help meet their goals and present themselves strategically to increase their chances of success. Success or failure in achieving these goals then has a decided impact on their self-concepts. When individuals fail to attain important objectives, they typically feel dejected, depressed, and less worthwhile, whereas success brings out feelings of pride and elation, accompanied by increases in self-esteem (Higgins, 1987).

Drawing on the pioneering work of Kelly and Erikson, Cantor and her colleagues (Cantor & Langston, 1989; Cantor & Norem, 1989; Cantor, Norem, Niedenthal, Langston, & Brower, 1987; Harlow & Cantor, 1994; Zirkel & Cantor, 1990) have conducted some noteworthy research in this area. They have focused on the **life tasks** of students at a critical transition period in their lives—namely, the movement from home and high school to college life. This transition is particularly jarring for many students, as you undoubtedly know. First-year students face the tasks of creating new groups of friends, forging new relationships with parents and family, learning new study habits to meet academic requirements, and taking care of themselves as newly independent adults (learning to eat the proper foods and to budget time and money). All of these tasks confront students during a period of time when they also need to make important decisions about the future (Zirkel & Cantor, 1990, p. 173).

Obviously, not all students see these tasks as equally important. For example, some students may be more concerned about meeting new friends, while others are more anxious about meeting academic requirements. Zirkel and Cantor (1990) found that students who were very absorbed in the task of "being on my own, away from my family" experienced more stress than students who were less absorbed with the struggle for independence. However, by the end of college, the absorbed students expected to find being on their own significantly more fun than did the less absorbed students. Absorbed students were also more likely to leave college with a future commitment to professional or graduate school than were less absorbed students. Apparently, the absorbed students had learned how to achieve independence while in college, even though it was very stressful at the time, and now felt better able to handle the rigors of professional or graduate school, in comparison to their less absorbed peers.

Cantor, Norem, Niedenthal, Langston, and Brower (1987) also found individual differences among students in the kinds of **cognitive strategies** they used to cope with threatening academic life tasks. Specifically, these investigators focused on students who used **defensive-pessimism strategies** or **defensive-optimism strategies** in examination situations to cope with anxiety and stress. Defensively pessimistic students set low expectations for success on exams, in spite of good past performances, and felt very anxious and out of control *before* their performances. Defensively optimistic students, in contrast, preferred not to think about possible negative outcomes before beginning a task. They set high expectations based on their successful past experiences and felt positive, calm, and in control when thinking about their upcoming performance.

Intuitively, we might expect defensive pessimists to be debilitated by their pessimistic outlook. In fact, however, they tend to do better on exams, to the extent that they are able to confront their anxieties in advance by planning ahead for (unlikely) negative outcomes. Interestingly, both types of individuals perform equally well. However, subsequent research by Cantor and Norem (1989) found that, although the strategy of defensive pessimism is effective in the short run, it may have some negative long-term side effects. Clearly, defensive pessimists are more distressed and experience less enjoyment than do optimists. Defensive pessimists report more fatigue than optimists in social situations when they let their guard down. They also experience more psychological symptoms of worry, sleeplessness, and hopelessness, especially by the end of their third year in college. In the long run, it seems, the emotional ups and downs that characterize defensive pessimists take a heavy toll on their well-being. The all-out efforts and excessive worrying to achieve success are disproportionate to the demands of the tasks.

Defensive optimism also has its costs, but they do not appear to be as severe. Because defensive optimists deny or avoid negative information, they may fail to notice when their routine ways of coping do not work. Thus, they may be relatively slow to adjust to changing circumstances and experience negative consequences as a result. However, they also have reserves of energy available for particularly bad times.

Finally, Harlow and Cantor (1994) showed that many students try to cope with threatening academic setbacks not by pursuing cognitive strategies directly related to the problem—for example, by redoubling their study efforts and/or seeking tutoring—but by using people in their social lives to help them with their feelings—that is, by seeking continual reassurance from their friends. This strategy tended to be adopted by those students who were more outcome-focused—that is, those most concerned with achieving good grades and avoiding failure. Unfortunately, this strategy was not very effective; over the course of a semester, outcome-focused students performed academically on a par with their less outcome-focused counterparts. Moreover, the reassurance-seeking strategy used by the outcome-focused students had deleterious effects on their friendships: it was very annoying to their friends to have to constantly encourage the outcome-focused students about their academic performances when others were busy socializing and seeking to establish or maintain romantic relationships. As a consequence, outcome-focused students and their friends reported less satisfying social lives and strains on their relationships.

NEW DEVELOPMENTS IN THE DISCIPLINE

Personality psychology has been undergoing some exciting changes in the past decade. These new developments have been based, to a large extent, on the wisdom embedded in many of the current theories of personality (Cantor & Kihlstrom, 1987, pp. 11–46). Personality psychology has also borrowed knowledge, principles, and procedures from other disciplines within psychology, including cognitive psychology, social psychology, developmental psychology, and biological psychology. By drawing on these sources, personality psychologists have gained a much-needed infusion of energy and enthusiasm and have expanded the range of phenomena that they study (Buss & Cantor, 1989).

In particular, personality psychologists have been paying more attention to the role of various cognitive concepts and processes in determining behavior. People are often flooded with situational information that somehow must be reduced and simplified to avoid overload. To predict individual differences in behavior, we need to know how individuals uniquely encode (interpret), store, and retrieve information in order to achieve their goals. We also need to know, as part of this cognitive process, how some people are able to develop cognitive strategies that enable them to cope effectively with the demands of various situations, while others are unable to generate tactics that work. This focus on cognitive concepts and processes promises to continue during the next decade.

The use of cognitive concepts suggests that people are aware of their experiences, can adequately categorize them, and as a consequence are in a position to act effectively. Yet we know that such a view is overly simplistic. Freud made us keenly aware that people are not always aware of their experiences, cannot always categorize them adequately, and often act ineffectively. Sometimes individuals are unaware of the actual determinants of their actions and attempt to account for them by invoking plausible (but false) explanations (Nisbett & Wilson, 1977; Wilson & Stone, 1985). Sometimes people may make good judgments and show effective behaviors, but the judgments are based on *implicit* information. In such cases, we talk about the role of intuition in determining behavior (Bowers, 1981). Clearly, an adequate understanding of personality will have to account for the roles played by both conscious *and* unconscious factors in the production of behavior.

Personality psychologists have become increasingly interested in the role of the unconscious and have utilized new methods to assess unconscious processes and to show how they relate to personal behavior (Westen, 1990, pp. 40–42). Research in cognitive psychology, for example, has led to the development of models that support the idea of information processing outside of conscious awareness (Brody, 1987, p. 293). Personality psychologists are just beginning to use these models. For example, Lewicki (1986) suggests that people learn general rules on a nonconscious level, on the basis of a few experiences and observations, often early in life. Later on, the right circumstances can evoke an immediate behavioral response, even though people cannot explain why they acted as they did. For example, many people know when a joke is funny, but they cannot tell you why. Individuals who cry in an emotionally touching situation often express surprise at their inability to control their reactions and cannot explain them. Similarly, people with psychological disorders often are perfectly aware that their strong negative emotional reactions to certain stimuli (such as being home alone) are unreasonable, yet believe that they cannot do anything to change their behavior (Lewicki & Hill, 1987). Lewicki and several other investigators are pursuing rigorous research to help us understand how these unconscious rules are learned and how they can be unlearned (Kihlstrom, 1990).

Personality psychologists also realize that an adequate understanding of personality requires some consideration of motivation, the well-spring of much behavior. To study motivation, psychologists examine people's emotions and moods as reactions to the fate of their goals in everyday living. Failure to attain important goals leads to negative emotions such as anger, envy, jealousy, and disgust; success in attaining them brings positive emotions such as happiness, pride, and love (Novacek & Lazarus, 1990, p. 694). Thus, there are strong links between cognitions and affect, as noted initially by Freud, and personality psychologists can be expected to continue to focus on the dynamic and complex interrelationships between the two (Singer & Bonanno, 1990, p. 420; Wakefield, 1992, pp. 86–89).

Individuals also have knowledge of their performances and values, their goals and motives, and their rules and strategies for regulating their own behavior. This self-knowledge is based in part on an organized understanding of their behaviors and the consequences of displaying them in various past situations. But self-knowledge is also organized in terms of possibilities. Individuals plan for the future; they hope and dream and strive to attain their ideals. At times, they also fear the future and thus avoid taking certain actions because they fear the consequences. Envisioning desired possible selves creates positive affect, and thereby energizes behavior and makes the attainment of the desired end-states (goals) more likely. For example, imagining our own successes on tests produces good feelings, and as a result our attention and energies are focused on the task at hand, and we are able to achieve excellent performances. Doubts and insecurities prompt us to envision negative possible selves—for example, to imagine our own failures on tests. The accompanying negative affect and negative thoughts consume attention and energy that could be devoted to task performances; the result could well be very poor grades. Personality psychologists are incorporating these new, richer conceptions of the self into their research programs (Markus, 1977, 1983; Markus & Cross, 1990; Markus & Nurius, 1986; Ruvolo & Markus, 1992).

Finally, there are some rumblings in the discipline about the need to more actively examine the special impact that different cultures have on the personality development and functioning of their citizens. In particular, in the United States we generally grow up in a highly individualistic culture, which places heavy emphasis on independence, self-reliance, ambition, determination, pleasure, the pursuit of happiness, and personal success. In other cultures—for example, in parts of Europe (southern Italy, rural Greece), much of

Africa, Asia, and Latin America—the primary orientation is collectivistic. Collectivistic cultures teach their members to be more harmoniously interdependent, to share resources, to see success as depending on help from others, and to focus largely on trying to satisfy the needs of the group (Triandis, 1994, pp. 165–172). These differences in orientation give rise to different motives, interests, attitudes, behavior, values, and ideas of mental health and psychopathology. For example, a small Texas corporation seeking to increase productivity told its employees to look in the mirror and say, "I am beautiful," 100 times before coming to work each day. In contrast, employees of a Japanese supermarket were instructed to begin the day by holding hands and telling each other, "You are beautiful" (Markus & Kitayama, 1991, p. 224).

Most of what we know about human personality in Western cultures is based on our view of individuals as independent, self-contained, autonomous beings whose unique configurations of traits, abilities, values, and motives influence their behavior. As a result, personality psychologists' views of human personality are unnecessarily limited (Markus & Kitayama, 1991, p. 224). For example, our models of psychological health tend to emphasize self-realization, self-fulfillment, fulfilling individual potential, and so forth. These models, in many respects, mirror the individualistic bias of our culture. Although they do point out that self-actualizing people care about others and are socially responsible, the primary emphasis appears to be on the glorification of the individual. Models that emphasize the role played in the development of optimal psychological health by harmonious interdependence, sharing resources, and caring about the welfare of others are relatively rare in Western cultures, although a good case could be made for the social interest model created by Adler. Even if we acknowledge that many subcultures within the United States value interdependence and that various religious denominations emphasize love and caring for others (Markus & Kitayama, 1991, p. 228), the fact remains that the overall cultural emphasis is on independence and personal success. In that context, it appears clear that personality psychologists need to expand their view, inquiries, and analyses beyond their own culture if they are to continue making progress toward an adequate theory of human personality.

In conclusion, the many interesting new developments in personality psychology pose numerous questions and challenges for personality psychologists in their quest for a fuller understanding of personality development and functioning. If the past few years of exciting growth are any indication, the future of the discipline as we approach the 21st century looks promising indeed.

DISCUSSION QUESTIONS

1. Why are the grand theories of personality generally still alive and well?
2. Do you agree or disagree with the evolutionary viewpoint that males tend to be more active, aggressive, and dominant, whereas females tend to be more sociable, nurturant, and fearful? State your reasons.
3. What are the implications for our well-being if we learn to minimize personality differences between the sexes?
4. What advantages do you see in constructing a taxonomy of personality traits?
5. Do we need to incorporate cognitive constructs in building an adequate view of human personality? Why?
6. From your own life, give some examples of occasions when it has been adaptive for you to maintain your behavior across several situations and occasions when it has not.
7. What kinds of cognitive strategies do you use to cope with the stresses of exams? Describe why they do, or do not, work.
8. Personality psychologists have reached tentative agreement on five basic dimensions of personality. Can you think of any dimensions that they have overlooked? What are they?
9. Have you set goals that you think you must attain before you graduate? What are they? What strategies have you devised for accomplishing them?
10. Do we generally overemphasize personal achievement and success in this culture? If so, what are some of the possible harmful consequences of such an orientation to ourselves and others? Is it possible to value achievement and personal success in a way that is psychologically healthy? Give reasons for your answer.

GLOSSARY

behavior genetics   Scientific discipline that seeks to document the relative influences of heredity and environment on behavior differences observed among individuals.

big five factors   Five major dimensions of personality, which have been derived largely from analyses of the terms people use to describe themselves and others.

cognitive strategies   The use of self-knowledge and knowledge about the social world to translate goals into reality; these strategies include individuals' patterns of appraisal, planning, and effort to attain valued goals while protecting their self-esteem.

conditional approach to dispositions   Theoretical model designed to account for individual differences in behavior by linking personality dispositions to a circumscribed set of situations.

defensive-optimism strategies   Attempts to cope with stress and anxiety by not thinking about possible negative outcomes before beginning a task.

defensive-pessimism strategies   Attempts to cope with stress and anxiety before a performance, by setting low expectations for success in spite of good past performances.

differential parental investment hypothesis   From an evolutionary perspective, the conjecture that males and females will employ different mating strategies because of their differential investments in parenting.

evolutionary theory   A theory that seeks to understand the development of human behavioral tendencies by focusing on our animal heritage.

grand theories of personality   Theories that cover a broad range of phenomena and seek to explain virtually all individual differences in behavior.

interactional model of personality   Position that seeks to explain personality functioning by examining the joint effects of person and situation variables on behavior.

interactional temperament model   The theory that temperament (traits) and environment affect each other.

life tasks   The consciously accessible goals that are important to people at a given point in time.

person variables   Internal characteristics of the person (cognitions, emotions, motives, traits, needs, urges) that are involved in the production of behavior.

person/situation debate   A longstanding controversy in personality psychology that focuses on the issue of whether behavior is stable despite situational fluctuations or variables in the face of situational changes.

purposive orientations   The view that human beings generate meaning for their lives by creating goals and pursuing them.

situation variables   The physical (temperature, lighting, size of room) and social (the number and different kinds of people) aspects of the environment that affect behavior.

SUGGESTED READINGS

Buss, D. M., & Cantor, N. (Eds.). (1989). *Personality psychology: Recent trends and emerging directions*. New York: Springer-Verlag.

Craik, K. H., Hogan, R., & Wolfe, R. N. (Eds.) (1993). *Fifty years of personality psychology*. New York: Plenum Press.

Pervin, L. A. (Ed.). (1989). *Goal concepts in personality and social psychology*. Hillsdale, NJ: Erlbaum.

Pervin, L. A. (Ed.). (1990). *Handbook of personality: Theory and research*. New York: Guilford Press.

REFERENCES

Alker, H. A. (1977). Beyond ANOVA psychology in the study of person-situation interactions. In D. Magnusson & N. S. Endler (Eds.), *Personality at the crossroads: Current issues in interactional psychology* (pp. 243–256). Hillsdale, NJ: Erlbaum.

Allport, F. H., & Allport, G. W. (1921). Personality traits: Their classification and measurement. *Journal of Abnormal and Social Psychology, 16,* 6–40.

Allport, G. W. (1955). *Becoming: Basic considerations for a psychology of personality*. New Haven, CT: Yale University Press.

Allport, G. W., & Odbert, H. S. (1936). Trait names: A psycholexical study. *Psychological Monographs, 47* (Whole No. 211).

Baumeister, R. F. (1989). The problem of life's meaning. In D. M. Buss & N. Cantor (Eds.), *Personality psychology: Recent trends and emerging directions* (pp. 138–148). New York: Springer-Verlag.

Borgatta, E. F. (1964). The structure of personality characteristics. *Behavioral Science, 9,* 8–17.

Bowers, K. S. (1981). Knowing more than we can say leads to saying more than we can know: On being implicitly informed. In D. Magnusson (Ed.), *Toward a psychology of situations: An interactional perspective* (pp. 179–194). Hillsdale, NJ: Erlbaum.

Bowers, K. S. (1987). Toward a multidimensional view of personality and health. *Journal of Personality, 55,* 343–349.

Briggs, S. R. (1989). The optimal level of measurement for personality constructs. In D. M. Buss & N. Cantor (Eds.), *Personality psychology: Recent trends and emerging directions* (pp. 246–260). New York: Springer-Verlag.

Brody, N. (1987). Some thoughts on the unconscious. In N. Brody (Ed.), The unconscious [Special Issue]. *Personality and Social Psychology Bulletin, 13,* 293–313.

Buss, A. H. (1988). *Personality: Evolutionary heritage and human distinctiveness.* Hillsdale, NJ: Erlbaum.

Buss, A. H. (1995). *Personality: Temperament, social behavior, and the self.* Boston: Allyn & Bacon.

Buss, A. H., & Plomin, R. (1975). *A temperament theory of personality development.* New York: Wiley.

Buss, D. M. (1989). Sex differences in human mate preferences: Evolutionary hypotheses tested in 37 cultures. *Behavioral and Brain Sciences, 12,* 1–49.

Buss, D. M. (1992). Manipulation in close relationships: Five personality factors in interactional context. *Journal of Personality, 60,* 477–499.

Buss, D. M. (1994). *The evolution of desire: Strategies of human mating.* New York: Basic Books.

Buss, D. M., & Cantor, N. (Eds.). (1989). *Personality psychology: Recent trends and emerging directions.* New York: Springer-Verlag.

Buss, D. M., & Dedden, L. A. (1990). Derogation of competitors. *Journal of Social and Personal Relationships, 7,* 395–422.

Buss, D. M., & Schmitt, D. P. (1993). Sexual strategies theory: An evolutionary perspective on human mating. *Psychological Review, 100,* 204–232.

Cantor, N., & Kihlstrom, J. F. (1987). *Personality and social intelligence.* Englewood Cliffs, NJ: Prentice-Hall.

Cantor, N., & Langston, C. A. (1989). "Ups and downs" of life tasks in a life transition. In L. A. Pervin (Ed.), *The goals concept in personality and social psychology* (pp. 127–167). Hillsdale, NJ: Erlbaum.

Cantor, N., & Norem, J. K. (1989). Defensive pessimism and stress and coping. *Social Cognition, 7,* 92–112.

Cantor, N., Norem, J. K., Niedenthal, P. M., Langston, C. A., & Brower, A. M. (1987). Life tasks, self-concept ideals, and cognitive strategies in a life transition. *Journal of Personality and Social Psychology, 53,* 1178–1191.

Cattell, R. B. (1943). The description of personality: Basic traits resolved into clusters. *Journal of Abnormal and Social Psychology, 38,* 476–506.

Cattell, R. B. (1950). *Personality: A systematic theoretical and factual study.* New York: McGraw-Hill.

Cattell, R. B. (1965). *The scientific analysis of personality.* Baltimore, MD: Penguin Books.

Cattell, R. B. (1979). *Personality and learning theory: Vol. 1. The structure of personality in its environment.* New York: Springer.

Cattell, R. B. (1980). *Personality and learning theory: Vol. 2. A systems theory of maturation and structured learning.* New York: Springer.

Digman, J. M., & Takemoto-Chock, N. K. (1981). Factors in the natural language of personality: Reanalysis and comparison of six major studies. *Multivariate Behavioral Research, 16,* 149–170.

Epstein, S. (1977). Traits are alive and well. In D. Magnusson & N. S. Endler (Eds.), *Personality at the crossroads: Current issues in interactional psychology* (pp. 83–98). Hillsdale, NJ: Erlbaum.

Epstein, S. (1983a). Aggregation and beyond: Some basic issues in the prediction of behavior. *Journal of Personality, 51,* 360–392.

Epstein, S. (1983b). The stability of confusion: A reply to Mischel and Peake. *Psychological Review, 90,* 179–184.

Epstein, S. (1984). The stability of behavior across time and situations. In R. Zucker, J. Aronoff, & A. I. Rabin (Eds.), *Personality and the prediction of behavior* (pp. 209–269). San Diego: Academic Press.

Feshbach, S. (1984). The "personality" of personality theory and research. *Personality and Social Psychology Bulletin, 10,* 446–456.

Funder, D. C. (1991). Global traits: A neo-Allportian approach to personality. *Psychological Science, 2,* 31–39.

Funder, D. C. (1993). Judgments of personality and personality itself. In K. H. Craik, R. Hogan, & R. N. Wolfe (Eds.), *Fifty years of personality psychology* (pp. 207–214). New York: Plenum Press.

Goldberg, L. R. (1981). Language and individual differences: The search for universals in personality lexicons. In L. Wheeler (Ed.), *Review of personality and social psychology* (Vol. 2, pp. 141–165). Beverly Hills, CA: Sage.

Goldberg, L. R. (1990). An alternative "description of personality": The Big Five factor structure. *Journal of Personality and Social Psychology, 59,* 1216–1229.

Graziano, W. G., & Ward, D. (1992). Probing the Big Five in adolescence: Personality and adjustment during a developmental transition. *Journal of Personality, 60,* 4425–4439.

Harlow, R. E., & Cantor, N. (1994). Social pursuit of academics: Side effects and spillover of strategic reassurance seeking. *Journal of Personality and Social Psychology, 66,* 386–397.

Higgins, E. T. (1987). Self-discrepancy: A theory relating self and affect. *Psychological Review, 94,* 319–340.

John, O. P. (1989). Towards a taxonomy of personality descriptors. In D. M. Buss & N. Cantor (Eds.), *Personality psychology: Recent trends and emerging directions* (pp. 261–271). New York: Springer-Verlag.

John, O. P. (1990). The "Big Five" factor taxonomy: Dimensions of personality in the natural language and in questionnaires. In L. A. Pervin (Ed.), *Handbook of personality: Theory and research* (pp. 66–100). New York: Guilford Press.

John, O. P., Caspi, A., Robins, R. W., Moffitt, T. E., & Stouthamer-Loeber, M. (1994). The "Little Five": Exploring the nomological network of the five-factor model of personality in adolescent boys. *Child Development, 65,* 160–178.

Kenrick, D. T., Sadalla, E. K., Groth, G., & Trost, M. R. (1990). Evolution, traits, and the stages of human courtship: Qualifying the parental investment model. *Journal of Personality, 58,* 97–116.

Kihlstrom, J. F. (1990). The psychological unconscious. In L. A. Pervin (Ed.), *Handbook of personality: Theory and research* (pp. 445–464). New York: Guilford Press.

Lewicki, P. (1986). *Nonconscious social information processing.* New York: Academic Press.

Lewicki, P., & Hill, T. (1987). Unconscious processes as explanations of behavior in cognitive, personality, and social psychology. *Personality and Social Psychology Bulletin, 13,* 355–362.

Maddi, S. R. (1993). The continuing relevance of personality theory. In K. H. Craik, R. Hogan, & R. N. Wolfe (Eds.), *Fifty years of personality psychology* (pp. 85–101). New York: Plenum Press.

Markus, H. (1977). Self-schemata and processing information about the self. *Journal of Personality and Social Psychology, 35,* 63–78.

Markus, H. (1983). Self-knowledge: An expanded view. *Journal of Personality, 51,* 543–565.

Markus, H., & Cross, S. (1990). The interpersonal self. In L. A. Pervin (Ed.), *Handbook of personality: Theory and research* (pp. 576–608). New York: Guilford Press.

Markus, H., & Kitayama, S. (1991). Culture and the self: Implications for cognition, emotion, and motivation. *Psychological Review, 98,* 224–253.

Markus, H., & Nurius, P. (1986). Possible selves. *American Psychologist, 41,* 954–969.

McCrae, R. R., & Costa, P. T., Jr. (1990). *Personality in adulthood.* New York: Guilford Press.

McCrae, R. R., & John, O. P. (1992). An introduction to the Five-Factor Model and its applications. In R. R. McCrae (Ed.), The Five-Factor Model: Issues and applications. *Journal of Personality, 60,* 175–215.

Mendelsohn, G. A. (1993). It's time to put theories of personality in their place, or, Allport and Stagner got it right, why can't we? In K. H. Craik, R. Hogan, & R. N. Wolfe (Eds.), *Fifty years of personality psychology* (pp. 103–115). New York: Plenum Press.

Mischel, W. (1968). *Personality and assessment.* New York: Wiley.

Mischel, W. (1977). The interaction of person and situation. In D. Magnusson & N. S. Endler (Eds.), *Personality at the crossroads: Current issues in interactional psychology* (pp. 333–352). Hillsdale, NJ: Erlbaum.

Mischel, W. (1983). Alternatives in the pursuit of the predictability and consistency of persons: Stable data that yield unstable interpretations. *Journal of Personality, 51,* 578–604.

Mischel, W., & Peake, P. K. (1983). Some facets of consistency: Replies to Epstein, Funder, and Bem. *Psychological Review, 90,* 394–402.

Moskowitz, D. S. (1982). Coherence and cross-situational generality in personality: A new analysis of old problems. *Journal of Personality and Social Psychology, 43,* 754–768.

Nisbett, R. E., & Wilson, T. D. (1977). Telling more than we can know: Verbal reports on mental processes. *Psychological Review, 84,* 231–259.

Norman, W. T. (1963). Toward an adequate taxonomy of personality attributes: Replicated factor structure in peer nomination personality ratings. *Journal of Abnormal and Social Psychology, 66,* 574–583.

Norman, W. T. (1967). *2800 personality trait descriptors: Normative operating characteristics for a university population.* Ann Arbor: University of Michigan, Department of Psychology.

Novacek, J., & Lazarus, R. S. (1990). The structure of commitments. *Journal of Personality, 58,* 693–715.

Olweus, D. (1977). A critical analysis of the "modern" interactionist position. In D. Magnusson & N. S. Endler (Eds.), *Personality at the crossroads: Current issues in interactional psychology* (pp. 221–233). Hillsdale, NJ: Erlbaum.

Plomin, R., Chipuer, H. M., & Loehlin, J. C. (1990). Behavioral genetics and personality. In L. A. Pervin (Ed.), *Handbook of personality: Theory and research* (pp. 225–243). New York: Guilford Press.

Ruvolo, A. P., & Markus, H. R. (1992). Possible selves and performance: The power of self-relevant imagery. *Social Cognition, 10,* 95–124.

Singer, J. L., & Bonanno, G. A. (1990). Personality and private experience: Individual variations in consciousness and inattention to subjective phenomena. In L. A. Pervin (Ed.), *Handbook of personality: Theory and research* (pp. 419–444). New York: Guilford Press.

Singer, J. L., & Kolligan, J., Jr. (1987). Developments in the study of private experience. *Annual Review of Psychology, 38,* 533–574.

Small, S. A., Zeldin, R. S., & Savin-Williams, R. C. (1983). In search of personality traits: A multimethod analysis of naturally occurring prosocial and dominance behavior. *Journal of Personality, 51,* 1–16.

Triandis, H. C. (1994). *Culture and social behavior.* New York: McGraw-Hill.

Tupes, E. C., & Christal, R. C. (1961). *Recurrent personality factors based on trait ratings* (Tech. Rep. No. ASDTR61–97). Lackland Air Force Base, TX: U.S. Air Force.

Wakefield, J. C. (1992). Freud and cognitive psychology: The conceptual interface. In J. W. Barron, M. N. Eagle, & D. L. Wolitzky (Eds.), *Interface of psychoanalysis and psychology* (pp. 77–98). Washington, DC: American Psychological Association.

West, S. G. (1986). Methodological developments in personality research: An introduction. *Journal of Personality, 54,* 1–17.

Westen, D. (1990). Psychoanalytic approaches to personality. In L. A. Pervin (Ed.), *Handbook of personality: Theory and research* (pp. 21–65). New York: Guilford Press.

Wilson, T. D., & Stone, J. I. (1985). Limitations of self-knowledge: More on telling more than we can know. *Review of Personality and Social Psychology, 6,* 167–183.

Wright, J. C., & Mischel, W. (1987). A conditional approach to dispositional constructs: The local predictability of social behavior. *Journal of Personality and Social Psychology, 53,* 1159–1177.

Wright, J. C., & Mischel, W. (1988). Conditional hedges and the intuitive psychology of traits. *Journal of Personality and Social Psychology, 55,* 454–469.

Zirkel, S., & Cantor, N. (1990). Personal construal of life tasks: Those who struggle for independence. *Journal of Personality and Social Psychology, 58,* 172–185.

Zuckerman, M. (1990). The psychophysiology of sensation-seeking. *Journal of Personality, 58,* 313–345.

Name Index

Bonarius, J., 419, 433
Bonett, R. M., 626, 642
Bordages, J. W., 457, 468
Borgatta, E. F., 656, 675
Boring, E. G., 532
Bornstein, R. F., 55–56, 67, 68, 74
Boss, M., 505, 508, 524
Bourne, E., 203, 222
Bower, G. H., 67, 74
Bowers, K. S., 662, 670, 675
Breiter, H. J., 172, 180
Breland, H. M., 128, 146
Brandtstadter, J., 592–593, 606
Brannon, R., 55, 76
Brennan, J. F., 123, 146
Brereton, K., 463, 469
Breuer, J., 34
Briggs, K. C., 99, 116
Briggs, S. R., 656, 675–676
Broca, P., 273–74
Brody, N., 670, 676
Brower, A. M., 667–668, 676
Brown, R. C., 491–492, 499
Brown, R. J., 105, 116
Brown, S. D., 626, 642
Brownell, K. D., 555, 577
Briggs, K. C., 99
Brucke, E., 33–34,
Buckley, F., 427, 434
Bullock, W. A., 373, 396
Burt, C., 358
Buss, A. H., 649–653, 655, 676
Buss, D. M., 653, 654, 660–661, 669, 676
Bussey, K., 614, 642
Butler, J. C., 153–154, 181
Butler, J. M., 488, 499
Byrne, D., 272, 277

Campbell, A., 375, 396
Campbell, J. B., 371, 396
Campbell, J. F., 12–13, 25
Camus, A., 505
Cann, D. R., 104–105, 116
Cantor, N., 667–669, 676, 677
Cantrell, P., 596–597, 608
Caplan, P. J., 167–168, 180
Carlson, R., 100–101, 116
Carpenter, F., 537–538, 547, 577
Carter, J. A., 489, 499
Carton, J. S., 592, 606
Caspi, 659, 677
Catanzaro, S. J., 586, 606
Cattell, R. B., 276–277, 307–356, 656, 661–662, 676
Cervone, D., 624, 643
Chance, J. E., 580, 581, 582, 583, 584–585, 586, 608
Chaplin, M. P., 138, 146
Charcot, J., 34, 525
Child, I. L., 275, 277
Chipuer, H. M., 649, 679
Chodorkoff, B., 482, 483, 499

Christal, R. C., 656, 679
Christie, R., 13, 25
Cofer, C. N., 370, 396
Cohen, J., 67, 74
Coles, R., 183, 184, 186, 187, 222
Cooper, C. R., 129, 146
Cooper, H. M., 593, 607
Cortes, J. B., 275, 277
Costa, P. T., Jr., 656, 659, 678
Cote, J. E., 206, 222
Cramer, P., 43, 74, 75
Crandall, J. E., 134, 142, 146
Crandall, V. C., 592, 606–607
Crandell, C. J., 172, 181
Crawford, M., 449, 468
Critelli, J. W., 249, 268
Cromwell, R. L., 429, 434
Cronbach, L. J., 10, 25
Cross, S., 671, 678
Crozier, W. J., 532, 533
Csikszentmihalyi, M., 452–455, 469
Curlette, W. L., 142, 148

D'Alelio, W. A., 173, 180
Dalton, P., 405, 434
Darwin, C., 27
Davies, D. R., 372, 396
Davies, J. D., 273, 277
DaVinci, L., 15–16,
Davis, C. M., 476–477, 499
Dedden, L. A., 654, 676
de St. Aubin, E., 209, 223
Diehr, P., 642
Dietch, J., 447, 469
Digman, J. M., 656, 676–677
Dion, K. K., 596, 607
Dion, K. L., 596, 607
Dobson, K. S., 172, 180
Dobson, W. R., 205, 224
Domino, G., 104, 116
Donderi, D. C., 104–105, 116
Donovan, D. M., 603, 607
Dosamantes-Alperson, E., 462, 469
Downs, A. F. D., 634–635, 642
Draffan, J., 427, 434
Dreger, R. M., 309,
Dreikurs, R., 135, 146
Dry, A. M., 88, 116
Durham, M., 642
Duster, T., 345, 346, 355

Eagle, M. N., 229, 268
Ee, J. S., 249, 268
Eidelson, R. J., 173, 180
Ellis, A., 142, 146, 173, 177, 180
Elmes, D. G., 12, 25
Epstein, N., 173, 180
Epstein, S., 663, 664, 664, 677
Erdelyi, M. H., 58, 59, 75
Erikson, E., 30, 182–225

Subject Index

Credits

These pages constitute an extension of the copyright page. We have made every effort to trace the ownership of all copyrighted material and to secure permission from copyright holders. In the event of any question arising as to the use of any material, we will be pleased to make the necessary corrections in future printings. Thanks are due to the following authors, publishers, and agents for permission to use the material indicated.

CHAPTER 2: **33,** photo: Courtesy, National Library of Medicine.

CHAPTER 3: **78,** photo: Courtesy, National Library of Medicine. **85:** Figure 3.1 adapted from *The Psychology of C. G. Jung,* by J. Jacobi, 1962, p. 126, Diagram 6. New Haven: Yale University Press. **92:** Figure 3.2 adapted from *The Psychology of C. G. Jung,* by J. Jacobi, 1962, p. 114, Plate 14. New Haven: Yale University Press. **99:** Table 3.1 reproduced by special permission from the Myers-Briggs Type Indicator, by Katherine C. Briggs and Isabel Briggs Myers. Copyright 1943, 1944, 1957, and 1976 by Consulting Psychologists Press, Inc., Palo Alto, CA.

CHAPTER 4: **118,** photo: Courtesy, Alfred Adler Institute of Chicago.

CHAPTER 5: **149,** photo: Bettman Archive. **153:** Table 5.1 adapted from "Construction of a Hypercompetitive Attitudes Scale," by R. M. Ryckman, M. Hammer, L. M. Kaczor, and J. A. Gold, 1990, *Journal of Personality Assessment, 55,* pp. 630–639. Reprinted by permission of Lawrence Erlbaum Associates, Inc.

CHAPTER 6: **182,** photo: Jon Erikson. **185:** Excerpt from *Erik H. Erikson: The Growth of His Work,* by R. Coles, 1970, pp. 157–158. Boston: Little, Brown. **190:** Table 6.1 adapted from *Childhood and Society,* by Erik H. Erikson, with permission of W. W. Norton & Company, Inc. Copyright 1950, 1963 by W. W. Norton & Company, Inc. **204:** Figure 6.1 adapted from "Identity Development from Adolescence to Adulthood: An Extension of Theory and a Review of Research," by A. S. Waterman, 1982, *Developmental Psychology, 18,* pp. 341–358. Copyright 1982 by the American Psychological Association. Adapted by permission.

CHAPTER 7: **226,** photo: Chicago Institute of Psychoanalysis.

CHAPTER 8: **279,** photo: W. H. Tobey/Courtesy of the Harvard University Archives. **297–299:** Excerpts from *Letters from Jenny,* by G. W. Allport, 1965. New York: Harcourt, Brace & World.

CHAPTER 9:   307, photo: Courtesy, University of Illinois. **311:** Figure 9. 1 adapted from *Handbook of Multivariate Experimental Psychology,* by J. R. Nesselroade and R. B. Cattell (Eds.), 1988, p. 17. New York: Plenum. **314:** Figure 9.2 and excerpt from *Personality and Motivation: Structure and Measurement,* by Raymond B. Cattell. Copyright © 1957 by Harcourt Brace & Company, reproduced by permission of the publisher. **319:** Table 9.3 adapted from *The Scientific Analysis of Personality,* by R. B. Cattell, p. 365. Baltimore: Penguin. **320:** Table 9.4 adapted from *The Scientific Analysis of Personality,* by R. B. Cattell, p. 70. Baltimore, Penguin. **322:** Figure 9.3 adapted from *The Scientific Analysis of Personality,* by R. B. Cattell, 1965, pp. 302–303. Baltimore: Penguin. **329:** Table 9.5 reproduced by special permission of the Institute for Personality and Ability Testing, Inc., 1602 Coronado Drive, Champaign, IL 61820. **332:** Figure 9.5 adapted from *Personality: A Systematic Theoretical and Factual Study,* by R. B. Cattell, 1950, p. 158. New York: McGraw-Hill.

CHAPTER 10:   357, photo: Courtesy, University of London, British Postgraduate Medical Federation. **362:** Figure 10.1 adapted from *The Biological Basis of Personality,* by H. J. Eysenck, 1967, p. 36. Courtesy of Charles C Thomas, Publisher, Springfield, Illinois. **363:** Table 10.1 adapted from the adult EPQ by H. J. Eysenck and S. B. G. Eysenck, © 1975, published by EdITS (Educational and Industrial Testing Service), San Diego, California. **363:** Figure 10.2 from *Personality and Individual Differences,* by H. J. Eysenck and M. W. Eysenck, p. 15. Copyright © 1985 by Plenum Publishing Corporation. Adapted by permission. **364:** Figure 10.3 from *Personality and Individual Differences,* by H. J. Eysenck and M. W. Eysenck, p. 15. Copyright © 1985 by Plenum Publishing Corporation. Adapted by permission. **364:** Figure 10.4 from *Personality and Individual Differences,* by H. J. Eysenck and M. W. Eysenck, p. 14. Copyright © 1985 by Plenum Publishing Corporation. Adapted by permission. **365:** Table 10.2 from *Greatness:Who Makes History and Why,* by D. K. Simonton, 1994, p. 287. New York: Guilford. **371:** Figure 10.5 from *Personality and Individual Differences,* by H. J. Eysenck and M. W. Eysenck, p. 249. Copyright © 1985 by Plenum Publishing Corporation. Adapted by permission. **375:** Figure 10.6 adapted from *The Biological Basis of Personality,* by H. J. Eysenck, 1967, p. 231. Courtesy of Charles C Thomas, Publisher, Springfield, Illinois. **382:** Figure 10.7 from *Personality and Individual Differences,* by H. J. Eysenck and M. W. Eysenck, p. 170. Copyright © 1985 by Plenum Publishing Corporation. Adapted by permission. **383:** Figure 10.8 from *Personality and Individual Differences,* by H. J. Eysenck and M. W. Eysenck, p. 171. Copyright © 1985 by Plenum Publishing Corporation. Adapted by permission.

CHAPTER 11:   403, photo: Courtesy, Brandeis University. **405–425:** Scattered quotations reprinted from *The Psychology of Personal Constructs,* by George A. Kelly, 1955, Volumes 1 and 2. Reprinted by permission of Routledge. **416:** Table 11.1 reprinted from *The Psychology of Personal Constructs,* by George A. Kelly, 1955, Volume 1, p. 270. Reprinted by permission of Routledge.

CHAPTER 12:   441, photo: Archives of the History of American Psychology. **451:** Table 12.1 adapted from "Whatever Turns You On: Triggers to Transcendent Experiences," by C. S. Keutzer, 1978, *Journal of Humanistic Psychology, 18,* p. 78. **460:** Table 12.2 adapted from Personal Orientation Inventory, by E. L. Shostrom. San Diego: EdITS/Educational and Industrial Testing Service, 1963. Reproduced with permission. All rights reserved.

CHAPTER 13:   471, photo: Courtesy, Carl Rogers Memorial Library. **477:** Table 13.1 adapted from "Self-Selection of Diet by Newly Weaned Infants," by C. M. Davis, 1928, *American Journal of Diseases of Children, 36,* p. 659.

CHAPTER 14:   501, photo: Stock, Boston.

CHAPTER 15:   531, photo: Courtesy, Julie Vargas. **560:** Table 15.2 adapted from "The Measurement and Reinforcement of Behavior of Psychotics," by T. Ayllon and N. H. Azrin, 1965, *Journal of the Experimental Analysis of Behavior, 8,* p. 360.

CHAPTER 16:   579, photo: Courtesy, University of Connecticut. **591:** Table 16.1 adapted from "Generalized Expectancies for Internal versus External Control of Reinforcement," by J. B. Rotter, 1966, *Psychological Monographs, 80* (Whole No. 609), p. 11. Copyright © 1966 by the American Psychological Association. Reprinted by permission.

CHAPTER 17:   610, photo: Chuck Painter, Stanford University. **620:** Figure 17.1 adapted from "Effects of Viewing Justified Real and Unreal Film Violence on Aggressive Behavior," by T. P. Meyer, 1972, *Journal of Personality and Social Psychology, 23,* p. 26. Copyright

Credits

© 1972 by the American Psychological Association. Reprinted by permission of the author. **632:** Figure 17.2 adapted from "Factors Determining Vicarious Extinction of Avoidance Behavior through Symbolic Modeling," by A. Bandura and F. L. Menlove, 1968, *Journal of Personality and Social Psychology, 8,* p. 102. Copyright © 1968 by the American Psychological Association. Reprinted by permission of the author. **633:** Figure 17.3 adapted from "Test Anxiety and the Self-Disclosing Coping Model," by I. G. Sarason, 1975, *Journal of Consulting and Clinical Psychology, 43,* p. 150. Copyright © 1975 by the American Psychological Association. Reprinted by permission of the author.

CHAPTER 18: 657: Table 18.1 adapted from "An Alternative 'Description of Personality': The Big Five Factor Structure," 1990, *Journal of Personality and Social Psychology, 59,* pp. 1224–1225. Copyright © 1990 by the American Psychological Association.